Gardening by Mail

Gardening by Mail

A SOURCE BOOK

Barbara J. Barton

Everything for the Garden and Gardener

A directory of mail-order resources for gardeners in the United States and Canada, including seed companies, nurseries, suppliers of all garden necessaries and ornaments, horticultural and plant societies, magazines, libraries, and a list of useful books on plants and gardening.

FOURTH EDITION
UPDATED AND REVISED

A Tusker Press Book

Houghton Mifflin Company
Boston • New York

Dedicated to my parents, Hildor and Marguerite Barton,
and to my aunt, Margit Barton McNulty;
they thought I could do anything, made it possible,
and it worked!

———————

For information about permission to reproduce selections from this book,
write to Permissions, Houghton Mifflin Company, 215 Park Avenue South,
New York, New York 10003.

Library of Congress Cataloging-in-Publication Data

Barton, Barbara J.
Gardening by mail : a source book : everything for the garden and
gardener / Barbara J. Barton. — 4th ed.
p. cm.
"A directory of mail-order resources for gardeners in the United States and Canada, including
seed companies, nurseries, suppliers of all garden necessaries and ornaments, horticultural and
plant societies, magazines, libraries, and a list of useful books on plants and gardening."
"A Tusker Press book."
Includes bibliographical references and index.
ISBN 0-395-68079-4
1. Gardening — United States — Directories. 2. Gardening equipment industry — United
States — Directories. 3. Gardening — Canada — Directories. 4. Gardening equipment
industry — Canada — Directories. 5. Mail-order business — United States — Directories.
6. Mail-order business — Canada — Directories. I. Title.
SB450.943.U6B37 1994   93-33278
635'.029'47 — dc20   CIP

Printed in the United States of America

BP 10 9 8 7 6 5 4 3

Originated and composed by Tusker Press
P.O. Box 1338
Sebastopol, California 95473
Phone and fax: (707) 829-9189
(*To send a fax, push "start" when the phone begins to ring.*)

TABLE OF CONTENTS

Introduction

Listings

Indexes

Practical Matters

A table of the symbols and abbreviations used in this book appears
on the bookmark inside the back cover.

Dear Gardener:

I don't know how you fell in love with growing things, but I came home from work one day to find a Wayside Gardens catalog in the mail. It was as fatal and irresistible as Cupid's dart -- soon I was carrying seed catalogs to read on the bus, rushing to secondhand book stores during my lunch hour, always trying to learn more.

As this insatiable habit was developing, one of my greatest frustrations was that there seemed to be no easy way to find out everything I wanted to know. If I saw a lovely plant, where could I get one to try to grow myself? Surely there must be wonderful gardening magazines, but there were very few on newsstands -- what did *real* gardeners do? Were there plant and horticultural societies? Would they allow *me* to join? Where might I find a horticultural library to browse in? Even though I'm a long time reference librarian myself, it all seemed so difficult! Only *old* gardeners knew -- and it took them years to find out.

When suddenly I had the time and the opportunity, I decided to "whip together" the ideal reference book for people like me -- full of sources of seeds, plants and garden supplies, societies to join, libraries to haunt, magazines to curl up with, and a list of good books on plants and practical gardening, "good reads" and books with inspiring pictures to feast the imagination.

My mind began to spin with grandiose ideas. I'd index everyone listed in many ways to make the book even more useful. I'd describe their catalogs, whether you could visit them and when, and whether they had display gardens to visit, and I'd list them by location so I could plan trips to include horticultural high spots! I'd mention their shipping seasons, whether they sold wholesale to the trade, what their minimum order was, whether they shipped to buyers overseas, and whether they listed their plants by botanical name. Every day I thought of some new and indispensable tidbit of information that the gardeners of North America just *had* to be told. This first "whipping together" took me three years!

Ten years after I first started collecting information, I'm much wiser and know that putting together the ideal reference book is nearly impossible. It's very difficult to get thousands of people to send back information promptly and in a standard format, and it's only current on the day they mail it! Most people are very helpful, some are very uncooperative, and a few will reply long after the book has gone to press, with a note saying "I just found this on my desk..."

Readers of the three earlier editions, the first two of which I published myself as Tusker Press, know the stirring saga of the plucky librarian who forged ahead, undeterred by rejection slips, with money cascading out of her pockets and double chins set at a determined angle. Three years ago I was lucky enough to get Houghton Mifflin as my publisher and Frances Tenenbaum as my editor; they've made everything much easier for me.

I can't help feeling as I write this introduction that I'm writing to many friends out there in the world of plants and gardening; many of you have written to me and I've talked to others on the telephone. Through my chats and contacts with people listed in this book and with my readers, I feel connected from my little spot in the country to the wide world of those who love plants. You can imagine my delight when one of "my people" writes a book or an article, or is the subject of a story in a magazine. I love hearing from you and encourage you to share information and your opinions and suggestions with me.

What's new? There are about three hundred new nurseries and seed companies, including a number of new bulb and seed sources from abroad; the variety of plants offered is much greater than ever before! I hope you'll find the new sources as exciting as I do. Sadly, the end of the "roaring eighties" has seen a number of nurseries and suppliers go out of business, and there has been more consolidation among the old-line mail order "garden emporiums." Some of my favorite specialty nurseries have stopped doing retail or mail order business, in spite of my wails of protest! There are about the same number of nurseries as before, but the number of suppliers is somewhat less; there seem to be fewer new suppliers to take the place of those that went out of business.

Here at Tusker Press World Headquarters things keep humming along. I spent one of the years between editions of *Gardening by Mail* gathering material and writing the *Taylor's Guide to Specialty Nurseries*, which Houghton Mifflin published in March, 1993. The garden is beginning to look pretty nice, and many of the tiny trees I planted when I moved here seven years ago have begun to look like more than dwarf shrubs. A very wet winter has made all the difference to my part of northern California, everything is flourishing this year. My beloved dog Alice has been joined by Sandy, a lively Australian shepherd; my cats Trout and Kelpie have made room, very grudgingly, for Phoebe. Kelpie comes and (mostly) goes, being gone at one point for a full year! Trout was chosen as one of the official spokespets for Medipet Insurance -- she's the beautiful cat in the grass in their brochure. I now have five little grandnieces and nephews, one of whom already has his own little radish patch. I'm still very happy in my little country house, and can't think of anywhere else I'd rather be.

Revising this book is always a flat out effort; in order for it to be current it has to be revised pretty much at the last minute, and then it needs more than one old librarian to get it all pulled together quickly. This time around I had the very able help of Ginny Hunt, whose horticultural knowledge has been a huge benefit. She's been very resourceful and full of good ideas, and what's more, lots of fun to work with: my gratitude to her is boundless. Computer problems and panics have been smoothed by the dear and patient Rick Ryall; I'm still a techno-dunce! As before, Kathy Spalding kept the flood of information organized and made our work much easier. My brilliant friend Nancy Jacobsen has gone on to programming glory and is writing books herself, but the program she wrote for me years ago still helps me get the job done. Many thanks to all the people who helped us track down addresses and information on elusive societies. And, as always, I'm very grateful to the businesses that let me use line drawings from their catalogs to decorate this book -- I think the drawings are just about the nicest part.

IMPORTANT INFORMATION FOR USING THIS SOURCE BOOK

This is an annotated directory of sources for everything that a gardener might want or need to purchase through the mail. My purpose is to provide you with information that will help you find what you want: this is not a "buyer's guide" which rates or recommends companies. I make every effort to describe the contents of catalogs or other sales material as fairly and accurately as I can.

This book is written primarily for gardeners in the US and Canada. You can imagine my excitement when people from all over the world began to call and write to find out how they could buy it. Because most of the readers are in North America, the information is still presented in a way which will be most useful to them, but we do give information on which companies will ship overseas, and how much gardeners overseas should send for a catalog. To reduce the confusion of foreign telephone numbers, we've tried to standardize them a bit.

WHO'S LISTED -- All of the mail-order garden businesses and organizations which met my criteria, and that I could locate and find enough information about by my cutoff date. A few previous listees have been dropped for a variety of reasons; some because of reader complaints, but most because they had gone out of business or their forwarding order had expired. In all but the few cases noted, everyone listed has been sent a questionnaire and letter asking for detailed information and their catalog or literature. For those who didn't reply fully, the notes give you all the information I could find; I'm sorry that it isn't always complete. I have always asked companies to let me know if they don't want to be listed; some companies I would love to include have asked not to be listed, or even more frustrating, have resisted all attempts to get them to reply to questionnaires and phone calls.

ADDRESSES -- When I know them, I have given both the mailing address and the sales location of the business (these are frequently the same). Please always use the first or top address given for inquiries by mail. When the nursery or shop is in a different town from the post office address, this is given in parentheses after the street address.

ABBREVIATIONS -- There's a list of the abbreviations used in the listings on the flap inside the back cover of the book; it's meant to be cut off and used as a bookmark. There is a list of state, provincial and country name abbreviations at the end of this introductory section.

CALL AHEAD or BY APPOINTMENT ONLY -- Many of the smaller businesses are run by one person who sometimes has a full-time job elsewhere and almost always has to run the mundane errands of us ordinary folk. Please honor their requests that you contact them before coming to visit, and please don't try to visit those companies that don't welcome visitors; if they don't give a sales location or other information on how to visit, they sell only by mail order.

RETAIL & WHOLESALE -- It is common for businesses to sell multiple items at a declining cost per item; many also sell "wholesale to the trade" (those who buy the merchandise for resale or other business uses). Unless I indicate that they will sell wholesale to anyone who will buy the minimum amount, do not ask to buy from a wholesale catalog unless you qualify. It's best to send your inquiry on your business letterhead.

TELEPHONE & FAX NUMBERS -- Many people have used this book as a sort of horticultural telephone directory; this year I have included many Fax numbers. Communicating by Fax is often easier and cheaper than using the phone. It lets you ask a simple question without having to call at the proper time, which is especially useful for overseas inquiries. The area code for the Fax line is the same as that for the local telephone number unless otherwise indicated. Where it says " FAX same," the Fax number is the same as the local telephone number.

TELEPHONE & FAX ORDERS -- Many companies will accept telephone or Fax orders with a credit card, which is especially convenient where foreign exchange is a problem. If you order by Fax, remember to include your credit card number, expiration date, your name and signature as they appear on the card, and your telephone number and/or Fax number. You could photocopy the blank order form from the catalog, fill it in and Fax that.

PAYMENT TO OTHER COUNTRIES -- I have tried to indicate where you may pay with international reply coupons, available at most post offices, or international money orders, available at larger post offices. Some overseas businesses and societies ask for US Bills, as the bank charges for changing foreign checks are sometimes more than the check is worth. Others will accept US personal checks, and will inform you of the amount to send. You can often charge purchases to your credit card, which automatically takes care of foreign exchange. Listed in the Suppliers section is a foreign exchange service which will issue checks in foreign currencies for a modest charge, and information on buying international money orders at the Post Office. Canadians can write checks in US dollars, and a check to Canada in US dollars is usually acceptable; you shouldn't worry about the different value of Canadian dollars for small amounts. Except as noted, all prices not in US or Canadian dollars are in the currency of the country where the business or organization is located. Orders to US or Canadian companies from overseas are usually paid by international money orders, checks in US dollars or by credit card.

SELF-ADDRESSED STAMPED ENVELOPES -- Always send a business size envelope (10 inches or 27 cm. long) as your SASE -- most of the lists will not fit into anything smaller. Also note if the business has requested more than the usual first-class postage; the list may well be too heavy for one stamp. Foreign companies that request a SASE should be sent a self-addressed long envelope and one or two international reply coupons.

PLANT AND AGRICULTURAL REGULATIONS -- You should check with local offices of your state or provincial agricultural authorities, the US Department of Agriculture or Agriculture Canada to see whether seeds, bulbs or plants from other states or countries may be imported and what permits are needed. You will notice that some companies will not ship to certain states because of agricultural regulations, and many companies will not ship to other countries for the same reason; I have tried to indicate where companies say they cannot ship. Because of regulations, companies are justified in charging a fee for the time-consuming preparation of export papers. Please do not ask companies to send you catalogs if they do not ship to your area.

ENDANGERED AND WILD-COLLECTED PLANTS -- In most cases, endangered plants are protected by state or federal laws or by international treaty. In addition to endangered and protected plants, many plants have been collected from the wild by "nurseries" specializing in "native plants." Many of these plants collected in the wild are slow to regenerate; their populations will gradually diminish because of collecting. Ethical companies indicate the sources of their rare and endangered seeds, bulbs and plants, and propagate native plants from seeds or cuttings. Look for companies that sell *nursery-propagated* native plants and bulbs -- if in doubt, ask; please don't encourage the collecting of wild or endangered species by buying suspect plants.

BOTANICAL AND COMMON NAMES -- After I've studied the catalog, I indicate whether botanical names are used, but I have not checked on the correctness or currency of the names. Some catalogs are maddeningly inconsistent, using botanical names for some plants and not for others, or making up their own fanciful common names.

It is common for herbs, fruits and vegetables to be listed by common and cultivar names, and many popular garden plants are listed by their cultivar names, frequently without botanical names. I have used the term "collectors' list" to indicate plant lists that assume knowledgeable buyers, usually listing plants only by botanical/cultivar name and having brief or no plant descriptions.

TRADE NAMES -- In the Product Sources Index I have identified trade names as either registered trademarks (R) or trademarks (TM).

NOTES ON CATALOGS -- The notes are based on a study of the catalog; if I have not received one, the notes are necessarily very brief. I have used the expressions "nice," "good," "wide," "broad" or "huge selection" to indicate the breadth of selection offered, **not** as a quality judgment on what's offered. I try to get as much information as I can into limited space, including items that cannot be included among the twelve specialties indexed. Many of these annotations don't change very much from one edition to the next -- it's so hard to cram so much information into a few lines that sometimes there's just no other way to say it. I think of myself as a master of annotation Haiku!

LISTINGS -- Being in *Gardening By Mail* costs nothing to those listed; these listing are **not** advertisements, and all the descriptions are mine, based on a study of catalogs or literature. I do ask every company that wants to be listed to fill out a detailed questionnaire every few years and to put me on their mailing list to receive a catalog every year; the choice of listings is mine alone. Companies that would like to be listed in future editions or the updates to this edition will find a form in the Practical Matters section at the back of the book. Please contact me and don't wait for me to hunt you down!

ORDERING CATALOGS or LITERATURE -- One thing businesses like to know is where their customers heard about them. To let people know that you found them in *Gardening By Mail*, I have included a form for ordering or requesting catalogs and information in Practical Matters. If you don't use the form, please tell them you read about them in *Gardening By Mail*.

Please keep in mind that catalogs and postage are expensive and request only catalogs for merchandise that is truly of interest to you, or from companies that will ship to your state or province. An avalanche of requests can be considered more disaster than benefit to a small business; please be patient and considerate of the effort that goes into offering something special and working without much help. One company asked not to be listed again because my readers "never" sent the SASE requested for a list; in such situations the company is perfectly justified in not replying to your request.

READER FEEDBACK -- Hearing from readers has been the greatest pleasure of working on this book -- you've given me both pats on the back and well aimed kicks when deserved, and a lot of good suggestions. One complaint I really don't deserve is that I enticed you into requesting more catalogs or ordering more plants than you really needed to have -- self-control is *your* problem! There's a Reader Feedback form in the Practical Matters section.

UPDATES -- We discovered with the first edition that companies constantly move, change their names and owners, or go out of business, so in order to keep the book as current as possible we started selling regular updates. For this fourth edition the updates will be issued three times a year, starting with September 1994 and ending with May 1996, for a total of six updates. The updates are cumulative, so you only need to order the most recent one. With each update ordered, you'll receive a separate sheet listing new sources, societies and magazines discovered and new books received; these are not cumulative. The Update order form is on the back of the Reader Feedback form -- see Practical Matters. Please be sure to put your name and address on the Reader Feedback/Update Order form -- I'm still holding a five dollar bill from someone in Waterbury, CT who ordered updates without putting a return address on either the form or the envelope! I marked the envelope "hold for complaint" and to my distress, I've never heard another peep.

REQUESTS FOR ADDITIONAL INFORMATION FROM TUSKER PRESS -- Tusker Press is only me, Barbara Barton, and not a huge enterprise with many researchers! I've tried to point you in the right direction with quite detailed plant and product indexing and a list of good plant finding books in the Books section. Please don't write or call to ask me where to find a specific plant or product, I just don't have the time to search them out for you.

Why do people order plants and seeds by mail? Many of us have local sources for ordinary or even unusual plants; but some of us live where few nurseries exist, others are so besotted by rarities that only specialist nurseries have what we want, and still others grow orchids or tropical fruit in greenhouses and need to order from other climates. Some of us order for reasons of perceived economy, and some for greater selection or just to have something exotic from a faraway source. Whatever the reason, there's a season of the year when only a good seed or nursery catalog can warm the gardener's heart.

I've been working with plant and seed catalogs for ten years now and have inadvertently become something of an expert on catalogs and what they convey to their readers. I'd like to share some thoughts and warnings so that you'll be happy with your purchases and avoid unpleasant experiences as much as possible.

There is a science to reading a catalog which will almost always repay you in good results. When you receive a catalog, don't go first to the plants and their prices; search first for information on the company. I always look to see if the catalog gives the name of the proprietor or someone to contact if need be; if there is no name and no telephone number, read on with increased caution. After all, these people are in business and should be willing to communicate with their customers. Some companies asked me not to put their phone numbers in this book, but most do put it on their catalogs.

Does the company list plants by correct botanical names and/or specific cultivar names? Does it guarantee that plants are true to name? Does it offer to replace plants that arrive in bad condition, and how long do you have to request a replacement? Does it tell you frankly what size the plants or bulbs you receive will be? If the plants are endangered or "native," does the company specify that their plants are nursery grown and propagated? When will it ship your plants? Beware of companies that ship live plants all year; harsh winters or hot summers can quickly ruin even healthy plants in transit, and companies shouldn't blame predictable weather problems on the carrier.

When you feel some confidence in the company, then you can study the plant lists. You will quickly notice that there are catalogs aimed at all levels of plant expertise, starting with those that list plants only by common name and topping off with catalogs that list plants only by botanical name. Each is meant for a particular audience. Catalogs aimed at unsophisticated gardeners have an obligation to give good descriptions of the plants and how to grow them; they can also educate their customers when they include the correct botanical names. Catalogs that make up fanciful common names such as "dainty little dancing alpine fairy bells" or are deliberately vague, using "Viburnum sp." for a plant they should easily be able to identify, should go to the bottom of your catalog pile.

I particularly like a catalog that gives good and honest plant descriptions. Some catalogs would have you believe that every plant they sell is perfect; the plain truth is that some varieties are much better behaved than others, some need special coddling, some reseed all over the garden, some smell not so sweet! The descriptions should offer the pros *and* the cons in addition to height and color of flower; they should also tell you something about growing the plant -- soil, exposure, hardiness, need for water, fertilizer, division and pruning; it simply isn't true that most plants will grow happily anywhere you live or under all conditions. Catalogs meant for sophisticated plant collectors do not go into such detail but can rely on the advanced knowledge of their readers.

Finally, the price! Which do you think is cheapest, the $8 plant from a reputable nursery that will replace it within a reasonable period, or the $3.95 runt that arrives half dead from a company that won't answer your letters of complaint or sends a plant in the same condition to replace it? This is an extreme example, and I hope I have eliminated companies like the latter, but we all know there's no free lunch. It's expensive to grow good plants, especially those that take years to reach shipping size.

Use your judgment about how difficult or expensive a plant is to grow. Daylilies are obviously easier to propagate than specially grafted dwarf conifers and are priced not by difficulty of propagation but by the newness and rarity of the cultivar. Plants are also priced by age and size, and if you are willing to take them small and grow them on yourself, you can save money.

When ordering plants, first try to pick a company you feel comfortable with, then place a small trial order. It's a good idea when ordering plants to be shipped at another season to include a self-addressed postcard with your order, already written for the company to fill in the blanks, stating when it received your order and confirming the amount of your payment, and when it expects to ship your order -- be sure to include the company's name and address so you won't confuse your orders.

There are fads in plants as in all things. People who enter flower shows or are hybridizers want only the newest and rarest and are willing to pay steep prices; there are usually older varieties on the same list that are just as lovely and cost a fraction of the price. If you're just starting out, or want to try a number of varieties to see what you like best, many nurseries offer special plant collections, which are usually bargains.

One reader complained because I did not describe the condition and size of plants received from each nursery. How could I possibly order a wide selection of plants from many hundreds of plant catalogs, then evaluate and grow them on to see how healthy they are? To be fair I would somehow have to order without giving my name, I'd have to have enormous test gardens and greenhouses, unlimited water and expert help; and I would have to be rich beyond my wildest dreams!

Finally, if you do have reason to complain, write to the company at once and detail your complaint. Be sure to mention the date of your order, when it was received, and what was wrong with the plant(s); keep a copies of all correspondence for your records. If you do not receive a reply within a few weeks, telephone, or photocopy your original letter and send it again with another letter. If you still receive no reply, or have ordered and paid for merchandise that did not arrive at the proper shipping season, write to the postal inspector in care of the post office where the business is located (check with the country's consulate or embassy in the case of foreign companies). I cannot straighten out consumer disputes, but I do drop companies about which I have received several complaints; please let me know of such instances. I would never knowingly list a company I suspect of being shady; such businesses don't belong in this book.

I'd love to see a day when all nursery catalogs are botanically correct, honest and forthcoming, informative, well illustrated and fun to read; in this book you'll find a good many that meet all or most of those criteria. When I'm doing the last minute scramble to pull all the last facts and details together and have a few momentary dark thoughts, I remind myself of all the dear people who answer my questionnaires and send their catalogs promptly, and of all the charming notes I've received from readers. In the end, this book is written for just two people: I include everything I'd want to find for *my own* use and pleasure, and that I'd want to pass on to *you*, my like-minded gardening friend. Enjoy this book -- you have my enthusiastic permission to mark it up and add your own notes to your heart's content! What's meant to be "beautiful" isn't always satisfying -- what's truly useful is always satisfying *and* beautiful!

© The Fragrant Path
Artist: Christine Rasmussen

State, Provincial and Country Abbreviations
Used in the Listings and Indexes

U.S. and Canada

AB	Alberta, Canada
AK	Alaska
AL	Alabama
AR	Arizona
BC	British Columbia, Canada
CA	California
CO	Colorado
CT	Connecticut
DC	District of Columbia
DE	Delaware
FL	Florida
GA	Georgia
HI	Hawaii
IA	Iowa
ID	Idaho
IL	Illinois
IN	Indiana
KS	Kansas
KY	Kentucky
LA	Louisiana
MA	Massachusetts
MB	Manitoba, Canada
MD	Maryland
ME	Maine
MI	Michigan
MN	Minnesota
MO	Missouri
MS	Mississippi
MT	Montana
NB	New Brunswick, Canada
NC	North Carolina
ND	North Dakota
NE	Nebraska
NF	Newfoundland, Canada
NH	New Hampshire
NJ	New Jersey
NM	New Mexico
NS	Nova Scotia, Canada
NV	Nevada
NY	New York

U.S. and Canada (continued)

OH	Ohio
OK	Oklahoma
ON	Ontario, Canada
OR	Oregon
PA	Pennsylvania
PE	Prince Edward Island, Canada
PQ	Province of Quebec, Canada
PR	Puerto Rico
RI	Rhode Island
SC	South Carolina
SD	South Dakota
SK	Saskatchewan, Canada
TN	Tennessee
TX	Texas
UT	Utah
VA	Virginia
VT	Vermont
WA	Washington
WI	Wisconsin
WV	West Virginia
WY	Wyoming

Overseas

Au	Australia
Cz	Czech Republic
En	England
Ge	Germany
In	India
Ja	Japan
Ne	New Zealand
No	Northern Ireland
So	South Africa
Sw	Switzerland
Wa	Wales

SAMPLE ENTRY FROM GARDENING BY MAIL

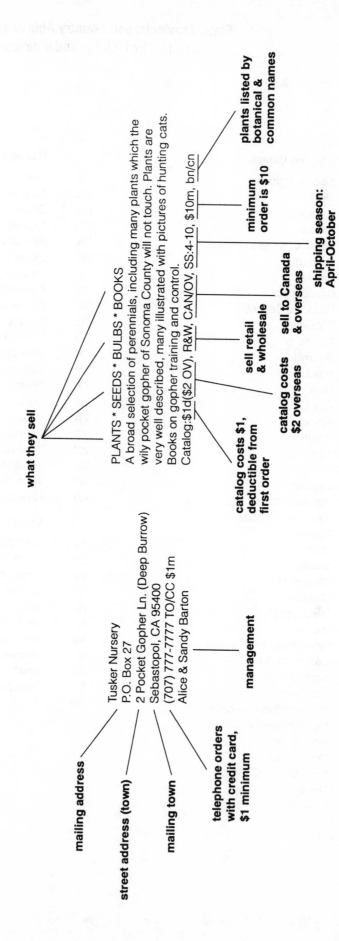

mailing address

street address (town)

mailing town

telephone orders
with credit card,
$1 minimum

management

what they sell

Tusker Nursery
P.O. Box 27
2 Pocket Gopher Ln. (Deep Burrow)
Sebastopol, CA 95400
(707) 777-7777 TO/CC $1m
Alice & Sandy Barton

PLANTS * SEEDS * BULBS * BOOKS
A broad selection of perennials, including many plants which the
wily pocket gopher of Sonoma County will not touch. Plants are
very well described, many illustrated with pictures of hunting cats.
Books on gopher training and control.
Catalog:$1d($2 OV), R&W, CAN/OV, SS:4-10, $10m, bn/cn

catalog costs $1,
deductible from
first order

sell retail
& wholesale

catalog costs
$2 overseas

sell to Canada
& overseas

minimum
order is $10

shipping season:
April-October

plants listed by
botanical &
common names

Plant and Seed Sources

Plant and seed sources are listed alphabetically; former company names or alternative names used in advertising are cross-referenced to the main listing. Specialties (plants, seeds, supplies, books, bulbs) are indicated on the top line of the notes on catalogs. If no shipping season information is given, the company will ship at any time during the year.

For display gardens, greenhouses, orchards and other plant displays, the months given are the best months to visit. Check to see whether you can visit at other times; if the nursery has regular hours, you can probably visit anytime it is open.

See the Index section for:

H. Plant Sources Index: an index of plant and seed sources by plant specialties. A two-letter code tells you which state/province/country the source is located in, so that you can order from the nearest source or a source in a similar climate zone if you like.

J. Geographical Index: an index of plant and seed sources by location. Sources in the U.S. and Canada are listed by state or province and then by city or post office; other sources are listed by country only. Symbols indicate which sources have nurseries or shops and plant displays; those without symbols sell by mail order only. Always check the main listing to see if you should call ahead or make an appointment to visit.

Other Sources of Seeds and Plants

In addition to using the sources listed, you can sometimes locate harder-to-find plants in the seed exchanges and plant sales of horticultural societies or botanical gardens. You can also place an advertisement in the "plants wanted" section of many society magazines. These are usually free, but the plant must be rare in commerce.

Many societies provide their members with lists of specialist nurseries, and there is a list of plant-finding source books in the Books section.

Finally, many gardeners are very generous with seeds and cuttings of their plants when they are properly asked—be you likewise!

A table of the symbols and abbreviations used in this book appears
on the bookmark inside the back cover.

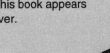

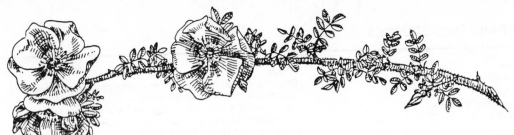

© Vintage Gardens   Artist: James Sagmiller

A & D Peony & Perennial Nursery
6808 180th S.E.
Snohomish, WA 98290
(206) 485-2487 or 668-9690 TO/CC
Don Smetana & Keith Abel

Plants
A & D Nursery is very popular with their customers in the spring when the
peonies are in bloom -- they grow about 500 cultivars, plus another 300
hostas and over 500 **daylilies**; other perennials are sold at the nursery.
Every year they list some of the many plants that they grow, a good selec-
tion with very good plant descriptions. (1969)
❐ Catalog: $1.50($2 OV), OV, SS:3-11, $30m
⌂ Nursery: Spring, daily; Summer & Fall, W-Su
♥ Garden: May-September, W-Su

A-mi Violettes
P.O. Box 630
75 Marier Street
St-Felix de Valois, PQ, Canada J0K 2M0
(514) 889-8673
MicheLyne Frechette

Plants Supplies
Specializes in **African violet leaves**, especially from hybridizers in Quebec
and Canada, but includes others; many are show winners for those who want
violets to show. Also listed are some **rex begonias and streptocarpus**, and
various growing supplies. (1987)
❐ Catalog: $2, US/OV, SS:5-10
⌂ Nursery: All year, daily, by appointment only

Abbey Gardens
4620 Carpinteria Avenue
Carpinteria, CA 93013
(805) 684-5112 or 1595, FAX 684-8235 TO/CC
Lem & Pat Higgs

Plants Books
Catalog offers a very broad selection of **cacti and succulents** to hobbyists
and collectors; some b&w photos, plants briefly described. I don't know why,
but I can't look at a cactus catalog without wanting one of everything --
they are very fascinating plants! The nursery also sells some books. (1968)
❐ Catalog: $2d, R&W, CAN/OV, SS:3-11, $20m, bn
⌂ Nursery: All year, Tu-Su
♥ Garden: March-October, Tu-Su

Abundant Life Seed Foundation
P.O. Box 772
1029 Lawrence Street
Port Townsend, WA 98368
(206) 385-5660 or 7192, FAX 385-7455
Collective

Seeds Books
"A non-profit educational foundation...raising and collecting open-pollinated
cultivars without chemicals." Offers a wide choice of seeds: **vegetables,
Northwestern native plants, Native American grains, garden flowers** and
books on many garden subjects. Bulk seed prices available. (1975)
❐ Catalog: $2, R&W, CAN/OV, bn/cn

Adagent Acres
2245 Floral Way
Santa Rosa, CA 95403
(707) 575-4459
Arnold Adams & Julius Sargent

Plants
A hobby started in 1965 with one **orchid** plant (the same old story); now
offering a good selection of paphiopedilum, cattleya, cymbidium and other
hybrids, each briefly to very well described.
❐ Catalog: $.50, CAN/OV, SS:W, $20m

Adamgrove
Route 1, Box 246
California, MO 65018
Eric Tankesley-Clarke

Plants
Catalog offers a huge selection of bearded, beardless, Siberian, arilbred,
Louisiana and species **irises**, all well described, with some cultural
information. Also offers a somewhat smaller selection of **daylilies**, both
diploid and tetraploid, and some **herbaceous peonies**, too. (1983)
❐ Catalog: $3d($6 OV), CAN/OV, SS:7-9, $15m

Adams County Nursery, Inc.
P.O. Box 108
26 Nursery Lane
Aspers, PA 17304
(717) 677-8105, FAX 677-4124 TO/CC
John H. Baugher

Plants
Offers a broad variety of **fruit** -- apples, pears, peaches and nectarines,
sweet and sour cherries, plums and apricots, on a variety of rootstocks for
various growing conditions, for both home gardeners and large commercial
growers. Informative catalog; no peaches, nectarines or plums to CA. (1905)
❐ Catalog: Free, R&W, CAN/OV, SS:11,3-5, $40m
⌂ Nursery: All year, M-F

Adventures in Herbs
P.O. Box 23240
Mint Hill, NC 28227
(704) 882-2669, 545-7665 TO/CC
Virginia Frazier & Brenda Dills

Plants
A small family business, offering a good selection of **herbs**, ornamental,
culinary, fragrant and medicinal, including scented geraniums. Plants are
listed by common name, with no plant descriptions: artemisias, lavenders,
mints, rosemarys, thymes and more. (1991)
❐ Catalog: Long SASE, R&W, CAN/OV, cn
⌂ Nursery: March-June, daily, call ahead
♥ Garden: June, September-October, call ahead

African Queen
2351 Ballycastle Drive
Dallas, TX 75228
(214) 320-4944, FAX 320-4944
Margery & Mark Clive

Plants
Offer a good selection of **African violets and other gesneriads**, mostly "diminutive" plants for terrariums and container gardens. They offer their own "Nubian" series, and represent local African violet hybridizers. Also sell small ficus plants and small leaved ivies. Brief descriptions. (1991)
❏ Catalog: $2, CAN, SS:4-10, $15m

Air Expose
4703 Leffingwell Street
Houston, TX 77026-3434
George Haynes III

Plants
Offers a wide selection of **hibiscus**, both subtropical and hardy, and **bougainvillea**, described only by size and color of flowers. (1981)
❏ Catalog: Long SASE, R&W, CAN/OV, $20m
⌂ Nursery: June-September, Sa-Su, by appointment only
▼ Garden: June-September, Sa-Su, by appointment only

Aitken's Salmon Creek Garden
608 N.W. 119th Street
Vancouver, WA 98685
(206) 573-4472, FAX 576-7012
Terry & Barbara Aitken

Plants
"Hybridize and sell all varieties of **bearded irises** in addition to a selection of Japanese, Siberians, Pacific Coast Natives and a few species irises." They will be offering orchids before long. A wide selection with plants very briefly described, some shown in color and b&w photos. (1978)
❏ Catalog: $2, R&W, CAN/OV, SS:7-9, $15m
⌂ Nursery: April-October, daily
▼ Garden: April-June, daily

Alberta Nurseries & Seed Company
P.O. Box 20
Bowden, AB, Canada T0M 0K0
(403) 224-3544, FAX 224-2455 TO/CC
Ed Berggren

Plants ∾ Seeds ∾ Supplies
Offers a good selection of **vegetable and flower seeds** to the US and Canada and general nursery stock only in Canada; varieties are specially selected for short-season climates. Also sells general growing supplies. (1922)
❏ Catalog: Free($2 US), US, SS:4-5
⌂ Nursery: All year, M-Sa

Alberts & Merkel Bros., Inc.
2210 S. Federal Highway
Boynton Beach, FL 33435-7799
(407) 732-2071
J. L. Merkel

Plants
Specializes in **orchids, bromeliads and other tropical foliage plants**. Issues three catalogs at $1 each; request catalog of orchids, bromeliads or other tropical plants. (1890)
❏ Catalog: See notes, CAN/OV
⌂ Nursery: All year, M-Sa
▼ Garden: All year, greenhouse

Alfrey Seeds -- Peter Pepper Seeds
P.O. Box 415
Knoxville, TN 37917
Hershel & Evelyn Alfrey

Seeds
List of **unusual hot and sweet peppers**, also okra, luffas and gourds, castor beans (as a deterrent to moles) and some **novelty tomatoes**; plants briefly described, some photographs. Offers a **pepper tomato** that looks like a bell pepper, but is hollow for stuffing. (1977)
❏ Catalog: Long SASE, CAN

Alice's Violet Room
Route 6, Box 233
Waynesville, MO 65583
(314) 336-4763 TO
Alice Pittman

Plants
List features **African violets** from many well-known hybridizers, both latest introductions and older favorites, including trailers, miniatures and semi-miniatures; a broad selection, plants are briefly described. Also sells leaves. (1980)
❏ Catalog: Long SASE, R&W, SS:5-10
⌂ Nursery: All year, daily, call ahead

Allen Plant Company
P.O. Box 310
Fruitland, MD 21826-0310
(410) 742-7123, FAX 742-7120 TO/CC
Richard & Nancy Allen

Plants
Color catalog of **strawberries, 'Jersey Knight' asparagus** (99.5% male), **raspberries, blueberries** and **thornless blackberries**; plants are well described with growing suggestions. Check with local agricultural authorities about ordering from out of state -- some have strict regulations. (1885)
❏ Catalog: Free, R&W, SS:11-6, $9m
⌂ Nursery: All year, M-F, call ahead

Allen, Sterling & Lothrop
191 US Route 1
Falmouth, ME 04105
Shirley Brannigan, Mgr.

Seeds ∾ Supplies
Catalog offers a good selection of **short-season vegetables**, annual and perennial flowers, all well described with cultural suggestions. They also sell growing and greenhouse supplies, fertilizers and supplies for canning and basket-making! (1911)
❏ Catalog: $1d
⌂ Nursery: All year, M-Sa

Allwood Bros.
Mill Nursery
Hassocks, W. Sussex, England BN6 9NB
(0273) 84-4229
W. Rickaby

Seeds
This firm is famous for its hybrid **dianthus and carnations**. Catalog lists
the seed of over 30 species and hybrids. Also offers a special plant support
for taller growing carnations and Rickaby's "Allwood's Guide to Perpetual
Flowering Carnations," a 22-page pamphlet (£1.65 ppd. OV). (1911)
❒ Catalog: $1(US Bills), cn/bn

Aloha Tropicals
13674 Soper Avenue
Chino, CA 91710
(909) 627-2007
Murray Laird

Plants
Small company offers **palms and cycads**, the palms divided into palms and
tender palms: no plant descriptions. Most plants available as seedlings and
in one gallon pots, some available in five gallon pots. (1990)
❒ Catalog: Long SASE, R&W, CAN, SS:3-11, $20m, bn

Alpen Gardens
173 Lawrence Lane
Kalispell, MT 59901-4633
(406) 257-2540 TO/CC
Bill & Lois McClaren

Plants
"Specializing in early varieties, new introductions and cream-of-the-crop
dahlias." A collectors' list that gives brief descriptions of each variety
and stars their top choices; plants listed by size and type of flower. (1979)
❒ Catalog: Free, CAN/OV
⌂ Nursery: All year, daily, call ahead
▼ Garden: August-September, growing area, call ahead

Alpine Gardens & Calico Shop
12446 County F
Stitzer, WI 53825
(608) 822-6382
Charlotte Nelson

Plants
A nice selection of sedums, sempervivums and jovibarbas and other **alpine
plants**, listed only by botanical name with no plant descriptions. All are
grown outside all year in Wisconsin, so they're very hardy. Cannot ship to
AZ, CA, OR or WA. (1976)
❒ Catalog: $2, R&W, SS:3-9, $15m
⌂ Nursery: March-October, daily, call ahead
▼ Garden: May-June, daily, call ahead

Alpine Valley Gardens
2627 Calistoga Road
Santa Rosa, CA 95404
(707) 539-1749
Wilbur & Dorothy Sloat

Plants
Alpine Valley Gardens is my local **daylily** nursery, and I've very much
enjoyed following Dolly Sloat through the fields with her digging fork. They
offer a good selection, nearly 500 varieties, very briefly described
in informative tables. (1979)
❒ Catalog: Long SASE, $10m
⌂ Nursery: June-July, daily, call ahead
▼ Garden: June-July, daily, call ahead

Alplains
32315 Pine Crest Court
Kiowa, CO 80117
(303) 621-2247
Alan D. Bradshaw

Seeds
A very good selection of hard-to-find **Rocky Mountain natives, alpine** and
rock garden plants and unusual **perennials**, each very well described.
Source location given for many of the habitat collected seeds. (1989)
❒ Catalog: $1d(2 IRC OV), CAN/OV, bn
▼ Garden: May-September, by appointment only

Jacques Amand, Bulb Specialists
P.O. Box 59001
Potomac, MD 20859
(301) 762-6601, (800) 452-5414
Elaine M. Wiggers, Mgr.

Bulbs
Now with an order department in the US, Amand is a well-known British supplier of **spring- and summer-blooming bulbs** offering a broad selection of
alliums, colchicums, crocus, cyclamen, fritillaries, hybrid and species
lilies, daffodils, tulips and others. Each plant is briefly described, some
shown in color. Orders shipped from England at no extra charge. (1930)
❒ Catalog: Free, R&W, CAN/OV, SS:9-12, $25m, bn

Amaryllis, Inc.
P.O. Box 318
1452 Glenmore Avenue
Baton Rouge, LA 70821
(504) 924-5560 or 4521 TO/CC
Ed Beckham

Bulbs
Offers a broad variety of named hybrid and species **amaryllis** from Holland
and India; some shown in color photos, very brief plant descriptions. (1942)
❒ Catalog: $1, R&W, CAN, SS:9-5, $15m
⌂ Nursery: All year, call ahead

Ambergate Gardens
8015 Krey Avenue
Waconia, MN 55387
(612) 443-2248, FAX same
Michael & Jean Heger

Plants
Small nursery specializing in **Martagon lilies** and other hardy **perennials,
native plants and ornamental grasses**, some of them unusual, as well as a
good selection of **hostas**; all plants are well described. They also supply
durable custom-engraved plastic plant labels. (1985)
❒ Catalog: $2, CAN, SS:4-5,8-9, $25m, bn/cn
⌂ Nursery: April-October, Tu-Su, call ahead
▼ Garden: May-September, Tu-Su, call ahead

Amberway Gardens
5803 Amberway Drive
St. Louis, MO 63128
(314) 842-6103
Sue & Ken Kremer

Plants
Offers a broad selection of **iris of all types**: tall, median and dwarf
bearded, Japanese, Siberian, and Louisiana, horned, reblooming and some
species. There's only room for the briefest descriptions. (1988)
◻ Catalog: $1.25d ($2 OV), CAN/OV, SS:7-9, $15m
▼ Garden: April-June, September-October, Sa-Su, call ahead

Ameri-Hort Research
P.O. Box 1529
Medina, OH 44258
(216) 723-4966
Peter & Karen Murray

Plants
Offers the **lilac** introductions of the late Fr. John Fiala of Falconskeape
Gardens. The plants are well described, and a number of them are shown in his
book "Lilacs: the Genus Syringa" (Timber Press, 1988). Twelve cultivars are
offered as liners or single potted plants.
◻ Catalog: $2

American Bamboo Company
345 W. Second Street
Dayton, OH 45402
Todd Mumma

Plants
Sells rhizomes of **timber bamboo** hardy in Northern climes -- Phyllostachys
bissettii and other species. Availability list issued in January. (1956)
◻ Catalog: Free, SS:4, bn

American Daylily & Perennials
P.O. Box 210
Grain Valley, MO 64029
(816) 224-2852, FAX 443-2849 TO/CC
Jack & Jo Roberson

Plants
Color catalog of **daylilies and cannas** (many are their own introductions)
and a nice selection of their hybrid **lantanas** in a variety of colors; all
varieties are illustrated and well described. They also offer some herbaceous peonies, and almost ever-blooming "Landscape Supreme" daylilies. (1976)
◻ Catalog: $3d, R&W, SS:4-11, $15m

American Forest Foods Corp.
P.O. Box 81
Townsville, NC 27584
(919) 438-2674
T.J. Farris & Marlene Smith

Seeds
This company sells certified and inspected spawn for growing **shiitake** and
oyster mushrooms; they have written a booklet, "Forest Mushroom Farming and
Gardening," on how to grow shiitake. They also buy mushrooms from growers
under contract and market dried mushrooms nationwide. (1982)
◻ Catalog: $1d, R&W, CAN/OV, SS:9-5
⌂ Nursery: All year, M-Sa, call ahead

Ames' Orchard & Nursery
18292 Wildlife Road
Fayetteville, AR 72701
(501) 443-0282
Guy & Carolyn Ames

Plants
Offers a variety of **fruit trees, grapes and berries** with emphasis on
disease resistance and tolerance in less than ideal growing conditions.
Customers are usually home gardeners or small orchardists trying to reduce
spraying. Very informative catalog: apples, pears, peaches, plums, sour
cherries and more. (1983)
◻ Catalog: 2 FCS, R&W, SS:11-4, $10m
⌂ Nursery: All year, call ahead

Anderson Iris Gardens
22179 Keather Avenue North
Forest Lake, MN 55025
(612) 433-5268 TO
Sharol Longaker

Plants
Offers a broad selection of hardy **tall bearded iris and herbaceous peonies**;
all plants are briefly described. Some iris are their own introductions,
many are recent award winners; they have added some daylilies. (1978)
◻ Catalog: $1, CAN/OV, SS:7-10, $10m
⌂ Nursery: April-October, F-Tu
▼ Garden: June-August, F-Tu

The Angraecum House
P.O. Box 976
Grass Valley, CA 95945
(916) 273-9426 TO
Fred Hillerman

Plants ⬿ Books
Specialist in **species and hybrid angraecum and aeranthes orchids** from
Africa and Madagascar. Offers two cultural manuals for $5.75 each postpaid,
as well as his own book, "Introduction to Cultivated Angraecoid Orchids of
Madagascar," for $32.95 autographed and postpaid.
◻ Catalog: Free, CAN/OV, SS:4-11, $20m, bn
⌂ Nursery: March-November, M-F, by appointment only

Annabelle's Fuchsia Garden

See Regine's Fuchsia Garden.

Antique Rose Emporium
Route 5, Box 143
Brenham, TX 77833
(409) 836-4293 or 9051, FAX 836-0928 TO/CC
Mike Shoup

Plants ⬿ Books
Color catalog offers a broad selection of **old garden roses**, each well
described, with a good deal of historical and cultural information. Roses
are grown on their own roots, selected for fragrance and long bloom in
Zones 6 and above. They also offer perennials, books and supplies. (1983)
◻ Catalog: $5, R&W, CAN/OV, SS:2-4,12
⌂ Nursery: All year, daily
▼ Garden: Spring & Fall, daily

Antonelli Brothers, Inc.
2545 Capitola Road
Santa Cruz, CA 95062
(408) 475-5222 or 8828 TO/CC $20m
Skip Antonelli

Plants ∾ Bulbs
Well known for their **tuberous begonias**, their lath houses are a glorious
sight in the summer. They offer a good selection, including hanging-basket
begonias and a number of collections. They also offer tigridias, fuchsias,
tuberoses, gladiolus, gloxinias, dahlias, ranunculus and anemones. (1935)
❑ Catalog: $1, R&W, CAN/OV, SS:1-6, $5m
⌂ Nursery: All year, daily
▼ Garden: July-September, daily

Apothecary Rose Shed
P.O. Box 194
Route 160
Pattersonville, NY 12137
(518) 887-2035
Shawn Schultz & Susan Cooper

Seeds
A nice selection of **herbs**, listed only by common name with brief plant
descriptions. At the nursery they give lectures and classes, sell herb
books, dried herbs and everlastings. (1986)
❑ Catalog: $2d, CAN, cn
⌂ Nursery: April-October, Tu-Su
▼ Garden: June-September, Tu-Su

Appalachian Gardens
P.O. Box 82
410 Westview Avenue
Waynesboro, PA 17268
(717) 762-4312, FAX 762-7532 TO/CC $25m
Tom McCloud & Ezra Grubb

Plants
Good list of **hardy ornamental trees** and **shrubs**: azaleas, holly, conifers,
dogwoods, box, berberis, viburnums, kalmias, rhododendrons; all plants very
well described, some harder to find, such as Franklinia alatamaha. (1986)
❑ Catalog: $2d, R&W, $5m, bn/cn
⌂ Nursery: All year, M-F, call ahead

Appalachian Wildflower Nursery
Route 1, Box 275A
Reedsville, PA 17084
Don Hackenberry

Plants
Small nursery specializes in **rock garden plants and garden perennials**, with
emphasis on local native plants descended from known wild colonies or plants
from Soviet Central Asia, China and Japan. Lists species iris, gentians,
phlox, primula, gaultheria, hellebores, dianthus and others. (1973)
❑ Catalog: $2d, SS:3-5,9-11, bn
⌂ Nursery: Spring to Fall, Sa, call ahead
▼ Garden: Spring to Fall, Sa, call ahead

Applesource
Route 1
Chapin, IL 62628
(217) 245-7589
Tom & Jill Vorbeck

Applesource is not a source of plants, but a service that will send you unusual varieties of both **new and antique apples** during harvest season so
that you can taste before you decide which cultivars to plant. A really
nifty idea -- even if you don't have room for a tree! Good holiday gift for
yourself or a friend. Catalog is mailed in September. (1983)
❑ Catalog: Free, SS:10-1, $18m

Arbor & Espalier
201 Buena Vista Avenue East
San Francisco, CA 94117
(415) 626-8880 or (707) 433-6420
John C. Hooper

Plants
Offers **espaliered fruit trees**; works with the Sonoma Antique Apple Nursery
and trains a wide variety of organically grown apples, pears, figs, stone
fruits, pomegranates, persimmons and guavas into classic shapes. (1985)
❑ Catalog: $2, R&W, CAN/OV, SS:1-3
⌂ Nursery: Call ahead, see notes

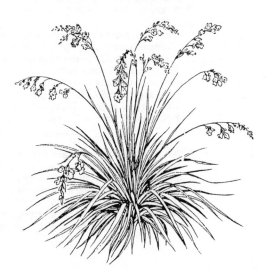

© Digging Dog Nursery
Artist: Marsha Mello

Arborvillage Farm Nursery
P.O. Box 227
Holt, MO 64048
(816) 264-3911
Lanny, Sue & Derrick Rawdon

Plants
Offers a good selection of **ornamental trees and shrubs**, including some hard to find elsewhere: species and Japanese maples, horse chestnuts, birches, hickories, real chestnuts, dogwoods, magnolias, flowering crabapples, oaks, lilacs, viburnums and conifers among others. Plants well described. (1978)
❑ Catalog: $1, CAN/OV, bn/cn
⌂ Nursery: All year, M-F, by appointment only

Archias' Seed Store
106 E. Main Street
Sedalia, MO 65301
(816) 826-1330
Henry & Nancy Stephens

Seeds ◈ Supplies
Wide selection of **vegetable seeds and some asparagus and vegetable plants**, all well described. They also sell flower seeds, plants and bulbs and **berry** plants, as well as a good selection of growing supplies, bird houses and feeders, fertilizers, insecticides and beekeeping aids. (1884)
❑ Catalog: Free, R&W, CAN/OV, SS:3-6, $5m

Jim & Jenny Archibald
"Bryn Collen"
Ffostrasol, Llandysul
Dyfed, Wales SA44 5SB

Seeds
The Archibalds are **roving seed collectors** who probably rarely get to rest their weary bones at "Bryn Collen." Their lists vary each year depending on where they've been, and what other collectors have been able to supply, but their list is always terrific, with good plant descriptions. Because they collect very carefully, seed is frequently in quite limited supply.
❑ Catalog: $3(US Bills), bn

Arena's Antique Roses
29 W. Thomas Road
Phoenix, AZ 85013
FAX (602) 230-8153
Sylvester Arena

Plants
Offers a nice selection of **old roses** suited to the hot climate of the Southwest; the roses are tested and then grafted onto Dr. Huey root-stocks. More varieties being tested for future catalogs. (1991)
❑ Catalog: Free, R&W, SS:12-4, $25m

Arrowhead Alpines
P.O. Box 857
Fowlerville, MI 48836
(517) 223-3581, FAX 223-8750
Bob & Brigitta Stewart

Plants ◈ Seeds
Life-Form Replicators married Perennial Plantation, so they picked a new name for their joint venture. This small nursery specializes in seeds and plants of **perennial and alpine plants**, and the list is broad and impressive. Some seed is imported from plant breeders in Britain, Europe and some Soviet bloc countries. (1982)
❑ Catalog: $2d, R&W, CAN, SS:W, bn
⌂ Nursery: All year, call ahead
♥ Garden: May-September, call ahead

Arrowhead Nursery
5030 Watia Road
Bryson City, NC 28713-9683
Linda Schneider

Plants
Small nursery specializing in hard-to-find **Southeastern flowering trees** and **shrubs**: redbuds, clethra, dogwoods, witch hazels, magnolias and stewartias. A growing and changing list, plants are well described. (1985)
❑ Catalog: 1 FCS, R&W, CAN/OV, bn

Artemis Gardens
170 Moss Bridge Road
Bozeman, MT 59715-9338
Cynthia E. Hyde

Plants ◈ Supplies
A Rocky Mountain nursery specializing in hardy miniature and small flowered **daylilies** and **standard dwarf bearded and dwarf bearded iris**; a very nice selection, with good plant descriptions. They also offer some nice songbird **whirligigs** that look like real birds. No shipping to AK or HI. (1989)
❑ Catalog: $1d, SS:5-8, $10m

Artistic Plants
608 Holly Drive
Burleson, TX 76028
(817) 295-0802 TO/CC $20m
Estella Flather

Plants ◈ Books ◈ Supplies ◈ Tools
A **bonsai** nursery, offering plants for bonsai, accent plants and some succulents and tropical plants for display with bonsai, all briefly described. Also sells bonsai tools, pots and books; finished bonsai, some "in training" for many years, are available at the nursery. (1985)
❑ Catalog: $1, R&W, $20m, bn
⌂ Nursery: All year, Th-Su, call ahead
♥ Garden: All year, Th-Su, call ahead

Ashwood Nurseries
Greensforge
Kingswinford, W.Mid., England DY6 0AE
(0384) 40-1996, 27-9139, FAX 40-1108
John Massey & Philip Baulk

Seeds
Seeds of **lewisia** species and hybrids; they have hybridized a number of colors not found in the species. Their catalog shows the plants in color and gives good cultural information. Also seeds of cyclamen, hellebores and auricula primulas. Seed list available in September. (1967)
❑ Catalog: $2(US Bills), R&W, US/CAN, bn
⌂ Nursery: Daily except December 25-26
♥ Garden: Daily except December 25-26

Avatar's World
9106 Hurd Road
Edgerton, WI 53534
(608) 884-4730, FAX 884-6920 TO/CC
John S. Hurd

Seeds ∾ Supplies
Offers a broad selection of seed for **cut and dried flowers**, and some really cute bird houses and other garden ornaments. They also sell dried flowers to the wholesale market. (1988)
❑ Catalog: Free, CAN/OV
⌂ Nursery: All year, M-F (Closed 12/22-1/1)
▼ Garden: Summer, M-F

Avid Gardener

See Springvale Farm Nursery.

Avon Bulbs
Burnt House Farm, Mid-Lambrook
South Petherton, England TA13 5HE
Chris Ireland-Jones

Bulbs
Source for many **spring and summer-blooming bulbs**: alliums, calanthe, crocosmia, galanthus, pleione, lilies, hardy cyclamen, arums, colchicums, crocus, fritillaries, erythronium, species gladiolus, irises, tulips, narcissus and trilliums. Plants well described, some shown in color; an import permit is needed for some, a CITES certificate needed for others. (1979)
❑ Catalog: $5(US Bills), OV, SS:3,10, $50m, bn

Aztekakti

see Desertland Nursery.

B & D Lilies
330 P Street
Port Townsend, WA 98368
(206) 385-1738, FAX 385-9996 TO/CC $20m
Bob & Dianna Gibson

Bulbs
Offers a broad selection of **hybrid and species lilies** and several special collections of lilies; each is well described, many are shown in color. A second catalog lists their "heirloom" collection, tried and true hybrids which perform well in home gardens. Also sells alstroemerias and daylilies.
❑ Catalog: $3d, R&W, CAN, SS:10-12, bn
⌂ Nursery: July-August, daily, call ahead
▼ Garden: July-August, daily, by appointment only

B & T World Seeds
Whitnell House, Fiddington
Bridgewater, Somerset, England TA5 1JE
(0278) 73-3209, FAX Same
David Sleigh

Seeds
Seed for thousands of species of **tropical and subtropical plants**: fruit, cactus, palms, proteas, bromeliads, carnivorous plants, flowering trees and shrubs. They publish seed lists in 160 categories; for two International Reply Coupons they'll send a list of seed lists. Their alphabetical species list with 25,000 entries sells for $20. Many seeds are collected to order and sent when viable; tell them what you're looking for. (1985)
❑ Catalog: 2 IRC, R&W, OV, $5m, bn

Bailey's
P.O. Box 654
Edmonds, WA 98020
(206) 774-7528
Larry A. Bailey

Plants
Small nursery specializes in **exhibition auriculas and Juliana hybrid primulas**; plants very briefly described. You can also make special requests for other hybrid and species primulas. (1981)
❑ Catalog: Free, SS:4-5,9-10, bn

Baker & Chantry Orchids
P.O. Box 554
18611-132nd Street N.E.
Woodinville, WA 98072
(206) 483-0345 TO/CC $20m
Gary Baker, Will Chantry & Dennis Kleinback

Plants
Offers many types of **hybrid orchids** -- masdevallia, paphiopedilum, miltonia, cattleya, brassia, dracula, pleurothallid -- and also many **species orchids**. List doesn't cover all the types, so send your "want list" for items not listed. (1978)
❑ Catalog: Long SASE w/ 2FCS, SS:W
⌂ Nursery: All year, daily
▼ Garden: All year, greenhouse, daily

Balash Gardens
26595 H Drive North
Albion, MI 49224
(517) 629-5997
Nicholas Balash

Plants
Nick Balash is a hybridizer and grower of "new and expensive" cultivars of **daylilies**, but don't be put off, he offers a number of daylilies at quite reasonable prices. too. Good brief plant descriptions, but no date of introduction given. (1984)
❑ Catalog: $1d, R&W, CAN, SS:4-5,8-10, $35m
⌂ Nursery: April-September, daily
▼ Garden: July, by appointment only

Bamboo Gardens of Washington
5016 192nd Place NE
Redmond, WA 98053-4602
(206) 868-5166
Daphne & Doug Lewis

Plants ∾ Supplies
Formerly Bamboo Brokerage, Inc., this nursery offers a nice selection of **bamboos** and **waterlilies**, all well described, as well as bamboo poles, fences and other products, and Japanese style stoneware and fountains. (1986)
❑ Catalog: $4, R&W, CAN/OV, bn
⌂ Nursery: All year, daily
▼ Garden: All year, daily

A Bamboo Shoot
1462 Darby Road
Sebastopol, CA 95472
(707) 823-0131
Richard Waters

Plants
Good selection of **bamboo**, both clumping and running, from timber to pygmy, hardy and tropical, listed by botanical and common name. Send $1 bill for catalog in the US. (1985)
❏ Catalog: $1($2 OV), R&W, CAN/OV, $50m, bn/cn

Bamboo Sourcery
666 Wagnon Road
Sebastopol, CA 95472
(707) 823-5866 or 1649, FAX 829-8106
Gerald Bol

Plants
Collectors' list of **bamboos** -- 100 varieties, listed by botanical and cultivar name with good descriptions and cultural information -- available in one-gallon or larger containers. Some are quite rare, some are non-invasive and make handsome garden ornamentals, others make good indoor plants. New introductions are available every year. (1985)
❏ Catalog: $2, CAN/OV, $20m, bn
⌂ Nursery: By appointment only
▼ Garden: By appointment only

The Banana Tree
715 Northampton Street
Easton, PA 18042
(215) 253-9589, FAX 253-4864 TO/CC $25m
Fred Saleet

Seeds
Seeds of a wide selection of **tropical plants** for collectors and "astute growers of tropicals"; offers many types of bananas and other tropical fruits, ferns and bromeliads, palms, gingers, proteas, phormiums, cashews carambola and much more; all plants are well described. Also rhizomes of **heliconia** and the "tuber-like bulbs" of **bananas**. Sells plants at the nursery. (1960)
❏ Catalog: $3, R&W, CAN/OV, $7m, bn
⌂ Nursery: All year, daily, by appointment only

Barber Nursery
13118 Pantano Drive
Houston, TX 77065
(713) 894-2430, 279-2074
William Barber

Plants
Nice selection of **seedling trees and shrubs** -- conifers, maples, oaks and ornamental southern species -- listed by botanical and common name only. Small plants at reasonable prices, most grown from seed collected in Texas, Louisiana and Arkansas; Bill says most are fairly hardy. (1978)
❏ Catalog: Free, R&W, CAN/OV, SS:11-4, $25m, bn/cn
⌂ Nursery: All year, daily, call ahead
▼ Garden: All year, daily, call ahead

Barnhaven Primroses
Langerhouad
Plouzelambre, France 22420
(33) 9635-3154, FAX 9635-3155
Angela Bradford

Seeds
Florence Bellis' **primroses** have moved from England to Normandy in France, but are still in good hands. Angela Bradford is still producing seed by hand-pollination, some from pure strains selected and bred over 50 years ago. The selection and plant descriptions are very good. Hurrah! Orders can be paid in British pounds, French francs or by credit card. (1990)
❏ Catalog: $1(US Bills), OV
⌂ Nursery: February-November, call ahead
▼ Garden: Spring, call ahead

Bastrop Botanical
P.O. Box 628
Bastrop, TX 78602
(512) 321-7161 or 4145
Dianna & Archie Butler, Richard Laird

Plants
An **orchid** seed flasking lab, which also does micropropagation of **carnivorous plants**; they're species specialists. Ask for the species list, flask list, or carnivorous plants and tropicals list. I saw only the flask list, which offers a good selection with very brief plant descriptions. (1992)
❏ Catalog: Free, R&W, CAN/OV, bn
⌂ Nursery: By appointment only

Bay Laurel Nursery
2500 El Camino Real
Atascadero, CA 93422
(805) 466-3406
Jim Patterson & Kristie Wells

Plants
Offers a broad selection of **fruit trees**, including many new varieties from Zaiger Genetics -- including their inter-specific hybrids: fruit trees available on a variety of rootstocks. Also lists **berries, wine and table grapes**, and some ornamental trees and shrubs. Good plant descriptions.
❏ Catalog: Free, SS:1-3
⌂ Nursery: All year, daily

Bay View Gardens
1201 Bay Street
Santa Cruz, CA 95060
Joseph Ghio

Plants ⬥ Seeds
A broad selection of **irises**: tall bearded, Louisiana, spuria and very special Pacific Coast Natives; plants are well described. Joe Ghio is a well-known hybridizer, and winner of many AIS awards. Also sells collections and even "surprise packages" at season's end. (1965)
❏ Catalog: $2($3 OV), CAN/OV, SS:7-10, $20m

Baycreek Gardens
P.O. Box 339
Grayson, GA 30221-0339
(404) 339-1600, 963-8227, FAX 339-0899 TO/CC
Andrew Reece, Mgr.

Plants
This is the retail arm of a wholesale nursery, specializing in landscape sized plants as well as smaller sizes; **azaleas, conifers, hollies, crape myrtles, flowering trees and shrubs** and some **perennials**. Also sells trays of 18 Zoysia grass plugs. Cannot ship to AZ, CA, OR or WA. (1990)
❏ Catalog: Free, R&W, $25m, bn/cn
⌂ Nursery: All Year, M-F, Sa in Spring & Fall
▼ Garden: All Year, M-F

Bear Creek Nursery
P.O. Box 411
Northport, WA 99157-0411
Donna & Hunter Carleton

Plants ∾ Tools
"**Hardy fruits, nuts, shrubs and rootstocks** for the home gardener and orchardist." Large selection of antique apples, berries and hardy nut trees; good plant descriptions and cultural information. Specializes in cold-hardy and drought-resistant stock -- trees and shrubs for windbreaks, wildlife and hardwood; also sells pruning tools. (1979)
❏ Catalog: Free, R&W, SS:2-5,10-11, cn/bn
⌂ Nursery: January-May, October-November, by appointment only

Beaver Creek Nursery
7526 Pelleaux Road
Knoxville, TN 37938
(615) 922-3961
Mike Stansberry

Plants
Specializes in collectors' **trees and shrubs**: species maples, stewartias, viburnums, magnolias, kalmias, hollies, mildew-resistant crape myrtles and other ornamental plants, most of them Southern natives. A good selection; each plant well described. Some of the plants are quite recent introductions. Cannot ship to CA, OR or WA. (1986)
❏ Catalog: $1, SS:W, $20m, bn/cn
⌂ Nursery: March-November, Th-Sa or by appointment
♥ Garden: March-November, Th-Sa

Becker's Seed Potatoes
RR 1
Trout Creek, ON, Canada P0H 2L0
(705) 724-2305
Murray & Sharon Becker

Plants ∾ Books
Offers 38 varieties of **seed potatoes**, listed by maturity date and well described by flavor and use. Also offers "garden packs" -- ten eyes each of four varieties that will mature over a long period, and a few books on potatoes. May resume shipping to the US in 1994; call and ask. (1985)
❏ Catalog: Free, R&W, SS:4, $6m

Bedford Dahlias
65 Leyton Road
Bedford, OH 44146
(216) 232-2852
Eugene A. Woznicki

Plants
Offers a good selection of **dahlias**, many of them newer introductions and show varieties, some imported from England and Japan. Most varieties are well described; they are shipped at the time you specify. (1980)
❏ Catalog: 1 FCS, CAN/OV, SS:1-5

Berton Seeds Company, Ltd.
151 Toryork Dr., Unit 20
Weston, ON, Canada M9L 1X9
(416) 745-5655, FAX same
Walter Berton

Seeds
A nice selection of **vegetable seed from Italy**, ask for their free packet list. Packets are $1.19 each, with a $2 handling charge for orders less than $10. Wholesale buyers should order their color catalog for $12. (1977)
❏ Catalog: See notes, R&W, US/OV, $10m

Betsy's Brierpatch
1610 Ellis Hollow Road
Ithaca, NY 14850
(607) 273-6266
Elizabeth Mann

Plants
Offers a variety of **cacti and succulents**; each plant is well described, with some cultural information. (1980)
❏ Catalog: Long SASE, SS:4-10, bn/cn

Big Sky Violets
10678 Schoolhouse Lane
Moiese, MT 59824
(406) 644-2296
Angelika Brooks

Plants ∾ Supplies
Offers a good selection of **African violet** hybrids, listed by hybridizer, with a few miscellaneous varieties, and some streptocarpus and episcias, all briefly described. In addition to plants and leaves, they offer growing supplies, pots and lighted plant stands. (1986)
❏ Catalog: $2d ($5 OV), R&W, CAN/OV, SS:5-10, $12m
⌂ Nursery: All year, call ahead

Big Tree Daylily Garden
777 General Hutchison Parkway
Longwood, FL 32750-3705
(407) 831-5430
Kathleen Chenet

Plants
Offers a large selection of **daylilies**, mostly recent introductions judging from the prices. They also offer a number of older varieties if you're not the sort who has to have the newest or the most fashionable, or want to use new introductions for hybridizing. All plants are briefly described. (1964)
❏ Catalog: $2($3 OV), CAN/OV, SS:3-10
⌂ Nursery: March-October, daily, call ahead
♥ Garden: Spring-Summer, call ahead

Bigfoot
P.O. Box 1025
324 Shamrock Lane
Blue Lake, CA 95525
(707) 668-4136
Robert Filbey & Catherine Zakoron

Plants
Small family nursery, "more a collection gone mad than a nursery!" Offers a very nice selection of **cacti and succulents, old garden roses, heaths** and **heathers** and some perennials. Will custom propagate from their collection. Plants briefly described, some may be in short supply. (1988)
❏ Catalog: $1, R&W, bn
⌂ Nursery: All year, daily, by appointment only

Bijou Alpines
13921 240th Street E.
Graham, WA 98338-8615
(206) 893-6191
Mark D. Dusek

Plants
A specialist in **rock garden and alpine plants**: herbaceous perennials, ferns, dwarf trees and shrubs, and dwarf and slow growing conifers. A good selection, all plants are well described with letter codes for appropriate use. Mark will also do custom propagation. (1989)
❑ Catalog: $1, SS:3-5,9-11, $15m, bn
⌂ Nursery: March-June, September-October, F-Sa, call ahead
▼ Garden: By appointment only

Bio-Quest International
P.O. Box 5752
Santa Barbara, CA 93150-5752
(805) 969-4072 TO
Dr. Richard Doutt

Bulbs
Specializes in **South African bulbs** -- collectors' list offers a good selection of bulbs, mostly from Cape Province. Small but choice selections -- babiana, lachenalia, ixia, moraea, gladiolus, watsonia and many more. Seed is collected on special order; archival collection is listed. (1980)
❑ Catalog: $2, OV, SS:6-9,11-12, $10m, bn
⌂ Nursery: All year, daily, by appointment only

Birch Farm Nursery
Gravetye
East Grinstead, England RH19 4LE
(0342) 81-0236
M. P. Ingwersen

Seeds
One of the best-known nurseries in England, specializing in **alpine and rock garden** plants. They publish a seed list, on which you would be sure to find desirable plants -- they also ship plants outside Great Britain, with $100 minimum. The seed list is 2 IRC to the US, 1 IRC to Europe; the plant catalog is £1, $2 or 5 IRC. Specify which list you want. (1926)
❑ Catalog: See notes, US/CAN, bn
⌂ Nursery: March-October, daily; November-February, M-F
▼ Garden: March-May, daily

Bird Rock Tropicals
6523 El Camino Real
Carlsbad, CA 92009
(619) 438-9393, FAX 438-1316 TO/CC
Pamela Koide

Plants
A collectors' list of species and hybrid **tillandsias**, and some **vrieseas**. A very broad selection, adding more all the time; no plant descriptions. Plants available individually or mounted in a variety of ways. (1981)
❑ Catalog: Long SASE, R&W, CAN/OV, $25m, bn
⌂ Nursery: All year, M-F
▼ Garden: Summer, M-F

Bisnaga Cactus Nursery

See New Mexico Cactus Research.

Black Copper Kits
111 Ringwood Avenue
Pompton Lakes, NJ 07442
Harold Welsh

Plants ⬿ Supplies
Offers a small selection of **carnivorous plants**, terrarium supplies, leaflets and growing supplies; plants not described. (1978)
❑ Catalog: 1 FCS, SS:2-11, $5m, cn/bn

Bloomingfields Farm
Route 55
Gaylordsville, CT 06755-0005
(203) 354-6951 TO/CC
Lee Bristol

Plants
Daylilies listed by color with an index of cultivar names; plants are very well described, with season of bloom and cultural hints given. Offers a broad selection, quantity discounts and several collections for a long season of bloom. (1969)
❑ Catalog: Free($1 OV), CAN/OV, SS:4-11
⌂ Nursery: June-August, F-Su pm
▼ Garden: July-August, F-Su pm

Blossom Valley Gardens
15011 Oak Creek Road
El Cajon, CA 92021-2328
Sanford & Patricia Roberts

Plants
Specializes in tetraploid **daylilies**, mostly his own and the recent introductions of other hybridizers whose daylilies are in demand for hybridizing; this is reflected in the prices. There is a great demand for these among the daylily underground; each is well described in a chatty list. (1982)
❑ Catalog: $1, SS:3-6,9-10, $25m

Blossoms & Bloomers
E. 11415 Krueger Lane
Spokane, WA 99207
(509) 922-1344
Geraldine Krueger

Plants
Gerry says she's "located in serious winter country" and has turned away from hybrid tea roses to the **hardy old roses**. She offers own-root plants from her collection of over 250 old roses, the list changes each year as she propagates different plants. Also offers a few honeysuckles for hummingbirds. All plants well described; can't ship to CA, FL or PR. (1988)
❑ Catalog: $1, SS:4-5
⌂ Nursery: May-June, F-Su, or by appointment
▼ Garden: May-June, F-Su, by appointment only

Blue Ridge Gardens
2770 Mattson Road
Coos Bay, OR 97420
Michael & Kathy Iler

Plants
A new nursery offering a good selection of hybrid **fuchsias**, both old and new cultivars, divided into "uprights" and "trailing." Each plant is well described, with name of hybridizer, country of origin and date of introduction. (1993)
❑ Catalog: $2d, CAN/OV, SS:4-10

Bluebird Haven Iris Garden
6940 Fairplay Road
Somerset, CA 95684
(209) 245-5017
Mary Hess

Plants
Small nursery in the California Mother Lode offers many types of **iris**, from dwarf to tall bearded, reblooming and horned, all briefly described. If you're interested in "antique iris" (pre-1964 varieties), send a long SASE with two first class stamps for a list -- offers many of these, too. (1980)
☐ Catalog: $1, SS:7-8, $10m
⌂ Nursery: April-May, July-September, Tu-Su
▼ Garden: April-May, Tu-Su

Bluebird Orchard & Nursery
429 E. Randall Street
Coopersville, MI 49404
(616) 837-9598
Timothy Strickler

Plants
Small nursery sells **new and antique apple varieties** grafted onto various rootstocks, and also offers scion wood for grafting. They have a collection of about 200 varieties, and will do custom grafting. (1982)
☐ Catalog: Long SASE, SS:3-4,10-11, $15m

Kurt Bluemel, Inc.
2740 Greene Lane
Baldwin, MD 21013
(410) 557-7229, FAX 557-9785
Kurt Bluemel

Plants
A very extensive list of **ornamental grasses, sedges and rushes**, as well as **perennials, bamboos, ferns and aquatic plants**, and some new imports. All very briefly described, with hardiness zones. There are also useful tables listing grasses by desirable traits and for specific purposes. (1964)
☐ Catalog: $3, R&W, CAN/OV, SS:3-5, $25m, bn/cn
⌂ Nursery: All year, by appointment only
▼ Garden: All year, by appointment only

Bluestem Prairie Nursery
Route 2, Box 106-A
Hillsboro, IL 62049
(217) 532-6344
Ken Schaal

Plants ⬿ Seeds
Specializes in **prairie plants** of the Midwest, especially Illinois; a good selection of plants, and a larger selection of seeds of prairie plants and grasses. No plant descriptions except for color of flower, height and preferred habitat. (1985)
☐ Catalog: Free, R&W, SS:3-5
▼ Garden: By appointment only

Bluestone Perennials
7211 Middle Ridge Road
Madison, OH 44057
(216) 428-7535, (800) 852-5243, FAX 428-7198
Richard & William Boonstra

Plants
A broad selection of **hardy perennials**. They seem to specialize in chrysanthemums, sedums and ground covers, but offer a choice of many other plants for a perennial border and some shrubs; good plant descriptions with cultural information and color photos. Small plants at moderate prices. (1972)
☐ Catalog: Free, R&W, SS:3-6,8-11, bn/cn
⌂ Nursery: March-June, August-October, M-F

Robert Bolton & Son
Birdbrook
Halstead, Essex, England CO9 4BQ
(0440) 85-246
C. M. & R. J. Bolton, E.M. Filbey

Seeds
Bolton's are **sweet pea** specialists and hybridizers; they offer a good selection of cultivars, each well described. They also offer a number of collections of favorite cultivars and mixed color packets. (1901)
☐ Catalog: Free, R&W, OV
▼ Garden: June-July, call for hours

Bonnie Brae Gardens
1105 S.E. Christensen Road
Corbett, OR 97019
(503) 695-5190
Frank & Jeanie Driver

Bulbs
A nice selection of show quality **novelty daffodils**; varieties described by name, class and hybridizer with very brief personal comments and descriptions of growth habit and season of bloom. Many of the varieties are good naturalizers. Seller pays postage in the US. (1984)
☐ Catalog: Long SASE, CAN/OV, SS:9-10, $10m
▼ Garden: March-April, call ahead

Bonsai Farm
13827 Highway 87 South
Adkins, TX 78101
(210) 649-2109 TO/CC $10m
Jerry A. Sorge

Plants ⬿ Books ⬿ Supplies ⬿ Tools
List offers a number of plants to use for **bonsai**, both indoor and outdoor, as well as a large selection of bonsai supplies -- pots, tools, planting supplies, soil amendments, bonsai display stands and books. Plants very well described. (1971)
☐ Catalog: $1d, $10m, cn/bn
⌂ Nursery: 2nd Sa-Su each month, daily in December, by appt.

The Bonsai Shop
43 William Street
Smithtown, NY 11787
Rhys & Kathy O'Brien

Plants ⬿ Supplies ⬿ Tools
Specialize in finished **bonsai**; several examples are shown in color, though not all plants will look just like them. They also have a video catalog available; it's $5.95, deductible from your first order. They sell many more bonsai at the nursery, along with books, tools and growing supplies. (1986)
☐ Catalog: $2d, R&W, CAN, SS:W, $50m, cn
⌂ Nursery: By appointment only
▼ Garden: By appointment only

Boothe Hill Wildflower Seeds
23 B Boothe Hill
Chapel Hill, NC 27514
(919) 967-4091
Nancy Easterling

Plants ～ Seeds
Boothe Hill bought the business of Passiflora, and specializes in nursery propagated plants and seeds of native and naturalized **wildflowers** which perform well in the Southeast; a nice selection with growing information.
❑ Catalog: $2d, R&W, CAN, cn/bn
⌂ Nursery: All year, M-F, by appointment only

Borbeleta Gardens
15980 Canby Avenue
Faribault, MN 55021-7652
(507) 334-2807, 685-4179, FAX 334-2395
Julius Wadekamper

Plants ～ Bulbs
"Introduce **daylilies, Siberian and bearded iris and lilies** developed by amateur gardeners who in the past have had no commercial outlet. We also develop and introduce our own originations." Plants are briefly described.
❑ Catalog: $3(4 IRC OV), R&W, CAN/OV, SS:4-10
⌂ Nursery: All year, M-F, call ahead
▼ Garden: April-September, growing area, call ahead

The Borneo Collection
"Treefarm"
El Arish, North QLD, Australia 4855
(070) 685-263
David K. Chandlee

Seeds
David Chandlee is a plant explorer in Borneo, and the author of a chapter in Glenn Tankard's book "Tropical Fruit." He offers a nice selection of **tropical fruit** seeds, most of which are shipped when fresh. No plant descriptions, so do your homework! He also sells the Tankard book, ask for information on price and postage. (1985)
❑ Catalog: $3(US Bills) OV, $15m, bn

Bottoms Nursery & Owens Vineyard
Route 1, Box 281
Concord, GA 30206
(706) 495-5661
Edward Bottoms

Plants
Offers a good selection of muscadine and other **grapes**, some of which they bought from Owens Vineyard; the catalog gives good information on growing, training, pruning and harvesting grapes. Also sells rabbiteye blueberries, blackberries, other berries, some fruit trees and flowering dogwoods.
❑ Catalog: Free, R&W, CAN/OV, SS:11-3

Bountiful Gardens
18001 Shafer Ranch Road
Willits, CA 95490
(707) 459-6410, FAX 459-6410 (6-10 PM PST)
Bill & Betsy Bruneau, Mgrs.

Seeds ～ Books ～ Supplies ～ Tools
Catalog offers a broad selection of **open-pollinated vegetable seeds** from Chase Seeds and the Henry Doubleday Foundation in England and other sources around the world, as well as seeds of herbs, flowers, green manure crops and grains; all well described in informative catalog. Also sells a wide selection of gardening books, tools and organic supplies. (1983)
❑ Catalog: Free($2 or 3 IRC OV), R&W, CAN/OV, cn/bn
⌂ Nursery: Common Ground Garden Supply, Palo Alto, CA

The Bovees Nursery
1737 S.W. Coronado
Portland, OR 97219
(503) 244-9341 TO/CC
Lucie Sorensen & George Watson

Plants
A collector's catalog of **species and hybrid rhododendrons**, as well as a good selection of vireya rhododendrons. A separate catalog lists Japanese maples, camellias, lilacs, clematis, dwarf conifers, alpine and rock garden plants, dwarf shrubs, ground covers and woodland plants -- all well described. (1953)
❑ Catalog: $2d($4 OV), CAN/OV, SS:9-11,2-4, $20m, bn/cn
⌂ Nursery: September-December, February-June, W-Sa, Su pm
▼ Garden: February-June, W-Su

S & N Brackley
117 Winslow Road, Wingrave
Aylesbury, Bucks., England HP22 4QB
(0296) 68 1384
S. & N. Brackley

Seeds
Specializes in **sweet peas**: offers many cultivars, including many old-fashioned sweet-smelling varieties. Sold by individual cultivar, each briefly described, or in several special mixes. Also sells seeds of those monster "exhibition" vegetables that the British love so well. (1890)
❑ Catalog: 2 IRC, R&W, OV
⌂ Nursery: All year, call ahead
▼ Garden: June-August, call ahead

Brand Peony Farm
P.O. Box 842
St. Cloud, MN 56302
Gerald Lund

Plants
A good selection of old and new herbaceous **peonies**, many developed by Ben Gilbertson. Plants well described, including P. tenuifolia flora plena, the fern leaf peony. They claim to be the oldest nursery in Minnesota. (1868)
❑ Catalog: $1d, CAN, SS:9-10

Brawner Geraniums
Route 4, Box 525 A
Buckhannon, WV 26201
(304) 472-4203
Faye Brawner

Plants
Faye Brawner is a **geranium** hybridizer and collector of rare **pelargoniums**; she offers a very broad selection of all types of geraniums and pelargoniums, grouped by type and very briefly described. (1970)
❑ Catalog: $2, CAN, SS:W, $10m
⌂ Nursery: By appointment only

Breck's
US Reservation Center
6523 North Galena Road
Peoria, IL 61632
Foster & Gallagher, Inc.

Bulbs
Color catalog offers a large selection of **spring-blooming bulbs** -- tulips, daffodils, alliums, iris and more; each plant glowingly described, some given rather fanciful names. No shipping to AK or HI. (1818)
❑ Catalog: Free, SS:8-11, cn

Breckinridge Orchids
6201 Summit Avenue
Brown Summit, NC 27214-9744
(910) 656-7991, FAX 656-7504 TO/CC
R. Mark Rose

Plants ⚘ Supplies
Because of rapid turnover they issue only a price list, not a catalog. Offer a good selection of **blooming orchids** all year; specialize in phalaenopsis, vanda, cattleya, dendrobium, oncidium, paphiopedilum and species orchids. Prices by size of pot and number of bloom spikes. Some supplies. (1957)
❑ Catalog: Long SASE, R&W, SS:3-11, $35m
⌂ Nursery: All year, M-Sa
▼ Garden: March-July, M-Sa

Briarwood Gardens
14 Gully Lane, RFD 3
East Sandwich, MA 02537
(508) 888-2146, FAX same
Jonathan Leonard

Plants
Nursery specializing in choice selections of **Dexter hybrid rhododendrons** which were originally bred in Sandwich, a few miles away. They also have other rhododendrons hybrids, as well as pieris, kalmia and holly at the nursery. Plants are very well described. (1984)
❑ Catalog: $1($2 CAN), R&W, CAN, SS:5-6,9-11
⌂ Nursery: May-September, Tu-Su
▼ Garden: Late May-mid-June, Tu-Su

Lee Bristol Nursery

See Bloomingfields Farm.

Brittingham Plant Farms
P.O. Box 2538
Salisbury, MD 21802
(410) 749-5153, FAX 749-5148 TO/CC
Wayne & Sylvia Robertson

Plants
Specializes in virus-free **strawberry** plants, as well as **asparagus** roots, **raspberries, blackberries, blueberries, rhubarb and grapes**; all very well described, with cultural and hardiness information. (1945)
❑ Catalog: Free, R&W
⌂ Nursery: All year, M-Sa

Broken Arrow Nursery
13 Broken Arrow Road
Hamden, CT 06518
(203) 288-1026
Richard & Sally Jaynes

Plants ⚘ Books
Specializes in **kalmias, species and hybrid rhododendrons** and a number of other choice **woodland trees and shrubs** -- fothergilla, pieris, Japanese lilac, enkianthus, deciduous azaleas, dawn redwood and others. Mr. Jaynes is the author of "Kalmia: The Laurel Book" ($32 postpaid); many of the kalmia are his own selections. Cannot ship to CA or AZ. (1984)
❑ Catalog: Long SASE w/3 FCS, SS:3-4,9-11, $20m, bn/cn
⌂ Nursery: Daily, call ahead
▼ Garden: May-June, September-October, call ahead

Brookside Wildflowers
Route 3, Box 740
Boone, NC 28607
(704) 963-5548
Jo Boggs

Plants ⚘ Books
Offer nursery-propagated **wildflowers**; a good selection, all very well described with good cultural information. Plants are one-year-olds and shipped in pots; cannot ship to CA. Also offer books on growing and identifying wildflowers and a line of bird houses. (1987)
❑ Catalog: $2, SS:3-5,9-11, $10m, bn/cn
⌂ Nursery: May-October, Th-Tu
▼ Garden: May-August, Th-Tu

Brown's Edgewood Gardens
2611 Corrine Drive
Orlando, FL 32803
(407) 896-3203, FAX 898-5792
Brandon Brown & Jean Dell

Plants ⚘ Books ⚘ Supplies
Offers a nice selection of **herbs**, organic gardening supplies, books on herbs and herb growing, herbal flea collars and other herbal items. (1987)
❑ Catalog: Long SASE, SS:W, $10m, cn
⌂ Nursery: All year, daily
▼ Garden: October-June, daily

Brown's Kalmia & Azalea Nursery
8527 Semiahmoo Drive
Blaine, WA 98230
(206) 371-2489, FAX 371-5551 TO/CC
Ed & Barbara Brown

Plants
Specialize in **kalmias**, offering a nice selection of hybrids from liners to blooming sizes with good plant descriptions. They sell azaleas and other garden plants at the nursery. (1983)
❑ Catalog: Long SASE($1 OV), R&W, CAN/OV, SS:3-6
⌂ Nursery: March-December, daily, call ahead
▼ Garden: May-June, call ahead

Brudy's Exotics
P.O. Box 820874
Houston, TX 77282-0874
(713) 963-0033, (800) 926-7333, FAX 960-7117
Michael & Deborah Stich

Plants ⚘ Seeds
The Stiches bought John Brudy's business in 1992 and moved it to Texas; still offer a nice selection of seeds for **tropical trees, shrubs** and **fruits**; each plant well described with germination instructions. Also offer plants of bananas, dwarf citrus, bougainvillea, plumeria, hibiscus, gingers and cannas. Seeds only outside the US. Very informative catalog. (1965)
❑ Catalog: Free, R&W, CAN/OV, $15m, cn/bn

Brussel's Bonsai Nursery
8365 Center Hill Road
Olive Branch, MS 38654
(601) 895-7457 TO/CC
Brussel Martin & Maury Straus

Plants ⬿ Books ⬿ Supplies ⬿ Tools
Grower and importer offers specimen finished **bonsai** and plants for bonsai, as well as books, plastic and clay bonsai pots, pruners and a soft spray nozzle for bonsai culture. Plants briefly described, some specimen plants illustrated. (1975)
❑ Catalog: $2d, R&W, $20m, cn/bn
⌂ Nursery: All year, M-F, Sa by appointment only
▼ Garden: All year, M-F, Sa by appointment only

Buckley Nursery Garden Center
646 North River Avenue
Buckley, WA 98321
(206) 829-1811 or 0734
Don & Penny Marlow

Plants
A good selection of **fruit for the Pacific Northwest**: apples, apricots, cherries, peaches, plums and prunes, Asian pears, nuts and many berries, and table and wine grapes. They have added French hybrid **lilacs** and other **flowering deciduous shrubs**; all plants briefly but well described.
❑ Catalog: Free, SS:2-4
⌂ Nursery: All year, daily
▼ Garden: March-November, daily

The Bulb Crate
2560 Deerfield Road
Riverwoods, IL 60015
(708) 317-1414, FAX same
Alice Hosford

Plants ⬿ Bulbs
Small company sells **hybrid lilies, peonies, tall and dwarf bearded iris,** and some **Japanese and Siberian iris, and tulips**; all are briefly described. Also offered are several collections for long seasons of bloom.(1987)
❑ Catalog: $1d, R&W, $10m

Bull Valley Rhododendron Nursery
214 Bull Valley Road
Aspers, PA 17304
(717) 677-6313
Faye & Ray Carter, Kim Altice

Plants
Specializes in Dexter and Wister-Swarthmore **hybrid rhododendrons**, "plants for the serious collector," described only by color of bloom. Have added Gable, Pride, Consolini and Leach hybrids and unnamed hybrids of Jack Cowles. They also offer a number of **hollies and magnolias**. (1979)
❑ Catalog: $2, SS:5-6,9, $30m
⌂ Nursery: All year, by appointment only
▼ Garden: May, by appointment only

Bundles of Bulbs
112 Green Springs Valley Road
Owings Mills, MD 21117
(410) 363-1371
Kitty Washburne

Bulbs
A broad selection of **spring-blooming bulbs**: tulips, daffodils, crocus, lilies and various small bulbs; all are well described and illustrated with nice block prints. Also offer "span" collections for a long season of bloom. Also offer hybrid **lilies and daylilies** and some flower arranging and growing supplies. (1984)
❑ Catalog: $2d, SS:10-11, $10m
⌂ Nursery: By appointment only
▼ Garden: March-June, by appointment only

Burford Brothers
Route 1 - Nursery
Monroe, VA 24574
(804) 929-4950
Thomas Burford

Plants ⬿ Supplies
Offer more than 300 varieties of **antique and modern apples**; their brochure, which sells for $2, describes 60 varieties by taste, appearance and time of ripening. They offer a hefty descriptive catalog for $15 which gives much fuller histories of the apples and includes more varieties. They also sell other types of fruit trees and orchard supplies, and offer seminars.
❑ Catalog: See notes, SS:3-4,11-12, $15m
⌂ Nursery: January-December, Tu-Sa, by appointment only
▼ Garden: September-October, by appointment only

Burk's Nursery
P.O. Box 1207
11020 Avilla West (Alexander)
Benton, AR 72015-1207
(501) 794-3266
Bob & Lois Burks

Plants
Former owners of California Epi Center have a new nursery specializing in **haworthias, gasterias and astrolobas**; a very broad selection with good brief plant descriptions and habitat information; all plants seed-grown or nursery-propagated. Serious collectors will crow! (1988)
❑ Catalog: $1d(3 IRC OV), CAN/OV, SS:4-11, $10m, bn
⌂ Nursery: By appointment only
▼ Garden: By appointment only

Burkey Gardens

See Hickory Hill Gardens.

Burnt Ridge Nursery
432 Burnt Ridge Road
Onalaska, WA 98570
(206) 985-2873
Michael & Carolyn Dolan

Plants
Small nursery specializes in **perennial crops** -- hardy and regular kiwis, as well as beeches, Asian pears, berries, dawn redwood, bald cypress, fig trees, hybrid chestnuts, walnuts and filberts and other **fruiting trees**; all plants well described. (1980)
❑ Catalog: Long SASE, R&W, CAN, $10m, cn/bn
⌂ Nursery: All year, call ahead

W. Atlee Burpee Company
300 Park Avenue
Warminster, PA 18974
(215) 674-4900, (800) 888-1447 TO/CC
Geo. J. Ball, Inc.

Plants ◈ Seeds ◈ Books ◈ Supplies ◈ Tools ◈ Bulbs
A **gardening fixture** for many years, they offer flowers, vegetables, perennial plants, berries and fruit trees in a fat color catalog; each plant well described. Offer spring bulbs in a separate summer catalog. Also carry many tools, supplies, some canning equipment and beekeeping supplies. (1876)
❒ Catalog: Free, cn/bn
⌂ Nursery: All year, daily

D. V. Burrell Seed Growers Co.
P.O. Box 150
Rocky Ford, CO 81067-0150
(719) 254-3318, FAX 254-3319
Bill & Rick Burrell

Seeds ◈ Books ◈ Supplies ◈ Tools
A good selection of **vegetable seed**, especially watermelons, cantaloupes, hot peppers, corn and popcorn, tomatoes and onions, as well as **annual flowers**. Also offers growing supplies and a good deal of growing information for their commercial grower customers. (1898)
❒ Catalog: $1, R&W, CAN/OV

Burt Associates
P.O. Box 719
Westford, MA 01886
(508) 692-3240
Albert Adelman

Plants
Offers 58 species of **bamboos**, 44 of which are hardy, but specialize in varieties which make dramatic indoor plants. They are adding plants for water and bog gardens; you know how bamboo spreads! (1990)
❒ Catalog: $2, R&W, CAN, bn
⌂ Nursery: May-October, W-Su
▼ Garden: May-October, W-Su

Bushland Flora
17 Trotman Crescent
Yanchep, WA, Australia 6035
(09) 561-1636
Brian Hargett

Seeds ◈ Books
Collectors' list with seeds of hundreds of **Australian plants**, each briefly described; also offers some color-illustrated books on these plants. Many acacias, banksias, eucalyptus, melaleucas, callistemons, helichrysums and helipterums (everlastings) and others; planting guides with orders. Send your "want list" for species not listed; they're sometimes available. (1972)
❒ Catalog: $2(US Bills or 3 IRC), OV, $12m, bn/cn
⌂ Nursery: By appointment only

Busse Gardens
13579 10th Street N.W.
Cokato, MN 55321-9426
(612) 286-2654, FAX 286-2654 TO/CC
Ainie H. Busse

Plants
A extensive catalog of **hardy perennials** of all types; offers an especially large selection of hostas, Siberian iris, daylilies, ferns, astilbes, phlox, heucheras, hardy geraniums, herbaceous peonies and wildflowers for rock gardens and woodland, well to briefly described. No shipping to CA. (1973)
❒ Catalog: $2d, R&W, SS:4-10, $25m, bn/cn
⌂ Nursery: May-October, M-F
▼ Garden: June-August, M-F

The Butchart Gardens
P.O. Box 4010
Victoria, BC, Canada V8X 3X4
(604) 652-4422
R. I. Ross

Seeds
Butchart Gardens in Victoria sells seed of many of the **annual and perennial flowers** grown in their famous gardens; plants are well described, and prices are very reasonable. They also sell a number of collections: cottage garden, window box, rock garden, children's and hanging baskets. (1904)
❒ Catalog: $1d, US/OV, $2m
⌂ Nursery: Gift shop, daily
▼ Garden: All year, daily, admission charge

© Tripple Brook Farm
Artist: Betty Stull Schaffer

Butterbrooke Farm
78 Barry Road
Oxford, CT 06478-1529
(203) 888-2000
Tom Butterworth

Seeds
Offers seed of **open-pollinated, short-season vegetables** for Northern climates, not treated chemically; priced at $.50 a packet. Sells booklets and a video cassette on organic vegetable growing; customers may join their seed co-op. (1979)
❒ Catalog: Long SASE(1 IRC OV), CAN/OV
⚲ Nursery: Daily, call ahead

C & C Nursery
Route 3, Box 422
Murray, KY 42071
(502) 753-2993
Cyndi & Charlie Turnbow

Plants
A small family nursery in western Kentucky which offers **daylilies, hostas** and herbaceous and tree **peonies**; all plants very well described. They grow many more than they list, so you might send your "want list." (1985)
❒ Catalog: $1d, R&W, CAN/OV, SS:3-10
⚲ Nursery: March-October, Th-Su, call ahead
▼ Garden: March-October, Th-Su, call ahead

C K S
P.O. Box 74
Ostrava-Poruba, Czech Republic 708 00
Milan Sembol

Seeds
Specializes in seeds of **alpine and bulbous plants**, as well as cactus and succulent seeds: specify which type of seed you're interested in. They will also try to find seed of plants on your "want-list." Catalog in English with brief plant descriptions. (1980)
❒ Catalog: $2(US Bills), OV, SS:6-7,11-2, $30m, bn
⚲ Nursery: By appointment only

CRM Ecosystems

See Prairie Ridge Nursery.

CTDA
174 Cambridge Street
London, England SW1V 4QE
(071) 821-1801
Dr. Basil Smith

Seeds
Dr. Smith collects and ships fresh seed from 12 species and 60 strains of hardy **cyclamen**, each well described on his list. He has many selections of C. hederifolium and C. coum, and tells me he also offers fresh seed of **hellebores**, 4 species and many color selections of H. orientalis. I didn't see the hellebore list, so be sure to ask for it if interested. (1989)
❒ Catalog: 2 IRC, OV, SS:7-2, $50m, bn

Cactus by Dodie
934 Mettler Road
Lodi, CA 95242
(209) 368-3692 TO/CC
Dick & Dodie Suess

Plants ⚘ Books ⚘ Supplies
A broad selection of **cacti and succulents** in a collectors' list: mammillaria, lobivia, gymnocalycium, echinocereus, coryphantha, notocactus, parodia, rebutia, aloes, agaves, crassulas, euphorbias and haworthias; no plant descriptions, a few illustrated in b&w photos. Also offer pots, labels, supplies and some books on cacti. (1981)
❒ Catalog: $2($2 OV), CAN/OV, SS:W, $20m, bn
⚲ Nursery: All year, Th-Sa
▼ Garden: All year, greenhouse, Th-Sa

Cactus by Mueller
10411 Rosedale Highway
Bakersfield, CA 93312
(805) 589-2674
Maria Piazza

Plants
A collectors' list of **cacti and succulents**: cereus, echinocereus, echinopsis, gymnocalycium, lobivia, mammillaria, notocactus, opuntia, rebutia, aloe, caralluma, crassula, echeveria, haworthia, huernia, senecio and many more. Also some **mesembs**. No plant descriptions, but some shown in color. (1966)
❒ Catalog: $2, R&W, SS:W, bn
⚲ Nursery: All year, Th-Tu
▼ Garden: Spring-Fall, Th-Tu

Cactus Farm
Route 5, Box 1610
Nacogdoches, TX 75961
(409) 560-6406
Fred Bright

Plants
Specialize in "free-flowering, easy-to-care-for hybrid **cacti**" as well as nursery propagated species which are also good bloomers. They suffered a terrible freeze in 1989-90, but are rebuilding stock as quickly as possible; offer echinopsis hybrids, opuntias and others. (1980)
❒ Catalog: Free, R&W, bn
⚲ Nursery: All year, call ahead
▼ Garden: May-September, call ahead

The Cactus Patch

See Midwest Cactus.

Caladium World
P.O. Drawer 629
Sebring, FL 33871
(813) 385-7661, FAX 385-5836 TO/CC
L. E. Selph

Bulbs
Specialize in **caladium bulbs**, those brilliantly colored fancy leaved plants that survive so well through the Southern summers. Several are illustrated in their color leaflet. (1979)
❒ Catalog: Free, R&W, OV, SS:1-7, $10m

California Carnivores
7020 Trenton-Healdsburg Road
Forestville, CA 95436
(707) 838-1630
Peter D'Amato & Marilee Maertz

Plants
Offers a good selection of **carnivorous plants**: droseras, sarracenias, utricularias, pinguiculas and nepenthes, all very well described in the catalog, which also gives a lot of growing information. Their greenhouse is located at a winery, where they have over 400 varieties on display; their growing guide is $2, the price list is free. (1989)
❒ Catalog: See notes, SS:3-11, $35m, bn
⌂ Nursery: April-November, daily; other months, call ahead
▼ Garden: April-November, daily

California Nursery Co.
P.O. Box 2278
Fremont, CA 94536
(510) 797-3311
Bruce Roeding

Plants
List offers a broad selection of **fruit and nut trees** for home gardeners and commercial orchardists, including kiwis, persimmons, pistachios, grapes, citrus, avocados, nut trees, bamboo; no plant descriptions. (1865)
❒ Catalog: Free, CAN/OV, $35m

Callahan Seeds
6045 Foley Lane
Central Point, OR 97502
(503) 855-1164
Frank T. Callahan II

Seeds
An extensive list of seeds of **native Northwestern trees and shrubs** as well as some from most other continents, about 600 species listed by botanical and common names only. They will also custom-collect seeds from "want lists" -- seeds available in small packets and in bulk. Small supplier, good list.
❒ Catalog: $1(3 IRC OV), R&W, CAN/OV, bn/cn
⌂ Nursery: All year, daily, by appointment only

Camellia Forest Nursery
125 Carolina Forest
Chapel Hill, NC 27516
Kai-Mei Parks

Plants
Camellias selected for hardiness and disease resistance, both species and unusual hybrids just being introduced; also species maples and rhododendrons, unusual **ornamental trees and shrubs**, dwarf conifers, holly and evergreen azaleas. Wide selection of collectors' plants; some are recent introductions from China and Japan. Plants are briefly described. (1978)
❒ Catalog: 4 FCS($2 OV), R&W, CAN/OV, SS:3-5,10-12, $20m
⌂ Nursery: All year, by appointment only
▼ Garden: Spring, Fall, by appointment only

Campanula Connoisseur
702 Traver Trail
Glenwood Springs, CO 81601
Janna Belau

Plants
Here's an amazing new nursery, specializing in **campanulas**, and offering over 60 varieties and adding more all the time. Each is very well described, and some come in several color forms. Isn't it great what people do? (1990)
❒ Catalog: $1, SS:4-6,9-10, bn

Campberry Farms
R.R.1
Niagara-on-the-Lake, ON, Canada L0S 1J0
(416) 262-4927
R. D. Campbell

Plants ⬿ Seeds
Specializing in extra hardy **nut trees, fruit trees, berries** and native trees; offers seeds of hardy trees in the fall. Also does consulting on commercial nut growing in the north, and sells several leaflets of cultural suggestions. Cannot ship to CA. (1972)
❒ Catalog: $2, R&W, US, SS:3-5
⌂ Nursery: All year, by appointment only
▼ Garden: Spring-Fall, by appointment only

Canyon Creek Nursery
3527 Dry Creek Road
Oroville, CA 95965
John & Susan Whittlesey

Plants
A good selection of **perennials**, including many violas and violets, species geraniums, the "chocolate" cosmos, euphorbias, salvias, campanulas, hardy fuchsias and many more; all very well described with cultural suggestions. Surely the chief attraction of the Oroville area! (1985)
❒ Catalog: $2, SS:2-6,9-11, bn
⌂ Nursery: All year, M-Sa

Cape Cod Violetry
28 Minot Street
Falmouth, MA 02540
(508) 548-2798
John & Barbara Cook

Plants ⬿ Supplies
A collectors' list of **African violets**, many from well-known hybridizers, and **episcias, sinningias and miniature streptocarpus**; all very briefly described and available as plants or by leaves and stolons. Also sells growing supplies and African violet gift items. (1969)
❒ Catalog: $2($4 OV), R&W, CAN/OV, SS:5-10

Cape Cod Vireyas
405 Jones Road
Falmouth, MA 02540
(508) 548-1613 (Su-M pm), FAX (617) 742-4749
Dr. Richard W. Chaikin

Plants
Offers a large selection of named cultivars of **vireya rhododendrons**, including cultivars from England, Australia and New Zealand. In all but the mildest areas, these are greenhouse plants, where they can grow in containers or hanging baskets; they come in many colors, and are well described. (1988)
❒ Catalog: $3d($4 OV), CAN/OV, SS:4-11, $8m
⌂ Nursery: All year, Su-Tu, by appointment only
▼ Garden: All year, Su-Tu, by appointment only

Cape Iris Gardens
822 Rodney Vista Blvd.
Cape Girardeau, MO 63701
(314) 334-3383
O. David Niswonger

Plants
Dave Niswonger is a hybridizer of **tall bearded, spuria, Siberian and median iris**, and offers a very good selection of all types, including his own introductions. Many varieties are fairly recent introductions, and are in demand by other hybridizers. (1963)
❐ Catalog: $1d, R&W, CAN/OV
❦ Garden: May, call ahead

Cape Seed & Bulb
P.O. Box 4063, Idasvalley
Stellenbosch, Cape, South Africa 7609
James L. Holmes

Bulbs
A source of **South African bulbs**, listed with only botanical names and flower color; a nice selection: babiana, geissorhiza, hardy gladiolus, bulbinella, mini agapanthus, lachenalia and others. Jim also does breeding and selection of rare bulbous plants. Sold only by 10's or 100's. (1981)
❐ Catalog: $1d(US Bills), R&W, OV, SS:12-3, $50m, bn

Caprice Farm Nursery
15425 S.W. Pleasant Hill Road
Sherwood, OR 97140
(503) 625-7241, FAX 625-5588 TO/CC $20m
Allan, Dorothy & Richard Rogers, Robin Blue

Plants
A good selection of **hostas, Japanese and Siberian irises, daylilies** and **peonies**, both herbaceous and tree cultivars, some quite rare. All plants are very well described, and some are illustrated in color; much here to gladden the heart! (1978)
❐ Catalog: $2d, R&W, CAN/OV, $10m
⌂ Nursery: All year, M-Sa, call ahead
❦ Garden: May-September, call ahead

Carino Nurseries
P.O. Box 538
Indiana, PA 15701
(412) 463-3350, (800) 223-7075, FAX 463-3050
James L. Carino

Plants
Specializes in **seedling trees** for windbreaks, wildlife food, Christmas trees and ornamental trees for garden use. Trees available as seedlings and as larger transplants. Minimum order varies. No shipping to AK, FL, HI or LA. (1947)
❐ Catalog: Free, R&W, SS:3-5,9-11, cn
⌂ Nursery: Call ahead
❦ Garden: Call ahead

Carlson's Gardens
P.O. Box 305
South Salem, NY 10590
(914) 763-5958
Bob & Jan Carlson

Plants
A broad selection of **azaleas and rhododendrons** for collectors: native and hybrid azaleas such as Knaphill-Exbury, Robin Hill, Gable, North Tisbury, Glenn Dale and their own "Face 'em Down" evergreens. Also large and small leafed hybrid rhododendrons (Dexter, Leach, Gable) and **kalmias**. No shipping to AK, CA or HI. (1970)
❐ Catalog: $3, SS:4-11, bn/cn
⌂ Nursery: Daily, by appointment only
❦ Garden: April-June, by appointment only

Carncairn Daffodils, Ltd.
Carncairn Lodge
Broughshane
Ballymena, Co. Antrim, No. Ireland BT43 7HF
(0266) 86-1216
Mrs. Kate Reade

Bulbs
Collectors' list of **daffodils**: a broad selection of types with division and color class given for each, along with a good description; many are their own introductions. Bulbs are shipped airmail.
❐ Catalog: Free, OV, $10m
❦ Garden: March-May, call ahead

Carroll Gardens
P.O. Box 310
444 E. Main Street
Westminster, MD 21158
(410) 848-5422, (800) 638-6334
Alan L. Summers

Plants ❧ **Books** ❧ **Tools**
Informative catalog lists a huge selection of **perennials, herbs, roses, vines, conifers, trees and shrubs and spring and summer bulbs**, all very well described with cultural information. Many hollies, lilies, yews, box, viburnums, clematis, species geraniums, dianthus, campanulas and much more; many fine woody plants suitable for small gardens.
❐ Catalog: $2d, CAN, SS:W, bn/cn
⌂ Nursery: All year, daily

Carter & Holmes, Inc.
P.O. Box 668
1 Old Mendenhall Road
Newberry, SC 29108
(803) 276-0579, FAX 276-0588 TO
Owen Holmes & Gene Crocker

Plants ❧ **Books** ❧ **Supplies**
A broad selection of **orchids**; they are especially well known for their cattleya and phalaenopsis hybrids, many of which are shown in color and are irresistible. Plants are listed by color, with good descriptions. (1948)
❐ Catalog: $1.50d, R&W, CAN/OV, SS:W
⌂ Nursery: All year, M-Sa
❦ Garden: September-March, M-Sa

Cascade Bulb & Seed
2333 Crooked Finger Road
Scotts Mills, OR 97375
Dr. Joseph C. Halinar

Seeds ❧ **Bulbs**
Small grower specializing in seed of **species and hybrid lilies, daylilies, Siberian irises and alliums** for hybridizers and collectors; brief plant notes include information on hybridizing qualities. Supplies limited; you'll have to choose substitutes, but they all sound desirable. Some plants available; list distributed in November. (1980)
❐ Catalog: Long SASE(2 IRC OV), R&W, CAN/OV, SS:3-5

Cascade Daffodils
P.O. Box 10626
White Bear Lake, MN 55110
David & Linda Karnstedt

Bulbs
A very broad selection of **novelty daffodils**, both standard and miniature categories. Each plant is described by name of hybridizer, class and brief comments; collectors will know and want them -- they sound delicious. Offers between 300 and 400 varieties for show and landscape use. (1986)
❒ Catalog: $2($3 OV), R&W, CAN/OV, SS:9-10, $15m
⌂ Nursery: April-August, Sa-Su, by appointment only
▼ Garden: April-May, by appointment only

Cascade Forestry Nursery
22033 Fillmore Road
Cascade, IA 52033
(319) 852-3042, FAX 852-3042
Leo Frueh

Plants
Offers **hardy nut trees, conifers and other trees and shrubs** primarily for reforestation, woodlots and windbreaks; plants not described, informative leaflet free of charge. Plants offered from seedling size to several feet tall, depending on variety. They help customers find buyers for veneer quality hardwoods, offer forestry consulting and planting services. (1973)
❒ Catalog: Free, R&W, CAN/OV, $20m, SS:4-5,9-10, cn/bn
⌂ Nursery: All year, M-F
▼ Garden: All year, M-F

Cedar Valley Nursery
3833 McElfresh Road S.W.
Centralia, WA 98531
(206) 736-7490
Charles C. Boyd

Plants
A tissue-culture lab which offers a good selection of red, yellow and black **raspberries**, and also a variety of **blackberry** cultivars. The advantage of tissue culture is the rapid propagation of new introductions, and disease free plants. They will also do custom propagation of your plants. (1978)
❒ Catalog: Free, R&W, CAN/OV, $25m

Chadwell Himalayan Seed
81 Parlaunt Road
Slough, Berks., England SL3 8BE
(0753) 54-2823
Christopher Chadwell

Seeds
Specializes in the **flora of the northwest Himalaya and the Orient**, seed available from expeditions and local collectors. List has section of easy seeds for beginners, good plant descriptions and line drawings of many of the plants. Also issuing a joint seed list with P. Kohli, which is inactive at present due to political unrest. Lists of Japanese and Mexican plants are a recent addition. (1984)
❒ Catalog: $3(US Bills), OV, bn
▼ Garden: April-November, by appointment only

Champlain Isle Agro Associates
East Shore
Isle La Motte, VT 05463
(802) 928-3425, FAX 928-3107
Randy McCoy

Plants
Propagators of virus-tested "Vermont Premium" **small fruit nursery stock**. Sixteen cultivars of raspberries, including red, yellow, black and thornless, and French tarragon; they are adding hardy table grapes and ornamentals. "Vermont Premium" stock meets stringent standards of certification for virus testing, are shipped direct from the greenhouse in a soilless medium. (1985)
❒ Catalog: Free, R&W, CAN/OV

Chehalem Creek Nursery
31677 N. Lake Creek Dr.
Tangent, OR 97389
Theresa Wagner

Plants
Offers **red and black currants, gooseberries, jostaberries**, ornamental **ribes**, hybrid **chestnuts** and, of all things, aquilegias. No plant descriptions. (1977)
❒ Catalog: $2d, R&W, CAN/OV, SS:12-3, $10m

Chehalem Gardens
P.O. Box 693
Newberg, OR 97132
(503) 538-8920
Tom & Ellen Abrego

Plants
A list for lovers of **Siberian and spuria irises.** They have "regular" and tetraploid Siberian irises; the latter are sturdier and richer in color with larger blooms. Each plant briefly but well described. A small nursery; stock may be limited on some plants. Can't ship to FL or HI. (1982)
❒ Catalog: Free, SS:8-9
▼ Garden: May, Sa-Su, by appointment only

Chehalis Rare Plant Nursery
2568 Jackson Highway
Chehalis, WA 98532
(206) 748-7627
Herbert Dickson

Seeds
Small specialty nursery offers only **primula** seed by mail: single, double, show and alpine auricula, florindae, some petite hybrids and mixed candelabra. Ask for seed list. At the nursery they sell miniature and unusual alpine and rock garden plants, dwarf conifers and trees and shrubs. (1968)
❒ Catalog: Long SASE, CAN/OV, $5m
⌂ Nursery: All year, call ahead

Chestnut Hill Nursery, Inc.
Route 1, Box 341
Alachua, FL 32615
(904) 462-2820, (800) 669-2067, FAX 462-4330
R. D. Wallace

Plants ✁ Books
Specialize in blight-resistant hybrid **chestnuts** -- Dunstan hybrids and the 'Revival,' 'Carolina' and 'Heritage' chestnuts -- all well described and illustrated in a color pamphlet. They also offer 34 varieties of **Oriental persimmons**, figs, hardy citrus and other fruit trees, and books on chestnut and persimmon orcharding in America. (1980)
❒ Catalog: Free, R&W, CAN/OV, SS:12-4
⌂ Nursery: All year, M-F, by appointment only
▼ Garden: November-March, orchard, by appointment only

Chieri Orchids
2913 9th Street North
Tacoma, WA 98406-6717
(206) 752-5510
Pat Pettit

Plants
"I sell cool-growing **orchids** from the cloud forests of Columbia, Ecuador and Peru, which like temperatures between 45F-80F. The west coast north of San Francisco is considered the ideal climate." Offered are masdevallias, odontoglossums, miltonopsis and mini-cattleya hybrids; brief descriptions.
❐ Catalog: Free, R&W, CAN/OV, $10, bn
⌂ Nursery: All year, Sa-Su, by appointment only
▼ Garden: February-May, Sa-Su, by appointment only

Chiltern Seeds
Bortree Stile
Ulverston, Cumbria, England LA12 7PB
(0229) 58-1137 (24 hrs.), FAX 54549
Mrs. B. S. Bowden

Seeds
Catalog is a sure delight; offers seed of about 4,000 plants for every purpose, each very well described. The catalog is a useful reference book containing **ornamental plants** from all over the world. Also sells seed of Oriental, unusual and common vegetables and herbs and British wildflowers.
❐ Catalog: $4(US Bills), OV, bn/cn

Choice Edibles
584 Riverside Park Road
Carlotta, CA 95528
(707) 768-3135
Dan Harkins

Seeds
A small company specializing in cultures and spawn of morel, shiitake, oyster and stropharia **mushrooms**; they will also do custom tissue culturing of customers' mushrooms. Will provide detailed indoor and outdoor growing instructions. Cannot ship to South Africa. (1985)
❐ Catalog: Long SASE(2FCS OV), R&W, CAN/OV, $10m

Christa's Cactus
529 W. Pima
Coolidge, AZ 85228
(602) 723-4185
Christa Roberts

Seeds
Offers a collectors' list of **cacti and succulents, desert trees and shrubs**; some quite rare, very briefly described in tiny print. A broad selection, including some caudiciforms and succulents used for bonsai; geographical sources of habitat-collected seed mentioned where known. Catalog available in English or German. (1979)
❐ Catalog: $1($3 US Bills or 4 IRC OV), R&W, CAN/OV, bn
⌂ Nursery: All year, M-F, call ahead
▼ Garden: March-June, M-F, call ahead

Paul Christian -- Rare Plants
P.O. Box 468
Wrexham, Clwyd, Wales LL13 9EP
(0978) 36-6399, FAX Same
Dr. P.J. Christian

Bulbs
Source of rare **bulbs, corms and tubers**: alliums, anemones, arums, colchicum, corydalis, crocus, erythroniums, fritillaria, galanthus, species irises, trillium, species tulips and more, from all over the world. Plants briefly described. Accepts credit card orders; £11 fee for health certificate and postage.
❐ Catalog: $3(US Bills), US, SS:9-4, bn

City Gardens
451 W. Lincoln
Madison Heights, MI 48071
(313) 398-2660
Bob Barnhart & Mike Stevenson

Plants ∾ Supplies
City Gardens have moved out of their seventy-five year old greenhouse to a more convenient location, and will henceforth be specializing in **bromeliads** and **miniature orchids**. I haven't seen their new plant list.
❐ Catalog: $2d, R&W, SS:3-10, $15m
⌂ Nursery: All year, M-Sa
▼ Garden: October-June, M-Sa

Clargreen Gardens, Ltd.
814 Southdown Road
Mississauga, ON, Canada L5J 2Y4
(416) 822-0992, FAX 822-7282 TO/CC
Mike Dytnerski, Mgr.

Plants ∾ Books ∾ Supplies ∾ Tools
Offers **orchids**: phalaenopsis, cattleyas and miniature cattleyas, vandas, paphiopedilums and other species, each very briefly described. Another catalog lists trees and conifers, tropical plants, roses, perennials, bonsai, general nursery stock and books, tools, supplies and pots. (1918)
❐ Catalog: $2, R&W, US, SS:5-11, $75m, bn/cn
⌂ Nursery: All year, daily
▼ Garden: All year, greenhouses, daily

Clifford's Perennial & Vine
Route 2, Box 320
East Troy, WI 53120
(414) 968-4040 April-Sept, 642-7156 Oct-March
Ken & Connie Clifford

Plants
"Suppliers of the Cottage Garden," offers a good selection of **perennials**, including iris, daylilies and clematis and other flowering vines; each plant very well described with cultural notes. (1982)
❐ Catalog: $1d, SS:4-5,9-10, $15m, bn/cn

Cloud Forest Orchids
P.O. Box 370
Honokaa, HI 96727
(808) 775-9850
Erik & Hillery Gunther

Plants
Small nursery specializes in **species and hybrid orchids** for the collector, offered as seedlings and mericlones in individual pots; plant list is a copy of their periodic availabilty ads in the AOS Journal. Ship around the world.
❐ Catalog: Free, R&W, bn
⌂ Nursery: By appointment only
▼ Garden: By appointment only

Cloud Mountain Nursery
6906 Goodwin Road
Everson, WA 98247
(206) 966-5859
Tom & Cheryl Thornton

Plants
Offers a nice selection of **fruit trees and berries**: apples, European and
Asian pears, plums, cherries, kiwis, peaches, table grapes and currants,
blueberries, raspberries and strawberries. They also offer filberts, walnuts
and chestnuts, some hardy bamboos and native plants. Informative catalog,
fruit growing and landscaping classes at the nursery.
☐ Catalog: Free, SS:2-5, $15m
⌂ Nursery: All year, F-Sa

Coastal Gardens & Nursery
4611 Socastee Boulevard
Myrtle Beach, SC 29575
(803) 293-2000 TO/CC $35m
Rudy & Ursula Herz

Plants
A large selection of **hostas**, as well as Japanese and Siberian irises, day-
lilies, ground covers, perennials, woodland, bog and aquatic plants. Plants
are well described, and sure to thrive in the Southeast. (1974)
☐ Catalog: $2d, R&W, CAN/OV, SS:3-11, $35m, bn
⌂ Nursery: All year, M-Sa, call ahead
▼ Garden: April-June, M-Sa, call ahead

Coburg Planting Fields
573 East 600 North
Valparaiso, IN 46383
(219) 462-4288
Philipp Brockington & Howard H. Reeve, Jr.

Plants
Small nursery offering **daylilies** -- a nice selection of both old and new
varieties, grown in the rich farm soil of Indiana; all are shipped with
double fans. Some varieties may be limited, so they suggest calling to check
on availability; each plant is briefly described by color, season of bloom
and name of hybridizer. (1984)
☐ Catalog: $2d, CAN, SS:5-9
⌂ Nursery: July-mid-August, daily
▼ Garden: July, call ahead

Coda Gardens
P.O. Box 8417
Fredericksburg, VA 22404
David & Colleen Turley

Plants
Formerly called Home-Grown Gesneriads, Coda Gardens offers a wide selection of **gesneriads**: sinningias, aeschynanthus, gloxinias, episcias,
achimenes and others, all well described. Also offers a good selection of
passion flowers, and expect to be adding more. (1988)
☐ Catalog: $2, CAN/OV, SS:4-6,9-10, $15m, bn

Coenosium Gardens
P.O. Box 847
Sandy, OR 97055
(503) 668-3574, FAX same
Robert & Dianne Fincham

Plants ⚘ Supplies
A collector of conifers who offers a very broad selection of **conifers, dwarf
conifers, Japanese maples, oaks, beeches, kalmias** and other plants for
bonsai. Each plant well described; some rarer items propagated to order.
Also available are video cassettes of collection and grafting methods. (1979)
☐ Catalog: $3d, CAN/OV, SS:6-10, bn

Cold Stream Farm
2030 Free Soil Road
Free Soil, MI 49411
(616) 464-5809 TO
Mike Hradel

Plants
Specializes in hybrid poplars for woodlots, wildlife habitat and erosion
control, other native **trees and shrubs** useful for woodland planting in
seedling size (including American chestnut), and mixed collections for
wildlife cover plantings; no descriptions. (1978)
☐ Catalog: Free, R&W, SS:9-7, $5m, cn

Collector's Nursery
16804 N.E. 102nd Avenue
Battle Ground, WA 98604
(206) 574-3832
Bill Janssen & Diana Reeck

Plants
Bill and Diana hasten to explain that they do not collect plants from the
wild, but that their nursery appeals to plant collectors; I heartily agree.
Offered are **perennials, hostas, beardless iris, saxifragas, tricyrtis**, and
choice trees and shrubs. Good selection, all plants well described. (1989)
☐ Catalog: $2, SS:3-5,9-11, bn
⌂ Nursery: All year, call ahead
▼ Garden: All year, call ahead

Color Farm Growers
2710 Thornhill Road
Auburndale, FL 33823
(813) 967-9895
Vern Ogren

Plants
Specializes in **old-fashioned heirloom types of coleus**, which they consider
superior garden plants -- some are even sun-tolerant. They have also hybridized these plants and offer a large selection; each plant well described in
all its glowing colors. New introductions yearly, and collections. (1985)
☐ Catalog: $1d, SS:W, $10m

Colorado Alpines, Inc.
P.O. Box 2708
41246 Highway 6 & 24
Avon, CO 81620
(303) 949-6464
Sandra Jones

Plants
Specializes in **alpine and rock garden plants** grown at 7,500 feet in the
Rocky Mountains. Offers a broad selection, plants well but briefly des-
cribed: androsaces, dianthus, erysimums, gentians, lewisias, penstemons,
phlox, primulas, saxifragas, sempervivums, and some dwarf conifers. (1986)
☐ Catalog: $2, CAN/OV, SS:4-6,9-10, $10m, bn
⌂ Nursery: All year, daily

Colvos Creek Farm
P.O. Box 1512
Vashon Island, WA 98070
(206) 441-1509, 463-9776
Mike Lee

Plants
A broad selection of unusual **trees and shrubs**: acacias, species maples, eucalyptus, conifers, flowering shrubs, oaks, palms and yuccas, among others. They are testing new introductions and listing new plants all the time and send out catalog supplements as new items are ready for sale. (1972)
❒ Catalog: $2d, R&W, CAN/OV, SS:W, $15m, bn
⌂ Nursery: By appointment only

Comanche Acres Iris Gardens
Route 1, Box 258
Gower, MO 64454
(816) 424-6436 TO
Jim & Lamoyne Hedgecock

Plants ⬤ Bulbs
Specializes in **tall bearded irises** and offers a selection that includes a number of award winners, all well described in a color catalog. Also offers a few dwarf bearded and border bearded irises, "horned" and Louisiana irises and **daylilies**. (1981)
❒ Catalog: $3(2 yrs.), R&W, OV, SS:7-9, $10m
⌂ Nursery: April-October, daily, call ahead
▼ Garden: April-May, daily

Companion Plants
7247 N. Coolville Ridge Road
Athens, OH 45701
(614) 592-4643 TO/CC $20
Peter & Susan Borchard

Plants ⬤ Seeds
Over 400 **herb** plants for sale and about 120 varieties of seed -- all very well described in an informative catalog. Selection includes **scented geraniums, everlastings, woodland plants** and a few books on herbs and herb growing. Will ship only seeds to Canada and overseas. (1982)
❒ Catalog: $2, R&W, CAN/OV, SS:W, $15m, cn/bn
⌂ Nursery: March-November, Th-Su (closed August 1-15)
▼ Garden: April-October, Th-Su

The Compleat Garden -- Clematis Nursery
217 Argilla Road
Ipswich, MA 01938-2614
Susan G. Austin

Plants
Offers nothing but **clematis**; a good selection of large flowered hybrids, and small flowered species and varieties, all briefly but well described. There may be some difficulty shipping to certain parts of Canada. (1985)
❒ Catalog: $1.50d, CAN, SS:3-4, $30m, bn
⌂ Nursery: June-September, daily, by appointment only

Comstock, Ferre & Co.
P.O. Box 125
263 Main Street
Wethersfield, CT 06109
(203) 529-3319
Pierre Bennerup

Seeds
Offer older varieties of **vegetables** and new varieties proven to be more disease-resistant and productive; plants are well described with some cultural information for each. Also offer seeds of annuals and perennials, a good selection including everlastings. (1820)
❒ Catalog: $3d, R&W, CAN, $10m, cn/bn
⌂ Nursery: All year, daily
▼ Garden: June-September, call ahead

Comstock Seed
8520 W. 4th Street
Reno, NV 89523
(702) 746-3681
Ed & Linda Kleiner

Seeds
Offers a nice selection of seed of **native grasses and native plants** of the Great Basin region; plants are listed by common and botanical names without descriptions, most are drought tolerant. Will try to locate seeds for you if they don't have what you want. (1992)
❒ Catalog: Free($1 OV), R&W, CAN/OV, $10m, cn/bn
⌂ Nursery: All year, call ahead
▼ Garden: Late spring, call ahead

Concord Nurseries, Inc.
10175 Mileblock Road
North Collins, NY 14111
(716) 337-2485, (800) 223-2211
David M. Taylor, Pres.

Plants
A wholesale nursery which offers a broad selection of **table and wine** grapes; they are categorized as American Grape varieties, French hybrid varieties, Florida bunch varieties, American premium seeded and seedless varieties, grafted Vinifera varieties and rootstocks; no descriptions. Minimum retail order is 25 vines or $50. Bought Foster Nurseries. (1894)
❒ Catalog: Free, CAN/OV, SS:10-5, $50m

Conley's Garden Center
145 Townsend Avenue
Boothbay Harbor, ME 04538
(207) 633-5020, (800) 334-1812, FAX 633-5961
Jane Conley

Plants ⬤ Seeds
Offers **native bulbs and orchids, ferns, wildflowers, vines and ground covers**. Some of the plants well described in catalog -- a larger selection is offered in the price list without descriptions. (1940)
❒ Catalog: $1.50, CAN, SS:W, $30m, bn/cn
⌂ Nursery: All year, daily
▼ Garden: Spring-Fall, "idea" garden, daily

Connell's Dahlias
10216 - 40th Avenue East
Tacoma, WA 98446
(206) 531-0292 TO/CC $20m
Les Connell

Plants
Offers a broad selection of **dahlias** (their own hybrids and selections from around the world), grouped by type; each briefly but well described, some illustrated in color. Several collections are available for those who want to start with only a few! Also offers **gladiolus** and the wonderful annual publication "Dahlias of Today." No shipping to England. (1973)
❒ Catalog: $2, CAN/OV, SS:4
⌂ Nursery: All year, daily, call ahead (10616 Waller Rd. E)
▼ Garden: August-September, daily

The Conservancy
51563 Range Road 212A
Sherwood Park, AB, Canada T8G 1B1
James Bowick

Seeds
Specializes in "seed of **trees, shrubs, perennials, wildflowers and grasses**
native to, or adapted to, climate zones 1 to 4." This includes conifers,
deciduous trees and shrubs, vines and herbaceous perennials for natural
landscaping; all from a private preserve and all well described. (1991)
❒ Catalog: $2, bn

The Cook's Garden
P.O. Box 535
Moffits Bridge
Londonderry, VT 05148
(802) 824-3400 or 3406, FAX 824-3027 TO/CC
Shepherd & Ellen Ogden

Seeds ∾ Books ∾ Supplies
Specializes in **vegetables and salad greens, edible flowers and ornamental
vegetables** for home gardeners/cooks and specialty market gardeners. A very
broad selection with good plant descriptions and growing hints; also some
seed starting supplies and books, including their "The Cook's Garden." (1977)
❒ Catalog: $1($2 OV), CAN/OV
⌂ Nursery: All year, M-F, call ahead
▼ Garden: June-August, by appointment only

Cooley's Gardens
P.O. Box 126
11553 Silverton Road N.E.
Silverton, OR 97381
(503) 873-5463 or 8537, FAX 873-5812 TO/CC
Richard C. Ernst

Plants
Color catalog offers large selection of **tall bearded irises**; most are shown
in photographs, all are well described. They also offer a number of irises
which can be selected as a your-choice collection at a good savings. (1928)
❒ Catalog: $4d, R&W, CAN/OV, SS:7-9, $15m
⌂ Nursery: All year, M-F; daily during bloomtime
▼ Garden: May, daily, call ahead

Cooper's Garden
2345 Decatur Avenue North
Golden Valley, MN 55427
(612) 591-0495
Penny Aguirre

Plants
New owner but the same name: specializes in species, Siberian and Louisiana
irises, daylilies, perennials and wildflowers. Offers a good selection,
particularly species irises; plants briefly to well described. (1975)
❒ Catalog: $1($2 OV), CAN/OV, SS:8-9, bn
⌂ Nursery: Call ahead
▼ Garden: June, call ahead

Coopers Nut House/Rancho Nuez Nursery
1378 Willow Glen Road
Fallbrook, CA 92028
(619) 728-6407, FAX 728-4690
Tom & Cindy Cooper

Plants
Specialize in **macadamia nuts** (the only edible protea!); grafted trees are
available. They also publish "The Macadamia Nut Grower Quarterly," consult
with growers and sell grafting supplies. Macadamias are hardy to 27F. (1970)
❒ Catalog: Free, R&W, OV
⌂ Nursery: September-July, daily, call ahead
▼ Garden: September-July, daily, call ahead

Copacabana Gardens
P.O. Box 323
234 Hall Drive
Moraga, CA 94556
(510) 254-2302 TO
Lee Anderson & James Larsen

Plants
Specializes in **tropical and subtropical plants** for collectors and land-
scapers; a good selection, each plant is very briefly described with notes on
minimum temperature. Among the offerings are eucalyptus, palms, tropical
fruit, proteas, bamboos, subtropical flowering trees, and drought tolerant
plants from South Africa and Australia. The catalog is not dated, but
updated from time to time. Send a "want list" to see what's in stock. (1980)
❒ Catalog: $2, R&W, SS:W, $25m, bn/cn
⌂ Nursery: By appointment only
▼ Garden: By appointment only

Cordon Bleu Farms
P.O. Box 2033
418 Buena Creek Road
San Marcos, CA 92079-2033
Bob Brooks

Plants
Offers a very broad selection of **daylilies** of all types -- tetraploids,
diploids, miniatures and doubles -- plus **spuria and Louisiana irises**;
plants well described, many illustrated in color. Many other plants are
offered at the nursery. No shipping to South Africa or New Zealand. (1970)
❒ Catalog: $1, CAN/OV, SS:2-5,7-11, $12m
⌂ Nursery: All year, W-Sa
▼ Garden: April-October, daily

Corn Hill Nursery
R.R. 5
Petitcodiac, NB, Canada E0A 2H0
(506) 756-3635, FAX 756-1087
Robert Osborne

Plants
A nursery selling **fruit trees and ornamental trees and shrubs** within
Canada, they specialize in own-root hardy modern shrub and old garden
roses, which they will ship to the US and overseas. The rose descrip-
tions are very good; for more information you should see Robert Osborne's
book "Hardy Roses" (Garden Way) on growing roses in the north. (1982)
❒ Catalog: $2, R&W, US/OV, SS:2-6,10-11
⌂ Nursery: April-November, daily; December-March, M-F
▼ Garden: May-September, daily

Cornelison Bromeliads
225 San Bernardino Street
North Fort Myers, FL 33903
(813) 995-4206
Frank Cornelison

Plants
A collector's list of **bromeliads**: aechmeas, billbergias, canistrums, cryptanthus, dyckias, guzmanias, neoregelias, nidulariums, orthophytums, quesnelias, tillandsias, and vrieseas. There are no plant descriptions; cannot ship to HI. (1963)
❐ Catalog: 1 FCS
⌂ Nursery: All year, daily

Cottage Gardens
266 17th Avenue
San Francisco, CA 94121
(415) 387-7145 or (916) 687-6134 (garden)
James McWhirter, Larry Lauer & A. Feuerstein

Plants
A small nursery caters to the "iris crowd" with a broad selection of recent and new **tall bearded and median irises**. Quite a few are their own introductions; new introductions are well described, all others are given brief descriptions. Elvis fans will find an iris named for The King. (1974)
❐ Catalog: Free ($2 OV), R&W, CAN/OV, SS:7-8, $20m
⌂ Nursery: April-May, call ahead (11314 Randolph Rd., Wilton)
▼ Garden: April-May, call ahead (11314 Randolph Rd., Wilton)

Country Bloomers Nursery
Route 2, Box 33-B
Udall, KS 67146
(316) 986-5518, FAX 986-5493
Mike & Sharon Morton

Plants
A good selection of **old garden and miniature roses**, listed by name, color, year of introduction and hybridizer (and old roses by type of rose). The old garden roses are available as liners or as year-old bare-root plants and should be reserved in advance of bare-root season. (1982)
❐ Catalog: Free, R&W, CAN/OV, $25m, bn

Country Cottage
10502 N 135 W
Sedgwick, KS 67135-9675
Micki Crozier

Plants
"Catering to the enthusiastic gardener," collectors' list of **sempervivums, sedums and jovibarbas**, well to briefly described, with some cultural notes. It makes you think that you must have room for a few of these plants, with their "flushes" of various colors -- they sound irresistible. Grow many more than they list, so you can send your "want list." (1983)
❐ Catalog: Long SASE, SS:4-9, bn
⌂ Nursery: April-September, by appointment only
▼ Garden: April-September, by appointment only

Country Heritage Nursery
P.O. Box 536
Hartford, MI 49057-0536
(616) 621-2491 or 2260
William & Marjorie Hall

Plants
Country Heritage offers various **fruit trees**, many kinds of **berries**, table **grapes, kiwis, asparagus, rhubarb, and other root vegetables**. Plants well described for flavor and best growing climates and conditions. (1986)
❐ Catalog: Free, R&W, CAN/OV, SS:1-7,9-11, $10m
⌂ Nursery: All year, M-Sa

The Country Mouse
11780 W. Hafeman Road
Orfordville, WI 53576
(608) 879-2270
Ron & Leigh Rawhoof

Plants
A small new nursery offers a good selection of **herbs and perennials**, with good brief plant descriptions and cultural suggestions, and information on traditional uses. They will help you locate rare and unusual herbs if they don't have them, and have a gift shop at the nursery. Ship only to the contiguous 48 states. (1991)
❐ Catalog: $1d, R&W, SS:5-10, $15m, bn/cn
⌂ Nursery: May-November, W-Sa
▼ Garden: Spring-Fall, W-Sa

Country Wetlands Nursery & Consulting
S. 75 W. 20755, Field Drive
Muskego, WI 53150
(414) 679-1268, FAX 679-1279
JoAnn Gillespie

Plants ⬿ **Seeds** ⬿ **Books** ⬿ **Supplies**
This nursery specializes in **wetland plants** and will help you create wild-life ponds and natural wetland habitats. They sell both plants and seeds (some habitat-collected), and some books on wetland plants. Plants given only a general description, listed by botanical and common names. (1986)
❐ Catalog: $2, CAN, SS:4-10, bn/cn
⌂ Nursery: April-November, M-F, call ahead
▼ Garden: May-September, M-F, call ahead

Craven's Nursery
1 Foulds Terrace
Bingley, W. Yorkshire, England BD16 4LZ
(0274) 56-1412
Stephen & Marlene Craven

Seeds
A specialist in **primula** seed, and offering a very good selection: auriculas, wandas, many species primulas, and mixes and selections of special show varieties. All plants are well described, some shown in charming drawings.
❐ Catalog: $2(US Bills), OV, £5m, bn

Creole Orchids
P.O. Box 24458
New Orleans, LA 70184-4458
(504) 282-5191, (800) 729-6804, FAX 827-5391
Harry A. Freiberg, Jr.

Plants
Hybrid orchids of all kinds: cattleya alliance, oncidium alliance, paphiopedilum alliance, dendrobium alliance and cymbidium alliance, both divisions and seedlings. Good selection, brief plant descriptions. (1981)
❐ Catalog: $1.75 ($2 OV), R&W, CAN/OV, $30m
⌂ Nursery: All year, by appointment only
▼ Garden: All year, by appointment only

Cricket Hill Garden
670 Walnut Hill Rd.
Thomaston, CT 06787
(203) 283-4707 or 1042
Kasha & David Furman

Plants

Cricket Hill imports and sells **tree peonies** from China; all are three years old or three branched. They have wonderful names: 'Intoxicated Celestial Peach,' 'Mixing Delicacy with Joy,' 'The Blossom that Greets the Day!' Expensive, but with names like that, think of the bragging rights! Color photos. (1988)
❒ Catalog: $2d, R&W, CAN/OV, $50
⌂ Nursery: All year, daily, call ahead
▼ Garden: May-June, call ahead

Cricklewood Nursery
11907 Nevers Road
Snohomish, WA 98290
(206) 568-2829
Evie Douglas

Plants

Small nursery specializes in old-fashioned "**English cottage border perennials**" and **rock garden plants** -- a very nice selection listed only by botanical name. Offers species geraniums, hebes, species primulas and many others. (1982)
❒ Catalog: $1, R&W, SS:3-5,9-10, bn
⌂ Nursery: April-June, F-Sa
▼ Garden: May-June, F-Sa

Crintonic Gardens
County Line Road
Gates Mills, OH 44040
(216) 423-3349
Curt Hanson

Plants

A **daylily** hybridizer who offers his own new and recent introductions, and recent tetraploid and diploid introductions of other prominent hybridizers. These are much sought after by other daylily hybridizers, but are too expensive for the ordinary gardener. New varieties well described. (1982)
❒ Catalog: $1d, R&W, CAN, SS:4-6, $50m
⌂ Nursery: May-September, daily, call ahead

C. Criscola Iris Garden
Route 2, Box 183
Walla Walla, WA 99362
(509) 525-4841
Carrie Criscola

Plants

Offers a good selection of bearded **irises**, listed only by name. The prices indicate that she offers both older and newer varieties.
❒ Catalog: 2 FCS

Crockett's Tropical Plants
P.O. Box 389
Harlingen, TX 78551-0389
(210) 423-1747, (800) 580-1747, FAX 423-1792
Stan & Allan Crockett

Plants ⁐ Supplies

Offers a very nice selection of **tropical and sub-tropical** plants: bougainvillea, citrus trees, gardenias, Chinese hibiscus, jasmines, lantanas, mandevillas, natal plums, oleanders, palms and others. Also sells their own tropical potting soil and tropical fertilizer. (1952)
❒ Catalog: $3, CAN/OV, cn/bn

Crosman Seed Corp.
P.O. Box 110
511 W. Commercial Street
East Rochester, NY 14445
(716) 586-1928 TO/CC
William & Justine Mapstone, Mgrs.

Seeds

Calling themselves "America's oldest packet seed house," they offer a good selection of **vegetable, herb and annual flower** seeds on a combined seed list/order form; no descriptions of plants, prices very reasonable. (1838)
❒ Catalog: Free, R&W, CAN/OV, $3m
⌂ Nursery: All year, M-F
▼ Garden: Spring-Fall, M-F

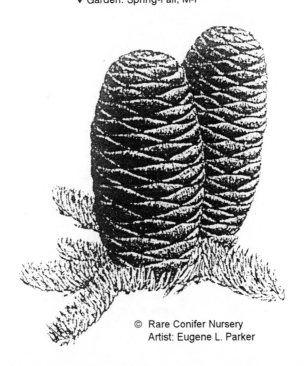

© Rare Conifer Nursery
Artist: Eugene L. Parker

Cross Seed Company
109 9th Street
Bunker Hill, KS 67626
(913) 483-6163
Dale K. Cross

Seeds
A small supplier of organic **grain, bean, sprouting and sunflower seeds**, most available organically grown. Offered are: lentils, adzuki, popcorn, mung beans, barley, rye, oats, wheat, buckwheat, millet, black and striped sunflower seeds and various seeds for sprouting. (1943)
❒ Catalog: $1d, R&W, CAN/OV, SS:6-9
⌂ Nursery: All year, M-F, Sa am
♥ Garden: Summer, M-F, Sa am

Crownsville Nursery
P.O. Box 797
Crownsville, MD 21032
(410) 923-2212
Charles Wasitis

Plants
Catalog offers a large selection of **perennials, ornamental grasses, herbs, wildflowers and ferns and some shrubs and azaleas** -- each very well described with cultural information. Many aquilegias, daylilies, dianthus, campanulas, species geraniums, phlox, and hostas. No shipping to AZ, CA or WA.
❒ Catalog: $2d, SS:3-5,9-11, $25m, bn/cn

Cruickshank's, Inc.
1015 Mount Pleasant Road
Toronto, ON, Canada M4P 2M1
(416) 488-8292, (800) 665-5605, FAX 488-8802
Laura Rapp, Linda Ledgett & Annette McCoubrey

Plants ❧ **Books** ❧ **Supplies** ❧ **Tools** ❧ **Bulbs**
Spring catalog offers a large selection of **summer-blooming bulbs**: begonias, gladiolus, dahlias, amaryllis, cannas, caladiums and lilies. Also offers **perennials** such as peonies, daylilies, clematis and many irises. Another catalog offers a broad selection of **spring bulbs**, major and minor. (1927)
❒ Catalog: $3d, R&W, US/OV, SS:W, $20m, bn/cn
⌂ Nursery: All year, M-Sa

Cumberland Valley Nurseries, Inc.
P.O. Box 471
McMinnville, TN 37110-0471
(615) 668-4153, FAX 473-4279
W. W. Bragg, Pres.

Plants
Specializes in **peaches, plums and nectarines** for larger plantings and home growers. Also offers apples (hardy and low-chill), cherries, pears, apricots and pecans. Informative leaflet -- a very large selection of peaches listed by ripening sequence. Can't ship to AZ, CA, OR or WA. (1902)
❒ Catalog: Free, R&W, SS:12-3, $25m
⌂ Nursery: All year, M-F, call ahead

The Cummins Garden
22 Robertsville Road
Marlboro, NJ 07746
(908) 536-2591 TO/CC
Elizabeth K. Cummins

Plants
Specialize in **dwarf and small leaved rhododendrons, azaleas and dwarf conifers** for the rock garden and bonsai, also kalmias, heathers, pieris, boxwood and other acid-loving plants; all well described. They are adding new varieties all the time and have an annual plant propagation workshop -- call for details. Can't ship to AZ, CA, OR, or WA. (1972)
❒ Catalog: $2, R&W, SS:3-6,9-11, $15m, bn/cn
⌂ Nursery: All year, daily, call ahead
♥ Garden: April-October, call ahead

Cycad Gardens
4524 Toland Way
Los Angeles, CA 90041
(213) 255-6651, FAX 344-0858
Loran M. Whitelock

Plants
Specializes in **cycad seedlings** -- bowenia, ceratozamia, cycas, dioon, encephalartos, lepidozamia, macrozamia, stangeria and zamia -- with notes on origins. Some plants also available in gallon sizes; you can send a "want list" for other rare items that may be available from time to time. (1978)
❒ Catalog: Long SASE, $30m, bn
⌂ Nursery: By appointment only

Dabney Herbs
P.O. Box 22061
Louisville, KY 40252
(502) 893-5198 TO/CC $20m
Davy Dabney

Plants ❧ **Books** ❧ **Supplies**
Offers a good selection of **herbs, scented geraniums, ginseng, perennials** and **wildflowers**, all well described, as well as books, potpourri supplies and cooking extracts in an informative catalog. (1986)
❒ Catalog: $2, R&W, SS:9-6, cn/bn

Dacha Barinka
46232 Strathcona Road
Chilliwack, BC, Canada V2P 3T2
(604) 792-0957
David Schmierbach

Seeds
Offers seeds for **everlasting flowers, vegetables, herbs** and Chinese vegetables, as well as seeds and starts of onions, garlic and chives. Also some table and wine grapes, the 'Holunder' German elderberry, which is a very heavy bearer, and nut trees and miscellaneous ornamental plants.
❒ Catalog: Long SASE, OV, SS:3-5

The Daffodil Mart
Route 3, Box 794
Gloucester, VA 23061
(804) 693-3966 FAX 693-9436 TO/CC $20m
Brent & Becky Heath

Books ❧ **Tools** ❧ **Bulbs**
A very extensive catalog of **spring bulbs** -- hundreds of varieties, as well as novelty, miniature and species daffodils. Request the specialty bulb catalog for less common bulbs, or the **summer bulb** catalog; between the three catalogs, over 1,000 species or cultivars of bulbs are offered. Offer growing supplies, tools and books; they also do consultation and give illustrated lectures on bulb plantings. Prices drop as quantity rises. (1935)
❒ Catalog: Free, R&W, CAN/OV, SS:9-11, $15m, bn
⌂ Nursery: By appointment only
♥ Garden: March-April, by appointment only

Daisy Fields
12635 S.W. Brighton Lane
Hillsboro, OR 97123-9051
JoAnn Wiltrakis

Plants
Here's a nursery after my own heart -- they named it after their beloved dog! The specialize in "**old-fashioned herbaceous perennials**," a nice selection with good plant descriptions. Keep up the good work, Daisy! (1989)
❒ Catalog: $1d, R&W, SS:4-6,9-10, bn/cn

William Dam Seeds
P.O. Box 8400
279 Highway 8 (Flamborough)
Dundas, ON, Canada L9H 6M1
FAX (905) 627-1729
René Dam

Seeds ∾ Books ∾ Supplies
Color catalog of short-season **vegetables, herbs, annuals and perennials**: varieties of European and Oriental vegetables and seeds for **houseplants**. Plants are well described; all seeds are untreated. Some organic growing supplies, propagation supplies and gardening books. (1949)
❒ Catalog: $2d, US/OV, SS:W
⌂ Nursery: All year, M-Sa
▼ Garden: Summer, M-Sa

Dan's Dahlias
1087 South Bank Road
Oakville, WA 98568
(206) 482-2607
Dan Pearson

Plants
Offers a nice selection of both "exhibition type" **dahlias** and varieties best for the cut flower market; all are well described, and quite a few are shown in color. (1983)
❒ Catalog: $2d, R&W, CAN/OV, SS:3-5, $10m
⌂ Nursery: August-October, daily, call ahead
▼ Garden: August-October, daily, call ahead

Dane Company
4626 Lamont Street
Corpus Christi, TX 78411
(512) 852-3806
Rosa Meilleur

Plants
A collectors' list of **bromeliads** -- aechmea, billbergia, cryptanthus, many neoregelias (including their own "neo" hybrids), tillandsia species and hybrids; no plant descriptions. Plants shipped bare-root by Priority Mail.
❒ Catalog: Long SASE, SS:W, $20m, bn
⌂ Nursery: All year, by appointment only
▼ Garden: April-September, by appointment only

Davidson-Wilson Greenhouses
RR 2, Box 168
Ladoga Road
Crawfordsville, IN 47933-9426
(317) 364-0556, FAX 364-0563
Barbara Wilson & Marilyn Davidson

Plants
Specializes in **geraniums, begonias, African violets and other gesneriads, ferns, cactus, ivy, hoyas, herbs, succulents, hibiscus** and much more; b&w photos illustrate many plants, each briefly to well described. They will sell wholesale to the public with a minimum of 100 plants ordered. (1980)
❒ Catalog: $2(4$ OV), R&W, SS:W
⌂ Nursery: All year, M-Sa
▼ Garden: May-September, M-Sa

B. & D. Davies
2 Wirral View, Connah's Quay
Deeside, Clwyd, Wales CH5 4TE
B. Davies

Seeds
A seed source for **conifers, trees and shrubs**: a nice selection, with no plant descriptions. They also offer mixed packets of conifer seeds. (1980)
❒ Catalog: 3 IRC, OV, $10m, bn

Corwin Davis Nursery
20865 Junction Road
Bellevue, MI 49021
(616) 781-7402
Corwin Davis

Plants ∾ Seeds
Sells plants and seeds of **pawpaw**; plants are either seedlings or grafts. He calls pawpaw the "forgotten fruit: edible and beautiful trees for landscaping, nothing bothers them, insects or pests or diseases." Sound terrific! Send SASE for price list; $4 for informational bulletin.
❒ Catalog: See notes, SS:4
⌂ Nursery: All year, call ahead

Daylily Discounters
1 Daylily Plaza
Alachua, FL 32615
(904) 462-1539, FAX 462-5111 TO/CC
Ara Das

Plants
A **daylily** nursery which offers varieties with a proven track record nationally; all are very well described, and many are illustrated in color photographs. Claim hardiness on all varieties to Zone 5. (1988)
❒ Catalog: $2d, R&W, CAN/OV, $25m
▼ Garden: April-May, call ahead

Daylily World
P.O. Box 1612
260 N. White Cedar Road
Sanford, FL 32772-1612
(407) 322-4034
E. David Kirchhoff

Plants
A very broad selection of **daylilies** in a catalog with color and b&w photos; new introductions well described, older varieties briefly described. They have many diploids and tetraploids, and many blooms seem to be double. Both David Kirchhoff and Mort Morss are award winners for hybridizing. (1971)
❒ Catalog: $5d, CAN/OV, $30m
⌂ Nursery: March-October, M-F, call ahead
▼ Garden: March-July, M-F, call ahead

Daystar
Route 2, Box 250
Litchfield-Hallowell Road (West Gardiner)
Litchfield, ME 04350
(207) 724-3369
Marjorie & George Walsh

Plants
A good selection of **alpine, rock garden and dwarf plants**; many are choice, including dwarf conifers and shrubs, daphnes, hardy ferns, ornamental grasses, heathers, dianthus, phlox, holly, azaleas, rhododendrons; plants are very briefly described. (1969)
❒ Catalog: $1d, R&W, CAN, SS:4-6,9-11, $15m, bn
⌂ Nursery: March-November, call ahead
▼ Garden: By appointment only

Peter De Jager Bulb Co.
P.O. Box 2010
188 Asbury Street
South Hamilton, MA 01982
(508) 468-4707, FAX 468-6642 TO/CC
Peter De Jager

Bulbs
A very good selection of **Dutch bulbs** -- tulips, daffodils, crocuses, alliums, amaryllis, hybrid lilies, hyacinths and other spring and fall bulbs. Well illustrated and described in a color catalog. (1954)
❒ Catalog: Free, R&W, SS:9-12, $10m

Deerwood Geraniums

See Brawner Geraniums.

DeGiorgi Seed Company
6011 'N' Street
Omaha, NE 68117-1634
(402) 731-3901, FAX 731-8475 TO/CC $10m
Duane & Monte Thompson

Seeds ❧ Books ❧ Supplies
A good old-fashioned catalog, offering a broad selection of garden **annuals, perennials, wildflowers, ornamental grasses and vegetables** for home and commercial growers. All varieties are well described, with cultural suggestions; also offers books and supplies. (1905)
❒ Catalog: $2($3 OV), R&W, CAN/OV, $10m, bn/cn
⌂ Nursery: January-November, daily
▼ Garden: June-September, daily

DeGrandchamp's Blueberry Farm
15575 - 77th Street
South Haven, MI 49090
(616) 637-3915, FAX (616) 637-2531
Mike DeGrandchamp

Plants
Specializes in **blueberries** -- 19 kinds by their count -- as well as some small and large leafed **rhododendrons, Northern Lights azaleas, pieris, kalmias, Meserve hollies and heathers**. They've added four cultivars of lingonberries: 'Sussi' and 'Sanna' from Sweden, and 'Splendor' and 'Regal' from the University of Winconsin.
❒ Catalog: Free, R&W, $25m
⌂ Nursery: March-December, M-F

Del's Japanese Maples
240 Irving Road
Eugene, OR 97404
(503) 688-2174, 688-5587
Delbert Loucks

Plants
Small nursery sells grafted **Japanese maples** as liners -- offers a good selection with Japanese cultivar names, no descriptions. Collectors and bonsai folks will be delighted; they grow more than 250 varieties. Some losses in "the big freeze" but stock is being built up again. (1979)
❒ Catalog: $1, R&W, CAN/OV, SS:W, $50m
⌂ Nursery: All year, by appointment only
▼ Garden: Spring-Fall, by appointment only

Delegeane Garlic Farms
P.O. Box 2561
Yountville, CA 94599
(707) 944-8019
James & Nyda Delegeane

Plants
Sells elephant, white and red **garlic** cloves for autumn planting, with growing and harvesting instructions. Also sells various seasonings, wildflower honey and garlic and shallots for cooking. (1979)
❒ Catalog: Free, CAN, SS:8-11, $3m

Desert Enterprises
P.O. Box 23
Morristown, AZ 85342
(602) 388-2448
Judith A. Clement

Seeds
Specializes in **native plants** for revegetation and erosion control; offers grass, shrub, tree and wildflower seed by the pound only. The also offer seeds of cacti, wildflower mixes, and custom desert revegetation mixes for your specific location requirement. No plant descriptions. (1972)
❒ Catalog: $1d, R&W, bn/cn

Desert Moon Nursery
P.O. Box 600
Veguita, NM 87062
(505) 864-0614
Theodore & Candace Hodoba

Plants ❧ Seeds
Offers a fine listing of nursery propagated **Southwestern native plants**; cactus and succulents, yuccas, agaves, and wildflowers, grown for their interesting shapes, lovely flowers, or utility (shade and windbreaks). All plants are well described, they will be listing seeds in 1994. (1987)
❒ Catalog: $1, R&W, $15m, SS:4-10, bn
⌂ Nursery: April-October, Sa; other days by appointment
▼ Garden: May-September, Sa; other days by appointment

Desert Nursery
1301 South Copper
Deming, NM 88030
(505) 546-6264
Shirley J. Nyerges

Plants
Small nursery offers a good selection of **cacti and succulents** for the collector, some very hardy; descriptions are sketchy but geographical origins are given. Plants include: echinocereus, opuntias, mammillarias, parodias, rebutias, euphorbias and haworthias. Hours vary, call ahead! (1977)
❒ Catalog: Free, SS:W, $20m, bn
⌂ Nursery: September-February, M-Sa, call ahead
▼ Garden: April-May, greenhouse, call ahead

Desert Theatre
17 Behler Road
Watsonville, CA 95076
(408) 728-5513, FAX 728-4091
Kate Jackson

Plants
A broad selection of **cactus and succulents** from South America and Africa, including aloes, lithops, notocactus, haworthias, echeverias, euphorbias, gymnocalyciums, mammillarias, rebutias and sulcorebutias, listed by botanical name; catalog gives brief descriptions. (1979)
☐ Catalog: $2d, R&W, SS:2-10, $20m, bn
⌂ Nursery: All year, Tu-Su
♥ Garden: April-June, Tu-Sa

Desertland Nursery
P.O. Box 26126
11306 Gateway East
El Paso, TX 79926
(915) 858-1130, FAX 858-1560 TO/CC
David & Lupina Guerra

Plants ⁓ Seeds
Specializes in rare and hard-to-find **Mexican and South American cactus** and some **succulents, desert and subtropical trees** -- plants and seeds, some habitat-collected. Seed list issued under name Aztekakti. Both are collectors' lists, just botanical names, but offer a very good selection. (1976)
☐ Catalog: $1, R&W, bn
⌂ Nursery: All year, daily, call ahead
♥ Garden: Spring-Summer, daily, call ahead

Dick's Flower Farm
N 5028 Delaney Road
Delavan, WI 53115
(414) 724-5682
Richard M. Hinz, Sr.

Bulbs
A new source of **summer blooming bulbs**: gladiolus, dahlias, hybrid lilies, and a few caladiums, cannas, and others. A nice selection, described only as to color. (1992)
☐ Catalog: $1, R&W, SS:4-5,9-10, $10m
⌂ Nursery: May-October, call ahead
♥ Garden: August-September, call ahead

Digging Dog Nursery
P.O. Box 471
Albion, CA 95410
(707) 937-1130, FAX 937-4389
Deborah Whigham & Gary Ratway

Plants
Offers a good selection of "good doers," **perennials, shrubs and trees** which they have grown for years on the northern California coast, many are cultivars I haven't seen listed elsewhere: artemisias, asters, campanulas, dianthus, eupatorium, species geraniums, penstemons, ornamental grasses and a number of good shrubs and a few trees. Good plant descriptions. (1980)
☐ Catalog: $2d, R&W, CAN, SS:2-5,9-11, $20m
⌂ Nursery: All year, M-Sa, by appointment only

Howard Dill Enterprises
RR 1
400 College Road
Windsor, NS, Canada B0N 2T0
(902) 798-2728, FAX 798-0842
Howard N. Dill

Seeds ⁓ Books
Sells seed of 'Dill's Atlantic Giant' **pumpkin**, which has obtained a world class weight of 827 pounds -- up 400 pounds just since I did the first edition of this book! Also offered are seeds of several other varieties of pumpkins, and a book about Howard, the "Sultan of Squash." (1979)
☐ Catalog: $1, R&W, US/OV
♥ Garden: August-October, call ahead

Dixondale Farms
P.O. Box 127
Carrizo Springs, TX 78834
(210) 876-2430, 876-2335, FAX 876-9640 TO/CC
Bruce Frasier

Plants
Offers a nice selection of **onion plants** for home gardeners: Texas Supersweet, Granex (yellow Granex also called Vidalia, Maui, Society or Noonday), White Bermuda, Walla Walla, Spanish and Sweet Flat Red. (1913)
☐ Catalog: Long SASE, R&W, SS:1-4, $8m

Dominion Seed House
P.O. Box 2500
Georgetown, ON, Canada L7G 5L6
(416) 873-3037 TO/CC

Seeds ⁓ Books ⁓ Supplies ⁓ Tools ⁓ Bulbs
A Canadian garden emporium selling seeds of **annuals, perennials and vegetables**, as well as summer-blooming bulbs, berries and seed potatoes; many illustrated in color and all well described. In addition, they sell tools, gardening supplies, canning equipment and books. (1927)
☐ Catalog: Free, R&W, SS:4-9, cn/bn

Donaroma's Nursery
P.O. Box 2189
Upper Main Street
Edgartown, MA 02539
(508) 627-8595 or 3036, FAX 627-7855 TO/CC
Michael Donaroma

Plants
Nursery on Martha's Vineyard that specializes in **perennials** and **wildflowers**; a very good selection, well described in their "listing of choice perennials." They send out availability lists in spring and fall. Broad choice of aquilegia, astilbe, campanula, delphinium, dianthus, inula, lupine, meconopsis, papaver, silene and veronica and many others.
☐ Catalog: $1, R&W, CAN/OV, SS:2-5,9-12, bn/cn
⌂ Nursery: All year, M-Sa
♥ Garden: Summer, M-Sa

Donnelly's Nursery
705 Charlotte Highway
Fairview, NC 28730
Russell Donnelly

Plants
A nice selection of **hosta**, all briefly but well described. (1975)
☐ Catalog: $1d, SS:4-10, $15m
⌂ Nursery: April-October, call ahead

Donovan's Roses
P.O. Box 37800
Shreveport, LA 71133-7800
(318) 861-6693, 865-3273
Tom Schimschock

Plants
Offers a nice selection of recently introduced **roses**, hybrid teas, flori-
bundas, shrubs, and climbers, many of which were All America Rose
Selections or World Class Roses -- many of these are the roses in
demand by rose show people. Good plant descriptions. (1982)
❒ Catalog: Long SASE, SS:1-4, $21m

Double D Nursery
2215 Dogwood Lane
Arnoldsville, GA 30619
(706) 742-7417, (800) 438-7685 TO/CC
Janet & David Duerk

Plants
A new mail-order source of **ground covers**: ajuga, hostas, honeysuckles, ivy,
jasmines, liriope, sedums, vincas and other vines, and more, including daylilies and some other perennials. Plants well described, and tables give
information on the best plants for various uses. (1992)
❒ Catalog: Free, $10m

Down on the Farm Seeds
P.O. Box 184
Hiram, OH 44234
Rose A. Guth

Seeds
A newish seed company run by an Ohio farm family, specializing in open-pollinated and heirloom varieties; all seeds are untreated. A good selection of
vegetables, including tomatoes and also some herbs and old fashioned garden
flowers. Each variety briefly described. (1990)
❒ Catalog: Free, CAN/OV, $1m

Jim Duggan Flower Nursery
1817 Sheridan
Leucadia, CA 92024
(619) 943-1658
Jim Duggan

Bulbs
Small nursery offers a nice selection of **South African bulbs** for container
growing, rock gardens, and for naturalizing in dry summer areas; these bulbs
need a Mediterranean climate. Brief plant descriptions; growing 200 species,
so choice will increase as he builds up stock. List mailed in June. (1991)
❒ Catalog: Long SASE($1 OV), CAN/OV, SS:7-9, $10, bn
▼ Garden: February-April, by appointment only

Dunford Farms
P.O. Box 238
Sumner, WA 98390
Donald Duncan & Warren Gifford

Plants ❧ Bulbs
Sells **agapanthus** 'Headbourne Hybrids' and **alstroemerias**; aurantiaca,
pelegrina, mongolica or 'Ligtu Hybrids,' their own re-selections, and two
hybrids, 'Kay Davis' and 'Walter Fleming.' They have added **cyclamen** coum
and hederifolium and some other perennials. (1973)
❒ Catalog: $1, SS:2-5

Dutch Gardens, Inc.
P.O. Box 200
Adelphia, NJ 07710
(908) 780-2713, FAX 780-7720 TO/CC
John & Nick Langeveld

Bulbs
Color catalog of spring-flowering **Dutch bulbs** offers all of the most popular hybrids, with some cultural information. They have bulk order plans and
another catalog of **summer-blooming bulbs** -- lilies, gladiolus, dahlias,
cannas, amaryllis and some perennials. Brief cultural hints. (1960)
❒ Catalog: Free, R&W, SS:2-5, $20m, cn/bn

Dyke Blueberry Farm & Nursery
Route 1, Box 251
Vincent, OH 45784
(614) 678-2192
James Armour

Plants
Offer four varieties of highbush **blueberries** -- 'Blueray,' 'Berkeley,'
'Colville' and 'Jersey.' Minimum order for blueberries is twelve plants;
varieties can be mixed. Blackberries available as single plants.
❒ Catalog: Long SASE, SS:W
⌂ Nursery: All year, call ahead
▼ Garden: Pick your own berries, call ahead

Early's Farm & Garden Centre, Inc.
2615 Lorne Avenue South
Saskatoon, SK, Canada S7J 0S5
(306) 931-1982 TO/CC
J. C. Bloski, Mgr.

Seeds ❧ Supplies ❧ Tools ❧ Bulbs
This old firm re-entered the mail order business in 1985 with a color catalog offering **garden flower and vegetable seeds, gladiolus bulbs** and a huge
selection of supplies and tools -- everything for Northern gardening. I love
the name Saskatoon, Saskatchewan -- say it slowly, with feeling. (1907)
❒ Catalog: $2d, R&W, US, $25m
⌂ Nursery: All year, M-Sa

Earthly Goods, Ltd.
903 E. 15th Street
New Albany, IN 47150
Stephen Brown & Ann Streckfus

Seeds ❧ Supplies
Offers a nice selection of **wildflower seeds**, both single species and mixes
for various regions; good plant descriptions and information on natural
habitat. Also offers bird houses and bat boxes, even squirrel feeders. (1992)
❒ Catalog: $2d, CAN, $8m, bn

Eastern Plant Specialties
P.O. Box 226
Georgetown, ME 04548
(207) 371-2888 TO/CC $25m
Mark Stavish

Plants ❧ Supplies
A broad selection of hardy **rhododendrons and azaleas**, unusual and dwarf
conifers, kalmias, pieris, holly, ornamental trees, dwarf shrubs and ground
cover plants; all well described, some illustrated. Catalog full of rare and
hardy collectors' plants; lists of plants for special uses. (1982)
❒ Catalog: $3d, R&W, CAN, SS:4-11, $15m, bn
⌂ Nursery: April-November, by appointment only
▼ Garden: May-June, by appointment only

Eclipse Farms
P.O. Box 459
2917 Hy Drive
High Ridge, MO 63049
(314) 677-3619, FAX 821-5632
Paula McWilliams & Verdell Brelje

Plants ⟡ Seeds
Offers a broad selection of seeds of **Australian plants**, both in packets and by the kilogram; listed only by botanical names. They have just started offering tube-grown Australian plants for both houseplants and garden use, but do your own research, no hardiness information is given in the brief plant descriptions. (1989)
☐ Catalog: $2d(2 IRC OV), R&W, CAN/OV, SS:3-5, bn
⌂ Nursery: January-September, M-F, call ahead
♥ Garden: April-June, M-F, call ahead

Eco-Gardens
P.O. Box 1227
Decatur, GA 30031
(404) 294-6468
Don L. Jacobs, Ph.D.

Plants ⟡ Books
Eco-Gardens is a private collection of **native and exotic plants** hardy in the Piedmont region; they sell surplus plants, some of their own breeding, to raise operating funds. Nice selection of **perennials, bog plants, trilliums, species iris, ferns and shrubs**; brief descriptions. Also offer plant books at a discount. (1976)
☐ Catalog: $2, CAN/OV, SS:3-6,9-1, $10m, bn
⌂ Nursery: All year, by appointment only
♥ Garden: March-May, by appointment only

Eden Exotics
Route 1, Box 201-C
Riggins Mill Road
Dry Branch, GA 31020
(912) 743-4098
Michael Kirk

Plants
Small nursery which specializes in **hardy palms, citrus, eucalyptus** and a few flowering sub-tropical trees and shrubs; all well described. Mike says most plants he offers are hardy to USDA zone 8, and some to zone 7. (1991)
☐ Catalog: Long SASE w/ 3 FCS, R&W, CAN, $15m, bn/cn
⌂ Nursery: All year, by appointment only
♥ Garden: March-November, by appointment only

Edge of the Rockies
133 Hunna Road
Bayfield, CO 81122-9758
Susan Komarek & Kevin Tonkin

Seeds
A small seed company which offers seeds of **native Rocky Mountain plants**, from desert canyons to alpine peaks. Some are habitat collected, others are from cultivated plantings; nice selection, all well described. (1991)
☐ Catalog: $2, OV, bn/cn

Edgewood Farm & Nursery
R.R. 2, Box 303
Stanardsville, VA 22973-9405
(804) 985-3782
Robert Cary & Norman Schwartz, Jr.

Plants
Offers a huge selection of **herbs and perennials**, including many catmints, origanums, germanders, thymes, salvias and about 30 old cultivars of dianthus. They grow 700 varieties of herbs and 1,500 perennials and a good number of **species iris**; send your "want list." No shipping to AZ, CA or OR. (1987)
☐ Catalog: $2d, R&W, SS:2-5,9, $10m, bn
⌂ Nursery: April-October, M-Sa
♥ Garden: April-October, M-Sa

Edible Landscaping
P.O. Box 77
Afton, VA 22920
(804) 361-9134 TO
Michael McConkey

Plants
A selection of **fruit for Mid-Atlantic gardens**, including Actinidia arguta (hardy kiwi), black currants, several gooseberries, Oriental persimmons, mulberries, jujube, pawpaw and grapes; most plants are well described in a charmingly hand-lettered and illustrated catalog. (1980)
☐ Catalog: $2, R&W, CAN/OV, $7m
⌂ Nursery: All year, M-F, call ahead

Edmunds' Roses
6235 S.W. Kahle Road
Wilsonville, OR 97070
(503) 682-1476, FAX 682-1275 TO/CC $10m
Philip & Kathy Edmunds

Plants ⟡ Supplies
An informative color catalog offers a broad selection of modern hybrid tea, floribunda, grandiflora and climbing **roses**, all well described with cultural suggestions. They have recently changed their name from Roses by Fred Edmunds (Fred has retired). They also offer goatskin gloves, leaky pipe and Felco pruning shears. (1950)
☐ Catalog: Free, R&W, CAN/OV, SS:11-5
⌂ Nursery: All year, M-F
♥ Garden: September, M-F, call ahead

Ellison Horticultural Pty., Ltd.
P.O. Box 365
Nowra, NSW, Australia 2541
(044) 21-4255, 21-6670, FAX 23-0859
Rhonda Lebrocque, Mgr.

Seeds ⟡ Books
Bulk suppliers of **Australian tree, shrub and palm seed**, a very broad selection, including some plants from other parts of the world, with very brief plant descriptions; many plants are shown in color. Offer a good selection of **passion flowers**, among other plants. The smallest packet of seed seems to be 25 grams. Also sell books on Australian plants and gardens. (1983)
☐ Catalog: $5(US Bills), R&W, OV, $30m, bn
⌂ Nursery: All year, M-F

Emlong Nurseries
P.O. Box 236
2671 W. Marquette Woods Road
Stevensville, MI 49127
(616) 429-3431 TO/CC $10m
C. R. Emlong, Pres.

Plants
Offers a broad selection of **fruit trees, roses and general nursery stock**; catalog shows many plants in color or b&w photographs. All plants are well described. Among those offered are many berries, grapes, flowering shrubs and other shrubs for hedging, and conifers.
❏ Catalog: Free, R&W, SS:4-6,10-11, $8m
⌂ Nursery: All year, daily, call ahead (closed Su in July)
♥ Garden: April-May, daily

Enchanted Valley Garden
9123 N. Territorial Road
Evansville, WI 53536
(608) 882-4200
Al Dahman & Steve Evers

Plants
Offers a nice selection of **daylilies**, including many old favorites and some landscaping collections; each is well described. They will be offering Siberian irises in future lists, offer only a few now. Also sell at the Dane County farmers market Saturdays in summer. No shipping to CA. (1984)
❏ Catalog: Free, R&W, SS:4-9, $25m
⌂ Nursery: May-September, by appointment only
♥ Garden: July, by appointment only

Englearth Gardens
2461 - 22nd Street
Hopkins, MI 49328
(616) 793-7196
Mary Englearth Herrema

Plants
Specializes in **perennials** -- daylilies, hostas, Japanese and Siberian iris -- and offers a good selection, especially of daylilies, as well as collections of hostas and daylilies for naturalizing. Each plant is briefly described. (1931)
❏ Catalog: $.50, R&W, SS:4-6,8-10, $10m
⌂ Nursery: April-October, M-Sa
♥ Garden: July, M-Sa

Enoch's Berry Farm
Route 2, Box 227
Fouke, AR 71837
(501) 653-2806
A. B. Enoch

Plants
Offers three **blackberries** released by the Arkansas Experimental Station: 'Navaho' (thornless), 'Choctaw' and 'Shawnee.' They claim that the fruit is of very high quality. (1980)
❏ Catalog: Free, R&W, SS:12-3, $8m
⌂ Nursery: All year, M-F, call ahead

Ensata Gardens
9823 E. Michigan Avenue
Galesburg, MI 49053
(616) 665-7500 TO
John Coble & Bob Bauer

Plants
Small nursery specializing in **Japanese and Siberian iris**. They have a very broad selection of Japanese iris, smaller selection of Siberian iris; all plants are well described, and some shown in color. Also have a Japanese garden display area, for those lucky enough to be close by. (1985)
❏ Catalog: $2($3 OV), R&W, CAN/OV, SS:5-10, $15m
♥ Garden: June-July, daily, call ahead

Epi World
10607 Glenview Avenue
Cupertino, CA 95014-4514
(408) 865-0566, FAX same TO/CC
Jim Pence

Plants
Offers a nice selection of **epiphyllums, schlumbergera, and rhipsalidopsis**, known respectively as orchid cactus, christmas cactus and easter cactus; each plant well described. Also offers some starter collections. (1989)
❏ Catalog: $2, R&W, SS:4-10, $15m
⌂ Nursery: Th-Su, call ahead
♥ Garden: March-June, Th-Su, call ahead

A. I. Eppler, Ltd.
P.O. Box 16513
Seattle, WA 98116-0513
(206) 932-2211
Alexander Eppler

Plants ⬿ Books
A specialist in **currents, gooseberries, and jostaberries**; offers a broad selection of each type, with only general descriptions and growing hints for each group. Also offers Cornelian Cherry for fruit and wine, and books on berry culture. (1986)
❏ Catalog: $3d($5 OV), R&W, CAN, SS:11-3, $12m
⌂ Nursery: All year, M-F, call ahead
♥ Garden: June-August, M-F, call ahead

Eric's Exotics
6782 Belvedere Road
West Palm Beach, FL 33413
(407) 687-7700, (800) ORCHIDS, FAX 687-3000
Ann & Eric Fishman

Plants
Offers a nice selection of **hybrid orchids**: asocendas, brassavolas, brassias, cattleyas, dendrobiums, doritaenopsis, encyclias, oncidiums, phalaenopsis, rhyncostylis, and vandas; all briefly described. You can also send or Fax your "want list."
❏ Catalog: $3d, R&W, SS:W, $50m
⌂ Nursery: All year, Tu-Su
♥ Garden: All year, Tu-Sa

Ericaceae
P.O. Box 293
Deep River, CT 06417
Mathias C. Zack

Plants
A small nursery which specializes in the hardy **rhododendron** hybrids of Dr. David Leach; offers about twenty cultivars, all well described, and several cultivars of **heather** and **kalmia**, which like the same growing conditions.
❏ Catalog: Free, SS:2-6,9-11
♥ Garden: Spring, by appointment only

Ernst Crownvetch Farms
R.D. 5, Box 806
Meadville, PA 16335
(814) 425-7276, (800) 873-3321, FAX 425-2228
Calvin Ernst

Plants ～ Seeds
Mail order farm seed house can supply many **grains**; also sells several fast-growing **trees, crownvetch and grasses** for erosion control, cover crops, reclamation and ground cover, and wetland plants and seeds. Seed sold by the pound, crownvetch plants in quantity.
❏ Catalog: Free, CAN/OV, SS:4-12
⌂ Nursery: March-November, M-F

Euroseeds
P.O. Box 95
Novy Jicin, Czech Republic 741 01
Mojmir Pavelka

Seeds
One of the great things about the opening of Eastern Europe is the number of new seed sources; Euroseeds specializes in rare **alpine and rock garden** plants from Romania, Bulgaria, Turkey, Slovenia and other parts of Europe. Campanulas, daphnes, gentians, flax, primulas on a list with brief plant descriptions. (1991)
❏ Catalog: $2(US Bills), OV, bn
⌂ Nursery: October-June, daily

Murray Evans Daffodils

See Oregon Trail Daffodils.

Evergreen Acres Dahlia Gardens
682 Pulaski Road
Greenlawn, NY 11740
(516) 262-9423 TO $50m
Joe & Nedra Marsh

Plants
Offers a good selection of **dahlias**, with new introductions from the US, Canada, Japan, England and New Zealand, as well as established cultivars. Plants are described by form and color in table form, no descriptions. (1975)
❏ Catalog: Long SASE w/2 FCS($1 OV), CAN/OV, SS:4-6
⌂ Nursery: May-November, daily, call ahead
▼ Garden: September-October, daily, call ahead

Evergreen Gardenworks
P.O. Box 1357
430 North Oak Street
Ukiah, CA 95482
(707) 462-8909 $25m
Brent Watson

Plants
A small nursery which specializes in **bonsai, dwarf shrubs, alpines,** Mediterranean species and plants which are drought-proof and deer-proof. A good selection: maples, hornbeams, flowering quinces and crabs, clematis, cotoneaster, dianthus, helianthemums, crape myrtles, conifers, flowering cherries and elms. No plant descriptions. No shipping to HI. (1989)
❏ Catalog: $1, R&W, CAN, $25m, bn
⌂ Nursery: March-November, call ahead
▼ Garden: March-November, call ahead

Evergreen Y. H. Enterprises
P.O. Box 17538
Anaheim, CA 92817-7538
Wen Hwang

Seeds ～ Books ～ Supplies
Offers a broad selection of **Oriental vegetables**, even that cute "baby corn!" Varieties listed in English and Chinese and well described. Sells Oriental gardening and cookbooks and oriental seasonings and sauces. (1978)
❏ Catalog: $2d($3 OV), R&W, CAN/OV, $5m

John Ewing Orchids, Inc.
P.O. Box 1318
487 White Road (Watsonville)
Soquel, CA 95073
(408) 684-1111
John & Loraine Ewing

Plants
Collectors' list of seedling phalaenopsis **orchids**, available in several sizes; in pink, white, yellow, tan and red stripes or spots on colored backgrounds; available in flasks, as stem propagations or seedlings. Also cymbidiums, miltonias and cattleyas in season.
❏ Catalog: Free, R&W, CAN/OV
⌂ Nursery: All year, M-Sa, call ahead
▼ Garden: March-June, greenhouse

Exotica Rare Fruit Nursery
P.O. Box 160
2508-B East Vista Way
Vista, CA 92085
(619) 724-9093
Steve Spangler & Jessica Leaf

Plants
Offers **tropical fruits and flowering trees and nuts**, Hawaiian ornamentals, palms and Mexican and South American fruit -- all for southern climates. Listed are bananas, figs, sapotes, annonas, low-chill apples and palms. They also do consultation on edible landscaping. (1975)
❏ Catalog: Long SASE, R&W, CAN/OV, cn/bn
⌂ Nursery: All year, daily
▼ Garden: All year, daily

Fairweather Gardens
P. O. Box 330
Greenwich, NJ 08323
(609) 451-6261 TO/CC
Robert Popham & Robert Hoffman

Plants
I have grown to love **viburnums**, and this nursery has a very good selection. They offer a fine selection of **ornamental trees and shrubs,** many are new or recent introductions, including **camellias, hollies, magnolias, oaks** and the aforementioned viburnums; the catalog is very informative. (1989)
❏ Catalog: $3($5 OV), CAN/OV, SS:9-5, bn/cn
⌂ Nursery: All year, daily
▼ Garden: All year, daily

Fairyland Begonia & Lily Garden
1100 Griffith Road
McKinleyville, CA 95521
(707) 839-3034
Winkey Woodriff

Bulbs
Hybridizes **lilies**, also sells acidanthera, hybrid calla lilies, amaryllis and amarine and nerines. Offers a nice selection, including mixed collections of lilies and "yearling" lilies which will bloom in two years; all plants well described, some new, rare or very fragrant. (1970)
❏ Catalog: $.50($1 OV), CAN/OV, SS:W, $10m
⌂ Nursery: All year, daily, call ahead

Fancy Fronds
1911 - 4th Avenue West
Seattle, WA 98119
(206) 284-5332, 483-0205 (Barfod's)
Judith I. Jones

Plants
A good selection of **hardy ferns**, including ferns from England, China, Japan and New Zealand and other temperate areas, all very well described and some illustrated with line drawings -- special requests invited. Judith now also sells ferns at Barfod's Hardy Ferns, 23622 Bothell Way, Bothell, WA. (1976)
❏ Catalog: $1d, R&W, CAN, SS:3-6,9-10, $10m, bn/cn
⌂ Nursery: See notes, call ahead
▼ Garden: May-October, by appointment only

Far North Gardens
16785 Harrison Street
Livonia, MI 48154
FAX (313) 522-9040
Karen J. Combs

Seeds ⚘ Books
An extensive list of seeds, offered in a confusing jumble of categories rather than alphabetically, but intriguing to the collector. Specialties include seed of Barnhaven primroses. They are adding more **perennials** and **rock garden** plants; brief to no plant descriptions. (1962)
❏ Catalog: $2d($3 OV), R&W, CAN/OV, SS:3-6,9, bn/cn

Farmer Seed & Nursery
P.O. Box 129
818 N.W. 4th Street
Faribault, MN 55021
(507) 334-1623 TO/CC $20m
Plantron, Inc.

Plants ⚘ Seeds ⚘ Supplies ⚘ Tools
A **garden emporium** in your mailbox: vegetable seeds, trees and shrubs, fruit and berries, roses, summer-blooming bulbs, tools, supplies, canning equipment. Color catalog offers broad selection of Northern-grown hardy stock, giant and midget vegetables and the gooseneck hoe that I still love! (1888)
❏ Catalog: Free, R&W, SS:3-5
⌂ Nursery: All year

Feathers Wild Flower Seeds
P.O. Box 13
Constantia, Cape, South Africa 7848
(021) 794-6432, FAX 21-7207
Rene & Alan Jeftha

Seeds
Seedsmen offering a good selection of **proteas, leucospermums, leuco-dendrons** and seeds of a few South African shrubs; very brief descriptions. Ask for the **erica** price list if you are interested. (1958)
❏ Catalog: $3(US Bills), R&W, OV, $30m, bn
⌂ Nursery: All year, M-F, call ahead
▼ Garden: All year, by appointment only

Fedco Seeds
52 Mayflower Hill Drive
Waterville, ME 04901
FAX (207) 426-9005
Cooperative

Plants ⚘ Seeds ⚘ Books ⚘ Supplies ⚘ Bulbs
Seeds of **short-season vegetables, herbs, annual and perennial flowers**. A very extensive list with every variety well described; they keep costs down by encouraging group orders. They also sell **hardy fruit and nut trees, berries and fruiting shrubs** ($50 minimum order) in the "Fedco Trees" list -- and some supplies and books on gardening. See also Moose Tubers. (1978)
❏ Catalog: $2d, SS:4,10, $25m (see notes)

Fedco Trees

See Fedco Seeds.

Fern Hill Farm
P.O. Box 185
Clarksboro, NJ 08020-0185
John F. Gyer

Seeds
Sells only **'Dr. Martin' Pole Lima Bean** seed; there's no description of this particular variety, but it must be heavy bearing and something special. Pre-germinated seed is available in April. (1971)
❏ Catalog: Long SASE, CAN/OV, $5m

Ferncliff Gardens
8394 McTaggart St.
Mission, BC, Canada V2V 6S6
(604) 826-2447, FAX 826-4316
David Jack

Plants
David Jack hybridizes "giant" **dahlias**, and introduces new varieties each year; in addition, he offers **herbaceous peonies, daylilies, gladiolus** and **tall and dwarf-bearded iris**, each briefly described. He'll ship only the dahlias to the US. (1920)
❏ Catalog: Free, R&W, US, SS:4-5,9-10, $20m
⌂ Nursery: April-September, M-Sa; October-March, M-F
▼ Garden: May-September, M-Sa

Field and Forest Products, Inc.
N3296 Kuzuzek Road
Peshtigo, WI 54157
(715) 582-4997, FAX 582-0181 TO/CC
Joseph H. Krawczyk & Mary Ellen Kozak

Seeds ⚘ Books ⚘ Supplies ⚘ Tools
Small company selling **shiitake mushroom spawn** (eleven strains for growing under various temperatures and conditions), **oyster mushroom spawn** and complete growing supplies, books and tools. Informative catalog; they also sell their own books on mushroom growing and some cookbooks. (1983)
❏ Catalog: $2d, R&W, CAN/OV
⌂ Nursery: All year, M-F
▼ Garden: By appointment only

Timothy D. Field Ferns & Wildflowers
395 Newington Road
Newington, NH 03801
(603) 436-0457
Timothy D. Field

Plants
Offers a good selection of **hardy ferns, native bulbs and perennials**, some of which have been wild collected with a permit. Plants listed by botanical and common names, with no plant descriptions.
⌂ Catalog: Free, SS:3-5,9-10, $25m
⌂ Nursery: By appointment only

Field House Alpines
6730 West Mercer Way
Mercer Island, WA 98040
June Skidmore, Agent

Seeds
Field House Alpines is a well-known British nursery specializing in seed of **alpine and rock garden plants** and **show auriculas and primulas**; they now have an agent in Washington who will send seed everywhere but England and Europe. A good selection with brief plant descriptions. (1940)
⌂ Catalog: $2, CAN/OV, $2, bn

Henry Field Seed & Nursery Co.
415 North Burnett
Shenandoah, IA 51602
(605) 665-9391 TO/CC $10m
Gurney's

Plants ⬿ Seeds ⬿ Supplies ⬿ Tools
A true **garden emporium**: vegetable and flower seeds, fruit and nut trees, grapes, berries, roses, ornamental flowering trees, shrubs and vines and growing supplies and tools. Field has been purchased by Gurney's, but still publishes a separate catalog; orders taken and shipped from Gurney's. (1892)
⌂ Catalog: Free, SS:2-6,10-11

Fieldstone Gardens, Inc.
620 Quaker Lane
Vassalboro, ME 04989-9713
(207) 923-3836
Steven D. Jones

Plants
Extensive list of **perennials and rock garden plants**: Japanese and Siberian irises, asters, astilbe, campanulas, clematis, delphiniums, epimediums, species geraniums, herbaceous and tree peonies, phlox and much more. Plants are well described, with cultural suggestions. Beautiful old farm. (1981)
⌂ Catalog: $2, CAN/OV, SS:4-6,9-11, bn/cn
⌂ Nursery: April-November, Tu-Su
▼ Garden: June-August, Tu-Su

The Fig Tree Nursery
P.O. Box 124
Gulf Hammock, FL 32639
(904) 486-2930
Gertrude Watson

Plants ⬿ Books
Offers a variety of **fig trees**, as well as **pears, muscadine grapes, mulberries and pomegranates**, each well but briefly described. Also sells her own book on "Growing Fruit Trees and Vines," ($3.45 postpaid). Can't ship plants to CA or AZ.
⌂ Catalog: $1, CAN, SS:10-3
⌂ Nursery: M-Sa, call ahead

Filaree Farm
Route 2, Box 162
Okanogan, WA 98840-9774
Ron & Watershine Engeland

Plants
Offers a huge selection of **garlic** varieties, all organically grown and lovingly described, as well as green manure crops, growing supplies for garlic growers, irrigation supplies, and Ron's book "Growing Great Garlic: the Definitive Guide for Organic Gardeners and Small Farmers." (1977)
⌂ Catalog: $2, R&W, SS:9-3, $7m
▼ Garden: May-June, call ahead

© Siskiyou Rare Plant Nursery
Artist: Baldassare Mineo

Finch Blueberry Nursery
P.O. Box 699
Bailey, NC 27807
(919) 235-4664, FAX 235-2411
Dan Finch

Plants
Offers a nice selection of northern highbush, southern highbush and rabbit-eye **blueberries**, each variety well described. Flier gives good information on blueberry culture; they sell mixed selections for cross-pollination and long bearing season. Prices are "wholesale to the public."
◻ Catalog: Free, SS:10-5
⌂ Nursery: All year, M-F

Fir Grove Perennial Nursury
19917 N.E. 68th Street
Vancouver, WA 98682
(206) 944-8384
Sheila Maynor

Plants
Everything grows in the Northwest, especially new nurseries! Fir Grove offers a good selection of **perennials and rock garden plants**: epimediums, species geraniums, the heuchera introductions of Dan Heims, and pulmonarias, among others. All plants are very well described. No shipping to AK or HI. (1991)
◻ Catalog: $2d, SS:3-6, $10m, bn
⌂ Nursery: Spring, Fall, Su-F; Summer, by appointment only
▼ Garden: Spring-Fall, Su-F, call ahead

Flickingers' Nursery
P.O. Box 245
Sagamore, PA 16250
(412) 783-6528, 397-4953, FAX 783-6528
Richard Flickinger

Plants
A wholesaler of **seedling trees** -- the same price to everyone, but a minimum of fifty trees of one variety. A nice selection of spruces, pines and firs and Canadian and Carolina hemlocks, birch and dogwood, as well as Vinca minor. (1947)
◻ Catalog: Free, SS:3-4, $50m
⌂ Nursery: All year, M-Sa

Floating Mountain Seeds
P.O. Box 1275
Port Angeles, WA 98362-1275
Roger Lemstrom

Seeds
A source of **antique and heirloom vegetable seeds** from the Pacific Northwest and elsewhere, some very intriguing such as broomcorn, Einkhorn wheat found in a Neolithic grave site (now that's antique!), and the "mortgage-lifter" tomato; all well described. Adding herbs and flowers. (1985)
◻ Catalog: $2($3 OV), CAN/OV

Floribunda Palms & Exotics
P.O. Box 635
Mt. View, HI 96771
(808) 968-8003, FAX 968-6921 (days)
Jeff Marcus

Plants
Jeff claims to grow 350 varieties of **palms** and 50 varieties of **cycads**; he specializes in Madagascan, Australian and South Pacific palms. List I received was not complete and listed plants only by botanical name. (1986)
◻ Catalog: Long SASE, R&W, SS:W
⌂ Nursery: By appointment only
▼ Garden: By appointment only

Florida Colors Nursery
23740 S.W. 147th Avenue
Homestead, FL 33032
(305) 258-1086, FAX Same
Luc & Carol Vannoorbeeck

Plants ⬿ Books
Offers a good selection of grafted hybrid **hibiscus**; plants are listed by cultivar name with only information on size and color of flower. For more complete information they sell a "Hibiscus Catalogue" for $7.50; it has 144 color photos. Also several other hibiscus books and a calendar. (1977)
◻ Catalog: Free, R&W, CAN/OV
⌂ Nursery: All year, M-Sa
▼ Garden: April-December, M-Sa

Florida Mycology Research Center
P.O. Box 8104
Pensacola, FL 32505
(904) 327-4378
Stephen L. Peele, Curator

Seeds ⬿ Supplies
Stephen Peele seems to be a true mushroom-wonk, he is interested in all phases of **mushroom** research and cultivation, edits "The Mushroom Culture," a periodic journal, and offers mushroom spore and growing supplies. He also writes and publishes treatises on mushrooms. Price list free. (1972)
◻ Catalog: $10d, R&W, CAN/OV, bn
▼ Garden: Summer, by appointment only

Floridel Gardens, Inc.
330 George Street
Port Stanley, ON, Canada N5L 1C6
(519) 782-4015 TO
Tom & Rosita Morgan

Plants ⬿ Supplies
Offers **phalaenopsis orchids**, as well as others, and orchid growing supplies; they send growing instructions with every purchase and will give personalized instructions and repotting demonstrations at the nursery.
◻ Catalog: $2d, SS:3-9, $20m
⌂ Nursery: All year, Tu-Sa, call ahead

Flowerplace Plant Farm
P.O. Box 4865
Meridian, MS 39304
(601) 482-5686
Gail Barton & Richard Lowery

Plants
"We sell only **perennials** which prove tough in [the South]. We like old-fashioned flowers and select those which tolerate drought and heavy clay soils and have few (if any) pests. We test each new addition before listing." Their nursery is small, but selection is increasing; plants are very well described. (1988)
◻ Catalog: $3, SS:3-6,9-11, $10m, bn/cn
⌂ Nursery: By appointment only
▼ Garden: Spring & Fall, by appointment only

Flowers & Greens
P.O. Box 1802
Davis, CA 95617
(916) 756-9238, FAX 756-1201
Roy & Sue Cartwright

Plants ⟨ Bulbs
Run by two horticultural scientists, Flowers & Greens has set themselves the task of developing improved **alstroemerias, gladiolus and freesias**. The alstroemerias are available by color or in mixes, as are the others; information on growing sent with the order. Great for cut flowers. (1990)
▢ Catalog: $2d, R&W, CAN/OV, $15m
▼ Garden: March-September, by appointment only

Flowery Branch Seed Company
P.O. Box 1330
Flowery Branch, GA 30542
(404) 536-8380, FAX 532-7825
Dean Pailler

Seeds
Flowery Branch bought the seed business of Catnip Acres Herb Farm, and has expanded the offerings of **herbs and everlastings** (some available by individual colors). They also offer hot peppers, alpine strawberries, and a good selection of garden **annuals and perennials**. Plants well described.
▢ Catalog: $2($4 OV), R&W, CAN/OV, bn/cn

Floyd Cove Nursery
725 Longwood-Markham Road
Sanford, FL 32771-8315
(407) 324-9229
Patrick M. Stamile

Plants
A very broad selection of **daylilies**, many of them the newest, most wanted cultivars, many diploids and tetraploids, as well as recent introductions and classics. Plants very briefly described, a few are shown in color. (1978)
▢ Catalog: $2d($4 OV), CAN/OV
▼ Garden: May, by appointment only

Foliage Gardens
2003 - 128th Avenue S.E.
Bellevue, WA 98005
(206) 747-2998
Sue & Harry Olsen

Plants
A very good selection of **ferns, both hardy and for greenhouses**, listed by botanical name with good plant descriptions. All plants grown from spore; new varieties added all the time. Harry Olsen is grafting Japanese maples, and is offering about 20 cultivars in limited quantities. (1976)
▢ Catalog: $2(2 IRC OV), CAN/OV, SS:4-6,9-11, $15m, bn
⌂ Nursery: All year, by appointment only
▼ Garden: April-June, by appointment only

Foothill Cottage Gardens
13925 Sontag Road
Grass Valley, CA 95945
(916) 272-4362
Carolyn Singer

Plants
Located in the Sierra foothills, this nursery offers tough **perennials** which can tolerate drought and the informative catalog notes which plants the deer (there, anyway) won't touch. A nice selection, including dianthus, achilleas, thymes, asters, herbs and daylilies. Gardening classes at the nursery. (1980)
▢ Catalog: $3, SS:3-5,9-11, $4m, bn
⌂ Nursery: February-November, Tu,Th,Sa am
▼ Garden: April-November, Tu,Th,Sa am

Fordyce Orchids
1330 Isabel Avenue
Livermore, CA 94550
(510) 447-7171, FAX 828-3211 TO/CC
Susan Fordyce, Mgr.

Plants
Specialists in **miniature cattleya orchid hybrids**, splashed-petal cattleyas and yellow and red cattleyas -- rooted seedlings in flasks or pots, many are their own hybrids. Offer a nice selection; all plants briefly described.
▢ Catalog: Free, CAN/OV, SS:3-11, $10m
⌂ Nursery: All year, Tu-Su
▼ Garden: All year, greenhouse, Tu-Su

Forest Seeds of California
1100 Indian Hill Road
Placerville, CA 95667
(916) 621-1551, FAX 626-6926
Bob Graton

Seeds
A California Registered Professional Forester who collects and sells seed of various **western conifers**; the geographical source of his seed is given for each selection: firs, incense cedar, cypress, sequoias, pines and Douglas firs, as well as some native hardwood trees and shrubs including oaks. (1980)
▢ Catalog: Free, R&W, CAN/OV, $10m, bn

Forestfarm
990 Tetherow Road
Williams, OR 97544
(503) 846-7269, FAX 846-6963
Ray & Peg Prag

Plants
A collectors' list of many interesting **Western natives, garden perennials** and **trees and shrubs**. Offers 2,000 + small plants at reasonable prices, some quite unusual; each plant well described. Also sells hardy eucalyptus, bee plants, conifers, species roses, woodland plants and much more -- a curl-up-with catalog! Starting to offer larger plants by popular request. This nursery has a model catalog and a fantastic selection. (1974)
▢ Catalog: $3, CAN, SS·W, bn/cn
⌂ Nursery: All year, daily, call ahead

Forevergreen Farm
70 New Gloucester Road
North Yarmouth, ME 04097
(207) 829-5830, FAX 829-6512
Suzy Verrier

Plants ⟨ Tools
Offers a good selection of old-fashioned, hardy and uncommon **roses**: old garden varieties and species roses, more modern shrub roses from Canada and the Midwest and some David Austin roses. Emphasis is on the hardy growers and roses which grow well organically and without "fussing." (1983)
▢ Catalog: $1, SS:11,4-5
⌂ Nursery: March-October, daily; other times by appointment
▼ Garden: May-September, daily

Forked Deer Farm
107 Gilmore Lane
Chattanooga, TN 37343
Dave Crisman

Plants
There are "experimental" gardeners who are always trying the limits of hardiness, wet and drought-tolerance of sub-tropical plants. This nursery offers some **palms, yuccas and other sub-tropicals** to experiment with. (1992)
❑ Catalog: Free, R&W, CAN/OV, bn
⌂ Nursery: All year, Sa-Su, by appointment only
▼ Garden: March-December, Sa-Su, by appointment only

Foster Nurseries

See Concord Nurseries, Inc.

Four Winds Growers
P.O. Box 3538
42186 Palm Avenue
Fremont, CA 94539
(510) 656-2591
Donald F. Dillon

Plants
Specializes in **dwarf citrus**: oranges, tangerines, mandarin oranges, limes, grapefruit, lemons, tangelos and kumquats -- 30 varieties in all. These are true dwarf trees, growing to only eight feet; informative leaflet tells how to grow them. Cannot ship to FL, TX or AZ. (1954)
❑ Catalog: Long SASE, R&W, SS:W, $20m
⌂ Nursery: All year, M-F

Fowler Nurseries, Inc.
525 Fowler Road
Newcastle, CA 95658
(916) 645-8191 FAX 7374 TO/CC
Robert & Richard Fowler, Nancy F. Johnson

Plants
Offers a broad selection of **fruit for the home garden**, including red and Asian "crunch" pears (first planted in California in the 1850's), European, Chinese and hybrid chestnuts, berries, table and wine grapes, pecans and walnuts. Price list is free; informative, descriptive catalog is $4. (1912)
❑ Catalog: See notes, R&W, SS:1-2
⌂ Nursery: All year, daily
▼ Garden: All year, daily

Fox Hill Farm
P.O. Box 9
440 W. Michigan Avenue
Parma, MI 49269-0009
(517) 531-3179 TO
Marilyn J. Hampstead

Plants ⚘ Books ⚘ Supplies
Broad selection of **herbs and scented geraniums, bee and dye plants**, some 350 varieties by their count -- listed only by common name. They also offer herbal products, books and videotapes about herbs and a computer program for making plant lists and printing plant labels. (1972)
❑ Catalog: $1, plant/price list free
⌂ Nursery: April-October, W-Sa
▼ Garden: April-October, W-Sa

Fox Hill Nursery
347 Lunt Road
Freeport, ME 04032
(207) 729-1511
Eric & Jennifer Welzel

Plants
Fox Hill offers a good selection of hardy **lilacs** grown on their own roots, each variety very well described with general cultural suggestions. (1986)
❑ Catalog: Free, R&W, CAN, SS:3-4,8-9, $25m, bn
⌂ Nursery: April-November, daily
▼ Garden: Spring, daily

Fox Hollow Herbs & Heirloom Seed Company
P.O. Box 148
McGrann, PA 16236
(412) 763-8247
Carol Porter

Plants ⚘ Seeds ⚘ Books
Small seed company offers open-pollinated varieties of **herbs and vegetables** and **garlic, shallot and Egyptian onion** sets, as well as some old-fashioned garden flowers. All plants are well described. (1987)
❑ Catalog: $1, CAN/OV, cn/bn
⌂ Nursery: All year, M-Sa

Fox Orchids, Inc.
6615 W. Markham Street
Little Rock, AR 72205
(501) 663-4246
John M. Fox

Plants ⚘ Books ⚘ Supplies
A very extensive list of cattleya hybrids and many other **hybrid orchids, bromeliads, ferns and other tropical plants**; all plants briefly described. Also sell orchid books and growing supplies which they ship at any time of the year. (1945)
❑ Catalog: Free, SS:3-11, bn
⌂ Nursery: All year, M-F, call ahead
▼ Garden: All year, greenhouse, call ahead

The Fragrant Path
P.O. Box 328
Ft. Calhoun, NE 68023
E. R. Rasmussen

Seeds
Catalog is devoted to seeds of **fragrant, rare and old-fashioned plants** of all kinds, with irresistible descriptions, literary quotations and charming sketches. A wide selection of annuals, perennials, herbs and even vines and shrubs; can you live without trying "Kiss-me-over-the-garden-gate?" Cottage gardeners beware! (1982)
❑ Catalog: $1($2 CAN), CAN, $5m, bn/cn

Fred's Plant Farm
P.O. Box 707
Dresden, TN 38225
(901) 364-3754, (800) 243-9377, FAX 364-3322
Fred C. Stoker

Plants
Sells only **sweet potato plants**, but fifteen kinds, all described by color of "meat." Cannot ship to AZ or CA. Fred's hats are not listed this year, sorry! If you have one, it's a collectors' item. (1947)
❑ Catalog: Free, R&W, SS:4-6, $11m
⌂ Nursery: April-June, daily, call ahead

French's Bulb Importer
P.O. Box 565
Pittsfield, VT 05762
(802) 746-8148
Robin Martin, Mgr.

Bulbs
Specializes in pre-cooled **spring-blooming bulbs** for indoor forcing: hyacinths, freesias, tulips, narcissus and lilies. They also offer a good selection of spring bulbs for the garden: tulips, daffodils, anemones, fritillaries, ranunculus, and some annual seeds for greenhouse growing. (1943)
❐ Catalog: Free, $6m

Freshops
36180 Kings Valley Highway
Philomath, OR 97370
(503) 929-2736
Dave Wills

Plants
Here's a specialist! Dave sells ten varieties of female **hop rhizomes**: why female -- because only female plants produce the flowers used in brewing. Each variety is described for growth habit and bitterness. No shipping to WA, shipping to Canada only with import permit. Sells dried hops, too. (1982)
❐ Catalog: $1, R&W, SS:3-5, $8m
⌂ Nursery: By appointment only

Frey's Dahlias
12054 Brick Road
Turner, OR 97392
(503) 743-3910
Bob & Sharon Frey

Plants
The Freys bought Hookland's Dahlias in 1992, and offer a nice selection of older varieties of **dahlia** and some dahlia collections by type. All cultivars are very briefly described. No shipping to AK or HI. (1993)
❐ Catalog: 1 FCS, R&W, CAN, SS:4-5
⌂ Nursery: March-October, M-Sa, call ahead
▼ Garden: August-October, call ahead

Friendship Gardens
2590 Wellworth Way
West Friendship, MD 21794
Joan & Ken Roberts

Plants
Recently opened iris nursery specializes in **reblooming iris**, but also offers tall bearded, dwarf bearded, horned (or "space age" in iris talk), and median bearded. Each plant is very well described, most are fairly recent introductions. (1991)
❐ Catalog: $1, SS:7-9, $10
▼ Garden: May, October, by appointment only

Frosty Hollow
P.O. Box 53
Langley, WA 98260
(206) 221-2332, 321-6456, FAX 321-6456 TO
Marianne Edain & Steve Erickson

Seeds
Small company does habitat collection of pre-ordered seeds; they offer a wide variety of **Northwestern native plants** for which they collect seed -- wildflowers, ornamental trees and shrubs and conifers. Will collect to order; also consult on landscape restoration and permaculture design. (1982)
❐ Catalog: Long SASE($1 OV), R&W, CAN/OV, $20m, bn/cn

Fruit Spirit Botanical Gardens
Dorroughby, NSW, Australia 2480
(066) 895-192
Paul Recher

Seeds
Here's something different: seeds of **exotic fruits and nuts**, more than 160 species, some collected fresh at a botanical garden which specializes in tropical plants. Also **Australian native plants, palms and ornamentals**. Seeds available in "home packs" and larger quantities; will also trade seed.
❐ Catalog: $2(US Bills), R&W, OV, A$15m, bn
⌂ Nursery: All year, daily
▼ Garden: All year, daily

Fungi Perfecti
P.O. Box 7634
Olympia, WA 98507
(206) 426-9292, FAX 426-9377 TO/CC
Paul Stamets

Seeds ∾ Books ∾ Supplies
Catalog offers **mushroom spawn**, growing kits, supplies and books for the amateur and commercial grower. Varieties include shiitake, oyster, button, enoki, Coprinus comatus and Stropharia rugoso-annulata. Paul is co-author of "The Mushroom Cultivator," and teaches mushroom seminars. (1980)
❐ Catalog: $3, R&W, CAN/OV, $10m, bn/cn

G & B Orchid Lab & Nursery
2426 Cherimoya Drive
Vista, CA 92084
(619) 727-2611, FAX 727-0017 TO/CC
Barry L. Cohen

Plants ∾ Supplies
Specializes in phaleneopsis, cymbidium, cattleya and dendrobium **orchids** in great variety, each briefly described. Also sells several types of flasking media, laboratory glassware and a variety of fertilizers and chemicals for orchid hobbyists and hybridizers. (1970)
❐ Catalog: Free, R&W, CAN/OV, $20m
⌂ Nursery: All year, M-Sa
▼ Garden: All year, glasshouse, M-Sa

Garden City Seeds
1324 Red Crow Road
Victor, MT 59875
(406) 961-4837, FAX 961-4877 TO/CC $15m
Down Home Project

Plants ∾ Seeds ∾ Books ∾ Supplies
A cooperative that offers heirloom and open-pollinated seeds for short growing seasons: **vegetables, flowers and herbs, and seed potatoes, garlic** and **onion sets and strawberries**, as well as books, organic pest controls and fertilizers. The catalog is informative, with good information on growing and seed saving.
❐ Catalog: $1, R&W, CAN/OV, SS:4
⌂ Nursery: February-June, M-Sa
▼ Garden: April-May, M-Sa

Garden of Delights
14560 S.W. 14th Street
Davie, FL 33325-4217
(305) 370-9004
Murray & Debra Corman

Plants & Seeds
Here's a list of **tropical fruits and nuts** so unusual that I've never heard of many of them -- collectors will swoon! A source of seeds and plants of cherimoyas, cashews, maya breadnut, jelly palm, star apple, governor's plum, lovi-lovi, ice cream bean and yam bean. Super stuff! Sells both seeds and small plants, some fruits by the dozen in season. (1975)
❒ Catalog: $2d, R&W, CAN/OV, $60m, bn/cn
⌂ Nursery: All year, daily, call ahead
▼ Garden: All year, daily, call ahead

Garden Perennials
Route 1
Wayne, NE 68787-9801
(402) 375-3615
Gail Korn

Plants
Sells a broad selection of **perennials**, including many daylilies; all plants are very well described with cultural symbols and information. Plants are field-grown clumps, most well-suited to do well in dry conditions. (1981)
❒ Catalog: $1d, SS:4-10, bn
⌂ Nursery: April-October, daily
▼ Garden: June-July, September, daily

Garden Place
P.O. Box 388
6780 Heisley Road
Mentor, OH 44061-0388
(216) 255-3705, FAX 255-9535 TO
John & Dave Schultz

Plants
A very large selection of **perennials**, each well but briefly described. The catalog gives growing tips and has informative tables of plants by color, height, use, exposure, etc. Plants sold singly or in groups of 3 or 12 and shipped bare-root. Selection too broad to describe! (1972)
❒ Catalog: $1, CAN/OV, SS:9-5, $10m, bn/cn
⌂ Nursery: Spring-Fall, M-F, call ahead

Garden Valley Dahlias
406 Lower Garden Valley Road
Roseburg, OR 97470
(503) 673-8521
Leon V. Olson

Plants
A collectors' list of **dahlias**, only briefly described as to color and form; some are Leon's own hybrids. (1969)
❒ Catalog: 1 FCS, CAN/OV, SS:4
⌂ Nursery: August-October, daily
▼ Garden: August-October, call ahead

Garden Valley Ranch
P.O. Box 750953
498 Pepper Road
Petaluma, CA 94975
(707) 795-5266 TO/CC
Rick Weeks, Manager

Plants
Offers a very nice selection of **roses**: hybrid teas, floribundas, grandifloras, climbers, and some old fashioned and shrub roses. All plants well described; they also offer some rose growing supplies, and owner Rayford Reddell's book "Growing Good Roses." (1989)
❒ Catalog: $1d, CAN, SS:12-2, $10m
⌂ Nursery: December-October, W-Su
▼ Garden: May-October, W-Su

Garden World
2503 Garfield Street
Laredo, TX 78043-3047
(210) 724-3951, FAX 724-4488
Tony Ramirez

Plants & Supplies
Bananas -- over 40 varieties -- and edible cactus, papayas and other tropicals, briefly well described. Also offer some growing supplies, including their own "Bio-Force" bio-catalyst, humic acids and seed inoculant. (1976)
❒ Catalog: $1($3 OV), R&W, CAN/OV, SS:W, $5m, cn/bn
⌂ Nursery: All year, by appointment only
▼ Garden: All year, by appointment only

Gardenimport, Inc.
P.O. Box 760
Thornhill, ON, Canada L3T 4A5
(416) 731-1950, FAX 881-3499 TO/CC
Dugald Cameron

Seeds & Supplies & Tools & Bulbs
Color catalog offers a broad selection of **garden annuals, perennials, summer-flowering bulbs**, Austin "English" **roses, clematis** and **vegetables** and imported garden tools; they are the distributors of Sutton's Seeds in Canada. A separate catalog offers **spring bulbs**. All plants are well described, many illustrated. Cannot ship to Italy. (1982)
❒ Catalog: $4, R&W, US/OV, SS:4-10, $20m, bn/cn
⌂ Nursery: All year, M-F; Sa in Spring and Summer, call ahead

Gardens North
34 Helena Street
Ottawa, ON, Canada K1Y 3M8
Kristl Walek

Seeds & Books
A new Canadian seed company offering a very good selection of **perennials** and **ornamental grasses**, primarily species and stable hybrids and varieties; most are hardy to USDA zone 4. Good plant descriptions and growing information. Also offers a nice selection of books on perennials. (1991)
❒ Catalog: $3($6 OV), R&W, US/OV, bn

Gardens of the Blue Ridge
P.O. Box 10
US 221 North
Pineola, NC 28662
(704) 733-2417, FAX 733-2417
Edward & Robyn Fletcher, Mgrs.

Plants
Catalog lists a good selection of **wildflowers, ferns, native orchids** and **native trees and shrubs**, all well described and some illustrated in color photos. Many are hard-to-find Southeastern native plants at reasonable prices, all are nursery-propagated. Great-grandsons of the founder have just taken over, and are happy to answer customers' questions. (1892)
❒ Catalog: $3d, R&W, CAN/OV, SS:9-5, $25m, bn/cn
⌂ Nursery: All year, M-Sa am, call ahead
▼ Garden: May-June, M-Sa am, call ahead

Garver Gardens
P.O. Box 609
Laytonville, CA 95454
(707) 984-6724
James Garver

Plants
A small nursery offers many selections of **Rhododendron occidentale**, the native Western azalea, which is deciduous, fragrant, hardy to 10F, and has the highest number of flowers in a truss of all the species azaleas. All plants well described in an informative catalog. (1982)
⬜ Catalog: Free, R&W, CAN/OV, SS:11-3, $23m
⌂ Nursery: By appointment only
❦ Garden: May-June, by appointment only

Louis Gerardi Nursery
1700 East Highway 50
O'Fallon, IL 62269
(618) 632-4456
Vernon Reinacher & David Frost

Plants
Scionwood of nuts for grafting: pecans and hicans, hickory, black walnuts, Carpathian walnuts, heartnuts, butternuts and Chinese chestnuts, as well as American persimmons and mulberries. Listed by size of nut, flavor, cracking ease, bearing habit and years to bearing. No shipping to CA. (1940)
⬜ Catalog: Long SASE, CAN/OV, SS:3-4, $10m
⌂ Nursery: Daily, except holidays
❦ Garden: Spring, daily

Gilson Gardens
P.O. Box 277
US Route 20
Perry, OH 44081
(216) 259-5252, FAX 259-2378
The Gilson Family

Plants
Specializes in plants for **ground cover** and offers a broad selection: many varieties of ivy, pachysandra, sedums, plumbago, primroses, vincas, lamiums and others. Each plant is well described, with good general cultural information. (1947)
⬜ Catalog: Free, SS:W, $10m, bn/cn
⌂ Nursery: Call ahead

Girard Nurseries
P.O. Box 428
6839 North Ridge East, Route 20
Geneva, OH 44041
(216) 466-2881, FAX 466-3999 TO/CC
Peter Girard, Jr.

Plants ❧ Seeds
Color catalog offers a broad selection of **rhododendrons and azaleas**: their own Girard Evergreen azaleas and Gable, Exbury, Knaphill, Ilam, Mollis and Ghent azaleas, as well as rhododendrons chosen for hardiness. Also sells a good selection of **conifers, flowering trees and shrubs, holly,** mixed collections of seedling trees and shrubs and seeds of trees, shrubs and conifers. Cannot ship to CA, HI, AK or Canada; no seeds to SD. (1946)
⬜ Catalog: Free, SS:4-6,10-11, $20m
⌂ Nursery: All year, M-Sa; Su spring only
❦ Garden: April-May, daily

Glasshouse Works
P.O. Box 97, Church Street
Stewart, OH 45778-0097
(614) 662-2142, FAX 662-2120 TO/CC $20m
Tom Winn & Ken Frieling

Plants
A very extensive list of **exotic and tropical plants** -- a list to thrill the collector with a greenhouse or tropical climate. Among the many: ferns, gingers, bromeliads, succulents, aroids, acanthus, cactus, euphorbias, all briefly described. Specialty is **variegated plants** of all kinds and plants for tropical indoor bonsai. (1973)
⬜ Catalog: $2($5 OV), CAN/OV, SS:W, $10m, bn/cn
⌂ Nursery: All year, Th-Sa
❦ Garden: All year, Th-Sa

Glecker Seedmen
Metamora, OH 43540
(419) 923-5463 or 644-4659
George L. Glecker

Seeds
Offer a broad selection of **heirloom and older non-hybrid vegetables**: tomatoes, peppers, American Indian squash, eggplant, gourds, melons and mustard greens, among others. Each is lovingly described. (1947)
⬜ Catalog: Free, R&W, CAN/OV, $3m

Gloria Dei
36 East Road
High Falls, NY 12440
(914) 687-9981
Marty & Norma Kelly

Plants
Specializes in new and recently introduced **miniature roses** from well-known hybridizers, plus old favorites; over 100 varieties, each well described.
⬜ Catalog: Free, SS:W, $15m
⌂ Nursery: All year, by appointment only
❦ Garden: April-September, by appointment only

Golden Bough Tree Farm
Marlbank, ON, Canada K0K 2L0
Josef Reeve

Plants
A good selection of **hardy fruit trees and grapes** for Northern climates, as well as **ornamental trees and conifers,** English oak, larch, birch and maples and plants for bonsai; all well described with cultural suggestions. (1973)
⬜ Catalog: $2(2 yrs.), R&W, US/OV, SS:W, $50m, bn/cn

Golden Lake Greenhouses
10782 Citrus Drive
Moorpark, CA 93021
FAX (805) 529-3620
Paula Lake

Plants ❧ Books
Specializes in **bromeliads**, offering a wide selection of tillandsias, aechmeas, billbergias, cryptanthus, dyckias, guzmanias, neoregelias and vrieseas; most with very brief descriptions. Also sells hoyas, ceropegias, rhipsalis and epiphyllums, as well as a few books on bromeliads. (1968)
⬜ Catalog: $2(2 IRC OV), CAN/OV, bn

Good Hollow Greenhouse & Herbarium
50 Slate Rock Mill Road
Taft, TN 38488
(615) 433-7640
Frank & Triss Peterson

Plants ✍ Supplies
A nice selection of **herbs, perennials, scented geraniums and wildflowers**; each well described. They also offer herb wreaths and topiaries, and a selection of dried herbs, spices, teas, essential oils and potpourris. (1986)
❒ Catalog: Free, SS:4-11, $10m, cn/bn
⌂ Nursery: By appointment only

Good Seed Co.
Star Route, Box 73 A
Oroville, WA 98844
Michael Guizar

Seeds ✍ Books ✍ Supplies
Good Seed has changed hands again -- in good hands, we trust; they offer the same broad selection of open-pollinated, untreated **heirloom vegetable** seeds in packets of three sizes. All varieties are well described, with good cultural and seed-saving information. They also offer some flower and herb seeds, cover crop seed, Oriental vegetables and books on gardening. (1980)
❒ Catalog: $3d($5 OV), R&W, CAN/OV, $10m, bn/cn

Goodness Grows
P.O. Box 311
Lexington, GA 30648
(706) 743-5055
Marc Richardson & Richard Berry

Plants
Specializes in **perennials and southeastern native plants**, offering a very good selection for all sorts of garden conditions; all plants are well described with cultural suggestions. All orders by credit card; they close on December 22nd, and reopen in March. (1977)
❒ Catalog: Free, R&W, bn
⌂ Nursery: March-December, M-Sa
▼ Garden: March-November, M-Sa

L.S.A. Goodwin & Sons
Goodwins Road
Bagdad So., Tasmania, Australia 7030
(002) 68-6233
Allen Goodwin

Seeds
Offer seed of **Australian plants**, but specialize in **hardy cyclamen** and **primroses**. Also offer a broad selection of tree, shrub and flower seeds, with very brief plant descriptions: that's what books are for! (1956)
❒ Catalog: $1(US Bills), OV, $10m, bn/cn
⌂ Nursery: All year, call ahead
▼ Garden: February-March, September-October, call ahead

Goodwin Creek Gardens
P.O. Box 83
Williams, OR 97544
(503) 846-7357, 488-3308
Jim & Dotti Becker

Plants ✍ Seeds ✍ Books
Sells plants and seeds of **everlasting annual and perennial flowers, herbs and wildflowers**. A good selection; plants are well but briefly described. They also sell their book, "A Concise Guide to Growing Everlastings," with illustrations and instructions on growing and drying many plants. They have opened a shop on Oak Street in Ashland for Shakespeare fans. (1978)
❒ Catalog: $1, SS:4-6,9-11, cn/bn
⌂ Nursery: All year, by appointment only
▼ Garden: By appointment only

Goravani Growers
1730 Keane Avenue
Naples, FL 33964
(813) 455-4287 TO/CC
Douglas Glick

Plants
Family nursery offers a good selection of **daylilies**, chosen for being "good doers," and many are award winners in competition. Evening bloomers are indicated; all plants well described and many shown in color. (1988)
❒ Catalog: $2d, R&W, CAN/OV, $25m
⌂ Nursery: All year, M-Th, call ahead
▼ Garden: March-June, M-Th, by appointment only

John Gordon Nursery
1385 Campbell Boulevard
Amherst, NY 14228-1404
(716) 691-9371
John Gordon

Plants ✍ Seeds
Offers **hardy nuts** for the western New York climate: heartnuts, walnuts, filberts, chestnuts, hickories, hicans and pecans. Also some tough **fruits** such as persimmons, pawpaws and mulberries. Many cultivars of nut trees are available, and seed nuts are available, too. No shipping to CA. (1980)
❒ Catalog: Long SASE, SS:4, cn/bn
⌂ Nursery: All year, by appointment only
▼ Garden: All year, by appointment only

Gossler Farms Nursery
1200 Weaver Road
Springfield, OR 97478-9691
(503) 746-3922
Marjory & Roger Gossler

Plants ✍ Books
A very large selection of **magnolias**, each well described. Also a number of **daphnes, stewartias, franklinia, hamamelis, kalmias, beeches, viburnums** and other unusual trees and shrubs, even some **perennials** have crept in. All plants well described with cultural suggestions. Collectors of very special trees and shrubs will be delighted! (1968)
❒ Catalog: $2, R&W, SS:10-12,2-4, bn/cn
⌂ Nursery: All year, by appointment only
▼ Garden: March-June, by appointment only

The Gourmet Gardener
4000 West 126th Street
Leawood, KS 66209
(913) 345-0490
Chris Combest

Seeds ✍ Books
The Gourmet gardener acquired the seed business of Herb Gathering and specializes in **vegetables from France**, as well as edible flowers, annuals and everlastings, and a selection of books on gardening and cooking. (1989)
❒ Catalog: $2d, CAN/OV

Gourmet Mushrooms
P.O. Box 515
Graton, CA 95444
(707) 829-7301, FAX 823-1507 TO/CC
James Malachowski

Plants
Another neighbor of Tusker Press, offering **mushroom spawn** for morels, shiitake, hericium and pleurotus mushroom -- several come in already planted pots, the morels are grown in "habitats" which they tell you how to create in your city or country garden. (1970)
❒ Catalog: $1, R&W, CAN/OV, $12m

Grace Gardens North
N 3739 County Highway K
Granton, WI 54436
(715) 238-7122
Mary Friesen

Plants
Mary Friesen's parents ran Grace Gardens in Baraboo, Wisconsin for thirty years; she's taken over their stock and is continuing on. She specializes in **daylilies and iris**, offers various bearded iris, including antiques, and older varieties of daylilies. Also sells plant labels. (1990)
❒ Catalog: Free, SS:7-9, $10m
⌂ Nursery: By appointment only

Russell Graham, Purveyor of Plants
4030 Eagle Crest Road N.W.
Salem, OR 97304
(503) 362-1135
Russell & Yvonne Graham

Plants ✍ Bulbs
A collectors' catalog, full of unusual plants such as **species bulbs** like lilies, iris, fritillaria, hardy cyclamen, as well as hardy ferns, trillium and ornamental grasses; all plants well described and sure to tempt plant fanatics. Small nursery with a good selection. (1980)
❒ Catalog: $2d, R&W, SS:8-11, $30m, bn/cn
⌂ Nursery: Sa, by appointment only
▼ Garden: Sa, by appointment only

Gray/Davis Epiphyllums
P.O. Box 710443
Santee, CA 92072
(619) 448-2540
Jean Gray & Michele Davis

Plants
Jean and Michele started out to perserve old varieties of **epiphyllums**, but found they couldn't resist the new varieties too. They grow over 2,000 hybrids at the nursery (get out your "want-list"), and offer a good selection of cuttings, and some rooted cuttings, all well described. (1988)
❒ Catalog: $2, R&W, SS:4-10, $10m
⌂ Nursery: All year, by appointment only
▼ Garden: April-June, by appointment only

The Green Escape
P.O. Box 1417
1212 Ohio Avenue
Palm Harbor, FL 34682
(813) 784-1991, FAX 787-0193
Joan & Marshall Weintraub

Plants ✍ Books ✍ Supplies
Offers close to 500 species of rare and uncommon **palms**: indoor and cold hardy species, many that do well in low light and others very hardy. List arecas, arenga, calamus, chamaedorea, gaussia, howea, licuala, pinanga, johannesteijsmannia (yes!), livistona, sabal, thrinax and veitchia; all well described. Each plant comes with specific cultural information; no shipping to HI. (1988)
❒ Catalog: $6d, R&W, CAN/OV, bn/cn
⌂ Nursery: All year, F-M
▼ Garden: All year, F-M

Green Horizons
218 Quinlan, #571
Kerrville, TX 78028
(210) 257-5141 TO/CC
Sherry Miller

Seeds ✍ Books
Devoted to preserving and protecting **Texas wildflowers**, company offers a number of them in small packets to bulk supplies. Also offers scarified blue-bonnet seeds for better germination and books on wildflowers and gardening in Texas and the South. Sells native plants and herbs at the nursery.
❒ Catalog: Long SASE, CAN/OV, cn/bn
⌂ Nursery: January-November, M-Sa, 145 Scenic Hill Road

Green Mountain Transplants
R.R. 1, Box 6c
East Monpelier, VT 05651
(802) 454-1533, (800) 258-5255, FAX 454-1204
Dexter R. Merritt

Plants
Offer **vegetable and flower transplants** in 40 or 98 cell flats; you can mix the varieties any way you want. A good selection of vegetables and some annual and perennial flowers, well described; also offer a video on growing vegetables, wooden harvest baskets, boxes and growing supplies. (1991)
❒ Catalog: Free, R&W, SS:5-6
⌂ Nursery: May-June, M-F pm, Sa-Su

Green Plant Research
P.O. Box 735
Kaaawa, HI 96730
(808) 237-8672
Ted Green

Plants
A broad selection of **hoyas, dischidias and other asclepiads**, each very well described, as well as species and hybrid **orchids**. These plants come from private collections and collecting trips in Samoa, Australia, New Guinea, the Solomon Islands, New Hebrides, Java, Singapore, Malaysia and the Philippines.
❒ Catalog: Free, R&W, CAN/OV, $25m, bn/cn
⌂ Nursery: By appointment only
▼ Garden: By appointment only

Green Valley Orchids
77200 Green Valley Road
Folsom, LA 70437
Don Saucier

Plants
Specialize in phalaenopsis and cattleya alliance **orchids**, most of their own hybridizing; they also sell ascocendas, vandas and dendrobiums. List is written in that secret code known to orchidists which always sounds like gossip, but has to do with pedigree; so does most gossip! (1979)
☐ Catalog: $1d($2 OV), R&W, CAN/OV, SS:W, $25m
⌂ Nursery: All year, F-Su, call ahead
♥ Garden: March-June, F-Su, call ahead

The Greenery
1451 W. Burdickville Road
Maple City, MI 49664
(616) 228-7037
Carole & Jim Roach

Plants
A small nursery specializing in very hardy, northern grown **azaleas, rhododendrons and kalmias**; a nice selection, listed by color, with good plant descriptions. Companion plants available at the nursery. (1990)
☐ Catalog: Free, SS:5-10
⌂ Nursery: May-October, M-Sa am
♥ Garden: May-October, M-Sa am

Greenfield Herb Garden
P.O. Box 9
Shipshewana, IN 46565
(219) 768-7110
arLene Shannon

Seeds ✿ Books
Offers a good selection of **herb seeds**, listed by common and botanical names; included are culinary herbs and everlastings. They also list many books on herbs, and hold classes and sell plants at the nursery. (1980)
☐ Catalog: $1.50, R&W, CAN, cn/bn
⌂ Nursery: All year, M-Sa
♥ Garden: May-October, M-Sa

GreenLady Gardens
1415 Eucalyptus Drive
San Francisco, CA 94132-1405
(415) 753-3332, FAX 665-3308
Anthony J. Skittone

Seeds ✿ Books ✿ Bulbs
Formerly listed as Anthony J. Skittone, they have a very good selection of **spring and summer bulbs**, many rare species from around the world, including South Africa. All varieties are very well described. Also offer seed of South African bulbous plants and Australian plants and books about these plants. Ask for seed or book list. (1980)
☐ Catalog: $3($5 OV), R&W, CAN/OV, SS:8-4, bn
⌂ Nursery: August-May, M-F, by appointment only

Greenlee Nursery
301 E. Franklin Avenue
Pomona, CA 91766
FAX (909) 620-6482
John Greenlee

Plants
Broad selection of **ornamental grasses**; the descriptive catalog costs $5, is very informative and gives good descriptions of each plant and its performance in the West, with cultural suggestions and tables of plants by use and best planting location. The brief catalog is free. See the books section for information on John's "Encyclopedia of Ornamental Grasses." (1986)
☐ Catalog: See notes, R&W, CAN, SS:9-6, $25m, bn/cn
⌂ Nursery: All year, M-F, by appointment only
♥ Garden: All year, M-F, by appointment only

Greenmantle Nursery
3010 Ettersburg Road
Garberville, CA 95542
(707) 986-7504
Ram & Marissa Fishman

Plants
Catalog packed with cultural information, offers **antique apples**, many collected from old homesteads in Humboldt County. Also pears, cherries, plums, quinces and disease-resistant chestnuts. On another list, about 200 old garden **roses**, many rare varieties and species imported from England. (1983)
☐ Catalog: $3, (rose list, long SASE), SS:1-3
♥ Garden: Late May, by appointment only

Greenwood Daylily Gardens
5595 East 7th St., #490
Long Beach, CA 90804
(310) 494-8944, FAX 494-0486 TO $50m
John Schoustra

Plants
A good selection of **daylilies**, each well described. They have a daylily display garden at Pacific View Nursery (698 Studebaker Road, East Long Beach) and have open houses there on the 1st and 3rd Saturday of each month; also have occasional open houses at their growing grounds in Riverside, which is an All American Daylily test site. (1989)
☐ Catalog: $5, CAN/OV, $25m
⌂ Nursery: All year, 1st & 3rd Sa, Pacific View Nursery
♥ Garden: April-June, 1st & 3rd Sa, Pacific View Nursery

Greer Gardens
1280 Goodpasture Island Road
Eugene, OR 97401
(503) 686-8266, FAX 686-0910 TO/CC
Harold E. Greer

Plants ✿ Books
Color catalog offers a very large selection of **rhododendrons and azaleas, vireyas**, and an ever-growing list of **ornamental trees**, maples (many palmatum cultivars), dwarf conifers, acid-loving shrubs and vines and bonsai materials; all well described in a very informative catalog (famous for its enthusiasm!). Also many books on trees and plants. (1955)
☐ Catalog: $3($5 OV), CAN/OV, bn
⌂ Nursery: All year, daily
♥ Garden: All year, March-June, daily

Grigsby Cactus Gardens
2326 Bella Vista Drive
Vista, CA 92084
(619) 727-1323 FAX 727-1578 TO/CC
Madelyn Lee, Mgr.

Plants
Catalog profusely illustrated with b&w photos -- a real collectors' list of
unusual **cacti & succulents**, all well described. They specialize in euphorbias, sansevierias, aloes, haworthias, mammillarias and other specimen plants
and rare succulents. Also send four or five "wish letters" to regular
customers each year, offering new, rare and unusual plants. (1965)
⊓ Catalog: $2, R&W, SS:W, $15m, bn
⌂ Nursery: All year, Tu-Sa
▼ Garden: April-August, Tu-Sa

Grimo Nut Nursery
RR 3, Lakeshore Road
Niagara-on-the-Lake, ON, Canada L0S 1J0
(416) 935-9773 TO
Ernest & Marion Grimo

Plants ⬿ Supplies
A selection of **hardy nuts** for Northern climates, seedlings and grafted
trees: persian walnuts, black walnuts, heartnuts, butternuts, Chinese chest-
nuts, apricots (sweet kernels), filberts, hickory and more -- well described
in an informative list. Sells supplies, seed nuts, does custom grafts. (1974)
⊓ Catalog: $2, R&W, US, SS:4, $7m
⌂ Nursery: All year, by appointment only
▼ Garden: July-August, by appointment only

Grootendorst Nurseries

See Southmeadow Fruit Gardens.

Growers Service Company
10118 Crouse Road
Hartland, MI 48353
John J. & John K. Riordan

Plants ⬿ Bulbs
John Riordan founded the International Growers Exchange (which ran aground
after he sold it and retired). He missed being in horticulture and started
this "wholesale bulb import club." He offers much the same good selection of
bulbs and exotics as he used to, and perennials, fruit and orchids. (1989)
⊓ Catalog: $5d, R&W, CAN/OV, bn/cn

Gurney's Seed & Nursery Co.
110 Capital Street
Yankton, SD 57079
(605) 665-1671, FAX 665-9718 TO/CC
Don Kruml, Pres.

Plants ⬿ Seeds ⬿ Supplies
Color tabloid catalog offers a very **broad selection of plants and seeds** for
the home gardener -- fruit trees, roses, flowering trees and shrubs, nuts,
berries, grapes and vegetable and flower seeds, all well described. Also
gardening and canning supplies and advice in an informative catalog. (1866)
⊓ Catalog: Free, SS:2-6, cn
⌂ Nursery: All year, daily

Hahn's Rainbow Iris Garden
200 N. School Street
Desloge, MO 63601
(314) 431-3342
Clyde & Anna Hahn

Plants
Offers a good selection of **irises**, both old favorites and many newer culti-
vars; brief plant desctitions. List includes tall bearded, intermediate and
dwarf bearded irises and also a good selection of **daylilies**. (1981)
⊓ Catalog: $1.50d, SS:4-7,8-9
⌂ Nursery: May-September, call ahead
▼ Garden: May-July, call ahead

Halcyon Gardens

See Kingfisher, Inc.

© Fairweather Gardens
Artist: Belva Prycl

Dr. Joseph C. Halinar

See Cascade Bulb & Seed.

Hammond's Acres of Rhodys
25911 - 70th Avenue N.E.
Arlington, WA 98223
(206) 435-9206 or 9232
David & Joan Hammond

Plants
Offer a broad selection of **rhododendrons and azaleas**, both hybrids and species, listed only by name, hardiness, season and color of bloom. They grow 3,000 hybrids and species, and list about 600; if you don't find what you want, send them your "want list." They offer other ornamentals at the nursery, will try to fill special requests if plants are available from other local nurseries. (1976)
❏ Catalog: $2, R&W, SS:W
⌂ Nursery: All year, daily
▼ Garden: April-May, daily

Hansen Nursery
P.O. Box 446
Donald, OR 97020
(503) 678-5409
Robin L. Hansen

Plants
A small nursery which specializes in seed grown species **cyclamen**; at present offers ten species and describes each very well, with notes on cultivation and hardiness. (1985)
❏ Catalog: Long SASE, R&W, SS:2-11, $15m, bn
⌂ Nursery: By appointment only

Hardscrabble Enterprises
HC 71, Box 42
Circleville, WV 26804
(304) 358-2921, (202) 332-0232
Paul Goland

Seeds ⌦ Books ⌦ Supplies
Sell spawn of **shiitake mushrooms** and all of the equipment necessary to grow them in your own woodlot. Price of the catalog includes growing instructions and their newsletter; they will buy dried shiitake mushrooms from organic growers. Also sell a professional dehydrator expandable to 35 trays. (1985)
❏ Catalog: $3, R&W

Hardy Roses for the North
P.O. Box 2048
Grand Forks, BC, Canada V0H 1H0
(604) 442-8442, FAX 442-2766
Barry Poppenheim

Plants
Offer the hardy Canadian Explorer and Parkland **roses**, bred in Canada for extreme hardiness, as well as some English roses, hybrid rugosas, miniatures and old garden roses: all are well described. Orders to the US are sent with a phytosanitary certificate by USPO Priority Mail or UPS. (1990)
❏ Catalog: Free, US/OV, SS:3-10, $35m
⌂ Nursery: April-September, Sa
▼ Garden: June-September, Sa

James Harris Hybrid Azaleas
538 Swanson Drive
Lawrenceville, GA 30243
(404) 963-7463

Plants
I received only the plant list, which offers **hybrid evergreen azaleas** and cutting-grown **native azaleas** (species). The hybrids are well described, with information on crosses, color, size of bloom and size of plant at maturity -- a nice selection. Ten species azaleas are offered. (1965)
❏ Catalog: Long SASE

Harris Seeds/Garden Trends, Inc.
60 Saginaw Drive
Rochester, NY 14623
(716) 442-0410, FAX 442-9386
Richard Chamberlain, Pres.

Seeds ⌦ Supplies ⌦ Tools
Color catalog offers a broad selection of **flower and vegetable seeds**, many developed by their own research staff and all well described. They list "special merit" vegetables which they feel perform best -- and have those cute "baby" pumpkins. They also sell some tools and growing supplies. (1879)
❏ Catalog: Free, R&W

Harrisons Delphiniums
Newbury Cottage, Playhatch
Reading, Berks., England RG4 9QN
(0734) 47-0810
Leonard Harrison

Seeds
Britain seems to be the home of beautiful **delphiniums** in mixed borders, and here's a source of hand-pollinated delphinium seed for cut flower and perennial growers. Also sell open-pollinated seed; altogether a good selection, briefly described, with instructions on growing from seed. (1990)
❏ Catalog: 2 IRC, R&W, US/CAN
⌂ Nursery: April-September, by appointment only
▼ Garden: June-July, by appointment only

Hartle-Gilman Gardens
R.R. 4, Box 14
Owatonna, MN 55060-9416
(507) 451-3191, 455-0087, FAX 451-2170
Dr. Robert Gilman, Dean & Marsha Hartle

Bulbs
Hartle-Gilman Gardens introduced their own hybrid **lilies**, and those of several other hybridizers in Minnesota, Wisconsin and Connecticut, and they also offer several older favorites. All lilies are well described. Canadians need an import permit to order, and must pay extra for a phytosanitary certificate. (1980)
❏ Catalog: Free, R&W, CAN/OV, SS:9-11
⌂ Nursery: June-November, call ahead
▼ Garden: June-July, call ahead

Hartman's Herb Farm
1026 Old Dana Road
Barre, MA 01005
(508) 355-2015 TO/CC
Lynn & Peter Hartman

Plants ⌖ Supplies
Offers a selection of **herb and scented geranium plants**, as well as essential oils, herb teas, potpourris, dried flower arrangements and wreaths, note papers and an herbal calendar. They also have herb classes and a Bed & Breakfast at the farm. (1980)
❏ Catalog: $2, CAN/OV, $15m, cn/bn
⌂ Nursery: All year, daily
▼ Garden: May-October, daily

Hartmann's Plantation, Inc.
310 - 60th Street
Grand Junction, MI 49056
(616) 253-4281 TO/CC $10m
Dan Hartmann

Plants ⌖ Supplies
Selection of **Northern and Southern blueberries**, as well as "Arctic" kiwis, pineapple guava, pawpaw, wintergreen, lemongrass and a new "Baba" berry, a red raspberry for the South. They also carry supplies for fruit growers, including bird repellent devices, and have recently added other ornamental plants and shrubs. (1942)
❏ Catalog: Free, R&W, CAN/OV
⌂ Nursery: All year, M-F, Sa am, call ahead

H. G. Hastings
P.O. Box 115535
2350 Cheshire Bridge Road (at Lindbergh)
Atlanta, GA 30310-5535
(404) 755-6580, FAX 755-6059 TO/CC
David Sills

Plants ⌖ Seeds ⌖ Supplies
A **regional garden emporium**: fruit and nut trees, berries, grapes, kiwis and seed for vegetables and garden annuals. Color catalog has good plant descriptions, also offers tools and supplies. They sell a broad selection of plants suitable for Southern gardens; no shipping to AK or HI. (1889)
❏ Catalog: Free, SS:1-4, cn/bn
⌂ Nursery: All year, daily

Hauser's Superior View Farm
Route 1, Box 199
Bayfield, WI 54814
(715) 779-5404 TO $25m
Jim Hauser

Plants
Offers a nice selection of hardy field-grown **perennials** -- sold only by the dozen or hundred; only name and flower color given. A good choice of chrysanthemums, lupines, sedums, delphiniums and others; also asparagus and rhubarb. Also offers homemade jams, jellies and apple butter. (1908)
❏ Catalog: Free, R&W, CAN, SS:4-6,9-11, $25m
⌂ Nursery: March-November, call ahead
▼ Garden: June-July, September, call ahead

Havasu Hills Herbs
20150-A Rough & Ready Trail
Sonora, CA 95370
(209) 536-1420
Cynthia Stratton

Plants ⌖ Books ⌖ Supplies
Offer a broad selection of organically grown **herbs and scented geraniums**; all plants are well described. They also sell herb and cookbooks and potpourri supplies and offer classes at their farm. (1984)
❏ Catalog: $1d, R&W, SS:9-6, $10m, cn/bn
⌂ Nursery: All year, daily, call ahead
▼ Garden: April-July, daily, call ahead

Heard Gardens, Ltd.
5355 Merle Hay Road
Johnston, IA 50131
(515) 276-4533, FAX 276-8322 TO/CC
Bob Rennebohm

Plants
Specialize in **lilacs** propagated on their own roots; some 50 varieties, each briefly described. They have the lovely variety, 'Primrose,' which is a soft pale yellow and hard to find. Also offered are several species lilacs, and three low-chill varieties which bloom in southern climates. (1959)
❏ Catalog: $2d($5 US Bills OV), CAN/OV, SS:3,10, $15m
⌂ Nursery: All year, M-Sa
▼ Garden: All year, M-Sa (special tours call ahead)

Heaths and Heathers
P.O. Box 850
1199 Monte-Elma Road
Elma, WA 98541
(206) 482-3258 TO/CC
Bob, Alice & Cindy Knight

Plants
A collectors' list of many species and cultivars of **erica, calluna** and **daboecia**, each described by color, season of bloom, size and color of foliage. Offers about 280 varieties; if you don't see what you want, write and ask if they have it. (1982)
❏ Catalog: Long SASE, CAN, SS:2-6,9-11, $12m
⌂ Nursery: All year, M-F, call ahead
▼ Garden: June-October, call ahead

Heirloom Garden Seeds
P.O. Box 138
Guerneville, CA 95446
Ariana Raysor

Seeds ⌖ Books
Offer over 400 varieties of **culinary herbs and heirloom flowers**, most very well described in an informative catalog. They also sell custom plant labels and books on growing and using herbs. (1979)
❏ Catalog: $2.50($3 OV), R&W, CAN/OV, cn/bn

Heirloom Old Garden Roses
24062 NE Riverside Drive
St. Paul, OR 97137
(503) 538-1576, FAX 538-5902
Louise & John Clements

Plants
Specializes in old garden and modern shrub **roses**, and offers a huge selection; all are very well described and some are shown in color in a very informative catalog. They have over 1,000 rose plants in their display.
❏ Catalog: $5, SS:W
⌂ Nursery: All year, daily
▼ Garden: May-July, daily

Heirloom Seed Project
  Landis Valley Museum
2451 Kissel Hill Road
Lancaster, PA 17601

Seeds
Landis Valley Museum is a living history museum recreating 18th and 19th century rural Pennsylvania German life. They have a seed preservation program to preserve **vegetables** with a history in their area, and also offer some antique apple scionwood. Catalog is informative and interesting. (1986)
❏ Catalog: $2($3 OV), CAN/OV
♥ Garden: Historical Gardens at Museum

Heirloom Seeds
P.O. Box 245
West Elizabeth, PA 15088-0245
Tom Hauch

Seeds
Small family business specializing in seeds of open-pollinated **heirloom tomatoes and vegetables** "that taste good." Catalog has good descriptions of each variety and some cultural information. They also offer a few "old-fashioned" annual flowers. (1988)
❏ Catalog: $1d, CAN

Hemlock Hollow Nursery & Folk Art
P.O. Box 125, Route 7-32
Sandy Hook, KY 41171
(606) 738-6285
Brent C. Conley

Plants
Small new nursery, offering **water lilies and lotus** at the present, and expects to expand to more water garden plants and ornamental trees within a year or two. They also plan to offer a catalog of Appalachian folk art before long. (1993)
❏ Catalog: Free, R&W, CAN/OV, SS:W, $15m, bn

Henrietta's Nursery
1345 N. Brawley Avenue
Fresno, CA 93722-5899
(209) 275-2166 TO/CC $20m
Jerry & Sylvia Hardaway

Plants ⬯ Seeds
A very large selection of **cactus and succulents**: euphorbias, cereus, caudiciforms, notocactus, mammillaria, crassula, sedum, rhipsalis, parodia and far too many more to list! Each plant is very well described, and some are shown in b&w photos; they offer a number of inexpensive collections to get you started, as well as mixed seeds. (1958)
❏ Catalog: $1, R&W, $15m, bn
⌂ Nursery: All year, M-Sa
♥ Garden: Growing area, M-Sa

The Herb Barn
HC 64, Box 435D
Trout Run, PA 17771
(717) 995-9327
Sandy Nelson

Plants
Offers a nice selection of **herb plants**, especially artemisia, mint, thyme and scented leaved geraniums; each plant very briefly described. Can't ship to AZ, CA, OR or WA, must ship bare root to some other states. (1977)
❏ Catalog: Long SASE, SS:W, $5m, cn/bn
⌂ Nursery: April-September, Sa-Su pm or call ahead

The Herb Farm
R.R. 4
Norton, NB, Canada E0G 2N0
(506) 839-2140
Joyce Belyea & Clinton Wiezel

Plants ⬯ Seeds
Small nursery offers plants and seeds of **herbs and everlasting**; a nice selection, with each plant well described. Also sells potpourri makings and dried flowers. (1976)
❏ Catalog: $5($6 OV), R&W, US/OV, SS:5-10, cn/bn
⌂ Nursery: May-September, Sa

The Herb Garden
P.O. Box 773
Pilot Mountain, NC 27041-0773
Ann Beall

Plants ⬯ Books ⬯ Supplies
Offers a very good selection of **herbs**, especially artemisias, basils, bee balms, lavenders, rosemarys, mints and thymes; all well described with some cultural information. Also sells dried herbs, teas and seasonings, potpourri supplies, books on herbs, and natural pest controls for your pets. Can't ship plants to HI, will ship dried products and supplies to HI and Canada.(1983)
❏ Catalog: $4, SS:4-10, $15m, cn/bn

Herb Gathering

See The Gourmet Gardener.

Herbs-Liscious
1702 S. Sixth Street
Marshalltown, IA 50158
(515) 752-4976
Carol Lacko-Beem

Plants ⬯ Supplies
Offers a good selection of **herb plants** with no plant descriptions; plants come at the end of a catalog packed with dried herbs for flavorings, herb baths, essential oils, porcelain garden markers, etc. They will search for and fill requests for more unusual herbs if asked. (1987)
❏ Catalog: $2d, R&W, CAN, $10m, cn
⌂ Nursery: All year, M-Sa, call ahead
♥ Garden: June-September, M-Sa, call ahead

Heritage Rosarium
211 Haviland Mill Road
Brookville, MD 20833
(301) 774-2806 (eves. and weekends)
Nicholas Weber

Plants
Offers a large selection of old garden, modern shrub and species **roses**, available on a custom-root basis. About 400 varieties are listed only by cultivar or species name, with symbols for type, color and date of introduction; get out your "old rose" books. They will also root or bud your own roses to increase old favorites, and help with rose identification. (1985)
❏ Catalog: $1, SS:W
⌂ Nursery: Sa-Su, by appointment only
♥ Garden: May-June, Sa-Su, by appointment only

Heritage Rose Gardens
16831 Mitchell Creek Drive
Ft. Bragg, CA 95437
Virginia Hopper & Joyce Demits

Plants ∾ Bulbs
A broad selection of **species and old garden roses**, including unidentified
roses found at old North Coast homesteads and named for the location found.
Specializes in teas/Chinas, ramblers/climbers and will do custom-rooting of
additional rare varieties. Garden visits in June and July, by appointment
only. Also offers bulbs of colchicums and Spanish bluebells. (1981)
❐ Catalog: $1.50, CAN/OV, SS:1-2, bn
▼ Garden: 40350 Wilderness Road, Branscomb, see notes

Heronswood Nursery
7530 - 288th Street N.E.
Kingston, WA 98346
(206) 297-4172
Daniel J. Hinkley & Robert L. Jones

Plants
Offers a broad selection of **ornamental woody plants**: maples, berberis, box,
callicarpa, cercidiphyllum, cotoneaster, daphne, eucryphia, hydrangea, holly,
mahonia, pernettya, pieris, rubus, sarcococca, viburnum, willows and coni-
fers. Also many choice **perennials**. Plants are very well described. (1987)
❐ Catalog: $4, SS:3-5,10-11, $25m, bn
⌂ Nursery: March-November, by appointment only
▼ Garden: May-October, by appointment only

Heschke Gardens
11503 77th Street S.
Hastings, MN 55033
(612) 459-8381
David Heschke

Plants ∾ Bulbs
Specializes in **hardy plants for northern gardeners**: hostas, daylilies,
bearded and Siberian iris, herbaceous peonies, astilbes, species geraniums, gladiolus and other perennials. A good selection, described in very
brief tables; there is a two acre display garden.
❐ Catalog: Free, R&W, SS:4-11, $25m
▼ Garden: May-August, by appointment only

Hickory Hill Gardens
RR 1, Box 11
Loretto, PA 15940
Clayton Burkey

Plants
A very broad selection of **daylilies**, each plant briefly but well described;
many are their own introductions. Also advertises as Burkey Gardens. (1981)
❐ Catalog: $2.50($5 OV), CAN/OV, SS:5-6,8-10, $20m
⌂ Nursery: June-October, by appointment only
▼ Garden: July-August, by appointment only

Hidden Garden Nursery, Inc.
13515 S.E. Briggs
Milwaukie, OR 97222-6117
Wayne & Kathy Lauman

Plants
A small family nursery which offers a nice selection of **miniature roses**,
each variety very well described. Plants are available "pre-finished" and
"finished," but there's no further explanation of what that means. They also
sell WaterWorks hydrogels to reduce watering, and some books. (1986)
❐ Catalog: $.50($1 OV), R&W, CAN/OV
⌂ Nursery: All year, M-Sa
▼ Garden: May-June, M-Sa

Hidden Springs Nursery -- Edible Landscaping
170 Hidden Springs Lane
Cookeville, TN 38501
(615) 268-9889
Hector Black

Plants
Offers plants for **edible landscaping** and low maintenance fruits for
sustainable agriculture, with emphasis on disease and pest resistance.
Antique apples, apricots, figs, grapes, mayhaws, hardy kiwis, medlars
and quinces, pears, plums, jujube, goumi and several nitrogen-fixing
shrubs for reclamation. (1978)
❐ Catalog: $1, R&W, CAN/OV, SS:11-5, $15m
⌂ Nursery: M-Sa, by appointment only
▼ Garden: M-Sa, by appointment only

High Altitude Gardens
P.O. Box 1048
308 S. River
Hailey, ID 83333
(208) 788-4363, FAX 788-3452 TO/CC
Bill McDorman

Seeds ∾ Books ∾ Supplies ∾ Tools
Seed of open-pollinated **gourmet and heirloom vegetables, herbs, wildflowers** and **native grasses**, adapted to the cold, short-season, high-
altitude climate of the mountain West. Informative catalog with cultural
suggestions; also sells tools, growing supplies and books. Price list free
with SASE. Also called Seeds Trust - High Altitude Gardens. (1984)
❐ Catalog: $3, R&W, CAN/OV, SS:5-8, cn/bn
⌂ Nursery: All year, M-F
▼ Garden: August, by appointment only

A High Country Garden
2902 Rufina Street
Santa Fe, NM 87501
(505) 438-3031, (800) 925-9387, FAX 438-9552
David M. Salman

Plants ∾ Supplies
Specializes in **perennials** for Southwestern growing conditions, plants are
generally drought tolerant and hardy; a good selection, including many native
plants, shown and well described in a color catalog. Good selections of
penstemons, artemisias, and dianthus; some hyper-tufa troughs, too. (1984)
❐ Catalog: Free, SS:3-5, $30m, bn/cn
⌂ Nursery: All year, daily
▼ Garden: April-September, daily

High Country Rosarium
1717 Downing Street
Denver, CO 80226
(303) 832-4026, FAX same
William Campbell

Plants
Very hardy old garden **roses** grown in the Rockies -- a good selection of species, old garden varieties and shrub roses, all well described. They have recently turned their focus to wholesale sales, but anyone may order if they order at least ten plants. (1971)
❒ Catalog: Free, R&W, SS:W, bn/cn
⌂ Nursery: All year, M-F
▼ Garden: May-June, M-F

Highland Succulents
1446 Bear Run Road
Gallipolis, OH 45631
(614) 256-1428, FAX 256-1454 TO/CC
William Ballard

Plants
"We specialize in hard-to-find **succulents** -- no common varieties." A quarterly collectors' list of new and unusual items; a very good selection which changes as new items are offered. Plants well described, many shown in color and b&w photographs.
❒ Catalog: $2, $20m, bn

Highlander Nursery
P.O. Box 177
Pettigrew, AR 72752
(501) 677-2300
Lee & Louise McCoy

Plants ∾ Supplies
Specializes in hardy and low-chill **blueberries**, a dozen varieties which bear from early to late in the season. Also offers one dwarf variety, 'Tophat,' which grows less than twenty-four inches high and makes a nice container, bonsai or border plant, and two ground cover varieties. (1986)
❒ Catalog: Free, R&W, SS:10-5
⌂ Nursery: All year, daily, call ahead
▼ Garden: May-June, October, daily, call ahead

Hildenbrandt's Iris Gardens
HC 84, Box 4
Lexington, NE 68850-9304
(308) 324-4334
Les & Tony Hildenbrandt

Plants
An extensive list of **tall bearded and dwarf irises**, each briefly described. Also offers a good selection of **herbaceous peonies, Oriental poppies, hostas** and a few hybrid **lilies**. The color selection of Oriental poppies seems wonderful! (1956)
❒ Catalog: $1(2 IRC OV), R&W, CAN/OV, SS:7-9, $15m
⌂ Nursery: May-September, call ahead
▼ Garden: May-June, call ahead

Hill 'n dale
6427 N. Fruit Avenue
Fresno, CA 93711
(209) 439-8249
Dale Kloppenburg

Plants ∾ Books
A very extensive list of **hoyas**, both species and named cultivars, with a number of **dischidias** and some **aeschynanthus**. Dale has added to his collection on trips to Australia, Guadalcanal, the Solomon Islands and the Philippines, so there are more to come. Cuttings only; three books. (1957)
❒ Catalog: $1(2 IRC OV), R&W, CAN/OV, $30m, bn
⌂ Nursery: All year, by appointment only
▼ Garden: April-September, by appointment only

Hillary's Garden
P.O. Box 378
Sugar Loaf, NY 10981-0378
John Russo

Plants
Another new source of **perennials**, a good selection with good plant descriptions, and informative tables to help you decide where and what to plant in your perennial beds. (1990)
❒ Catalog: $2d, R&W, CAN, SS:3-10, bn

Hillhouse Nursery
90 Kresson-Gibbsboro Road
Voorhees, NJ 08043
(609) 784-6203 TO/CC $10m
Theodore S. Stecki

Plants
Specializes in the **Linwood hardy azaleas**, hybridized by the late G. Albert Reid -- all either double, semi-double or hose-in-hose varieties, which come in a range of habits from prostrate and compact to tall -- all very hardy. Very brief descriptions; plants grown in 3" pots. (1968)
❒ Catalog: Free, R&W, SS:4-9
⌂ Nursery: Sept-June, evenings & weekends, call ahead
▼ Garden: April-June, Sept-October, call ahead

Hilltop Herb Farm
P.O. Box 325
Chain-O-Lakes Resort
Romayor, TX 77368
(713) 592-5859
Beverly Smith

Plants ∾ Seeds ∾ Books
Hilltop Herb Farm is well known in Texas for its restaurant, for which reservations are necessary. They sell **herb plants, scented geraniums** and herb seeds; a nice selection with no plant descriptions. Also sell their famous "Tranquility Tea" and gift baskets of preserves.
❒ Catalog: Free, SS:W, $20m
⌂ Nursery: All year, daily

Historical Roses
1657 W. Jackson Street
Painesville, OH 44077
(216) 357-7270
Ernest J. Vash

Plants
Small nursery offers a good selection of **old garden roses** of all kinds, some fragrant hybrid teas and the very hardy shrub roses of Griffith Buck. All plants very briefly described; over 100 in all. Ships only to the lower forty-eight states. (1982)
❒ Catalog: Long SASE, SS:3-4,10-1, $8m
⌂ Nursery: All year, M-Sa, by appointment only

Hobbs and Hopkins
1712 SE Ankeny
Portland, OR 97214
(503) 239-7518, FAX 230-0391
Keith Hopkins

Seeds
Offers seed mix for "Fleur de Lawn," a low-growing **flowering lawn mixture**.
Also offers other lawn grass seed. (1979)
❐ Catalog: Free, R&W

Holbrook Farm & Nursery
P.O. Box 368
115 Lance Road
Fletcher, NC 28732-0368
(704) 891-7790, FAX 891-1505 TO/CC $25m
Allen W. Bush

Plants
Offers a broad selection of **garden perennials, native wildflowers, hardy
geraniums, hostas, grasses, and trees and shrubs**; all are very well described, with cultural information. The catalog has a homey touch which
enhances the grand selection of fine perennials, a number of which are new
introductions. Cannot ship to AK, HI or PR. (1980)
❐ Catalog: Free, SS:3-5,9-11, $15m, bn/cn
⌂ Nursery: April-October, M-Sa
♥ Garden: April-October, M-Sa

Holden Clough Nursery
Holden, Nr. Bolton-by-Bowland
Clitheroe, Lancs., England BB7 4PF
(020 07) 615
Peter J. Foley

Seeds
Offers a good selection of seeds of **alpine and rock garden plants**; good
but very brief descriptions. Listed are: alliums, androsace, anemones, aquilegias, campanulas, drabas, gentians, meconopsis, potentillas, primulas,
saxifragas, violas and much more. (1927)
❐ Catalog: $3(US Bills), OV, bn

Holladay Jungle
P.O. Box 5727
1602 E. Fountain Way
Fresno, CA 93755
(209) 229-9858
Barbara Holladay

Plants
A broad selection of **tillandsias** available bare-root; there are no plant
descriptions, but you should be able to find them in a good book. They
"grow on trees and rocks without soil and all flower." They also have a
bromeliad list which I did not see. (1984)
❐ Catalog: Free, R&W, CAN/OV, $15m, bn
⌂ Nursery: All year, by appointment only
♥ Garden: All year, by appointment only

Holland Gardens
29106 Meridian East
Graham, WA 98338-9032
(206) 847-5425
Martin S. Holland

Plants
Talk about specialized! Martin Holland grows only one old **iris**, which his
mother grew since 1917, and it is registered as 'Sweet Lena' with the American Iris Society after her. Pale blue with white trim, it has a very strong,
sweet fragrance and 5 to 7 blooms on a stalk.
❐ Catalog: Free, CAN/OV, $10m

Holland Wildflower Farm
290 O'Neal Lane
Elkins, AR 72727
(501) 643-2622 TO/CC $15m
Bob & Julie Holland

Plants ⚘ Seeds
Small nursery sells plants and seeds of **prairie wildflowers** ideal for harsh
winters and hot summers. Send long SASE with 2 FCS for price list; they also
sell a booklet on growing wildflowers in which each plant is well described,
with cultural suggestions and a nice sketch for $4.25. (1985)
❐ Catalog: See notes, R&W, CAN, $15m, bn/cn
⌂ Nursery: Mid-March-November, Th-Sa, by appointment only
♥ Garden: May-June, Th-Sa, by appointment only

Holly Haven Hybrids
136 Sanwood Road
Knoxville, TN 37923-5564
(615) 690-3410
Harold L. Elmore

Plants
Harold is a **holly** collector with over 700 varieties planted out. Each year
he lists about 70 unusual varieties for sale, but he'll also custom propagate
from your "want list" if you're willing to wait a while. Varieties listed are
usually newer introductions; each is well described. (1972)
❐ Catalog: Long SASE, R&W, CAN
⌂ Nursery: All year, daily, by appointment only
♥ Garden: December-February, by appointment only

Holly Lane Iris Gardens
10930 Holly Lane
Osseo, MN 55369
Jack J. Worel

Plants
Formerly Worel Iris Gardens: offers a broad selection of **bearded irises**:
tall, border and dwarf bearded, as well as Siberians and some species. Also
daylilies, hostas and peonies; each plant briefly described. (1983)
❐ Catalog: Long SASE w/2 FCS, CAN, SS:7-9, $10m
⌂ Nursery: May-August, Tu-Su
♥ Garden: June-August, Tu-Su

Holly Ridge Nursery
1570 Compton Road
Cleveland Heights, OH 44118
(216) 321-5608, 466-0134
Paul Hanslik & Lucinda Little

Plants
A new source of **hollies, lilacs and viburnums**; a good selection of hollies,
and they are adding plants from their collection of more than 60 varieties of
American hollies. These are very hardy, and have red, yellow and orange
berries. Plants well described; no shipping to AZ, CA, OR or WA. (1991)
❐ Catalog: Free, R&W, $5m
⌂ Nursery: By appointment only

Hollydale Nursery
P.O. Box 68
Pelham, TN 37366
(615) 467-3600, (800) 222-3026, FAX 467-3062
Dale M. Bryan

Plants
Offers a very broad selection of **peaches** (some low-chill), **nectarines** and **plums** and a few **apples and pears**. They sell mostly to orchardists, but will also sell in small quantities. Trees grown on 'Nemaguard' and 'Lovell' rootstock in fumigated soil. No shipping to CA or WA. (1983)
◻ Catalog: Free, CAN/OV, SS:12-2, $35m

Hollyvale Farm
P.O. Box 69
Humptulips, WA 98552
Bonnie L. Heintz & Alice M. Reid

Plants
Offer 28 varieties of **holly**, all the hybrids of John Wieman: 'Wieman's Crinkle Variegated,' 'Goldburst,' 'Moon Bright,' 'Oriental Queen' and others. Mr. Wieman and his wife, both in their 90's, have registered more holly varieties than anyone else in the US. (1979)
◻ Catalog: Long SASE, R&W, CAN/OV, $10m

Homan Brothers Seed
P.O. Box 337
Glendale, AZ 85311-0337
(602) 244-1650, FAX same
Nathan Young

Seeds
Formerly Hubbs Brothers Seed, this company specializes in habitat collected seed of **native plants of the Sonoran and Mojave Deserts**; they offer native grasses, wildflowers and shrubs; described in brief tables. (1991)
◻ Catalog: 2 FCS, R&W, CAN/OV, $25m, bn/cn
⌂ Nursery: All year, M-F, by appointment only
▼ Garden: April-May, by appointment only

Homeplace Garden Nursery
P.O. Box 300
Harden Bridge Road
Commerce, GA 30529
(706) 335-2892
Willis Harden

Plants
Specializing in **rhododendron** species and hybrids and evergreen and deciduous **azaleas**, also offers a much smaller selection of companion plants as well: Japanese maples, dwarf conifers, kalmias, magnolias, and hostas, ferns and other ground covers. A broad selection of rhododendrons and azaleas, briefly described. No shipping to AK, CA or HI. (1985)
◻ Catalog: $2, R&W, SS:10-5
⌂ Nursery: April-May, October, daily

Homestead Division of Sunnybrook Farms
9448 Mayfield Road
Chesterland, OH 44026
(216) 729-9838
Peter & Jean Ruh

Plants ⟳ Seeds ⟳ Tools
A retirement business of the founders of Sunnybrook Farms -- huge selection of **hostas** (and hosta seeds), also a number of **ivies, epimediums, daylilies** and a Japanese fern -- some retirement! Plants briefly to well described. They also offer a few of their favorite hand tools and plant labels. (1980)
◻ Catalog: $2($3 OV), CAN/OV, SS:4-10, $25m
⌂ Nursery: April-October, daily, by appointment only
▼ Garden: June-September, by appointment only

Homestead Farm
P.O. Box 946
Idaho Springs, CO 80452
(303) 567-4886
David & Sarah Beth Snyder

Plants
Specializes in organically grown **herbs, Siberian tomatoes, wildflowers**, and hardy **native trees, shrubs and ground covers**, all grown at 9,000' in the Rocky Mountains. The catalog is very informative, with recipes, and each plant is very well described. Also sell honey and bee products. (1992)
◻ Catalog: $4d, CAN, SS:4-11, $16m, cn/bn
⌂ Nursery: By appointment only
▼ Garden: June-September, by appointment only

Homestead Farms
Route 2, Box 31A
Owensville, MO 65066
(314) 437-4277
Ronald & Brett Vitoux

Plants
Offers a nice selection of **daylilies, hostas, clematis, peonies**, and **daffodils**, with some Siberian and reblooming iris and wild collected ferns. While the choice is not large, the plants are well described and many are award winners, both old and new. (1983)
◻ Catalog: Free, SS:3-10
⌂ Nursery: March-October, M-Sa
▼ Garden: May-September, M-Sa

Homestead Gardens
125 Homestead Road
Kalispell, MT 59901
(406) 756-6631 TO/CC
Ray & Iris Jones

Plants
Offers a very nice list of **dahlias**, grouped by size or type, and very briefly described. Many are described as winners, so they must have many dahlia exhibitors as customers. (1989)
◻ Catalog: Free, CAN,SS:1-5, $20m
▼ Garden: July-August, daily

Honeysong Farm
51 Jared Place
Seaford, DE 19973
Mark Silva

Plants
Mark Silva owns and operates the retail sales of Honeysong Farm, the huge **hosta** collection (1,500+) of Alex Summers, four times the president of the American Hosta Society. Offerings vary from well-known varieties to the newest introductions; all plants are well described. (1993)
◻ Catalog: $1d, SS:4-10, $25m

Honeywood Lilies
P.O. Box 68
Parkside, SK, Canada S0J 2A0
(306) 747-3296, FAX 747-3395
Allan B. Daku

Plants ∿ Bulbs
Specializes in **lilies**, offering a nice variety of all types and some collections, shipped all over the world. Also offers herbaceous peonies and iris, alliums, species tulips, hardy daylilies and a few "minor bulbs," for shipment only in Canada; sells **sedums and sempervivums** as well, which can be shipped anywhere.
❒ Catalog: $2d, R&W, US/OV, SS:4-5,9-11, $25m, cn/bn
⌂ Nursery: April-October, M-Sa
▼ Garden: July-September, M-Sa

Hookland's Dahlias

See Frey's Dahlias.

Hoosier Orchid Company
8440 West 82nd Street
Indianapolis, IN 46278
(317) 291-6269
William A. Rhodehamel

Plants
Specializes in seed grown **orchid species**, a very good selection with excellent plant descriptions; they also offer their own inter-specific hybrids. They have a orchid species seed propagation program, and will grow yours from seed and share the plants with you. (1988)
❒ Catalog: $1d, R&W, CAN/OV, SS:3-11, bn
⌂ Nursery: All year, Tu-Sa
▼ Garden: All year, Tu-Sa

Jerry Horne -- Rare Plants
10195 S.W. 70th Street
Miami, FL 33173
(305) 270-1235
Jerry Horne

Plants
A collectors' list of rare and exotic **tropical plants**. A good selection of bromeliads, platyceriums, ferns, palms, cycads, aroids and others, all briefly described with cultural suggestions. (1975)
❒ Catalog: Long SASE($1 OV), CAN/OV, $15m, bn
⌂ Nursery: All year, by appointment only
▼ Garden: All year, by appointment only

Hortico, Inc.
723 Robson Road, RR 1
Waterdown, ON, Canada L0R 2H1
(416) 689-6984 or 3002, FAX 689-6566
William Vanderkruk

Plants
A very broad selection of garden **perennials**, hardy ornamental **trees** and **shrubs, roses, lilacs, ferns, wildflowers and conifers**, briefly described. Essentially a wholesale nursery, but will sell in small quantities to home gardeners at retail prices. Ask for rose, shrub or perennial list, $3 each.
❒ Catalog: See notes, R&W, US/OV, SS:9-5, bn

Horticultural Enterprises
P.O. Box 810082
Dallas, TX 75381-0082
John A. Mako

Seeds
"Chiles are our business." **Chiles and sweet peppers** from around the world -- each briefly described and illustrated as to size and shape. Also a few **Mexican herbs and vegetables**. Included is a bibliography of cookbooks with publishers' addresses -- uses galore for your harvest! (1973)
❒ Catalog: Free, CAN

Spencer M. Howard Orchid Imports
11802 Huston Street
North Hollywood, CA 91607
(818) 762-8275, FAX 505-9902
Spencer M. Howard

Plants
Only **species orchids**, collected from all over the world. A collectors' list offers dendrobium, epidendrum, angraecum, oncidium, laelia, rhyncostylis, paphiopedilum, phalaenopsis, cirrhopetalum, pleurothallis and many others; very brief descriptions -- get out your reference books and dream. (1957)
❒ Catalog: Long SASE w/3 FCS, R&W, CAN/OV, SS:W, $35m, bn
⌂ Nursery: All year, by appointment only
▼ Garden: Spring, by appointment only

J. L. Hudson, Seedsman
P.O. Box 1058
Redwood City, CA 94064
J. L. Hudson

Seeds ∿ Books
"Specialize in **rare seeds** from all over the world -- except Antarctica." Now called the "Ethnobotanical Catalog of Seeds," it's informative, with a broad selection, historic, cultural and literary references and current scientific information, illustrated with old prints. More than a catalog, it's an education. Also offers some books. (1911)
❒ Catalog: $1($4 OV), R&W, CAN/OV, bn/cn

Huff's Garden Mums
P.O. Box 187
617 Juniatta
Burlington, KS 66839-0187
(316) 364-2765, (800) 279-4675
Harry & Charles Huff

Plants
A huge selection of **chrysanthemums** -- a collectors' list -- each very briefly described and organized by type. Still carries some old favorites, and offers a number of collections by type or use for those who are bewildered by the choice. Cannot ship to England. (1955)
❒ Catalog: $1d, R&W, CAN/OV, SS:3-6, $5m
⌂ Nursery: Mid-September-June, M-Sa
▼ Garden: September-October, call ahead

Huggins Farm Irises
Route 1, Box 348
Hico, TX 76457
(817) 796-4041
Pete & Mary Huggins

Plants
Broad selection of **bearded irises**: tall bearded, reblooming, intermediate, border, dwarf, horned, "space age" and "antique" (before 1950 -- by which measure, I'm an antique, too). The "antiques" are often used for landscaping restored older homes.
☐ Catalog: $1d, CAN/OV, SS:7-10, $10m
⌂ Nursery: Weekends & eves, call ahead
♥ Garden: March-May, Sept.-Nov., weekends & eves, call ahead

Hughes Nursery
1305 Wynooche West
Montesano, WA 98563
(206) 249-3702, FAX same
Howard Hughes

Plants
A collectors' list of **Japanese maples**, mostly listed by their Japanese cultivar names, and a few other species maples; all are well described with cultural suggestions. A good selection of hard-to-find trees, listed by shape and leaf color/character. (1964)
☐ Catalog: $1.50d, CAN/OV, SS:10-3
⌂ Nursery: All year, by appointment only
♥ Garden: June, by appointment only

Hungry Plants
1216 Cooper Drive
Raleigh, NC 27607
(919) 851-6521, 829-3751, FAX 755-0173
Ron Gagliardo

Plants
Back in business after a hiatus, Hungry Plants specializes in **carnivorous plants**: droseras, pygmy droseras, Venus flytrap, pinguiculas on a brief list -- the names used are either common or botanical, so it's a bit confusing. Expects to be adding plants on new list. (1983)
☐ Catalog: $2, R&W, CAN/OV, $15m
♥ Garden: June-August, by appointment only

Brenda Hyatt
1 Toddington Crescent, Bluebell Hill
Chatham, Kent, England ME5 9QT
(0634) 86-3251
Brenda Hyatt

Seeds
Specializes in **Auricula primroses**, both Alpine and show varieties; sells seeds of both types in packets of mixed colors. She now keeps the National Collection of P. auricula, including the collection of Gordon Douglas; seeds available of cowslips, candelabras, double Jack-in-the-Green and double and single gold-laced. She's written a book on auriculas. Catalog 40p in UK.
☐ Catalog: 2 IRC, OV, $5m
⌂ Nursery: By appointment only

Indiana Berry & Plant Co.
5218 W. 500 S.
Huntingburg, IN 47542
(812) 683-3055, FAX 683-2004 TO/CC $25m
James W. Erwin

Plants ～ **Books** ～ **Supplies**
Informative color catalog offers 30 varieties of **strawberries** and other **bramble berries and blueberries, asparagus and rhubarb**, as well as specialized supplies and machinery for the commercial strawberry grower.
☐ Catalog: Free, R&W
⌂ Nursery: All year, M-F

Ingraham's Cottage Garden Roses
P.O. Box 126
Scotts Mills, OR 97375
(503) 873-8610
Jill Ingraham

Plants
Offers a nice selection of **old garden and modern roses**, some grafted and some on their own roots. Each rose is well described, with notes on fragrance and rebloom, and whether it's budded or own-root. (1989)
☐ Catalog: $1d(1 IRC OV), CAN/OV, SS:2-3, $10m
⌂ Nursery: February-September, call ahead
♥ Garden: June-September, call ahead

W. E. Th. Ingwersen, Ltd.

See Birch Farm Nursery.

Intermountain Cactus
1478 North 750 East
Kaysville, UT 84037
(801) 546-2006, 487-3041
Robert A. Johnson

Plants
Offers a selection of **very hardy cactus** (some to -20 to -50F), most of which are profuse bloomers, including opuntia, pediocactus, echinocereus, coryphantha and neobesseya. Opuntias sold by pad or by clump. Each plant well described. (1976)
☐ Catalog: Long SASE, SS:4-11, $20m, bn/cn
⌂ Nursery: May-October, M-Sa, call ahead
♥ Garden: May-October, M-Sa, call ahead

Iris & Plus
P.O. Box 903
1269 Route 139
Sutton, PQ, Canada J0E 2K0
(514) 538-2048, FAX 538-0448
Danielle Paquette & John Salisbury

Plants
Offers a nice selection of **daylilies, hostas, iris and astilbes**: bearded iris of all types, Japanese and Siberian iris. Catalog is in English and in French, plants are briefly described. (1990)
☐ Catalog: $2d, R&W, US/OV, SS:5-10
⌂ Nursery: May-September, daily, by appointment only
♥ Garden: May-July, call ahead

Iris Acres
Route 4, Box 189
Winamac, IN 46996
(219) 946-4197
Thurlow & Jean Sanders

Plants
A very extensive list of "winter tested" **bearded irises in all sizes**, including reblooming and "space age" types; all plants briefly described. List offers general information on planting and care of irises. (1959)
❑ Catalog: $1d, CAN, SS:7-9
⌂ Nursery: April-September, call ahead
▼ Garden: May-June, call ahead

Iris Country
6219 Topaz Street N.E.
Brooks, OR 97305
(503) 393-4739 (evenings)
Roger R. Nelson

Plants
I'm happy to have found Roger Nelson again -- I lost track of him when he moved to Oregon. Roger's specialty is **tall and border bearded iris** selected for maximum vigor and hardiness, he tests them all over the country. Also listed are some older favorites; all are well described. (1968)
❑ Catalog: $1.50, R&W, CAN/OV, $10m
⌂ Nursery: By appointment only
▼ Garden: May-October, by appointment only

The Iris Pond
7311 Churchill Road
McLean, VA 22101
Clarence & Suky Mahan

Plants
Offers tall bearded, Japanese, Siberian, reblooming and species **irises** and a large selection of miniature tall bearded irises; good selection, plants very briefly described. Also have a locator service for out-of-print books on irises. (1985)
❑ Catalog: $1, CAN/OV, SS:7-9, $25m
▼ Garden: May-June, by appointment only

Iris Test Gardens
1010 Highland Park Drive
College Place, WA 99324
(509) 525-8804
Austin & Ione Morgan

Plants
A nice selection of "novelty" tall bearded **irises**; brief descriptions. Some of the offerings are their own hybrids, including 'Morgan's Double Rimmers,' which have double bands of color around the falls. Prices very modest. (1977)
❑ Catalog: $.50, SS:7-9, $5m
⌂ Nursery: July-September, call ahead
▼ Garden: May, daylight hours

Iron Gate Gardens
Route 3, Box 250
Highway 216
Kings Mountain, NC 28086
(704) 435-6178, FAX 435-4367
Van Sellers & Vic Santa Lucia

Plants
A well-known **daylily** nursery, introducing their own hybrids and those of Pauline Henry (Siloam names) and Virginia Peck. All of their listings are recent introductions, which are pricier than older varieties. They also list both new and older **hostas**; all plants well described. (1960)
❑ Catalog: $3d, CAN/OV, SS:4-10, $50m
⌂ Nursery: March-October, daily
▼ Garden: April-July, daily

Ison's Nursery
P.O. Box 190
8544 Newnan Highway
Brooks, GA 30205
(404) 599-6970
William G. Ison

Plants
Specialize in **muscadine-scuppernong grapes**; offer many varieties and are working on a seedless muscadine. They also sell many other fruits -- blackberries, blueberries, raspberries, apricots, low-chill apples, plums, figs, pomegranates, nut trees; well described, with cultural hints. (1936)
❑ Catalog: Free, R&W, SS:11-4
⌂ Nursery: September-June, M-F
▼ Garden: Orchard, M-F

© Seeds of Change
Artist: Helen Beck

It's About Thyme
11726 Manchaca Road
Austin, TX 78748
(512) 280-1192, FAX 280-6356
Diane Winslow

Plants
Offers a good selection of **herbs**, including Southwestern herbs and peppers, and scented geraniums, all briefly described. They will be adding old garden roses to coming lists; these are limited in quantity at present. (1979)
❑ Catalog: $1, SS:3-6,9-11, $20m, cn/bn
⌂ Nursery: All year, daily
▼ Garden: All year, daily

Ivies of the World
P.O. Box 408
Highway 42 (2 miles East)
Weirsdale, FL 32195-0408
(904) 821-2201 or 2322 TO/CC
Tim & Judy Rankin

Plants
Offers more than 250 cultivars of **ivy**, mainly rooted cuttings; plants are grouped by type and well described. This nursery was formerly Tropexotic Growers, and before that The Alestake of Elkwood, VA (for those of you who haven't been keeping track). Adding new varieties all the time. (1986)
❑ Catalog: $1.50, CAN, $20m
⌂ Nursery: All year, M-F, by appointment only

J & L Orchids
20 Sherwood Road
Easton, CT 06612
(203) 261-3772, FAX 261-8730 TO/CC
C. Head, M. Webb & L. Winn

Plants ⟋ Books
A broad selection of **species orchids** from all over the world, as well as hybrids; all well described with lovely illustrations. Specializes in rare and unusual species and miniatures which can be grown in the home under lights or on the windowsill; also offers "beginners' specials." (1960)
❑ Catalog: $1($4 OV), CAN/OV, SS:3-11, bn
⌂ Nursery: All year, M-Sa
▼ Garden: December-April, M-Sa

J. E. M. Orchids
6595 Morikami Park Road
Delray Beach, FL 33446
(407) 498-4308, FAX same
Gene Monnier

Plants
Offers **hybrid orchids and new world species**: oncidium intergenerics, minicattleyas, paphiopedilums, phalaenopsis, dendrobiums, catasetum, zygopetinae and others, each very briefly described with information on crosses. A separate species list is available for $1. (1974)
❑ Catalog: $2d, R&W, CAN/OV, SS:W
⌂ Nursery: September-July, M-Sa
▼ Garden: September-July, M-Sa

Jackson & Perkins Co.
2518 S. Pacific Highway
Medford, OR 97501
(800) 292-4769, 872-7673, FAX (800) 242-0329
Bear Creek Corporation

Plants ⟋ Bulbs
Color catalogs offer a wide selection of modern hybrid tea, grandiflora, floribunda and climbing **roses**, mostly of their own breeding, as well as perennials, hybrid lilies and other summer-blooming bulbs. Another catalog offers spring bulbs, and another offers garden ornaments and gifts. (1872)
❑ Catalog: Free, CAN
▼ Garden: May-August, Rose Test Garden

Jasperson's Hersey Nursery
2915 - 74th Avenue
Wilson, WI 54027
Lu Jasperson

Plants
Small nursery specializes in tall bearded **irises, gladioli and daylilies**, listed only by color and cultivar name. Fresh cut flowers and vegetable plants are available at the nursery, where you can choose and dig other perennials on the spot. (1987)
❑ Catalog: Long SASE, R&W, SS:4,7,9, $15m
⌂ Nursery: April-October, M-Sa
▼ Garden: April-October, M-Sa

**The Thomas Jefferson Center
for Historic Plants**
Monticello
P.O. Box 316
Charlottesville, VA 22902
FAX (804) 977-6140
Peggy C. Newcomb, Dir.

Seeds
Seeds from the **historic flowers and vegetables** grown at Monticello and at Tufton Farm. The center is a force in the preservation of garden plants grown in the 18th century. They also offer books on historic or old-fashioned flowers, including reprints of early books, and books by and about Jefferson as a gardener. Other historic plants are sold at Monticello. (1987)
❑ Catalog: Long SASE, CAN, $2m, bn/cn
⌂ Nursery: April-October, daily
▼ Garden: April-June, October, daily

Jelitto Staudensamen GmBH
P.O. Box 1264
Am Toggraben 3
D 3033 Schwarmstedt, Germany
(05071) 4085, FAX 4088
Klaus Jelitto & Christian Baltin

Seeds
A very broad selection of **rock garden and alpine plants, perennials and ornamental grasses** listed by botanical name. Catalog is in German, with cultural instructions for germinating seeds in English and French, symbols for use and some color photographs. (1957)
❑ Catalog: Free, R&W, OV, $20m, bn
⌂ Nursery: September-July, M-F

Jernigan Gardens
Route 6, Box 593
Dunn, NC 28334
(919) 567-2135
Bettie Jernigan

Plants
Long collectors' list of **daylilies**, very briefly described, with concise
tables of information. Also offers a good selection of **hostas** and some
irises by mail; other perennials are available only at the nursery.
❑ Catalog: Long SASE, R&W, SS:4-11, $15m
⌂ Nursery: April-October, daily, call ahead
▼ Garden: April-July, daily, call ahead

Jersey Asparagus Farms
RD 5, Box 572
Newfield, NJ 08344
(609) 358-2548, FAX 358-6127
Samuel Walker

Plants ⬿ Seeds
Specialize in the Jersey male hybrid **asparagus**, which are very tolerant to
fusarium diseases, resistant to rust, and are much higher yielding than the
older Washington varieties. They offer plants and seeds of nine varieties,
all well described as to flavor, appearance and growing conditions. (1985)
❑ Catalog: Free, R&W, CAN/OV, SS:11-5, $5m
⌂ Nursery: All year, M-F

Joe's Nursery
P.O. Box 1867
Vista, CA 92085-1867
Joseph W. Kraatz

Plants
A collector's list of **palms, cycads, aloes, agaves, euphorbias, bromeliads,**
yuccas, dyckias, dasylirions, nolinas, puyas, pachypodiums, species ficus,
various succulents and other sub-tropicals; no plant descriptions, but a
nice selection. (1986)
❑ Catalog: $2d, SS:W, $15m, bn

Johnny's Selected Seeds
Foss Hill Road
Albion, ME 04910-9731
(207) 437-9294, FAX 437-2165 TO/CC $15m
Robert L. Johnston, Jr.

Seeds ⬿ Books ⬿ Supplies
Catalog lists a broad selection of **vegetables, herbs and garden annuals**, as
well as specialty grains and seed for commercial crops; also a good selection
of growing supplies and books. All plants are very well described, with
cultural suggestions and germination guides; particularly suited to Northern
growing. (1973)
❑ Catalog: Free, R&W, CAN/OV
⌂ Nursery: Mid-March-December, M-Sa
▼ Garden: July-September, call ahead

Johnson Nursery
Route 5, Box 29-J
Highway 52 E.
Ellijay, GA 30540-9294
(706) 276-3187 TO $20m
Elisa S. Ford

Plants ⬿ Supplies ⬿ Tools
Catalog offers a good selection of **fruit trees** -- apples, old peach vari-
eties, pears, plums, cherries, nuts, many kinds of berries and some grapes --
all well described, with b&w photos. Also sells supplies and tools. (1981)
❑ Catalog: Free, R&W, SS:12-4, $5m
⌂ Nursery: All year, M-Sa

Jordan Seeds
6400 Upper Afton Road
Woodbury, MN 55125
(612) 738-3422, 739-9578, FAX 731-7590
Dan, Jake & Nancy Jordan

Seeds ⬿ Supplies
Offer a broad variety of **vegetable seeds**, each very briefly described by
days to maturity, size and appearance. Seeds are sold in bulk, with one
ounce being the smallest size. Also sell some growing and marketing
supplies and mechanical transplanters for bigger operations. (1979)
❑ Catalog: Free, R&W, CAN
⌂ Nursery: All year, M-Sa
▼ Garden: Summer-Fall, M-Sa

JoS Violets
2205 College Drive
Victoria, TX 77901
(512) 575-1344
Joanne Schrimsher

Plants ⬿ Supplies
List of standard, miniature, semi-miniature and trailing **African violets**
for sale as plants or leaves; each briefly described. Also sells some
growing supplies and Oyama Texas-style pots. (1983)
❑ Catalog: Long SASE, R&W, SS:4-10, $5m
⌂ Nursery: All year, Sa-Su, by appointment only

Joy Creek Nursery
20300 N.W. Watson Road
Scappoose, OR 97056
(503) 543-7474, 227-2160
Mike Smith & Maurice Horn

Plants
A small new nursery offering a very nice selection of **perennials**, including
some usually hard to find, like meconopsis, penstemons, Pacific Coast iris
hybrids, species iris, species clematis, and some Northwestern native plants.
All plants well described, and new varieties being added all the time. (1992)
❑ Catalog: $2d ($5 OV), R&W, CAN/OV, SS: 2-5,8-11, bn
⌂ Nursery: March-October, Sa
▼ Garden: May-October, Sa

Joyce's Garden
64640 Old Bend Redmond Highway
Bend, OR 97701
(503) 388-4680
Joyce Macdonald

Plants
Offers "ultra-hardy" **perennials, ground covers and herbs**; Bend gets
freezes even in July and August! Good selection of plants for good drain-
age, including achillea, asters, campanulas, dianthus, helianthemums, phlox,
veronicas, sages and more; plants are briefly described. (1987)
❑ Catalog: $2, R&W, SS:4-6,9-10, bn/cn
⌂ Nursery: February-November, M-Sa, call ahead
▼ Garden: June-September, M-Sa, call ahead

J. W. Jung Seed Co.
335 S. High Street
Randolph, WI 53957-0001
FAX (414) 326-5769
Richard Zondag & Peter Jung

Plants ⁊ Seeds ⁊ Supplies ⁊ Bulbs
Color catalog offers a broad selection of seeds for the flower and vegetable garden, as well as nursery stock -- **fruit trees, roses, perennials, ornamental trees, shrubs and vines.** Also issues a bulb catalog in the summer. Carries tools and supplies, too. (1907)
❐ Catalog: Free, R&W, SS:3-6,8-10
⌂ Nursery: All year, M-Sa
♥ Garden: August-September (Randolph trial garden)

Jungle Gems, Inc.
300 Edgewood Road
Edgewood, MD 21040
(410) 676-0672 TO/CC
Dr. Charles Williamson

Plants
Sells **phalaenopsis orchids** from blooming size to seedlings, as well as miltonopsis, cattleyas, tillandsias, species orchids and mericlones in mini-flasks. All plants are very briefly described. (1975)
❐ Catalog: Free, R&W, CAN/OV, SS:W
⌂ Nursery: All year, M-Sa
♥ Garden: All year, glasshouse, M-Sa

Just Enough Sinningias
P.O. Box 560493
Orlando, FL 32856
(407) 423-4750
Patti Schwindt

Plants
Patti specializes in **miniature sinningias**, offering a nice selection in an informative catalog with lots of information on ancestry. These little plants are great houseplants, and are frequently used in terrariums. (1990)
❐ Catalog: $2($3 OV), R&W, CAN/OV

Just Fruits
Route 2, Box 4818
Crawfordville, FL 32327
(904) 926-5644
JJ & Brandy Cowley

Plants
Specializes in **fruits for the Southeast** and fruits which thrive under "low chill" conditions: figs, kiwi, bananas, peaches and nectarines, grapes, Asian and regular pears, mayhaws, apples, plums, berries, hardy citrus and much more. All fruits well described; can't ship to CA or HI. (1983)
❐ Catalog: $3d
⌂ Nursery: September-April, Th-Su
♥ Garden: All year, Th-Su, call ahead

Justice Miniature Roses
5947 S.W. Kahle Road
Wilsonville, OR 97070
(503) 682-2370
Jerry, June & Tara Justice

Plants
A broad selection of **miniature roses**, all very well described, with some growing advice. In 1987 they started introducing varieties hybridized in Ireland by Sean McCann, and they also hybridize roses themselves. (1982)
❐ Catalog: Free, R&W, CAN/OV
⌂ Nursery: All year, daily

K & L Cactus & Succulent Nursery
9500 Brook Ranch Road East
Ione, CA 95640
(209) 274-0360 TO/CC $25m
Keith & Lorraine Thomas

Plants ⁊ Seeds ⁊ Books ⁊ Supplies
Color and b&w catalog offers extensive list of **flowering desert and jungle cacti, succulents** and some seed; each well but briefly described. Also sells some cactus books and a few supplies, including handsome pots. (1971)
❐ Catalog: $2d, CAN/OV, SS:4-11, $20m, bn

KSA Jojoba
19025 Parthenia Street
Northridge, CA 91324
(818) 701-1534, FAX 993-0194
Kathie Aamodt

Plants ⁊ Seeds ⁊ Supplies
Sells only **jojoba** -- seeds, seedlings and rooted cuttings of Simmondsia chinensis, and a variety of jojoba products such as soap, shampoos, lotions and automotive products. Cuttings, seedlings may be purchased in bulk; no plant descriptions. (1979)
❐ Catalog: Long SASE w/2 FCS, R&W, CAN/OV
⌂ Nursery: All year, M-F, call ahead

Kalmia Farm
Route 1, Box 149
Esmont, VA 22937
Ken Klotz

Plants
Sell only varieties of **garlic, shallots and onions** -- but some interesting onions: potato onions, bird's nest onions, Egyptian top onions; all well described. The potato onions are an old variety which they say is perennial. No shipping to certain counties in Oregon and Idaho. (1982)
❐ Catalog: Free, SS:9-11

Karleens Achimenes
1407 W. Magnolia
Valdosta, GA 31601-4235
(912) 242-1368
Karleen Lane

Plants ⁊ Seeds
A small hobby business, but offers a wide selection of achimenes and other **gesneriads** -- sinningias, gloxinias, smithiantha, eucodonias and kohlerias. Also offers **variegated plants**; most briefly but well described. Sells seeds she collects in her garden, and brugmansia plants. (1978)
❐ Catalog: $1.50, CAN/OV, SS:1-5, $12m, bn
⌂ Nursery: By appointment only
♥ Garden: April-September, by appointment only

Kartuz Greenhouses
1408 Sunset Drive
Vista, CA 92083-6531
(619) 941-3613
Michael J. Kartuz

Plants
The catalog, a collectors' dream, offers flowering plants for the home,
greenhouse and outside in warm areas -- **begonias, gesneriads** and
species **African violets** and many other rare flowering plants and vines --
all very well described. Even more plants available at the nursery. (1960)
❑ Catalog: $2, CAN, $20m, bn
⌂ Nursery: All year, W-Sa, call ahead
❦ Garden: All year, W-Sa, call ahead

Kasch Nursery
2860 N.E. Kelly Place
Gresham, OR 97030-2793
(503) 661-0357
Lorry & Tim Kasch

Plants
Offers a good selection of rooted and grafted **conifers**, both "regular" big
ones and dwarfs; plants are briefly described by growth habit, hardiness,
and size at maturity. (1983)
❑ Catalog: Free, R&W, CAN/OV, $5m, bn
⌂ Nursery: All year, by appointment only

Kawamoto Orchid Nursery
2630 Waiomao Road
Honolulu, HI 96816
(808) 732-5808, FAX 732-5572 TO/CC $25m
Leslie Kawamoto

Plants
Color catalog of **hybrid and species orchids** -- cattleyas, oncidiums, den-
drobiums, vandas -- many illustrated, all briefly described. A number of
mericlones are listed. They also have three orchid-of-the-month clubs with
various offerings. A wide selection, available in various sizes. (1947)
❑ Catalog: $2d, R&W, $25m, bn
⌂ Nursery: All year, M-Sa
❦ Garden: All year, M-Sa

Kay's Greenhouses
207 W. Southcross
San Antonio, TX 78221
Kay Tucker

Plants
A broad selection of **rhizomatous and cane begonias**, both plants and
cuttings. Each plant is briefly described by color of leaves and bloom.
Ask if you're looking for something rare, she has more plants than she
lists. No shipping to Australia. (1987)
❑ Catalog: $2, R&W, CAN/OV, SS:W, $10m
⌂ Nursery: Daily, by appointment only
❦ Garden: January-May, by appointment only

Kelleygreen Rhododendron Nursery
6924 Highway 38
Drain, OR 97435
(503) 836-2290 TO/CC
Jan Kelley

Plants ❧ **Supplies**
Collectors' list -- a huge selection of **species and hybrid rhododendrons**,
and they have added **azaleas, pieris and kalmias** to the 1,450 rhododen-
drons they offer. All varieties are well described, and there is good gen-
eral cultural information. (1978)
❑ Catalog: $1.25($3 OV), CAN/OV, SS:9-6, $13m, bn
⌂ Nursery: All year, by appointment only
❦ Garden: May, by appointment only

Kelly's Plant World
10266 E. Princeton
Sanger, CA 93657
(209) 294-7676
Herbert Kelly, Jr.

Plants ❧ **Bulbs**
Summer-blooming bulbs: crinums, amarcrinums, amaryllids, cannas, nerines,
irises, daylilies, hymenocallis and more. He lists 115 varieties of canna,
and has a broad selection of crinums, and has added aspidistras from Japan.
He also collects trees, shrubs, bamboos, palms and other plants; you can call
and ask him what's available.
❑ Catalog: $1

Kensington Orchids
3301 Plyers Mill Road
Kensington, MD 20895
(301) 933-0036, FAX 933-9441
Merritt W. Huntington

Plants ❧ **Books** ❧ **Supplies**
List offers phalaenopsis, doritaenopsis and oncidium hybrids, cattleyas,
"Cambria types," miltonias and paphiopedilum **orchids** in seedling and
flowering sizes, very briefly described. Also sells books and orchid grow-
ing supplies. (1946)
❑ Catalog: $1d, R&W, CAN/OV, SS:W, $25m
⌂ Nursery: All year, daily
❦ Garden: All year, greenhouses, daily

Kent's Flowers
2501 East 23rd Avenue
Fremont, NE 68025
(402) 721-1478 TO/CC
Kent & Joyce Stork

Plants
New and recent **African violets** from various leading hybridizers, including
their own prize winners; plants well described. Sell both plants and leaves.
❑ Catalog: $.50, SS:9-10, $13m, bn
⌂ Nursery: All year, M-Sa, call ahead
❦ Garden: All year, M-Sa, call ahead

Keith Keppel
4020 Cordon Road N.E.
Salem, OR 97305
(503) 391-9241
Keith Keppel

Plants
Keith has retired and moved to Oregon: he issues an extensive list of **tall
bearded irises**, many his own introductions; plants very well described,
with very good information on parentage. He caters to the "iris crowd," which
means he has the latest and most desirable new iris. (1955)
❑ Catalog: $1d($2 OV), CAN/OV, SS:7-8, $10m
⌂ Nursery: Daily, during bloom season
❦ Garden: May, daily during daylight hours

Kester's Wild Game Food Nurseries
P.O. Box 516
4582 Highway 116 East
Omro, WI 54963
(414) 685-2929, FAX 685-6727 TO/CC
David & Patricia Kester

Plants & Seeds
A wide selection of **plants to feed wildlife**: plants for ponds, various grains and wild rice (including an edible variety). The catalog offers a lot of cultural and wildlife food management information, lists seed and plants, including **aquatic plants**, and seed for feeding pet birds. (1899)
❏ Catalog: $2, R&W, CAN/OV, SS:2-10
⌂ Nursery: All year, M-Sa, call ahead

Kilgore Seed Company
1400 W. First Street
Sanford, FL 32771
(407) 323-6630
J. H. Hunziker

Seeds & Supplies & Tools
A regional seed company, offering **vegetables and flowers** for the Gulf Coast area of the US, but suited to any subtropical or tropical climate. A wide selection, each very well described, with cultural suggestions; they also sell gardening supplies and tools. (1918)
❏ Catalog: $1d($2 OV), CAN/OV
⌂ Nursery: All year, M-F

Kilworth Flowers
RR 3
County Road 14
Komoka, ON, Canada N0L 1R0
(519) 471-9787
Jim & Jo-Anne Eadie

Plants & Books & Supplies
Seedling to blooming size **orchids**: cattleya, phalaenopsis, dendrobium, ascocendas, cymbidium and paphiopedilum hybrids and sophronitis, paphiopedilium and other species; all briefly described. Also orchid books and growing supplies. (1983)
❏ Catalog: $1d, R&W, SS:3-10
⌂ Nursery: All year, Tu-Su, call ahead
▼ Garden: March-June, Tu-Su, call ahead

King's Mums
P.O. Box 368
20303 E. Liberty Road
Clements, CA 95227
Ted & Lanna King

Plants
Color catalog offers wide choice of **chrysanthemums** -- a real collectors' list; all plants well described, with cultural information. Sells collections of mums and the handbooks of the National Chrysanthemum Society. (1964)
❏ Catalog: $2d, SS:2-6, $10m
⌂ Nursery: October-November, daily
▼ Garden: October-November, daily

Kingfisher, Inc.
P.O. Box 75
Wexford, PA 15090-0075
(412) 935-2233, FAX 935-5515 TO/CC $15m
Elizabeth Bair

Seeds
Offers a nice selection of **herb** seeds; each plant very well described with germination and cultural information. They also sell a few seed collections for various uses and a kit for growing culinary herbs at home. Formerly Halcyon Gardens. (1989)
❏ Catalog: $1d, R&W, CAN, cn/bn

Kirkland Daylilies
P.O. Box 176
Newville, AL 36353
(205) 889-3313
Marjorie C. Kirkland

Plants
Specializes in large-flowered **daylilies**; almost all of them have flowers seven inches or more across. Plants are listed in an informative table. Also offers hybrid **amaryllis**, described by color. (1990)
❏ Catalog: Free, SS:4-8, $25m
⌂ Nursery: All year, daily
▼ Garden: May-June, daily

Kitazawa Seed Co.
1111 Chapman Street
San Jose, CA 95126
Sakae Komatsu

Seeds
A good selection of seeds for **Oriental vegetables**; plants are briefly described. Eleven varieties of daikon, the Japanese radish, and eleven kinds of mustard, squash, melons, greens, eggplants, beans and more. (1917)
❏ Catalog: Free, R&W, CAN/OV

Arnold J. Klehm Grower, Inc.
44 W 637 State Route 72
Hampshire, IL 60140
(708) 683-4761, FAX 683-4766 TO/CC
Arnold J. Klehm

Plants
A nice selection of **orchids**, mostly hybrid seedlings of phalaenopsis, but also vandaceous, cattleya alliance, paphiopedilums, ascocenda and species; some are their own "Meriklehms." All plants are briefly described, some special collections, too. (1980)
❏ Catalog: Free, R&W, CAN/OV, SS:W, bn
⌂ Nursery: All year, M-Sa, call ahead
▼ Garden: All year, M-Sa, call ahead

Klehm Nursery
4210 N. Duncan Road
Champaign, IL 61821
(217) 359-2888, (800) 553-3715, FAX 373-8403
Kit Klehm

Plants & Books
Offers a broad selection of **hosta, daylilies, irises** and herbaceous and tree **peonies, ferns, ornamental grasses and perennials**; all plants well described, with general cultural information, many are their own hybrids. They also offer a few books on the plants which are their specialty. (1852)
❏ Catalog: $4d, R&W, CAN/OV, SS:W, bn
▼ Garden: May-August, M-F, call ahead

Kline Nursery Co.
P.O. Box 23161
Tigard, OR 97281-3161
(503) 244-3910
Phil Parker

Plants
Offers **perennials, hardy cyclamen, hardy ferns and species lilies**; good general information and very brief plant descriptions. Also listed are species irises, rock garden narcissus, trilliums. This was the Edgar L. Kline Nursery for many years. (1987)
☐ Catalog: $2d, R&W, CAN/OV, $15m
⌂ Nursery: All year, Tu-Sa, by appointment only
♥ Garden: September-May, Tu-Sa, by appointment only

Gerhard Koehres Cactus & Succulent Nursery
Wingertstrasse 33
Erzhausen/Darmstadt, Germany D-6106
(0 61 50) 7241, FAX 84168
Gerhard Koehres

Seeds
A very extensive list of **cactus and succulent** seeds, as well as some tillandsias and palms, listed by botanical name; no plant descriptions, but sure to please collectors. Offered are aylostera, copiapoa, frailea, gymnocalyciums, parodia, agaves, aloes, euphorbias, mesembs and many more!
☐ Catalog: $1(US Bills), R&W, OV, bn

P. Kohli & Co.

See Chadwell Himalayan Seed.

V. Kraus Nurseries, Ltd.
P.O. Box 180
1380 Centre Road
Carlisle, ON, Canada L0R 1H0
(416) 689-4022, FAX 689-8080
Victor & Eva Kraus

Plants
A broad selection of hardy flowering and ornamental **trees and shrubs**, including many hybrid tea roses, grandifloras, floribundas, climbers, modern shrub and miniature **roses**. Also sells fruit trees, including many apples and plums, grapes, berries, rhubarb and asparagus. No descriptions. (1951)
☐ Catalog: $1, R&W, US/OV, SS:4,11, bn/cn
⌂ Nursery: All year, M-F, Sa in Spring & Fall
♥ Garden: June-August, M-F

L. Kreeger
91 Newton Wood Road
Ashtead, Surrey, England KT21 1NN
L. Kreeger

Seeds
A good selection of seeds of **alpine and rock garden** plants; all plants well described, with country and site of origin of wild-collected seed and type of growing conditions which suit them best. Be sure to send US$ bills only for list, no checks. (1985)
☐ Catalog: $2(US Bills), OV, bn

Michael & Janet Kristick
155 Mockingbird Road
Wellsville, PA 17365
(717) 292-2962
Michael & Janet Kristick

Plants
The sort of catalog that makes a collector's heart sing! Hundreds of cultivars: **conifers**, including many dwarfs, and **Japanese and species maples**. No descriptions, just pages and pages of names. Japanese maples listed by Japanese cultivar names. (1970)
☐ Catalog: Free, CAN/OV, SS:4-12, bn
⌂ Nursery: All year, daily, by appointment only
♥ Garden: May-October, daily, by appointment only

Krohne Plant Farms
Route 6, Box 586
Dowagiac, MI 49047
(616) 424-3450 or 5423
William & Shiela Krohne

Plants
Fifteen varieties of **strawberries** which will produce in Northern climates; informative leaflet. Will sell in quantities as low as 25 per customer; quantity discounts for commercial growers. Also offers two kinds of asparagus crowns and horseradish. (1974)
☐ Catalog: Free, R&W, SS:3-6, $7m
⌂ Nursery: All year, M-Sa, call ahead
♥ Garden: June, M-Sa, call ahead

Kuk's Forest Nursery
10174 Barr Road
Brecksville, OH 44141-3302
(216) 526-5271
Robert Kuk

Plants
Not a source of mighty trees, Robert Kuk is a **hosta** hybridizer who offers his own introductions as well as other new and old varieties. A good selection, each variety is well described. (1986)
☐ Catalog: $2d, R&W, CAN/OV, SS:5-10, $30m
⌂ Nursery: May-October, Sa-Su, call ahead
♥ Garden: June-September, Sa-Su, call ahead

Kumar International
Ajitmal
Etawah (U.P.), India 206121
Mrs. Meera Agarwal

Seeds
Offers a good selection of seeds of **conifers, ornamental trees and shrubs, palms, bamboos, and tropical fruit trees**; no plant descriptions, only botanical names. Ask for price list, which is not included in catalog. (1976)
☐ Catalog: $1(US Bills), OV, $50m, bn

Kusa Research Foundation
P.O. Box 761
Ojai, CA 93024
Lorenz Schaller

Seeds
Non-profit group devoted to seedcrops of folk origin, especially **cereal grains**. Sells seed of crops which can be grown by home gardeners and small-scale farmers: special strains of millet, hull-less barley, Swiss gourmet baking wheat, lentils, sesame, oats and others; all well described. For membership information, see The Kusa Society in Section D. (1980)
☐ Catalog: $1($3 OV), R&W, CAN/OV

Lady Bug Beautiful Gardens
857 Leopard Trail, Tuscawilla
Winter Springs, FL 32708
Ra Hansen

Plants
Offers a wide selection of **daylilies**, some of which are their own intro-
ductions; cultivars are both new introductions and older varieties, all are
well described in a friendly, chatty catalog. (1976)
❐ Catalog: $2d, R&W, SS:3-11, $35m
▼ Garden: May-August, by appointment only

LaFayette Home Nursery, Inc.
RR 1, Box 1A
Lafayette, IL 61449
(309) 995-3311
Corliss Jock Ingels

Seeds
Broad selection of **prairie grasses, forbs, trees, shrubs and wildflowers**
for prairie restoration and development; all plants listed by botanical and
common name. They also offer a number of grass and wildflower mixes
for various growing conditions and do consulting and installation. (1887)
❐ Catalog: Free, R&W, bn/cn

Lake Odessa Greenhouse
1123 Jordan Lake Street
Lake Odessa, MI 48849
(616) 374-8488
Mark Potter

Plants
They offer a large selection of **geraniums** -- scented, brocade, rosebud,
zonal, "tulip" and ivy types -- as well as a variety of houseplants such as
ivies, wandering jews, peperomias and more. All plants well but briefly
described.
❐ Catalog: Free, R&W, SS:5-10
⌂ Nursery: All year, M-Sa
▼ Garden: All year, greenhouse, M-Sa

Lakeside Acres
8119 Roy Lane
Ooltewah, TN 37363
(615) 238-4534
Mary H. Chastain

Plants
Offers a very nice selection of **hostas and daylilies**, and some hardy
ferns, some of the hostas and daylilies are their own introductions. All
plants briefly described. Other shade plants available at the nursery. (1960)
❐ Catalog: $2d, CAN/OV, SS:5-10, $35m
⌂ Nursery: All year, M-Sa, call ahead
▼ Garden: May-June, M-Sa, call ahead

Lamb Nurseries
E. 101 Sharp Avenue
Spokane, WA 99202
(509) 328-7956
Nicola Luttropp

Plants
Catalog packed with **rock garden and perennial plants, vines, ground
covers, succulents, clematis, violets and flowering shrubs**; a wide selec-
tion of collectors' plants, each very well described with cultural notes.
They supply many botanical gardens, as well as people like us. (1938)
❐ Catalog: $1($2 OV), R&W, CAN/OV, SS:W, bn/cn
⌂ Nursery: February-October, F-Sa

Lamtree Farm
Route 1, Box 162
2323 Copeland Road
Warrensville, NC 28693
(910) 385-6144 TO/CC
Lee A. Morrison

Plants
My heart leaps at the word "Franklinia," and here it is! Small nursery sells
a limited but choice selection of **trees and shrubs**: franklinia, leucothoe,
native rhododendrons and azaleas, kalmia, styrax, halesia, seedling maples
and conifers and 'Lu shan' (Rhododendron fortunei); good plant descriptions.
Also sells Christmas wreaths and garlands, lovely gifts for city folk! Can't
ship to CA, OR or WA. (1979)
❐ Catalog: $2, R&W, SS:W, bn
⌂ Nursery: By appointment only

Landis Valley Museum

See Heirloom Seed Project, Landis Valley Museum.

D. Landreth Seed Company
P.O. Box 6426
180-188 W. Ostend Street
Baltimore, MD 21230
(410) 727-3922 or 3923, FAX 244-8633

Seeds
"America's oldest seed house" -- George Washington and Thomas Jefferson
were early customers. Offers a broad selection of new and old varieties of
vegetables, all well described with cultural information, as well as a
smaller selection of **herbs** and **garden annuals**. (1784)
❐ Catalog: $2, R&W, CAN/OV, $25m
⌂ Nursery: All year, M-F

Landscape Alternatives, Inc.
1465 North Pascal Street
691 W. Larpenteur Avenue (Roseville)
St. Paul, MN 55108
(612) 488-1342
Karl Ruser & Roy Robison

Plants
Specializes in nursery-propagated native **Minnesota wildflowers** and prairie
and other ornamental **grasses** for distinctive low-maintenance landscapes. A
good selection, with very brief plant descriptions. They also offer a few
garden perennials. Cannot ship to CA. (1986)
❐ Catalog: $1, SS:5-9, $25m, cn/bn
⌂ Nursery: Mid-April-October, M-Sa, by appointment only
▼ Garden: May-September, M-Sa, by appointment only

D.E. Lark Seeds
P.O. Box 12243
Santa Rosa, CA 95406
(707) 584-3679
David Lark

Seeds
A small mail order **vegetable** seed company, offers reasonable prices and
same day shipping; a nice selection with brief descriptions. (1992)
❐ Catalog: Free, CAN

Larner Seeds
P.O. Box 407
Bolinas, CA 94924-0407
(415) 868-9407
Judith Larner Lowry

Seeds ~ Books
Seed for the Western landscape -- a good selection of **native wildflowers**, annual and perennial, and **trees, shrubs, vines and grasses**. Catalog emphasizes use in natural landscaping and offers several mixes for various habitats. Also offers books on natural landscaping and their own series of pamphlets on growing native plants. (1978)
☐ Catalog: $3($4 OV), R&W, CAN/OV, $6m, bn/cn
⌂ Nursery: All year, M-Sa, call ahead
▼ Garden: All year, by appointment only

Las Pilitas Nursery
Star Route, Box 23 X
Las Pilitas Road
Santa Margarita, CA 93453
(805) 438-5992
Bert & Celeste Wilson

Plants ~ Seeds ~ Bulbs
A very extensive list of **California native plants** of all kinds, including a few wildflower seeds. Price list gives the number of plants available -- a good indication of what's rare or hard to propagate; list gives botanical and common name only. The catalog has become a very useful and extensive treatise on growing our Western native plants -- a bargain at $4! (1979)
☐ Catalog: $4 (price list free), R&W, bn/cn
⌂ Nursery: All year, Sa or by appointment only
▼ Garden: All year, Sa or by appointment only

Lauray of Salisbury
432 Undermountain Road (Route 41)
Salisbury, CT 06068
(203) 435-2263
Judy Becker

Plants
A very extensive collectors' list of **begonias, gesneriads, cacti, succulents, epiphyllums and hybrid and species orchids**, all well but briefly described, with some cultural notes on genera.
☐ Catalog: $2, SS:4-10, $10m, bn
⌂ Nursery: All year, daily, call ahead
▼ Garden: All year, glasshouse, call ahead

Laurie's Garden
41886 McKenzie Highway
Springfield, OR 97478
(503) 896-3756
Lorena M. Reid

Plants
Specializes in **beardless irises** -- Western natives, Japanese, Evansia, Sino-Siberian, water irises and other species and crosses between Pacific Coast and Siberian irises; broad selection including many of her own hybrids, all briefly described. Also lists a few other hardy perennials. (1964)
☐ Catalog: Long SASE, SS:8-10, bn/cn
⌂ Nursery: April-October, call ahead
▼ Garden: May-July, call ahead

Laurie's Landscaping
2959 Hobson Road
Downers Grove, IL 60517
(708) 969-1270
Laurie Skrzenta

Plants
A nice selection of **hostas, herbaceous peonies**, and a few **perennials** and ornamental trees and shrubs; plants are very briefly described. No shipping to AZ, CA, OR or WA. (1988)
☐ Catalog: Long SASE, SS:5-11, $25m
⌂ Nursery: May-October, by appointment only
▼ Garden: May-June, August, by appointment only

Lawson's Nursery
Route 1, Box 472
Yellow Creek Road
Ball Ground, GA 30107
(404) 893-2141 TO/CC
Jim & Bernice Lawson

Plants ~ Books
A good selection of **antique apple and pear trees**; all well described with historical background -- even a 14th century apple called "Rambo"! They've added **blueberries, grapes, plums, peaches, apricots and nuts**. Sell the Potter Walnut Cracker and books on fruit growing and cookbooks. (1968)
☐ Catalog: Free, R&W, CAN/OV, SS:11-3
⌂ Nursery: August-May, M-Sa
▼ Garden: September-October, M-Sa

Le Jardin du Gourmet
P.O. Box 75
St. Johnsbury Center, VT 05863
(802) 748-1446, FAX 748-9592 TO/CC $15m
Paul Taylor

Plants ~ Seeds ~ Books
Still going strong, I lost track of them last time. They offer a good selection of **herb and vegetable** seeds in both regular and $.25 sample packets. Ship herb plants only in the US, as well as garlic and shallots. Also sell books on herbs, and some pates, teas, and other gourmet supplies. (1954)
☐ Catalog: $.50, R&W, CAN/OV, SS:3-10
⌂ Nursery: All year, M-Sa

Orol Ledden & Sons
P.O. Box 7
Center & Atlantic Avenues
Sewell, NJ 08080-0007
(609) 468-1000, (800) 783-7333, FAX 464-0947
Don & Dale Ledden

Seeds ~ Supplies ~ Tools ~ Bulbs
Catalog offers over 600 varieties of **flowers, vegetables, grasses** and **cover crops** and some summer-blooming **bulbs**, all well described; varieties are both hybrid and open-pollinated, and most seed is available untreated if desired. Also sells a full line of growing supplies and tools, organic pest controls and fertilizers. (1904)
☐ Catalog: $1d, R&W, CAN/OV, SS:3-9, $5m
⌂ Nursery: All year, daily
▼ Garden: April-September, daily

Ledgecrest Greenhouses
1029 Storrs Road
Storrs, CT 06268
(203) 487-1661 TO/CC $20m
Paul L. Hammer, Jr.

Plants
Offers a good selection of **hardy perennials** in three-inch pots, each briefly described. Also offers collections of 24 plants for specific growing conditions: sun, shade, or sun and shade. Plants in larger sizes are available at the nursery, as are general growing supplies. (1974)
❑ Catalog: Free, R&W, SS:4-10, bn/cn
⌂ Nursery: All year, daily
▼ Garden: May-June, daily

Lee's Botanical Garden
P.O. Box 669
LaBelle, FL 33935
(813) 675-8728
Bruce Lee Bednar

Plants
Collectors' list of **carnivorous plants** -- sarracenia, nepenthes, dionaea, drosera, pinguicula, utricularia, catopsis; no plant descriptions, but collectors will know them -- some are his own hybrids. Also offers some **ferns** and **terrestrial orchids**. No shipping to Mexico. (1980)
❑ Catalog: Free($1 OV), R&W, OV, $10m, bn
⌂ Nursery: By appointment only
▼ Garden: By appointment only

Lee's Gardens
P.O. Box 5
25986 Sauder Road
Tremont, IL 61568
(309) 925-5262
Janis Lee

Plants
Hostas, iris, daylilies, wildflowers and other sun and shade-loving **perennials**, both common and rare; a good selection with very brief plant descriptions. (1988)
❑ Catalog: $2d, SS:W, $25m, bn
⌂ Nursery: Mid-April, May, daily; June-October, M-Sa am
▼ Garden: May-September, M-Sa am

Lenette Greenhouses
1440 Pom Orchid Lane
Kannapolis, NC 28081
(704) 938-2042
K. G. Griffith

Plants
Catalog offers cattleya and phalaenopsis **hybrid orchids**, in community pots, flasks and blooming sizes, even "stud plants." Plants very briefly described. Also offers miniature cymbidium crosses and a few oncidiums, vandas and paphiopedilums, dendrobiums and laelia species. Most are their own hybrids.
❑ Catalog: Free, R&W, SS:4-8, $25m
⌂ Nursery: All year, M-Sa
▼ Garden: All year, greenhouses, M-Sa

Les Violettes Natalia
124 Ch. Grapes
Sawyerville, PQ, Canada J0B 3A0
(819) 889-3235
Roch & Natalie Pineault

Plants ⚘ Supplies
A huge selection of **African violets** from many prominent hybridizers -- standards, miniatures and semi-miniatures and trailers, all well described, with a "!" for nearly every one! They also offer a broad selection of other **gesneriads** -- sinningeas, columneas, kohlerias, streptocarpus, gloxinias, achimenes, episcias and aeschynanthus -- and indoor growing supplies. US orders can be sent to P.O. Box 206, Beecher Falls, VT 05902. (1987)
❑ Catalog: $2, US/OV, SS:4-11, $20m
⌂ Nursery: All year, Tu-Su
▼ Garden: All year, Tu-Su

W. O. Lessard Nursery
19201 S.W. 248th Street
Homestead, FL 33031
(305) 247-0397, 248-2666, FAX 246-4497
William O. Lessard

Plants
Catalog lists 36 varieties of **bananas** -- even more sold at the nursery. Some available as corms or plants, some plants available as large specimens; each plant is very well described. (1978)
❑ Catalog: $1, R&W, CAN, SS:3-11
⌂ Nursery: M-Sa, by appointment only
▼ Garden: Summer-Fall, by appointment only

Henry Leuthardt Nurseries, Inc.
P.O. Box 666
Montauk Highway
East Moriches, NY 11940
(516) 878-1387
Henry P. Leuthardt

Plants
A selection of **fruit trees, berries and grapes**, including some old varieties; all briefly to well described. This nursery is also a source of espaliered apple and pear trees in several styles. Their "handbook" is $1, gives more information than the free catalog.
❑ Catalog: Free, R&W, SS:10-12,3-5
⌂ Nursery: All year, daily, call ahead

Lewis Mountain Herbs & Everlastings
2345 State Route 247
Manchester, OH 45144
(513) 549-2484
Judy Lewis

Plants ⚘ Books ⚘ Supplies
Offers a nice selection of **herbs, scented geraniums and everlastings**, listed by common and botanical name, but with no plant descriptions. Also sells some books, dried everlastings, and baskets for gathering. (1985)
❑ Catalog: $1, R&W, CAN, SS:4-10, $50m, cn/bn
⌂ Nursery: All year, M-Sa
▼ Garden: June-October, M-Sa

Lewis Strawberry Nursery
P.O. Box 24
Rocky Point, NC 28457
(919) 675-2394, (800) 453-5346, FAX 675-2394
C. E. Lewis

Plants
Over 30 "scientifically grown" varieties of **strawberries**, sold in
quantities of 100 and up; no descriptions. Most of the plants are
June-bearers; they also carry 5 everbearing kinds, and 5 day-neutral
varieties; ship all over the East and Midwest. (1954)
❒ Catalog: Free, R&W, CAN/OV, SS:11-6, $12m

Liberty Seed Company
P.O. Box 806
128 - 1st Drive S.E.
New Philadelphia, OH 44663
(216) 364-1611, FAX 364-6415 TO/CC $20m
William & Connie Watson

Seeds ❧ Supplies
Color and b&w catalog offers a broad selection of garden **annuals** and
perennials, **vegetables** (including heirloom and open-pollinated varieties), giant pumpkins and super sweet corn; all well described and adapted
to the Midwest. Also offers a broad selection of propagation and growing
supplies. (1981)
❒ Catalog: Free, R&W, OV, SS:3-4
⌂ Nursery: All year, M-F; February-June, Sa
❦ Garden: July-September, M-F

Life-Form Replicators

See Arrowhead Alpines.

Lily of the Valley Herb Farm
3969 Fox Avenue
Minerva, OH 44657
(216) 862-3920
Paul & Melinda Carmichael

Plants ❧ Books ❧ Supplies
Offers a broad selection of **herbs and everlastings**, each briefly described,
as well as dried herbs and flowers, potpourri makings, and books on herbs
and herb growing. Can't ship to CA. (1982)
❒ Catalog: $1d, R&W, CAN, SS:4-9, $15m, cn/bn
⌂ Nursery: All year, M-Sa; May-June, M-Su pm
❦ Garden: May-August, M-Sa

The Lily Pad
5102 Scott Road
Olympia, WA 98502
(206) 866-0291, FAX 866-7128
Jan Detwiler

Bulbs
A family-run bulb company; they started out selling cut flowers and found
that more people wanted their **lily** bulbs. Offer a good selection of newer
hybrids, many are shown in color; good plant descriptions. (1984)
❒ Catalog: $2d, R&W, SS:10-5, $5m
❦ Garden: June-August, by appointment only

Lilypons Water Gardens
P.O. Box 10
6800 Lilypons Road
Buckeystown, MD 21717-0010
(301) 874-5133, (800) 723-7667, FAX 874-2959
Charles B. Thomas

Plants ❧ Books ❧ Supplies
Color catalog offers a broad selection of **water lilies, lotus, bog plants**,
garden ponds, statues, fountains, fish and water gardening supplies. They
also have a nursery in Texas, at 839 FM 1489 (P.O. Box 188), Brookshire, TX
77423, (713) 934-8525, with a display garden, too. The photographs are
irresistible! (1917)
❒ Catalog: Free, R&W, CAN/OV, cn/bn
⌂ Nursery: March-October, daily; November-February, M-Sa
❦ Garden: May-September, daily

Limerock Ornamental Grasses
RD 1, Box 111C
Port Matilda, PA 16870
(814) 692-2272 TO/CC $20m
Norman Hooven III

Plants
Offers a broad selection of **ornamental grasses**, each well described, with
a list of grasses for various growing conditions and uses. There is a nice
introduction to grasses with comments on form, color, texture and motion.
They've recently added some fall blooming perennials. No shipping to CA.
❒ Catalog: $3, R&W, CAN/OV, SS:W, bn/cn
⌂ Nursery: March-November, M-Sa
❦ Garden: September-October, M-Sa

© Northwest Mycological Consultants
Artist: Annette Simonson

Lindel Lilies
5510 - 239th Street
Langley, BC, Canada V3A 7N6
(604) 534-4729, FAX 534-4742
Linda & Del Knowlton

Bulbs
Offers a broad selection of **hybrid lilies**: trumpets (including sunburst forms), Oriental hybrids, Asiatic hybrids (including Columbia-Platte Asiatics) and some species lilies; all are well described. (1986)
❑ Catalog: Free, R&W, US, SS:Fall
⌂ Nursery: June-October, Su-F, call ahead
▼ Garden: June-August, Su-F, call ahead

Little River Farm
7815 NC 39
Middlesex, NC 27557
(919) 965-9507 TO/CC
Melvin Oliver, Jr.

Plants
Offers a good selection of **daylilies**, listed in a table format with brief information on each cultivar: hybridizer, height, season, flower size and color. Both old and newer varieties offered. No shipping to CA. (1980)
❑ Catalog: $2, R&W, SS:4-10, $25m
⌂ Nursery: All year, call ahead
▼ Garden: June, call ahead

Little Valley Farm
Route 3, Box 544
Spring Green, WI 53588
(608) 935-3324
Barbara Glass

Plants ❧ Seeds ❧ Books
Small nursery specializes in **native plants of the Midwest** -- wildflowers, trees, shrubs and vines for woods, wetlands and prairie; a nice selection, all plants well described. Also offers some seeds, plant collections, books on prairie plants and local workshops on prairie planting. Can't ship to CA.
❑ Catalog: 1 FCS, R&W, SS:4-6,9-11, cn/bn
⌂ Nursery: May-October, call ahead
▼ Garden: May-October, call ahead

Live Oak Nursery
P.O. Box 815
Knights Ferry, CA 95361
(209) 881-0228, (800) 870-6257
Jack & Mary Tune

Plants
Small nursery in the Sierra Foothills offers seedlings of California native **oaks, pines, redwoods**, and other native trees and shrubs; all plants are well described with information on habitat. (1992)
❑ Catalog: Free, R&W, SS:10-5, cn/bn

Living Stones Nursery
2936 N. Stone Avenue
Tucson, AZ 85705
(602) 628-8773 TO/CC
Jane Evans & Gene Joseph

Plants
I've had several inquiries about Ed Storms' Living Stones Nursery, which was listed in earlier editions. Jane Evans & Gene Joseph took over the very large **lithops** collection, and also offer other **cacti and succulents, aloes** and others. A good selection; some plants described. (1987)
❑ Catalog: $2d, R&W, CAN/OV, $15m, bn
⌂ Nursery: All year, W-Sa, call ahead
▼ Garden: All year, W-Sa, call ahead

Living Tree Centre
P.O. Box 10082
Berkeley, CA 94709
(510) 420-1440
Dr. Jesse Schwartz

Plants
Historic **apples** from England, France, Russia and California's pioneering days, including some "highly aromatic" apples -- over 80 kinds, all well described, with cultural information on apple growing. Also offers apple scion wood, apricots, quince and pears, and fruits mentioned in the Bible. (1979)
❑ Catalog: $4($5 OV), R&W, CAN/OV, SS:1-4
⌂ Nursery: By appointment only

Lochside Alpines Nursery
Lochside, Ulbster
Caithness, Scotland KW2 6AA
(095 585) 320
Terry & Jane Clarke

Seeds
A nice list of **alpines**, including some aquilegias, cyclamen, gentians, potentillas, and primulas; plants very briefly described.
❑ Catalog: $1(US Bills), OV, bn

Lockhart Seeds
P.O. Box 1361
3 North Wilson Way
Stockton, CA 95201
(209) 466-4401 TO/CC
Lockhart Family

Seeds ❧ Supplies
Color catalog with a broad selection of **vegetables** (both hybrid and open-pollinated) and **Oriental vegetables**, with comparative tables on size, season and disease resistance. Specializes in crops for central California; also offers some growing supplies. (1948)
❑ Catalog: Free, R&W, CAN, $10m, cn/bn
⌂ Nursery: All year, M-F

Loehman's Cactus Patch
P.O. Box 871
Paramount, CA 90723
(310) 428-4501
Tom Loehman

Plants
Offers a good selection of **cacti and succulents**: echinocereus, ferocactus, gymnocalyciums, mammillarias, notocactus, dorstenias, echeverias, euphorbias, haworthias and more. Plants listed only by botanical names. (1975)
❑ Catalog: $1d, SS:W, $10m, bn
⌂ Nursery: By appointment only

Logee's Greenhouses
141 North Street
Danielson, CT 06239
Joy Logee Martin

Plants ⌖ Books
A very extensive list of **begonias and other greenhouse and exotic plants** --
many are outdoor plants in warmer climates; all well described with some
cultural suggestions, many illustrated in color. It's impossible to convey
the variety -- a collector's dream, a houseplant lover's candy store. Catalog
published every other year, with sales lists in spring and fall. (1892)
❒ Catalog: $3d, CAN/OV, SS:W, $20m, bn/cn
⌂ Nursery: All year, daily
♥ Garden: All year, daily

Lon's Oregon Grapes

See Lon J. Rombough.

Lone Pine Connection
P.O. Box 1338
Forestville, CA 95436
Joan Humberstone

Plants ⌖ Supplies
Lone Pine Nursery is a fine (non mail-order) nursery in my neighborhood, Joan
Humberstone is a former employee who ships **plants for bonsai** and Chinese
bonsai pots from Lone Pine. All plants are well described, many are quite un-
usual; finished bonsai, penjing and saikei are also available. (1991)
❒ Catalog: $3, CAN/OV, bn/cn

Long Hungry Creek Nursery
P.O. Box 163
Red Boiling Springs, TN 37150
Jeff Poppen

Plants
Specializing in antique **apples**, as well as newer, hardy, disease-resistant
varieties with great taste -- about 40 varieties, including 'Liberty,' 'Ar-
kansas Black,' 'Griffith,' 'Grimes Golden,' 'Spigold,' 'Jonagrimes,' 'Mollies
Delicious' -- very brief descriptions. (1976)
❒ Catalog: Long SASE, R&W, CAN/OV, SS:10-4, $20m
♥ Garden: All year, write ahead

Long Island Seed Company
1368 Flanders Road
Flanders, NY 11901
(516) 369-0257
Ken Ettlinger

Seeds
I lost this seed company the last time around, but they have such a good idea
that I'm glad I found them again. They offer mixed packets of various open-
pollinated **vegetable seeds** so that you can try various kinds which won't
all ripen at once. A good selection of heirloom tomatoes, too. (1982)
❒ Catalog: Free, CAN

Long's Gardens
P.O. Box 19
3240 Broadway
Boulder, CO 80306
(303) 442-2353
Catherine Long Gates

Plants
List offers broad selection of hardy **tall bearded irises**, with several collections and progressive savings on larger purchases; some are introductions by Colorado hybridizers. During blooming time you can select your
favorites and dig them up on the spot. Sells a few border, intermediate
and dwarf bearded irises as well; brief plant descriptions. (1905)
❒ Catalog: Free, SS:7-8
⌂ Nursery: May-June, daily, call ahead
♥ Garden: May-June, daily, call ahead

Loucks Nursery
P.O. Box 102
Cloverdale, OR 97112
Mert & Marjorie Loucks

Plants
Specializes in **Japanese maples** for bonsai and container growing. Offers
a broad selection of cultivars by their Japanese cultivar names; each plant
well described. Small nursery offers over 100 cultivars. (1955)
❒ Catalog: $1, R&W
⌂ Nursery: All year, call ahead
♥ Garden: April-May, September-October, call ahead

Louisiana Nursery
Route 7, Box 43
Highway 182
Opelousas, LA 70570
(318) 948-3696, FAX 942-6404
Ken, Albert & Dalton Durio

Plants
Magnolias -- 350 cultivars -- and many other unusual trees, shrubs, vines
and other collectors' plants in catalog (M); catalog (D) has a huge selection
of daylilies, Louisiana, spuria and pseudacorus irises, cannas, ginger,
liriope and related plants. Catalog (C) lists **crinums** and other bulbs.
Catalog (F) has fruiting trees, shrubs & vines. Overseas the catalogs cost:
(M) $15, (D)$12.50, (C)$10, and (F)$10. Endless choices; plants are briefly
but well described. (1950)
❒ Catalog: $6(M), $3.50(D), $3(C), $3(F), R&W, CAN/OV, bn/cn
⌂ Nursery: All year, M-Sa, Su in Spring
♥ Garden: By appointment only

Paul P. Lowe
5741 Dewberry Way
West Palm Beach, FL 33415
(407) 686-9392
Paul P. Lowe

Plants
A collectors' list of **begonias**: rhizomatous, shrub, cane and "vining"
types. Plants are very briefly described, offered as leaf or stem cuttings.
Listed are many of Paul's own hybrids; cuttings available singly or in collections of 50 or 100 mixed cuttings. Wide selection; you might send a
"want list" for special items. (1970)
❒ Catalog: Long SASE, SS:W, $10m

Lowe's own-root Roses
6 Sheffield Road
Nashua, NH 03062
(603) 888-2214
Malcolm (Mike) Lowe

Plants
A catalog of old **roses**; a huge selection of many types, including species roses and some of the modern shrub roses of contemporary hybridizers in Europe and the US. All roses are custom propagated on their own roots to order; these take 18 months to deliver. The whole collection is over 4,000 plants, so you might want to send your "want list." (1979)
❏ Catalog: $2($3 OV), CAN/OV, SS:10-11, $10m, bn/cn
⌂ Nursery: Mid-April-October, call ahead
▼ Garden: June, September, call ahead

Lyndon Lyon Greenhouses, Inc.
14 Mutchler Street
Dolgeville, NY 13329-1358
(315) 429-8291, FAX 429-3820 TO/CC $20m
Paul Sorano

Plants
This firm is the originator of many favorite **African violets** and also sells **streptocarpus, episcias, columneas, rex begonias** and other house-plants; many are illustrated in color photographs, with good brief plant descriptions and some cultural information. (1954)
❏ Catalog: $2(6 IRC OV), R&W, OV, SS:5-10, $14m
⌂ Nursery: All year, daily
▼ Garden: March-May, daily

McAllister's Iris Gardens
P.O. Box 112
Fairacres, NM 88033
Sharon McAllister

Plants
New nursery specializing in **aril iris**, listed as three-quarter breds and half-breds, quarter-breds, and "airlbredmedians." All are well described, and customers may request a list of arils and species in the summer. No shipping to CA. (1991)
❏ Catalog: $1d, CAN/OV, SS:7-9, $15m
▼ Garden: March-May, by appointment only

McClure & Zimmerman
P.O. Box 368
108 W. Winnebago
Friesland, WI 53935
(414) 326-4220 FAX 326-5769 TO/CC
J. W. Jung Seed Co.

Books ⬤ Bulbs
A very large selection of **bulbs**, both the common spring Dutch bulbs and a wide selection of species bulbs not so easy to find -- species tulips, bulbous irises, hardy cyclamen, summer-blooming bulbs; all very well described, many charmingly illustrated. Books on bulbs, too. (1980)
❏ Catalog: Free, SS:8-12, bn

McDaniel's Miniature Roses
7523 Zemco Street
Lemon Grove, CA 91945-4062
Earl & Agnes McDaniel

Plants
List offers about a hundred **miniature roses**, listed by color; all briefly described, petal count frequently given. Many are their own hybrids; they cannot ship to FL. (1973)
❏ Catalog: Free
⌂ Nursery: All year, M-Sa, call ahead
▼ Garden: April-September, call ahead

Mark McDonough
30 Mt. Lebanon Street
Pepperell, MA 01463

Plants ⬤ Seeds
Mark specializes in "seeds and plants of correctly named **allium** species and cultivars, including many items that are rare or new and unavailable elsewhere." He offers nearly 100 on his list, and is eagerly searching for more; plants are very well described. Seeds only to Canada and Overseas. (1990)
❏ Catalog: $1, R&W, CAN/OV, SS:5-10, bn

McFayden Seeds
P.O. Box 1800
Brandon, MB, Canada R7A 6N4
(204) 725-7300, FAX 725-1888
Randy Mowat, Marketing Mgr.

Plants ⬤ Seeds ⬤ Books ⬤ Supplies ⬤ Tools ⬤ Bulbs
Offers a broad selection of **general nursery stock**, flower and vegetable seeds, spring-blooming bulbs and perennials; color catalog also offers tools and supplies as well as kitchen and canning items. (1910)
❏ Catalog: $2, SS:4-5,9

McKinney's Glasshouse
89 Mission Road
Wichita, KS 67207
(316) 686-9438
James McKinney & Charles Pickard

Plants ⬤ Supplies
"We are **gesneriad specialists**, with a large supply of African violets, episcias and diminutive terrarium plants." Also lists growing supplies and terrariums in many styles. (1946)
❏ Catalog: $2, CAN/OV, bn/cn
⌂ Nursery: By appointment only

Rod McLellan Co.
1450 El Camino Real
South San Francisco, CA 94080
(415) 871-5655, (800) 237-4089, FAX 583-6543
Karen Kerby, Cust. Service Mgr.

Plants ⬤ Books ⬤ Supplies
Color catalog offers many types of **orchids**. Nursery specializes in hybridizing cattleyas and cymbidiums, but also offers miltonias, oncidiums, brassias, odontoglossums, phalaenopsis and more. Also sells books on orchids, orchid food and potting mixture. They have daily tours of the nursery. (1895)
❏ Catalog: $2($5 OV), R&W, CAN/OV, SS:4-10, $10m
⌂ Nursery: All year, daily
▼ Garden: All year, greenhouses, tours

McMillen's Iris Garden
RR 1
Norwich, ON, Canada N0J 1P0
(519) 468-6508
Gloria McMillen

Plants
Offers a very large selection of **irises** and some **daylilies**; they grow
over 1,000 irises, 100 daylilies in their gardens. Tall, border and dwarf
bearded, "novelty" and Siberian irises; good plant descriptions. (1973)
❒ Catalog: $2, R&W, US/OV, SS:8-10
⌂ Nursery: April-October, call ahead
▼ Garden: May-June, August, call ahead

Mad River Imports
RR 1, Box 1685
Rankin Road
Moretown, VT 05660
(802) 496-3004, FAX same
Jeffrey M. Rice

Plants ⬗ **Bulbs**
Offers a wide selection of **spring-flowering bulbs** -- tulips, daffodils,
crocus and the "minor bulbs" in a fall catalog; sold in quantities of five,
ten and twenty-five. They also sell hybrid Asiatic lilies and bare root
perennials in their spring catalog; all plants briefly described. (1985)
❒ Catalog: Free, SS:5,9, cn/bn

Ann Mann's Orchids
9045 Ron-Den Lane
Windermere, FL 34786-8328
(407) 876-2625
Ann Mann

Plants ⬗ **Books** ⬗ **Supplies**
Very large selection of **orchids, bromeliads, hoyas, anthuriums, alocasias**
and other exotic plants, all briefly described with cultural notes. Also
sells books, water purifiers, charcoal and other growing supplies, including
their own potting fiber, "Husky-Fiber," and New Zealand sphagnum moss. (1969)
❒ Catalog: $1, R&W, CAN, SS:W, $20m, bn
⌂ Nursery: By appointment only
▼ Garden: By appointment only

Maple Tree Gardens
P.O. Box 547
Ponca, NE 68770-0547
Larry L. Harder

Plants
Bearded irises: standard tall, miniature and standard dwarf, intermediate, miniature tall and border, as well as arilbred and Siberian irises and
daylilies. A real collectors' list; a broad selection with brief plant
descriptions. (1961)
❒ Catalog: $.50($1 CAN), CAN, SS:7-9, $10m
▼ Garden: May, July, by appointment only

Mar-Low Epi House
31527 Oakridge Crescent, RR #5
Abbotsford, BC, Canada V3S 4N5
(604) 850-9588
Marie K. Lowen

Plants
An **epiphyllum** collector who offers plants and cuttings from her collection;
described only by color; there will be new offerings each year. Americans can
request catalogs from P.O. Box 1940, Sumas, WA 98295. (1988)
❒ Catalog: $2d, US/OV, SS:4-10, $15m
⌂ Nursery: Summer, T-Sa; Winter, F, call ahead
▼ Garden: April-June, call ahead

Marilynn's Garden
13421 Sussex Place
8184 Katella Ave (Stanton)
Santa Ana, CA 92705
FAX (714) 633-1375
Marilynn Cohen

Plants
Offers a nice selection of **drought-tolerant plants** and **bromeliads** on two
separate lists; no plant descriptions. The drought-tolerant list offers cras-
ulas, aloes, agaves, euphorbias, kalanchoe, opuntias, epiphyllums, hoyas
and rhipsalis. Also offers **plumerias** and **epidendrum orchids**. (1972)
❒ Catalog: $2, R&W, CAN/OV, $50m, bn
⌂ Nursery: By appointment only

Mary's Plant Farm
2410 Lanes Mill Road
Hamilton, OH 45013
(513) 894-0022
Mary E. Harrison

Plants
Offer a wide selection of **perennials**, including species geraniums, irises,
ornamental grasses, herbs and hostas. Also sell a number of **trees and
shrubs**, many good for smaller gardens: berberis, hydrangeas, spireas,
lilacs, viburnums, amelanchier, dogwood and crabapples, as well as some
wildflowers and ferns. Plants very briefly described. (1976)
❒ Catalog: $1, SS:3-11, bn/cn
⌂ Nursery: March-October, Tu-Sa
▼ Garden: April-October, Tu-Sa

Maryland Aquatic Nurseries
3427 N. Furnace Road
Jarrettsville, MD 21084
(410) 557-7615, FAX 692-2837 TO/CC $25m
Richard J. Schuck

Plants ⬗ **Supplies**
Good selection of **plants for ponds, pools and bogs**: water lilies, Japan-
ese and Louisiana irises, ornamental grasses. All plants are well but brief-
ly described. Also sell fish, supplies and water garden ornaments. (1986)
❒ Catalog: $5d, R&W, CAN/OV, $25, bn
⌂ Nursery: March-September, M-Sa
▼ Garden: May-September, M-Sa

Maryott's Gardens
1073 Bird Avenue
San Jose, CA 95125
(408) 971-0444 TO/CC $15m
Bill Maryott

Plants
A good choice of tall, intermediate and standard dwarf bearded **irises** for
collectors; most are new or recent introductions, all are briefly described.
They also offer several collections of special irises. (1978)
❒ Catalog: Long SASE w/2 FCS, R&W, SS:7-8, $15m
⌂ Nursery: April-May, daily
▼ Garden: April-May, daily

Matsu-Momiji Nursery
P.O. Box 11414
410 Borbeck Street
Philadelphia, PA 19111
(215) 722-6286 (after 4 pm)
Steve Pilacik

Plants ⚭ Supplies ⚭ Tools
A collectors' list of many cultivars of Japanese black pine (Pinus thunber-gii), spruces, Japanese maples and other **plants for bonsai**, each fairly briefly described. Also finished bonsai, pots, supplies and bonsai classes at the nursery. (1980)
❑ Catalog: $2, R&W, CAN/OV, $50m
⌂ Nursery: All year, daily, by appointment only
▼ Garden: April-September, daily, by appointment only

Matterhorn Nursery Inc.
227 Summit Park Road
Spring Valley, NY 10977
(914) 354-5986 FAX 354-4749
Matt & Ronnie Horn

Plants ⚭ Books ⚭ Supplies ⚭ Tools
Renowned for their beautiful display gardens, Matterhorn will sell **peren-nials, ornamental grasses, hostas, aquatic plants and dwarf conifers** by mail; they offer a very good selection with each plant well described. Be sure to ask for the price list when you write for the catalog. (1981)
❑ Catalog: $5, R&W, SS:W, $20m, bn/cn
⌂ Nursery: All year, daily
▼ Garden: All year, daily

Maxim's Greenwood Gardens
2157 Sonoma Street
Redding, CA 96001-3008
(916) 241-0764
Georgia Maxim

Plants ⚭ Bulbs
A huge selection of **irises**: bearded in various sizes, Japanese and Siberian irises, Pacific Coast Hybrids, arilbreds, spuria and Louisiana irises. Also some tetraploid and diploid daylilies and a broad selection of novelty daffo-dils (daffodils offered every three years). All briefly described. (1955)
❑ Catalog: $1, CAN, SS:7-11, $10m
⌂ Nursery: All year, by appointment only
▼ Garden: March-June, by appointment only

Meadowbrook Herb Garden
93 Kingstown Rd. (Route 138)
Wyoming, RI 02898
(401) 539-7603
Marjory & Tom Fortier

Seeds ⚭ Supplies
Offer a nice selection of **herbs,** and several collection of seed packets; very, very brief plant descriptions. Also offer dried herbs and spices, and herb teas; sell herb plants and hold herb workshops at the nursery. (1967)
❑ Catalog: Long SASE

Meadowbrook Hosta Farm
81 Meredith Road
Tewksbury, MA 01876-1333
(508) 851-8943
Jay C. Gilbert

Plants ⚭ Supplies
Jay is the editor of The Hosta Digest, and has a small **hosta** nursery as well; he offers a nice selection of newer varieties, with some of the old favorites. Each variety is very briefly described. (1989)
❑ Catalog: Free, R&W, CAN, SS:5-10

Meadowlake Gardens
Route 4, Box 709
Walterboro, SC 29488
(803) 844-2524 or 2359 (eves) TO/CC $50m
John Allgood

Plants
Offer a wide selection of **daylilies**, including a number of new introduc-tions from various hybridizers. Plant descriptions vary from very detailed to good but brief. (1960)
❑ Catalog: $2d, R&W, CAN/OV, SS:4-5,8-10, $20m
▼ Garden: May 22-June 30

Mellinger's, Inc.
2310 W. South Range Road
North Lima, OH 44452
(216) 549-9861, FAX 549-3716 TO/CC
Jean Steiner

Plants ⚭ Seeds ⚭ Books ⚭ Supplies ⚭ Tools ⚭ Bulbs
Catalog is a large general store of home and commercial gardening supplies, books, **seeds and plants of all kinds** -- impossible to fit into any cate-gory. It's hard to believe that they can carry so many items -- 4,000 by their count! It's a jumble, with plants in no logical order and brief plant descriptions, but you get used to it. (1927)
❑ Catalog: Free($2 OV), R&W, CAN/OV, $10m, cn/bn
⌂ Nursery: All year, M-Sa
▼ Garden: Spring-Fall, M-Sa

Mendocino Heirloom Roses
P.O. Box 670
Mendocino, CA 95460
(707) 877-1888, 937-0963, FAX 937-0963
Gail Daly & Alice Flores

Plants
An effort of two gardening friends who fell in love with old garden **roses**: they offer a nice selection, and will custom root others if they are on your "want list." All roses are well described, all are propagated on their own roots. (1991)
❑ Catalog: $1, SS:12-3, $10m
⌂ Nursery: All year, Sa-Su, by appointment only

Merry Gardens
P.O. Box 595
Mechanic Street
Camden, ME 04843
(207) 236-9064 TO/CC $25m
Mary Ellen Ross

Plants
Catalog lists **herbs**, scented and miniature **geraniums**, many **ivy** culti-vars and **fuchsias**, as well as flowering vines, ferns, succulents and other foliage plants for home and conservatory. Collectors' list; plants very briefly described. (1947)
❑ Catalog: $2, CAN, SS:W, $20m, bn/cn
⌂ Nursery: All year, M-Sa
▼ Garden: May-October, M-Sa

Mesa Garden
P.O. Box 72
Belen, NM 87002
(505) 864-3131, FAX 864-3124 TO/CC $5m
Steven Brack

Plants ⬿ Seeds
A very extensive collectors' list of **cacti and succulents**, both seed and
seed-grown plants, with very brief descriptions including habitat data on
wild-collected seed. Seed list in January, plant list in spring; guaranteed
to thrill collectors! (1976)
❏ Catalog: 2 FCS(2 IRC OV), R&W, CAN/OV, SS:3-11, bn
⌂ Nursery: By appointment only
▼ Garden: By appointment only

Messelaar Bulb Co.
P.O. Box 269
County Road, Route 1-A
Ipswich, MA 01938
(508) 356-3737
Pieter Messelaar

Bulbs
Importer of **spring- and summer-flowering Dutch bulbs** sells in quantities
from five to hundreds; plants are briefly described, and many are illustrated
in color. (1946)
❏ Catalog: Free, R&W, SS:9-12,2-5, $10m
⌂ Nursery: September-December, M-Sa, Su pm

Meyer Seed Company
600 S. Caroline Street
Baltimore, MD 21231
(410) 342-4224

Seeds ⬿ Supplies ⬿ Tools ⬿ Bulbs
Specializes in **vegetable and flower** seeds which do well in the Baltimore-
Washington, DC area. Catalog is informative to the home or commercial grow-
er and also offers supplies, equipment and summer-blooming **bulbs**. (1910)
❏ Catalog: Free, R&W

Miami Water Lilies
22150 S.W. 147th Avenue
Miami, FL 33170
(305) 258-2664 TO/CC
Milton Millon

Plants
Miami Orchids was put out of business by Hurricane Andrew, as were several
nearby nurseries with big greenhouses. They've dug ponds and started over
again with **water lilies**, listing about 35 varieties. (1987)
❏ Catalog: Free, R&W, $30m
⌂ Nursery: All year, M-Sa
▼ Garden: All year, M-Sa

Michael's Bromeliads
1365 Canterbury Road North
St. Petersburg, FL 33710
(813) 347-0349
Michael H. Kiehl

Plants
"Specializes in providing specific plants and new varieties for the **bromeliad** collector, but also provide starter collections and growing information for the beginner." Offers aechmeas, billbergias, guzmanias, vriesias,
tillandsias, cryptanthus, neoregelias; no plant descriptions. (1987)
❏ Catalog: Long SASE($2 OV), CAN/OV, $20m, bn
⌂ Nursery: Sa-Su, call ahead, or evenings by appointment

Mid-America Iris Gardens
3409 N. Geraldine Avenue
Oklahoma City, OK 73112-2806
(405) 946-5743
Paul W. Black

Plants
Color catalog offers a very broad selection of **bearded and reblooming
irises** in several sizes; each plant very briefly described, but new intro-
ductions and current favorites get lots of ink. Many of Paul's intro-
ductions have won national and international awards. (1978)
❏ Catalog: $2($4 OV), CAN/OV, SS:5-10, $10m
⌂ Nursery: April-October, Tu,Th pm, Sa-Su
▼ Garden: April-September, Tu,Th pm, Sa-Su

Midwest Cactus
P.O. Box 163
New Melle, MO 63365
(314) 828-5389, FAX Same
Chris Smith

Plants
Specializes in cold hardy **opuntia cacti** for year-round outdoor gardens;
plants are shown in b&w photographs, briefly described with good grow-
ing information. Also offers some sedums and yuccas. Bought the collection
of The Cactus Patch in 1993. (1984)
❏ Catalog: $1, R&W, CAN/OV, SS:5-9, $5m, bn
⌂ Nursery: By appointment only
▼ Garden: June-August, by appointment only

Mighty Minis
7318 Sahara Court
Sacramento, CA 95828
Jean Stokes

Plants
A small nursery selling miniature **African violets** (plants and leaves) and
mini-sinningias and other miniature **gesneriads**. A broad selection; each
gets a brief description. (1982)
❏ Catalog: $2d, CAN/OV, SS:5-10, $30m
⌂ Nursery: All year, by appointment only
▼ Garden: January-February, by appointment only

Milaeger's Gardens
4838 Douglas Avenue
Racine, WI 53402-2498
(414) 639-2371, FAX 639-1855 TO/CC
Kevin D. Milaeger

Plants
A broad selection of **perennials**, including a good selection of mostly
modern **roses**, clematis, shade plants, prairie wildflowers and ornamental
grasses; all very well described, many illustrated in color photographs.
The catalog is accurately called "The Perennial Wishbook." (1960)
❏ Catalog: $1, SS:3-6,8-10, bn/cn
⌂ Nursery: All year, daily
▼ Garden: Spring-Summer, daily

Millar Mountain Nursery
5086 McLay Road, RR 3
Duncan, BC, Canada V9L 2X1
(604) 748-0487
Kathy Millar

Plants
A source of Japanese, Siberian, Pacific Coast Native hybrids, Evansia and species **iris**, including some water and bog iris. A nice selection, with each plant briefly described. Payment may be made by check in US$. (1989)
❑ Catalog: $2, US/OV, SS:8-10, $15m
▼ Garden: May-June, by appointment only

Miller Nurseries, Inc.
5060 West Lake Road
Canandaigua, NY 14424
(716) 396-2647, (800) 836-9630 TO/CC $10m
John & David Miller

Plants ≈ Supplies
Color catalog offers a broad selection of **fruit and nut trees, berries** of all kinds, **grapes, ornamental trees** and supplies; each plant well describ-ed, many illustrated. Can't ship certain plants to AZ, CA, ID, or WA, no ribes to ME, NH, NC, or VT. (1936)
❑ Catalog: Free, SS:2-6,10-11, cn
⌂ Nursery: All year, M-F, March-May, daily
▼ Garden: April-May, growing area, daily

Miller's Manor Gardens
3167 East US 224
Ossian, IN 46777
(219) 597-7403, 433-3432
Lynda Miller

Plants
Offers **bearded irises** of all types: an extensive list featuring newer med-ian and dwarf irises, each very briefly described. Also offers a number of **Siberian iris** cultivars, as well as a nice selection of **daylilies**. Have added some perennials, which can't be shipped to AZ, CA, OR or WA. (1976)
❑ Catalog: $1d, R&W, CAN/OV, SS:7-9, $10m
⌂ Nursery: April-October, M-Tu, Th-Sa
▼ Garden: May, M-Tu, Th-Sa

The Mini-Rose Garden
P.O. Box 203
Austin Street
Cross Hill, SC 29332-0203
(803) 998-4331 TO/CC
Michael & Betty Williams

Plants
List offers a selection of award-winning **miniature roses** chosen for best performance; each briefly but well described, a few illustrated in color, including their own introductions. (1983)
❑ Catalog: Free, R&W
⌂ Nursery: All year, daily, call ahead
▼ Garden: June-September, daily, call ahead

Miniature Plant Kingdom
4125 Harrison Grade Road
Sebastopol, CA 95472
(707) 874-2233
Don Herzog

Plants
Offers a good selection of **miniature roses**, including their own hybrids, as well as **Japanese maples, conifers and plants for bonsai**. The bonsai list has grown to take over most of the catalog; these are desirable plants, many of which have fruit and/or flowers. (1965)
❑ Catalog: $2.50, R&W, SS:W, $7m
⌂ Nursery: All year, Th-Su
▼ Garden: Spring-Summer, Th-Su

Miree's
70 Enfield Avenue
Toronto, ON, Canada M8W 1T9
(416) 251-6369
Mrs. M. Lex

Plants
Sells cane, rex, rhizomatous, shrub and semi-tuberous **begonias**, a good selection with good plant descriptions. Also offers some **episcias**, miniature **sinningias** and other **gesneriads**.
❑ Catalog: $2, US, SS:5-9, $20m
⌂ Nursery: By appointment only

Misty Hill Farms - Moonshine Gardens
5080 West Soda Rock Lane
Healdsburg, CA 95448
(707) 433-8408
Jack & Phyllis Dickey

Plants
The Dickeys took over the **iris** of the late Monty Byers of Moonshine Gar-dens, and will continue to offer his selection of reblooming iris and intro-duce his crosses. They also offer "space-age" and antique iris. All varieties are well described. Orders taken at the garden during April and May. (1985)
❑ Catalog: Free($1 OV), CAN/OV, SS:7-9, $10m
⌂ Nursery: April-May, Sa-Su

Grant Mitsch Novelty Daffodils
P.O. Box 218
Hubbard, OR 97032
(503) 651-2742 (evenings)
Dick & Elise Havens

Bulbs
Specialize in rarer hybrids of **daffodils**, including those of Elise Havens' father Grant E. Mitsch, as well as many others; each plant is very well des-cribed, and many are illustrated in color in an informative catalog. Grant Mitsch was introducing new cultivars until the time of his death at 81; the Havens carry on the family tradition. (1927)
❑ Catalog: $3d, CAN/OV, SS:9-10
▼ Garden: Spring, call ahead

Mohns Nursery
P.O. Box 2301
Atascadero, CA 93423
(805) 466-4362
Jim DeWelt, Mgr.

Plants
Offer their own 'Minicaps' strain of perennial **Oriental poppies**, bred especially for the warm winter climate of central and southern California. They come in a choice of several shades of red, pink and orange and in dwarf, standard and tall heights. (1983)
❑ Catalog: 1 FCS, SS:3-4, $5m

Monashee Perennials
Site 6, Box 9, RR 7
Vernon, BC, Canada V1T 7Z3
(604) 542-2592
John & Margaret Montgomery

Plants
Offers a nice selection of **daylilies, dwarf bearded irises, Siberian irises, hostas and hybrid lilies**; plants are well described. (1988)
❐ Catalog: $2d, US, SS:4-10

Monocot Nursery
Jacklands, Tickenham
Clevedon, Avon, England BS21 6SG
Mike Salmon

Seeds
Oh, what a wonderful list! **Seeds of bulbous plants** from all over Europe and the Mediterranean world: narcissus, leucojum, sternbergia, arums, crocus, species iris, lapeirousia, romulea, moraea, alliums, colchicums, fritillaria, scilla, species tulips and cyclamen. All are species, with site of original seed collection given - read it with a good bulb book at your side! (1960)
❐ Catalog: $3(US Bills), OV, SS:3,8-9, $25m, bn

Moon Mountain Wildflowers
P.O. Box 725
Carpinteria, CA 93014-0725
(805) 684-2565 TO/CC
Becky Lynn Schaff

Seeds ⬿ Books ⬿ Supplies
Informative catalog lists **annual and perennial wildflowers and grasses** of many areas, including mixes suitable for many habitats or uses, sold in packets and in bulk. Plants well described with cultural suggestions. Also sells the lovely wildflower posters of the California Native Plant Society and some wildflower books, as well as seed starting kits. (1981)
❐ Catalog: $2, R&W, CAN/OV, bn/cn
⌂ Nursery: All year, M-F, call ahead

Moonshine Gardens

See Misty Hill Farms/Moonshine Gardens.

Moore Water Gardens
P.O. Box 70
Port Stanley, ON, Canada N5L 1J4
(519) 782-4052, FAX 782-3139
Sue See

Plants ⬿ Books ⬿ Supplies
A good selection of **water lilies, lotus, aquatic plants**, supplies and ponds for water gardens, all well described in an informative catalog, some illustrated in color. Also a number of books on water gardening. (1930)
❐ Catalog: Free, R&W, SS:4-9, bn/cn
⌂ Nursery: All year, call ahead
▼ Garden: May-August, call ahead

Moose Tubers
P.O. Box 520
Waterville, ME 04903-0520
FAX (207) 426-9005
Bill Getty & Gene Frey

Plants ⬿ Bulbs
Moose Tubers is part of Fedco Seeds/Fedco Trees, and puts out a separate list of **seed potatoes, onion sets and Jerusalem artichokes** and spring and summer blooming **bulbs and perennials**, such as gladiolus, begonias and lilies. Each variety is well described. No shipping to AZ or CA.
❐ Catalog: Free, SS:4, $25m, bn

Morden Nurseries, Ltd.
P.O. Box 1270
Morden, MB, Canada R0G 1J0
(204) 822-3311
Els Temmerman

Plants
A good selection of **hardy fruit trees, ornamental trees and shrubs, roses, and perennials**. Color catalog, some plants illustrated. Offers fruiting and ornamental crabapples, apples, plums, apricots and berries -- all very hardy; plants briefly described. (1964)
❐ Catalog: $2
⌂ Nursery: All year, M-F; hours vary, call ahead

Mostly Natives Nursery
P.O. Box 258
27235 Highway 1
Tomales, CA 94971
(707) 878-2009
Margaret Graham & Walter Earle

Plants
A small nursery specializing in **West Coast natives and grasses**; a nice selection, with some good plant descriptions. Their own introductions have "Tomales Bay" names. At the nursery they offer a good selection of drought tolerant plants of all kinds. (1984)
❐ Catalog: $3, SS:3-5,9-11, $21m, bn
⌂ Nursery: All year, Tu-Sa
▼ Garden: April-October, Tu-Sa

Mt. Leo Nursery
Route 9
603 Beersheba Street
McMinnville, TN 37110
(615) 473-7833
Virginia Pearsall

Plants
List offers a nice selection of **evergreens, flowering trees and shrubs, ground covers and fruit and nut trees**; sizes listed but no descriptions. List includes thorn-free blackberries, apples, apricots, pears, peaches, plums, berries and grapes, and some ornamental trees and shrubs. (1982)
❐ Catalog: Free, R&W, CAN/OV, SS:10-4, cn
⌂ Nursery: All year, daily

Mt. Tahoma Nursery
28111 - 112th Avenue East
Graham, WA 98338
(206) 847-9827 TO/CC
Rick Lupp

Plants
Small nursery offers a very nice selection of **alpine plants** for collectors, as well as a number of **small shrubs and dwarf conifers** ideal for gardeners with limited space. All plants very well described, with brief indications as to culture. Troughs for alpines available at the nursery. (1985)
❐ Catalog: $1, R&W, CAN, bn
⌂ Nursery: September-June, weekends or by appointment
▼ Garden: Weekends, April-May, by appointment only

Mountain Maples
5901 Spy Rock Road
Laytonville, CA 95454-1329
(707) 984-6522
Don & Nancy Fiers

Plants
Offer over a hundred **Japanese maple** cultivars, and some **species maples**, each very well described for either bonsai or landscape use. Many listed by their Japanese cultivar names -- it would be ideal to have Vertrees' book on hand as you read the catalog. Offer a few books, and redwood planters. (1985)
❏ Catalog: $1, R&W, SS:2-6,10-11, bn
⌂ Nursery: February-November, by appointment only
❦ Garden: April-June, October-November, by appointment only

Mountain Valley Growers, Inc.
38325 Pepperweed Road
Squaw Valley, CA 93675
(209) 338-2775, FAX same
V. J. Billings

Plants ❧ Books
A very good selection of **herbs**, including some new cultivars and hard to find varieties; all plants are well described with information on height at maturity and garden or culinary uses. Listed are **everlastings** and many good garden plants. Also offer many books on herbs, and an herb newletter. No shipping to AK or HI.
❏ Catalog: Free, R&W, SS:W, $15m, bn

Charles H. Mueller Co.
7091 N. River Road
New Hope, PA 18938
(215) 862-2033, FAX 862-3696
Charles Fritz, III & Nancy Gregory

Bulbs
Offers a good selection of spring and summer blooming **bulbs**: the fall planting catalog offers novelty daffodils, tulips, alliums, crocus and other "little" bulbs. The summer blooming list offers lilies, daylilies, dahlias, cannas, tuberous begonias, gladiolus, caladiums and autumn crocus. (1935)
❏ Catalog: Free($2 OV), R&W, CAN/OV, SS:3-11, $20
⌂ Nursery: All year, M-F
❦ Garden: April-May, daily

Mums by Paschke
12286 East Main Road
North East, PA 16428
(814) 725-9860
Jack Paschke

Plants
A good selection of hybrid **chrysanthemums** available to home gardeners from a large wholesaler. Pamphlet gives good plant descriptions, offers 78 varieties to choose from, listed by color. (1933)
❏ Catalog: Free, R&W, SS:3-6, $10m
⌂ Nursery: May-November, daily
❦ Garden: September-October, daily

Mushroompeople
P.O. Box 220
560 Farm Road
Summertown, TN 38483
(615) 964-2200, FAX same
Frank Michael

Seeds ❧ Books ❧ Supplies ❧ Tools
Specializes in spawn of **shiitake mushrooms**, both cold and warm weather strains, for log or sawdust cultivation. Also offers complete growing supplies, books on mushroom growing, hunting and cooking, and video cassettes of mushroom conferences and on shiitake growing in Japan. (1976)
❏ Catalog: Free, CAN/OV, cn/bn
⌂ Nursery: All year, M-F, call ahead

Musser Forests Inc.
P.O. Box 340
Route 119 North
Indiana, PA 15701
(412) 465-5686, FAX 465-9893 TO/CC
Fred A. Musser

Plants
Supplies a broad selection of ornamental trees and shrubs in transplant sizes: **conifers**, flowering **trees and shrubs**, hedging plants and ground covers for the home gardener and commercial grower. Good descriptions, some color photographs. (1928)
❏ Catalog: Free, R&W, CAN/OV, SS:3-5,9-12, $10m, cn/bn
⌂ Nursery: March-November, daily
❦ Garden: April-May, daily

NWN Nursery
P.O Box 1143
DeFuniak Springs, FL 32433
(904) 638-7572
John & Kathy Foster

Plants ❧ Seeds
A good selection of **Southeastern native plants**, and a few others: trees and shrubs, vines, bulbs and tubers. They will provide germination advice for the seeds, and give some cultural advice for most of the plants. Plants are especially suited to the Southeast, USDA zones 7b - 9a. (1989)
❏ Catalog: Free, R&W, bn
⌂ Nursery: All year, M-Sa

Native American Seed
3400 Long Prairie Road
Flower Mound, TX 75028
(214) 539-0534, FAX (817) 464-3897
Jan & Bill Neiman

Seeds
The Neiman's main line of work is prairie restoration in the Blackland Prairie of Texas; they also harvest seeds of **wildflowers and native grasses** with permission of landowners. Their seeds are specifically for use in Texas, where they do well. Also sell some organic garden products. (1988)
❏ Catalog: $1, R&W, $15m, cn/bn

Native Gardens
5737 Fisher Lane
Greenback, TN 37742
(615) 856-0220, 856-3550
Meredith & Ed Clebsch

Plants ❧ Seeds
Nursery-propagated **native plants** (and seeds) for meadows and natural landscaping. Tables in the catalog give good information on growing conditions, season and color of flower, habitat and soil, with very concise comments. Ship only seeds to Canada and Overseas, and to AZ, CA, OR or WA. (1983)
❏ Catalog: $2($3 OV), R&W, $10m, cn/bn
⌂ Nursery: By appointment only
❦ Garden: By appointment only

Native Oak Nursery
20316 Fallen Leaf Drive
Tehachapi, CA 93561
(805) 822-4746, (800) 949-6257
Michael & Suzann Chesebrough

Plants ⬥ Supplies
A small family nursery which offers some seedling **native California oaks** grown in deep treepots to develop deep root systems; also offered are a few non-native oaks, a book on California oaks, and Tubex(R) tree shelters to protect the trees while they become established. (1991)
☐ Catalog: Free, R&W, CAN, SS:11-4, bn
⌂ Nursery: By appointment only

Native Seeds, Inc.
14590 Triadelphia Mill Road
Dayton, MD 21036
(301) 596-9818 TO
Dr. James A. Saunders

Seeds
Offers seed of a nice selection of individual **wildflowers**, chosen to flourish in many regions of the country. Also offers seed mixes with a broad variety of wildflowers and seeds in bulk: all plants well described.
☐ Catalog: Free, R&W, CAN/OV, bn/cn

Native Seeds/SEARCH
2509 N. Campbell Avenue, #325
Tucson, AZ 85719
Kevin Dahl, Assoc. Dir.

Seeds ⬥ Books ⬥ Supplies
Non-profit group offers traditional **Southwestern native crops**, many by Spanish names, as well as **wild food plants**; all plants briefly described, with cultural suggestions. Offers a few related publications, occasional workshops and Indian seed-drying baskets. A wide selection of open-pollinated corn, beans, amaranth, gourds, squash and hot peppers. (1983)
☐ Catalog: $1, CAN/OV, $2m
⌂ Nursery: September-July, Tu-Th, call ahead
▼ Garden: Summer, Tu-Th, call ahead

Nature's Curiosity Shop
3551 Evening Canyon Road
Oceanside, CA 92056
Rick Nowakowski

Plants
Offers **variegated plants** of all types, especially **succulents**: aeoniums, agaves, aloes, crassulas, gasterias, haworthias, aspidistras, agapanthus, crinums and cannas, and a variety of others, each briefly described. (1970)
☐ Catalog: $1d, R&W, CAN, $15m, bn/cn
⌂ Nursery: By appointment only

Nature's Garden
40611 Highway 226
Scio, OR 97374-9351
Frederick W. Held

Plants ⬥ Bulbs
A good selection of plants for the woodland, shady or sunny garden, including some **sedum and sempervivums, hardy ferns, gentians and hellebores, species primulas, violas** and other choice rock garden plants, each very briefly described. Also sells some daffodil bulbs. (1974)
☐ Catalog: Long SASE w/2 FCS, R&W, CAN/OV, SS:2-6,9-12, bn

E. B. Nauman & Daughter
688 St. Davids Lane
Schenectady, NY 12309
(518) 276-6726
E. B. Nauman

Plants
"We specialize in broadleaf evergreens which are hardy in the Northeast and Midwest: **rhododendrons, azaleas and mountain laurels**, featuring young plants of quality, named varieties." A brief list; each plant is well described, with detailed cultural notes. (1973)
☐ Catalog: $1, SS:4-6,9-11, $10m

© Mountain Maples
Artist: Carolyn Carpenter

Neon Palm Nursery
3525 Stony Point Road
Santa Rosa, CA 95407
(707) 585-8100
Dale & Cindy Motiska

Plants
A good selection of **hardy subtropical plants**: many palms, cycads, winter-hardy cactus, yuccas, agaves, ferns, bamboos, conifers and others. There are no plant descriptions, but there are notes as to hardiness. (1983)
❐ Catalog: $1, CAN/OV, SS:4-10, $50m, bn
⌂ Nursery: All year, Tu-Su
▼ Garden: All year, Tu-Su

New Mexico Cactus Research
P.O. Box 787
1132 E. River Road
Belen, NM 87002
(505) 864-4027
Horst Kuenzler

Plants ⚭ Seeds
A very extensive collectors' list of **cacti and succulent** seeds and mixtures of seeds by genus, listed by botanical name only, with very brief notes on origin. Many of the seeds are habitat-collected; no plant descriptions for most, brief notes on some. Also sel's winter-hardy cactus; seeds only overseas. (1955)
❐ Catalog: $1, R&W, CAN/OV, $5m, bn
⌂ Nursery: By appointment only
▼ Garden: By appointment only

The New Peony Farm
P.O. Box 18235
St. Paul, MN 55118
(612) 457-8994
Kent Crossley

Plants
Catalog lists about 75 of the 350 varieties of herbaceous **peonies** which they grow; each plant well described. They are particularly interested in offering fine older cultivars in danger of being lost in commerce; they also offer single and double fernleaf peonies, mixed assortments by color. (1980)
❐ Catalog: Free($1 OV), R&W, CAN/OV, SS:9-11
▼ Garden: June, by appointment only

New York State Fruit Testing Coop. Assn.
P.O. Box 462
Geneva, NY 14456-0462
(315) 787-2205, FAX 787-2216
Elizabeth Munzer, Gen. Mgr.

Plants
For a $5 membership fee, fruit testers may buy a large selection of new and older varieties of **hardy fruit**. They must agree not to distribute the new varieties, as well as to report on how their choices perform. All plants are well described; prices seem about average. (1918)
❐ Catalog: Free

Niche Gardens
1111 Dawson Road
Chapel Hill, NC 27516
(919) 967-0078
Kim Hawks

Plants
Small nursery specializing in **Southeastern wildflowers and native plants**, **perennials, ornamental grasses and herbs** for rock gardens, bogs and dry areas. Plants are well described, with notes on use and placement, and come in four-inch, quart or gallon pots; all are nursery-propagated. Workshops are held at the nursery during the year, call for dates. (1986)
❐ Catalog: $3, R&W, SS:W, $15, bn/cn
⌂ Nursery: March-May, Tu-Sa, other times by appointment only
▼ Garden: September, by appointment only

Nicholls Gardens
4724 Angus Drive
Gainesville, VA 22065
(703) 754-9623 TO
Diana Nicholls

Plants
Small nursery sells a good selection of **irises** -- Siberian, Japanese, Louisiana, species and bearded, dwarf to tall -- as well as **daylilies** and **dahlias**. All plants are briefly described -- and would provide something in bloom from early spring to late fall. They are an official display garden for the Society for Japanese Iris; it looks very beautiful. (1984)
❐ Catalog: $1d($2 OV), CAN/OV, SS:4-5,7-9, $10m
⌂ Nursery: April-September, daily, call ahead
▼ Garden: April-September, daily, call ahead

Nichols Garden Nursery, Inc.
1190 N. Pacific Highway
Albany, OR 97321-4598
(503) 928-9280, FAX 967-8406 TO/CC $10m
Rose Marie McGee

Plants ⚭ Seeds ⚭ Books ⚭ Supplies
An extensive selection of **herbs, and vegetable and flower** seeds; many vegetables selected for coastal Northwestern conditions. Plants well described with cultural hints -- also garden, herbal and winemaking supplies and books. They've introduced a lovely lavender, 'Sharon Roberts,' reblooming, very hardy and a deep lavender-blue. They also specialize in elephant garlic. No roots, plants or bulbs to Canada or HI. (1950)
❐ Catalog: Free, R&W, CAN, SS:4-5,9-10
⌂ Nursery: All year, M-Sa, 1190 Old Salem Road N.E.
▼ Garden: Spring-Summer, M-Sa

Nindethana Seed Service

See Eclipse Farms.

Nolin River Nut Tree Nursery
797 Port Wooden Road
Upton, KY 42784
(502) 369-8551
John & Lisa Brittain

Plants
Formerly the Leslie Wilmoth Nursery, specializing in grafted **nut trees** -- pecans, hicans, hickories, heartnuts, butternuts, black and Persian walnuts, chestnuts -- over 175 varieties; also grafted **persimmons**. Listed by variety name; very brief plant descriptions. No shipping to CA or AZ. (1985)
❐ Catalog: 2 FCS, SS:3-4, cn/bn
⌂ Nursery: All year, M-Sa, by appointment only
▼ Garden: June-September, by appointment only

Nor'East Miniature Roses
P.O. Box 307
58 Hammond Street
Rowley, MA 01969
(508) 948-7964, FAX 948-5487
John Saville

Plants
Color catalog of **miniature roses**, including "mini" tree roses and climbers, both single plants and collections. Nice selection, plants well described. Another office at P.O. Box 473, Ontario, CA 91762, (909) 984-2223. (1972)
❑ Catalog: Free, R&W, $6m
⌂ Nursery: Daily, call ahead
▼ Garden: May-September, AARS Display Garden, call ahead

North Coast Rhododendron Nursery
P.O. Box 308
Bodega, CA 94922
(707) 829-0600
Parker Smith

Plants
Rhododendron nursery specializes in plants for mild coastal climates, and for greenhouses in cold climates. They offer Maddenii hybrids (very fragrant) and other hybrids and species, and deciduous **azaleas**; all plants are very well described. (1986)
❑ Catalog: $1, SS:W, $25m

North Pine Iris Gardens
P.O. Box 595
308 No. Pine Street
Norfolk, NE 68701
Chuck & Mary Ferguson

Plants
Specializes in bearded **irises** of all sizes, a broad selection with brief plant descriptions. Also sells some **hosta**, as well as windsocks, wind chimes and other iris ornaments in wood.
❑ Catalog: $1, CAN/OV, SS:4-9, $10m
⌂ Nursery: By appointment only

North Pole Acres
P.O. Box 56822
North Pole, AK 99705
(907) 488-3940
Ed Bostrom

Plants
Offers very, very hardy **strawberries, raspberries, asparagus** for the sub-arctic climate of Alaska; all plants have over wintered on their farm where temperatures have fallen to minus 70F. (1986)
❑ Catalog: $1, R&W, SS:5-7
⌂ Nursery: May-July, call ahead
▼ Garden: June-July, call ahead

North Star Gardens
2124 University Avenue W.
St. Paul, MN 55114-1838
(612) 659-2515, FAX 659-2464
Kyle D. Haugland, Mgr.

Plants ❧ Books ❧ Supplies
"We are the **raspberry** specialists," and they offer over 30 cultivars: each variety compared by qualities and very well described. Also offer the new European "Jostaberry," a cross between a currant and gooseberry; minimum order on all plants is 25. Sell books, growing and marketing supplies. (1987)
❑ Catalog: Free, R&W, CAN, SS:2-6, $50m
⌂ Nursery: All year, M-Sa

Northern Groves
P.O. Box 86291
Portland, OR 97286-0291
(503) 774-6353
Rick Valley

Plants
A source of **hardy bamboos**, a good selection with good plant descriptions for each plant. The catalog also has extensive information on growing bamboos. Rick can also supply cuttings of basket willows, ask for that list if you're interested. Can ship to HI only with a quarantine permit. (1981)
❑ Catalog: $1($2 OV), R&W, CAN/OV, SS:6-11, $6m, bn

Northern Kiwi Nursery
RR 3, 181 Niven Road
Niagara-on-the-Lake, ON, Canada L0S 1J0
Peter & Paul Klassen

Plants
A Canadian source for fifteen varieties of very **hardy kiwis**; list gives good information on each variety and on general culture. (1985)
❑ Catalog: $1d, R&W, US, SS:4-6, $15m
⌂ Nursery: April-October, M-Sa, call ahead
▼ Garden: June-October, M-Sa, call ahead

Northland Gardens
315-A West Mountain Road
Queensbury, NY 12804
(518) 798-4277, (800) 4-BONSAI, FAX 798-9004
Tracy Tabor & Drew Monthie

Plants ❧ Books ❧ Supplies ❧ Tools
A one-stop "bonsai centre"; **pre-bonsai and finished plants**, books, tools, pots and growing supplies. Plants available for both temperate and tropical bonsai, and some unusual plants at the nursery; no plant descriptions. (1986)
❑ Catalog: $2, CAN, $10m, cn
⌂ Nursery: All year, daily
▼ Garden: Spring-Fall, daily

Northplan/Mountain Seed
P.O. Box 9107
Moscow, ID 83843-1607
(208) 882-8040 TO/CC
Loring M. Jones

Seeds
Seeds of **native trees and shrubs** for disturbed land restoration, erosion control and highway landscaping; **wildflower** mixes for various habitats and **range and reclamation grasses**. Garden seed catalog lists **short-season vegetables and annuals**. Garden seed catalog $1d; send long SASE for native plant list. (1975)
❑ Catalog: See notes, R&W, CAN/OV
⌂ Nursery: By appointment only

Northridge Gardens
9821 White Oak Avenue
Northridge, CA 91325
(818) 349-9798 TO/CC
Arnie & Susan Mitchnick

Plants ◈ Books
Northridge Gardens bought the business of Singer's Growing Things, and will be combining the offerings of the two nurseries: caudiciforms, **unusual succulents**, plants for bonsai, brachychitons, euphorbias, monadeniums, pachypodiums and sansevierias, all briefly described. (1991)
❐ Catalog: Free, R&W, $20m, bn
⌂ Nursery: All year, F-Sa, or by appointment
▼ Garden: All year, F-Sa, or by appointment

Northwest Epi Center
2735 S.E. Troutdale Rd.
Troutdale, OR 97060-9438
(503) 666-4171 TO/CC
Robert A. Buroker

Plants ◈ Supplies
Offers a good selection of **epiphyllums** or "orchid cacti"; Bob says his greenhouse looks like a tropical rainforest from April to August. They grow over 300 varieties and list around 100; well described. Also offer a special growth enhancer called "Proyield-H" for rainforest plants. (1967)
❐ Catalog: $2, R&W, CAN/OV, SS:3-10, 15m
⌂ Nursery: February-November, Tu-Su
▼ Garden: March-June, Tu-Su

Northwest Mycological Consultants
702 N.W. 4th Street
Corvallis, OR 97330
(503) 753-8198, FAX 753-8198 TO/CC $20m
Annette Simonson, Lab. Dir.

Seeds ◈ Supplies ◈ Tools
Offer a good selection of **mushroom spawn**: shiitake, enoki, reiski, morel and black morel, several types of oyster and several others such as "hen of the woods" and "shaggy mane." They also sell books and mushroom growing supplies and consult with growers. (1985)
❐ Catalog: $2, R&W, CAN/OV, $2m

Northwest Native Seed
915 Davis Place South
Seattle, WA 98144
(206) 329-5804
Ron Ratko

Seeds
Ron collects seed and offers **native plants and wildflowers** from all over the Northwest, species listed each year depend on where he's been collecting the summer before; he will also collect requested seed when he can. It's important to order early in the year, late requests can be delayed. A good selection, with good plant descriptions, location and habitat information.
❐ Catalog: $1, CAN/OV, bn

Northwind Nursery & Orchards
7910 335th Avenue N.W.
Princeton, MN 55371
(612) 389-4920
Frank Foltz

Plants
Small family nursery offers a nice selection of hardy organically grown **fruit trees**: apples, plums, pears, cherries, crabapples, mulberries, as well as wine grapes, raspberries, filberts and miscellaneous fruiting trees and shrubs for **edible landscaping**, each well described. Also sells books, tools, and organic growing supplies; gives classes in fruit culture. (1983)
❐ Catalog: $1d, R&W, SS:4-5,10, cn/bn
⌂ Nursery: April-May, October, F-Sa
▼ Garden: June-September, call ahead

Northwoods Retail Nursery
27635 S. Oglesby Road
Canby, OR 97013
(503) 266-5432, FAX 266-5431 TO/CC $10m
Kathy Fives

Plants ◈ Books ◈ Supplies ◈ Tools
Offers **hybrid chestnuts, berries, apples, figs, hardy kiwis, pawpaws** and **oriental pears**, grown by organic methods "as much as possible." A good variety of kiwis, other fruits and nuts and many ornamental shrubs and trees which do well in the Northwest and which are, in many cases, suited to the urban-sized lot. (1979)
❐ Catalog: Free, CAN, SS:1-5, $10m
⌂ Nursery: January-May, Tu-Su
▼ Garden: January-May, Tu-Su

Nourse Farms, Inc.
RFD, Box 485
River Road (Whately)
South Deerfield, MA 01373
(413) 665-2658, FAX 665-7888
Tim Nourse

Plants
Growers of tissue-cultured **strawberries** as a means of producing "virus-free" plants -- 31 varieties. They also sell **blackberries, raspberries, rhubarb, horseradish** and the Rutgers University "all-male" **asparagus** hybrids -- more vigorous and they do not set seed. Seedling conifers, too. Informative catalog with cultural suggestions. (1933)
❐ Catalog: Free, R&W, CAN/OV, SS:3-6
⌂ Nursery: April-May, M-Sa
▼ Garden: May-September, growing area, call ahead

Nuccio's Nurseries
P.O. Box 6160
3555 Chaney Trail
Altadena, CA 91003
(818) 794-3383
Julius, Tom & Jim Nuccio

Plants
A huge selection of **camellias and azaleas**; all plants well to briefly described. Camellias include japonica, sasanqua, reticulata, rusticana and higo hybrids and a number of species; some camellia scions are also available. Azalea hybrids of many types, including many of their own and a huge selection of Japanese satsukis, and a few gardenias. No shipping to LA. (1935)
❐ Catalog: Free, R&W, SS:10-4
⌂ Nursery: All year, F-Tu; June-December, closed Su

Nurseries at North Glen
Route 2, Box 2700
Glen St. Mary, FL 32040
(904) 259-2754
Kyle E. Brown

Plants
Offers about 28 species of **hardy palms and cycads**, listed only by botanical name, including several species of butia, livistona, sabal, and trachycarpus. No plant descriptions. (1976)
❒ Catalog: Free, R&W, $10m, bn
▼ Garden: All year, call ahead

Oak Hill Farm
204 Pressly Street
Clover, SC 29710
(803) 222-4245 (6-8 am) TO
Betsy Johnson

Plants
Small nursery offers **species azaleas** -- arborescens, atlanticum, austrinum, bakeri, prunifolium, slippenbachi, roseshell, canescens, vaseyi, and crosses of native azaleas; some hardy to -10F, container-grown from seed. Also lists about 50 evergreen azaleas; no plant descriptions. (1977)
❒ Catalog: $1d, R&W, CAN, SS:11-3, $25m, bn
⌂ Nursery: All year, call ahead
▼ Garden: April-May, call ahead

Oak Hill Gardens
P.O. Box 25
37W 550 Binnie Road
Dundee, IL 60118-0025
(708) 428-8500, FAX 428-8527 TO/CC
Hermann & Dorothy Pigors

Plants ⬿ Books ⬿ Supplies
Informative catalog offers a broad selection of **species and hybrid orchids**, as well as **bromeliads** and other flowering and foliage indoor plants; each plant briefly described in table format. Also offers growing supplies and books on orchids and houseplants. (1973)
❒ Catalog: $1, R&W, CAN, SS:W, bn
⌂ Nursery: All year, M-Sa
▼ Garden: All year, M-Sa

Oakes Daylilies
8204 Monday Road
Corryton, TN 37721
(615) 687-3770
Stewart Oakes

Plants
Just **daylilies**, a collectors' list of hundreds of varieties from many noted hybridizers and AHS award winners. Color catalog offers most popular varieties, with concentration on award winners; plants are well described. They also issue a Collector's Catalog listing 1,000 cultivars for $1. (1979)
❒ Catalog: $2, R&W, CAN/OV
▼ Garden: AHS Display Garden, call for open dates

Oakridge Nursery
P.O. Box 182
East Kingston, NH 03827
(603) 642-8227, FAX 778-3004
Richard Marcella & Glen Taylor

Plants
Small nursery offers nice selection of **ferns and wildflower plants**, mature and ready for planting. Plants are well but briefly described, a few shown in color photographs. Some plants are rescued from sites about to be developed or logged over; they say they're very careful in their collecting! (1971)
❒ Catalog: Free, R&W, CAN/OV, SS:3-5,9-10, $15m, cn/bn

Oikos Tree Crops
P.O. Box 19425
Kalamazoo, MI 49019-0425
(616) 624-6233, 342-6504, FAX 342-2759
Ken Asmus

Plants
Offers "native, naturalized and exotic species for human and wildlife use:" **nuts, fruits and berries**, including chestnuts, hickories, walnuts, many oaks, and some magnolias, lilacs and other ornamentals. Offers drought hardy species from the Southwest and hybrid oaks. (1985)
❒ Catalog: $1, R&W, SS:3-12, $20m, cn/bn
⌂ Nursery: All year, by appointment only
▼ Garden: June-September, by appointment only

Olallie Daylily Gardens
HCR 63, Box 1
Marlboro Branch Road
South Newfane, VT 05351
(802) 348-6614
Christopher & Amelia Darrow

Plants ⬿ Seeds
Christopher inherited his **daylilies** and interest in hybridizing from his grandfather, Dr. George Darrow, who was a plant breeder with the USDA. He offers a good selection of their own introductions and other favorite daylilies, and a few garden perennials. (1982)
❒ Catalog: Free, R&W, SS:4-10, $20m
⌂ Nursery: May-September, W-Su
▼ Garden: July-August, W-Su

Old House Gardens
536 Third Street
Ann Arbor, MI 48103-4957
(313) 995-1486
Scott G. Kunst

Bulbs
Scott Kunst is a consultant on historic garden restoration, and has started to sell **historic bulbs**, many from the 19th and early 20th century. All the bulbs offered are well researched for date of introduction; the catalog is very informative and fun to read. Offered are tulips, narcissus, hyacinths and others. (1993)
❒ Catalog: $1, SS:9-11, $20m

Onion Man

See Mark McDonough.

Ontario Seed Company, Ltd.
P.O. Box 144
16 King Street South
Waterloo, ON, Canada N2J 3Z9
(519) 886-0557 or 2990, FAX 886-0605 TO/CC
Scott Uffelman

Seeds ❧ Books ❧ Supplies
Offer a wide selection of **vegetables, annuals and perennials** for Canadian gardens; each variety well described with some seed starting suggestions. They also offer general gardening supplies, seeders, row covers, some books and bird feeders. They have acquired Tregunno Seed Company. (1899)
❐ Catalog: Free, R&W, cn

Orchid Gardens
2232 - 139th Avenue N.W.
Andover, MN 55744
Carl Phillips

Plants
Collectors' list of **Midwestern wildflowers and hardy ferns**; a good selection with good descriptions and concise cultural notes in an informative catalog. Most plants are native to northern Minnesota, including native orchids, violets, ferns, vines, club mosses and some trees and shrubs. (1945)
❐ Catalog: $.75, SS:4-5,9-10, cn/bn
⌂ Nursery: April-May, September-October, M-F

Orchid Species Specialties
42314 Road #415
Raymond Road
Coarsegold, CA 93614
(209) 683-3239 TO
Walter J. Rybaczyk

Plants ❧ Supplies
Extensive collectors' lists of **species orchids**, collected by the proprietors or other well-known jungle collectors; no descriptions. Award-winning species cattleya and laelia clones a specialty, much wanted by hybridizers. Three lists: general botanical, laelia and species cattleya, $1 each. They also sell some growing supplies. (1972)
❐ Catalog: See notes, CAN/OV, SS:W, $50m, bn
⌂ Nursery: All year, daily, call ahead
▼ Garden: All year, daily, call ahead

Orchid Thoroughbreds
731 W. Siddonsburg Road
Dillsburg, PA 17019
(717) 432-8100, FAX 432-1199 TO/CC $25m
Diane Vickery

Plants
Offers a good selection of **species and hybrid orchids** of all kinds, with emphasis on easy to grow orchids for beginners and those which make good houseplants. They have a cypripedium breeding program and will be listing them as they become available. Most plants are briefly described. (1984)
❐ Catalog: Free, R&W, CAN/OV
⌂ Nursery: By appointment only

Orchids by Hausermann, Inc.
2N134 Addison Road
Villa Park, IL 60181
(708) 543-6855, FAX 543-9842 TO/CC
Eugene Hausermann

Plants ❧ Books ❧ Supplies
Color catalog gives brief descriptions of hundreds of **species and hybrid orchids**: asocendas, cattleyas, dendrobiums, miltonias, oncidiums, phalaenopsis and vandas, among others, described in informational tables. Offers cultural suggestions, orchid growing supplies and books about orchids. (1920)
❐ Catalog: $1, R&W, CAN/OV, SS:3-12, $10m, bn
⌂ Nursery: All year, daily
▼ Garden: January-May, greenhouses, daily

Oregon Exotics Rare Fruit Nursery
1065 Messinger Road
Grants Pass, OR 97527
(503) 846-7578, FAX same
Jerry Black, Paulette Pratschner, Thane Caro

Plants
"Specializes in rare fruits, with emphasis on **hardy subtropical fruits** and their culture in Northern climates." Offers hardy citrus (citranges), ichandarins, hardy grapefruit relatives, dwarf citrus, feijoas, hicans, bananas, jujubes, loquats, low-chill apples, hardy kiwis and many varieties of figs. All are very well described. (1983)
❐ Catalog: $2, R&W, CAN/OV, SS:W, $15m

Oregon Miniature Roses
8285 S.W. 185th Avenue
Beaverton, OR 97007
(503) 649-4482 TO/CC
Ray Spooner

Plants
Color catalog offers a good selection of **miniature roses**, each well described and many illustrated. Sells a few of their own hybrids, miniature tree roses and roses for hanging baskets. (1978)
❐ Catalog: Free, R&W, CAN, $10m
⌂ Nursery: All year, daily, call ahead

Oregon Trail Daffodils
41905 S.E. Louden Road
Corbett, OR 97019
(503) 695-5513
Bill & Diane Tribe

Bulbs
Specializing in the **novelty daffodils** of the late Murray Evans and new cultivars of Bill Pannill, a broad selection of specialty daffodils. Each variety is well described by class, breeding and seedling number; the owners are the fourth generation of the Evans family in the daffodil trade. (1989)
❐ Catalog: Free, R&W, CAN/OV, SS:9-10, $5m
⌂ Nursery: All year, call ahead
▼ Garden: April, call ahead

Orgel's Orchids
18950 S.W. 136th Street
Miami, FL 33196-1942
(305) 233-7168
Orgel C. Bramblett

Plants
Collectors' list of **carnivorous plants** -- an especially large selection of nepenthes, droseras, sarracenias and pinguiculas -- and **species orchids** -- dendrobiums, vandas, aerides, cymbidiums, ascocentrums, phalaenopsis and more. Will export plants covered by CITES convention. (1972)
❐ Catalog: Free, CAN/OV, bn
⌂ Nursery: All year, by appointment only
▼ Garden: All year, growing area, by appointment only

Ornamental Edibles
3622 Weedin Court
San Jose, CA 95132
Joyce W. McClellan

Seeds
Offers a good selection of **vegetable, herbs and edible flowers** for the
"edible landscape and the gourmet table." Varieties from around the world,
well described for flavor and appearance. Alpine strawberries, too. (1988)
❐ Catalog: $2, R&W, CAN/OV

D. Orriell -- Seed Exporters
45 Frape Avenue, Mt. Yokine
Perth, WA, Australia 6060
FAX (619) 344-8982
Patricia B. Orriell

Seeds
Very extensive list of **Australian native plants** for collectors or botanical
gardens; each plant briefly described. Includes hardy eucalyptus, wildflowers, ferns, palms, proteas, banksias and cycads, acacias and many trop-
ical/greenhouse plants. Also has list of native plants for bonsai. (1978)
❐ Catalog: $6(US Bills), R&W, OV, $25m, bn/cn

Otter Valley Native Plants
P.O. Box 31, R.R.1
Eden, ON, Canada N0J 1H0
Gail Rhynard

Plants
Specializes in **native plants and meadow species** of Ontario, and can only
ship plants within Ontario. Plants are raised from locally collected seed, a
nice selection listed in an informative table. (1992)
❐ Catalog: $2, SS:4-5,10-11, $20, bn/cn
⌂ Nursery: May-September, Th-F, Su
❦ Garden: June-September, Tu-F, Su

Our Orchids
23113 S.W. 156th Avenue
Miami, FL 33170
(305) 852-1824, 242-1317, FAX 242-1317
Richard C. Paull

Plants
Offers a very nice selection of **species orchids**: aerides, brassavolas, cat-
tleyas, dendrobiums, epidendrums, laelias, oncidiums, phalaenopsis, rhyn-
costylis and vandas -- no plant descriptions. No shipping to CA. (1987)
❐ Catalog: Long SASE w/ 2 FCS, SS:W, bn
⌂ Nursery: All year, Tu-F, call ahead

Owen Farms
Route 3, Box 158-A
2951 Curve-Nankipoo Road
Ripley, TN 38063-9420
(901) 635-1588 (6-9 pm CST)
Edric & Lillian Owen

Plants
Offers a nice selection of collectors' **trees, shrubs and perennials**: birch,
dogwood, hydrangea, crape myrtle (including mildew-resistant cultivars),
Satsuki azaleas and garden perennials. All plants are very well described.
Finished bonsai are available at the nursery. (1985)
❐ Catalog: $2(2 IRC OV), R&W, CAN/OV, SS:W, bn/cn
⌂ Nursery: All year, W-Su, call ahead
❦ Garden: April-November, W-Su, call ahead

Owen's Vineyard & Nursery

See Bottoms Nursery & Owens Vineyard.

Owens Orchids
P.O. Box 365
18 Orchidheights Drive
Pisgah Forest, NC 28768-0365
(704) 877-3313 TO/CC
William & Joyce Owens

Plants
Good selection of **orchids** -- phalaenopsis and cattleya hybrids, many
meristems and some seedlings, briefly described. Also offers an orchid-a-
month plan and starter collections for beginners. Several lists a year.
❐ Catalog: Free, SS:W
⌂ Nursery: All year, M-Sa
❦ Garden: All year, greenhouse, M-Sa

P & P Seed Company
14050 Route 62
Collins, NY 14034
Ray Waterman

Seeds
Specialize in **giant vegetable** seed: pumpkins, squash, watermelons, gourds,
cabbage and others, used by people growing for competition. They are one of
the sponsors of the World Pumpkin Confederation, which hopes for a 1,000 lb.
(half ton!) pumpkin by the turn of the century. (1984)
❐ Catalog: Long SASE, R&W, CAN/OV, $3m
❦ Garden: July-October, by appointment only

Ben Pace Nursery
Route 1, Box 925
Pine Mountain, GA 31822
(706) 663-2346
Benjamin H. Pace

Plants
Offers a nice selection of **Southeastern native plants**, ornamental trees
and shrubs, and perennials. Listed are baptisias, clethras, hollies, leuco-
thoes, crested irises, species azaleas and viburnums among others; plants
listed by botanical name without descriptions. (1977)
❐ Catalog: Free, R&W, SS:10-2, bn
⌂ Nursery: October-June, M-Sa am, or by appointment
❦ Garden: March-May, M-Sa am

Pacific Coast Hybridizers
P.O. Box 972
1170 Steinway Avenue
Campbell, CA 95009-0972
(408) 370-2955
Bryce Williamson

Plants
Hobbyist hybridizers turned nurserymen; the catalog a wide selection of tall
bearded, reblooming, "space age," median and Louisiana **irises**. Plants well
but briefly described. (1970)
❐ Catalog: $1d, CAN/OV, SS:7-9
⌂ Nursery: April 15-May 15, by appointment only
❦ Garden: April 15-May 15, by appointment only

Pacific Coast Seed Company
3999 Chestnut, Suite 256
Fresno, CA 93726
FAX (209) 225-5606
David B. Recor

Seeds
Formerly Recor Tree Seed, this small company offers seed of **conifers** and **maples**, from packets to pounds; most of the plants are well described, and many would be of interest to bonsai or Christmas tree growers. They also offer some birch seed in larger quantities. (1986)
❑ Catalog: $1d, CAN/OV, $10m, cn/bn

Pacific Southwest Nursery
P.O. Box 985
National City, CA 91951
(619) 477-5333, FAX 447-1245
R. Mitch Beauchamp

Plants
A new mail order venture combining two disparate collections: Catalog A will list **drought tolerant native plants** for the Southern California climate, Catalog B lists a huge selection of greenhouse and tropical plants. I haven't yet seen Catalog A, but Catalog B lists **gesneriads, vines, jasmines, passion flowers, carnivorous plants and indoor bonsai** from the collection of nursery manager Patrick Worley. Specify Catalog A or B.
❑ Catalog: $3, R&W, $20m, bn
⌂ Nursery: All year, W-Su (2565 Cactus Rd., San Ysidro)

Pacific Tree Farms
4301 Lynwood Drive
Chula Vista, CA 91910
(619) 422-2400 TO/CC
William L. Nelson

Plants ❧ Books ❧ Supplies ❧ Tools
A broad selection of **fruit, nut and ornamental trees** (including 90 varieties of pine), California native trees and shrubs and tender warm-climate fruits like banana, cherimoya, lychee, date palm, pistachio and more; good selection, no plant descriptions. Adding new trees all the time. Also books, grafting supplies and fertilizers. (1970)
❑ Catalog: $2($4 OV), R&W, CAN/OV, bn/cn
⌂ Nursery: All year, W-M
▼ Garden: All year, W-M

Palestine Orchids
Route 1, Box 312
Palestine, WV 26160
(304) 275-4781
Betty & Philip Lower

Plants
Specializes in fragrant **orchids**, and they put "sniffability" first, then beauty and ease of culture. Offers hybrid and species cattleyas, and many other species orchids, each briefly described; they like helping beginners get started and seeing them succeed. (1991)
❑ Catalog: Free, bn
⌂ Nursery: By appointment only
▼ Garden: By appointment only

Carl Pallek & Son Nurseries
P.O. Box 137
1567 Highway 55
Virgil, ON, Canada L0S 1T0
Otto Pallek

Plants
An extensive list of hybrid tea **roses**, as well as floribunda, grandiflora, climbing and a selection of old garden roses, each briefly described. Ships in Canada only, but Americans may pick up orders at the nursery; order 2 weeks early to allow preparation of inspection papers. (1959)
❑ Catalog: Free, SS:11-12,3-4
⌂ Nursery: March-December, M-Sa
▼ Garden: July-September, M-Sa

Palms for Tropical Landscaping
6600 S.W. 45th Street
Miami, FL 33155
(305) 666-1457
Carol Graff

Plants ❧ Seeds
Small nursery offer a wide selection of **palms**; over 130 individual species and varieties listed only by botanical name. They can be shipped in three inch, one or three gallon pots. Seeds are available for some species, but supplies might be limited. Plants not listed might be available. (1983)
❑ Catalog: Long SASE($2 OV), CAN/OV, SS:3-11, $100m, bn
⌂ Nursery: Daily, by appointment only
▼ Garden: Daily, by appointment only

Pampered Plant Nursery
P.O. Box 3
Bourbonnais, IL 60914-0003
(815) 937-9387 (evenings & weekends)
Douglas Armstrong

Plants
Small nursery offfers a selection of hardy **nut and fruit trees**: walnuts, pecans, hickories, filberts, Chinese and Korean chestnuts, persimmons, paw paw, jujube, Japanese raisin tree, kiwis and more. Also offers **tropical fruits** to be grown in greenhouses; all plants briefly described. (1992)
❑ Catalog: Long SASE, SS:3-4,10-11, $10m, cn/bn

Paradise Water Gardens
14 May Street
Whitman, MA 02382
(617) 447-4711, FAX 447-4591 TO/CC $10m
Paul Stetson

Plants ❧ Books ❧ Supplies
Specializes in plants and supplies for **water gardens** -- water lilies, aquatic and bog plants, fish for garden ponds, books on water gardening and supplies for pools and ponds. (1950)
❑ Catalog: $3d, R&W, CAN, SS:4-10, $10m, cn/bn
⌂ Nursery: All year, daily
▼ Garden: May-September, daily

Park Seed Company, Inc.
P.O. Box 46
Highway 254 North
Greenwood, SC 29648-0046
(803) 223-7333 TO/CC $20m
Park Family

Plants ～ Seeds ～ Books ～ Supplies ～ Tools ～ Bulbs
Park offers a huge selection of plants, seeds and bulbs for the home garden-er, many illustrated in color. In addition to **flowers and vegetables**, also sells propagating supplies and some books. The catalog seems to arrive short-ly after Christmas to help fight the post-holiday blues (it works!). (1868)
□ Catalog: Free, R&W, CAN, cn/bn
⌂ Nursery: All year, M-F
▼ Garden: May-July, M-F

Parsley's Cape Seeds

See Silverhill Seeds.

Patio Garden Ponds
7919 S. Shields Blvd.
Oklahoma City, OK 73149
(405) 634-7663, (800) 487-5459, FAX 631-5459
Joe Villemarette, Jr.

Plants ～ Supplies
Offers a full line of **water garden plants and supplies**, including the var-ious water treatments and water filters that they manufacture themselves. The catalog is informative; both plants and products well described. (1986)
□ Catalog: $3d, R&W, CAN/OV, SS:4-10, $30m
⌂ Nursery: All year, daily
▼ Garden: April-November, daily

Theodore Payne Foundation
10459 Tuxford Street
Sun Valley, CA 91352
(818) 768-1802
Dr. Holliday Wagner, Exec. Dir.

Seeds ～ Books
This non-profit foundation honors the work of Theodore Payne, who made **California wildflowers and native plants** admired the world over. They sell seeds by mail and plants at their headquarters; no plant descriptions. They also sell many books on native flora -- including Payne's original 1956 cata-log with good plant descriptions (ask for price). From March to May call their southern California wildflower viewing hotline, (818) 768-3533. (1963)
□ Catalog: $3($5 OV), R&W, CAN/OV, $3m, bn/cn
⌂ Nursery: All year, Tu-Sa
▼ Garden: March-May, Tu-Sa

Peace Seeds

See Seeds of Change.

Peekskill Nurseries
P.O. Box 428
Shrub Oak, NY 10588
(914) 245-5595
L. Gary Lundquist

Plants
Specializes in **ground covers**: pachysandra, vinca minor, euonymus, Baltic ivy and Bar Harbor juniper. Plants well described and sold in quantities from ten to thousands. (1937)
□ Catalog: Free, R&W, CAN, SS:3-11, $20m
⌂ Nursery: March-November, call ahead

Pen Y Bryn Nursery
R.R. 1, Box 1313
Forksville, PA 18616
(717) 924-3377
Charlie Howell

Plants ～ Books ～ Supplies ～ Tools
Specializes in **pre-bonsai plants**, especially oriental varieties; a good selection of conifers and broadleaf trees, Japanese azaleas, and even bamboos and moss, most well described. Also offers some bonsai books and growing supplies, including a rotating work station to make grooming easier. (1946)
□ Catalog: Free, R&W, CAN, $25m, bn/cn
⌂ Nursery: April-December, Sa-Su
▼ Garden: May-October, Sa-Su

Penn Valley Orchids
239 Old Gulph Road
Wynnewood, PA 19096
(215) 642-9822, FAX 649-4230
William W. Wilson

Plants
A very broad selection of **hybrid orchids**, some one of a kind, with some **species orchids** as well; most well but briefly described. Offers a huge list of paphiopedilums, also cattleya alliance and others. Sells antique orchid prints; ask for special list of prints and old journals. (1946)
□ Catalog: $1, R&W, CAN/OV, SS:W, bn
⌂ Nursery: All year, by appointment only

Pense Nursery
Route 2, Box 330-A
Mountainburg, AR 72946
(501) 369-2494
Phillip D. Pense

Plants
Specializes in **berries and table grapes** -- boysenberries, youngberries, raspberries, blackberries, gooseberries, blueberries and grapes. Berry plants available in quantities of 12, 25, 50 and up; single grapevines and elderberries available with orders of berry plants. (1981)
□ Catalog: Free, R&W, SS:10-4, $11m
⌂ Nursery: October-May, call ahead

The Pepper Gal
P.O. Box 23006
Fort Lauderdale, FL 33307-3006
(305) 537-5540, FAX 566-2208
Betty Payton

Seeds
There's a new "Pepper Gal." The new gal, Betty, still has an extensive list of lively **ornamental, hot and sweet peppers**, 200 varieties by her count, with brief plant descriptions. (1978)
□ Catalog: Free($1 OV), CAN/OV

Perennial Plantation   See Arrowhead Alpines.

Perennial Pleasures Nursery
2 Brickhouse Road
East Hardwick, VT 05836
(802) 472-5512, 472-5104
Rachel Kane

Plants ～ Seeds ～ Books ～ Supplies
Offers a very good selection of **perennials and herbs**, but listed with a
twist: they specialize in plants for historical restoration, so their plants
are listed by period of introduction into gardens. Informative catalog; they
sell "period" plant collections, books on restoration, and some garden ornaments and herb products. No plants to CA, Canada or OV. To top it off, they
serve English Cream Teas, and have a Bed & Breakfast. (1980)
❏ Catalog: $2d, SS:4-5,8-10, bn/cn
⌂ Nursery: May-October, Tu-Su
▼ Garden: June-September, Tu-Su

Perpetual Perennials
1111 Upper Valley Pike
Springfield, OH 45504
(513) 325-2451
Anthony & Brenda Pennington

Plants
Perpetual Perennials specialize in starter sized **perennials**, offering about
2,000 varieties by their count. The catalog is a hodge-podge of categories,
with only a sketchy index, but there are lots of good plants if you have the
patience to search for them. Brief plant descriptions. (1988)
❏ Catalog: $2d, R&W, SS:4-11, bn
⌂ Nursery: April-November, M-Sa
▼ Garden: May-July, M-Sa

W. H. Perron & Co., Ltd.
2914 Labelle Blvd., Chomedey
Laval, PQ, Canada H7P 5R9
(514) 332-3619 TO/CC
Dominion Seed Co.

Plants ～ Seeds
The catalog, all in French, offers a broad selection of seeds for garden
annuals, perennials, and vegetables, and **shrubs, bulbs, vines, roses** and
more; all well described and many shown in color. Also sells gardening books
in French, and gardening supplies.
❏ Catalog: $3d, SS:4-5,9-10

Peter Pauls Nurseries
4665 Chapin Road
Canandaigua, NY 14424-8713
(716) 394-7397 TO/CC
James Pietropaolo

Plants ～ Seeds ～ Books
A good selection of **carnivorous plants**, and seeds thereof, as well as
growing supplies, terrarium kits, plant collections and their book, "The
Carnivorous Plants of the World," on how to identify and grow carnivorous
plants from seed to maturity. Featured are Venus's-flytrap, sarracenias,
droseras, darlingtonia and pinguiculas. (1955)
❏ Catalog: Free(3 IRC OV), R&W, CAN/OV, SS:4-11, bn

Phedar Nursery
Bunkers Hill, Romiley
Stockport, Cheshire, England SK6 3DS
(061) 430-3772, FAX same
Will McLewin

Seeds
Here's one of the world experts on **hellebores**, who offers fresh seed from
48 species and varieties, another 10 spotted types by background flower
color, and 6 seed mixtures. Sowing instructions are sent with the seed; he
also sells "Hellebore Notes," very interesting information, $5 ppd. (1989)
❏ Catalog: $2(US Bills), OV, SS:8-9, bn
⌂ Nursery: By appointment only
▼ Garden: Spring, by appointment only

Pickering Nurseries, Inc.
670 Kingston Road (Highway 2)
Pickering, ON, Canada L1V 1A6
(416) 839-2111, FAX 839-4807
Joseph & Joel Schraven

Plants
A very extensive list of **roses** -- hybrid tea, floribunda and many old gar-
den roses, with tables of information for size, ARS rating, fragrance and
color and a section on how to winterize roses in very cold climates.
Many of the roses are shown in color photographs. (1956)
❏ Catalog: $3, R&W, US/OV, SS:2-4,11, $24m
⌂ Nursery: All year, call ahead

Picov Greenhouses
380 Kingston Road East
Ajax, ON, Canada L1S 4S7
(416) 686-2151, (800) 663-0300, FAX 686-2183
Barry Picov

Plants ～ Books ～ Supplies
Offers a broad selection of **aquatic and bog plants**, poolside perennials,
ferns and grasses, water garden supplies and even crabs for your pond. At the
nursery they also sell garden ornaments, plants for bonsai and bonsai tools
and supplies. (1985)
❏ Catalog: Free, R&W, $25m, bn/cn
⌂ Nursery: All year, daily
▼ Garden: April-October, daily

Piedmont Plant Company
P.O. Box 424
807 N. Washington Street
Albany, GA 31703
(912) 435-0766, 883-7029 TO/CC $10m
DuVernet, Jones & Parker

Plants
Offers 60 varieties of **vegetable plants** -- onions, cabbage, lettuce, broccoli, cauliflower, tomatoes, peppers and eggplant, some illustrated in color,
all well described. Can't ship to Western and Gulf states, AK or HI. (1906)
❏ Catalog: Free, R&W, SS:4-6

Pine Heights Nursery
Pepper Street
Everton Hills, QLD, Australia 4053
(07) 353-2761
Donald V. Rix

Bulbs
An Australian source of **spring and summer-blooming bulbs**: alliums, cri-
nums, gingers, haemanthus, hymenocallis, kaempferia, moraea, sprekelia,
veltheimia, watsonia and many more. Also specialize in species and hybrid
hippeastrum (amaryllis), both bulbs and seeds. Brief plant descriptions.
❑ Catalog: $1(US Bills), OV, $25m, bn/cn
⌂ Nursery: All year, call ahead
▼ Garden: September-November, call ahead

Pineapple Place
3961 Markham Woods Road
Longwood, FL 32779
(407) 333-0445
Carol & Jeff Johnson

Plants
Offers a very broad selection of **bromeliads**: aechmeas, billbergias,
nidulariums, neoregelias, dyckias, pitcairnia, tillandsias, guzmanias,
vrieseas and others, listed only by botanical names, but collectors
will know them. They are inspected to ship anywhere.
❑ Catalog: Long SASE, SS:W, $20m, bn
⌂ Nursery: All year, M-Sa, call ahead
▼ Garden: All year, M-Sa, call ahead

Pinecliffe Daylily Gardens
6604 Scottsville Road
Floyds Knob, IN 47119
(812) 923-8113 or 8132, FAX 923-9618
Don & Kathy Smith

Plants
Huge selection of **daylily** cultivars; plants are very briefly described in
informative tables, many are recent or brand new introductions. They have
250,000 seedlings in their trial beds, 2,000 cultivars on display. (1982)
❑ Catalog: $2, R&W, CAN/OV, SS:4-11, $25m
⌂ Nursery: March-October, daily, by appointment only
▼ Garden: June-September, daily, call ahead

Pinetree Garden Seeds
Box 300
New Gloucester, ME 04260
(207) 926-3400, FAX 926-3886
Dick Meiners

Seeds ❧ Books ❧ Supplies ❧ Tools ❧ Bulbs
Catalog offers a very broad selection of **vegetable, flower, herb** and **ever-
lasting** seed in smaller, less expensive packets. Offers a good selection of
heirloom and ethnic vegetables; all well described in an informative catalog.
Also sells organic gardening supplies, spring and fall bulbs, tools and 250
books on gardening and self-sufficiency. (1979)
❑ Catalog: Free, CAN/OV, bn
⌂ Nursery: All year, M-F

Pinky's Plants
P.O. Box 126
442 G Street
Pawnee City, NE 68420
(800) 94-PINKY
Harriett Dokken

Plants
Specializes in **perennials, ornamental grasses, shade plants and ground
covers**, more than 850 kinds in a very informative catalog. Plants are
grouped by growing conditions, so there are several alphabetical sections.
Pinky is testing new plants from several countries for introduction. (1979)
❑ Catalog: $3.50, R&W, bn

Pixie Treasures Miniature Roses
4121 Prospect Avenue
Yorba Linda, CA 92686
(714) 993-6780 TO/CC $20m
Dorothy Crale & Laurie Chaffin

Plants
A huge selection of **miniature roses** -- over 125 varieties, including their
own hybrids. Many are illustrated in the color catalog; all are well de-
scribed, and a number are their own introductions. (1972)
❑ Catalog: $1d, $20m
⌂ Nursery: All year, M-Sa
▼ Garden: April-November, M-Sa

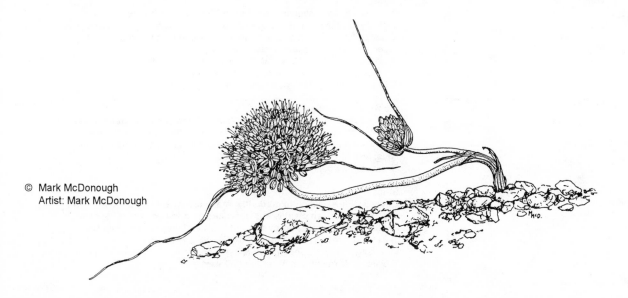

© Mark McDonough
Artist: Mark McDonough

Plant Delights Nursery
9241 Sauls Road
Raleigh, NC 27603
(919) 772-4794
Tony & Michelle Avent

Plants
This catalog has a warning label on it, and it's true, opening the catalog is "highly addictive" -- they offer a broad selection of **perennials**, with particular strengths in hostas, ornamental grasses, asarums, heucheras and pulmonarias; also some dwarf conifers. Good plant descriptions. (1988)
❒ Catalog: $2, SS:3-11, $25m, bn/cn
▼ Garden: March-November, by appointment only

Plant Hideaway
Route 3, Box 259
Franklinton, NC 27525
(919) 494-7178
Nancy Huber

Plants
Someday they'll invent a really effective snail killer, and I'll try growing some **hostas** -- they're wildly popular where snails can't overwinter. Plant Hideaway offers a nice selection of hostas, no plant descriptions. They also offer ferns and other shade plants at the nursery. (1990)
❒ Catalog: Free, SS:5-8, $20m
⌂ Nursery: May-June, September, F-Sa

Plant it Hawaii, Inc.
P.O. Box 388
Kurtistown, HI 96760
(808) 966-6633, FAX 966-6900
Eric Weinert

Plants
Specializes in **tropical fruit trees**: citrus, dwarf citrus, avocados, breadfruit, cherimoya, guavas, loquats, longans, lychees, mangos, starfruit, and seedlings of other unusual fruits, very briefly described. There is a ten plant minimum, only certain plants can be sent to CA, LA and TX. (1978)
❒ Catalog: $1, R&W, CAN/OV
⌂ Nursery: All year, M-F, by appointment only
▼ Garden: All year, M-F, by appointment only

Plant World
St. Marychurch Road
Newton Abbot, Devon, England TQ12 4SE
(0803) 87-2939
Ray & Lin Brown

Seeds
Offers seed of **perennials, alpine and rock garden plants**: aquilegia, digitalis, gentians, lewisias, meconopsis, primulas (including double auriculas), saxifragas, silenes and violas. Please note that they don't sell plants by mail. Visitors to the garden will find a giant floral map of the world.
❒ Catalog: 4 IRC, OV, bn
▼ Garden: All year, daily

Plantasia Cactus Gardens
867 Filer Avenue W.
Twin Falls, ID 83301
(208) 734-7959
LaMar N. Orton

Plants
A new source of **winter hardy cactus**, grown outdoors in Idaho where it sometimes goes down to -20F, and it can go over 100F in the summer. Listed are a very good selection of opuntias, and some cylindropuntia and corynopuntias (chollas) and one coryphantha. (1992)
❒ Catalog: 2 FCS, CAN/OV, SS:4-11, $10m, bn
⌂ Nursery: April-November, Sa, by appointment
▼ Garden: May-June, Sa, by appointment only

Plants of the Southwest
Route 6, Box 11A, Agua Fria
Santa Fe, NM 87501
(505) 471-2212, 438-8888 TO/CC $20m
Gail Haggard

Plants ⌇ **Seeds** ⌇ **Books**
Catalog full of landscaping and cultural information, with the object of suggesting water-saving gardens. Offers seeds of **native trees and shrubs, wildflowers, grasses, cacti and succulents** -- also native **vegetable** seeds and some plants. Informative catalog is $3.50, price list is free. (1977)
❒ Catalog: See notes, R&W, SS: 5-6, bn/cn
⌂ Nursery: April-October, daily; other months, M-F
▼ Garden: May-October, daily

Plants of the Wild
P.O. Box 866
Tekoa, WA 99033
(509) 284-2848, 291-5411, FAX 284-6464
Kathy Hutton, Mgr.

Plants
Broad selection of seedling **Western native trees and shrubs**, all well described with notes on uses. Minimum order is 20 plants of each species and a total of 100 plants; plants are useful for natural landscaping, wildlife cover, erosion control and reclamation.
❒ Catalog: $1, R&W, CAN/OV, SS:spring,fall, $10m, bn/cn
⌂ Nursery: All year, M-F, by appointment only
▼ Garden: Spring, M-F, by appointment only

Pleasant Hill African Violets
Route 1, Box 73
Brenham, TX 77833
(409) 836-9736 TO/CC
Ruth Goeke

Plants ⌇ **Supplies**
"**African violet** leaves and plants, episcia stolons and other **gesneriads**: aeschynanthus, nematanthus and columnea cuttings, and at the moment we have many varieties of episcias." Large selection, brief plant descriptions. Also offer growing supplies. (1980)
❒ Catalog: $1.50, R&W, SS:4-10

Pleasant Valley Glads and Dahlias
P.O. Box 494
Agawam, MA 01001
Gary Adams

Bulbs
Offers a wide selection of **gladiolus**; many are recent introductions and prize winners. Each plant is well described. In addition, a number of **dahlias** are offered, listed by size of bloom and very briefly described.
❒ Catalog: Free ($2 OV), R&W, CAN/OV, SS:3-6, $15m
⌂ Nursery: Call for appointment & directions
▼ Garden: August-frost, by appointment only

Pleasure Iris Gardens
425 East Luna
Chaparral, NM 88021
(505) 824-4299 after 6 pm
Luella Danielson

Plants
A very extensive list of **irises** for collectors, including a number of their own hybrids -- bearded of all types, Japanese and Siberians, aril and arilbred, Louisiana, Sino-Siberian and spuria, oncocylus and regelia species and hybrids -- all briefly described with cultural notes. (1981)
❒ Catalog: $1, SS:7-9
▼ Garden: April, by appointment only

The Plumeria People
P.O. Box 820014
Houston, TX 77282-0014
(713) 496-2352
Mary Helen Eggenberger

Plants ↷ Books ↷ Supplies ↷ Bulbs
Tropical plant specialists: plumerias, bougainvillea, gingers, hibiscus, tender bulbs, flowering vines and shrubs, heliconias and more; a good selection, all very well described. Also books on growing tropical plants, including their "Handbook on Plumeria Culture," and growing supplies. (1981)
❒ Catalog: $2, R&W, CAN/OV, SS:3-10, $12m, cn/bn
⌂ Nursery: All year, M-F, call ahead
▼ Garden: Spring-Summer, M-F, call ahead

Plumtree Nursery
387 Springtown Road
New Paltz, NY 12561
(914) 255-0417
Lee Reich

Plants
Small nursery offers **unusual fruit and vegetable plants**: musk and yellow alpine strawberries, 'Consort' European and clove currants, chuffa and skinless garlic, each well described. They also offer soil testing kits and organic pest controls by mail. (1984)
❒ Catalog: $1, SS:4,10-11
⌂ Nursery: By appointment only

Pond Doctor
HC 65, Box 265
Kingston, AR 72742
(501) 665-2232
Hal Reiss

Plants ↷ Books ↷ Supplies
Offers a nice selection of **water lilies and aquatic plants** and water gardening supplies. The farm, in a rural mountain setting, has 20 ponds filled with water lilies, lotus, koi and goldfish -- it sounds wonderful.
❒ Catalog: $2d, R&W, SS:W, $25m
⌂ Nursery: By appointment only
▼ Garden: May-June, September-October, by appointment only

Pony Creek Nursery
Tilleda, WI 54978
(715) 787-3889 TO/CC
Jenny Schultz

Plants ↷ Seeds ↷ Books ↷ Supplies
Tabloid catalog lists a wide selection of **fruit and nut trees**, ornamental shrubs, berries, flower and vegetable seeds, books, growing supplies and beneficial insects; all well described. Plants best suited to the Midwest; cannot ship to CA. (1950)
❒ Catalog: Free, SS:5-10, cn/bn
⌂ Nursery: April-May, daily; June-October, M-Sa
▼ Garden: Growing area, same hours as nursery

Portable Acres
2087 Curtis Drive
Penngrove, CA 94951
Colin Rigby

Plants
A small nursery specializing in **Pacific Coast Native irises** and beardless **species irises**; a very good selection, each plant briefly described with some cultural information. (1984)
❒ Catalog: Long SASE w/2 FCS, SS:11-4

Porter & Son
P.O. Box 104
1510 E. Washington Street
Stephenville, TX 76401-0104
Alice J. Porter

Seeds ↷ Books ↷ Supplies
A long-time family business offering a good selection of **vegetable and flower** seeds for the South, especially melons, tomatoes and hot peppers; each variety very well described. Also a good selection of gardening tools and supplies, drip irrigation supplies and gardening books. (1912)
❒ Catalog: Free, SS:1-4, $3m
⌂ Nursery: All year, M-F

Porterhowse Farms
41370 S.E. Thomas Road
Sandy, OR 97055
(503) 668-5834, FAX same
Don Howse & Lloyd Porter

Plants
A fine source of **dwarf conifers, trees and shrubs, sedums, sempervivums** and **jovibarbas**, saxifragas and other rock garden plants, Japanese and Siberian iris; a good selection, well described. Also offer "Collector's Cases," boxes of mixed plants by type for various uses, pots for bonsai and alpines, and some potted bonsai and alpine plants. (1979)
❒ Catalog: $4d, R&W, CAN/OV, bn
⌂ Nursery: All year, call ahead
▼ Garden: All year, call ahead

Potterton & Martin
The Cottage Nursery
Moortown Road, Nettleton
Caistor, Lincs., England LN7 6HX
(472) 85-1792
Mr.& Mrs. R. Potterton, Alan Martin

Books ↷ Bulbs
A British bulb specialist offering **dwarf bulbs**, which we would call the "little bulbs" -- a good selection of alliums, anemones, corydalis, crocus, cyclamen, erythronium, fritillaria, species iris, narcissus, oxalis and pleione, among others. Good plant descriptions; some books. (1971)
❒ Catalog: $3(US Bills), US, SS:8-10, bn
⌂ Nursery: Daily, call ahead
▼ Garden: Daily, call ahead

Powell's Gardens
9468 U.S. Highway 70 E.
Princeton, NC 27569
(919) 936-4421
Loleta R. Powell

Plants
A huge selection of **irises**, many **daylilies and hosta**, and a broad selection of perennials, dwarf conifers and some ornamental trees and shrubs; the pages are tightly packed, with only the briefest of descriptions -- a true collectors' list. The gardens look beautiful, too. (1953)
☐ Catalog: $3($5 OV), CAN/OV, bn/cn
⌂ Nursery: All year, M-Sa
▼ Garden: All year, M-Sa

Prairie Grown Garden Seeds
P.O. Box 118
Cochin, SK, Canada S0M 0L0
(306) 386-2737
Jim Ternier

Seeds
A regional seedsman, serving the Canadian prairie provinces and offering **vegetables for short-season growing** (100 frost free days) and a dry climate. All seeds are open-pollinated and grown without chemicals, and quite a few are older varieties. All well described. (1985)
☐ Catalog: $1, US
▼ Garden: July-September, call ahead

Prairie Moon Nursery
Route 3, Box 163
Winona, MN 55987
(507) 452-1362
Alan L. Wade

Plants ∿ Seeds ∿ Books
A good selection of **grasses and wildflowers** for prairie restoration and wild gardens, both plants and seeds, listed by botanical and common name and habitat only, with coded information on germination. Also sells books on prairie gardening. (1983)
☐ Catalog: $2, R&W, CAN, SS:4-5,10-11, bn/cn
⌂ Nursery: All year, by appointment only
▼ Garden: June-August, restored prairie, by appointment only

Prairie Nursery
P.O. Box 306
Westfield, WI 53964
(608) 296-3679, FAX 296-2741 TO/CC
Neil Diboll

Plants ∿ Seeds
A small nursery specializing in **prairie plants and seed, grasses and forbs** (flowering herbaceous plants other than grasses); all plants well described, some color pictures and some line drawings. Also a list of plants to feed birds and butterflies. Sells only seeds overseas. (1974)
☐ Catalog: $3, R&W, CAN/OV, SS:4-6,9-10, $25m, cn/bn
⌂ Nursery: All year, M-F, call ahead
▼ Garden: Dates of nursery tours in catalog

Prairie Ridge Nursery/CRM Ecosystems, Inc.
9738 Overland Road
Mt. Horeb, WI 53572
(608) 437-5245, FAX 437-8982 TO/CC $45m
Joyce Powers

Plants ∿ Seeds
Specializing in **prairie wildflowers, grasses and forbs**, both plants and seeds; plant information given in concise tables. They also sell plant and seed collections for various growing conditions and do consulting on the establishment of low-maintenance erosion-control plantings. (1974)
☐ Catalog: $3d, R&W, CAN/OV, SS:5-6,9-10, bn/cn
⌂ Nursery: M-F, by appointment only
▼ Garden: All year, call ahead

Prairie Seed Source
P.O. Box 83
North Lake, WI 53064-0083
Robert Ahrenhoerster

Seeds
Another company striving to recreate prairie ecosystems and to encourage people to create their own. Offers seed of S.E. Wisconsin **prairie plants**, with very brief information in table form and outlines showing size and form of each plant. They also rent slide sets on prairie plants and restoration.
☐ Catalog: $1, CAN/OV, bn/cn
⌂ Nursery: Write for appointment
▼ Garden: Write for appointment

Prairie State Commodities
P.O. Box 6
Main Street
Trilla, IL 62469
(217) 235-4322 FAX 235-3246
Charles L. Stodden

Seeds ∿ Supplies
Seeds for agriculture, including **open-pollinated corn, alfalfa, clovers, soybeans, buckwheat, sorghum, lawn grasses and cover crops**; also sell grain mills and used seed cleaners, can supply "organically grown" on some items. All items sold in fairly large quantities. (1975)
☐ Catalog: $1, R&W, $5m
⌂ Nursery: All year, M-Sa, call ahead

Prentiss Court Ground Covers
P.O. Box 8662
Greenville, SC 29604
(803) 277-4037 TO/CC $15m
Lesesne & Gene Dickson

Plants
A small family enterprise offers **ground cover plants**: ajuga, cotoneaster, euonymous, ivy, hypericum, liriope, jasmine, daylilies, vincas, sedums and more. Plants offered bare-root or in pots, in quantities of fifty or more; no plant descriptions. (1978)
☐ Catalog: $.25, R&W, SS:4-10, $15m, bn

The Primrose Path
R.D. 2, Box 110
Scottdale, PA 15683
Charles & Martha Oliver

Plants
A broad selection of **perennials**, including rock garden and woodland plants, all well described and with lists of plants for special uses. They have an active hybridization and selection program in phlox, heuchera, tiarella and primula; good selection of primulas, aquilegias, phlox and hardy ferns. No shipping to HI. (1985)
☐ Catalog: $2d, R&W, SS:3-5,9-11, bn/cn
⌂ Nursery: October-March, F-Sa
▼ Garden: April-September, M-Sa, by appointment only

The Propagator's Private Stock
8805 Kemman Road
Hebron, IL 60034
Elaine & Phill King

Plants
A source of new introductions of hardy **shrubs**: selection on their first
list is good but not large. They also run The Wildflower Source, which
offers hardy native orchids, asarums and trilliums, **native woodland plants**
and **hardy ferns**; all plants very well described, with cultural suggestions.
They offer nine trilliums and other charmers for shady acid soil. (1984)
❑ Catalog: $1d, R&W, SS:4-5,9-11, bn

Putney Nursery, Inc.
P.O. Box 265
Route 5
Putney, VT 05346
C. J. & Ruth Gorius

Seeds
Offers seeds of **wildflowers, herbs, perennials and alpines**; the wildflowers
are sold in seed mixes for various growing conditions, as well as seeds of
individual plants. Seed list has no plant descriptions. Also sells Christmas
greens by mail; request Christmas greens brochure separately. (1928)
❑ Catalog: Free, CAN, $10m, bn/cn
⌂ Nursery: April-December, M-Sa
▼ Garden: May-June, September-October, M-Sa

Qualitree Nursery
11110 Harlan Road
Eddyville, OR 97343
(503) 875-4192
Donna Frank

Plants
"We sell one and two year old **conifers and deciduous seedlings** for Christ-
mas tree growers, reforesters and small woodlot owners. We will grow almost
any species on contract." Sells only in quantity. (1981)
❑ Catalog: Free($1 OV), R&W, CAN/OV, SS:11-2, $30m
⌂ Nursery: All year, by appointment only

Railway Design & Landscape Company
4228 Church Street
Parish, NY 13131-9640
(315) 625-4380, FAX same
Donald Weeks

Plants ↝ Supplies
Specializes in **dwarf and semi-dwarf plants** for landscaping garden railways,
one of the hottest fads in garden design; all plants are very well described.
They also offer water garden supplies and watercourses, and miniature wooden
fencing in several styles, and also offer railway design services. (1993)
❑ Catalog: $3d, SS:4-10, $25m, bn/cn

Rainbow Acres
P.O. Box 1362
Avon Park, FL 33825-1362
(813) 382-4449, 382-1011
Donald W. Dittmar

Bulbs
Sells bulbs of **fancy leaf caladiums** by named variety or in mixes of reds,
pinks or whites or mixed colors. No plant descriptions, about 20 varieties
shown in color on their brochure. Ships only to contiguous 48 states. (1978)
❑ Catalog: Free, SS:1-6, $17m

Rainbow Gardens Nursery & Bookshop
1444 E. Taylor Street
Vista, CA 92084-3308
(619) 758-4290, FAX 945-8934 TO/CC
Charles H. Everson

Plants ↝ Books ↝ Supplies
Specializes in **epiphyllums and other rainforest cacti, hoyas, haworthia**;
a large selection. Plants well described, many shown in color photos. Book-
shop has a separate catalog offering a huge selection of books on cacti, suc-
culents, bromeliads, ferns and greenhouse propagation. Bought out California
Epi Center, the greatest nursery name ever! (1977)
❑ Catalog: $2(6 IRC OV), CAN/OV, SS:4-11, $15m, bn/cn
⌂ Nursery: All year, Tu-Sa, by appointment only
▼ Garden: All year, Tu-Sa, by appointment only

Rainbow Tropicals, Inc.
P.O. Box 4038
Hilo, HI 96720
(808) 959-4565, FAX 959-7294
Jules Gervais

Plants
Growers of **tropical plants**, which are shipped bare root, in soil-free media
or as cuttings all over the world: heliconias, gingers, anthuriums, bananas,
and cordylines. A nice selection, each very briefly described. Formerly
Kuaola Farms. (1971)
❑ Catalog: Free, R&W, CAN/OV, bn

Rainforest Flora, Inc.
1927 W. Rosecrans Avenue
Gardena, CA 90249
(310) 515-5200, FAX 515-1177
Paul Isley

Plants
Offers bromeliads, tillandsias, platyceriums, cycads, neoregelia and other
tropical plants. Send long SASE for price list, or $2 for color brochure.
Paul Isley is the author of "The Genus Tillandsia." (1976)
❑ Catalog: See notes, R&W, CAN/OV, $30m
⌂ Nursery: All year, M-Sa
▼ Garden: All year, M-Sa

Rainforest Gardens
13139 - 224th Street, R.R. 2
Maple Ridge, BC, Canada V2X 7E7
(604) 467-4218
Elke & Ken Knechtel

Plants
Specializes in **herbaceous perennials**, especially plants for the shade: this
is British Columbia, don't forget! Offers a good selection of species geran-
iums for sun and shade, hostas, astilbes, ferns, primulas, beardless iris,
native plants, and many others, all very well described. (1986)
❑ Catalog: $2d, US, SS:3-5,9-10, $20m, bn
⌂ Nursery: March-October, Sa, call ahead
▼ Garden: June-August, Sa, call ahead

Rainforest Plantes et Fleurs, Inc.
1550 Rycroft Street
Honolulu, HI 96814
(808) 942-1550, FAX same
Michael Miyashiro

Plants ✑ Seeds
Growers and shippers of **hoyas**; list has good plant descriptions of rare species and hybrid varieties -- they can also provide seeds. (1985)
❑ Catalog: $1d (2 IRC OV), R&W, CAN/OV, $30m, bn
⌂ Nursery: All year, M-Sa
♥ Garden: By appointment only

Rainforest Seed Company
P.O. Box 241
San Jose, Costa Rica 1017
Joe Azaria, Mgr.

Seeds
A seed company which harvests seed from their own 1,500 acre protected rainforest: offers a nice selection of **trees and shrubs**, listed by common and botanical names. Each is very well described, though eventual size is not mentioned; I guess "majestic" = very large! Many would make fine greenhouse plants. You can send a personal check for the catalog. (1981)
❑ Catalog: $5d, R&W, OV, $3m, cn/bn

Raintree Nursery
391 Butts Road
Morton, WA 98356
(206) 496-6400, FAX 496-6465 TO/CC
Sam Benowitz

Plants ✑ Books ✑ Supplies
Offer edible plants, many **fruit and nut** varieties in an informative catalog full of orchard lore, edible landscaping and cultural suggestions. They also offer some ornamental trees and shrubs, grafting and pruning supplies and books on fruit growing and edible landscaping. (1974)
❑ Catalog: Free, R&W, SS:1-4, $10m, cn/bn
⌂ Nursery: Daily, December-May
♥ Garden: June-November, 1st Sa of month, 12-4

Ramona Gardens
2178 El Paso Street
Ramona, CA 92065
(619) 789-6099
Linda Moore

Plants
Offers bearded **irises and daylilies**; a good selection, each well but briefly described. Linda also raises black Arabian horses, who provide her with lots of "free" fertilizer; a symbiotic brace of interests. (1985)
❑ Catalog: $2d ($3 OV), CAN/OV, SS:3-11, $15m
⌂ Nursery: All year, by appointment only
♥ Garden: April-June, by appointment only

Rancho Nuez Nursery

See Coopers Nut House.

Rarafolia
16 Beverly Drive
Kintnersville, PA 18930
(215) 847-8208 TO/CC $30m
Skeeter & Beth Rodd

Plants
Offers a broad selection of **dwarf conifers**, over 400 cultivars, and another 100 cultivars of **Japanese maples**; they also offer 11 European beech cultivars and some companion trees and shrubs. Most of their plants are suited for bonsai or for gardens. No shipping to CA, HI, OR or WA. (1986)
❑ Catalog: $3d, R&W, SS:4-6,9-11, $25m, bn
⌂ Nursery: By appointment only
♥ Garden: May-October, by appointment only

Rare Conifer Nursery
P.O. Box 100
Potter Valley, CA 95469
FAX (707) 462-5936
John Mayginnes

Plants
A new nursery specializing in **conifers**, some of them hard to find; all are seedling grown from seed collected all over the world, and they plan seed collecting expeditions to many countries over the next few years. Offers a good selection of abies, piceas, pinus, larix and many others; each conifer is briefly described with eventual size and country of origin. (1992)
❑ Catalog: Free, R&W, CAN/OV, SS:10-4, $25m, bn
♥ Garden: Spring, Fall, by appointment only

Rare Plant Research
9527 S.E. Wichita
Milwaukie, OR 97222
FAX (503) 652-1471
Burl L. Mostul, PhD.

Plants
Their "primary goal is to research **rare succulents** through botanical exploration...work has been done in Mexico, Costa Rica, Malaysia, Borneo and the US. The sale of propagated plants supports our botanical research and explorations." Adeniums, aloes, euphorbias, jatropas, monadeniums and many others, including a few hardy plants; notes as to source, very brief plant descriptions. (1988)
❑ Catalog: Long SASE ($2 OV), R&W, CAN/OV, $20m, bn
⌂ Nursery: By appointment only

Rare Seed Locators, Inc.
2140 Shattuck Avenue, Drawer 2479
Berkeley, CA 94704
Abdal Singh

Seeds
If you are looking for a **really rare species**, you may send for their "want list" form; they correspond with seed and spore suppliers all over the world, and are eager to hear from wholesale and retail sources of seeds of rare and endangered plants to put them into cultivation and preserve them from extinction.
❑ Catalog: Long SASE (2 IRC OV), CAN/OV

Rasland Farm
NC 82 at US 13
Godwin, NC 28344-9712
(919) 567-2705
Sylvia Tippett

Plants ⟋ Supplies
A good selection of **herb** plants and **scented geraniums**; good but brief
plant descriptions. Also a broad selection of herbal products: teas, pot-
pourri supplies, cooking herbs, wreaths and more. No shipments to HI. (1981)
▢ Catalog: $2.50, SS:4-6, $15m, cn/bn
⌂ Nursery: All year, M-Sa
▼ Garden: May-September, M-Sa

Rawlinson Garden Seed
269 College Road
Truro, NS, Canada B2N 2P6
(902) 893-3051
Bill Rawlinson

Seeds
Catalog offers seeds for a broad selection of **vegetables, some herbs** and
flowers, all very well described. Included is the spotted heritage baking
bean called 'Jacob's Cattle;' it's got to be good! Cultural instructions are
sent with each seed order. (1979)
▢ Catalog: Free

Steve Ray's Bamboo Gardens
909 - 79th Place South
Birmingham, AL 35206
(205) 833-3052
Steve Ray

Plants
Specializes in **hardy bamboos**; 35 varieties listed in the informative cata-
log, all very well described, with many culms shown in b&w photographs.
They have more varieties planted on 50 acres in the country, new varieties
will be available; larger plants can be dug from the country grove. (1976)
▢ Catalog: $2, SS:9-2, bn/cn
⌂ Nursery: All year, by appointment only
▼ Garden: Summer-Fall, by appointment only

Rayner Bros.

See Brittingham Plant Farms.

Reasoner's, Inc.
P.O. Box 1881
2501 - 53rd Avenue East (Bradenton)
Oneco, FL 34264-1881
(813) 756-1881
Bud Reasoner

Plants ⟋ Books
Here's a source for **hibiscus**; not hardy, but the lovely, tender kind that
grows in Florida and Hawaii. They have a very large selection, described only
by letter codes; scionwood also available. Also sell an American Hibiscus
Society book on growing hibiscus, and a book on the history of their 112 year
old nursery business. No plants to AZ, CA or TX. (1881)
▢ Catalog: $1, CAN/OV, SS:W, $25m
⌂ Nursery: All year, daily

Reath's Nursery
County Road 577, Box 247
Vulcan, MI 49892
(906) 563-9777
David Reath

Plants
Offers herbaceous and tree **peonies**, including hybrids of Daphnis, Saunders
and their own. Japanese tree peonies listed by Japanese cultivar name -- a
true collectors' list; catalog has color photographs and good plant descriptions. Have started selling **Siberian iris**, too.
▢ Catalog: $1, SS:9-10

Recor Tree Seed

See Pacific Coast Seed Company.

Red's Rhodies
15920 S.W. Oberst Lane
Sherwood, OR 97140
(503) 625-6331 TO
Dick & Karen Cavender

Plants ⟋ Books
In a change of direction, "Red" now specializes in **vireya rhododendrons** and
pleiones; he has a good selection of species and hybrids, each well des-
cribed. He is actively hybridizing rhododendrons and pleiones, and will be
offering other terrestrial orchids soon. Also sells some books. (1977)
▢ Catalog: Long SASE w/2 FCS, R&W, CAN/OV, SS:W, bn/cn
⌂ Nursery: All year, daily, call ahead
▼ Garden: April-June, call ahead

Redlo Cacti
2315 N.W. Circle Boulevard
Corvallis, OR 97330
(503) 752-2910
Lorne & Lola Hanna

Plants
Good selection of **cacti, succulents** and some **lithops and lewisias**; each
given a good, brief description, many available in more than one size. There
are several pages of detailed cultural information. (1984)
▢ Catalog: $2d, bn
⌂ Nursery: All year, daily, by appointment only

Redwood City Seed Co.
P.O. Box 361
Redwood City, CA 94064
(415) 325-SEED
Craig & Sue Dremann

Seeds ⟋ Books
Old-fashioned open-pollinated **vegetables and herbs**, mostly developed before
1906; unusual varieties, including Oriental types and Native American beans,
corn, hot peppers and squash. These and other "useful" plants are very well
described, with growing hints. Books on plants and organic gardening. (1971)
▢ Catalog: $1($2 OV), R&W, CAN/OV, cn/bn

Regine's Fuchsia Garden
32531 Rhoda Lane
Fort Bragg, CA 95437
Bruce & Regine Plows

Plants
Offer a very large selection of hybrid **fuchsias**, from the old tried and
true to the most recent, and some species fuchsias, each briefly described
and rooted to order. They also offer **orchids**, particularly paphiopedilums,
at the nursery, and will be issuing a list soon. No shipping to HI. (1979)
▢ Catalog: $1, SS:12-6
⌂ Nursery: March-October, W-Su; other months call ahead
▼ Garden: July-October, W-Su

Rhapis Palm Growers
P.O. Box 84
31350 Alta Vista Drive
Redlands, CA 92373
(909) 794-3823 TO
Leland & Anna Hollenberg

Plants
"We offer more than 50 named varieties of **Rhapis excelsa and R. humilis**
palms, imported from Japan -- including variegated and all-green varieties."
Tender plants for indoors or mild climates; some in very short supply. (1976)
❏ Catalog: Long SASE($1 OV), R&W, CAN/OV
⌂ Nursery: All year, by appointment only
▼ Garden: All year, by appointment only

Richardson's Seaside Banana Garden
6823 Santa Barbara Avenue
Ventura, CA 93001
(805) 643-4061
Doug Richardson

Plants
Offers corms of **bananas**, 40 varieties, each very well described for habit
of growth and flavor of fruit, with good cultural information. They also
sell bananas to eat, so you can taste several varieties before investing in
a plant. (1985)
❏ Catalog: $2, R&W, $20m
⌂ Nursery: All year, daily, call ahead
▼ Garden: April-December, daily, call ahead

Richters Herbs
357 Highway 47
Goodwood, ON, Canada L0C 1A0
(416) 640-6677, FAX 640-6641 TO/CC
Otto Richter & Sons, Ltd.

Plants ❧ Seeds ❧ Books ❧ Supplies ❧ Tools
Catalog offers seed and plants of many **herbs, wildflowers and everlast-
ing** flowers, as well as dried herbs and spices, herbal gifts and books and
posters on herbs; ships plants in Canada and by UPS to the US. Over 600 herbs
are well described, with information on culture and traditional uses. (1971)
❏ Catalog: $2($4 OV), R&W, US/OV, SS:4-10, cn/bn
⌂ Nursery: January-October, daily
▼ Garden: January-October, daily

Rider Nurseries
Route 2, Box 78
Farmington, IA 52626
(319) 878-3313 TO/CC
Geri & William Rider

Plants
Specializes in **strawberries**. Also offers asparagus, horseradish, rhubarb,
grapes, raspberries, blackberries and hardy blueberries, some roses, fruit
trees, dwarf fruit trees and ornamental shrubs. Very brief plant descriptions. Offers several "collections" of fruit, berries and roses. (1930)
❏ Catalog: Free, R&W, SS:3-5
⌂ Nursery: March-May, M-Sa, call ahead

Riverbend Orchids
14220 Lorraine Road
Biloxi, MS 39532
(601) 392-2699 TO/CC
Morton Engelberg & James Phillips

Plants ❧ Supplies
List offers a number of **phalaenopsis orchids**, both hybrids and species;
all briefly described. Sold in flasks, community pots and individually when
available.
❏ Catalog: Free, R&W, $25m
⌂ Nursery: All year, M-F, call ahead
▼ Garden: All year, M-F, call ahead

Riverdale Iris Gardens
P.O. Box 524
Rockford, MN 55373
(612) 477-4859
Tracy W. Jennings

Plants
Specializes in dwarf and median **iris** and some aril-median crosses, and
offers a very good selection. The plants are listed by type, and very well
described. Tracy bought the business from Zula Hansen and carries on
with enthusiasm. (1988)
❏ Catalog: $1d, CAN/OV, $10m, SS:7-9
⌂ Nursery: By appointment only
▼ Garden: By appointment only

Riverhead Perennials
5 Riverhead Lane
East Lyme, CT 06333
(203) 437-7828, 447-1558, FAX 437-0342
Tom & Nancy Kalal

Plants
A new source of **perennials**, a good selection of well-established plants,
all very well described. They also sell plants at their Jordan Brook
Nursery, located at 368 Boston Post Road, Waterford, CT.
❏ Catalog: Free, R&W, CAN, SS:3-12, $15m, bn/cn
⌂ Nursery: March-December, daily
▼ Garden: April-November, daily

Riverside Gardens
RR 5
Saskatoon, SK, Canada S7K 3J8
Art Delahey

Bulbs
Offers a nice selection of hybrid Asiatic **lilies**, listed in table format
with information on color, bloom type, height and bloom season. (1968)
❏ Catalog: Free, SS:9-10, $15m
⌂ Nursery: July-October, daily
▼ Garden: July, daily

Rob's Mini-o-lets
P.O. Box 9
7209 County Road 12
Naples, NY 14512
(716) 374-8592
Ralph Robison

Plants
Rob is a hybridizer of miniature **African violets and streptocarpus**, and has
won awards for "best new cultivar" three times. He lists his own
introductions, and some favorites from others: a nice selection, well
described. (1986)
❏ Catalog: $1d, R&W, CAN/OV, SS:W
⌂ Nursery: All year, call ahead
▼ Garden: All year, call ahead

Clyde Robin Seed Co.
3670 Enterprise Avenue
Hayward, CA 94545
(510) 785-0425, FAX 785-6463 TO/CC $5m
Steve Atwood

Seeds
Color catalog offers a broad selection of **wildflower mixes** formulated for various regions and climates, as well as some individual flowers for those who want to make their own mixes: available in packets or in bulk. (1934)
❑ Catalog: $2, CAN/OV, cn
⌂ Nursery: All year, M-F

Robinett Bulb Farm
P.O. Box 1306
Sebastopol, CA 95473-1306
(707) 829-2729
Jim Robinett

Seeds ⬿ Bulbs
Seeds and bulbs of **West Coast native bulbs**: alliums, brodiaea, calochortus, species lilies, fritillaries, erythroniums and others; also alstroemerias. Bulbs are nursery-grown and, because the business is small, may be in short supply; new list every August. Minimum overseas order is $20. (1983)
❑ Catalog: Free, R&W, CAN/OV, SS:9-11, $10m, bn/cn

Robyn's Nest Nursery
7802 N.E. 63rd Street
Vancouver, WA 98662
(206) 256-7399 TO/CC $50m
Robyn Duback

Plants
A small nursery offering a good selection of **perennials and rock garden plants**, particularly astilbes, ferns, species geraniums, epimediums, ornamental grasses, and many hostas; each plant well described, some of them hard to find. Charming animal illustrations, too! Cannot ship to TX. (1982)
❑ Catalog: $2d, CAN, SS:spring,fall, bn/cn
⌂ Nursery: April-June, September, Th-Sa
▼ Garden: May-September, call ahead

Rock Spray Nursery
P.O. Box 693
Depot Road
Truro, MA 02666
(508) 349-6769 TO/CC
Kate Herrick

Plants
Suppliers of **heaths and heathers**; they offer a number of species and varieties of erica and calluna, briefly described by size, color and season of bloom, habit and color of foliage. They sell other seaside plants at the nursery. (1981)
❑ Catalog: $1, R&W, CAN, $4m, bn
⌂ Nursery: Summer, daily; November-March, by appointment only
▼ Garden: April-October, daily

Rocknoll Nursery
7812 Mad River Road
Hillsboro, OH 45133
(513) 393-5545, FAX 393-8159 TO/CC $25m
Jan & Jerry Hopkins

Plants ⬿ Seeds
Catalog offers a broad selection of **rock garden plants**, shade and native plants, some dwarf evergreens and flowering shrubs and perennials; very brief plant descriptions. Features hostas, dianthus, phlox, penstemons, irises, daylilies, epimediums. Separate seed list available. (1928)
❑ Catalog: $1, R&W, SS:3-6,9-11, bn/cn
⌂ Nursery: March-June, September-November, by appointment
▼ Garden: April-May, by appointment only

Rocky Meadow Orchard & Nursery
360 Rocky Meadow Road N.W.
New Salisbury, IN 47161
(812) 347-2213
Ed Fackler

Plants ⬿ Supplies
Specializes in apples, pears and Oriental pears, cherries and plums and rootstocks for these **fruit trees**; some trees available as espaliers. Also does custom propagation, sells grafting supplies and does consultation on fruit culture. All fruit varieties are chosen with flavor as first priority. Informative catalog. (1975)
❑ Catalog: $1, R&W, SS:11-4
⌂ Nursery: All year, daily, by appointment only
▼ Garden: August-October, by appointment only

Rollingwood Gardens
21234 Rollingwood Trail
Eustis, FL 32726
(904) 589-8765
Elizabeth & Jeff Salter

Plants
Elizabeth's the niece of Bill Munson of Wimberlyway, so you know she's into **daylilies**. Jeff hybridizes large flowered forms, and Elizabeth does miniature and small flowered forms; also offers many recently introduced daylilies; all well to briefly described, some color photos. (1989)
❑ Catalog: $3d, R&W, CAN/OV
⌂ Nursery: All year, by appointment only
▼ Garden: April-June, by appointment only

Lon J. Rombough
13113 Ehlen Road
Aurora, OR 97002-9746
(503) 678-1410

Plants
Lon is a fruit researcher who grows many old and new varieties of **wine and table grapes**, and will provide cuttings; you won't see many of these varieties on other lists. Can't ship to Canada or overseas, but will provide the names of sources in Canada and other countries. Send $1 and a long SASE for the list. Formerly listed as Lon's Oregon Grapes.
❑ Catalog: See notes

Ronniger's Seed Potatoes
Star Route, Road 73
Moyie Springs, ID 83845
FAX (208) 267-3265
David Ronniger

Plants ∾ Books ∾ Supplies ∾ Tools
Offer a broad selection of **seed potatoes**: 27 early-maturing varieties, 36 that mature in mid-season, 21 late-maturing varieties and 15 varieties of fingerlings, and samples of several dozen new and heirloom varieties. Each variety is well described by color, flavor, disease resistance and keeping qualities. They also offer sunchokes, garlic, onions, shallots, cover crop seed, books and growing supplies, as well as lots of information. No shipping to AK. (1988)
❒ Catalog: $1, R&W, SS:2-6,9-11, $7m

Roris Gardens
8195 Bradshaw Road
Sacramento, CA 95829
(916) 689-7460, FAX 689-5516
Joseph B. Grant II, Mgr.

Plants
Offer a good selection of tall bearded **irises**, all shown in color photographs, with good plant descriptions.
❒ Catalog: $2d, CAN/OV, SS:6-9, $10m
⌂ Nursery: All year, M-F
▼ Garden: Late March-early May, daily

Rose Acres

See Roses & Wine.

Rose Hill Herbs and Perennials
Route 4, Box 377
Amherst, VA 24521
Joan Rothemich

Plants
A good selection of **herbs, perennials, scented geraniums and everlastings**; plants briefly to well described. They also offer several collections of plants for salad lovers and vinegar makers. Good selections of rosemary, mints, basils, sages and thymes.
❒ Catalog: $2, SS:4-6,9-10, $15m

The Rose Ranch
P.O. Box 10087
240 Cooper Road
Salinas, CA 93912
(408) 758-6965
Alice & Anthony Hinton

Plants
Alice Hinton and her son Anthony offer old garden and some modern **roses**; most of the older roses are own-root, some old roses and the modern roses are budded onto virus-free understock. They are also hybridizing and hope to introduce their own roses soon. A good selection, all well described. (1992)
❒ Catalog: $3($4 OV), CAN/OV, $9m
⌂ Nursery: All year, daily, call ahead
▼ Garden: April-October, daily, call ahead

Rosehill Farm
P.O. Box 188
Gregg Neck Road
Galena, MD 21635
(410) 648-5538 TO/CC
Patricia Berlen

Plants
Color catalog offers a good selection of **miniature roses** and several collections; each plant well described. Also sells books on rose growing. (1977)
❒ Catalog: Free, R&W
⌂ Nursery: All year, M-Sa
▼ Garden: May, September, M-Sa

The Rosemary House
120 South Market Street
Mechanicsburg, PA 17055
(717) 697-5111 TO/CC
Bertha Reppert

Plants ∾ Seeds ∾ Books ∾ Supplies
Offers a good selection of **herb** seeds, some herb plants, **scented geraniums** and herbal gifts, supplies, teas, books, cards and kitchenware. Also cookbooks, herb garden plans, and makings for potpourri. Bertha's written a nice book, "Growing & Using Herbs with Confidence." Can't ship plants to CA, or mints to MT. (1968)
❒ Catalog: $2($4 OV), R&W, CAN/OV, SS:4-6,9-11, $10m, cn
⌂ Nursery: All year, Tu-Sa
▼ Garden: April-October, Tu-Sa

Roses & Wine
6260 Fernwood Drive
Shingle Springs, CA 95682
(916) 677-9722, FAX 676-4560
Barbara Procissi

Plants
Barbara Procissi has taken over the shipping of **roses** for Muriel Humenick of Rose Acres in Diamond Springs; Rose Acres will still sell roses on site by appointment (916) 626-1722. They offer a good selection of old garden roses, as well as some miniatures and modern roses -- no descriptions. Muriel has a large number of stock plants, and will propagate desired plants to order.
❒ Catalog: Long SASE

Roses by Fred Edmunds

See Edmunds' Roses.

Roses of Yesterday & Today
803 Brown's Valley Road
Watsonville, CA 95076-0398
(408) 724-3537 or 2755, FAX 724-1408
Patricia Stemler Wiley

Plants
Informative catalog lists a broad selection of "old garden" and many other types of **roses** -- modern shrubs, climbers and ramblers, hybrid teas and species roses; plants very well described, some illustrated in b&w photos. Included are rare, highly perfumed and some very hardy roses. (1946)
❒ Catalog: $3, CAN/OV, SS:1-5, $20m
⌂ Nursery: All year, M-F
▼ Garden: May-June, daily

Roses Unlimited
Route 1, Box 587
Laurens, SC 29360
(803) 682-2455 or 9112, FAX 682-2455
Bill Patterson & Pat Henry

Plants
Offers old garden, species, miniature and modern shrub and hybrid **roses**,
container grown on their own roots, listed only by type and name, with date
of introduction. A good selection, but some sell out very quickly, so order
early. No shipping to AZ, CA, or OR. (1988)
❒ Catalog: Long SASE, SS:3-5, $30
⌂ Nursery: All year, M-Sa, by appointment only
▼ Garden: May-June, September, by appointment only

Roslyn Nursery
211 Burrs Lane
Dix Hills, NY 11746
(516) 643-9347, FAX 484-1555 TO/CC
Philip Waldman

Plants ～ Books
Collectors' list of hybrid and species rhododendrons, evergreen and decidu-
ous azaleas, dwarf conifers, ferns, hollies, pieris, kalmias, other **orna-
mental shrubs and trees and perennials**; each plant briefly described, with
some color photographs. A large selection of choice landscape plants. (1980)
❒ Catalog: $3($5 OV), CAN/OV, SS:4-6,9-12, $20m, bn
⌂ Nursery: All year, M-Sa; April-May, Tu-Su
▼ Garden: April-May, growing area, daily

Roswell Seed Co.
P.O. Box 725
115-117 South Main Street
Roswell, NM 88202-0725
(505) 622-7701, FAX 623-2885 TO/CC $5m
Walter & Jim Gill

Seeds ～ Supplies
Regional seed company sells **vegetables, grains and grasses** for New Mexico,
Arizona, Oklahoma and Utah. Hybrid and open-pollinated crops well described;
offers a good variety of grains, cover crops, native grasses, some annual
flowers and growing supplies. (1900)
❒ Catalog: Free, R&W, CAN/OV, $5m
⌂ Nursery: All year, M-Sa

Doug & Vivi Rowland
200 Spring Road, Kempston
Bedford, England MK42 8ND

Seeds
The ultimate collectors' list -- thousands of **cactus, succulents** and other
desert plants, densely typed in tiny print; no descriptions, enough to make
your heart sing! They specialize in desert plant seed of all kinds, including seed of **carnivorous plants** and **South African bulb** seed. (1971)
❒ Catalog: Free, OV, bn

Jim & Irene Russ - Quality Plants
HCR 1, Box 6450
Buell Road (Ono)
Igo, CA 96047
(916) 396-2329 (evenings)
Jim & Irene Russ

Plants
A broad selection of **sedums, sempervivums, jovibarba and heuffeliis**,
well described in a tightly packed collectors' list, with good cultural information (they are happy to help with specific cultural questions). Most
of the plants are hardy to Zone 1 and come in many colors, leaf textures,
even cobweb types. They also offer four **lewisias**. (1956)
❒ Catalog: 2 FCS, SS:5-9, $10m, bn
⌂ Nursery: April-September, by appointment only
▼ Garden: April-June, by appointment only

Rust-En-Vrede Nursery
P.O. Box 753
Brackenfell, South Africa 7560
(27 21) 981-4515, FAX 981-0050
A. M. Horstmann

Seeds ～ Books ～ Bulbs
Rus-En-Vrede Nursery has recently changed hands, but still offers seeds and
bulbs of **South African bulbous plants** for serious collectors. They issue an
Amaryllid list and a Liliaceae and Iridaceae list; some of the seed is viable
for only a short period, and orders are held until seed is ripe and ready to
plant. A nice selection with no plant descriptions. Books on SA bulbs, too.
❒ Catalog: $1(US Bills), OV, $30m, bn

© Robyn's Nest Nursery
Artist: Mari Eggebraaten

St. Lawrence Nurseries
RD 5, Box 324
Potsdam-Madrid Road
Potsdam, NY 13676
(315) 265-6739
Diana & Bill MacKentley

Plants ❧ Books
A broad selection of organically grown cold-hardy **fruit and nut** trees, other **edible fruits, berries** and scionwood; plants very well described, with comparative tables on hardiness, fruit color and harvest season in an informative catalog. Books on fruit culture and pruning tools available.
❒ Catalog: $1, R&W, CAN/OV, SS:4,11, cn/bn
⌂ Nursery: M-Sa, call ahead
▼ Garden: Call ahead

Salt Spring Seeds
P.O. Box 33
Ganges, BC, Canada V0S 1E0
Dan Jason

Seeds
Offers only their own organically grown and untreated **vegetable** seeds, they "feature high protein, good tasting and high-yielding crops...all adapted to northern climates." Each variety is well described, all open-pollinated.
❒ Catalog: $2, US/OV
▼ Garden: Summer, by appointment only

Saltspring Primroses
2426 W. 47th Avenue
Vancouver, BC, Canada V6M 2N2
John Kerridge

Seeds
Offer seeds of **primroses**: primulas and polyanthus, including auriculas, gold-laced polyanthus and their own lines of Wanda hybrids, polyanthus hybrids and the Cowichan strain. They also offer seed of Asiatic species and candlabras; a good selection with very brief plant descriptions.
❒ Catalog: $1, US/OV

Sandy Mush Herb Nursery
Route 2, Surrett Cove Road
Leicester, NC 28748
(704) 683-2014 TO $25m
Fairman & Kate Jayne

Plants ❧ Seeds ❧ Books
A very broad selection of **herbs**, both seeds and plants, all very well described in a lovely italic hand. Also offers scented geraniums, irises, ornamental grasses, primulas, heathers, other perennials, herbal gifts and books. Many salvia, lavender, rosemary, thyme, mints and more. (1978)
❒ Catalog: $4d, R&W, CAN, $10m
⌂ Nursery: All year, Th-Sa, call ahead
▼ Garden: May-October, Th-Sa, call ahead

Santa Barbara Orchid Estate
1250 Orchid Drive
Santa Barbara, CA 93111
(805) 967-1284, (800) 553-3387, FAX 683-3405
Anne P. Gripp

Plants ❧ Supplies
Offers many **cymbidium orchids** which do well outdoors in coastal California, as well as a good selection of **species orchids** -- too many to list! Each is briefly described; get out your orchid reference books. (1957)
❒ Catalog: Free, R&W, CAN/OV, SS:W
⌂ Nursery: All year, daily
▼ Garden: March-April, daily

Santa Barbara Water Gardens
160 E. Mountain Drive
Santa Barbara, CA 93108
(805) 969-5129
Stephne Sheatsley

Plants ❧ Books ❧ Supplies
A nice selection of water lilies, lotus, **aquatic and bog plants**, each briefly described, with some cultural information. Also sells books and supplies for water gardening and does local water garden design, construction and maintenance. (1980)
❒ Catalog: $2d, SS:W, $30m, cn/bn
⌂ Nursery: All year, W,Sa
▼ Garden: June-August, W,Sa

Savory's Gardens, Inc.
5300 Whiting Avenue
Edina, MN 55439-1249
(612) 941-8755, FAX 941-3750 TO/CC $35m
Arlene, Robert & Dennis Savory

Plants
Around 200 varieties of **hosta** are listed. Plants are briefly but well described, some illustrated in color; many are their own introductions. They also have a daylily list. They grow over 800 varieties of hosta at the nursery, and sell ground covers and other perennials there. (1946)
❒ Catalog: $2($3 OV), R&W, CAN/OV, SS:4-5,9-10, $25m, bn
⌂ Nursery: April-October, M-Sa
▼ Garden: June-August, M-Sa

Saxton Gardens
1 First Street
Saratoga Springs, NY 12866
(518) 584-4697
Stanley Saxton

Plants ❧ Bulbs
A broad selection of **daylilies, lilies and hostas** -- their own "Adirondack" daylily introductions, which are extra-hardy, as well as others. Plants well described, some illustrated in color; also sell daylily seed. Send a long SASE for the lily or hosta lists; they aren't in the daylily catalog. (1945)
❒ Catalog: $.50, R&W, CAN, SS:4-5,9-10, $10m
⌂ Nursery: May-October, daily, call ahead
▼ Garden: July-August, call ahead

John Scheepers, Inc.
P.O. Box 700
Bantam, CT 06750
(203) 567-0838 FAX 567-5323
Jan Ohms, Pres.

Bulbs
Issues catalog offering spring and summer-blooming **bulbs**, many illustrated in color, all well described: daffodils, tulips, crocus, species narcissus, alliums, and other spring bulbs, amaryllis and hybrid lilies. (1910)
❒ Catalog: Free

S. Scherer & Sons
104 Waterside Road
Northport, NY 11768
(516) 261-7432, FAX 261-9325 TO/CC $20m
Robert W. Scherer

Plants ❧ Supplies
Offers everything necessary for a garden pool or pond: **water lilies** and
other **aquatic plants**, fiberglass pools, pool liners, fountain heads, pumps
and low-voltage garden lights. Everything briefly but well described. (1907)
❒ Catalog: $1d, R&W, CAN/OV, SS:4-12, $20m, cn/bn
⌂ Nursery: All year, daily
▼ Garden: April-October, daily

Schild Azalea Gardens & Nursery
1705 Longview Street
Hixson, TN 37343
(615) 842-9686
Joseph E. Schild, Jr.

Plants
Specializes in species **azaleas**, both from the Southeastern US and Asia,
and evergreen azaleas,as well as **kalmias**, species and hybrid **rhododen-
drons**; all well described. There are also Joe's own crosses between
species and hybrid azaleas; these are limited in quantity.
❒ Catalog: $1d, SS:9-5, $25m
⌂ Nursery: By appointment only
▼ Garden: By appointment only

Schipper & Co.
P.O. Box 7584
Greenwich, CT 06836-7584
(203) 625-0638, (800) 877-8637, FAX 862-8909
Timothy P. Schipper

Bulbs
Offers a nice selection of spring flowering bulbs, but specializes in "Color-
blends," **bulbs** chosen to complement each other when planted in groups.
The pictures look quite smashing, so it works! No schipping to HI. (1947)
❒ Catalog: Free, R&W, $50m

Schreiner's Gardens
3625 Quinaby Road N.E.
Salem, OR 97303
(503) 393-3232, (800) 525-2367, FAX 393-5590
Schreiner Family

Plants
Color catalog describes tall bearded **irises**, "lilliputs" and intermediates
and offers a number of collections; a very large selection. All plants very
well described, with cultural advice. Can't ship to FL or HI. (1925)
❒ Catalog: $4d($10 OV), R&W, CAN/OV, SS:7-9, $10m
▼ Garden: Late May, daily

Schulz Cactus Growers
1095 Easy Street
Morgan Hill, CA 95037
(408) 683-4489
Ernst Schulz

Plants
A broad selection of **cactus** -- coryphanthus, echinocereus, escobaria, fero-
cactus, matucana, neochilenia, neoporteria, parodia and others, as well as a
very large number of mammillaria; listed by botanical name only. (1979)
❒ Catalog: Free, bn
⌂ Nursery: All year, call ahead
▼ Garden: All year, call ahead

F. W. Schumacher Co., Inc.
36 Spring Hill Road
Sandwich, MA 02563-1023
(508) 888-0659, FAX 833-0322
Donald H. Allen

Seeds ❧ Books
A very broad selection of seeds of **trees, shrubs, conifers, rhododendrons**
and **azaleas** listed by botanical and common name, and with geographical
source where important. Offers species maples, birches, dogwoods, cotoneas-
ters, crabapples, hollies, species roses, viburnums and much more; they will
also buy seed of rare plants. Some books on propagation, too. (1926)
❒ Catalog: Free, R&W, bn

Scottsdale Fishponds
6915 E. Oak Street
Scottsdale, AZ 85257
(602) 946-8025
Scott A. Butler

Plants ❧ Supplies
Offers a good selection of **water lilies, lotus, and aquatic and bog plants**,
each well described. They also sell supplies for water gardening and pond
making, and fish, snails and frogs to keep your pond clean. (1986)
❒ Catalog: $2, R&W, CAN/OV, SS:W, $10m, cn/bn
⌂ Nursery: All year, daily, by appointment only
▼ Garden: March-October, by appointment only

Scotty's Desert Plants
P.O. Box 1017
Selma, CA 93662-1017
(209) 891-1026 TO/CC $20m
Mel & Mike Scott

Plants
Offers a good selection of **cacti and succulents**, many types, as well as
epiphyllums: plants are briefly described, many illustrated in b&w or color
photographs. Formerly Altman's Specialty Plants. (1974)
❒ Catalog: $1, SS:W, $15m, cn/bn

Sea-Tac Dahlia Gardens
20020 Des Moines Memorial Drive
Seattle, WA 98198
(206) 824-3846
Louis Eckhoff

Plants
Collectors' list of **dahlias**, with information given in a compact table;
a good selection, especially for cut flowers. Louis's a dahlia hybridizer,
his hybrids begin with 'Sea' -- as in 'Sea-Miss' -- a real winner. (1978)
❒ Catalog: Long SASE, SS:2-4, $10m
⌂ Nursery: March-October, daily
▼ Garden: August-September, daily

Seagulls Landing Orchids
P.O. Box 388
Glen Head, NY 11545
(516) 367-6336 TO/CC $20
Shell Kanzer

Plants ⚘ Supplies
Original hybridizers of "**Mini Cats**" and "**Compact Cats**" -- cattleya hybrids which will bloom two to four times a year and make good houseplants. They also sell **cattleyas, dendrobiums and phalaenopsis** and other hybrids; all plants well described. Supplies and a special potting mix, too. (1972)
❑ Catalog: $2.50($3 OV), R&W, CAN/OV, SS:4-11
⌂ Nursery: All year, Tu-Su, 1702 Route 25A (Laurel Hollow)
▼ Garden: All year, Tu-Su

Seaside Banana Garden

See Richardson's Seaside Banana Garden.

R. Seawright
P.O. Box 733
Carlisle, MA 01741-1747
(508) 369-2172
Robert D. Seawright

Plants
A collectors' list of **daylilies** -- both diploids and tetraploids -- a wide selection; each very well described, with good general cultural advice. Also offers **hostas**, some available in specimen size. (1976)
❑ Catalog: $1d($2 OV), R&W, CAN/OV, SS:5-9, $15m
⌂ Nursery: May-August, daily
▼ Garden: June-July, daily (134 Indian Hill Road)

The Seed Shop
Tongue River Stage
Miles City, MT 59301-9804
Barbara Linaburg

Seeds
Small company offering seeds of **cactus** of many kinds and a few **succulents** -- a nice selection. Also lists seeds of some endangered or threatened species, habitat-collected from privately owned land and in compliance with all federal and state laws. Plants well described. (1988)
❑ Catalog: $2, CAN/OV, bn/cn

Seedalp
P.O. Box 282
Meyrin, Geneva, Switzerland CH 1217
FAX (022) 782-2741
André Kroner

Seeds
Broad selection of **alpine and rock garden plants**, listed by botanical name; color descriptions and brief information in French, key to symbols in French, German and English. Anemones, aquilegias, campanulas, dianthus, digitalis, gentians, hellebores, irises, poppies, primulas, pulsatillas. (1981)
❑ Catalog: 2 IRC, R&W, OV, $35m, bn

Seeds Blum
Idaho City Stage
Boise, ID 83706
FAX (208) 338-5658
Jan Blum

Seeds ⚘ Books
Pronounced "Seeds Bloom" -- their catalog is informative, fun and helpful. They offer a number of **vegetables, annuals and perennials** for various conditions, and advice on saving seed. Unlike most seed companies, they insist that you order your seeds **the summer before you need them**, many months in advance of planting. They also sell books -- "fireside friends." (1982)
❑ Catalog: $3, CAN/OV, cn/bn

Seeds of Alaska
P.O. Box 3127
Kenai, AK 99611
(907) 262-5267, FAX 262-3755
Richard L. Baldwin

Seeds
Small seed company offers seed of **Alaskan wildflowers**, and arctic and subarctic species from Siberia and the Russian Far East. I've seen only a brief list, but they say the next catalog will have good plant descriptions.
❑ Catalog: $3, CAN/OV, bn

Seeds of Change
621 Old Santa Fe Trail, #10
Santa Fe, NM 87501
(505) 438-8080, FAX 438-7052 TO/CC $10m
Nina Simons, Pres.

Seeds
Seeds of Change has merged with Peace Seeds, and offers a huge selection of **organically grown and open-pollinated vegetable** seed, including heirloom and Native American varieties. Over 500 varieties, including grains, herbs and garden flowers. All varieties are very well described for flavor, with growing suggestions. (1989)
❑ Catalog: $3d, R&W, CAN/OV

Seeds Trust

See High Altitude Gardens.

Seeds West Garden Seeds
P.O. Box 1739
El Prado, NM 87529
(505) 758-7268
Ken & Jane Winslow

Seeds
Specializes in **heirloom, hybrid and rare vegetable** varieties for difficult Western growing conditions: drought and poor soils. Some are native crops in the Southwest, such as blue and black corns. All varieties are well described, with growing suggestions. Also offers some flower seed. (1988)
❑ Catalog: $3, CAN/OV

Select Seeds -- Antique Flowers
180 Stickney Hill Road
Union, CT 06076-4617
(203) 684-9310, FAX same
Marilyn Barlow

Seeds ⚘ Books ⚘ Supplies
This seed business grew out of an old garden restoration project; they specialize in **old-fashioned and heirloom perennials** found in cottage and period gardens, chosen for fragrance and flower cutting. Plants are well described -- there's not a "cultivar" on the list. Also offers books on traditional flower gardening, and old-fashioned cedar garden markers. (1986)
❑ Catalog: $2, R&W, CAN, cn/bn

Sequoia Nursery -- Moore Miniature Roses
2519 E. Noble Avenue
Visalia, CA 93292
(209) 732-0190 TO/CC $20m
Ralph S. Moore

Plants
Specializes in the hybrids of Ralph Moore, a **miniature rose** pioneer who
has patented over 150 cultivars. Color catalog introduces new varieties once
a year and offers popular varieties for sale, including an increasing number
of old garden roses and some new non-mini Moore hybrids. (1937)
❒ Catalog: Free, R&W
⌂ Nursery: All year, daily
▼ Garden: March-June, September, daily

Sevald Nursery
4937 3rd Avenue South
Minneapolis, MN 55409
(612) 822-3279
Alvin Sevald

Plants
Offers herbaceous **peonies** in a color catalog; they grow around 400
cultivars and list about 40 each year. You could send your "want list" to
find out if they have varieties you're looking for. Phone early in the
morning or in the evening. (1986)
❒ Catalog: $1d, R&W, CAN/OV, SS:8-10
⌂ Nursery: June, daily, call ahead
▼ Garden: June, daily, call ahead

Shackleton's Dahlias
30535 Division Drive
Troutdale, OR 97060
(503) 663-7057
Linda Shackleton

Plants
"Heavy emphasis is placed on quality exhibition **dahlia** varieties -- we
carry newer show varieties." A real collectors' list; information given in
concise tables, with only color descriptions. (1981)
❒ Catalog: 1 FCS, CAN/OV, SS:12-5
⌂ Nursery: August-October 10, daily, call ahead
▼ Garden: September, daily, call ahead

Shady Hill Gardens
821 Walnut Street
Batavia, IL 60510
FAX (708) 879-5679
Chuck Heidgen

Plants ❧ Seeds
Sells over 1,100 **geraniums and pelargoniums**, some of their own hybridiz-
ing. The selection is huge -- plants of all sizes, indoor and out, scented,
variegated, stellar, ivy, dwarf and a nice selection of species geraniums.
All plants briefly but well described; also sells geranium seed. Nursery is
also open on Sundays during April-June and Thanksgiving-Christmas. (1974)
❒ Catalog: $2d, R&W, SS:3-5,10-11, cn
⌂ Nursery: All year, M-Sa; see notes
▼ Garden: All year, glasshouses, M-Sa

Shady Oaks Nursery
112 10th Avenue S.E.
Waseca, MN 56093
(507) 835-5033, FAX 835-8772
Clayton & Gordon Oslund

Plants ❧ Books
This nursery specializes in **plants which grow well in shade** and offers a
good selection of perennials, ferns, wildflowers, ground covers, hostas and a
number of shrubs which tolerate shade; each plant well described. Also offers
several books on shade gardening and woodland plants. Can ship only bare
root hostas to CA. (1979)
❒ Catalog: $1, R&W, SS:4-5,9-10, bn/cn
⌂ Nursery: April-October, M-F, call ahead; Sa by appointment
▼ Garden: June-September, call ahead

Shanti Bithi Nursery
3047 High Ridge Road
Stamford, CT 06903
(203) 329-0768 FAX (203) 329-8872
Jerome Rocherolle

Plants ❧ Books ❧ Supplies ❧ Tools
Importers of finished **bonsai**, some quite mature; various plants are shown
in color photos. Also sell bonsai tools, pots, supplies and books and two
styles of stone lantern. (1970)
❒ Catalog: $3, SS:W, $35m, bn
⌂ Nursery: All year, M-Sa
▼ Garden: May-September, M-Sa

Sharp Brothers Seed Company
P.O. Box 140
Healy, KS 67850
(316) 398-2231, FAX 398-2220
Gail Sharp

Seeds
Sharp Bros. specializes in **native grasses and wildflowers for the midwest**:
offers a good variety of grasses, and various wildflower mixes for prairie
plantings, and also a number of lawn grasses including buffalo grass. (1958)
❒ Catalog: $5, R&W, CAN/OV, cn/bn

Sheffield's Seed Co., Inc.
273 Route 34
Locke, NY 13092
(315) 497-1058, FAX 497-1059
Rick Sheffield

Seeds ❧ Books
Seed company specializing in seeds of woody plants: **conifers, ornamental
trees and shrubs, and species roses**, over 1,000 species altogether, including some **perennials and herbs**. Plants are listed only by botanical
name, with no descriptions. Minimum seed order is 2 grams per species, with a
$2 handling charge per order. Also sells some books on propagation. (1978)
❒ Catalog: Free, R&W, CAN/OV, bn
⌂ Nursery: All year, M-F

Shein's Cactus
3360 Drew Street
Marina, CA 93933
(408) 384-7765
Rubin & Anne Shein

Plants

A collectors' list of **cactus and succulents** by botanical name; no descriptions, but a large selection of rare and unusual plants. Offered are copiapoa, coryphanthas, echinocereus, lobivia, gymnocalycium, parodia, rebutia, sulcorebutia, weingartia, haworthias and many mammillarias; all plants seed-grown or nursery-propagated. (1977)
❑ Catalog: $1d, SS:2-10, $20m, bn
⌂ Nursery: March-November, call ahead
▼ Garden: May-July, call ahead

Shelldance Nursery
2000 Highway 1
Pacifica, CA 94044
(415) 355-4845, FAX 355-4931 TO/CC
Michael Rothenberg & Nancy Davis

Plants ⬿ Books ⬿ Supplies

Offer a nice selection of **bromeliads**, primarily tillandsias, in a collectors' list; no plant descriptions. They suggest sending a "want list," as sizes and varieties available change so rapidly. Sell aechmea, billbergia, guzmania, neoregelia, nidularium, vriesea and many tillandsias. Also sell some books and supplies. (1976)
❑ Catalog: $1, R&W, CAN/OV, bn
⌂ Nursery: All year, M-F
▼ Garden: All year, M-F

Shepard Iris Garden
3342 W. Orangewood Avenue
Phoenix, AZ 85051
(602) 841-1231 TO/CC $20m
Don & Bobbie Shepard

Plants

A collectors' list offers a very large selection of tall bearded, aril and arilbred, Louisiana, spuria and median **irises**; each plant briefly described with useful cultural notes. (1969)
❑ Catalog: 2 FCS, CAN, SS:7-10
⌂ Nursery: April; by appointment only in other months
▼ Garden: April, open daily

Shepherd Hill Farm
200 Peekskill Hollow Road
Putnam Valley, NY 10579
(914) 528-5917, FAX 528-8343
Gerry Bleyer

Plants

Gerry Bleyer fell in love with rhododendrons in our very own Golden Gate Park, so he's got to be a nice guy! He offers a good selection of cold hardy **rhododendrons and azaleas** for the East and Midwest, and some **kalmias** and **pieris**; all plants well described. No shipping to AZ, CA, OR or WA. (1985)
❑ Catalog: Free, R&W
⌂ Nursery: All year, call ahead
▼ Garden: May, call ahead

Shepherd's Garden Seeds
6116 Highway 9
Felton, CA 95018
(408) 482-6910, (203) 482-3638 TO/CC $15m
Renee Shepherd

Seeds

European **vegetables, salad and herb varieties** for the cooking gardener and collections of seeds for various cuisines: Italian, French, Oriental and Mexican. Each vegetable is lovingly described, with cultural information and recipes. Also sells annual, everlasting and edible flowers, growing supplies and "fresh from the garden cookbooks." Easterners can order catalogs from 30 Irene Street, Torrington, CT 06790. (1983)
❑ Catalog: $1, R&W, CAN, cn/bn
⌂ Nursery: All year, M-F, call ahead

Sherry's Perennials
P.O. Box 39
Cedar Springs, ON, Canada N0P 1E0
(519) 676-4541
Sherry Godfrey

Plants

Offers a good selection of hardy **perennials and herbs**, with good plant descriptions and cultural information, and suggestions for plant combinations. (1986)
❑ Catalog: $4d, SS:4-5,9, $20m, bn/cn
⌂ Nursery: April-October, W-M
▼ Garden: April-October, W-M

Sherwood's Greenhouses
P.O. Box 6
Sibley, LA 71073
(318) 377-3653
Sherwood Akin

Plants

Small nursery sells a selection of **unusual fruits**: mayhaws (hawthorne), jujubes, pawpaw, keriberry, citrange and other citrus, chinknut and goumi. Among the more common fruits are hardy kiwis, pears, grapes and blackberries; all plants very briefly described on one page. No shipping to CA or FL.
❑ Catalog: Long SASE, SS:12-2
⌂ Nursery: All year, M-Sa, call ahead
▼ Garden: Spring, M-Sa

Shooting Star Nursery
444 Bates Road
Frankfort, KY 40601-9446
(502) 223-1679
Sherri Evans, Mgr.

Plants ⬿ Seeds

Specializes in "nursery grown plants native to regions east of the Rocky Mountains, including **forest, prairie and wetland plants** and seeds." Each plant and its habitat are well described; they also offer a number of wildflower seed mixes, and do consulting on habitat restoration. Plants shipped to CA, OR or WA must be bare-root. (1989)
❑ Catalog: $2d($4 OV), CAN/OV, SS:4-10, $10m, cn/bn
⌂ Nursery: May-October, M-Sa, call ahead

R. H. Shumway Seedsman
P.O. Box 1
Route 1, Whaley Pond Road
Graniteville, SC 29829
(803) 663-9771, FAX 663-9772 TO/CC $15m
J. Wayne Hilton

Seeds
Catalog offers a very good selection of open-pollinated **vegetables, annual**
and **perennial** flowers, green manure crops, **fruit trees and berries**,
illustrated with old-style line art. Also offers growing supplies. (1870)
❐ Catalog: Free ($2 OV), R&W, CAN, SS:1-5
⌂ Nursery: All year, M-F

Siegers Seed Co.
8265 Felch Street
Zeeland, MI 49464
(800) 962-4999, FAX (616) 772-0333
Richard L. Siegers

Seeds
Offers a wide selection of **vegetable** seed, both hybrid and open-pollinated,
and herbs as well. All seeds sold in bulk; minimum seems to be based on size
of seed. Also offers some growing supplies and seeders. (1957)
❐ Catalog: Free, R&W, CAN
⌂ Nursery: All year, M-F

Silvaseed Company, Inc.
P.O. Box 118
317 James Street
Roy, WA 98580
(206) 843-2246, FAX 843-2239
David & Mike Gerdes

Plants ∿ Seeds
Sell seed of **Pacific Northwest conifer species**; minimum order is one pound
of seed. List includes abies, chamaecyparis, pinus, pseudotsuga, sequoia,
picea, thuja and tsuga species; no plant descriptions. They do custom seed
collecting and seed stratification; sell seedling conifers in bulk. (1968)
❐ Catalog: $1d, R&W, CAN/OV, bn/cn
⌂ Nursery: All year, M-F, call ahead

Silver Springs Nursery
HCR 62, Box 86
Moyie Springs, ID 83845
(208) 267-5753
James Kramer

Plants
Offers a number of **native plants as ground covers**: Arctostaphylos uva-ursi,
Ceanothus prostratus, Cornus canadensis, Gaultheria ovatifolia, Linnaea bore-
alis and Mahonia repens; each plant is well described. Offers Red German
garlic also, very cold hardy for northern gardens. (1987)
❐ Catalog: $.50d, R&W, SS:4-10, $10m, bn/cn

Silverhill Seeds
18 Silverhill Crescent
Kenilworth, Cape, South Africa 7700
(021) 762-4245, FAX 797-6609
Rachel Saunders

Seeds
Formerly Parsley's Cape Seeds, Silverhill specializes in seeds of South
African plants: **geraniaceae, ericaceae, proteaceae, carnivorous plants,**
succulents, bulbous plants, as well as annuals, perennials and ornamental
shrubs and trees. Large selection, no plant descriptions. (1953)
❐ Catalog: $1d, R&W, OV, bn

Singers' Growing Things

See Northridge Gardens.

Sir Williams Gardens
2852 Jackson Boulevard
Highland, MI 48356
(313) 887-4779, 533-1827, FAX 889-2466
William G. Toll, IV

Plants
Sir William is a hybridizer of **daylilies and iris**: he also offers **hostas**.
His iris are tall bearded, median bearded, reblooming and Siberian.
Plants are listed in concise tables. He claims to offer generous bonuses,
and says he ships two year field grown plants. (1988)
❐ Catalog: $2d ($3 OV), R&W, CAN/OV, SS:4-9
⌂ Nursery: April-September, M-Sa
▼ Garden: July-August, by appointment only

Siskiyou Rare Plant Nursery
2825 Cummings Road
Medford, OR 97501
(503) 772-6846
Baldassare Mineo

Plants ∿ Books
A collectors' catalog of **alpine and rock garden plants** offers about 1,500
plants, with rarer items available in small quantities; all very well described with cultural information. Fall supplement with plants for fall planting. Also sells books on alpine and rock garden plants, and Baldassare has
a color encyclopedia of alpine plants coming from Timber Press. (1964)
❐ Catalog: $2d ($5 OV), CAN, SS:W, bn
⌂ Nursery: All year, M-F, by appointment only
▼ Garden: April-May, by appointment only

Sisters' Bulb Farm
Route 2, Box 170
Gibsland, LA 71028
(318) 843-6379
Celia Jones & Jan Jones Grigsby

Bulbs
This business was started by the grandmother of the Jones sisters; they offer
"heirloom" **daffodils** only, varieties introduced before 1940, a nice selec-
tion, briefly described. Also sell several other spring bulbs. (1918)
❐ Catalog: Free, R&W, CAN, SS:6-11, $25m
▼ Garden: March, by appointment only

Anthony J. Skittone

See GreenLady Gardens.

Skolaski's Glads & Field Flowers
4821 County Highway Q
Waunakee, WI 53597
(608) 836-4822 TO/CC
Stan & Nancy Skolaski

Bulbs
Offer **gladiolus, pixiolas, hybrid lilies** and other summer-blooming bulbs,
mostly plants suitable for cut flowers. Each variety is very well described.
They also offer collections of bulbs. (1967)
❐ Catalog: Free, R&W, CAN/OV, SS:2-6
⌂ Nursery: All year, M-Sa, call ahead
▼ Garden: August, M-Sa, call ahead

Skyline Nursery
4772 Sequim-Dungeness Way
Sequim, WA 98382
Herb Senft

Plants
Small nursery offers a good selection of **perennials, alpines and rock garden plants**: anemones, aquilegias, astilbes, campanulas, dianthus, gentians, hellebores, heucheras, penstemons, saxifrages, sisyrinchiums, violets and grasses. No plant descriptions. (1985)
❒ Catalog: $2, SS:3-6, $20m, bn
⌂ Nursery: All year, Tu-Sa
▼ Garden: June-October, Tu-Sa

Sleepy Hollow Herb Farm
568 Jack Black Road
Lancaster, KY 40444-9306
(606) 792-6183, (800) 726-1215
Steve & Julie Marks

Plants ⚬ Seeds
Offers a wide selection of organically grown **herb plants** and perennials, each very well described; good choices of lavenders, scented geraniums, mints, rosemary, salvias and thymes, among others. Also some seeds of culinary herbs, everlastings and herb teas and other herbal items. No shipping to HI. (1984)
❒ Catalog: $1, R&W, CAN, SS:3-11, $10m, cn/bn
⌂ Nursery: March-December, Tu-Sa

Slocum Water Gardens
1101 Cypress Gardens Boulevard
Winter Haven, FL 33884-1932
(813) 293-7151, FAX 299-1896 TO/CC $25m
Peter D. Slocum

Plants ⚬ Books ⚬ Supplies
Color catalog offers a wide selection of **water lilies and lotus**, aquatic and bog plants and aquarium plants, all well described. Also offers growing supplies and books for water gardening. (1938)
❒ Catalog: $3, R&W, CAN/OV, SS:4-10, $25m
⌂ Nursery: All year, M-Sa
▼ Garden: May-October, M-Sa

Smith Nursery Co.
P.O. Box 515
Charles City, IA 50616
(515) 228-3239
Bill Smith

Plants ⚬ Seeds
A good selection of **ornamental shrubs and trees** in small sizes. The list I received had a jumble of common and botanical names -- dogwoods, linden, elderberries, lilacs, euonymus, sumacs, birch, locust, species maples, viburnums, poplars and willows, among others; no plant descriptions. Seed, too.
❒ Catalog: Free, R&W, CAN, SS:1-6,9-12, cn
⌂ Nursery: All year, M-Sa, call ahead

Winn Soldani's Fancy Hibiscus(R)
1142 S.W. 1st Avenue
Pompano Beach, FL 33060-8706
(305) 782-0741
Winn Soldani

Plants
Offers a good selection of **hibiscus**, the tropical kind, all grafted and some shown in a color brochure; all briefly described. Winn encourages you to send your "wish list," he grows more than he lists, and knows many other sources. No shipping to CA. (1986)
❒ Catalog: $2, CAN/OV, $25m
⌂ Nursery: All year, by appointment only
▼ Garden: All year, by appointment only

Sonoma Antique Apple Nursery
4395 Westside Road
Healdsburg, CA 95448
(707) 433-6420 TO/CC $10m
Carolyn & Terry Harrison

Plants
Offer old English and American cider **apples**, and other varieties for cooking or eating, a good selection. Will select trees suitable for espalier or train them for you through their affiliate, Arbor & Espalier. They have added more fruits: antique and Oriental pears, figs, peaches and plums.
❒ Catalog: $2d, R&W, SS:1-4, $10m
⌂ Nursery: January-April, Tu-W,F-Sa; all year, W

Sonoma Grapevines
1919 Dennis Lane
Santa Rosa, CA 95403
(707) 542-5510, FAX 542-4801
Rich Kunde

Plants
A source of **varietal wine, raisin and table grafted grapevines**, grafting scions and rootstocks; you have to start your vineyard on a scale of at least 25 plants of a variety or have like-minded neighbors. Chardonnay, semillon, cabernet sauvignon, merlot, pinot noir and chenin blanc from excellent sources. (1972)
❒ Catalog: Long SASE, R&W, CAN/OV, SS:1-6, $25m
⌂ Nursery: All year, M-Sa

Sorum's Nursery
18129 S.W. Belton Road
Sherwood, OR 97140
(503) 628-2354
Glenn Sorum

Plants
Offer large leaf, dwarf and small leaf **rhododendrons** and **pieris**; the list groups plants by type and color, with no descriptions. They offer about 100 cultivars, most in several sizes. Also offer several varieties of **figs** from the old Willamette Fig Gardens.
❒ Catalog: Long SASE

Soules Garden
5809 Rahke Road
Indianapolis, IN 46217
(317) 786-7839
Clarence Soules

Plants
I sometimes wonder if anyone grows anything but daylilies and hosta! Yet their popularity means there are lots of fans: Soules Nursery offers a good selection of new and recently introduced **daylilies** and **hostas**, all plants well to briefly described. Ferns and perennials available at the nursery.
❒ Catalog: $1d, SS:4-9, $10m
⌂ Nursery: May-August, W-Sa, call ahead
▼ Garden: May-August, W-Sa, call ahead

Sourdough Iris Gardens
109 Sourdough Ridge Road
Bozeman, MT 59715
Maurine K. Blackwell

Plants
Offers hardy older, often hard-to-find, varieties of tall bearded, inter-
mediate and dwarf **irises**; plants briefly described, prices very reason-
able.
❑ Catalog: Long SASE, R&W, SS:7-8, $6m
⌂ Nursery: June-August, by appointment only
▼ Garden: June, by appointment only

South Cove Nursery
P.O. Box 615
Yarmouth, NS, Canada B5A 4B6
(902) 742-3406
David & Carla Allen

Plants
Offers a good selection of **herbs and perennials**; the owner is a garden
columnist, so the plant descriptions are very informative. They'll ship
all over Canada except to the Yukon and Northwest Territories. (1985)
❑ Catalog: $1, SS:5-6, $12m, bn/cn
⌂ Nursery: April-August, daily
▼ Garden: April-August, daily

Southern Exposure
35 Minor Street (at Rusk)
Beaumont, TX 77702
(409) 835-0644, FAX 835-5265 TO/CC $25m
Bob Whitman

Plants
Offers a huge selection of **cryptanthus**: 300 hybrids from Europe, Australia,
the Orient and the US, as well as Brazilian species. Also sells aroids, bro-
meliads, platyceriums, rhipsalis, epiphyllums and philodendrons, and many
variegated plants. Very brief plant descriptions. (1981)
❑ Catalog: $5d, R&W, CAN/OV, SS:W, bn
⌂ Nursery: April-October, daily, by appointment only
▼ Garden: April-October, daily, by appointment only

Southern Exposure Seed Exchange(R)
P.O. Box 158
North Garden, VA 22959
(804) 973-4703, FAX same TO/CC
Jeff McCormack

Seeds ॐ Books ॐ Supplies
Not a seed exchange in the swapping sense, this is a seed company offering
many **heirloom and open-pollinated vegetables**, a broad selection in a very
informative catalog with good variety descriptions and cultural information.
Also offered are herbs, grains, gourds, annual flowers and sunflowers, and
books, growing and seed saving supplies. An offshoot, Seed Shares(tm) sells
endangered varieties to be sure that they don't disappear forever. (1982)
❑ Catalog: $3d, R&W, CAN

Southern Plants
P.O. Box 232
Semmes, AL 36575
Don Whiddon

Plants
A small nursery which specializes in native and unusual plants for the
Southeast: **azaleas and rhododenrons, hollies, magnolias, conifers**, and a
nice selection of flowering shrubs and trees. Plants briefly described.
❑ Catalog: $1.50d, R&W, SS:4-10, $25m, bn
⌂ Nursery: All year, Sa-Su, by appointment only

Southern Seeds
The Vicarage, Sheffield
Canterbury, New Zealand 8173
NZ 318-3814
Malvern Anglican Parish

Seeds
Specializes in **alpine and rock garden plants of New Zealand**, collected from
the scree and tussock-grassland of the Waimakariri Catchment. Plants listed
by botanical name only; list of reference books on New Zealand plants is
included. Hebes, celmisias, coprosmas, fuchsias, schizeilemas, more. (1982)
❑ Catalog: $5(US Bills), OV, NZ$25m, bn
⌂ Nursery: By appointment only
▼ Garden: November-February, by appointment only

Southern Seeds
P.O. Box 2091
Melbourne, FL 32902-2091
(407) 727-3662 TO
Wae & Kathy Nelson

Seeds ॐ Books
A source of **open-pollinated vegetables** for really hot climates; they offer
grain, amaranth, beans, Cuban squash, carrots, Hawaiian sweet corn, gourds,
eggplant, lettuce, okra, onions, peas, tomatoes and peppers. But that's not
all -- also bananas, chayote, jicama, papaya, passionfruit, peanuts and
roselle. All very well described in an informative catalog. (1987)
❑ Catalog: $1, CAN/OV, $3m

Southmeadow Fruit Gardens
15310 Red Arrow Highway
Lakeside, MI 49116
(616) 469-2865
Theo Grootendorst

Plants ॐ Books
Offers a huge selection of **fruit trees**, many of them antique varieties --
apples, pears, peaches, plums, cherries, grapes, gooseberries, even medlars;
no descriptions. Sells a detailed reference guide to antique fruit varieties
for $9 (the price list is free); offers "conservation fruits" for wildlife,
and under the name Grootendorst Nurseries sells a wide variety of rootstocks
for fruit trees.
❑ Catalog: See notes, OV, SS:10-5, $15m
⌂ Nursery: All year, M-F, call ahead

Southwestern Exposure
10310 East Fennimore
Apache Junction, AZ 85220
(602) 986-7771
Leonard & Bernice Bruens

Plants ⬙ Seeds ⬙ Supplies
Specialize in larger-sized arid land plants, and seeds of **southwestern native plants**; they also offer special soil mixes for cactus, and will search among other Arizona nurseries for plants on your "want list." A nice selection, all plants well described; some may be habitat collected. (1990)
☐ Catalog: 2 FCS, R&W, cn/bn

Southwestern Native Seeds
P.O. Box 50503
Tucson, AZ 85703
Sally & Tim Walker

Seeds
Collectors' list of about 385 species of **Western, Southwestern and Mexican natives** "for gardens, nurseries, rock gardens, landscaping, botanical gardens and for many other uses." Information on type, outstanding qualities, size, hardiness and rarity are given in concise tables; many seeds are habitat-collected, listed by state of origin. (1975)
☐ Catalog: $1, CAN/OV, $11m, bn

Spangle Creek Labs
W. 2802 Depot Springs Road
Spangle, WA 99031
William & Carol Steele

Plants
Talk about specialization: Spangle Creek Labs sells only laboratory grown seedlings of **cypripediums** -- four species, each very well described and with detailed growing instructions. These are best for experienced wild-flower growers or rock gardeners. (1990)
☐ Catalog: $2, CAN/OV, SS;2-11, $10m, bn

Spring Hill Nurseries Co.
6523 North Galena Road
Peoria, IL 61632
Foster & Gallagher, Inc.

Plants ⬙ Bulbs
Color catalog offers a broad selection of **perennials, flowering shrubs, ground covers and some roses, summer-blooming bulbs and house-plants**, all glowingly described. No shipping to AK or HI. (1849)
☐ Catalog: Free, SS:2-5,9-11, cn/bn

Springvale Farm Nursery
Mozier Hollow Road
Hamburg, IL 62045
(618) 232-1108
Will & Jeanne Gould

Plants ⬙ Supplies ⬙ Tools
This nursery, which also advertises as "Avid Gardener(TM)," offers a nice selection of **rock garden plants, dwarf conifers and shrubs** for bonsai and small gardens, as well as **ground covers and perennials**. All plants container-grown and well described; they also sell bonsai supplies and tools and bird houses and feeders. No plants shipped to AK, AZ, CA or HI. (1980)
☐ Catalog: $2, SS:3-11, $25m, bn/cn
⌂ Nursery: April-September, Sa, call ahead
❦ Garden: April-September, Sa, call ahead

Springwood Pleiones
35, Heathfield
Leeds, England LS16 7AB
(0532) 61-1781
Ken Redshaw

Bulbs
Small family business specializing in **pleione species and cultivars**; offers about sixteen, each briefly described by color and growth habit. Catalog gives good cultural information, too. (1986)
☐ Catalog: $1 or 2 IRC, OV, SS:12-1, £50m, bn
❦ Garden: March-May, by appointment only

Spruce Gardens
RR 2, Box 101
Wisner, NE 68791-9527
(402) 529-6860
Calvin Reuter

Plants
Offers a broad selection of **tall bearded irises**, about 1,000 cultivars, with a few median bearded irises as well, all very briefly described. (1987)
☐ Catalog: $1d, CAN/OV, SS:7-8, $10m
⌂ Nursery: May-June, daily
❦ Garden: May-June, daily

Squaw Mountain Gardens
36212 S.E. Squaw Mountain Road
Estacada, OR 97023
(503) 630-5458
Joyce Hoekstra, Janis & Arthur Noyes

Plants
A broad selection of **sedums, sempervivums** and some **arachnoideums, calcareums, ciliosums, jovibarbas, mamoreums and tectorums**; all briefly described with general cultural instructions. They have added some perennials, ground covers, hardy ferns, dwarf evergreens, azaleas and hardy ivy. (1983)
☐ Catalog: Free, R&W, CAN/OV, SS:3-9, $15m, bn
⌂ Nursery: January-October, M-F, call ahead
❦ Garden: April-August, call ahead

Stallings Nursery
910 Encinitas Boulevard
Encinitas, CA 92024
(619) 753-3079
Dale Kolaczkowski, Mgr.

Plants ⬙ Bulbs
Hold your breath -- hibiscus, jasmines, gingers, ornamental grasses and bamboos, lilies, heliconias, bananas, palms, abutilons and bougainvilleas. They grow about 1,000 **tropical and subtropical plants**; all well described with growing suggestions. A collector's feast! (1945)
☐ Catalog: $3d(US$5 CAN), CAN, SS:1-11, $30m, bn
⌂ Nursery: All year, daily except Dec 25-Jan 1 & rainy days
❦ Garden: All year, same days as nursery

Stanek's Garden Center
2929 - 27th Avenue East
Spokane, WA 99223
(509) 535-2939
Tim & Steve Stanek

Plants
Offers a wide selection of **hybrid roses**, including floribundas, grandifloras, climbers and standard tree roses, all briefly described with ARS
ratings. They also offer table grapes, raspberries, hardy kiwis, semi-dwarf
fruit trees, nut trees, gladiolus and tuberous begonias. (1913)
❐ Catalog: Free, SS:4-5
⌂ Nursery: All year, daily; July-August, M-Sa

Starhill Forest Arboretum
Route 1, Box 272
Petersburg, IL 62675
Guy & Edie Sternberg

Seeds
Guy & Edie Sternberg are private collectors of **oaks** who offer seed acorns
of species and hybrid oaks in their collection, as well as mixed packets of
acorns from the oaks around Lincoln's tomb, a surprise packet and a sampler
of oaks for your area. They also offer seed of some companion trees and
shrubs, all of them interesting. No plant descriptions. (1976)
❐ Catalog: Long SASE, R&W, SS:10-12, $5m, bn
▼ Garden: Spring, Fall, by appointment only

Stark Bro's Nurseries & Orchards Co.
P.O. Box 10
Louisiana, MO 63353-0010
(314) 754-5511, FAX 754-5290 TO/CC
Clay Logan, Pres.

Plants ⚘ Supplies
This firm -- made famous by the 'Delicious' apples they developed many years
ago -- offers **fruit trees, grapes, ornamental trees and shrubs and roses** in
a color catalog, including good plant descriptions and some cultural hints.
Lots of mouth-watering pictures of pies! (1816)
❐ Catalog: Free, R&W, SS:2-5,10-12, cn
⌂ Nursery: February-December, M-Sa

Steele Plant Company
P.O. Box 191
212 Collins Street
Gleason, TN 38229
(901) 648-5476
Ken Sanders

Plants
They offer eleven varieties of **sweet potato** plants, yam plants and other
vegetable plants such as onions, cabbage, brussels sprouts, broccoli and
cauliflower. Plants are available in quantities from a dozen to hundreds.
Can't ship to CA. (1952)
❐ Catalog: 2 FCS, SS:4-6

Arthur H. Steffen, Inc.
P.O. Box 184
Fairport, NY 14450
(716) 377-1665, FAX 377-1893
Arthur Steffen, Jr.

Plants
A large wholesale grower of **clematis**, sells well-rooted plants of over 200
varieties by mail order if you order several plants. Catalog gives very good
cultural and pruning information and shows many species and cultivars in
color; be sure to ask for the mail order price list with the catalog. (1949)
❐ Catalog: $2, R&W, CAN, SS:10-5, $30m, bn

Stewart Orchids, Inc.
P.O. Box 550
3376 Foothill Road
Carpinteria, CA 93013-3053
(805) 684-5448, FAX 566-6609 TO/CC $10m
Ned Nash, Mgr.

Plants ⚘ Books ⚘ Supplies
Color catalog of **hybrid orchids**, also special lists of paphiopedilums,
cattleyas and phalaenopsis; a broad selection, all plants well described.
They also offer several "orchid-of-the-month" plans, orchid growing supp-
lies and orchid books. (1926)
❐ Catalog: $2, R&W, CAN/OV
⌂ Nursery: All year, M-Sa
▼ Garden: Sales area, M-Sa

© Siskiyou Rare Plant Nursery
Artist: Baldassare Mineo

Stigall Water Gardens
7306 Main Street
Kansas City, MO 64114
(816) 822-1256
Trent & Pam Stigall

Plants ⟋ Supplies
Early in this century the Missouri Botanic Garden was the world center of water lily culture and hybridization, so it feels good to list an aquatic nursery in Missouri. Stigall Water Gardens offers a good selection of **water lilies and other aquatic plants** and all the supplies you'll need. (1990)
❒ Catalog: $3d, R&W, CAN/OV, SS:4-9, $25m, bn/cn

Stock Seed Farms, Inc.
28008 Mill Road
Murdock, NE 68407-2350
(402) 867-3771, (800) 759-1520, FAX 867-2442
Stock Family

Seeds
Offers seed of **prairie wildflowers and grasses native to the Midwest**; all plants are well described in a pamphlet which contains good information on how to get started. They also sell wildflower mixes and literature. (1958)
❒ Catalog: Free, R&W, cn/bn

Stoecklein's Nursery
135 Critchlow Road
Renfrew, PA 16053
(412) 586-7882
Marc & Carol Stoecklein

Plants
This nursery offers a very good selection of plants for use in shade and woodlands: **daylilies, hostas, ornamental grasses, ivy, irises** and other **perennials**. Each plant is briefly described, with information on culture and use in the landscape. (1977)
❒ Catalog: $1d, R&W, SS:4-9, bn/cn
⌂ Nursery: March-November, Tu-Sa, call ahead
▼ Garden: May-September, Tu-Sa, call ahead

Stokes Seed Company
P.O. Box 548
Buffalo, NY 14240
(416) 688-4300 FAX (716) 695-9649 TO/CC
Wayne Gale

Seeds ⟋ Supplies
This large Canadian company publishes a very informative catalog aimed at commercial farmers and growers, but also sells smaller packets to home gardeners; each plant is well described, with a lot of cultural information. They offer a huge selection of **vegetable and flower** seeds, some available precision-sized or pelleted, and some supplies. Canadian customers should write to Box 10, St. Catharines, ON, Canada L2R 6R6. (1881)
❒ Catalog: Free, R&W, CAN/OV, bn/cn
▼ Garden: July-August, M-F, trial gardens, call ahead

Story House Herb Farm
Route 7, Box 246
Murray, KY 42071
(502) 753-4158 TO/CC
Cathleen Lalicker & Judy Taylor-Clark

Plants
Offers nearly a hundred varieties of **herbs**, selected to perform well in the kitchen garden. All are certified organically grown, and well described; there is a concise cultural instructions chart. They also offer several collections for specific culinary uses. No shipping to HI or WA. (1990)
❒ Catalog: $2d, SS:3-5,9-10, $16m
⌂ Nursery: April-May, F-Sa, other times by appointment

Strong's Alpine Succulents
P.O. Box 2264
Flagstaff, AZ 86003-2264
(602) 526-5784
Shirley Strong

Plants
Shirley Strong lives at 7,000 feet in the mountains of Arizona, so her **sempervivums and jovibarbas** are very hardy; she offers about a hundred varieties with good, brief descriptions -- there's even a sheet of leaf shapes and sizes for the very selective. (1989)
❒ Catalog: Long SASE, CAN/OV, SS:6-9, $15m, bn/cn
⌂ Nursery: June-October, by appointment only
▼ Garden: June-July, by appointment only

Stubbs Shrubs
23225 S.W. Bosky Dell Lane
West Linn, OR 97068
(503) 638-5048
Arthur & Eleanor Stubbs

Plants
Small nursery specializes in newer hybrid **evergreen azaleas** -- Kurume, Satsuki, Gable, Glenn Dale, Beltsville Dwarfs, Back Acres, Robin Hill, Linwood Hardy, Harris, North Tisbury and Greenwood; plants well described in an informative catalog. Offers about 400 varieties. (1977)
❒ Catalog: $2d, R&W, $25m
⌂ Nursery: All year, call ahead
▼ Garden: Spring, daily, call ahead

Succulenta
P.O. Box 480325
Los Angeles, CA 90048
(213) 933-1552 or 8676
Deborah Milne & Lykke Coleman

Plants
Collectors' lists of **cactus and succulents**, including rare haworthias, euphorbias and caudiciforms; plants briefly described in their lists of new offerings. No longer publish a catalog, but send periodic lists; you can always send a "want list." Plants are nursery-propagated. (1978)
❒ Catalog: $1, SS:3-10, bn

Alex Summerville
RD 1, Box 449
Glassboro, NJ 08028
(609) 881-0704
Alex Summerville

Plants
Offers a broad selection of **gladiolus**; new varieties from well-known hybridizers and many favorites both new and old, including some miniatures and collections for cutting and show; larger quantities at wholesale prices.
❒ Catalog: Free($2 OV), R&W, CAN/OV, SS:2-5
▼ Garden: Mid-July-August, call ahead

Sunburst Bulbs C.C.
P.O. Box 183
Howard Place, Cape, South Africa 7450
(021) 531-9829, FAX 531-3181 TO/CC $20m
Waldo Van Essen

Bulbs
Offers indigenous **bulbs from southern Africa**, all nursery propagated; a very nice selection, most shown in color and briefly described. Bulbs are shipped with instructions on how to adapt them to your conditions. (1987)
❒ Catalog: $1(US Bills), US/OV, SS:5-7, $20m, cn/bn
⌂ Nursery: January-November, M-F
▼ Garden: January-November, M-F

Sunlight Gardens
Route 1, Box 600-A
Hillvale Road
Andersonville, TN 37705
(615) 494-8237
Andrea Sessions & Marty Zenni

Plants
Specializes in nursery-propagated **wildflowers of southeastern and northeastern North America**; a nice selection, very well described, and with the easy ones pointed out. Also offers collections for special conditions. No shipping to AZ, CA, OR or WA. (1984)
❒ Catalog: $3, R&W, SS:9-5, $15m, bn
⌂ Nursery: All year, call ahead
▼ Garden: Spring-Fall, call ahead

Sunnybrook Farms Nursery
P.O. Box 6
9448 Mayfield Road
Chesterland, OH 44026
(216) 729-7232 TO/CC
Timothy Ruh

Plants ⬿ Books ⬿ Supplies
Specializing in **herbs, perennials, scented geraniums, hostas, ivies**; a very good selection in each category, each well described. They also offer herb books, dried herbs and essential oils and hold herb workshops and an Herb & Garden Fair (September) at the nursery. No shipping to CA. (1928)
❒ Catalog: $1d, SS:3-10, $15m, cn/bn
⌂ Nursery: All year, daily
▼ Garden: June-September, daily

Sunnyridge Gardens
1724 Drinnen Road
Knoxville, TN 37914
(615) 933-0723
John B. Couturier

Plants
The Couturiers grow 3,700 **daylilies** and 1,500 **irises**; their garden is both an official AHS and a Historical Iris Preservation Society display garden. They offer a broad selection of both daylilies and iris, including some Japanese and Siberian iris; plants are briefly described. (1983)
❒ Catalog: $1d, R&W, SS:4-10, $20
⌂ Nursery: April-October, daily, call ahead
▼ Garden: May-July, daily, call ahead

Sunnyslope Gardens
8638 Huntington Drive
San Gabriel, CA 91775
(818) 287-4071, FAX 287-4120
Phil Ishizu

Plants
Color catalog offers a large selection of **chrysanthemums** of many types, including spiders, cascades, brush, spoon, anemones, cushion types and even mums for bonsai culture. Also sells a selection of giant everblooming **carnations**; brief descriptions with some cultural suggestions.
❒ Catalog: Free, SS:mums 3-6; carnations 2-9, $5m

Sunrise Nursery
13705 Pecan Hollow
Leander, TX 78641
(512) 259-1877
Kathy & Tim Springer

Plants
Specializes in nursery-propagated **cactus and succulents** from all over the world, grown from seed or cuttings, and some hard to find: coryphanthus, echinocereus, escobaria, ferocactus, mammillarias, agaves, aloes, euphorbias, haworthias, lithops and pachypodiums, all briefly described. (1991)
❒ Catalog: $1, SS:3-11, $15m, bn
⌂ Nursery: By appointment only
▼ Garden: By appointment only

Sunrise Oriental Seed Co.
P.O. Box 330058
West Hartford, CT 06133-0058
(203) 666-8071, FAX 665-8156
Lucia Fu

Plants ⬿ Seeds ⬿ Books
Catalog, in both Chinese and English, offers over a hundred varieties of **Oriental vegetables**; also some flowers, sprouting seeds and gardening and cookbooks in Chinese and English. This year they have added a few hard-to-germinate houseplants, including several jasmines. They send information sheets with their seeds and will answer questions from customers on growing and serving Oriental vegetables. (1976)
❒ Catalog: $2d, R&W, CAN, SS:4-10, $5m, cn/bn

Sunshine Farm & Gardens
Route 5
Renick, WV 24966
(304) 497-3163, FAX 497-2698 TO/CC $64m
Barry Glick

Plants
Barry Glick's a manic plant collector who's decided to go into business since he already spends most of his time on plants; he'll even cheerfully swap wanted plants with his customers. His first list has a nice selection of **species geraniums, heucheras, polemoniums, tiarellas, violas and tricyrtis**. He ships 32 2½" pots in a box for $64 plus shipping. (1993)
❒ Catalog: Free, R&W, CAN/OV, $64m, bn
⌂ Nursery: By appointment only
▼ Garden: By appointment only

Sunswept Laboratories
P.O. Box 1913
Studio City, CA 91614
(818) 506-7271, FAX 506-4911 TO/CC
Robert C. Hull

Plants
Good selection of **hybrid and species orchids**; flask list includes brough-
tonias, catasetums, cattleyas, epidendrums, laelias, miltonias, oncidiums,
paphiopedilums, phalaenopsis, stanhopeas and other rare and endangered
orchids from seed or tissue culture, each briefly described. (1980)
❒ Catalog: $2d, CAN/OV, $18m, bn
⌂ Nursery: All year, daily, call ahead
▼ Garden: All year, daily, call ahead

Surry Gardens
P.O. Box 145
Surry, ME 04684
(207) 667-4493 or 5589 TO/CC
James M. Dickinson

Plants
Offers a good selection of **perennials and rock garden plants**, listed in
compact tables with zone, bloom season, exposure, height, soil needs and a
very brief description given; gentians, campanulas, primulas, asters, dian-
thus, platycodon, thyme and veronica. No shipping to CA, OR or WA. (1978)
❒ Catalog: Free, R&W, SS:5-6,9-11, $20m, bn
⌂ Nursery: All year, daily
▼ Garden: May-September, daily

Suttons Seeds (England)

See Gardenimport, Inc.

Swallowtail Garden & Nursery
475 Lightwood Knot Road
Woodruff, SC 29388
(803) 439-0328
Edmund & Abigail Taylor

Plants
A new source of **ornamental trees and shrubs**, including maples, camellias,
conifers, dogwoods, hydrangeas, hollies, crape myrtles, magnolias, nandinas,
and some rhododendrons, daylilies, ferns and other perennials. A good
selection, no plant descriptions. Can't ship to CA or OR. (1992)
❒ Catalog: Long SASE w/ 2 FCS, CAN, SS:10-3, $25m, bn
⌂ Nursery: All year, Tu-Sa, call ahead
▼ Garden: April-June, October, call ahead

Swan Island Dahlias
P.O. Box 700
995 N.W. 22nd Avenue
Canby, OR 97013-0700
(503) 266-7711, FAX 266-8768 TO/CC $19m
Nicholas & Ted Gitts

Plants
Color catalog offers a broad selection of **dahlias**, many shown in photos
and all well described. They offer several collections and, for the dahlia
fanatic, a powdered drink made from dahlia tubers (caffeine-free). Good
cultural and historical information on dahlias. (1930)
❒ Catalog: $3d, CAN/OV, SS:3-6, $15m
⌂ Nursery: All year, M-F
▼ Garden: August-September, daylight hours

Alfred Swanson
General Delivery
Challis, ID 83226-9999

Seeds
Swanson collects wild seed from over 100 acres of private land within the
White Cloud Peaks area of Idaho; he offers about 60 varieties of **alpines,
perennials and woody plants**, with no descriptions. He charges $50 for
your choice of 15 packets of seed; he will also custom collect.
❒ Catalog: Long SASE($3 OV), R&W, CAN/OV, $50m

T & T Seeds, Ltd.
P.O. Box 1710
Winnepeg, MB, Canada R3C 3P6
(204) 943-8483 TO/CC
P. J. & Kevin Twomey

Plants ❧ Seeds ❧ Supplies ❧ Bulbs
Color catalog offers good selection of **vegetables, annuals and perennials**,
summer-blooming bulbs, trees, shrubs, vines, fruit trees and berries, all
well described. They also carry a broad selection of growing supplies. Ship
only seeds to the US. (1946)
❒ Catalog: $2, US, SS:W
⌂ Nursery: All year, M-Sa

Talavaya Seeds
P.O. Box 707, Santa Cruz Station
Santa Cruz, NM 87567
Carol Underhill, Dir.

Seeds ❧ Books
A non-profit organization devoted to seed preservation and research in
sustainable agriculture. To raise funds, they sell organic, open-pollinated
native seed: **corn, beans, melons, squash, amaranth, peppers and quinoa**.
Varieties well described with information on dry land culture. (1984)
❒ Catalog: $1($2 OV), R&W, CAN/OV, cn/bn
⌂ Nursery: All year, M-Sa, by appointment only
▼ Garden: July-August, by appointment only

Dave Talbott Nursery
4038 Highway 17 South
Green Cove Springs, FL 32043
(904) 284-9874
David L. Talbott

Plants
Specialize in **daylilies**, including award winning hybrids of their own. New
introductions shown in color; all plants well described, some in glowing
prose! A wide selection of recent introductions and older favorites. Sell
flowering shrubs and perennials for northern Florida at the nursery. (1974)
❒ Catalog: $2d, CAN, $25m
⌂ Nursery: All year, M-Sa; May-July, daily
▼ Garden: May-June, daily

Tasmanian Forest Seeds
Summerleas Farm
Kingston, Tasmania, Australia 7050
(002) 29-6387
T. Walduck

Seeds
Specializes in seeds of **Tasmanian trees**, many of which come from mountains in Australia's coldest state and are quite hardy: acacias, callitris, eucalyptus, eucryphia, leptospermum, melaleuca, richea and others. There are only letter codes for plant type and hardiness, no descriptions. (1964)
❒ Catalog: $1 (US Bills), OV, $10m, bn
⌂ Nursery: All year, call ahead

Tate Rose Nursery
10306 FM Road 2767
Tyler, TX 75708-9239
(903) 593-1020
Otis & Bobbie Tate

Plants
A small family nursery offers a nice selection of modern hybrid **roses**: hybrid teas, floribundas, grandifloras and climbers. Can't ship to CA. (1942)
❒ Catalog: Free, R&W, SS:1-4, $19m
⌂ Nursery: December-April, M-F, call ahead

Taylor's Herb Gardens
1535 Lone Oak Road
Vista, CA 92084
(619) 727-3485, FAX 727-0289
Michele Andre, Mgr.

Plants ⬿ **Seeds**
A wide selection of **herb plants and seeds**, each well described in an informative catalog with recipes; some plants illustrated in color. (1947)
❒ Catalog: $3, R&W, CAN, cn/bn
⌂ Nursery: All year, M-Sa
▼ Garden: All year, M-Sa

Territorial Seed Company
P.O. Box 157
Cottage Grove, OR 97424
(503) 942-9547, FAX 942-9881 TO/CC
Tom & Julie Johns

Seeds ⬿ **Books** ⬿ **Tools** ⬿ **Bulbs**
Informative catalog specializes in **vegetables** for the maritime climate areas of Oregon, Washington, British Columbia and northern California. Also offers sprinklers, tools, books and a list of local organic fertilizer suppliers. Also lists seeds of annuals, herbs and green manure crops. (1979)
❒ Catalog: Free, R&W
⌂ Nursery: All year, M-F; Summer, daily
▼ Garden: July-August, Sa

Terrorchids
Am Atzumer Weg 18
Wolfenbuttel, Germany 38300
(05331) 62-999, FAX 63-040
Tanja Pinkepank

Plants
Specializes in "nearly" **hardy orchids**: cypripediums, dactylorhiza, orchis, ophrys, himantoglossum, calanthe, platanthera and pleione. The pleione list, which has no plant descriptions, lists both species (16) and hybrids (21). Write for information on import permits, etc. All plants are laboratory propagated; they will also raise difficult plants from seed for you. (1990)
❒ Catalog: 2 IRC, OV
⌂ Nursery: By appointment only

Thomasville Nurseries
P.O. Box 7
1842 Smith Avenue
Thomasville, GA 31799-0007
(912) 226-5568
A. Paul Hjort

Plants
All sorts of modern **roses, native deciduous and evergreen azaleas, daylilies, liriope and ophiopogon**; each well described and illustrated in color or b&w. Also has a large ARS test garden next to the nursery. (1898)
❒ Catalog: Free, R&W, SS:W
⌂ Nursery: All year, M-Sa am; December-May, Sa & Su pm
▼ Garden: April-November, daylight hours

Thompson & Morgan
P.O. Box 1308
Farraday & Gramme Avenues
Jackson, NJ 08527-0308
(908) 363-2225, (800) 274-7333, FAX 363-9356
Bruce J. Sangster, Pres.

Seeds
Color catalog with a huge selection of **plants of all types**. Good descriptions of plants and good germination and cultural information; the catalogs and color photographs create yearnings on a grand scale. (1855)
❒ Catalog: Free, CAN/OV, bn/cn
⌂ Nursery: All year, M-F

The Thyme Garden Seed Company
20546 Alsea Highway 34
Alsea, OR 97324
(503) 487-8671
Rolfe & Janet Hagen

Seeds
Family run seed company offers about 200 varieties of **herbs and everlasting flowers**, many of them grown organically on their farm in the mountains of western Oregon. Good selection and plant descriptions. (1990)
❒ Catalog: $1.50d ($2 OV), R&W, CAN/OV, SS:4-9, cn/bn
⌂ Nursery: May-September, F-M
▼ Garden: May-August, F-M

Tiki Nursery
P.O. Box 187
Fairview, NC 28730
(704) 628-2212
Jack & Claire Pardo

Plants
Offers a wide selection of **African violets**, sinningias, achimenes, streptocarpus and **other gesneriads** as well as begonias, fuchsias and a few other exotic houseplants. Each plant very briefly described. Plants must be shipped bare-root to CA. (1977)
❒ Catalog: $2, CAN, SS:4-10, $15m, bn
⌂ Nursery: All year, W-M, call ahead

Tile Barn Nursery
Standen Street, Iden Green
Benenden, Kent, England TN17 4LB
Peter Moore

Plants
Specialists in **hardy cyclamen**, offering many varieties, each very well
described; their focus is on the rarer types. There is a mandatory CITES
and Health Certificate Fee added to the price of the tubers, in addition to
the cost of postage.
❐ Catalog: $1(US Bills) or 2 IRC, US/CAN, SS:6-8, $50m, bn

Tilley's Nursery/The WaterWorks
111 E. Fairmount Street
Coopersburg, PA 18036
(215) 282-4784, FAX 282-1262 TO/CC
Tom Tilley

Plants ⚘ Books ⚘ Supplies
Good selection of **water lilies, bog and aquatic plants**, all well described.
They also sell pools, pond liners, fish and snails, water gardening supplies
and books on how to go about it. (1975)
❐ Catalog: $2, R&W, SS:4-10, cn/bn
⌂ Nursery: March-December, daily, call ahead
▼ Garden: July-September, daily, call ahead

Tinari Greenhouses
2325 Valley Road, Box 190
Huntingdon Valley, PA 19006
(215) 947-0144
Frank & Anne Tinari

Plants ⚘ Seeds ⚘ Books ⚘ Supplies
A good selection of **African violets** -- many are their own hybrids; all
briefly described, many illustrated in color. To my delight, they carry a
green African violet called 'Kermit'! Also sell seeds, books and growing
supplies, including plant stands and carts, and Anne Tinari's book on the
development of African violets, "Our African Violet Heritage." (1945)
❐ Catalog: $.50, CAN, SS:5-10
⌂ Nursery: All year, M-Sa; October-May, Su pm
▼ Garden: All year, M-Sa; October-May, Su pm

Tinmouth Channel Farm
RR 1, Box 428B
Tinmouth, VT 05773
(802) 446-2812
Carolyn Fuhrer & Kathleen Duhnoski

Plants ⚘ Seeds
Small nursery offers more than 80 varieties of annual and perennial **herbs**
and hardy plants, all organically grown; each plant well described. Cultural
hints are offered, including the formula of their own insecticide -- secret
ingredients are red pepper and garlic -- don't see how it could fail! (1987)
❐ Catalog: $2, SS:4-10, $18m, cn/bn
⌂ Nursery: April-December, F-Sa
▼ Garden: May-September, F-Sa

Tiny Petals Nursery
489 Minot Avenue
Chula Vista, CA 91910
(619) 422-0385 TO
Patrick & Susan O'Brien

Plants
A broad selection of **miniature roses**, featuring the hybrids of Dee Bennett:
minis, micro-minis, trailers and climbers, all well described; they offer 300
cultivars, and list 125 in the catalog. Can't ship to HI or AK. (1973)
❐ Catalog: Free, SS:W
⌂ Nursery: All year, W-M
▼ Garden: Spring-Summer, W-M

Tomato Growers Supply Company
P.O. Box 2237
Fort Myers, FL 33902
(813) 768-1119, FAX 332-5375 TO/CC
Linda & Vincent Sapp

Seeds ⚘ Books ⚘ Supplies
Over 200 varieties of **tomato** seed, growing supplies and books; all plants
well described, with good general cultural instructions and days to maturity
for each variety -- oh, the agony of choices, but they all sound so good it
must be hard to go wrong! They offer hot and sweet peppers, too. (1984)
❐ Catalog: Free

The Tomato Seed Company, Inc.
P.O. Box 1400
Tryon, NC 28782
Martin Sloan

Seeds
The ultimate in a world of specialization: **tomato** seed only. Varieties are
listed by type and shape and are well described in a hand-lettered catalog;
over 300 varieties -- hybrid, heirloom, red, yellow, large and small, round
and plum -- I'm suddenly starving! Adding some other vegetables and edible
flowers in 1994. (1983)
❐ Catalog: Free, CAN/OV

Torbay's Plant World

See Plant World.

Totally Tomatoes
P.O. Box 1626
Augusta, GA 30903
(803) 663-0016 TO/CC $15m
Randy Peele

Seeds
A new seed company, offering 250 varieties of **tomatoes** and 50 varieties of
peppers. You can buy from a 30-seed packet to seeds by the pound. I saw a
varieties list, but starting in 1994 they'll issue a real catalog. (1992)
❐ Catalog: Free, R&W, CAN

Tradewinds Nursery
28446 Hunter Creek Loop
Gold Beach, OR 97444
(503) 247-0835, FAX same
Gib & Diane Cooper

Plants ⚘ Books
Offers a nice selection of **bamboos** -- Phyllostachys pubescens (moso or
giant timber bamboo) and several other genera -- arundinaria, chimono-
bambusa, pleioblastus, sasa, bambusa, chusquea and fargesia; briefly des-
cribed. Also offers several books on bamboo and bamboo construction. (1986)
❐ Catalog: Long SASE(2 IRC OV), CAN/OV, bn
⌂ Nursery: February-November, Tu-Sa, call ahead
▼ Garden: February-November, Tu-Sa, call ahead

Tranquil Lake Nursery
45 River Street
Rehoboth, MA 02769-1395
(508) 252-4002, FAX 252-4310
Warren P. Leach & Philip A. Boucher

Plants
Catalog offers a good selection of **daylilies, Japanese and Siberian irises**
and two good border **sedums**; plants well described. Many more are available
at the nursery; they grow many older varieties, so send a "want list." Sell
other perennials at the nursery. (1958)
❑ Catalog: $1, CAN/OV, SS:4-6,8-10, $10m
⌂ Nursery: April-November, W-Su, call ahead
▼ Garden: June-September, W-Su, call ahead

Trans Pacific Nursery
16065 Oldsville Road
McMinnville, OR 97128
(503) 472-6215, 434-1505 TO/CC $20m
Jackson Muldoon

Plants
A wide selection of **trees, shrubs, vines and perennials** from all over the
world, many not easy to find; each plant well described. Among the plants
are anigozanthos, banksia, carex, clianthus, cotula, huernia, hardenbergia,
kennedia, moraea, pleione, parahebe, rhodohypoxis, violas, South African
bulbs and Japanese maples. (1982)
❑ Catalog: $2($3 OV), R&W, CAN/OV, SS:W, $10m, bn
⌂ Nursery: All year, call ahead
▼ Garden: All year, call ahead

Transplant Nursery
Parkertown Road
Lavonia, GA 30553
(706) 356-8947, FAX 356-8842
Mary, Jeff & Lisa Beasley

Plants
Collectors' list of Dexter and other **rhododendrons**, rare **native deciduous
azaleas** and **hybrid azaleas** of James Harris, Robin Hill, Ralph Pennington,
North Tisbury and several others; brief descriptions and a few color photo-
graphs. Many are suitable for bonsai. Also offer camellias, kalmias and some
other companion plants. No shipping to CA, OR or WA. (1975)
❑ Catalog: $1, R&W, SS:9-11,2-4, $25m, bn
⌂ Nursery: April-May, M-F, by appointment in other months
▼ Garden: April-May, M-F, call ahead

Travis' Violets
P.O. Box 42
Ochlochnee, GA 31773-0042
(912) 574-5167 or 5236 TO/CC $25m
Travis Davis

Plants ⬿ **Supplies**
African violets, including their own hybrids and many others: Hortense's
Honeys, Lyon's, Betty Bryant's and Fredettes included. Sell both leaves and
plants; all are well described. They also sell pots, fertilizer and a violet
potting mix. (1980)
❑ Catalog: $1d($3 OV), R&W, CAN/OV, SS:W, $15m
⌂ Nursery: All year, daily, call ahead
▼ Garden: April-June, daily, call ahead

Trees by Touliatos
2020 Brooks Road
Memphis, TN 38116
(901) 345-7361, FAX 398-5217
Greg Touliatos

Plants ⬿ **Supplies**
Offers a nice selection of hardy and tropical **water lilies and lotus**,
floating, bog and marginal plants, and all the necessary supplies and
wildlife to set up a successful pond. At the nursery they sell other
ornamental plants and trees. (1962)
❑ Catalog: Long SASE, R&W, $30m
⌂ Nursery: All year, M-Sa
▼ Garden: All year, M-Sa

Tregunno Seeds

See Ontario Seed Company.

William Tricker, Inc.
7125 Tanglewood Drive
Independence, OH 44131
(216) 524-3491, FAX 524-6688
Richard Lee

Plants ⬿ **Books** ⬿ **Supplies**
Color catalog of **water lilies and other aquatic and bog plants**, even a
Victoria trickeri with leaves up to 6 feet across. In addition to a broad
selection of plants, they sell books and videos on water gardening, fancy
fish, pool supplies and remedies in an informative catalog. (1895)
❑ Catalog: $3, R&W, CAN/OV, cn/bn
⌂ Nursery: All year, daily
▼ Garden: May-August, daily

Tripple Brook Farm
37 Middle Road
Southampton, MA 01073
(413) 527-4626 (evenings)
Stephen Breyer

Plants
Small nursery with a good selection of **Northeastern native plants**, hardy
bamboos, fruiting mulberries and hardy kiwi, irises, flowering shrubs and
more -- catalog full of good cultural information, as well as drawings of
many plants and the nursery cat and dog -- a delight!
❑ Catalog: Free, R&W, CAN/OV, SS:4-11, bn
⌂ Nursery: By appointment only
▼ Garden: Growing area, by appointment only

Tropiflora
3530 Tallevast Road
Sarasota, FL 34243
(813) 351-2267, FAX 351-6985
Dennis & Linda Cathcart

Plants
Tropiflora offers a huge selection of **bromeliads**, including over 400 **til-
landsias**, many aechmeas, guzmanias, vrieseas, and neoregelias, as well
as caudiciforms, cycads, palms, and cryptanthus. They publish the "Cargo
Report" which describes new introductions. Some plants are wild collected.
Also offer books and growing supplies. (1976)
❑ Catalog: Free, R&W, CAN/OV, $25m, bn
⌂ Nursery: All year, M-Sa

Tsolum River Fruit Trees
P.O. Box 1271
Ganges, BC, Canada V0S 1E0
(604) 537-4191, FAX 537-4615
Michael McCormick, Mgr.

Plants
Taken over by the Heritage Seed Program, this non-profit organization offers a very broad selection of hardy organically grown **heirloom fruit trees** -- apples, pears, plums, crabapples, medlars and quinces, each very well described in an informative catalog. Ships only within Canada. (1983)
❒ Catalog: $3.75, SS:12-4
⌂ Nursery: By appointment only
♥ Garden: Spring-Fall, by appointment only

Turner Seed Company
Route 1, Box 292
Breckenridge, TX 76424
(817) 559-2065, (800) 722-8616, FAX 559-8076
Bob Turner

Seeds
Offers a good selection of seed for **native grasses, wildlife food** and **forbs** for reclamation, grazing and pastureland. List is by common name, with no descriptions.
❒ Catalog: Long SASE, R&W, cn
⌂ Nursery: All year, M-Sa

Otis Twilley Seed Co.
P.O. Box 65
Trevose, PA 19053
(800) 622-7333, (800) 232-7333 (PA) TO/CC
Arthur Cobb Abbott, Pres.

Seeds ⌘ Supplies
Color catalog offers a large selection of **vegetables and garden flowers** -- all very well described and with growing suggestions -- available in packets or in bulk. Also offers growing supplies and the new seed company status symbols, tee-shirts and caps. FAX number is (215) 245-1949. (1920)
❒ Catalog: Free, R&W, CAN/OV

Twombly Nursery
163 Barn Hill Road
Monroe, CT 06468-2029
(203) 261-2133, FAX 261-9230
Ken & Priscilla Twombly

Plants
This nursery carries an excellent selection of **ornamental trees and shrubs, perennials, grasses and ferns**, all plants well described. Their minimum mail order is high, but if you live nearby, they have a beautiful five acre display garden. No shipping to AL, AZ, CA, FL, OR, SC, TN or WA. (1970)
❒ Catalog: $4, R&W, SS:3-5,9-10, $250m, bn
⌂ Nursery: All year, daily; July-August, M-Sa
♥ Garden: All year, daily; July-August, M-Sa

Upper Bank Nurseries
P.O. Box 486
670 S. Ridley Creek Road
Media, PA 19063
(215) 566-0679
Wirt L. Thompson, Jr.

Plants
A nursery selling a nice selection of ornamental trees and shrubs, but they ship only **bamboo**: phyllostachys, pleioblastus, arundinaria, sasa, semi-arundinaria, pseudosasa, shibataea. No plant descriptions. (1925)
❒ Catalog: Long SASE, R&W, SS:3-4,10-11, bn
⌂ Nursery: All year, M-F
♥ Garden: Spring-Summer, M-F

Valente Gardens
RFD 2, Box 234
Dillingham Road (North Berwick)
East Lebanon, ME 04027
(207) 457-2076
Ron & Cindy Valente

Plants
Small family-run nursery, shipping only **daylilies** at present; broad selection of newer hybrids and miniatures, briefly described. Visitors to the nursery can buy and dig other perennials, including Siberian and Japanese irises and hostas. Daylilies shipped when it's nice weather in Maine. (1983)
❒ Catalog: 2 FCS, SS:5-9
⌂ Nursery: May-September, Sa-Su; July-August, W-Su
♥ Garden: July-August, W-Su

Valley Nursery
P.O. Box 4845
2801 N. Montana Avenue
Helena, MT 59604
(406) 442-8460
Clayton Berg

Plants
"Best of the old plus newer, hardier plants for cold climates." A good selection of ornamental and berrying **trees, conifers and shrubs** are listed by size or use, then by common or botanical name. Prices not shown on list but will be quoted on available plants as requested. (1961)
❒ Catalog: $1 or 2 FCS, R&W, CAN/OV, SS:3-11, $15m, cn/bn
⌂ Nursery: All year, daily
♥ Garden: June-October, daily

Valley Vista Kiwi
16531 Mt. Shelly Circle
Fountain Valley, CA 92708
(714) 839-0796 (5-11pm PST)
Roger & Shirley Meyer

Plants
Small nursery offers scionwood of thirty varieties of **kiwi and hardy kiwi**, ten varieties of **jujube** (bare-root jujube trees available from January to March), and other **unusual fruits** such as Surinam cherry, lychee, Mexican yellow guava and dwarf banana. No plant descriptions. (1975)
❒ Catalog: Long SASE($1 OV), CAN/OV, cn
⌂ Nursery: By appointment only
♥ Garden: By appointment only

Van Bourgondien Bros.
P.O. Box 1000
245 Farmingdale Road
Babylon, NY 11702
(516) 669-3500, FAX 669-1228 TO/CC
Debbie Van Bourgondien

Plants ⌘ Bulbs
Color catalogs offer **spring and summer-blooming bulbs and perennials**; each plant briefly described, with cultural information given in symbols. Large selection, especially of bulbs, all shown in color; catalogs sent in fall and spring. No shipping to AK, HI, PR or Guam. (1919)
❒ Catalog: Free, SS:2-6,9-12, cn/bn
⌂ Nursery: All year, M-F, call ahead

Van Dyck's Flower Farms, Inc.
P.O. Box 430
Brightwaters, NY 11718
(916) 422-4782, (800) 248-2852
Jan Van Dyck

Bulbs
A new source of **spring-blooming bulbs**; the gimmick is that each package of bulbs is $5 -- number of bulbs varies by variety. Offered are tulips, daffodils, hyacinths, Dutch iris, crocus and other "little" bulbs, and some hybrid lilies. Ships only to contiguous 48 states. (1992)
❐ Catalog: Free, R&W, SS:9-12,3-6, $25m

Van Engelen, Inc.
313 Maple Street
Litchfield, CT 06759
(203) 567-5662, 567-8734, FAX 567-5323 TO/CC
Jan S. Ohms

Bulbs
Sells **Dutch bulbs** in quantities of 50 and 100 per variety, but anyone who orders a minimum of $50 may take advantage of their bulk prices. Offers a broad selection; brief plant descriptions, cultural suggestions. (1946)
❐ Catalog: Free, R&W, SS:9-12, $50m, cn/bn

Van Ness Water Gardens
2460 N. Euclid Avenue
Upland, CA 91786
(909) 982-2425, FAX 949-7217 TO/CC $15m
William C. Uber

Plants ❧ Books ❧ Supplies
Color catalog offers **everything for water gardens** -- water lilies and other aquatic plants, fish, ponds and supplies and books on water gardening, as well as a lot of information on how to do it. They also consult worldwide on fresh-water ecosystems and water gardens. (1932)
❐ Catalog: $4, CAN/OV, SS:W, $15m, cn/bn
⌂ Nursery: All year, Tu-Sa, call ahead in December & January
❦ Garden: June-September, Tu-Sa

Mary Mattison van Schaik
P.O. Box 32
Cavendish, VT 05142
(802) 226-7653
Paula M. Parker

Bulbs
Mary's long time assistant has bought the company, an importer of **spring-blooming Dutch bulbs** -- hybrid and species tulips, daffodils, hyacinths, crocus and other "little" bulbs. Very brief plant descriptions.
❐ Catalog: $1, R&W, SS:8-12, $10m

Van Well Nursery, Inc.
P.O. Box 1339
Wenatchee, WA 98807
(509) 663-8189, FAX 662-9336 TO/CC
Peter Van Well

Plants
A broad selection of **fruit trees**: apples, cherries, pears, peaches, plums and prunes, apricots, berries, walnuts and grapes. Some apple trees are available on standard-to-dwarf rootstocks, other dwarf fruit trees are available. (1946)
❐ Catalog: Free($1 OV), R&W, CAN/OV, SS:11-6, $15m
⌂ Nursery: All year, M-Sa
❦ Garden: July-September, M-Sa

Varga's Nursery
2631 Pickertown Road
Warrington, PA 18976
(215) 343-0646
Barbara L. Varga

Plants
Very wide selection of **hardy and greenhouse ferns**, listed only by botanical and common name, with brief notes on size or use. A list of source books is given to help you work your way through the jungle. They have added a tissue-culture lab and are propagating more difficult ferns. (1975)
❐ Catalog: $1, R&W, SS:W, $25m, bn
⌂ Nursery: All year, daily, by appointment only
❦ Garden: Spring & Fall, greenhouse, by appointment only

Veldheer Tulip Gardens
12755 Quincy Street
Holland, MI 49424
(616) 399-1900, FAX 399-1270 TO/CC
Vernin Veldheer

Bulbs
Specializes in **spring- and summer-blooming Dutch bulbs** -- tulips, daffodils, crocus, hyacinths, lilies, alliums and others -- all briefly described in a color catalog. (1950)
❐ Catalog: Free, R&W, CAN, SS:4-10
⌂ Nursery: All year, M-Sa
❦ Garden: April-September, daily, call ahead

Vermont Bean Seed Co.
Garden Lane
Fair Haven, VT 05743
(802) 273-3400 TO/CC
Wayne Hilton

Seeds ❧ Supplies ❧ Tools
Specializes in **bean and vegetable seeds**; informative catalog with good descriptions, growing instructions, even a number to call when customers need help! Also a selection of growing supplies, some annual, herb and perennial seeds; company acquired by Wayne Hilton, the owner of Shumway's. (1975)
❐ Catalog: Free($2 OV), CAN

Vermont Wildflower Farm
Route 7
Charlotte, VT 05445
(802) 425-3500 or 3931, FAX 425-3504 TO/CC
Chy & Ray Allen

Seeds
The garden is a tourist attraction in Vermont; they have seeded "thousands" of wildflower species in their six-acre test garden. Offer **wildflower seeds and seed mixes** for sun or shade, regionalized for the entire US. Color catalog gives basic how-to information on getting started. Also offer wildflower gifts: notecards, placemats, books and more. (1981)
❐ Catalog: Free, R&W, CAN/OV, $7m, cn/bn
⌂ Nursery: May-October, daily
❦ Garden: July-August, daily

Vesey's Seeds, Ltd.
P.O. Box 9000, York
Charlottetown, PE, Canada C1A 8K6
(902) 386-7333, FAX 566-1620 TO/CC $20m
B. E. & S. F. Simpson

Seeds ⚘ Books ⚘ Supplies
A broad selection of **vegetables and flowers**, all well described with cultural information. Specializes in short-season varieties for Canada and New England (request catalog from Box 9000, Calais, ME 04619). Also offers growing supplies, gardening books and hand-made white ash baskets. (1939)
❏ Catalog: Free, R&W, US
⌂ Nursery: All year, M-Sa
▼ Garden: July-September, M-Sa

Vicki's Exotic Plants
522 Vista Park Drive
Eagle Point, OR 97524
(503) 826-6318
Vicki Graves

Plants
Offers a broad selection of **fibrous and rhizomatous begonias and hoyas**, as well as some other **gesneriads and dischidias**. All plants are lovingly described, it's obviously collecting taken to the max.
❏ Catalog: $1($2 OV), R&W, CAN/OV, SS:W, $15m
⌂ Nursery: All year, F-Tu, call ahead
▼ Garden: All year, F-Tu, call ahead

Andre Viette Farm & Nursery
Route 1, Box 16
State Route 608
Fishersville, VA 22939
(703) 942-2118, 943-2315, FAX 943-0782 TO/CC
Andre Viette

Plants
A very broad selection of **garden perennials**; very brief plant descriptions. Plants are grouped by use or cultural conditions, shade or sun, or by type. Many daylilies, irises, hostas, peonies, ornamental grasses, epimediums, astilbes, liriopes, Oriental poppies and more. Cannot ship to CA. (1929)
❏ Catalog: $3, R&W, SS:3-11
⌂ Nursery: April-October, M-Sa, Su pm
▼ Garden: May-July, M-Sa, Su pm

Village Arbors
1804 Saugahatchee Road
Auburn, AL 36830
(205) 826-3490
J. Frandsen, Betty Breyer & Bill Carpenter

Plants
Specializing in **plants that do well in the Gulf South**: herbs, perennials and scented geraniums; each plant very well described. They offer nice selections of rosemary, thyme, salvia, basil and mint.
❏ Catalog: $1, R&W
⌂ Nursery: All year, M-Sa
▼ Garden: May, M-Sa

Vintage Gardens
3003 Pleasant Hill Road
Sebastopol, CA 95472
(707) 829-5342
Gregg Lowery

Plants
Offers a very good selection of "antique and extraordinary" **roses**, listed by type and each lovingly described; there are beautiful color paintings of some of the roses in the informative catalog. They seem to list some roses I've never seen listed anywhere else. Their availability list is free. (1992)
❏ Catalog: $4, R&W, CAN, SS:12-3, $50m, bn
⌂ Nursery: All year, M-F, by appointment only
▼ Garden: May, Open Garden, call for date

Violet Creations
5520 Wilkins Road
Tampa, FL 33610
(813) 626-6817, 963-7424, FAX 621-5093 TO/CC
Jo Anne Martinez & Cheryl Hukle

Plants ⚘ Supplies
Offers over 500 varieties of **African violets and some other gesneriads**: aeschynanthus, columneas, episcias, kohlerias, sinningias, streptocarpus and others. Also some books, growing supplies, tee shirts and note cards. (1989)
❏ Catalog: Free, R&W, CAN/OV, SS:W
⌂ Nursery: All year, M-Sa, by appointment only
▼ Garden: All year, M-Sa, by appointment only

Violet Express
1440-41 Everett Road
Eagle River, WI 54521
(715) 479-3099
Genola B. Cox

Plants ⚘ Supplies
Offers over 600 varieties of **African violets**, all listed by hybridizer or by type, with very good plant descriptions: plants and leaves are available. Also sells pots and other growing supplies. Ships all over the world, but shipping is not possible to the Middle East. (1986)
❏ Catalog: $2.50($4 OV), CAN/OV, SS:5-10, $15m
⌂ Nursery: All year, Tu-Sa
▼ Garden: All year, Tu-Sa

The Violet Showcase
3147 South Broadway
Englewood, CO 80110
(303) 761-1770
Douglas & Barbara Crispin

Plants ⚘ Seeds ⚘ Books ⚘ Supplies
A broad selection of **African violets**, each well described; also lists some other **gesneriads**. Their supplies catalog offers a wide selection of growing supplies: lights, plant carts, books, pots, fertilizers (supplies are sold in bulk to clubs or hobbyists gone mad). (1969)
❏ Catalog: $1($2 OV), CAN/OV, SS:5-10
⌂ Nursery: All year, M,W-Sa
▼ Garden: All year, M,W-Sa

Violets Collectible
1571 Wise Road
Lincoln, CA 95648
(916) 645-3487
Jeani Hatfield

Plants
Fanatic's list of **African violets**; a very large selection -- regular, mini-
ature, semi-miniature and trailers -- with good brief plant descriptions.
The list is tightly packed; settle down with your reading glasses. Big
display at the greenhouse; available as either plants or leaves. (1981)
❑ Catalog: $2, R&W, CAN/OV, SS:4-10, $15m
⌂ Nursery: All year, daily, call ahead
❤ Garden: Growing area, call ahead

Volkmann Bros. Greenhouses
2714 Minert Street
Dallas, TX 75219
(214) 526-3484
Henry & Walter Volkmann

Plants ∿ Supplies
A nice selection of **African violets**, many of their own hybridizing, each
briefly described and some shown in color. Also offer growing supplies,
equipment and plant stands. (1949)
❑ Catalog: Free, R&W, SS:3-11, $10m
⌂ Nursery: All year, M-F, Sa am
❤ Garden: January-June, M-F, Sa am

Washington Evergreen Nursery
P.O. Box 388
Brooks Branch Road
Leicester, NC 28748
(704) 683-4518
Jordan Jack

Plants
A collectors' dream catalog of **dwarf conifers and kalmias**; all very well
described, with cultural information and estimated size after ten years.
Included for beginners is a good reading list and a list of dwarf conifer
collections to visit. Cannot ship to CA. (1978)
❑ Catalog: $2d, CAN/OV, SS:4-6,9-10, $20m, bn
⌂ Nursery: April-October, by appointment only
❤ Garden: May-October, by appointment only

Water Ways Nursery
Route 2, Box 247
Lovettsville, VA 22080
(703) 822-5994 TO
Sarah R. Kurtz

Plants
Small nursery on a historic Virginia farm offers **waterlilies, lotus** and
aquatic plants. Plants are sold bare-root or potted; brief plant descrip-
tions in table format. (1989)
❑ Catalog: $2d, R&W, CAN/OV, SS:3-9, $50m, cn/bn
⌂ Nursery: March-October, Th-F
❤ Garden: June-August, Th-F

Waterford Gardens
74 E. Allendale Road
Saddle River, NJ 07458
(201) 327-0721, FAX 327-0684 TO/CC
James A. Lawrie, Mgr.

Plants ∿ Books ∿ Supplies
Complete selection of **water lilies, lotus and other aquatic and bog plants**,
as well as pools, supplies, fish, pumps, filters, remedies and books on water
gardening. Many color photographs and good descriptions. They have
greenhouses, ponds and display gardens to give you good ideas. (1985)
❑ Catalog: $5, R&W, CAN/OV, SS:4-8, cn/bn
⌂ Nursery: All year, M-Sa
❤ Garden: June-August, M-Sa

The WaterWorks

See Tilley's Nursery.

© Shepherd's Garden Seeds
Artist: Mimi Osborne

John Watson & Anita Flores
24 Kingsway
Petts Wood
Orpington, Kent, England BR5 1PR
(0689) 82-2494

Seeds
Seed collectors who specialize in **seeds from South America.** The list varies
from year to year as they move from region to region, but the list I saw had
a good selection, with the plants well described, good source and habitat
information, and some notes on germinating difficult genera. Specialize in
alpines; it may take a while to get a reply - they travel 6 months a year.
❏ Catalog: $1(US Bills), US/CAN, $12m, bn

The Waushara Gardens
N5491 5th Drive
Plainfield, WI 54966
(715) 335-4462 or 4281
George & Robert Melk

Plants ⌖ Books ⌖ Supplies ⌖ Bulbs
Color brochure offers a wide selection of gladiolus and pixiolas, hybrid
lilies, dahlias, callas and other **summer-blooming bulbs**, well described.
Sold in quantities suitable for the cut flower trade as well as for the home
gardener. Also some books on glads and lilies, and growing supplies. (1924)
❏ Catalog: $1, R&W, $18m, SS:1-6
⌂ Nursery: January-September, M-Sa, call ahead
❦ Garden: August-September, M-Sa, call ahead

Wavecrest Nursery & Landscaping Co.
2509 Lakeshore Drive
Fennville, MI 49408
(616) 543-4175
Carol T. Hop

Plants
Offers a very nice selection of **ornamental trees and shrubs** -- Japanese
maples, berberis, hollies, larch and other conifers -- with brief plant des-
criptions. They also have a shop called The Barn Owl which sells a broad
selection of bird houses and feeders and books about birds. (1955)
❏ Catalog: $1d, CAN, SS:W, $10m, bn
⌂ Nursery: March-December, daily
❦ Garden: Spring-Fall, daily

Wayside Gardens
P.O. Box 1
Hodges, SC 29695-0001
(800) 845-1124 TO/CC $25m
William J. Park

Plants ⌖ Supplies
Color catalog of **ornamental trees and shrubs, perennials and roses**, all
well described and illustrated, with good cultural information and a cultural
card with each plant purchased. A Wayside catalog that chanced my way
started my passion for ornamental garden plants and was my first tutor. Wide
selection; they introduce many new cultivars from Europe and England.
❏ Catalog: $1d, SS:1-5,9-11, bn/cn

We-Du Nurseries
Route 5, Box 724
Marion, NC 28752-9338
(704) 738-8300
Dr. Richard Weaver & Rene Duval

Plants
A collectors' catalog of **rock garden and woodland plants**, Southern natives,
American, Japanese, Korean and Chinese wildflowers; some are very unusual.
Each plant lovingly described; it's almost impossible to convey the pleasure
of reading such a catalog and looking up the new plants. No shipping to AZ,
CA or HI. (1981)
❏ Catalog: $2, CAN, $15m, bn
⌂ Nursery: All year, M-Sa, call ahead
❦ Garden: April-May, M-Sa, call ahead

Wedge Nursery
Route 2, Box 114
Albert Lea, MN 56007
(507) 373-5225
Donald & Bradford Wedge

Plants
Specializing in own-root **lilacs**, both "French lilacs" and other hybrids
such as 'Josiflexa' (S. josikaea X S. reflexa), 'Hyacinthiflora' (S. vulgaris
X S. oblata) and 'Prestoniae' (S. reflexa X S. villosa), as well as some spe-
cies and miscellaneous hybrids. Each plant very well described. (1878)
❏ Catalog: Free, R&W, SS:3-5, $10m

Chris Weeks Peppers
P.O. Box 3207
Kill Devil Hills, NC 27948
Chris Weeks

Seeds
New small supplier of **hot pepper** seeds, he lists 60 varieties, some of
which he claims are quite rare. Calculating his profits at a dime an hour,
he does it for the desire to distribute peppers to the other folks who appreciate the beauty, taste and pizzazz that hot peppers add to life. (1983)
❏ Catalog: $1($2 OV), CAN/OV, $2m

Weiss Brothers Nursery
11690 Colfax Highway
Grass Valley, CA 95945
(916) 272-7657, FAX 272-3578 TO/CC
Weiss-Baldoni Nurseries, Inc.

Plants ⌖ Books
Offer a good selection of **perennials and herbs**, each briefly but well des-
cribed, and some shown in color. Many achilleas, asters, coreopsis, del-
phiniums, monardas, and veronicas among others. No shipping to AK or HI.
❏ Catalog: Free, SS:3-6,8-10, bn/cn
⌂ Nursery: Daily

Well-Sweep Herb Farm
317 Mt. Bethel Road
Port Murray, NJ 07865
(908) 852-5390 TO/CC $40m
Louise & Cyrus Hyde

Plants ⌖ Seeds ⌖ Books ⌖ Supplies
A very broad selection of **herb plants, perennials and scented geraniums**;
brief plant descriptions. Also offers some herb seeds, dried flowers and
other herb gifts, supplies and books. Lectures and open houses in the spring
and fall; the garden looks charming. (1971)
❏ Catalog: $2, SS:4-10, $5m, cn/bn
⌂ Nursery: April-December, Tu-Sa, January-March, call ahead
❦ Garden: July-August, Tu-Sa

Bob Wells Nursery
P.O. Box 606
Lindale, TX 75771
(903) 882-3550, 882-8030
Bob Wells

Plants
Now run by the fourth generations of Wellses, offering **fruit, nut and shade trees, berries, grapes, roses and ornamental shrubs**, all briefly described. A good selection, all best suited to the South. (1913)
❏ Catalog: Free, R&W, CAN/OV, SS:11-4, $50m
⌂ Nursery: November-April, M-Sa
▼ Garden: November-March, M-Sa

Ken West Orchids
P.O. Box 1332
Pahoa, HI 96778
(808) 965-9895 TO/CC
Ken & Jean West

Plants
Offer a number of **cattleya hybrids**, listed by color, either in small pots or in community pots; each thoroughly described. Some of their hybrids have won awards from the American Orchid Society. They also offer a few other hybrids, and catasetinae hybrids bred by Wes Ramsey. (1979)
❏ Catalog: Free, R&W, SS:W

Western Biologicals, Ltd.
P.O. Box 283
Aldergrove, BC, Canada V0X 1A0
(604) 856-3339 FAX same
William Chalmers

Seeds ❧ Books ❧ Supplies
Offer live cultures and granular spawn for a broad selection of **mushrooms**, with pages of cultural instructions. They also offer complete growing supplies and books for commercial or home growers. Offer a tissue culture service and hold workshops in tissue culture and mushroom growing. (1983)
❏ Catalog: $3, R&W, US/OV, bn
⌂ Nursery: All year, M-Sa, call ahead

Western Native Seed
P.O. Box 1281
Canon City, CO 81215
(719) 275-8414, FAX 269-3423
Lynne Steinman & Mark Dalpiaz

Seeds
Small seed company offers **trees, shrubs and Western native plants** as well as **wildflowers and native grasses**; a good selection with no plant descriptions. Some of the seed is habitat collected, and they also offer several wildflower mixes. May be charges on foreign orders for a phytosanitary certificate; ask if your agricultural authorities require one. (1988)
❏ Catalog: Long SASE($1 OV), R&W, CAN/OV, $10m, bn

Westgate Garden Nursery
751 Westgate Drive
Eureka, CA 95503
(707) 442-1239 TO $100m
Catherine Weeks

Plants
Catalog offers a large selection of **species and hybrid rhododendrons and azaleas**, with good plant descriptions, and some unusual ornamental shrubs and trees as companion plants -- crinodendron, eucryphia, halesia, kalmia, stewartia, styrax, some dwarf conifers -- a real collectors' list. (1965)
❏ Catalog: $4d, SS:10-4, bn/cn
⌂ Nursery: All year, Th-Tu
▼ Garden: March-May, Th-Tu

Westside Exotics Palm Nursery
P.O. Box 143
Westley, CA 95387
Daniel and Susan Lara

Plants ❧ Seeds
A selection of **palms**, available as seedlings or small plants; no plant descriptions. A small nursery; not all palms available at all times; palm seed available in season only. Also a few tropical palms; everything withstood the 1990 freeze of two weeks below 15F. (1983)
❏ Catalog: $1($2 CAN), CAN, SS:W, $25m, bn

White Flower Farm
Route 63
Litchfield, CT 06759-0050
(203) 496-9600, FAX 496-1418 TO/CC
Eliot Wadsworth II

Plants ❧ Books ❧ Supplies ❧ Tools ❧ Bulbs
Color catalog offers a broad selection of **shrubs and perennials** in the spring; very good plant descriptions and detailed cultural suggestions. They offer many **spring and summer-flowering bulbs** in their fall catalog. Also offer books, supplies and tools and they have a staff horticulturist who will consult with customers over the phone. (1950)
❏ Catalog: Free, CAN, SS:W, bn/cn
⌂ Nursery: April-October, daily
▼ Garden: May-September, daily

White Oak Nursery
6145 Oak Point Court
Peoria, IL 61614
(309) 693-1354
Bob Keller

Plants
Offers a nice selection of **hostas**, field-grown and mature plants; some are shown in a color flyer, all are well described. They are gradually adding more ground cover plants and perennials. (1984)
❏ Catalog: Long SASE, R&W, CAN, SS:4-5, $20m
▼ Garden: June, by appointment only

Whitman Farms
3995 Gibson Road N.W.
Salem, OR 97304-9527
(503) 585-8728
Lucile Whitman

Plants
Grafted trees, including **species maples and magnolias, and nut trees**, also rooted cuttings of **currants, gooseberries, raspberries**. On another list, they offer **ornamental trees** in wholesale quantities, some quite desirable.
❏ Catalog: $1d, SS:11-5, $10m, bn

Whitney Gardens & Nursery
P.O. Box F
31600 Highway 101
Brinnon, WA 98320
(206) 796-4411, (800) 952-2404
Anne Sather

Plants
Offers a large selection of **hybrid and species rhododendrons and azaleas**, **kalmias** and other ornamental trees and shrubs: some plants illustrated in color, all very well described, with cultural information. There's a seven-acre display garden; sounds lovely in spring and fall. (1955)
❐ Catalog: $4, CAN/OV, SS:W, bn/cn
⌂ Nursery: February-November, daily
▼ Garden: April-June, daily

Wicklein's Water Gardens
P.O. Box 9780
1820 Cromwell Bridge Road (Baltimore)
Baldwin, MD 21013
(410) 823-1335, FAX 823-1427 TO/CC
Walt Wicklein

Plants ⚬ Supplies
Offers a good selection of **water lilies, lotus and other aquatic and bog plants**, all well to briefly described. Also sells fiberglass ponds, PVC pond liners, pumps and other supplies and fancy goldfish and koi. (1954)
❐ Catalog: $2, R&W, CAN/OV, $25m
⌂ Nursery: April-October, daily; other months, call for hours
▼ Garden: April-October, daily

Gilbert H. Wild & Son, Inc.
P.O. Box 338
1112 Joplin Street
Sarcoxie, MO 64862-0338
(417) 548-3514, FAX 548-6831 TO/CC
John Huitsing & Greg Jones

Plants
Color catalog offers a large selection of **daylilies and herbaceous peonies**; all plants very well described, many illustrated. Offers a number of collections and several your-choice collections at considerable savings. They will be adding iris in 1994. Many of the plants are their own hybrids. (1885)
❐ Catalog: $3d, R&W, CAN/OV, SS:4-11
⌂ Nursery: January 15-December 15, M-F
▼ Garden: May-July, M-F

Wild and Crazy Seed Company
P. O. Box 895
Durango, CO 81302
(303) 259-6385
Christine Hunt

Seeds
Offers **wildflower seeds** of the Southwest, Colorado and northern New Mexico; plants are well described with good cultural and habitat information. A nice selection. (1990)
❐ Catalog: $2d, R&W, CAN/OV, $3m, bn/cn

Wild Earth Native Plant Nursery
49 Mead Avenue
Wright DeBow Road (Jackson)
Freehold, NJ 07728
(908) 780-5661
Richard L. Pillar

Plants
Specializes in **native plants** of the mid-Atlantic region; the owner is a landscape architect working in natural landscapes and restoration projects. Offers a good selection of **wildflowers, grasses, ferns and perennials**, well described with growing suggestions. No shipping to AZ, CA, OR or WA. (1991)
❐ Catalog: $2d, R&W, SS:4-10, $15m, bn
⌂ Nursery: April-October, by appointment only
▼ Garden: April-October, call ahead

Wild Seed
P.O. Box 27751
Tempe, AZ 85285
(602) 345-0669
Rita Jo Anthony

Seeds
Specialize in **Southwestern wildflowers and native plants**, some of the seed is habitat collected. There are no plant descriptions, but they offer a very nice selection of desert wildflowers, trees and shrubs, and native grasses, and several wildflower mixes for various Southwestern habitats. (1982)
❐ Catalog: Free, R&W, CAN/OV, cn/bn
⌂ Nursery: By appointment only
▼ Garden: March-April, by appointment only

Wildflower Nursery
1680 Highway 25-70
Marshall, NC 28753
(704) 656-2681, 656-2091
Maggie Griffey

Plants ⚬ Bulbs
Specializing in **Southeastern native plants**, a nice selection of hardy native orchids and ferns, violas, trilliums, bog plants, lilies and other bulbous plants, perennials and some desirable native trees and shrubs; each plant briefly described. Formerly Griffey's Nursery. (1968)
❐ Catalog: $1d, R&W, CAN/OV, bn
⌂ Nursery: All year, M-Sa

Wildflower Seed Company
P.O. Box 406
St. Helena, CA 94574
Michael Landis

Seeds ⚬ Books
Specialize in **wildflower** seed for the home landscape; collections for a cottage garden, cutting garden, dried flowers, patio gardens and for dry places, as well as mixtures for every region of the country. They also offer a few books on wildflowers and gardening. (1988)
❐ Catalog: $1d, R&W, CAN, $15m

The Wildflower Source

See The Propagator's Private Stock.

Wildginger Woodlands
P.O. Box 1091
Webster, NY 14580
Phyllis Farkas

Plants ⚬ Seeds
A collectors' list of **rock garden and woodland plants**, including Northeastern native plants, shrubs, trees and ferns, offered as plants or seeds; no descriptions of plants, but many choice items such as trillium and violas. She's had great success germinating fringed gentian: instructions with the seed. Cannot ship to IL. (1983)
❐ Catalog: $1d, SS:4,10, $10m, bn/cn

Wildlife Nurseries
P.O. Box 2724
Oshkosh, WI 54903-2724
(414) 231-3780, FAX 231-3554
James Lemberger

Plants ⌇ Seeds ⌇ Supplies
Offers **native grasses, perennials and annuals for wildlife food**, wetlands
and reclamation projects; brief plant descriptions in an informative catalog.
Also aquatic plants, pond creatures, wood duck houses, pond supplies and
even wild ducks and pheasants for release into your new habitat. (1896)
⬜ Catalog: $2, R&W, CAN/OV, $20m, cn/bn
⌂ Nursery: All year, M-F, call ahead

Wildseed Farms
P.O. Box 308
Eagle Lake, TX 77434-0308
(409) 234-7353, (800) 848-0078, FAX 234-7407
Tom Kramer

Seeds
Wildflower seed for every region; many plants are illustrated in a color
catalog, with plant descriptions and growing instructions, and illustrations
of the seedlings. They list all of the plants in each regional seed mix and
the percent of each plant in the mix by weight. (1983)
⬜ Catalog: Free($3 OV), R&W, CAN/OV, cn/bn
⌂ Nursery: All year, M-F, call ahead
▼ Garden: April, daily tours of display fields

The Wildwood Flower
Route 3, Box 165
Pittsboro, NC 27312
(919) 542-4344
Thurman Maness

Plants
Nursery-propagated **wildflowers**, including crosses between Lobelia cardinalis and L. siphilitica which have created several new color forms, as well
as L. cardinalis in white and pink forms. Also **hardy ferns, hydrangeas,**
and other perennials and ornamental shrubs; all plants well described. (1975)
⬜ Catalog: Long SASE, SS:4-5, bn

Wildwood Gardens
14488 Rock Creek Road
Chardon, OH 44024
(216) 286-3714 TO
Mrs. Anthony J. Mihalic

Plants
A nice selection of **dwarf conifers and other dwarf shrubs**, primarily for
bonsai, both indoor and outdoor, as well as a few ferns, ground covers and
rock garden plants; each plant is very briefly described. They also import
bonsai specimens from Japan and the Far East, and sell pots and supplies.
⬜ Catalog: $1, SS:4-5,9-11, $25m, bn
⌂ Nursery: March-December, daily
▼ Garden: March-December, daily

Wiley's Nut Grove Nursery
2002 Lexington Avenue
Mansfield, OH 44907-3024
(419) 756-0697
Christ Pataky, Mgr.

Plants
Offers a nice selection of **hardy nut trees**, as well as some **pawpaws** and
persimmons. Listed are Chinese chestnuts, filberts, black and Persian
walnuts, butternuts, hickory nuts and hardy pecans, as well as grafted
chestnuts; there are no plant descriptions. (1918)
⬜ Catalog: 1 FCS, SS:5-6,9-10, cn
⌂ Nursery: By appointment only, 1116 Hickory Lane
▼ Garden: By appointment only

Wilk Orchid Specialties
P.O. Box 1177
45-212 Nohonani Place
Kaneohe, HI 96744
(808) 247-6733
Alice & Chet Wilk

Plants
Offer hybrids of many types of **orchid**: cattleyas, dendrobiums, ascocendas,
phalaenopsis, vanda, oncidiums and others; each very briefly described. Also
offer a number of mericlones. They will try to locate any orchid, not just
those listed. (1978)
⬜ Catalog: Free, R&W, CAN/OV, bn
⌂ Nursery: By appointment only
▼ Garden: By appointment only

Willamette Valley Gardens Nursery
P.O.Box 285
Lake Oswego, OR 97034
(503) 636-6517
Julie Rigby

Plants
Small new nursery offers a nice selection of **perennials and rock garden
plants**, including a very good selection of species geraniums; all plants
well described. They invite your "want lists," as they grow many other
plants in quantities too small to list. (1991)
⬜ Catalog: 1 FCS($1 OV), CAN/OV, SS:W, bn

Willhite Seed Co.
P.O. Box 23
Poolville, TX 76487
(817) 599-8656, FAX 599-5843 TO/CC $25m
Don Dobbs

Seeds
Color catalog features **watermelons, melons, pumpkins huge and small**, and
a broad line of **garden vegetables** -- all very well described. Broad selection of corn, tomatoes, cowpeas, peppers, cucumbers, gourds and squash,
including many favorite old varieties. Varieties especially suited to the
South, with some from France and the Indian subcontinent. (1920)
⬜ Catalog: Free, R&W, CAN/OV

Willow Oak Flower & Herb Farm
8109 Telegraph Road
Severn, MD 21144
(410) 551-2237
Maria Price

Plants ⌇ Supplies
Offers a nice selection of **herbs**: artemisias, basils, lavenders, mints,
salvias, thymes and everlastings. Plants listed by common name with no plant
descriptions. They also sell herb crafts and potpourri supplies.
⬜ Catalog: 1 FCS($1 OV), R&W, CAN/OV, SS:5-8, $25m, cn
⌂ Nursery: March-December, M-Sa
▼ Garden: May, M-Sa

Nancy Wilson Species & Miniature Narcissus
6525 Briceland-Thorn Road
Garberville, CA 95440
(707) 923-2407
Nancy Wilson

Bulbs
A very small nursery specializing in **species and miniature narcissus**. Each well described, but stock is limited; these are real collectors' items. She is looking for collectors willing to trade unusual items and wants to create a gene bank and recover old varieties. These are delightful plants. (1980)
❐ Catalog: $1d, CAN/OV, SS:9, $10m, bn

Wimberlyway Gardens
7024 N.W. 18th Avenue
Gainesville, FL 32605-3237
(904) 331-4922
R. W. "Bill" Munson, Jr. & Betty Hudson

Plants
A very broad selection of **daylilies**; most plants very well described, many shown in color photos. Many are Bill Munson's introductions (many tetraploids) and those of his sister, Betty Hudson, who specializes in doubles.
❐ Catalog: $3, CAN/OV
⌂ Nursery: May-September, call ahead

Windmill Point Farm & Nursery
2103 Perrot Boulevard
N.D. Ile Perrot, PQ, Canada J7V 8P4
(514) 453-9757
Lorraine & Ken Taylor

Plants
Offers a broad selection of **fruit trees and other edible fruited plants**, some selected for hardiness and others suitable for a northern greenhouse; all plants are well described and organically grown. Also offer a number of hardy ornamental trees and shrubs, and some interesting odds-and-ends. (1974)
❐ Catalog: $3, R&W, US/OV, SS:4-5,10-11
⌂ Nursery: September-June, Th-Su
▼ Garden: July-September, call ahead

Windrose Ltd.
1093 Ackermanville Road
Pen Argyl, PA 18072-9670
M. Nigel Wright

Plants
A new nursery specializing in **trees and shrubs** which are usually hard to find because they don't transplant well; Windrose is growing them in deep treepots. Offers oaks, hickories, horse chestnuts, species maples, birches and some fine flowering trees and shrubs. Each is briefly described. (1992)
❐ Catalog: Free, CAN, SS:3-4,9-10, bn
⌂ Nursery: April-October, Sa-Su, by appointment only
▼ Garden: May-September, Sa-Su, by appointment only

Windsong Orchids
14N456 Factly Road
Sycamore, IL 60178
(708) 683-2139
Mark Hippler & Stuart Baxter

Plants ⬥ Supplies
A newish small nursery offering **species and hybrid orchids**: phalaenopsis, paphiopedilums and phragmipediums, vandas and ascocendas, cattleya hybrids and mericlones, and some orchid growing supplies. They do most of their own breeding and have a tissue culture lab. Only flower color described. (1990)
❐ Catalog: Free, R&W, CAN/OV, SS:3-11, bn
⌂ Nursery: All year, M-Sa
▼ Garden: March-May, M-Sa

Windy Oaks Daylilies & Aquatics
W 377 S 10677 Betts Road
Eagle, WI 53119
(414) 594-2803, FAX 547-7831
Marilyn Buscher

Plants
Small nursery specializing in **pond and bog plants**: hardy waterlilies and marginal plants, some tropical marginal plants, koi and water gardening supplies and books. Nice selection, no plant descriptions. (1982)
❐ Catalog: Free, R&W, CAN/OV, SS:W, bn
⌂ Nursery: May-August, Sa-Su; September-April, call ahead
▼ Garden: May-September, Sa-Su

Windy Ridge Nursery
Box 12, Site 3
Hythe, AB, Canada T0H 2C0
(403) 356-2167, FAX 356-3694 TO/CC $10m
John & Carol Jones

Plants
Hardy and native fruit and ornamental trees, shrubs and perennials; all briefly to well described. Offer apples, saskatoons, raspberries and strawberries, Nanking cherries, currants and gooseberries. (1979)
❐ Catalog: $2d, R&W, US, SS:4-5,9-10, $10m
⌂ Nursery: April-October, daily
▼ Garden: July-August, daily

Wirth's Herbs
4037 Penn Avenue
Pittsburgh, PA 15224
Edward J. Wirth

Plants ⬥ Books
Offers a good selection of **scented geraniums**, each well described as to scent, leaf and flower; cannot ship plants to CA or HI. Also offers books on herbs and scented geraniums. (1990)
❐ Catalog: Long SASE, R&W, SS:4-10, $10m

Wisley Dahlia Farm
9076 County Road 87
Hammondsport, NY 14840
(607) 569-3578
Jim Embrey

Plants
Specializes in "top show **dahlias**," a nice selection on a concise list which indicates how many prizes each variety won two summers ago. Also offers several collections to hook you on growing and maybe even showing. (1986)
❐ Catalog: Free($1 OV), R&W, CAN/OV, $10m
⌂ Nursery: March-January, call ahead
▼ Garden: August-September, call ahead

Womack's Nursery Co.
Route 1, Box 80
Highway 6 between De Leon and Gorman
De Leon, TX 76444-9649
(817) 893-6497, FAX 893-3400
Larry J. Womack

Plants ❧ Supplies
Specialist in **fruits and nuts for the Southwest**: pecans, peaches, pears, apricots, apples, wine and table grapes, as well as shade and flowering trees, shrubs and roses; all plants well described. They also sell pruning and propagation tools and supplies, and sprayers. No shipping to CA. (1937)
❒ Catalog: Free, R&W, SS:12-3, $25m
⌂ Nursery: Mid-December-March, M-Sa

Tom Wood, Nurseryman
P.O. Box 100
Archer, FL 32618
(904) 495-9168
Tom Wood

Plants
A very good selection of **gingers**: alpinias, costus, curcumas, globbas, kaempferias, hedychiums, zingibers and his own hybrids; also lists bamboos. Plants are listed by common and botanical names with very brief but informative descriptions. He has a collection of 150 species and hybrids and will trade for new kinds. Some problems shipping to AZ, CA, LA or TX.
❒ Catalog: Free, R&W, CAN/OV, SS:W, $20m
⌂ Nursery: By appointment only
▼ Garden: By appointment only

Woodlanders, Inc.
1128 Colleton Avenue
Aiken, SC 29801
(803) 648-7522
Robt. & Julia Mackintosh, Robt. McCartney

Plants ❧ Books
A collectors' list of **Southeastern native trees, vines, shrubs, ferns, ground covers and perennials** and new or hard-to-find exotics; briefly described, with sources of further information. Looking up the plants is well worth the trouble, the list contains many treasures. Also sells books on plants and field guides. (1980)
❒ Catalog: $2($3 OV), R&W, CAN/OV, SS:10-3, $15m, bn
⌂ Nursery: All year, M-F, by appointment only
▼ Garden: April, October, by appointment only

Worcester County Horticultural Society
Tower Hill Botanic Garden
11 French Drive
Boylston, MA 01505-1008
(508) 869-6111, FAX 869-0314

Plants
Maintains a preservation orchard, from which they offer **scions of heirloom apple varieties**; over 100 pre-twentieth century varieties. Here's your chance to get 'Sops of Wine,' 'Crow Egg,' 'Utter,' 'Pomme Grise' and other tasties.
❒ Catalog: Long SASE, SS:3, $10m
▼ Garden: Preservation orchard, April-October, daily

Wrenwood of Berkeley Springs
Route 4, Box 361
Berkeley Springs, WV 25411
(304) 258-3071
Flora & John Hackimer

Plants
Large selection of **herbs, perennials, scented geraniums, sedums and rock garden plants,** listed in an informative catalog. Many thymes, dianthus, salvias, oreganos, mints, basils and other temptations -- so many herbs are also wonderful garden perennials. No shipping to CA. (1981)
❒ Catalog: $2, R&W, SS:4-10, $30m, bn/cn
⌂ Nursery: All year, W-Su
▼ Garden: May-September, W-Su

Wrightman Alpines
R.R. 3
Kerwood, ON, Canada N0M 2B0
(519) 247-3751
Harvey & Irene Wrightman

Plants
Small nursery which specializes in **alpine plants**, "especially new introductions from seed collections in the American West and Central Asia." A nice selection, with brief plant descriptions; Harvey says the list will change as new introductions become available. (1985)
❒ Catalog: $2, US/OV, SS:4-5,9-10, $40m, bn
⌂ Nursery: May-June, Sa-Su, call ahead
▼ Garden: May-June, Sa-Su, call ahead

Guy Wrinkle Exotic Plants
11610 Addison Street
North Hollywood, CA 91601
(310) 670-8637, FAX 670-1427
Guy Wrinkle

Plants ❧ Bulbs
Specializes in **collectors' plants** -- haworthia, species pelargoniums, species bulbs from South Africa, euphorbias, species orchids and a large selection of cycads and rare succulents from trips to Africa and Mexico. Some are rare and in short supply; no plant descriptions. Guy has written a book, "Cycad Culture and Propagation." (1980)
❒ Catalog: $1d($2 OV), R&W, CAN/OV, SS:W, $15m, bn
⌂ Nursery: All year, by appointment only

York Hill Farm
271 N. Haverhill Road
Kensington, NH 03833
(603) 772-8567
Darlyn C. Springer

Plants
A specialty nursery offering the "very newest" in **Japanese and Siberian irises,** and **hostas and daylilies,** with some other irises, companion perennials and ornamental grasses; most plants well described. Some of the Japanese iris and daylilies are their own introductions. (1990)
❒ Catalog: $1, SS:4-5,9-10, $20m, bn
⌂ Nursery: May-October, Th-Sa
▼ Garden: June-September, Th-Sa, call ahead

Roy Young, Seedsman
23, Westland Chase, West Winch
King's Lynn, Norfolk, England PE33 0QH
(0553) 84-0867
Mr. & Mrs. Roy Young

Seeds
"List of approximately 2,000 different **cactus and succulent** seeds obtained from either my own hand-pollinated plants or direct from habitat. Includes a guaranteed accurately named selection of every known lithops." (1984)
❒ Catalog: $2 or 3 IRC, R&W, OV, $10m

Yucca Do Nursery
P.O. Box 655
Waller, TX 77484-0655
(409) 826-6363
John Fairey & Carl Schoenfeld

Plants
Two plant explorers who introduce unusual **trees, shrubs and perennials** for Zones 7 to 9: species maples, cercis, styrax, salvias, conifers, yuccas, agaves and much more, all well described. Also listed are garden perennials that grow well in their tough summer climate: mostly native Texas plants and their Mexican, Asian and southeastern US counterparts. (1986)
❒ Catalog: $3, SS:10-12,1-3, $25m, bn
▼ Garden: By appointment only; write for information

© Bio-Quest International
Artist: Shari Smith

Garden Suppliers and Services

Sources of garden supplies are listed alphabetically. Their specialties (furniture, ornaments, supplies, tools, books, and services) are indicated at the top of the notes on catalogs.

See the Index section for:

K. Product Sources Index: an index of suppliers and services listed by specialties. This index also includes nurseries and seed companies that offer products or services. Within categories, sources are listed by location, and a symbol indicates whether they have a sales location or shop to visit.

Other Sources of Garden Supplies and Services

For tools and garden ornaments, keep your eye on garage sales, salvage yards and dumps—and always be alert for old houses and gardens being demolished for "progress." These are good sources of old bricks and paving stones, gates, fences, trellises, benches and more. Sometimes you can strike a deal with the wreckers and haul it away yourself, as I did with a thousand bricks on the hottest day of the year!

For books, see the many sources of new and used books listed in this section. Also, it's wise to check used bookstores and the remainder tables of new bookstores routinely. Many of the societies listed in Section D sell books to their members; some of these books are highly specialized and hard to find elsewhere.

For garden tours, also check the tour programs of horticultural and plant societies; many have excellent offerings. Several horticultural magazines, such as *Pacific Horticulture* and *Horticulture,* offer tours to their readers, as do several specialist nurseries.

A table of the symbols and abbreviations used in this book appears
on the bookmark inside the back cover.

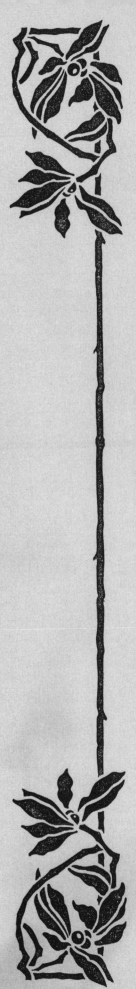

A & L Analytical Laboratories, Inc.
411 N. Third Street
Memphis, TN 38105
(901) 527-2780, FAX 526-1031
Richard Large

Services
A **testing laboratory** which will perform soil tests by mail; they also
perform plant analysis, pesticide, fertilizer and feed analysis, and water
and wastewater analysis, as well as other tests. (1971)
❒ Catalog: Free

Abracadata, Ltd.
P.O. Box 2440
Eugene, OR 97402
(503) 342-3030, (800) 451-4871 TO/CC
Customer Service

Services
"Design your own home landscape," a **computer program** that draws landscape plans, positions trees, shrubs and hard features, allows you to view
plans from different angles and plants at four different sizes. They also
have a program for vegetables gardens, called Sprout!, and a railway design
program in 8 different scales, to help you design your garden railway.
❒ Catalog: Free, R&W, CAN/OV

Acorn Services Corporation
P.O. Box 2854
40 Giddiah Hill Rd. (Orleans)
Brewster, MA 02631
(508) 240-0072, (800) 472-4957
Warren Smith

Furniture ⌘ Supplies
Sell **garden furniture, potting benches, plant stands, patio carts** and
trellises, all made of redwood for strength and durability. They also sell
a cold frame and long-lasting redwood flats for starting seeds; all products
have a lifetime money-back guarantee. (1982)
❒ Catalog: Free, R&W, CAN/OV
⌂ Shop: All year, M-Sa

Acres, U.S.A. -- Book Sales
P.O. Box 9547
Kansas City, MO 64133
(816) 737-0064, FAX 737-3346 TO/CC
Charles Walter, Jr.

Books
Books on **gardening and bio-dynamic farming**, the environment, herbs and
health, and political matters connected with those subjects. Acres, U.S.A. is
actually a periodical; this is their book sales division.
❒ Catalog: Free, CAN/OV
⌂ Shop: All year, M-F

Adams & Adkins
104 South Early Street
Alexandria, VA 22304
(703) 823-3404, FAX 823-5367
Dorcas Adkins & Bob Adams

Ornaments
Offers the Water Flute(TM), a self-contained **Japanese style fountain** which
comes in several sizes. They also make a matching red cedar planter, a cute
little bench, and a hanging "potting shed" for your garden supplies. (1983)
❒ Catalog: Free, R&W, CAN/OV
⌂ Shop: February-December, Sa, call ahead

Adirondack Designs
350 Cypress Street
Fort Bragg, CA 95437
(707) 964-4940, (800) 222-0343 TO/CC
George Griffith, Mgr.

Furniture
Sell the **Adirondack chair**, a garden classic, as well as a similar love-
seat, sun lounge and swing, potting bench and side and coffee tables;
all made of California redwood for durability. (1981)
❒ Catalog: Free, CAN/OV
⌂ Shop: All year, M-F

agAccess
P.O. Box 2008
603 Fourth Street
Davis, CA 95616
(916) 756-7177, FAX 756-7188 TO/CC
David Katz & Karen Van Epen

Books ⌘ Services
A source for new books in all areas of **agriculture and horticulture**, from
water and irrigation to specialty crops. While leaning toward agriculture,
they also carry books on forestry, natural history and gardening; books in
the catalog are reviewed in some detail. They stock over 12,000 titles, and
also have an agricultural research service. (1979)
❒ Catalog: Free, R&W, CAN/OV
⌂ Shop: All year, M-Sa

Age-Old Organics
P.O. Box 1556
Boulder, CO 80306
(303) 499-0201, FAX 499-3231 TO/CC $20m
Christ Burke & Chris Munley

Supplies
Offers **organic fertilizers**, including bat guano, greensand, kelp meal and
soluble seaweed and fish powders for foliar feeding; also compost tumblers
and composting aids, earthworms and beneficial insects. Products and their
uses well described in an informative list. (1988)
❒ Catalog: Free, R&W, CAN/OV
⌂ Shop: By appointment only

Albiflora, Inc.
P.O. Box 24, Gyotoku
Ichikawa, Chiba, Japan 272-01
(0473) 58-7627, FAX same
Mah Yanagisawa

Books
A **Japanese book store**, specializing in new books on Japanese plants and
gardens, and books on bonsai and native orchids, as well as used, out-of-
print and antiquarian books published in Japan. Catalog indicates which books
have Latin botanical or English cultivar names. (1984)
❒ Catalog: 2 IRC, R&W, OV
⌂ Shop: By appointment only

Alpine Millworks Company
1231 W. Lehigh Place
Englewood, CO 80110
(303) 761-6334
Kent Struble

Furniture
Sells **garden furniture** manufactured in Colorado. Two styles are offered: classic British and Adirondack chairs, benches, dining, coffee and end tables, and planters; all styles offered in either teak or mahogany. (1989)
❑ Catalog: Free, R&W, CAN

Alsto's Handy Helpers
P.O. Box 1267
Route 150 East
Galesburg, IL 61401
(309) 343-6181, FAX 343-5785 TO/CC
Mike Voyles, Mgr.

Furniture ❧ Ornaments ❧ Supplies ❧ Tools
Offers a broad selection of **gadgets for garden and home**: garden carts, tools, supplies, watering equipment, bird houses and bird feeders, animal traps, lawn furniture, and many items for auto, home and kitchen.
❑ Catalog: Free, CAN/OV

Alternative Garden Supply, Inc.
297 N. Barrington Road
Streamwood, IL 60107
(708) 885-8282, (800) 444-2837 TO/CC
David Ittel

Supplies ❧ Tools
The company has changed its focus to **hydroponic systems**; offers a good selection of plant lights, growing supplies, fertilizers and insect controls for the indoor grower. The shop is called Chicago Indoor Garden Supply.
❑ Catalog: Free, R&W
⌂ Shop: All year, daily

Amaranth Stoneware
P.O. Box 243
Sydenham, ON, Canada K0H 2T0
(800) 465-5444, FAX (613) 541-0799 TO/CC
Paul & Marilyn King

Ornaments ❧ Supplies
Stoneware and terra cotta **garden signs** for herb and vegetable gardens; available for a number of popular plants, as well as for "weeds," "cat crossing" and "thank you for not smoking." Other choices available. (1986)
❑ Catalog: Free, R&W, US/OV

American Arborist Supplies
882 South Matlack Street
West Chester, PA 19382
(215) 430-1214, (800) 441-8381, FAX 430-8560
Richard W. Miller, Pres

Books ❧ Supplies ❧ Tools
A very broad selection of **tools and supplies** for the "Green Industry:" chain saws, pruning tools, sprayers, climbing and safety equipment, shovels, rakes, picks and mattocks and much more. They also sell books on tree pruning and care. (1967)
❑ Catalog: $4d, CAN/OV

The American Botanist
P.O. Box 532
1103 West Truitt
Chillicothe, IL 61523
(309) 274-5254 TO/CC $25m
Keith Crotz

Books ❧ Services
Specialize in **rare, used and out-of-print books** in all areas of agriculture, horticulture and botany. Also offer collection development and book search services and appraisals, and will buy book collections in their field. Have published fine replicas of historical 19th century books. (1983)
❑ Catalog: $2, R&W, CAN/OV
⌂ Shop: All year, call ahead

American Standard Co.
157 Water Street
Southington, CT 06489
(203) 628-9643, (800) 275-3618, FAX 628-6036
Florian Family

Tools
Florian Rachet-Cut **pruning tools** with ratchet action have increased leverage and need less hand-power; they offer hand pruners, loppers and pole pruners. I have a pair of the hand pruners and love them -- they're sharp and lightweight, and really do the work I ask of them.
❑ Catalog: Free, R&W, CAN/OV
⌂ Shop: All year, M-F

American Weather Enterprises
P.O. Box 1383
Media, PA 19063
(215) 565-1232 TO/CC $25m
Ti Richard Sanders

Supplies
A nice selection of **weather instruments**: hygrometers, thermometers, barometers, anemometers, recording equipment, remote weather stations, sundials and weathervanes. They also offer books on the weather and computer software for weather forecasting and hurricane tracking. (1980)
❑ Catalog: Free, CAN/OV

Aquacide Company
P.O. Box 10748
1627 9th Street
White Bear Lake, MN 55110-0748
(612) 429-6742, (800) 328-9350, FAX 429-0563
Francis P. Markoe

Supplies
Offer a variety of **products to control algae and underwater weeds** in lakes and ponds; supposed to be harmless to fish. Another product, Mosquito Beater, is a safe dry powder which keeps mosquitoes away for days. They also sell some special tools for cutting and gathering weeds from ponds. (1956)
❑ Catalog: Free
⌂ Shop: All year, M-F

Aquamonitor
P.O. Box 327
Huntington, NY 11743
(516) 427-5664
Robert & Velma Whitener

Supplies
Complete **mist irrigation systems** and/or automatic controls to monitor soil moisture for propagation in greenhouses; useful for any greenhouse plants, seedlings or cuttings which need constant moisture. Because the system monitors the soil, it waters when needed, not on an automatic timer. (1971)
❑ Catalog: Free, R&W, CAN/OV

Arbico, Inc.
P.O. Box 4247 CRB
Tucson, AZ 85738-1247
(602) 825-9785, (800) 827-2847, FAX 825-2038
Rick & Sheri Frey

Supplies
Specialize in "sustainable environmental alternatives" and offer **organic** growing supplies, beneficial insects, fertilizers, pest barriers and traps, and free consultation to customers. Informative catalog. (1979)
❐ Catalog: Free, R&W, CAN/OV

Arborist Supply House, Inc.
P.O. Box 23607
215 S.W. 32nd Street
Fort Lauderdale, FL 33307
(305) 561-9527, (800) 749-9528, FAX 524-2210
Geraldine Hoyt

Books ❧ **Tools**
Offers specialized **equipment for arborists**, some of which is also useful to less specialized folk: pruning tools, safety equipment, deep-root barriers and a nice little tree guard to protect from weed-whackers. Also sells books for tree workers, and books on tropical plants. (1984)
❐ Catalog: Free, R&W, CAN/OV
⌂ Shop: All year, M-F

The Artisans Group
1039 Main Street
Dublin, NH 03444
(603) 563-8782, (800) 528-2035, FAX 563-7157
Craig Wentworth

Ornaments
Represents a number of artisans making **garden ornaments**: historical reproductions of bird houses and feeders, arbors, plant stands and more. All are charming, but they aren't cheap -- they'd make lovely gifts. (1991)
❐ Catalog: $1d, CAN
⌂ Shop: All year, Tu-Su

Asian Artifacts
P. O. Box 2494
Oceanside, CA 92051
(619) 723-3039, 967-3850
Soon & Frederick Krause

Ornaments
Specialize in hand crafted granite **Japanese garden ornaments**: water basins, lanterns, pagodas and figures. These are beautifully made and not cheap, but perfect as a finishing touch to your Japanese garden. (1986)
❐ Catalog: $2, R&W, CAN/OV, $100m
⌂ Shop: By appointment only

Astoria-Pacific, Inc.
P.O. Box 830
Clackamas, OR 97015
(503) 655-7470, (800) 536-3111, FAX 655-7367
Donna Kopman

Supplies
Offers Dip 'n Grow(R) liquid **rooting hormone** in 2 oz. bottles for the home gardener. It contains both IBA and NAA, frequently recommended in propagation manuals.
❐ Catalog: Free, R&W, $10m

Avant Horticultural Products
5755 Balfrey Drive
West Palm Beach, FL 33413
(407) 683-0171, (800) 334-7979
C. Wyclif Head II

Supplies
Manufacturers of **reacted liquid plant foods**, which they claim are more immediately available to plants. There are several formulas -- for roses, blooming plants and agricultural plants, growth hormones, and a formula compatible with fungicides and insecticides. Avant Thermo-Chem offers winter protection to plants and is an antidesiccant. (1985)
❐ Catalog: Free, CAN

David Bacon Woodworking
P.O. Box 1034
Nevada City, CA 95959
(916) 273-8889

Ornaments
A one-man woodworking shop that builds window boxes and planters (with liners to make them last longer), a garden gate, and a handsome cherry wood library bookstand for reading at the table or admiring a good illustration. (1977)
❐ Catalog: Free, R&W, CAN/OV, $45m

Baker's Lawn Ornaments
R.D. 5, Box 265
Somerset, PA 15501
(814) 445-7028
Valerie & Michael Baker

Ornaments
Manufacture and sell **gazing globes**, a Victorian garden ornament popular in period garden restorations or used just for fun. They are either 10 or 12 inches in diameter, and come in red, green, blue, gold, silver and purple.
❐ Catalog: Long SASE, R&W, $19m
⌂ Shop: All year, daily

Bamboo & Rattan Works Inc.
470 Oberlin Avenue S.
Lakewood, NJ 08701
(908) 370-0220, FAX 905-8386
Arthur L. Maison

Ornaments
Offers **bamboo and reed fencing** to give gardens an oriental look; fencing is available in several styles and you can buy the materials and make your own. Also offers reed matting, and material for caning chairs. (1880)
❐ Catalog: Long SASE w/2 FCS, CAN/OV
⌂ Shop: All year except Dec. 26-January 1, M-F

Bruce Barber Bird-Feeders, Inc.
928 West 19th Street
Erie, PA 16502
(814) 459-1406, FAX 459-5802
Melanie Butts

Ornaments
Sells **bird and squirrel feeders** in several appealing styles made of red cedar for durability. My favorite is the "flying squirrel feeder" made like a little airplane.
❐ Catalog: Free

The Barn Owl

See Wavecrest Nursery & Landscaping Co. in Section A.

Carol Barnett -- Books
3562 N.E. Liberty Street
Portland, OR 97211-7248
(503) 282-7036
Carol Barnett

Books ✍ Services
Specializes in **used, rare and out-of-print books** on gardens, horticulture and botany, with brief descriptions of contents as well as notes on condition. Occasionally reprints small books of historical horticultural interest, such as "Pearson on the Orchard House, 1867." She will also do book searches if you send her a "want list." (1983)
❒ Catalog: Free, CAN/OV

J. F. Beattie Book Co.
105 N. Wayne Avenue
Wayne, PA 19087
(215) 687-3347, FAX 687-5495
Jim Beattie

Books
Offers old, rare and collectible **books on gardening**, and issues catalogs once or twice a year. All subjects, including agriculture, landscape architecture, and many plant monographs from the early 20th century. (1976)
❒ Catalog: $2d, R&W, CAN/OV, $35m

Leona Bee Tours & Travel
9550 Bay Harbor Terrace, Suite 211
Bay Harbor Islands, FL 33154
(305) 861-8274 FAX 861-0707

Services
Travel agency specializing in **horticultural tours**, including special tours for orchid-lovers to various habitats of species orchids.
❒ Catalog: Free

Bell's Book Store
536 Emerson Street
Palo Alto, CA 94301
(415) 323-7822 TO/CC $10m
Mrs. Herbert Bell

Books
Offer a good selection of **new, used and out-of-print books** on gardening. They have a good annotated book list on "Old Garden Roses" ($2.50), but no regular catalog. Send a "want list" to see if they have what you want. (1935)
❒ Catalog: See notes, CAN/OV
⌂ Shop: All year, M-Sa

Berry Hill Limited
75 Burwell Road
St. Thomas, ON, Canada N5P 3R5
(519) 631-0480, FAX 631-8935 TO/CC
Ken Fox

Books ✍ Supplies ✍ Tools
Here's a wonderful old-time **farm equipment and country kitchen** catalog: full of canning supplies, equipment for dairy and poultry yards, garden bells, weather vanes, a cider press and tools and equipment for the garden. They also sell many practical "how-to" books. (1948)
❒ Catalog: Free($2 OV), R&W, US/OV, $5m

Better Yield Insects
R.R. 3, Site 4, Box 48
Belle River, ON, Canada N0R 1A0
(519) 727-6108, FAX 727-5989 TO/CC
Mrs. Patricia Coristine

Supplies
Supplier of **beneficial insects**: whitefly parasites, spider mite predators, aphid predators, thrip predators and nematodes. They also sell sticky traps, strips and insect barriers. No shipping to HI. (1977)
❒ Catalog: $1, US/OV, SS:W, $10m
⌂ Shop: All year, daily, call ahead

B. L. Bibby Books
1225 Sardine Creek Road
Gold Hill, OR 97525-9730
(503) 855-1621
George A. Bibby

Books
Offers **used and out-of-print books** on plants and horticulture, gardening, flower arranging and other natural history subjects. (1963)
❒ Catalog: $3d, CAN/OV

Dorothy Biddle Service
HC 01, Box 900
Greeley, PA 18425-9799
(717) 226-3239, FAX 226-0349
Lynne Dodson

Books ✍ Supplies ✍ Tools
A broad selection of **supplies and equipment for flower arrangers** which would be useful to all who cut and bring flowers indoors. Books on arranging and drying flowers, tools, and some houseplant growing supplies. (1936)
❒ Catalog: $.50, R&W, CAN/OV

Bio-Control Co.

See The Lady Bug Company.

Bio-Gard Agronomics
P.O. Box 4477
Falls Church, VA 22044
(800) 673-8502 or 1703, FAX (703) 536-2528
Dr. Andrew J. Welebir

Supplies
Offer their Calcium-25(TM), a completely **organic foliar fertilizer**, which they say will increase yield 20% to 50%, and can be used on ornamental plants as well as food crops. (1987)
❒ Catalog: Free, R&W, CAN/OV, $10m

BioLogic
P.O. Box 177
Springtown Road
Willow Hill, PA 17271
(717) 349-2789 or 2922, FAX 349-2789
Dr. Albert Pye, Jr.

Supplies
Sells Scanmask -- a strain of **beneficial, insect-eating nematodes** to control soil and boring pest insects such as black vine weevils, white grubs, cutworms, caterpillars and fly maggots; harmless to beneficial insects. Let them know if you are a home gardener or commercial grower. (1985)
❒ Catalog: Long SASE, R&W, CAN/OV, $17m
⌂ Shop: All year, call ahead

BioTherm Hydronic, Inc.
P.O. Box 750967
Petaluma, CA 94975
(707) 762-8425, (800) GET-HEAT, FAX 762-9628
Jim Rearden

Supplies
Manufacturers and sells **heating systems for greenhouses**, mostly for warming benches by radiant heat. While most of their systems are for commercial growers and not inexpensive, they may have just what you need. (1989)
❒ Catalog: $2($3 OV), R&W, CAN/OV

Geo. C. Birlant & Co.

See Charleston Battery Bench, Inc.

Blue Planet, Inc.
P.O. Box 1500
Princeton, NJ 08542
(718) 428-3627, (800) 777-9201, FAX 423-9223
Frank Chester

Supplies
Manufactures the COMPOsift **composting machine**, which tumbles and sifts compost, and which is powered by electricity, eliminating the effort of turning the drum. It will hold 33 cubic feet of raw materials. (1992)
❐ Catalog: Free, R&W, CAN/OV

Bodoh, Inc.
P.O. Box 248
488 Albion Road
Edgerton, WI 53534
(608) 884-8848
Ron Bodoh

Ornaments
A group of four artists who make **garden ornaments** out of recycled copper, brass and iron. They include whimsical sculptures, lanterns, bird houses, wind chimes, even some jewelery. Their studio is an old schoolhouse. (1987)
❐ Catalog: Free($1 OV), R&W, CAN/OV
⌂ Shop: All year, M-Sa

Bonide Products, Inc.
2 Wurz Avenue
Yorkville, NY 13495
(315) 736-8233 or 8246, FAX 736-7582 (orders)
Jim Wurz

Supplies
Offers a complete line of **home, garden and lawn pesticides**, including the organic products Rotenone, Dipel, Bacillus thuringiensis, dormant oil, oil and lime sulfur spray and many more. (1926)
❐ Catalog: $2d, R&W, CAN, $10m

Bonsai Associates, Inc.
3000 Chestnut Avenue
Baltimore, MD 21211
(410) 235-5336 TO/CC
Barbara Bogash & Arschel Morell

Books ❧ Supplies ❧ Tools ❧ Services
A wide selection of **bonsai books, tools and supplies**; they also sell some starter plants for bonsai, each plant well described. They repot, re-fine and board bonsai for local enthusiasts, and offer bonsai classes. (1979)
❐ Catalog: $2d, CAN/OV
⌂ Shop: All year, W-Sa, call ahead

Bonsai Northwest
5021 South 144th Street
Seattle, WA 98168
(206) 242-8244, FAX 244-2301
Sharon & John Muth

Books ❧ Supplies ❧ Tools ❧ Services
A broad selection of **bonsai pots, tools, supplies** and some books; they offer Kaneshin bonsai tools and Tokoname bonsai pots. They also offer classes on bonsai, plants, and repotting and styling services at the shop.
❐ Catalog: $2, R&W, CAN
⌂ Shop: All year, Th-Sa

Book Arbor
P.O. Box 20885
Baltimore, MD 21209-9998
(410) 367-0338
Judith M. Bloomgarden

Books ❧ Services
Offers **antiquarian and out-of-print books** on horticulture, landscape architecture, garden history and 19th century American agriculture. They will also search for books on your "want-list." (1990)
❐ Catalog: Free, CAN/OV

Book Orchard
1379 Park Western Dr., Suite 802
San Pedro, CA 90732
(310) 548-4279, FAX same
Raminta Jautokas

Books
Specializes in **books for the Western gardener**: books on regional gardening in California, the Southwest and Northwest, as well as books of general interest. Also sells books on cooking from the garden. (1991)
❐ Catalog: Free, CAN/OV, $6m

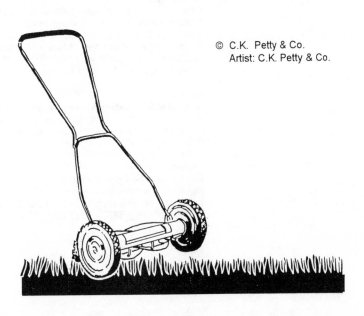

© C.K. Petty & Co.
Artist: C.K. Petty & Co.

The Book Tree
12 Pine Hill Road
Englishtown, NJ 07726
(908) 446-3853, FAX 446-5610 TO/CC
Anne & John Haines

Books & Services
Offer **new and recent books** on landscape architecture, horticulture, plants and gardening; over 600 titles. They will also try to locate current books for you. They have added a line of horticulturally inspired jewelry for gardeners in pewter, silver plate and enamel. (1986)
❑ Catalog: Free, R&W, CAN/OV
⌂ Shop: All year, call ahead

Bookfinders General, Inc.
Box G, Madison Square Station
New York, NY 10159-1056
(212) 689-0772, FAX 481-0552

Books & Services
A free **book-finding** service: send your "want list," and they will search for any book and send you a price quote when they find it. (1963)
❑ Catalog: Free

Bow House, Inc.
P.O. Box 900
92 Randall Road
Bolton, MA 01740
(508) 779-6464 or 2271, FAX 779-2272
John J. Rogers

Ornaments
Offer **gazebos and garden structures** of classic design; the Belvedeary can be finished in several styles, even cut in half for a bay window. Also sell a domed temple, arbors, a pergola, changing structures, a Japanese tea house, bridges up to 40 feet, even a dog house. All very elegant. (1971)
❑ Catalog: $3, R&W, CAN/OV
⌂ Shop: All year, M-F or by appointment

Bozeman Bio-Tech
P.O. Box 3146
1612 Gold Avenue
Bozeman, MT 59772
(406) 587-5891, (800) 289-6656, FAX 587-0223
Dr. W. Wayne Vinje

Supplies
"Producers and distributors of natural products for least-toxic, long-term protection from insect pests." Offer **pheromone traps, beneficial insects**, soaps, botanical extracts, fungicides and sprayers; catalog is very informative. (1986)
❑ Catalog: Free, R&W, CAN/OV
⌂ Shop: All year, M-F

Bramen Company, Inc.
P.O. Box 70
Salem, MA 01970-0070
(508) 745-7765, FAX 745-7425 TO/CC
Robert Strom

Books & Supplies & Tools
Automatic Thermafor **ventilation controllers** open and close hinged windows as heavy as 30 pounds -- adjustable for temperatures from 55F to 105F -- and they work without electricity. Also offer many **hand tools**, growing supplies, garden furniture, books, garden carts and much more.
❑ Catalog: Free, R&W, CAN/OV

Bridgeworks
306 East Lockwood St.
Covington, LA 70433
(504) 893-7933, 892-6640
Paul Swain

Ornaments
Builders of **bridges** in several designs; you can have them customized to your length if the standard sizes won't fit your needs. They also make arbors and garden benches. (1991)
❑ Catalog: Free, CAN/OV

Brighton By-Products Co., Inc.
P.O. Box 23
New Brighton, PA 15066
(800) 245-3502, (800) 642-2668 TO/CC $50m
Nathan Ortinberg, Pres.

Supplies
A very broad selection of **growing and landscaping supplies,** sold to anyone by mail; especially good on greenhouse and propagation supplies, irrigation and horticultural chemicals -- including DuPont Landscape Fabric, a non-chemical mulch/weed barrier. Call for price of catalog.
❑ Catalog: See notes, CAN/OV, $50m

Andy Brinkley Studio
P.O. Box 10282
Hickory, NC 28603
(704) 462-1137, FAX 462-4647 TO/CC
Andy Brinkley

Ornaments
Offers a variety of **garden sculptures and fountains** with plant, animal and flower themes; most are made of brass, copper or bronze, some with verdigris finish. The animals are fanciful, and the flower and tree sculptures are very handsome; some can be used as light fixtures. (1976)
❑ Catalog: Long SASE w/ 2 FCS, R&W, $39m
⌂ Shop: All year, M-F, call ahead

Warren F. Broderick -- Books
P.O. Box 124
Lansingburgh, NY 12182
(518) 235-4041
Warren F. Broderick

Books
A select stock of **used, some rare, and out-of-print books** on garden design and history, plant monographs, general gardening books, garden art and architecture and botanical illustration. Catalog is mailed in the fall. (1977)
❑ Catalog: $1, R&W, CAN/OV

Bronwood Worm Gardens
P.O. Box 28
Bronwood, GA 31726-0028
(912) 995-5994
J. F. Seymour

Supplies
Specialize in **bed-run redworms** in mixed sizes for composting and gardening; they also have gray nightcrawlers (Georgia wigglers). All shipments are by Air Mail or UPS; include instructions for doing your own worm farming.
❑ Catalog: Long SASE, R&W, CAN, $15m

Brooks Books
P.O. Box 21473
Concord, CA 94521-0473
(510) 672-4566, FAX same TO/CC
Philip & Martha Nesty

Books ⌖ Services
Sells **horticultural and botanical books; new, used and out-of-print** and **rare**. Specializes in cacti, succulents, ornamental horticulture, floras and botanicals, plant monographs, fruit, Australian and South African plants, trees and shrubs. Offers a search service; buys book collections. (1986)
⬜ Catalog: $1, R&W, CAN/OV
⌂ Shop: By appointment only

Brushy Mountain Bee Farm, Inc.
Route 1, Box 135
Moravian Falls, NC 28654
(919) 921-3640, (800) BEESWAX, FAX 921-2681
Steve & Sandy Forrest

Books ⌖ Supplies ⌖ Tools
Everything for the beekeeper: books, bees, hives, supplies and equipment, including supplies for selling honey -- an informative catalog. Recent additions are video cassettes and slide shows on bees and beekeeping. Can't ship to Nigeria. (1983)
⬜ Catalog: Free, R&W, CAN/OV
⌂ Shop: April-July, M-Sa; August-March, M-F

Builders Booksource
1817 Fourth Street
Berkeley, CA 94710
(510) 845-6874, (800) 843-2028 TO/CC
George & Sally Kiskaddon

Books
A very broad selection of **books on architecture and design, construction, interior design, landscaping and gardening** -- everything from start to finish; the store is a delight! They have added a branch store at 300 De Haro St at 16th St., San Francisco, (415) 575-3980. They produce a yearly catalog and send irregular newsletters about new books.
⬜ Catalog: Free, CAN/OV
⌂ Shop: All year, daily

Bulb Savers
P.O. Box 3024
Princeton, NJ 08543-3024
(609) 883-6250, (800) 472-3284
Alicia A. Magee

Supplies
Offers a **mesh bag with attached label** for planting and identifying bulbs when the time comes to find them again. They come in two depths, 8 inches and 16 inches, and expand to hold quite large bulbs.
⬜ Catalog: Free, R&W, CAN/OV, $4m

A.C. Burke & Co.
2554 Lincoln Blvd., Suite 1058
Marina Del Ray, CA 90291
(310) 574-2770, FAX 574-2771
Andrew Burke

Books ⌖ Supplies
"Our goal is to bring user-friendly technology into the garden." They specialize in videos, software, books and accessories for the garden; cover a range of subjects from vegetables to bonsai. (1991)
⬜ Catalog: Free($1 OV), CAN/OV

Calendula Horticultural Books
P.O. Box 930
Picton, ON, Canada K0K 2T0
(613) 476-3521, FAX 476-1085
Heiko Miles

Books
Offers **rare, used and out-of-print books** on flowers and gardens, landscape architecture, flower arranging, pomology, floriculture and wildflowers. Ask for the horticultural catalog; most books are pre-1950. (1987)
⬜ Catalog: Free, R&W, US/OV

Capability's Books
2379 Highway 46
Deer Park, WI 54007
(715) 269-5346, (800) 247-8154, FAX 269-5531
Pauline Rickard & Kristen Gilbertson

Books
A very broad selection of **horticultural and gardening books**, new or recently published in the US or England. They have nearly 1,000 books in 84 categories -- something for any special interest; they will accept credit card orders by Fax from overseas. They have recently published several fine gardening books themselves. (1978)
⬜ Catalog: Free, R&W, CAN/OV
⌂ Shop: All year, M-F

Cape Cod Worm Farm
30 Center Avenue
Buzzards Bay, MA 02532
(508) 759-5664
Maggie Pipkins

Supplies
Sells **earthworms and worm castings**.
⬜ Catalog: Free, SS:W

Carruth Studio
1178 Farnsworth Road
Waterville, OH 43566
(419) 378-3060, (800) 225-1178, FAX 878-3261
George & Deborah Carruth

Ornaments
Offer cast concrete and terra cotta **wall plaques, bird feeders, birdbaths, statues, planters and garden accessories**. They say, "Plant a smile in your garden." All have a charming, whimsical feeling, some are slyly medieval! Great gifts. No shipping to Taiwan, Korea or Mexico. (1975)
⬜ Catalog: Free, R&W, CAN/OV
⌂ Shop: All year, M-F; April-December, Sa am

Cart Warehouse
P.O. Box 3
Point Arena, CA 95468
(800) 852-2588, FAX (707) 882-2488
Peter Reimuller

Supplies
Sells major brands of **garden carts** at a discount; brands include Garden Way, Foldit, Homestead and Carry-It; prices include shipping. They have added another business, California Tanks Distributors, which sells water storage tanks, pumps and fittings for home and garden water systems. (1984)
⬜ Catalog: Free, R&W, CAN
⌂ Shop: All year, M-F

Catamount Cart
P.O. Box 365
Shelburne Falls, MA 01370
(413) 625-0284, (800) 444-0056
Jim Picardi

Supplies
The Catamount Cart is a **hybrid between an old-fashioned wheelbarrow and a big-wheeled garden cart**. Hand-built of oak, with stainless steel hardware, it's made to last; comes in two sizes to hold 300 or 400 pounds. (1991)
❏ Catalog: Free($2 OV), R&W, CAN/OV

Charleston Battery Bench, Inc.
191 King Street
Charleston, SC 29401
(803) 722-3842, FAX 722-3846 TO/CC
Andrew B. Slotin, Mr. & Mrs. Phil H. Slotin

Furniture
Sells only the **Charleston Battery Bench**, made using the mold patterns of the original maker; the bench has been in use in Charleston since the 1880s. It has cast iron sides painted in traditional green, and cypress wood slats.
❏ Catalog: Free, R&W, CAN
⌂ Shop: All year, M-Sa

Charley's Greenhouse Supply
1569 Memorial Highway
Mt. Vernon, WA 98273
(206) 428-2626 TO/CC
Charles & Carol Yaw

Books ❧ Supplies ❧ Tools
A broad selection of **growing supplies, tools, plant lights, drip** and **misting systems, shade fabric, books** and many other items. They also sell greenhouses and greenhouse materials and accessories, and have 11 hobby greenhouses on display on their property. (1975)
❏ Catalog: $2, CAN/OV
⌂ Shop: All year, M-F

Chestnut Lane
24 Lightcap Road
Latrobe, PA 15650
(412) 539-8605, (800) 584-1653
Dominic Demangone

Supplies
Offer "Havahart" **live animal traps** in several sizes to "move animals harmlessly from yard or garden." Just where you move them to is not mentioned; call the Humane Society and ask. (1990)
❏ Catalog: Free, R&W, CAN

Chicago Indoor Garden Supply

See Alternative Garden Supply, Inc.

Cieli
P.O. Box 151
La Honda, CA 94020
FAX (415) 369-2082
Joyce E. Converse

Ornaments
I've fallen in love with these enchanting **garden fairies** that look as if they came from Edwardian children's books. They're made from recycled aluminum with a slightly luminous finish, and should bring good luck and perfect plants to any garden. (1989)
❏ Catalog: Long SASE($1 OV), R&W, CAN/OV, $33m

Classic & Country Crafts
5100-1B Clayton Road, Suite 291
Concord, CA 94521
(510) 672-4337
Sue Siekierski

Ornaments
Makes very handsome **copper landscape lights** in several styles; these lights are on standards for use along paths or near parking areas, and will weather to an attractive patina over time.
❏ Catalog: Free, R&W, CAN

Clothcrafters, Inc.
P.O. Box 176
Elkhart Lake, WI 53020
(414) 876-2112 TO/CC
John & Karen Wilson

Supplies
Sell **clothing for gardeners**: gloves, kneepads and aprons. In addition, they sell Poly Ban row covers, mosquito netting, cloth wares for the home and kitchen items. (1936)
❏ Catalog: Free, CAN/OV

Robert Compton, Ltd.
R.D. 3, Box 3600
Bristol, VT 05443
(802) 453-3778 TO/CC
Christine Homer & Robert Compton

Ornaments
Sells **stoneware fountains** in a variety of configurations and will make custom orders. Fountains come with submersible pump, ready to plug in and fill; they are completely self-contained and can be used indoors or out. Also sells hand made pottery at the studio; planters, birdbaths, feeders.
❏ Catalog: $2d, R&W, CAN/OV
⌂ Shop: All year, by appointment only

Computer Junction

See Infopoint Software.

Computer/Management Services
1426 Medinah Court
Arnold, MD 21012
Charles W. Barbour

Services
Custom **computer programs** for orchid lovers and the nursery trade; both run on IBM or compatible computers. "Orchidata" is software for keeping track of an inventory of orchids; "Collector" makes an inventory of any type of collectible, including plants. Your chance to organize books or photos! Also sales and inventory programs for commercial nurseries. (1982)
❏ Catalog: Free, CAN/OV, $50m

Conservatory Greenhouse

See Santa Barbara Greenhouses.

Cook's Consulting
RD 2, Box 13
Lowville, NY 13367
(315) 376-3002
Peg Cook

Services
A **soil testing service** for agriculture that also serves home gardeners. They offer organic or chemical fertilizer and soil amendment recommendations depending on the preference of the customer. (1983)
❏ Catalog: Free, CAN

Coopersmith's England
6441 Valley View Road
Oakland, CA 94611
(510) 339-2499, FAX 339-7135
Paul Coopersmith

Services
Offer **garden tours** to England, Scotland, France, Italy, Spain, and in the US; groups are small, pace is relaxed, with several nights at each country inn or stately home. Most tours seem to include a few historical sites and private gardens; offer a tour of literary England, as well.
❐ Catalog: Free

Country Casual
17317 Germantown Road
Germantown, MD 20874-2999
(301) 540-0040, 428-3434 TO/CC
Mrs. Bobbie Goldstein

Furniture
Offer Lister and Verey British **teak benches and tables** in a variety of styles and sizes, as well as their own Chippendale II designs; also several styles of garden swing, trellis work, wooden planting tubs and deck chairs. Suppliers have Friends of the Earth (UK) approval. They pay the freight on purchases. (1977)
❐ Catalog: $3($6 OV), R&W, CAN/OV
⌂ Shop: All year, M-F, Sa call ahead

Country House Floral Supply
P.O. Box 4086, Bvl. Station
Andover, MA 01810
(508) 475-8463, FAX 475-2039 TO/CC $20m
Helga Frazzette

Ornaments ⬿ Books ⬿ Supplies ⬿ Tools
Offers **flower arranging supplies**, a very broad selection, including many styles of vases, "frogs" (flower holders), bonsai stands, pruning tools and a number of books on flower arranging. (1974)
❐ Catalog: $1, CAN/OV

The Crafter's Garden
P.O. Box 3194
Peabody, MA 01961-3194
(508) 535-1142
Debra Crowell

Supplies ⬿ Tools
Offers a good selection of garden **tools, watering and composting supplies**, organic insecticides and fertilizers, plant labels and garden markers, and flower arranging equipment. (1992)
❐ Catalog: Free

Creative Playgrounds, Ltd.
P.O. Box 10
McFarland, WI 53558
(608) 838-3326, (800) 338-0522, FAX 838-9595
Jim Lee, V.P., Sales

Furniture
Sells TimberGym **play structures**, which can be put together in several configurations of various complexity, depending on space and size of family. Even comes with a tented clubhouse for secret meetings. (1974)
❐ Catalog: Free, R&W, CAN/OV

Cropking, Inc.
P.O. Box 310
4930 Chippewa Road
Medina, OH 44258
(216) 725-5656, FAX 722-3958 TO $25m
Dan J. Brentlinger

Supplies
Specialize in **greenhouses and supplies** and equipment for hydroponic growers. They have added a "gardening catalog" for home gardeners; they offer everything for indoor growing and propagation. They also sell rockwool, the latest word in growing media. (1981)
❐ Catalog: $3d, R&W, CAN/OV
⌂ Shop: All year, M-F, Sa am

Cross VINYLattice
3174 Marjan Drive
Atlanta, GA 30340
(404) 451-4531, (800) 521-9878, FAX 457-5125
Susan M. Boyd

Ornaments
Here's a great idea! **Lattice** made of vinyl in nine colors; they say it never needs painting, it's impact resistant, it won't rot, it has no staples to rust and termites won't eat it. They will only sell by mail if you're not near one of their dealers; call or write for information. (1981)
❐ Catalog: Free, R&W, CAN/OV

Cumberland Woodcraft
P.O. Drawer 609
Carlisle, PA 17013
(717) 243-0063, (800) 367-1884, FAX 243-6502
Randolph Reese

Ornaments
Offers a broad line of Victorian gingerbread for remodeling, but also two charming **gazebos**, garden benches and other nice historical reproductions.
❐ Catalog: $5, R&W, CAN/OV

D.I.G. Corporation
130 Bosstick Boulevard
San Marcos, CA 92082
(619) 727-0914, (800) 322-9146, FAX 727-0282
Rick Heenan, Dir. of Sales

Supplies
Drip and mist irrigation supplies for the do-it-yourselfer -- including micro-sprinklers for indoors and out. Informative brochure gives basics on how to get started and what you'll need. (1982)
❐ Catalog: Free, R&W, CAN/OV
⌂ Shop: All year, M-F, call ahead

Dalton Pavilions, Inc.
20 Commerce Drive
Telford, PA 18969-1030
(215) 721-1492, FAX 721-1501
James E. Dalton, Sr.

Ornaments
Offers Western red cedar **gazebos** in various sizes and several styles -- Victorian, classic, Colonial or Victorian pagoda -- all available with screening. Also sells benches and tables to fit each size, architectural bird houses, and a handsome pergola seat. (1967)
❐ Catalog: $3d, R&W, CAN/OV

Dave's Aquariums & Greenhouse
RR 1, Box 97
Kelley, IA 50134
(515) 769-2446 TO/CC
Dave Lowman

Books ♠ Supplies ♠ Tools
The name will fool you -- they sell **bonsai pots, books and tools**; a good selection of their own pots and imported pots as well. They also offer Artstone slabs and planting stones for bonsai and can make them to order from your sketch. Also sell plants for bonsai and finished bonsai. (1981)
❐ Catalog: 4 FCS, R&W, CAN/OV, $10m
⌂ Shop: All year, daily, call ahead

Day-Dex Co.
4725 N.W. 36th Avenue
Miami, FL 33142
(305) 635-5241
Ernie & Kim Motsinger

Supplies
Offer **galvanized steel tiered benches** in several styles and sizes for orchids and other indoor and patio plants; also sell shade canopies with 55% to 80% shade. In addition, they manufacture and sell Kinsman carts, dollies and flat barrows for moving heavy nursery loads.
❐ Catalog: Free, R&W, CAN/OV
⌂ Shop: All year, M-F, call ahead

De Van Koek
3100 Industrial Terrace
Austin, TX 78758
(512) 339-0009, (800) 992-1220, FAX 832-5329
Andrew Cook

Supplies ♠ Tools
Importer of European, mainly Dutch, **garden tools and accessories**; many of the digging tools have "T" handles. Also offer watering cans, gloves and gauntlets, wheelbarrows, pruning tools, bird feeders and more. A good selection, most shown in the catalog. (1988)
❐ Catalog: Free, R&W, CAN/OV
⌂ Shop: All year, M-F, call ahead

Denman & Co.
187 West Orangethorpe Avenue
Placentia, CA 92670
(714) 524-0668, FAX 524-3208
Bob & Rita Denman

Supplies ♠ Tools
Manufacture and sell **gardening pants** with pockets for knee pads, called Greenknees (TM). Their line has expanded to garden chaps, picking aprons, holsters for trowels and shears; and several **tools** that they've adapted from old faithfuls; they'll adapt tools for the handicapped, too. (1987)
❐ Catalog: Free, CAN/OV
⌂ Shop: All year, M-F, call ahead

Diamond
628 Lindaro Street
San Rafael, CA 94901
(415) 459-3994, (800) 331-3994, FAX 453-8311
Steve Stragnola

Supplies
Specialists in high intensity discharge (HID) **lighting for indoor gardening**, as well as hydroponic gardening supplies, greenhouse controls and accessories, fertilizers and indoor growing supplies. (1983)
❐ Catalog: Free, R&W, CAN/OV
⌂ Shop: All year, M-Sa

Digger's Product Development Co.
P.O. Box 1551
Soquel, CA 95073
(408) 462-6095
Wayne Morgan

Supplies
Ever notice that every letter to the editor about pocket gophers comes from Sebastopol, CA? This might be the answer -- prefabricated **wire gopher baskets**, which are shipped flat but pop open easily for planting. They come in three sizes, and Sebastipudlians can buy them by the case. (1988)
❐ Catalog: Free, R&W, CAN/OV, $100m

Double-Pawed Software
432 Bigelow Hollow
Eastford, CT 06242-9302
Lawrence & Madelyn Truett

Services
Double-Pawed Software (cat on cover of manual) is a **perpetual garden journal** and reminder system for IBM compatibles. It's designed to be easy to use for computer novices, and I can attest to that! It lets you go back and forth, and has a search feature to find important entries. (1988)
❐ Catalog: Free, R&W, CAN/OV

The Dramm Corporation
P.O. Box 1960
Manitowoc, WI 54221-1960
(414) 684-0227, FAX 684-4499 TO/CC
Kurt Dramm

Supplies ♠ Tools
Known for the Dramm Water Breaker nozzles which break water flow into a gentle shower, offers other **watering equipment**, including watering cans. Also sells a pair of handy folding "Schnippers." (1945)
❐ Catalog: Free, R&W, CAN/OV, $10m

Drip Irrigation Garden

See D.I.G. Corporation.

DripWorks
380 Maple Street
Willits, CA 95490
(707) 459-6323, (800) 522-3747, FAX 459-6323
E. Glassey, J. Jordan & L. Springer

Supplies
"We make it simple" say these **drip irrigation** specialists; they put out an informative catalog to help you design and install drip irrigation. Also sell pond liners for farm and irrigation ponds, and water storage tanks. (1992)
❐ Catalog: Free, R&W, CAN/OV
⌂ Shop: All year, M-F, call ahead

Duncraft, Inc.
33 Fisherville Road
Penacook, NH 03303
(603) 224-0200, FAX 226-3735 TO/CC
Mike Dunn

Books ♠ Supplies
Broad selection of **bird feeders, bird houses and other bird-related items**, including birdbaths. Also offer specialized bird seed mixes, depending on the birds you want to attract, and some other pet supplies. (1952)
❐ Catalog: Free, R&W

Dutch Trader

See De Van Koek.

Earlee, Inc.
2002 Highway 62
Jeffersonville, IN 47130-3556
(812) 282-9134 TO/CC $5m
Earl, Mary & Brent Stewart

Supplies
A broad selection of **organic products** for farmer and gardener; they manufacture Nature's Way growing supplies and sell many soil amendments, fertilizers, live animal traps, pest controls and bird repellents. They have a branch in New Albany, IN, call (812) 944-0751 for location and hours.
❑ Catalog: Free, R&W, CAN/OV, $3m

Earthworks
P.O. Box 67
Hyattville, WY 82428
Leonard Sherwin, Mgr.

Ornaments
Earthworks makes hand-cast **hypertufa troughs** for growing alpine and rock garden plants, herbs and small perennials or shrubs. They are available in rectangular or oval shapes and come in three colors. (1990)
❑ Catalog: Long SASE, R&W, CAN

Eco Enterprises
1240 N.E. 175th Street, Suite B
Seattle, WA 98155
(206) 363-9981, (800) 426-6937, FAX 363-9983
Terri Mitchell

Supplies
Specialists in **hydroponic garden supplies**: offer fertilizers, growing supplies, books and technical papers, growing media, and anything else you might need. Catalog is very helpful and informative. (1972)
❑ Catalog: Free($1 OV), CAN/OV
⌂ Shop: All year, M-Sa

EcoHealth, Inc.
110 Broad Street
Boston, MA 02110
(617) 742-2400, FAX 350-6260 TO/CC $22m
Christian Nolen, Dir. of Marketing

Supplies
Manufactures Damminix(R), a **pesticide** specifically targeted at the ticks that carry Lyme Disease; impregnated cotton attracts tick carrying field mice, they collect the cotton as nesting material -- clever! They do not issue a catalog, but will send descriptive literature, and take orders over the phone. (1986)
❑ Catalog: See notes.

Economy Label Sales Co., Inc.
P.O. Box 350
Daytona Beach, FL 32115
(904) 253-4741, (800) 874-4465, FAX 238-1410
John Powell

Supplies
Various styles of **plastic, paper and metal plant and garden labels**, label printers and custom labels to customer design, computer labels and software. Minimum order for most items is 1,000 blank or printed of any one style, but you can get your friends or club to share an order.
❑ Catalog: Free, R&W, CAN/OV

Editions
Route 28A, Oak Mtn. Farm
Boiceville, NY 12412
Norman Levine

Books
A dealer in **used and out-of-print books** in many fields; each catalog has a nice selection of books on gardening and horticulture. (1948)
❑ Catalog: $2, CAN/OV

Elemental Software
2218 N 1200 E
Logan, UT 84321
(801) 755-0701, FAX same
Debra Spielmaker

Services
Offers "The Plant Doctor," a **computer program** that diagnoses over 200 plant disorders caused by nutrients, water, light and other factors, and identifies over 85 common insects of the garden. It's food garden oriented; for IBM compatible computers. (1991)
❑ Catalog: Free, R&W, CAN/OV

Elgin Landscape & Garden Center
1881 Larkin Avenue
Elgin, IL 60123
(708) 697-8733

Supplies
Supplies **organic gardening** supplies in an informative catalog; they offer an extensive line of "Nature Guard" products. (1990)
❑ Catalog: $2, R&W, CAN
⌂ Shop: Call ahead, hours change seasonally

EnP, Inc.

See Smith Greenhouse & Supply.

Environmental Concepts
710 N.W. 57th Street
Ft. Lauderdale, FL 33309
(305) 491-4490 TO/CC $20m
AMI Medical Electronics, Inc.

Supplies
Meters to measure pH, soil salts, temperature, moisture, light intensity or soil fertility. Each comes with a comprehensive book on use. Recently introduced is a light meter which measures all types of light: sun, fluorescent, grow lights and high-intensity discharge lights. (1975)
❑ Catalog: Free, R&W, CAN/OV, $20m

Eon Industries
P.O. Box 11
Liberty Center, OH 43532
(419) 533-4961
Dale E. Leininger

Supplies
Offer all-metal **plant and flower markers** -- zinc name plates will last for many years; galvanized wire standards are rust-resistant. Can be written on with pencils and markers which they also sell. Name plates are sold separately, because the standards are reusable. (1936)
❑ Catalog: Free, R&W, CAN/OV

Erth-Rite, Inc.
RD 1, Box 243
Gap, PA 17527
(717) 442-4171, (800) 332-4171, FAX 442-8997
Floyd H. Ranck, Gen. Mgr.

Supplies
Offers Erth-Rite **fertilizers and soil amendments** in several formulations
for lawn and garden, roses, vegetables, trees, shrubs and bulbs; also greensand, bone meal, compost starter, diatomaceous earth, Maxicrop and other
organic products. (1962)
❐ Catalog: Free, R&W, CAN/OV
⌂ Shop: All year, M-F

Escort Lighting
201 Sweitzer Road
Sinking Spring, PA 19608
(215) 670-2517, FAX 670-5170
Michael Hartman

Ornaments
Makes and sells **copper garden light fixtures** in several charming mushroom
and toadstool designs, and they will make light fixtures and other garden
ornaments such as birdbaths and bird houses to your designs. (1989)
❐ Catalog: Free, R&W, CAN/OV

Evergreen Garden Plant Labels
P.O. Box 922
Cloverdale, CA 95425
Gary Patterson

Supplies
Sell **metal plant label holders with metal name plates** for all types of
plants, available 13 inches, 20 inches and 26 inches high. Also sell 30 inch
Bloomstalk Supports for taller flowers and rose-pegging hooks. (1970)
❐ Catalog: 1 FCS, $12m

Exaco USA, Ltd.

See De Van Koek.

Expo Garden Tours
145 4th Avenue, Suite 4A
New York, NY 10003
(212) 677-6704, (800) 448-2685, FAX 260-6913
Michael Italiaander

Services
A travel agency which offfers **garden tours** both internationally and in the
US. The flier I saw had tours to Costa Rica, the "Old South," Pacific North-
west, Holland and the Chelsea Flower Show. They'll also arrange custom
tours for small groups. (1988)
❐ Catalog: Free

EZ Soil Co.
Route 3, Box 176
Idabel, OK 74745
(405) 286-9447, (800) 441-3672, FAX 286-2141
Tim Sharp

Supplies
Manufactures a **compressed potting mix** made of coir pith, water holding
polymers and peat moss that expands up to 14 times its size. Available in
packets of 40 pellets or 5 packets of seed starter mix for $19.95 postpaid.
❐ Catalog: Free, R&W, CAN/OV

Fairfax Biological Laboratory, Inc.
P.O. Box 300
Clinton Corners, NY 12514
(914) 266-3705, FAX 266-5390
David A. Chittick

Books ⬿ Supplies
Sell two **organic pest controls** -- Doom(R) milky disease spore powder and
Japidemic(R) milky disease spore powder for use against Japanese beetles;
these are harmless to humans and animals. Also sell two books on pest
control. (1945)
❐ Catalog: Free, R&W, $10m

Barbara Farnsworth, Bookseller
P.O. Box 9
West Cornwall, CT 06796
(203) 672-6571, FAX 672-3099 TO/CC $25m

Books
A large general antiquarian and out-of-print bookstore in a tiny village in
the country, with 40,000 books on all subjects; a specialty is **horticul-
tural books**. Sounds great, I'm on my way! (1978)
❐ Catalog: $5d, R&W, CAN/OV
⌂ Shop: All year, Sa, or by appointment

Cliff Finch's Zoo
P.O. Box 54
16923 N. Friant Road
Friant, CA 93626
(209) 822-2315
Cliff & Joan Finch

Ornaments
Cliff's made **topiary frames** for the San Diego Zoo and Longwood Gardens, and
his work has been featured in magazines. He offers a good selection of frames
in animal shapes, some other designs, and he will do custom work. (1985)
❐ Catalog: Long SASE($1 OV), R&W, CAN/OV
⌂ Shop: All year, M-Sa (closed December 24-January 1)

Flora & Fauna Books
121 First Avenue South
Seattle, WA 98104
(206) 623-4727, FAX 623-2001
David Hutchinson

Books
Offers a good selection of **new, used, rare and out-of-print books** in
horticulture and botany, and welcomes your "want lists." They will also
purchase used books and collections. (1983)
❐ Catalog: Free, CAN/OV
⌂ Shop: All year, M-Sa

Floracolour
21 Oakleigh Road, Hillingdon
Uxbridge, Middlesex, England UB10 9EL
(0895) 25-1831
Bill Shaw

Services
Here's the answer to my perennial problem of loading the film incorrectly:
Mr. Shaw offers sets of **slides of famous gardens**, the Chelsea Flower Shows,
interesting plants and flowers in England and abroad, "stately" homes and
even the Pasadena Rose Parade -- and he can wait for the sun! (1960)
❐ Catalog: 1 IRC, R&W, CAN/OV
⌂ Shop: All year, daily

The Floral Mailbox
P.O. Box 235
Lombard, IL 60148-0235
Gail Pabst

Supplies
Supplier of **professional floral supplies**: cut flower preservatives, flower drying compound and arranging supplies, bouquet holders, baskets, tools and indoor plant care products such as leaf gloss and sheet moss. (1987)
❏ Catalog: Free, CAN

Floralight Gardens Canada, Inc.
5-620 Supertest Road
North York, ON, Canada M3J 2M5
(416) 665-4000, FAX 665-1106 TO/CC
Alan Patté

Supplies
Manufactures and sells Floralight **plant stands** -- multitiered systems for propagation or for indoor growing of African violets, orchids and other houseplants; can also be used for hydroponics.
❏ Catalog: Free, R&W, US/OV

Florapersonnel
2180 West S.R. 434, Suite 6152
Longwood, FL 32779
Robert F. Zahra, Mgr.

Services
A **horticultural employee seach and placement firm** which lists many types of jobs: managers of commercial operations, florists, landscape architects, estate managers, nursery supply and management, import and export -- you name it! A good way to find a job or a qualified worker. (1982)
❏ Catalog: Free

Florentine Craftsmen, Inc.
46-24 - 28th Street
Long Island City, NY 11101
(718) 937-7632, (800) 876-3567, FAX 937-9858
Graham Brown

Furniture ❧ Ornaments
A wide selection of fine **lead statuary, fountains, cast aluminum and cast iron furniture** in classic styles. Also sundials, birdbaths, weathervanes, planters and cherubs and many animals of the most appealing sort. (1928)
❏ Catalog: $5d($7 OV), R&W, CAN/OV

Florist Products, Inc.
2242 North Palmer Drive
Schaumburg, IL 60173
(312) 885-2242
Paul Lange

Supplies ❧ Tools
A broad selection of **gardening supplies, tools and equipment, pots, fertilizers and mist systems**; also sell the Wonder Garden, a lighted plant stand for indoor light gardening. They have another catalog for commercial growers with a complete line of supplies; send a request on your letterhead.
❏ Catalog: Free, R&W, CAN
⌂ Shop: All year, M-F (closed first two weeks of July)

Foothill Agricultural Research, Inc.
510-1/2 W. Chase Drive
Corona, CA 91720
(714) 371-0120 TO
Joe Barcinas & Harry Griffiths

Supplies
Offers a wide selection of **beneficial insects**: parasitic wasps, fly parasites, ladybugs, predatory mites, green lacewings, preying mantids and decollate snails. (1978)
❏ Catalog: Free, CAN/OV, $50m
⌂ Shop: All year, daily, call ahead

Four Seasons Solar Products
5005 Veterans Memorial Highway
Holbrook, NY 11741-4516
(516) 563-4000, (800) FOURSEA

Supplies
Sells **greenhouses and lean-to solariums.**
❏ Catalog: Free

Fox Hill Farm/Hoophouse
20 Lawrence Street
Rockville, CT 06066
(203) 875-6676
Patti Pleau

Supplies
Offers "Hoophouse" **greenhouses** which have solid ends and hoops covered with plastic sheeting; they've sold them all over the country. Also offers growing and propagation supplies and greenhouse accessories. (1985)
❏ Catalog: Free, R&W, CAN/OV, $15m
⌂ Shop: All year, daily, call ahead

French Wyres(R)
P.O. Box 131655
Tyler, TX 75713-1655
(903) 597-8322, FAX 597-8322
Paul & Terri Squyres

Ornaments
Make a variety of Victorian-style **wire plant stands and garden accessories**, including trellises, window boxes, cachepots, arbors and topiary frames. They will also do custom work. (1989)
❏ Catalog: $3, R&W, CAN/OV

The Garden Architecture Group
631 North Third Street
Philadelphia, PA 19123
(215) 627-5552
Brian Foster

Ornaments
Makers of **garden trellis** in several styles -- especially modular arches and panels which can be used in several combinations. Each is hand made of cedar, and they will work with you to customize your project. (1989)
❏ Catalog: $3d, R&W, CAN/OV, $200m
⌂ Shop: All year, daily, by appointment only

The Garden Book Club
3000 Cendel Drive
Delran, NJ 08370-0001
(609) 786-1000, FAX 786-7888
Newbridge Communications

Books
Just like those other **book clubs**, which have monthly selections and alternates. They've had the ineffable good taste to offer this book each time it comes out, so you know they're good pickers! They advertise good introductory offers in major gardening magazines -- watch for them.
❏ Catalog: Write for information, CAN/OV

The Garden Concepts Collection
P.O. Box 241233
6621 Poplar Woods Cir. S., (Germantown)
Memphis, TN 38124-1233
(901) 756-1649, FAX 755-4564
John B. Painter

Furniture ∾ Ornaments
A broad selection of upscale **ornaments and furnishings** for the garden --
pavilions, arbors, pergolas, bridges, gates, trellis-work, lighting systems,
planters, plant stands, garden furniture in a variety of historical styles.
Customers may submit designs for pricing and construction. (1985)
❐ Catalog: $5, R&W, CAN/OV
⌂ Shop: All year, M-F

Garden Fonts
RFD 1, Box 54
Barnstead, NH 03218
Bruce Cormier

Supplies
Custom print **plant markers and labels** to your specific plant list; the
labels come as self-stick or mounted on metal markers. I've been testing a
couple over a very wet winter and they still look new. (1989)
❐ Catalog: Free, CAN/OV, $4m

Garden Street Books
P.O. Box 1811
Geelong, Victoria, Australia 3220
(052) 291-667, (03) 529-6850, FAX 529-1256
Elizabeth Kerr

Books
Elizabeth Kerr has recently bought the book business of Andrew Isles and
specializes in **new, used and antiquarian books on gardening** from all over
the world. FAX (03) 529-1256 (1993)
❐ Catalog: 4 IRC, OV

Garden Works
31 Old Winter Street
Lincoln, MA 01773
(617) 259-1110
Robin Wilkerson

Books ∾ Services
Formerly Wilkerson Books, they have a good selection of **used and out-
of-print books** on gardening and horticulture, herbs, plant exploration,
garden history and design. Some are fairly recent; they will search for
out-of-print titles. Shop is in a Victorian farmhouse with gardens. (1977)
❐ Catalog: $1, R&W, CAN/OV
⌂ Shop: By appointment only

Garden-Ville of Austin
8648 Old Bee Caves Road
Austin, TX 78735
(512) 288-6113, FAX 892-0704
John Dromgoole

Books ∾ Supplies ∾ Tools
A complete **organic gardening supplier**: from books to fertilizers, tools to
Bag Balm, organic pest control to products for the home. A good selection
in a friendly and informative catalog. (1985)
❐ Catalog: Free, R&W, CAN
⌂ Shop: All year, daily; closed Su in January

Gardener's Eden
Box 7307
San Francisco, CA 94120-7307
(800) 822-9600 TO/CC
Williams-Sonoma

Furniture ∾ Ornaments ∾ Supplies
Offers a broad selection of **tools, equipment and gadgets** for gardening,
including garden ornaments, planters, furniture and many unusual and
appropriate gifts for gardeners.
❐ Catalog: Free

Gardener's Kitchen
P.O. Box 412
Farmington, CT 06034
Betty J. Rafferty

Supplies
Offer canning lids, rings and press-on labels; they sell the #63 small canning lid which they say is still sought by many people. Also sell other
canning supplies and equipment. (1976)
❐ Catalog: Free, CAN/OV

Gardener's Supply Company
128 Intervale Road
Burlington, VT 05401
(802) 660-3500, FAX 660-3501 TO/CC $25m
Will Raap

Ornaments ∾ Supplies ∾ Tools
A broad selection of **tools and equipment, organic fertilizers and pesticides, tillers and food preservation supplies**, most illustrated in a color
catalog. They also sell greenhouses, composters, irrigation equipment,
shredder/chippers, carts, sprayers, knee pads and much more.
❐ Catalog: Free, R&W
⌂ Shop: All year, M-Sa

Gardeners Bookshelf
P.O. Box 16416
Hooksett, NH 03106-6416
Barbara Hermann

Books
Offers a very broad selection of **new books** on gardening, covering almost
every garden subject. They also have discount programs for clubs. Catalogs
are published in sections, so specify subjects of interest. (1990)
❐ Catalog: $2, R&W, CAN/OV

Gardenfind
P.O. Box 2703
Lynnwood, WA 98036
(206) 743-6605
Judy Magelssen

Services
Gardenfind is a **computerized magazine index** which indexes the six most
popular gardening magazines; it is cumulative and updated yearly in January.
They also produce a computer index to woodworking magazines. Program will
run on IBM compatibles, or on a Mac if you use a conversion program. (1989)
❐ Catalog: Free, R&W, CAN/OV

Gardens Alive!
5100 Schenley Place
Lawrenceburg, IN 47025
(812) 537-8650, FAX 537-8660 TO/CC
Niles Kinerk

Supplies
Natural insect and disease controls, supplies and equipment for organic
gardening; all explained in an informative catalog. Offers organic insect
controls, beneficial insects, fertilizers and drip irrigation systems. There
are color pictures of insects and their damage in the catalog. (1984)
❐ Catalog: Free
⌂ Shop: All year, M-Sa

Gardens for Growing People
P.O. Box 630
Point Reyes Station, CA 94956-0630
(415) 663-9433
Ruth Lopez

Supplies
Specializes in **children's gardening supplies** and backyard nature study; they publish a quarterly catalog/newsletter that costs $4 a year, but will send a free sample. They offer books, tools, games and other garden items that will appeal to children, and suggestions for garden projects. (1991)
❒ Catalog: Free, R&W

V. L. T. Gardner Botanical Books
625 E. Victoria Street
Santa Barbara, CA 93103
(805) 966-0246, FAX 969-4787
Virginia L. T. Gardner

Books
Offers **used, out of print, and antiquarian books** on horticulture, gardening, botany, landscape architecture and plants and new books on gardens appropriate to southern California and other dry areas; and will search for out-of-print books on those subjects. No catalog at present; call or send a "want list." (1982)
❒ Catalog: See notes, R&W, CAN/OV
⌂ Shop: By appointment only

Gateways
849 Hannah Branch Road
Burnsville, NC 28714
(704) 675-5286
Richard Kennedy

Ornaments
Offers garden **sculpture and ornaments** made of hand-cast stone; includes statues of St. Fiacre, the patron saint of gardens (with his shovel), St. Francis, and Pan, as well as wall sculptures, side tables and candle holders; prices generally upscale. (1989)
⌂ Shop: April-December, M-F, by appointment only

Genie House
P.O. Box 2478
139 Red Lion Road
Vincentown, NJ 08088
(609) 859-0600, (800) 634-3643, FAX 859-0565
Lloyd E. Williams, Sr.

Supplies
Hand-crafted brass, copper and tin reproduction **light fixtures** in classic styles for gardens and house exteriors; they will also do custom work. (1967)
❒ Catalog: $3, R&W, CAN
⌂ Shop: All year, M-F

Geostar Travel
1240 Century Court
Santa Rosa, CA 95403
(707) 579-2420, (800) 624-6633 (CA)
Barbara & John Hopper

Services
A travel agency which specializes in **horticultural, botanical and natural history tours** to England, Europe, Central and South America, Hawaii and Australia. The tours are led by experts; some are organized for various societies or special interest groups.
❒ Catalog: Free
⌂ Shop: All year, M-F

Gladstone & Jones
Old Stable Yard
Hawarden Castle
Hawarden, Clwyd, Wales CH5 3NY
(244) 52-0369, FAX (244) 52-0427
Francis & Josephine Gladstone

Ornaments
A source of antique and reproduction **botanical prints**, especially of gesneriads, orchids, roses, bromeliads, rhododendrons, fruits and native flowers of various continents. You can also write and ask if they have prints of particular plant types or styles of print. (1986)
❒ Catalog: $7(US Bills or PC), OV
⌂ Shop: September-July, Tu-Sa, call ahead

© Janco II Products
  Artist: James Gosewisch

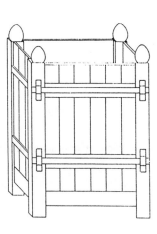

Good Directions
24 Ardmore Road
Stamford, CT 06902
(203) 348-1836, (800) 852-3002, FAX 357-0092
Michael Lodato

Ornaments
"**Weathervanes**: the good old-fashioned kind." True! Trotting horses, roosters, eagles and ducks, sheep and other animals, sailboats, Indians, locomotives and much more. They even sell a cupola to mount them on; or you can buy the figures without the swinging vane mechanism. (1976)
❒ Catalog: Free, R&W, CAN

Gothic Arch Greenhouses
P.O. Box 1564
Mobile, AL 36633-1564
W. H. Sierke, Jr.

Supplies
Redwood or red cedar **greenhouses** with fiberglass glazing in a pointed-arch style, either attached or free-standing. Also sells heating/cooling systems, shade cloth, benches and supplies. (1945)
❒ Catalog: $5, R&W, CAN/OV
⌂ Shop: All year, M-F, call ahead

Granite Impressions
342 Carmen Road
Talent, OR 97540
(503) 535-6190
Bob & Belinda Vos

Ornaments
Offer hand-crafted **Japanese lanterns and other ornaments**: water basins, signposts, pedestals, birdbaths or sundials, and bonsai pots. They are cast concrete made to look like granite, and quite handsome. (1990)
❒ Catalog: $1, R&W, CAN/OV
⌂ Shop: All year, by appointment only

Great American Rain Barrel Co.
295 Maverick Street
East Boston, MA 02128
(617) 569-3690, FAX same
George Gebelein

Supplies
Manufacturers a large and durable **rain barrel** with a capacity of 60 gallons; unconditionally guaranteed and made from recycled barrels. It has a spigot 14 inches above the ground to make room for a watering can. (1990)
❒ Catalog: Free, R&W

Great Lakes IPM
10220 Church Road N.E.
Vestaburg, MI 48891
(517) 268-5693 or 5911, FAX 268-5311
James Hansel

Supplies
A good selection of **supplies and equipment for integrated pest management**; they offer insect traps of all kinds, and live animal traps, as well as controlled-release pheromone dispensers, described in an informative catalog.
❒ Catalog: Free, R&W, CAN/OV
⌂ Shop: All year, M-F, 7563 N. Crystal Road

Green Enterprises
43 South Rogers Street
Hamilton, VA 22068
(703) 338-3606
Dwight Green

Furniture
Make Victorian style **porch swings, gliders, garden benches and dining tables**, all great complements to a period house and garden; made of oak with a natural finish, or maple painted white.
❒ Catalog: $1, R&W, CAN/OV

Green Thumb Industries
2400 Easy Street
San Leandro, CA 94578
(510) 276-0252
Paul & Janet Gordon

Supplies
Offers an English vertical **cold frame** for starting seedlings and growing tender plants; two models, a lean-to and a double depth model accessible from both sides. They are five feet high and have three shelves. (1987)
❒ Catalog: Free, R&W, CAN

Greenleaf Industries
1200 S.W. Spruce Street
Grants Pass, OR 97526
(503) 474-0571
David James, Director

Ornaments
A sheltered workshop which has a year-round horticultural training program. For Christmas they make and sell 22-inch **Christmas wreaths**, which they'll ship in the US except to AK or HI; orders must be placed by December 5.
❒ Catalog: Free, SS:11-12

Greenlist Info Services
12 Dudley Street
Randolph, VT 05060-1202
Cathy Czapla

Services
Greenlist is a **plant finding service** offering two different services. For $1, they'll send you a leaflet listing sources of plants such as old garden roses or heirloom vegetables. They'll also search for specific plants for a modest fee. Also known as Greenlist Gardeners Reference Service. (1992)
❒ Catalog: Long SASE

Grosoke, Inc.
7415 Whitehall Street #119
Ft. Worth, TX 76118
(817) 284-0696, (800) 522-0696 TO/CC

Supplies
Sell Agrosoke **hydrogels** for reducing water needs of plants and Agrodip root-protecting gel to keep cuttings and bare-root stock from drying out. They also sell Aquarius, a potting soil with hydrogels already mixed in.
❒ Catalog: Free, R&W, CAN/OV, $10m

Guano Company International, Inc.
3562 E. 80th Street
Cleveland, OH 44105
(216) 641-1200, (800) 424-8266, FAX 641-1310
Larry Pozarelli

Supplies
A source of **seabird guano** in several formulations for various uses, as well as "bat guano" and worm castings; literature gives good information on the benefits and use of each. Larry insists that only seabird droppings are guano, a word from the Inca civilization; he says "bat guano" is a misnomer.
❒ Catalog: Free, R&W, CAN/OV

Halcyon Laboratories
2627 North Baldwin
Portland, OR 97217
(503) 240-1724
Richard Harding

Services
A custom tissue culture laboratory specializing in **orchid seed flasking**, as well as stem propagation and tissue culture, and replating (something to do with seed flasking). Non-orchid species can also be tissue cultured. (1991)
❐ Catalog: Free, R&W, CAN/OV, SS:3-10

Hall Enterprises

See S & D Enterprises.

Hangouts
P.O. Box 148
1328 Pearl Street Mall
Boulder, CO 80306
(303) 442-2533, (800) HANGOUT, FAX 442-2610
Beto Goldberg

Furniture
Offers handwoven **hammocks** in a variety of styles, materials and colors; all call out to you in insistent voices, saying, "Why not have a little lie-down now and finish that later when it's cooler?"
❐ Catalog: Free, R&W, CAN/OV
⌂ Shop: All year, daily

Happy Valley Ranch
Route 2, Box 83
Paola, KS 66071-9516
(913) 849-3103, FAX 849-3104 TO/CC
Ray & Wanda Stagg

Supplies
Offer **cider and wine presses** for the home orchardist or winemaker: single and double presses and presses in kit form, as well as separate apple grinders and picking bags, loppers, pole saws and pruners. They also sell a cider cookbook.
❐ Catalog: $1, CAN/OV
⌂ Shop: All year, M-F, call ahead

Harlane Company, Inc.
266 Orangeburgh Road
Old Tappan, NJ 07675
Frank & June Benardella

Supplies ⟁ Tools
Sells **rose growing supplies**: garden markers with removable name plates, marking pens, Felco pruning shears, a rose pruning saw, and goatskin gloves. They will custom-print rose nameplates. (1964)
❐ Catalog: Free

Harmony Farm Supply
P.O. Box 460
3244 Highway 116 North (Sebastopol)
Graton, CA 95444
(707) 823-9125, FAX 823-1734
Kate Burroughs & David Henry

Books ⟁ Supplies ⟁ Tools
Only a mile or so from Tusker Press World Headquarters; I know it well! It's a real **emporium**, serving organic farmers/gardeners with a huge selection of drip and regular irrigation supplies, tools, organic pest controls, books, traps, fertilizers and soil amendments, grass and cover crop seed, beneficial insects and canning supplies. A very informative catalog. (1980)
❐ Catalog: $2d, R&W, CAN/OV
⌂ Shop: All year, daily

Harper Horticultural Slide Library
219 Robanna Shores
Seaford, VA 23696
Pamela Harper

Services
Huge selection of **photographic slides of plants, gardens, landscaping and natural scenery**, available for sale for publication. Also sells set of slides by subject. Ms. Harper is a well-known photographer and garden writer, with two fine books on perennials. (1973)
❐ Catalog: Long SASE w/ 2 FCS, CAN/OV

Karen Harris
200 East Genesee St.
Fayetteville, NY 13066

Ornaments
Offers **handmade hypertufa garden troughs**, distressed to look like weathered stone and very well done, approximate size is 21" x 11". (1991)
❐ Catalog: Long SASE, $60m

Hatchard's
187 Piccadilly
London, England W1V 9DA
(01) 439-9921, FAX 494-1313

Books
Long-established bookseller issues a periodic catalog offering a broad selection of **gardening and horticultural books** -- and will accept credit card orders from overseas. The Royal Horticultural Society was founded in the back room.
❐ Catalog: Free, OV
⌂ Shop: All year, M-Sa

Heritage Garden Furniture
1209 E. Island Highway, #6
Parksville, BC, Canada V9P 1R5
(604) 248-9598, FAX same
Karen Porter

Furniture
Garden furniture made of cedar, and available in kit form: they make gliders, lounges, Adirondack chairs, arbors, gates, swings and benches in rustic styles. Other items available at the shop. (1990)
❐ Catalog: Free, R&W, US/OV, $50m
⌂ Shop: All year, call ahead for hours

Heritage Garden Houses
311 Seymour Avenue
Lansing, MI 48933
(517) 372-3385, 484-3374
Robert Morris & Linda Peckham

Supplies
Sell **gazebos and other garden structures** in a variety of historical styles; they can be adapted to harmonize with the style of your own particular house. They also offer cupolas, spires and gates to fit your needs. (1991)
❐ Catalog: $3d, R&W, CAN/OV
⌂ Shop: All year, M-F, call ahead

Heritage Lanterns
70A Main Street
Yarmouth, ME 04096
(207) 846-3911, (800) 544-6070 TO/CC
H. William Geoffrion

Ornaments
Beautiful hand-crafted **lanterns and light fixtures in copper, pewter and brass**, available in a variety of classic styles for outdoors and indoors. They will also do custom work.
❑ Catalog: $3, R&W, CAN/OV
⌂ Shop: All year, M-F

Hermitage Gardens
P.O. Box 361
Canastota, NY 13032
(315) 697-9093, FAX 697-8169 TO/CC $25m
Russell Rielle

Ornaments
Sell a number of fiberglass **fountains, pools, waterfalls**, redwood water-wheels and equipment for water gardening such as pumps and lights; many of their illustrations show indoor installations. They also sell ornamental **bridges** in several styles. (1946)
❑ Catalog: $1($2 OV), R&W, CAN/OV
⌂ Shop: All year, daily, call ahead

Hollister's Hydroponics
P.O. Box 16601
Irvine, CA 92713
(714) 551-3822 TO/CC
Steve & Jorgeen Hollister

Supplies
Offer **hydroponic kits and supplies** in an informative catalog which explains how to create a system for your specific situation; they also sell books on hydroponics for those who want to plunge in. (1975)
❑ Catalog: $1, CAN/OV

Hollowbrook Pottery and Tile
26 Anton Place
Lake Peekskill, NY 10537
Roger L. Baumann

Ornaments
Stoneware planters for indoors and outdoors (frostproof to withstand harsh winters); available in handsome colors -- green, "shino," white, oxblood, celadon, stoney and woodfire; also tiles for floors, walls and patios. (1976)
❑ Catalog: Free, R&W, CAN/OV
⌂ Shop: By appointment only

Home Canning Supply & Specialties
P.O. Box 1158
2117 Main Street
Ramona, CA 92065
(619) 788-0520, 789-2125
Hugh & Myra Arrendale

Books ❧ **Supplies**
A good selection of **home canning supplies and equipment**, as well as food dehydrators, books on canning, pectin and spices, and some baking supplies. I'm just delighted to think that people are canning food again; I've paid my dues peeling and cutting up fruit. (1991)
❑ Catalog: $1, CAN/OV, $10m
⌂ Shop: All year, Tu,Th,Sa; Summer, daily; call ahead

Home Harvest(R) Garden Supply, Inc.
13426 Occoquan Road
Woodbridge, VA 22191
(703) 494-5980, (800) 348-4769 TO/CC
Jeff Edwards & Wallace Farrish

Supplies
Offers a range of **organic indoor gardening products**, including fertilizers, pest controls, plant lights and some hydroponic supplies. (1988)
❑ Catalog: Free, CAN/OV
⌂ Shop: All year, daily

Honingklip Book Sales
13 Lady Anne Avenue
Newlands, Cape Town, South Africa 7700
(021) 64-4410, FAX (021) 64-3460
Mrs. E. R. Middelmann

Books ❧ **Services**
Offer a broad selection of **books on southern African plants and gardens**; they also will search for used and out-of-print books. Prices given in US$ and may be paid in personal checks drawn on US, British or German banks.
❑ Catalog: Free, R&W, OV
⌂ Shop: By appointment only

Hortulus
139 Marlborough Place
Toronto, ON, Canada M5R 3J5
(416) 920-5057
Bruce & Linda Marshall

Books
Sell a broad selection of **used, out-of-print and rare books** on gardening, landscape architecture, herbs, garden history, floral art and design, and specific plants; prices are in US dollars. (1976)
❑ Catalog: $2, US/OV
⌂ Shop: By appointment only

Hurley Books
RR 1, Box 160
Westmoreland, NH 03467-9736
Henry Hurley

Books
Historical or textual **books on agriculture and horticulture**, animal husbandry, cottage industry and rural miscellany. They also have older seed catalogs and 19th century horticultural periodicals; more than 2,000 titles.
❑ Catalog: $1, CAN
⌂ Shop: All year, call ahead

Hyde Bird Feeder Co.
P.O. Box 168
Waltham, MA 02254
Jim Flewelling, Mgr.

Ornaments ❧ **Supplies**
Sells **bird houses, feeders, bird seed and gifts for the bird-lover**. A good selection, in a color catalog. (1942)
❑ Catalog: Free, R&W

Hydro-Farm West
3135 Kerner Boulevard
San Rafael, CA 94901
(415) 459-6095, (800) 634-9999 TO/CC
Peter Wardenburg

Supplies
Offering Hydrofarm **hydroponic systems**, as well as supplies and other equipment, and metal halide and high-pressure sodium **light systems**. Also carbon dioxide enrichment systems for home gardeners. They now have retail stores in Columbus, OH and Bristol, PA, in addition to mail order; call for information and locations. (1977)
❑ Catalog: Free($1 OV), R&W, CAN/OV
⌂ Shop: All year, M-Sa

Hydro-Gardens, Inc.
P.O. Box 25845
Colorado Springs, CO 80936
(719) 495-2266, (800) 634-6362 TO/CC $25m
Mike Morton

Supplies
Greenhouse and hydroponic vegetable growing supplies of all kinds for the home grower or commercial operator, including their Chem-Gro Nutrient. A very broad selection; including beneficial insects and even boxes and labels to take the produce to market. (1972)
❒ Catalog: Free, R&W, CAN/OV, $25m
⌂ Shop: All year, M-F

I.F.M.

See Integrated Fertility Management.

Idaho Wood
P.O. Box 488
Sandpoint, ID 83864-0488
(208) 263-9521, (800) 635-1100, FAX 263-3102
Leon Lewis & Jerry Luther

Ornaments
Natural wood garden lights, mostly lights on standards for paths and gardens; they have a number of handsome styles made of either cedar or oak. Also sell handsome indoor and outdoor wall and ceiling fixtures in natural wood and wooden bathroom accessories. (1975)
❒ Catalog: Free, R&W, CAN/OV

Indoor Gardening Supplies
P.O. Box 40567
Detroit, MI 48240
(313) 426-9080 TO/CC $20m
Tina Havro

Supplies
Offers a good selection of **growing supplies** for indoor and light gardening and plant propagation: lighted plant stands, plant lights, capillary matting, meters, timers, pots, trays and more. (1973)
❒ Catalog: Free, CAN

Infopoint Software
P.O. Box 83
Arcola, MO 65603
(417) 424-3424 or 3327
Dorothy Nichols

Services
Offers three MS DOS **computer programs** for hobbyists and commercial greenhouses and nurseries: these programs help you find the right flower, bulb or shrub for various uses and give germination and growing information (you can add your own information, too). A cost analysis program helps growers keep track of costs for pricing. (1988)
❒ Catalog: Free, R&W, CAN/OV

Integrated Fertility Management
333 Ohme Gardens Road
Wenatchee, WA 98801
(509) 662-3179, (800) 332-3179 TO/CC
Phillip Unterschuetz

Supplies ⟐ Services
Organic garden products and pest controls: a good selection, with products and their uses well described. They are specialists in organic fruit production and toxic residue testing. They offer soil amendments, natural pest controls, beneficial insects, traps and baits, soaps and green manure seed.
❒ Catalog: Free, R&W, CAN/OV
⌂ Shop: All year, M-F

International Irrigation Systems
P. O. Box 360
Niagara Falls, NY 14304
(416) 688-4090, FAX 688-4093
Robert L. Neff

Supplies
Irrigro **drip irrigation systems** based on microporous tubing, for watering, either above or below ground, from a gravity flow tank or house faucet with low pressure. Water filters are not needed. Canadian buyers may request a catalog from Irrigro, P.O. Box 1133, St. Catharines, ON, Canada L2R 7A3.
❒ Catalog: Free, R&W, OV

International Reforestation Suppliers
P.O. Box 5547
2100 West Broadway
Eugene, OR 97405
(503) 345-0597, (800) 321-1037
Steve Counard, Mgr.

Supplies ⟐ Tools
Tools and equipment for gardeners, foresters, Christmas tree growers and surveyors: weather instruments, safety equipment, pruning tools, supplies for wreath makers, sprayers, animal traps and tree planting supplies. They have a second location at P.O. Box 4195, Pineville, LA 71361.
❒ Catalog: Free, R&W, CAN/OV

InterNet, Inc.
2730 Nevada Avenue North
Minneapolis, MN 55427
(612) 541-9690, (800) 328-8456, FAX 541-9692
William Richardson & Ted Burchell

Supplies
Offers two weights of black polypropylene **bird netting** with an ultraviolet inhibitor, used by farmers and home gardeners and to keep birds from nesting on buildings. Also sells clips to attach the panels to buildings or cables.
❒ Catalog: Free, R&W, CAN/OV
⌂ Shop: All year, M-F, by appointment only

Irrigro

See International Irrigation Systems.

Ivywood Gazebo
P.O. Box 9
Fairview Village, PA 19403
(215) 584-0206, FAX 631-0846
John L. Huganir

Ornaments
Manufacture **gazebos** of red cedar or pressure-treated Southern pine in four sizes from nine to fifteen feet across; another model is available with screening. (1981)
❒ Catalog: $3, R&W, CAN/OV

Janco Greenhouses
9390 Davis Avenue
Laurel, MD 20723
(301) 498-5700, (800) 323-6933, FAX 497-9751
J. A. Nearing Co., Inc.

Supplies
Offers **greenhouses and greenhouse additions** in a variety of configurations for home and commercial uses. Also sells accessories, controls and ventilators for greenhouses.
❒ Catalog: $5, R&W, CAN/OV

Janziker
P.O. Box 957
Davis, CA 95617
Kathy Huntziker & Janet Ferrari

Supplies
Distributors of SuperSorb Crystals -- **water-absorbing acrylic polymer** particles that slowly release water to plants. Will reduce watering needs by 30% to 50%, can be used for garden or potted plants. (1988)
❒ Catalog: Free, CAN/OV, $6m

Jasco Distributing
P.O. Box 520
30 Depot Street
Lancaster, NH 03584
(603) 788-4744, FAX 788-4529
Barbara Hampton

Supplies
Offers the "Aqua Spike," which turns a two liter plastic soda bottle into a **slow release watering reservoir** for plants. (1990)
❒ Catalog: Free, CAN/OV, $5m

Kadco USA
27 Jumel Place
Saratoga Springs, NY 12866
(518) 587-2224, (800) 448-5503, FAX 587-9346
Thomas G. Petherick

Supplies
Offers the Carry-It cart, a **garden cart** made of one piece of molded polyethylene which will not rust or rot and can carry liquids or wet materials without leaking. Extension sides are available to increase the capacity, and a hitch converts it to a trailer for a tractor. (1986)
❒ Catalog: Free, R&W, CAN/OV

Kate's Garden & Studio
4721 Murphy School Road
Durham, NC 27705
(919) 383-7588, (800) Stone-4-U
Andy & Kate Fleishman

Ornaments
Kate says "Why pussyfoot around?" She and her husband make **stepping stones** in many sleeping cat styles, and also fish, snails, flowers, and other farm animals; I guess it's not bad luck to walk on them. (1990)
❒ Catalog: Free, R&W

Walter T. Kelley Co.
P.O. Box 240
Clarkson, KY 42726-0240
(502) 242-2012, FAX 242-4801
Sarah L. Manion, Pres.

Supplies
Huge selection of **supplies for beekeepers**, from a "beginner's outfit" with your first swarm of bees to professional honey-producing equipment. They also offer books and take subscriptions to beekeeping periodicals. (1924)
❒ Catalog: Free, CAN/OV

Kemp Company
160 Koser Road
Lititz, PA 17543
(717) 627-7979, (800) 441-5367 TO/CC

Supplies
Offer **shredder/chippers** in various models, depending on the volume of material to be handled. Also sell two **compost-tumblers**, which they claim make compost in two weeks, and the Yarkvark(TM), a hybrid yard vacuum, blower and chipper/shredder.
❒ Catalog: Free, CAN/OV, $10m
⌂ Shop: All year, M-F

The Ken-L-Questor
32255 N. Highway 99 West
Newberg, OR 97132
(503) 538-2051
Kenneth M. Lewis

Books
Specializes in **used, rare and out-of-print books** on cacti and succulents, ferns, lilies, mushrooms and fungi, lichens and natural dyes. Each category is on a separate list; please specify which list you want. (1935)
❒ Catalog: Free, R&W, CAN/OV

Myron Kimnach
5508 N. Astell Avenue
Azusa, CA 91702
(818) 334-7349, FAX 334-0658
Myron Kimnach

Books
Specializes in **new, used and out-of-print books** on cacti and succulents -- quite a large selection, including back issues of journals. (1984)
❒ Catalog: Free, CAN/OV

Kinsman Company, Inc.
River Road
Point Pleasant, PA 18950
(215) 297-5613, (800) 733-5613, FAX 297-0210
Graham & Michele Kinsman

Ornaments ⌇ Supplies ⌇ Tools
Importers of English **garden tools and equipment**, electric and hand-powered shredders, compost bins, sieves, strawberry tubs and modular arbors. It's always fun to see what they've added. Offer capillary matting, cold frames, rain gutter guards, great weathervanes and much more. (1981)
❒ Catalog: Free($2 CAN), R&W, CAN
⌂ Shop: All year, daily

Kitchen Krafts
P.O. Box 805
Mt. Laurel, NJ 08054
(609) 778-4960, FAX 234-3690 TO/CC
Dean Sorensen

Books ⌇ Supplies
"Supplies for your summer kitchen." **Home canning supplies**, food dehydrators, bottles and caps for your home-made beer, books on canning, cake baking and decorating equipment. It reminds me of the zillions of jars of fruit and apple butter that we used to put up every summer. (1989)
❒ Catalog: $1($3 OV), CAN/OV

Kosmolux & LP, Inc.
3616 Highland Avenue
Niagara Falls, NY 14303
(716) 282-0923, (800) 567-8383, FAX 282-0934
Vincent Cox

Ornaments
Offers **statues and other garden ornaments** made of bonded Carrara marble which does not deteriorate in cold winter climates. Offered are fountains, statues, table bases, plant stands and other ornaments in various classical styles. There's an office in Toronto at 50 Prince Andrew Place, Toronto, ON, Canada M3C 2H4, (416) 444-0403. (1985)
❒ Catalog: Free, R&W, CAN/OV
⌂ Shop: All year, M-F, Sa by appointment

Kunafin Trichogramma
Route 1, Box 39
Quemado, TX 78877
(210) 757-1181, (800) 832-1113, FAX 757-1468
Frank & Adele Junfin

Supplies
Specialists in biocontrol of insects and suppliers of **beneficial insects**: trichogramma wasps, fly parasites, Pymotes tritici and lacewings. They also supply Sitotroga cerella, a food source for beneficial insects. They consult with farmers about livestock operations (up to 10,000 head). (1959)
☐ Catalog: Free
⌂ Shop: All year, M-F

The Lady Bug Company
8706 Oro-Quincy Highway
Berry Creek, CA 95916
(916) 589-5227
Julie Steele

Supplies
Ladybugs, green lacewings, trichogramma, praying mantis egg cases, fly parasites and Bio-Control Honeydew to attract **beneficial insects**. An informative leaflet explains the use of these biological insect controls. (1959)
☐ Catalog: Free, R&W, CAN
⌂ Shop: All year, M,W,F, call ahead

Landscape Books
P.O. Box 483
Exeter, NH 03833
(603) 964-9333
Jane W. Robie

Books ~ Services
A very broad selection of **books on garden history, landscape architecture** and **city planning**: books are new, used, out-of-print and rare; all are well described as to contents and condition. Will do book searches, and assist with building collections and with garden history research. (1972)
☐ Catalog: $3, CAN/OV

Langenbach Fine Tool Co.
P.O. Box 453
Blairstown, NJ 07825
(800) 362-1991, FAX (201) 383-0844 TO/CC
Paul Langenbach

Tools
Offers imported **garden tools** from many countries: spades and forks, hoes, pruning and weeding tools, watering cans, sprinklers, axes and machetes, sprayers and a reel mower. (1986)
☐ Catalog: Free($2 OV), R&W, CAN/OV

LaRamie Soils Service
P.O. Box 255
Laramie, WY 82070
(307) 742-4185
Michael McFaul

Services
Soil testing by mail for organic and non-organic gardeners, with suggestions for amendments, crop suitability and rotation -- designed to build organically rich soils as quickly as possible. They do not send a catalog, but mail you collection instructions for soil samples.
☐ Catalog: See notes, CAN/OV

Laurelbrook Book Services
5468 Dundas Street West, Suite 600
Toronto, ON, Canada M9B 6E3
David Andrews

Books
Offers a good selection of new **horticultural and gardening books**. (1988)
☐ Catalog: $3d, US
⌂ Shop: All year, M-F

Lazy Hill Farm Designs
P.O. Box 235
Colerain, NC 27924
(919) 356-2828, FAX 356-2109 TO/CC
Betty Baker

Ornaments
Hand-crafted **bird houses, feeders** and a figure of St. Francis which also serves as a small feeder. All are charmingly designed with little shingled roofs; not cheap, but perfect for period or cottage gardens. (1987)
☐ Catalog: $1, R&W, CAN

Lee Valley Tools, Ltd.
1080 Morrison Drive
Ottawa, ON, Canada K2H 8K7
(613) 596-0350, FAX 596-3073
Leonard G. Lee

Supplies ~ Tools
Offers a good selection of imported **garden tools and growing supplies**, composting equipment, pruning tools, reel mowers and other useful items for home and garden. (1978)
☐ Catalog: Free, R&W, US/OV
⌂ Shop: All year, M-Sa

Lehman Hardware & Appliances, Inc.
P.O. Box 41
4779 Kidron Road
Kidron, OH 44636-0041
(216) 857-5441, FAX 857-5785
J. E. Lehman

Supplies ~ Tools
Lehman's is famous for its' "**non-electric**" catalog, most of their local customers are Amish farmers. They offer tools, oil lamps, canning supplies, wood and gas-burning cook stoves and refrigerators, homesteading and farming equipment of all kinds. A good source of old-fashioned farm tools. (1955)
☐ Catalog: $2, R&W, CAN/OV
⌂ Shop: All year, M-Sa

A. M. Leonard, Inc.
P.O. Box 816
6665 Spiker Road
Piqua, OH 45356-0816
(513) 773-2694, (800) 543-8955

Supplies ~ Tools
A very broad selection of **tools, supplies and equipment** for home and commercial gardeners -- almost everything for gardening and growing. They specialize in supplies for commercial operators, so some of the supplies come in large quantities. Most orders shipped UPS within 24 hours. (1885)
☐ Catalog: $1d, R&W, CAN, $20m
⌂ Shop: All year, M-F, Sa am

Linden House
148 Sylvan Avenue
Scarborough, ON, Canada M1M 1K4
(416) 261-0732, 830-9766
Gerda Rowlands & Evelyn Wolf

Books
A new mail order bookshop, offering a good selection of **books on gardening**, including books on related crafts; over 700 titles in their first catalog.
❒ Catalog: Free, US

Little's Good Gloves
P.O. Box 808
Johnstown, NY 12095
(518) 736-5014, FAX 762-8051 TO/CC $15m
Mark & Beth Dzierson

Supplies
"We specialize in **garden gloves** that fit, especially for ladies." They make four styles, including gauntlets that shield the arm up to the elbow for working around roses or other thorny plants. (1893)
❒ Catalog: Free, R&W, CAN/OV, $12m

Lloyds' of Kew
9, Mortlake Terrace
Kew, Surrey, England TW9 3DT
(01) 940-2512 TO/CC
Daniel Lloyd

Books ❧ Services
A very broad selection of **used and out-of-print books** on gardening and horticulture, with many new and recent books; they will search for wanted items not on their list. Shop is very near to Kew Gardens and fun to include on a visit there -- or to the Maids of Honour tea shop down the road.
❒ Catalog: $1d(US Bills or 2 IRC), OV
⌂ Shop: All year, M-Tu, Th-Sa

The Loken Company
P.O. Box 435
Crosby, ND 58730
(701) 965-6566 TO/CC
Mike & Gennie Loken

Supplies
The Lokens offers a personalized **five year garden diary** in a looseleaf binder; it includes a universal calendar for each month of each year, pages for records of what you've ordered, plant performance records and garden layout, and for garden photos, with room for your own additions. The calendar costs $19.45 postpaid, plus $1.17 tax in ND. (1992)
❒ Catalog: See notes; CAN/OV

Lord & Burnham

See Under Glass Manufacturing Corporation.

Kenneth Lynch & Sons, Inc.
P.O. Box 488
Wilton, CT 06897
(203) 762-8363, FAX 762-2999
Timothy A. Lynch

Furniture ❧ Ornaments
Offers a huge selection of **garden ornaments**: furniture, statues, planters and urns, gates, topiary frames, weathervanes, fountains and pools. Over 10,000 different items. Heaven must look like the Lynch catalog! (1930)
❒ Catalog: $9.50($15 OV), R&W, CAN/OV

MAC Industries
8125 South I-35
Oklahoma City, OK 73149
(405) 631-8553, (800) 654-4970
Billy Teague

Supplies
Offer **purple martin houses** in several styles, made of outdoor-sign plastic, which is easy to keep clean. They also sell several styles of bird feeder.
❒ Catalog: $.50, R&W

MN Productions
P.O. Box 577
Freeland, WA 98249
(206) 331-7995 TO/CC
Michael A. Nichols

Supplies
Offers **gardening and "chore" sweat pants** called Iron-Neezers, with padded knees and a drawstring waist, made from a polyester/cotton blend. Also offers Iron-Kneez padded knee dungarees manufactured by OshKosh in two styles. Useful for gardeners, painters and carpenters, too. (1987)
❒ Catalog: Free, R&W, CAN/OV

McQuerry Orchid Books
5700 W. Salerno Road
Jacksonville, FL 32244-2354
(904) 387-5044 (8-8 EST) TO/CC
Mary Noble McQuerry

Books
Specialize in **new, used, out-of-print and rare books on orchids** and also offer back issues of orchid magazines, old plant catalogs (orchids only) and antique orchid prints. They also publish and sell the "You Can Grow Orchids" series by Mary Noble. (1973)
❒ Catalog: Free, CAN/OV
⌂ Shop: By appointment only

Maestro-Gro
P.O. Box 6670
Springdale, AR 72766-6670
(501) 361-9155
Gary D. DeMasters

Supplies
Sells several **organic fertilizers**: Super-Plus, Pride-of-the-Bloom, Pride-of-the-Garden, Pride-of-the-Lawn, bone, blood, kelp, fish and feather meals, greensand, rock phosphate, agricultural limestone and diatomaceous earth for pest control. (1986)
❒ Catalog: Free, R&W, CAN/OV

Mainline of North America
P.O. Box 526
Junction of US 40 & State Route 38
London, OH 43140
(614) 852-9733 or 9734, FAX 852-2045 TO/CC
Paul A. Sullivan

Supplies
Offer Mainline(R) and Goldoni **tillers, sickle-bar mowers, rotary and power lawnmowers**; many models to choose from. They also offer a cider and wine press. (1938)
❒ Catalog: Free, R&W, CAN/OV
⌂ Shop: All year, M-Sa

Malley Supply
7439 LaPalma Ave., Suite 514
Buena Park, CA 90620-2698
Allan Garofalow

Supplies
Suppliers of **plastic pots and growing containers**; bowls, pots, flats and seedling trays, packs for bedding plants and plant labels. Most are sold individually, by 10's or by 100's. (1987)
❒ Catalog: $1d

Mantis Manufacturing Co.
1458 County Line Road
Huntingdon Valley, PA 19006
(215) 355-9700, (800) 366-6268 TO/CC
HJS Enterprises, Inc.

Supplies
Offer a small, lightweight garden **tiller**, with attachments which convert it to a lawn dethatcher or aerator, edge-cutter or hedge-trimmer; both gas and electric models. They also sell a **portable power sprayer** and both small and large **chipper/shredders**.
❒ Catalog: Free, CAN/OV
⌂ Shop: All year, M-F

Marck Wines
3119 Skyview Avenue
Pueblo, CO 81008
(719) 543-6940
Ronny Marck

Supplies
Supply gardeners with **beer and wine making equipment and supplies** "to get more enjoyment from the fruits of their labors." They offers a good selection of what you'll need to make a little pilsner, elderberry wine, or even carbernet sauvignon. (1978)
❒ Catalog: $2d ($5 OV), R&W, CAN/OV, $5m
⌂ Shop: All year, M-F, call ahead

The Marugg Company
P.O. Box 1414
Tracy City, TN 37387
(615) 592-5042
John Baggenstoss

Tools
The ultimate in weed whacking, a silent and efficient **Austrian scythe** with a metal or hickory snath (handle); you can order your scythe with a grass or bush blade. Marugg also offers sickles, and whetstones, anvils and hammers to sharpen your scythe.
❒ Catalog: Free

The Matrix Group
P.O. Box 1176
Southport, CT 06490
James Orrico

Services
Sells **video cassettes** of "The Home Gardener," John Lenaton's popular series of 30 gardening programs organized by subject. Also offers a **videodisc**, "Gardening at Home," a complete A-to-Z of gardening basics coordinated with Lenaton's book, "The Home Gardener." He's lively and fun. (1985)
❒ Catalog: Free, R&W, CAN/OV, $30m

Don Mattern
267 Filbert Street
San Francisco, CA 94133
(415) 781-6066
Don Mattern

Supplies
Offers the HERRmidifier, a **humidifier** with humidistat for greenhouse and orchid growers, available in 110 or 220 volts.
❒ Catalog: Free, CAN/OV, $20m

Maximum, Inc.
30 Samuel Barnet Boulevard
New Bedford, MA 02745
(508) 995-2200 TO/CC
Nat Bishop

Supplies
Offers **wind and weather instruments** in solid brass cases; catalog includes "complete weather stations" and wood panels on which to mount them. These are high-tech and high quality instruments for years of use.
❒ Catalog: Free, R&W, CAN/OV

Emi Meade, Importer
16000 Fern Way
Guerneville, CA 95446-9611
(707) 869-3218
Emi & Eugene Meade

Supplies
Offers two styles of Jollys, **waterproof garden clogs** from Europe in six colors; soft and comfortable, easy to rinse clean. The color goes all the way through, so they don't show wear easily. Also sells replacement insoles, and Atomocoll(R) for buffing rough skin, it really works! (1981)
❒ Catalog: Free, R&W, CAN/OV
⌂ Shop: Call ahead

Medina Agricultural Products Co.
P.O. Box 309
Hondo, TX 78861
(210) 426-3011 or 3012, FAX 426-2288 TO/CC
Stuart Franke

Furniture ⌖ Supplies
Sell the Medina **soil activator**, which they claim is like "yogurt for the soil," and Medina Plus, which contains micronutrients and growth hormones from seaweed extract for foliar feeding. They also offer HuMate humic acid to build soil, HastaGro fertilizers and other products. Informative flier.
❒ Catalog: Free, R&W

Mindsun
RD 2, Box 710
Andover, NJ 07821
(201) 398-9557 TO/CC
Edgar L. Owen

Services
"Gardenview" software for IBM and compatible computers: a **garden design program** in 136 colors which lets you see what your garden would actually look like every day of the year in a three-dimensional model. It can be rotated and viewed from any vantage point. Perfect for landscape architects and garden/computer fanatics! Also a program for home interiors. (1984)
❒ Catalog: Free, R&W, CAN/OV

Mitchells & Son
13558 Sunrise Drive N.E.
Bainbridge Island, WA 98110
(206) 842-9827
Jeannine & Deryl Mitchell

Supplies
Small family business sells **cedar planters** which fit onto porch or fence railings up to six inches wide. They come in 24, 30 or 36-inch lengths, with a planting depth of nearly 7 inches. The Rail Hanger(R) brackets are installed according to the width of your railing, they have a leveling bar to insure good drainage. They also sell removable window boxes. (1987)
❒ Catalog: Free, R&W, CAN

Morco Products
P.O. Box 160
Dundas, MN 55019
(507) 645-4277
Robert C. Morrow

Supplies
Offers the "Turn Easy **Composter**," a compost drum holding 55 gallons of waste for composting, plenty to accomodate the average household. All the drums are new to prevent contamination from previous contents. (1991)
❒ Catalog: Free, CAN

Mother Nature's Worm Castings
P.O. Box 1055
Avon, CT 06001
(203) 673-3029
Hazel & Ed Saillant

Supplies
Offers **worm castings**, an environmentally safe, nontoxic and organic fertilizer, high in phosphorus, potassium, magnesium, calcium and nitrate and low in ammonium. Aristotle called worms "the intestines of the earth."
❒ Catalog: Long SASE, R&W, $50m

Multiple Concepts
P.O. Box 4248
Chattanooga, TN 37405
(615) 266-3967, FAX 267-5436
Jim Crumley, Pres.

Supplies
Sells Moisture Mizer **hydrogels** that slowly release water to potted and other plants. Available in several sizes; clubs could order larger sizes as a group and divide them among members.
❒ Catalog: Long SASE w/ 2 FCS($2 OV), R&W, CAN/OV, $3m

Native Nurseries
1661 Centerville Road
Tallahassee, FL 32308
(904) 386-2747 or 8882
Donna Legare & Judy Walthall

Supplies
Their catalog, called "Southern Naturalist" specializes in backyard birding supplies: **bird feeders and food, bird houses**, and some nice nature jewelry and garden ornaments. No shipping to AK or HI. (1980)
❒ Catalog: Free
⌂ Shop: All year, M-Sa

The Natural Gardening Company
217 San Anselmo Avenue
San Anselmo, CA 94960
(415) 456-5060, FAX 721-0642 TO/CC
David Baldwin & Karin Kramer

Books ⚭ Supplies ⚭ Tools
Offer a nice selection of **imported garden tools**, books, supplies and a **copper snail barrier** which gives the little devils a mild shock -- they won't cross it. Also sell organic "gourmet" vegetable and herb seedlings, and drip irrigation systems to keep them growing. (1986)
❒ Catalog: Free, CAN
⌂ Shop: All year, daily

Natural Gardening Research Center

See Gardens Alive!

Natural Solutions

See Necessary Trading Company.

Naturally Free/Bug-Off, Inc.
Route 3, Box 248C
Lexington, VA 24450
(703) 463-1760
Mirabai McLeod

Supplies
Offer a natural **alternative to chemical insect repellents**: no alcohol, perfumes or dyes, made from essential herbal oils. They claim it can also be used for insect control on pets and around the home. (1985)
❒ Catalog: Long SASE($1 OV), R&S, CAN/OV

Nature's Control
P.O. Box 35
400 Morton Way (Jacksonville)
Medford, OR 97501
(503) 899-8318, FAX 899-9121
Don Jackson

Supplies
Predator mites, ladybugs, whitefly traps and parasites, mealybug predators and insecticidal soap for **natural pest control**; all especially useful for indoor or greenhouse growing. Stress helpful advice and fast service. (1980)
❒ Catalog: Free, R&W
⌂ Shop: All year, call ahead

Necessary Trading Co.
One Nature's Way
New Castle, VA 24127-0305
(703) 864-5103, FAX 864-5186 TO/CC
Bill Wolf

Books ⚭ Supplies ⚭ Tools
Large selection of **organic insect controls, tools, books and soil amendments** for "biological agriculture." The catalog's very informative; they also offer organic pest controls for pets and traps for insect pests. (1979)
❒ Catalog: Free, R&W, CAN
⌂ Shop: All year, M-F

Nichols Industries

See Infopoint Software.

The Walt Nicke Company
P.O. Box 433
Topsfield, MA 01983
(508) 887-3388, (800) 822-4114, FAX 887-9853
Katrina Nicke

Books ⚭ Supplies ⚭ Tools
Garden tools, gadgets and supplies, many imported from Europe; a broad selection. One of my favorite tools is a heavy-duty steel trowel with a long handle which I bought from them many years ago. There's much in the catalog which is useful, decorative or just desirable for yourself or for gifts.
❒ Catalog: Free, CAN/OV

Nitron Industries, Inc.
P.O. Box 1447
4605 Johnson Road (Johnson)
Fayetteville, AR 72702
(501) 750-1777, (800) 835-0123, FAX 750-3008
Frank & Gay Finger

Supplies
Offers a good selection of **organic growing supplies**: fertilizers, soil amendments including their own Nitron brand, and Wet Flex porous hose. Catalog gives good information on soil building, also offers composting supplies, water purifiers, even a deodorizer for pets called Sweet Pea. (1977)
❒ Catalog: $1($4 OV), R&W, CAN/OV
⌂ Shop: All year, M-F, Sa am

Niwa Tool Co.
2661 Bloomfield Court
Fairfield, CA 94533
(707) 422-0734, (800) 443-5512, FAX 524-3423
Ms. Kayoko Kuroiwa

Tools
Imports a good selection of **Japanese garden and bonsai tools**, kitchen knives and flower arranging frogs. Each tool is illustrated in the catalog, some of the tools are unusual, such as the bamboo splitters, and several styles of short handled garden hoes. (1992)
❒ Catalog: $2, R&W, CAN/OV

North American Kelp
P.O. Box 279A
Cross Street
Waldoboro, ME 04572
(207) 832-7506
Robert C. Morse & George Seaver

Supplies
Offer Sea Crop, Sea Life Soil Conditioner and other **soil conditioners** made from kelp; the only US manufacturer of seaplant products for gardening and agriculture. Their catalog has detailed information on use, even as a supplement to livestock feed. (1971)
❒ Catalog: Free, R&W, CAN, $10m

Northern Greenhouse Sales
P.O. Box 42
Neche, ND 58265
(204) 327-5540
Bob Davis & Margaret Smith

Supplies
Offer **woven polyethylene** and other supplies for making your own green-house, plus advice from the Far North on how to make it. The plastic poly is 9.5 mils thick and very strong, with an average life of 3 years; they will sell small amounts. Canadian address: Box 1450, Altona, MB, R0G 0B0. (1979)
❒ Catalog: 2 FCS, R&W, CAN/OV
⌂ Shop: All year, daily, call ahead

Northwest Eden Sales, Inc.
15103 N.E. 68th Street
Redmond, WA 98052
(800) 545-3336 TO/CC $20m
Bruce Moulton

Supplies
Offers aluminum and glass **greenhouses and kits**, lean-tos, extensions and a selection of greenhouse accessories, from small home installations to huge commercial greenhouses. (1981)
❒ Catalog: Free, R&W, CAN/OV, $4m

Norway Industries
143 West Main
Stoughton, WI 53589
(608) 873-8664 TO/CC
Brian Hanson

Supplies
Sells two models of **garden cart** -- the Carryall, 42 inches wide, and the Carryette, 32 inches wide for access through doorways; sold complete or as kits for you to put together with your own wood.
❒ Catalog: Free, R&W, CAN/OV
⌂ Shop: All year, M-F, call ahead

Nova Sylva, Inc.
1587 Denault Street
Sherbrooke, PQ, Canada J1H 2R1
(819) 821-4617, (800) 561-2963, FAX 821-4671
Pierre Roy

Supplies ⟳ Tools
Offers a good selection of **tools and equipment for foresters**: specialized tools and equipment for tree work and planting, pruning tools, sprayers, safety equipment, even cookshack and shower tents for forest camps. Also composting equipment, weather instruments, plastic mulch and more. (1985)
❒ Catalog: Free, R&W, US/OV, $25m
⌂ Shop: All year, M-F

© French Wyres (R)
Artist: Carol Levy

OFE International, Inc.
P.O. Box 161302
12100 S.W. 129th Court
Miami, FL 33186
(305) 253-7080, FAX 251-8245 TO/CC
Jose Hortensi

Supplies ⚭ Tools
Offers **growing supplies for orchids and bromeliads**: clay orchid pots, wood and wire plant baskets, fertilizers, sprayers, watering accessories, growing media, plant labels, plant stands and books about orchids. (1980)
❒ Catalog: $2d, R&W, CAN/OV, $20m
⌂ Shop: All year, M-Sa

O'Brien Ironworks
1760 Monrovia Ave., Suite B3
Costa Mesa, CA 92627
(714) 646-3290, FAX 646-1464
John Kalkanian & Denis O'Brien

Ornaments
Here's a great idea -- they manufacture **antique reproduction urns, planters** and **pedestals** out of recycled automobile engine blocks. They also make a number of reproduction planters and other decorative items, all made from recycled metals, including an "English garden bench." (1989)
❒ Catalog: $1($3 OV), R&W, CAN/OV

Ohio Earth Food, Inc.
5488 Swamp Street NE
Hartville, OH 44632
(216) 877-9356
Larry & Cynthia Ringer

Supplies ⚭ Services
Offer a broad selection of **natural soil conditioners and amendments**, including Erth-Rite and Maxicrop, insect controls and dormant oils; they also will do soil testing and make suggestions for which natural products to use. Farmers may request their quantity prices. (1972)
❒ Catalog: Free, R&W, CAN/OV
⌂ Shop: All year, M-Tu, Th-F; March-May, W & Sa am

Old World Garden Troughs(R)
P.O. Box 1253
Carmel, IN 46032
Rod Butterworth, Mgr.

Ornaments
Offers **alpine garden troughs** in two styles, rectangular or square with flaired sides, each in three sizes and a choice of four colors. Useful for alpine and rock garden plants, herbs or bonsai. Shipped by UPS. (1988)
❒ Catalog: $2d, R&W, $25m

One Up Productions
P.O. Box 410777
San Francisco, CA 94141
(415) 777-1964, (800) 331-6304 TO/CC
Hamilton V. Bryan

Supplies
Company specializing in **videos** for the gardener; they cover a number of subjects, from "how to" to landscaping and armchair tours of famous gardens.
❒ Catalog: Free, R&W, CAN, $16m

Orchis Laboratories
4820 Mason Road
Burdett, NY 14818
(607) 546-2072

Services
Will do **virus testing** (CYMV and ORSV) and **tissue culture on orchids**; also sell a home virus-testing kit and a home seed-sowing kit for orchid lovers.
❒ Catalog: Free, R&W, CAN/OV

Oregon Timberframe
1389 Highway 99 N.
Eugene, OR 97402
(503) 688-4940, FAX 688-5469
Jim Home

Ornaments
Oregon Timberframe builds **garden structures** of all kinds; gazebos, arbors, pergolas, bridges, greenhouses and storage buildings. They'll build a frame structure without nails in traditional mortise and tenon style to your design and specifications. Call for information. (1985)
❒ Catalog: See notes; CAN/OV

Organic Control, Inc.
P.O. Box 781147
Los Angeles, CA 90016
(213) 937-7444
Steve Hazzard

Supplies
Suppliers of **beneficial insects** for nontoxic pest control and of organic pesticides and fungicides. They also sell worm castings. (1973)
❒ Catalog: Free, R&W, CAN/OV
⌂ Shop: All year, M-F

Organic Gardening Book Club
P.O. Box 4515
Des Moines, IA 50336-4514
Rodale Press, Inc.

Services
Garden book club run by Rodale Press; they offer their own books as well as those of other publishers. Write for information.

The Original Bug Shirt(R) Company
P.O. Box 127
Trout Creek, ON, Canada P0H 2L0
(705) 729-5620, FAX same
Bob Meister & Sara Callaway

Supplies
Offer a lightweight **bug-proof garment** which is both cool to wear and protects your arms and whole upper body from biting insects and ticks; it has long sleeves, a hood with a mesh face protector, and plenty of air vents. Americans can write to 908 Niagara Falls Blvd., No. Tonawanda, NY 14120.
❒ Catalog: Free, R&W, CAN/OV

Original Home Gardener's Video Catalog

See One Up Productions.

Out of the Woods
P.O. Box 214
Citrus Heights, CA 95611
(916) 722-3691
Ernie & Philippa Platt

Ornaments
Offers a sleeve that fits around standard two gallon or five gallon nursery pots and looks like a **planter**; they're made of redwood, and since the soil does not touch them, they will last for a very long time. They also sell a redwood doormat. (1989)
❒ Catalog: Free, CAN/OV

Ozark Handle & Hardware
P.O. Box 390
91 S. Main Street
Eureka Springs, AR 72632
Eddie Silver

Supplies
Offers a very broad selection of **hardwood replacement handles** for tools of all sorts -- who else has wooden plow handles? Also has a space-age divining rod for finding cables and pipes and sells woven poly tarps. (1977)
❐ Catalog: $2d, R&W, CAN, $20m

P&R International, Inc.
P.O. Box 939
Norwalk, CT 06852-0939
(203) 846-2989 TO/CC
Ted Prahlow, Pres.

Ornaments
Offers a variety of **statues, planters, birdbaths, fountain heads** and other garden ornaments in various classical styles and in a number of finishes to suit your garden design. (1987)
❐ Catalog: $3d, CAN, $12m
⌂ Shop: All year, M-F

Pacific Coast Greenhouse Mfg. Co.
P.O. Box 2130
Petaluma, CA 94953-2130
(800) 227-7061
JoAnn West

Supplies
Manufacture **redwood greenhouses** in kit form; bought the company of the same name in 1991 and moved it from Cotati to Petaluma. Also offer greenhouse equipment and accessories. (1928)
❐ Catalog: $2d, R&W, CAN/OV
⌂ Shop: All year, M-F

Pacific Greenhouse
25550 Rio Vista Drive
Carmel, CA 93923
(408) 622-9233
Dick & Marilyn Sargent

Supplies
Offers redwood **greenhouses and garden rooms** in kits; they are easy to expand, as Dick says that most people start out with too small a greenhouse and then want to expand. Also sells greenhouse equipment. (1982)
❐ Catalog: Free, CAN/OV, $200m
⌂ Shop: All year, by appointment only

John Palmer Bonsai
P.O. Box 29
Sudbury, MA 01776
(617) 443-5084
W. John Palmer

Books ⬯ Supplies ⬯ Tools
Specializes in **bonsai books, tools, pots and supplies** -- with many books on Japanese gardens and bonsai techniques.
❐ Catalog: Free, CAN/OV
⌂ Shop: By appointment only

Paradise Information, Inc.
P.O. Box 1701
East Hampton, NY 11937
(800) 544-2721, FAX same TO/CC
Jim Owen

Services
Offers "CHIP2" **databases** with over 5,000 plant descriptions; the program includes five databases, intended for gardeners and landscape architects; for IBM and Macintosh computers. It finds plants by color, foliage, form, tolerances, height, zones, flowers, light, berries, wildlife, problems, etc.
❐ Catalog: Free, R&W, CAN/OV

Park Place
2251 Wisconsin Avenue N.W.
Washington, DC 20007
(202) 342-6294, FAX 342-9255 TO/CC
C. Philip Mitchell

Furniture ⬯ Ornaments
Offer many types of **garden furniture, light fixtures, street lamps, urns, rockers, swings and gliders**; styles are elegant and the very thing for your stately home. Carry products from many manufacturers; I didn't see their price list, and suspect prices are definitely "upscale." (1979)
❐ Catalog: $2, R&W, CAN/OV
⌂ Shop: All year

Paul Products
2200 Sangamon Avenue
Springfield, IL 62702
(217) 544-6141

Supplies
Offers a "mini seeder", a little device which will drop several small seeds at a time, just where you want them. It comes with several sizes of hole so that you can choose the right one for your seed. It's $9.50 postpaid.

Paw Paw Everlast Label Co.
P.O. Box 93
Paw Paw, MI 49079-0093
Arthur & Dorothy Arens

Supplies
Manufacture and sell "Everlast" **metal plant and garden labels** with zinc nameplates. They offer styles to put in the ground and to hang on the plant; also sell special marking pencils and crayons to write on the labels. (1962)
❐ Catalog: Free, R&W, CAN/OV

Peaceful Valley Farm Supply
P.O. Box 2209
125 Springhill Blvd.
Grass Valley, CA 95945
(916) 272-4769, FAX 272-4794
Mark & Kathleen Fenton

Supplies ⬯ Tools
Offers a very broad selection of **organic growing supplies**, as well as flower and vegetable seed, seed potatoes and garlic, cover crop seed, and spring blooming bulbs. They will do soil testing by mail, offer row covers and beneficial insects, garden tools of every kind; in fact, a complete emporium in a very informative catalog. (1976)
❐ Catalog: $2d, R&W, CAN/OV, $20m
⌂ Shop: All year, M-Sa, call ahead

PeCo, Inc.
P.O. Box 1197
100 Airport Road
Arden, NC 28704
(704) 684-1234, (800) 438-5823, FAX 684-0858
Brenda Hall

Supplies
Sell a completely self-contained **12-volt electric sprayer** which runs up to five hours on its rechargeable battery. It features a cart with big wheels to make it easy to move around and has a plug-in charger, an 8-foot hose and an opaque tank to keep track of fluid level. Also sell **lawn vacs**. (1971)
❐ Catalog: Free, R&W, CAN/OV, $15m

Peerless Products, Inc.
P.O. Box 2469
Shawnee Mission, KS 66201
(913) 432-2232, FAX 432-3004
Dick Rippey, Retail Sales Mgr.

Supplies
Manufactures and sells aluminum **greenhouse windows** in eleven sizes, in bronze or white finishes. Primarily sold through dealers, they will sell direct if there's no dealer near you.
❏ Catalog: Free, R&W, CAN/OV

C. K. Petty & Co.
203 Wildemere Drive
South Bend, IN 46615
(219) 232-4095, FAX 288-3211
Christopher K. Petty

Supplies
Offers a **reel lawn mower**, which he says he sells to a lot of women who've inherited power mowers that they won't touch; he says it only has five moving parts, including yourself. Also offers some nice small furniture. (1990)
❏ Catalog: Free

Phero Tech, Inc.
7572 Progress Way
Delta, BC, Canada V4G 1E9
FAX (604) 940-9433
Stephen Burke, Sales Mgr.

Supplies
A source of state-of-the-art pheromone **insect traps** for garden, forest and agricultural applications; they are also doing research on animal repellents and sell flea, yellowjacket and mouse traps. Garden clubs or neighbors can band together to place orders. (1981)
❏ Catalog: Free, US/OV, $100m

Pine Garden Bonsai Company
20331 State Route 530 N.E.
Arlington, WA 98223
(206) 435-5995, FAX same
Kate Bowditch & Max Braverman

Supplies
Offer hand-made wheel-thrown ceramic **bonsai containers** (glazed or unglazed, in many styles), and their own cast containers in the Japanese style. They also offer some plants suitable for bonsai; ask for their plant list. No plants shipped to Canada, HI or PR. Also known as Pine Garden Pottery. (1971)
❏ Catalog: $2, R&W, CAN, $25m
⌂ Shop: All year, daily, call ahead

Plant Collectibles
103 Kenview Avenue
Buffalo, NY 14217
(716) 875-1221 TO/CC
Marseille Luxenberg

Supplies
Growing and propagating supplies for indoors and out; pots in many sizes, fertilizers, potting soil, hanging baskets, peat pots and pellets, nozzles, plant lights and stands, propagating supplies and more. (1983)
❏ Catalog: 3 FCS($3 OV), R&W, CAN/OV, $10m

Planters International
2635 Noble Road
Cleveland Heights, OH 44121
(216) 382-3539, (800) 341-2673, FAX 382-2743
John Black & Laurence Schwartz

Supplies
Make a **self-watering ceramic planter** which needs filling only every few weeks, a hole in the bottom allows fertilizer salts to wash through, and prevents root rot. Available in several colors and sizes. (1990)
❏ Catalog: Free, R&W, CAN/OV
⌂ Shop: All year, call ahead

Plastic Plumbing Products, Inc.
P.O. Box 186
17005 Manchester Road
Grover, MO 63040
(314) 458-2226, FAX 458-2760
Craig Pisarkiewicz

Supplies
Sell supplies for **drip and mist irrigation** systems, and will develop custom-designed systems for customers in the Midwest. Also carry a large selection of drip and mist parts and fittings from several manufacturers. (1979)
❏ Catalog: $1d, R&W, CAN/OV
⌂ Shop: All year, M-F, Sa am

The Plow & Hearth
P.O. Box 830
Orange, VA 22960-0492
(703) 672-1712, (800) 627-1712, FAX 672-3612
Peter G. Rice

Furniture ❧ Ornaments ❧ Tools
Color catalog offers **goods for home and garden**: tools, garden furniture, ornaments, bird houses, fireplace accessories, pet supplies and other useful home goods -- even an "indestructible" rural mailbox. (1980)
❏ Catalog: Free, CAN/OV
⌂ Shop: All year, daily, 1107 Emmet St. (Charlottesville)

Pomona Book Exchange
P.O. Box 111
Rockton, ON, Canada L0R 1X0
(519) 621-8897
Fred & Walda Janson

Books ❧ Services
Offer **new, out-of-print and rare books** on plants, botany, gardening and horticulture, landscape design, fruit growing and related fields and will search for hard-to-find books. They also have a museum orchard and can supply propagation materials for several hundred varieties of apples to local Canadian collectors!
❏ Catalog: Free, US/OV
⌂ Shop: By appointment or by chance

Pompeian Studios
90 Rockledge Road
Bronxville, NY 10708
(914) 337-5595, (800) 457-5595, FAX 337-5661
Pamela Humbert

Ornaments
Marble, bronze, limestone, mosaic and wrought iron **garden ornaments**, made to order in Italy and hand-carved or hand-finished; the styles are classic and charming. Prices are very upscale and vary with the exchange rate for the lira. Statues and fountains, mostly -- all elegant and lovely. (1904)
❏ Catalog: $10d, R&W, CAN/OV

Popovitch Associates, Inc.
346 Ashland Avenue
Pittsburgh, PA 15228
(412) 344-6097
Don & Rose Popovitch

Ornaments
Offers **light fixtures** for gardens in eight natural styles, hand-crafted in copper and ceramic. Most of the styles are flower-shaped; one is shaped like a mushroom. All are elegant ornaments by day as well as functional at night.
❒ Catalog: Free, R&W

Pot Lock
1032 - 21st Street
Rock Island, IL 61201
Charles J. White

Supplies
Offer a unique **device to lock bonsai and other pots** to your shelf -- good insurance for tempting or valuable specimens! They do not have a catalog; they charge $10 for four, including postage and handling. (1984)
❒ Catalog: See notes, R&W, CAN/OV, $10m

Larry W. Price Books
353 N.W. Maywood Dr.
Portland, OR 97210-3333
(503) 221-1410

Books
Larry is a college professor who loves books; he specializes in **rare, old** and **collectible books** on natural history, botany and all types of plants and gardening. He insists that many of the books are useful, too! Tell him what interests you. (1985)
❒ Catalog: $1d, CAN/OV

A Proper Garden
225 S. Water Street
Wilmington, NC 28401
(919) 763-7177, (800) 626-7177, FAX 762-4096
Peg Beam

Furniture ❧ Ornaments
A charming catalog of **gifts for gardeners**, ranging from bird houses to benches, faucet handles, croquet sets, windvanes, stepping stones and lots more; a very nice selection. (1989)
❒ Catalog: $1d
⌂ Shop: January-March, M-Sa, April-December, daily

Public Service Lamp Corp.
410 W. 16th Street
New York, NY 10011
(212) 989-1694, (800) 221-4392, FAX 924-2708
Les Deutsch, Mgr.

Supplies
Sells Wonderlites, a self-ballasted **mercury vapor flood lamp** for any screw-socket -- excellent for growing plants indoors, even those with higher light requirements. (1950)
❒ Catalog: Free, R&W, CAN/OV, $70m

Purple Sage Productions
531 Corralitos Road, #130
Corralitos, CA 95076
(408) 724-1787
Chris Bryan & M. Nevin Smith

Services
Specialize in video-taping **horticultural symposia**; currently have videos on an Australian plants symposium at U.C. Santa Cruz, and a California native plant symposium at the Rancho Santa Ana Botanic Garden. They're working on instructional videos on low-maintenance plants (perennials, bulbs, shrubs and trees) for Western gardens. (1991)
❒ Catalog: Free, R&W, CAN/OV, $20m

Qualimetrics, Inc.
P.O. Box 230
Princeton, NJ 08542
(609) 924-4470 TO $50m
Thomas Tesauro

Supplies
Offers a large selection of **weather instruments**; those of special interest to gardeners are a temperature-time indicator, growing degree-day totalizers, humidity indicators and recorders for greenhouses, wind speed indicators, soil thermometers and rain gauges. Even sells complete weather stations.
❒ Catalog: Free, CAN/OV, $50m
⌂ Shop: All year, by appointment only

Quest Rare Books
774 Santa Ynez
Stanford, CA 94305
(415) 324-3119
Gretl Meier

Books
A specialist in **old and rare books** on gardening, landscape design and history and botany; she will also search for books worldwide and buy collections or single volumes. (1986)
❒ Catalog: $3, CAN/OV
⌂ Shop: All year, by appointment only

RNM Sales
P.O. Box 666
Jacksonville, OR 97530
(503) 899-7117 TO
Richard N. Maudlin

Tools
Offers a **stand-up weeder** called the Weed Twist which pulls weeds by the roots and can be used in lawns, as it leaves a small hole which quickly fills in with grass. A trigger releases the weeds. Saves sore backs and knees.
❒ Catalog: Free, R&W, CAN, $20m

Rainbow Gardens Bookshop

See Rainbow Gardens Nursery & Bookshop in Section A.

Rainbow Red Worms
P. O. Box 278
Lake Elsinor, CA 92531-0278
(909) 674-7041
Jonne Stauffers

Supplies
Offers **redworms**, shipped by Priority Mail, and **worm castings**. Great for the new rage for worm composting boxes in your basement.
❒ Catalog: Free, R&W, CAN

Raindrip, Inc.
P.O. Box 2173
21305 Itasca Street
Chatsworth, CA 91313-2173
(818) 718-8004, (800) 222-3747, FAX 407-1345
Ruth Mehra, Mgr.

Supplies
Sell Raindrip **drip irrigation systems and supplies**; informative booklet tells you how to get started and what you'll need. They have a multiplex dripper which will go on the sprinkler fittings of existing underground systems. They also sell a video cassette on how to do it. (1975)
❏ Catalog: Free, R&W, CAN/OV, $10m
⌂ Shop: All year, M-F

Bargyla Rateaver
9049 Covina Street
San Diego, CA 92126
(619) 566-8994
Dr. Bargyla Rateaver

Supplies
A source for **organic growing supplies and pest controls**: sabadilla dust, ryania, BT, fish meal, compost starter, BX, nematode remedy, Maxicrop seaweed powder and more. Also sells some organic gardening literature. (1973)
❏ Catalog: Long SASE, CAN/OV
⌂ Shop: Call ahead

Redwood Arts
P.O. Box 419
Airway Heights, WA 99001
(509) 244-9669
Chuck & Beryl Lohr

Supplies
Make three sizes of handsome and long-lasting **redwood planters** so carefully fitted together that they have no nails; they somewhat resemble "Versailles boxes." They plan to add furniture, bird houses and feeders soon. (1992)
❏ Catalog: Free($1 OV), CAN/OV, $45m

Reimuller's Cart Warehouse

See Cart Warehouse.

Reotemp Instrument Corporation
11568 Sorrento Valley Rd., #10
San Diego, CA 92121
(619) 481-7737, (800) 648-7737, FAX 481-7150
Kathy Martin, Sales Mgr.

Supplies
Offers bi-metal dial **thermometers**, including one specifically for measuring the heat in backyard compost piles with a 20 inch probe. (1963)
❏ Catalog: Free, R&W, CAN/OV

Resource Conservation Technology
2633 N. Calvert St.
Baltimore, MD 21218
(410) 366-1146

Supplies
Fabricates and sells **pond liners** of Butyl and EPDM synthetic rubbers; they come in several thicknesses, and they also sell the supplies you need to do the job or fix punctures. Catalog is full of how-to information. (1984)
❏ Catalog: Free($3 OV), R&W, CAN/OV
⌂ Shop: All year, M-F, call ahead

Richardson-Allen Furniture
P.O. Box 701
Cape Porpoise, ME 04014
(207) 967-8482
Samuel R. Butler

Furniture
Manufacture "estate" **garden furniture**, hand made in Maine of mahogany or teak (or painted) and in a variety of classic styles. Also offer planters, bedroom furniture and tables of various sizes. (1989)
❏ Catalog: $2, R&W, CAN/OV

Rocky Mountain Insectary
P.O. Box 152
Palisade, CO 81526
Linda Mowrer

Supplies
Sells **Pedio wasps** for control of the Mexican bean beetle; informative leaflet explains how to get them established. (1983)
❏ Catalog: Free, SS:5-8

Rodco Products Co., Inc.
2565 - 16th Avenue
Columbus, NE 68601
(402) 563-3596, (800) 323 2799 TO/CC
Rodney F. Bahlen

Supplies
Computemp **temperature monitor and alarm**: takes Fahrenheit or Celsius readings, both indoors and out; records high and low of the day; will monitor air, soil or water at up to nine locations; will sound an alarm at a pre-set temperature -- does everything but get up at midnight to fix things! They are offering a new Rain-O-Matic electronic rain gauge, too. (1977)
❏ Catalog: Free, R&W, CAN/OV
⌂ Shop: All year, M-F

A. I. Root Company
P.O. Box 706
Medina, OH 44258-0706
(216) 725-6677 TO/CC $10m
Kim Flottum & Diana Sammataro

Books ～ Supplies
Everything for the home or commercial beekeeper and honey producer, even bee toys -- they've been in business since 1869 and have branches in three states. Also publish "Gleanings in Bee Culture," the monthly magazine of the beekeeping industry. (1869)
❏ Catalog: Free, R&W, CAN/OV
⌂ Shop: All year, M-Sa; branches listed in catalog

Rosebud
3707 S.W. Coronado Street
Portland, OR 97219
(503) 245-0546
Jeremy Grand

Services
"Just the Right Rose!" is a **catalog of roses for the personal computer**. It has a database of over 700 roses, from old garden roses to modern hybrid teas, and will sort on color, fragrance, height, disease resistance, awards and more. Yearly upgrades are available; for IBM compatibles. (1990)
❏ Catalog: Free, R&W, CAN/OV

Rudon International Trading Company
P.O. Box 331104
Ft. Worth, TX 76163
(817) 292-8485, FAX 292-0950
John D. Croslin

Tools
Sells the EZ-Digger, a traditional **hand tool** from the Orient; it is a combination of weeder, hand hoe and trowel that comes with short or long handle. They've added a "disk hoe" for weeding and cultivating. (1988)
❏ Catalog: Free, R&W, CAN/OV

Ruesch International Financial Services
1350 Eye Street, N.W.
Washington, DC 20005
(202) 408-1200, (800) 424-2923, FAX 408-1211

Services
Here's an answer to the problem of sending payments to societies or suppliers in foreign countries: you call them and tell them how much you want to send and to "lock in" the exchange rate; they'll tell you the US dollar equivalent. Then send a personal or cashier's check for that amount plus $2 for a check, $15 for a wire transfer. There is no minimum amount necessary. They have offices in Washington, New York, Atlanta, Chicago and Los Angeles.
❏ Catalog: Free

S & D Enterprises
1280 Quince Drive
Junction City, OR 97448
(503) 998-2060
Stan Hall

Supplies
Offer anodized aluminium **plant labels** on which you can write with a #2 pencil for a lasting name. (1988)
❏ Catalog: Long SASE, R&W, CAN/OV
⌂ Shop: All year, call ahead

San Luis Video Publishing
P.O. Box 6715
Los Osos, CA 93401
(805) 528-8322, FAX 528-7227 TO/CC
Joe & Jora Clokey, Jodi Kinzler

Supplies
A broad selection of **environmental horticultural videos** on garden design, sustainable landscaping and agriculture, greenhouse and nursery safety, integrated compost systems, and plant selection. For professional and serious gardeners; libraries sometimes have these to loan. (1989)
❏ Catalog: Free, R&W, CAN/OV

Santa Barbara Greenhouses
1115-J Avenida Acaso
Camarillo, CA 93012
(805) 482-3765, (800) 544-5276 TO/CC $100m
Robert West Solakian

Supplies
Offer redwood and fiberglass prefabricated **greenhouses** in various sizes, as well as all of the accessories to fit them out, such as benches, mist systems, heaters and fans. Also have a line of deluxe redwood and glass greenhouses and sunrooms, which are shipped in preglazed sections. (1972)
❏ Catalog: Free, R&W, CAN/OV
⌂ Shop: All year, M-F

Santa Barbara Orchid Garden & Library
1350 More Ranch Road
Santa Barbara, CA 93111
(805) 967-9798
Paul Gripp

Services
A retired orchid nurseryman who offers five-day **orchid study vacations** in Santa Barbara, with tours of nurseries, etc., and native orchid hunts in other parts of California. Santa Barbara is a great orchid center, with many other attractions. He also provides an **orchid advice service. (1986)**
❏ Catalog: Free

Saroh
P.O. Box 8375
Springfield, IL 62791
George L. Lang

Services
Offers a **computer database** on the care, use and propagation of more than 9,500 plants; information given is fairly detailed. Used by home gardeners as well as commercial growers and landscape designers and architects; codes comply with the American Nurseryman's format for bar codes. IBM/DOS compatible, it needs 10MB of hard disk storage. (1988)
❏ Catalog: Free, CAN/OV

Savoy Books
P.O. Box 271
Lanesboro, MA 01237
(413) 499-9968
Robert Fraker

Books
Specializes in American, English and French **books on agriculture and horticulture**, mostly old and rare, for collectors. Also old botanical prints, nursery catalogs and other ephemera related to the history of gardening and agriculture. Material generally covers the 16th to 19th centuries. (1971)
❏ Catalog: Free, CAN/OV
⌂ Shop: By appointment only

Scanmask

See BioLogic.

Science Associates or Scientific Sales

See Qualimetrics, Inc.

Sea Born/Lane, Inc.
P.O. Box 204
Charles City, IA 50616
(515) 228-2000, (800) 457-5013 TO/CC $25m
Warren K. Dunkle, Mgr.

Supplies
Offers a variety of **seaweed fertilizers and other organic garden products**; the seaweed products are manufactured from Norwegian seaweed. Also offers fish meal, blood meal, bone meal, green sand, rock phosphates, some tools and technical crop data sheets. (1960)
❏ Catalog: Free, R&W, CAN/OV, $10m

Seed Saver(R)
P.O. Box 2726
Idaho Falls, ID 83403
(208) 522-2224, FAX same
Kristi Appelhans

Supplies
The Seed Saver(R) is a **seed file** for saving and storing seeds; a plastic storage box with resealable airtight bags for seed packets, it comes in several sizes with different capacities. For those with large amounts of seed, they sell a storage unit that fits in a standard hanging file drawer. (1990)
❒ Catalog: Free, R&W, CAN/OV, $2m

SeedScapes
P.O. Box 295
Edwardsburg, MI 49112
(616) 663-8601
Karen Tefft & Kathryn Alexander

Services
Offers **garden plans** for herb, vegetable and flower gardens; included with each design are growing tips for each plant, a general gardening manual, a monthly gardening calendar and sources of recommended seeds. Plans are based on your desires and situation. (1986)
❒ Catalog: $1d ($2 OV), CAN/OV, $6m

Robert Shuhi -- Books
P.O. Box 268
Morris, CT 06763
(203) 567-5231 or 9384

Books
Offers an extensive list of **used and out-of-print books**, covering a broad selection in the fields of travel, archaeology, nature, science and, of course, plants and gardening.
❒ Catalog: Free

Slugbuster
827 Albemarle Avenue
Cuyahoga Falls, OH 44221
(216) 923-0631
Earl Kull

Supplies
Earl Kull guarantees that Slugbuster(TM) will **kill slugs and snails** in your yard; you add it to a hose end sprayer or put it in a spray bottle, and it will kill them in minutes, with minimal harm to plants. It sounds wonderful, I'm tempted! Next to gophers, snails are my greatest problem. (1991)
❒ Catalog: Free, CAN/OV

Edward F. Smiley, Bookseller
43 Liberty Hill Road
Bedford, NH 03110
(603) 472-5800

Books ⬥ Services
Offers **used and out-of-print books** on gardening and horticulture, including a few rarities and some less-available new books. He also provides book search services for customers. (1977)
❒ Catalog: Free, CAN/OV

Smith & Hawken
117 East Strawberry Drive
Mill Valley, CA 94941
(800) 776-3336
CML Corporation

Furniture ⬥ Ornaments ⬥ Books ⬥ Tools
Offer a very broad selection of **garden tools**, many imported from England or Japan, irrigation supplies, composting equipment, books, garden furniture, housewares and many items suitable for gifts. (1979)
❒ Catalog: Free, R&W
⌂ Shop: All year, daily

Smith Greenhouse & Supply
P.O. Box 618
603 14th Street
Mendota, IL 61342
(815) 539-6768, (800) 255-4906, FAX 538-6981
Tom Smith

Supplies
Offer various **seed treatments, soil amendments, wetting agents, seaweed concentrate and humic acid products**. Informative leaflet explains purpose and use of each product manufactured by EnP, another branch of the same company. Also sell **propagation supplies and greenhouse equipment.** (1987)
❒ Catalog: Free
⌂ Shop: All year, M-Sa

Solarcone, Inc.
P.O. Box 67
Seward, IL 61077-0067
(815) 247-8454, FAX 247-8443 TO/CC $10m
Lloyd & Dale Falconer

Supplies
Distributors in the US of the Green Cone(TM) and the Green Keeper(TM), **composting containers**; the Green Cone breaks down kitchen waste, and produces small amounts of compost, the Green Keeper composts yard wastes. They sell direct to gardeners as well as to other suppliers. (1989)
❒ Catalog: Free, R&W, $5m

Spalding Laboratories
760 Printz Road
Arroyo Grande, CA 93420
(800) 845-2847 TO/CC $14m
Pat Spalding

Supplies
Sells Fly Predators(R), **beneficial insects** for fly control, useful wherever flies are a problem -- around indoor plants, animals, farm buildings, greenhouses, compost piles, etc., (who doesn't have flies?). (1976)
❒ Catalog: Free, R&W, $14m

Spray-N-Grow, Inc.
20 Highway 35 South
Rockport, TX 78382
(512) 790-9033, FAX 790-9313 TO/CC
Bill Muskopf

Supplies
Offer Spray-N-Grow, a micronutrient **growth stimulant** which they say will make all plants grow better, and produce better and more fruit or flowers. Also sell Triple Action 20, a **fungicide** which controls bacteria, mold, fungus, germs, and mildew in home or garden. (1982)
❒ Catalog: Free, R&W, CAN/OV, $12m

Stone Forest
P.O. Box 2840
Santa Fe, NM 87504
(505) 986-8883, FAX 982-2712
Michael Zimber

Ornaments
Offer hand-carved granite **garden ornaments**: lanterns, fountains and water basins, bridges, pedestals and lovely spheres. The designs are Japanese in feeling, but not strictly traditional. (1989)
❏ Catalog: $3d, R&W, CAN/OV
⌂ Shop: All year, M-Sa, by appointment only

Stuewe and Sons, Inc.
2290 S.E. Kiger Island Drive
Corvallis, OR 97333
(503) 757-7798, (800) 553-5331, FAX 754-6617
Eric, Shelly, Vern & Gladys Stuewe

Supplies
Stuewe is essentially a wholesale company, offering **forest seedling and deep nursery containers** and other tree propagation supplies, but anyone may buy from them; if you want less than a full case, they will charge you a modest repacking fee. Offered are expanded polystyrene seedling blocks, "Cone-tainers," "Multi-pots," "Deepots," and "Treepots." (1981)
❏ Catalog: Free, CAN/OV, $5m
⌂ Shop: All year, M-F

Sturdi-Built Mfg. Co.
11304 S.W. Boones Ferry Road
Portland, OR 97219
(503) 244-4100, (800) 722-4115
Rick & Bill Warner

Supplies
Offers redwood **greenhouses** in a number of styles, both free-standing and lean-to; also sells accessories and equipment. One model is round. They can be single or double-glazed and customized to fit your exact space. (1952)
❏ Catalog: Free($3 OV), CAN/OV, $10m
⌂ Shop: All year, M-F, or by appointment

Submatic Irrigation Systems
P.O. Box 246
719 26th Street
Lubbock, TX 79408
(806) 747-9000, (800) 692-4100, FAX 747-1800
Gene Brown

Supplies
A broad selection of supplies for **drip and mist irrigation systems**, sub-surface lawn irrigation and mini-sprinklers for a variety of uses -- for home gardeners and commercial use; they'll help you design your system. (1970)
❏ Catalog: Free, R&W, CAN/OV
⌂ Shop: All year, M-F

Sun Garden Specialties
P.O. Box 52382
Tulsa, OK 74152-0382
Tony Bishop

Ornaments
Offers custom made **ornaments for the Japanese garden**: signs and signposts in Japanese, a rustic Samurai seat, and sake barrel round signs in Japanese, all with your choice of text. (1990)
❏ Catalog: Free($2 OV), R&W, CAN/OV, $30m

Sunglo Solar Greenhouses
4441 - 26th Avenue West
Seattle, WA 98199
(206) 284-8900, (800) 647-0606 TO/CC
Robert & Ron Goldsberry

Supplies
Manufacture and sell **greenhouses in kit form**, either freestanding or lean-to, with double or triple-wall construction; also offer greenhouse accessories.
❏ Catalog: Free, CAN/OV
⌂ Shop: All year, M-F

Sunstream Bee Supply
P.O. Box 225
Eighty Four, PA 15330
(412) 222-3330
Francis Yost

Books ∾ Supplies
Offers a complete line of **beekeeping supplies and equipment**: bees, books, hives, honey-extracting equipment, clothing and gloves, even seeds of plants attractive to bees. You can buy a complete beginner's outfit -- with or without bees.
❏ Catalog: $1, CAN/OV, $10m
⌂ Shop: April-October, M,W,F,Su

Superior Autovents
17422 LaMesa Lane
Huntington Beach, CA 92647-6111
FAX (714) 848-0412
Donald Morris

Supplies
Sells the Bayliss MK.7, a solar-powered **automatic vent opener** for green-houses and coldframes; it can be set to open at temperatures between 55F and 75F and will lift up to 32 pounds in weight. No shipping to Europe.
❏ Catalog: Free, R&W, CAN, $45m

Raymond M. Sutton, Jr.
P.O. Box 330
430 Main Street
Williamsburg, KY 40769
(606) 549-3464, FAX 549-3469
Raymond M. Sutton, Jr.

Books
Specializes in **rare, out-of-print and new books** on gardening, botany and natural history, with over 7,000 books in stock; send your "want list" if there's something you've been looking for. (1986)
❏ Catalog: Free, CAN/OV
⌂ Shop: All year, M-F; other times by appointment only

TFS Injector Systems
211 West Maple Avenue
Monrovia, CA 91016
(818) 358-5507, FAX 358-0357 TO/CC
Tom Strong

Supplies
A broad selection of **supplies for drip irrigation systems** and free design advice for the customer; they sell a "Drip Irrigation Design Manual" for $4.95 ppd. -- 26 pages of practical advice. Also sell the Add-It(R) ferti-lizer injector for either drip systems or any garden hose bib. (1977)
❏ Catalog: Long SASE, R&W, CAN/OV, $20m
⌂ Shop: All year, M-F

Taxonomic Computer Research
P.O. Box 12011
Raleigh, NC 27605
(919) 856-0995
Larry Hatch

Services
They specialize in **horticultural library information systems**, including 28 horticultural and botany software programs. Emphasize plant selection, identification, and reference databases on specific groups of plants. Catalog on IBM/MS-DOS 5¼" disk: $3, Catalog disk with sample program: $5.
❒ Catalog: See notes; CAN/OV

Taylor Ridge Farm
P.O. Box 222
Saluda, NC 28773
(704) 749-4756
Gunnar Taylor

Ornaments
Make hand-crafted **arbors and trellises** of steel or copper in simple country-garden designs. Shipped by UPS and easy to assemble. (1991)
❒ Catalog: $3d, R&W
⌂ Shop: All year, Sa-Su, by appointment only

Tec Laboratories, Inc.
P.O. Box 1958
Albany, OR 97321
(800) ITCHING

Supplies
Tecnu **Poison Oak-n-Ivy Cleanser** really works! If you wash at once you can avoid the rash, and if you're too late, it lessens the rash and itch; it sits on my kitchen sink. They also make a venom remover for insect bites and stings and a 10-hour insect repellent which repels ticks. Call and they'll tell you where to buy their products in your Zip Code.
❒ Catalog: Free, R&W, $5m

Terrace Software
P.O. Box 271
Medford, MA 02155-0002
(617) 396-0382, FAX same
Roberta Norin

Services
"Mum's the Word" integrated **garden planning software** for the Macintosh; it "combines object-oriented drawing tools with a horticultural database." Search the database for plants meeting your needs (or add your own plants), then "plant" it on your plan, automatically labeling the drawing. (1986)
❒ Catalog: Free, R&W, CAN/OV

Texas Greenhouse Co.
2524 White Settlement Road
Ft. Worth, TX 76107
(817) 335-5447, (800) 227-5447 TO/CC
Kathy Carlisle, Pres.

Supplies
Sells **greenhouses and lean-tos** with curved glass eaves, automatic venting and aluminum or redwood frames in a variety of sizes; also a complete line of greenhouse equipment and accessories. (1948)
❒ Catalog: $4, R&W, CAN/OV
⌂ Shop: All year, M-F

Tiny Trees Book Sales
P.O. Box 5834
Hauppauge, NY 11788-0170
Tim Novak

Books
Offers a large selection of **books on bonsai**; some of the books described with quotations from reviews. Also bonsai notecards and Christmas cards.
❒ Catalog: Free, CAN

Topiaries Unlimited
RD 2, Box 40C
Pownal, VT 05261
(802) 823-5536, FAX 823-5080
Joyce & Ken Held

Ornaments
The Helds offer **topiary frames** in a number of animal and other designs, and will work with you to create frames for your own ideas or designs. Joyce in on the Board of the American Ivy Society, and may be able to suggest special planting and foliage effects. (1986)
❒ Catalog: Long SASE, R&W, $25m

Topiary, Inc.
41 Bering Street
Tampa, FL 33606
Carole Guyton & Mia Hardcastle

Ornaments
Painted galvanized wire **topiary frames** in many animal and other shapes, many available already planted. They also sell books, "The Complete Book of Topiary," and "The New Topiary" to help you get started. (1981)
❒ Catalog: Long SASE, R&W

Touchwood Books
P.O. Box 610
Hastings, New Zealand
(06) 874-2872, FAX 874-2701 TO/CC
Peter & Diane Arthur

Books ⌘ Services
A broad selection of over 2,000 **new and used books** from all countries on plants, trees and gardening; they will search for books on request. (1987)
❒ Catalog: Free, US/OV
⌂ Shop: All year, call ahead

Trans-Sphere Corp.

See Gothic Arch Greenhouses.

Treesentials
P.O. Box 7097
St. Paul, MN 55107
(612) 228-0535, (800) 248-8239, FAX 228-0554
Lawrence King & Joseph Lais

Supplies
If you've traveled in England recently, you've seen thousands of seedling trees along the railway lines planted in **tree shelter tubes**. Treesentials supplies these tubes, called Tubex; they offer seedling trees protection from animals and sunburn, provide good light and reduce moisture loss from transpiration. (1989)
❒ Catalog: Free, R&W

Trickle Soak Systems

See TFS Injector Systems.

Tropical Plant Products, Inc.
P.O. Box 547754
Orlando, FL 32854
Kenneth & Janet Lewis

Supplies
Sells **orchid growing supplies**: fertilizers, wire hanging baskets, coconut
fiber, fir bark, moss, tree fern baskets, sphagnum moss and osmunda fiber,
totems and plaques for mounting bromeliads, fertilizers and more. (1974)
❒ Catalog: Long SASE, R&W

Tumblebug
2029 N. 23rd Street
Boise, ID 83702
(208) 368-7900, (800) 531-0102, FAX 368-7900
Henry Artis

Supplies
The Tumblebug(R) is a rolling **compost tumbler**, with angled sides so
that it will stay where you put it -- you can roll it to where you want it,
fill it, and then let your kids roll it around to make compost. (1991)
❒ Catalog: Free, R&W, CAN/OV
⌂ Shop: All year, M-Sa

Turner Greenhouses
P.O. Box 1260
Highway 117 South
Goldsboro, NC 27533-1260
(919) 734-8345, (800) 672-4770, FAX 736-4550
Gary Smithwick

Books & Supplies
Galvanized-steel-framed **greenhouses** in various sizes and configurations,
available with fiberglass or polyethylene coverings, as well as a full line
of equipment, accessories and books on propagation and gardening. (1939)
❒ Catalog: Free, R&W, CAN, $10m
⌂ Shop: All year, M-F

Twinholly's
3633 Northeast 19th Avenue
Portland, OR 97212
Sandra H. Nigro

Supplies
Twinholly's has no catalog, but sells glassine **seed storage envelopes** useful for saving and sending seeds to gardening friends. They cost $4 for a
package of 50 envelopes, and each package contains three sizes. Available
in bulk for growers, or presumably, to clubs for seed exchanges. (1991)
❒ Catalog: See notes

U. S. Post Office
Every Town, USA

Services
You can purchase **international money orders** through your local post office:
ask for an "Application for International Money Order." The post office will
collect the money for payment and a fee, and a money order will be forwarded
to the payee from St. Louis -- it will indicate who is sending the money.

Under Glass Mfg. Corp.
P. O. Box 323
Wappingers Falls, NY 12590
(914) 298-0645, FAX 298-0648
William D. Orange, Mgr.

Supplies
Manufacturers of **greenhouses and solariums**, they are the successors to
Lord & Burnham and continue with their designs and features. They will put
you in touch with a distributor if you live near one, or will sell to you
direct if there's no distributor nearby. (1989)
❒ Catalog: $3, R&W, CAN/OV

Unique Insect Control
5504 Sperry Drive
Citrus Heights, CA 95621
(916) 961-7945, FAX 967-7082
Pete & Mary Foley, Jeanne Houston

Supplies
Offers several types of **beneficial insects**: ladybugs, green lacewings,
trichogramma wasps, praying mantis, fly parasites, white-fly parasites,
predatory mites, mealybug predators and earthworms. Their flier is very
informative. (1980)
❒ Catalog: Free, R&W, CAN

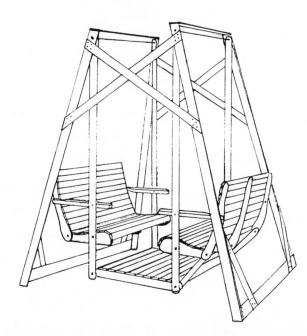

© Heritage Garden Furniture
Artist: Greger McLean

The Urban Farmer Store
2833 Vicente Street
San Francisco, CA 94116
(415) 661-2204, FAX 661-7826 TO/CC $10m
Tom Bressan & John Stokes

Supplies
Specialize in **drip and automatic irrigation systems**; catalog is a good all-around introduction to the subject and offers all the necessary parts and equipment. Carry products of thirty manufacturers and kits of their own; also offer a wide selection of low voltage **outdoor lighting** systems.
❏ Catalog: $1d, R&W, CAN/OV
⌂ Shop: All year, M-Sa

V-Base
920 Leland Avenue
Lima, OH 45805
Mike Schoenberger

Services
"V-Base is a **plant finding database** for varieties and commercial growers of African violets." It's $7 for the 5¼" disc, and it's updated yearly. IBM compatibles only, it runs on "X-Base" database programs, or comes with a shareware database program, for which you pay the shareware provider. (1992)
❏ Catalog: See notes, CAN/OV

Valley Oak Tool Company
448 West 2nd Avenue
Chico, CA 95926
(916) 342-6188
David Grau

Tools
Valley Oak makes a **wheel hoe**, an updated version designed to reduce back strain and be easy to use; a four-tine cultivator and "sweep cultivator" attachments are available. Also sells stake pounders and pullers. (1990)
❏ Catalog: Free, R&W, CAN/OV

Verilux, Inc.
P.O. Box 7633
Vallejo, CA 94590
(800) 786-6850, FAX (707) 544-8370 TO/CC
Nicholas Harmon

Supplies
Full spectrum Verilux TruBloom **fluorescent plant lights** are balanced to promote normal, compact growth and blooming -- long-lasting and available in various sizes for home or commercial use. (1956)
❏ Catalog: Free($2 OV), R&W, CAN/OV, $32m

Victory Garden Supply Co.
1428 E. High Street
Charlottesville, VA 22902
(804) 293-2298 or 9188, FAX 977-4362 TO/CC
John R. Corle

Supplies
Offers several models of aluminum **greenhouses**, as well as heaters, benches, vent openers, shades and ventilated shelving. Several complete kits available; the greenhouses have roof drains to keep the glass clean. (1987)
❏ Catalog: Free, CAN/OV, $10m
⌂ Shop: All year, M-F, Sa am

Vintage Wood Works
P.O. Box R
Highway 34 South
Quinlan, TX 78624
(903) 356-2158, FAX 356-3023 TO/CC
Gregory & Roland Tatsch

Ornaments
Offers a charming Victorian **gazebo**, as well as a broad selection of Victorian and period millwork trim for houses, including porch turnings, gables, fret brackets, window cornices, shelves and more -- a terrific way to perk up a lackluster house or turn a shed into a decorative cottage! (1978)
❏ Catalog: $2, CAN/OV
⌂ Shop: All year, M-F

The Violet House
P.O. Box 1274
Gainesville, FL 32602
(904) 377-8465
Dick & Lois Anne Maduro

Supplies
Offer **indoor growing supplies** -- plastic pots, wick-watering reservoirs, fertilizers, pesticides and potting materials for growing African violets and other houseplants. They also sell sinningia seed from Jeannie Moe, and seed of African violet hybrids from the Nadeau Seed Company. (1975)
❏ Catalog: Long SASE($1 OV), CAN/OV, $8m
⌂ Shop: All year, M-F, call ahead

Vista Products
1245 Prairie Dog Place
Ventura, CA 93003
(805) 659-4389
Gerry & Ritva Vadeboncoeur

Supplies
They invented and manufacture the Eezy Picker(TM), a **pole picker** that cuts the fruit and catches it in a cloth bag so that it isn't dropped or bruised; replacement blades and bags are available. (1990)
❏ Catalog: $1d, R&W, CAN/OV

Visual Education Productions
Cal Poly State University
San Luis Obispo, CA 93407
(805) 756-2295, (800) 235-4146, FAX 756-5550
Rick Smith, Dir.

Supplies
Produces a wide variety of **landscape/horticultural videotapes** for schools, landscape professionals, greenhouse and nursery operators and serious gardeners. Academic and practical, with safety a top consideration. Also sell some books. (1954)
❏ Catalog: Free, CAN/OV

Vixen Hill Gazebos
Main Street
Elverson, PA 19520
(215) 286-0909, (800) 423-2766, FAX 286-2099
Douglas Jefferys & Christopher Peeples

Ornaments
Make easy-to-assemble **prefabricated gazebos**, available in four sizes, Victorian or Colonial in style, even glassed-in, made of cedar and assembled with brass acorn nuts. They also make benches and tables to fit. (1981)
❏ Catalog: $3d, CAN/OV
⌂ Shop: All year, M-F, call ahead

Gary Wayner -- Bookseller
Route 3, Box 18
Fort Payne, AL 35967-9501
(205) 845-7828, FAX 845-2070 TO/CC $20m
Gary Wayner

Books
Specializes in scholarly **out-of-print books** on botany, gardening and
natural history. (1976)
❒ Catalog: $1, CAN/OV
⌂ Shop: By appointment only

Wheeler Arts
66 Lake Park
Champaign, IL 61821-7101
(217) 359-6816, FAX 359-8716 TO/CC
Paula & Stephen Wheeler

Services
For those caught up in the home-publishing frenzy, here is a source of nice
horticultural clip art called "Quick Art," both printed and on computer
disk and CD-ROM. There is a nice variety of subjects, both horticultural and
agricultural, and they send a free sample with each catalog order. (1973)
❒ Catalog: $3, R&W, CAN/OV, $30m

Wheldon & Wesley
Lytton Lodge, Codicote
Hitchin, Herts., England SG4 8TE
(0438) 82-0370, FAX 82-1478
Christopher K. Swann, Mgr.

Books
Dealers in **new, secondhand, old and rare books** on botany, flora of Britain
and other countries and gardening books, as well as books in other fields of
natural history. Books can be purchased with credit cards to save the hassle
of exchange rates; catalogs available by Air Mail at £6 per year. (1843)
❒ Catalog: Free, OV
⌂ Shop: All year, M-F, by appointment only

Wikco Industries, Inc.
4931 N. 57th Street, #1
Lincoln, NE 68507
(402) 464-2070, (800) 872-8864, FAX 464-2289
Brandon S. Ideen, Sales Manager

Furniture ∾ Tools
Offer the Clear Creek **garden bench** in turn-of-the-century wrought iron
style, with green, black or white enamel finish. Also sell the Super Spear
Log Splitter for splitting firewood without an ax. They also have a "Grounds
Maintenance Catalog" of tools and power equipment. (1979)
❒ Catalog: Free, CAN/OV

Willsboro Wood Products
P.O. Box 509
S. AuSable Street
Keeseville, NY 12944
(518) 834-5200, (800) 342-3373, FAX 834-5219

Furniture
Adirondack-style **cedar furniture** for indoors and out -- chairs, chaises,
settees, tables, picnic tables and benches; also planters. (1982)
❒ Catalog: Free, R&W, CAN/OV
⌂ Shop: All year, M-F

Wind & Weather
P.O. Box 2320
Albion Street Watertower
Mendocino, CA 95460
(707) 964-1284, FAX 964-1278 TO/CC
Mary Latko

Ornaments ∾ Books ∾ Supplies
Everything you need to enjoy and record the weather: **weather instruments**,
shelters for weather stations, weathervanes, wind chimes, sundials and lots
of books on weather -- even books for children. (1974)
❒ Catalog: Free, CAN/OV
⌂ Shop: All year, daily

Windleaves
7560 Morningside Drive
Indianapolis, IN 46240
(317) 251-1381 TO/CC
Bart Kister

Ornaments
Manufacture and sell **windvanes** sculpted in the shapes of leaves -- several
styles, such as tuliptree, dogwood, ginkgo and maple; they can be stuck in
the ground in the garden or mounted on a roof. (1983)
❒ Catalog: Free($1 OV) R&W, CAN/OV
⌂ Shop: By appointment only

Windsor Designs
37 Great Valley Parkway
Malvern, PA 19355
(215) 640-1212, (800) 783-5434, FAX 640-5896
Don Flanderd, Jr. & Bruce Bassett-Powell

Furniture
Offers **garden furniture** in shorea, teak and cast aluminum; classic designs
in a variety of styles, including the lovely teak deckchairs I read my way to
Europe and back on several times. Give up? Shorea is an Indonesian hard wood
which is in abundant supply. Formerly Brandywine Garden Furniture.
❒ Catalog: Free, CAN/OV, $100m

Winterthur Museum & Gardens
  Catalogue Division
100 Enterprise Place
Dover, DE 19901
(800) 767-0500, FAX (302) 676-3299 TO/CC $10m
Anne B. Coleman, Mgr.

Ornaments
Catalog from the Winterthur Museum & Gardens offers beautiful **reproductions**
of items on display both in the gardens and in the house, as well as special
plants from the gardens. A good selection of **gifts and garden ornaments**
for any garden or gardener -- many tempting items.
❒ Catalog: Free
⌂ Shop: Museum shop, Tu-Su

Wisconsin Wagon Co.
507 Laurel Avenue
Janesville, WI 53545
(608) 754-0026 TO/CC
Albert & Lois Hough

Supplies
Make wooden children's toys, including **wheelbarrows**, sleds and great
Janesville wagons. They also make an awning-covered **patio cart**, and have
added an adult-size wheelbarrow, probably because the little one is so cute
that grown-ups had to have their own. Baby and doll cradles, too. (1979)
❒ Catalog: Free, R&W
⌂ Shop: February-Christmas, M-F; Sa-Su by appointment only

Womanswork
P.O. Box 543
York, ME 03909-0543
(207) 363-0804, FAX 363-0805
Nancy Phillips

Supplies
Specialize in **gardening and work gloves** made to fit women's hands; they come in many styles and several weights, and in four sizes. Also gauntlet gloves for working around roses. They also make a practical work-apron, sun visors, and have designed a pair of heavy work boots for women. (1985)
❒ Catalog: Free, R&W, CAN/OV

Wood Classics
Osprey Lane
Gardiner, NY 12525
(914) 255-7871 or 5599, FAX 255-7881 TO/CC
Eric & Barbara Goodman

Furniture
Nicely crafted American-made **wooden outdoor (and indoor) furniture** in rustic and classic styles -- tables, chairs, lounges, porch swings and rockers, made of mahogany or teak; all available finished or in kit form. They are adding planters to their line. (1983)
❒ Catalog: Free, CAN/OV
⌂ Shop: All year, M-Sa

Wood Innovations of Suffolk
265 Middle Island Road
Medford, NY 11763
(516) 698-2345, FAX 698-2396
Henry Harms

Ornaments
Offers cedar **arbors, wishing wells, bridges, trellises and planters**, all made to order to your measurements; they will also assist you with your own design ideas. (1990)
❒ Catalog: Free, R&W, CAN/OV

Wood Violet Books
3814 Sunhill Drive
Madison, WI 53704
(608) 837-7207, 825-3073
Debra S. Cravens

Books ✍ Services
New and used books, specializing in books on herbs and other garden subjects, including cookbooks for garden produce; they will search for hard-to-find books, and special order books you can't find. (1983)
❒ Catalog: $2, CAN/OV
⌂ Shop: All year, by appointment only

Woodbrook Furniture Manufacturing Co.
P.O. Box 175
Trussville, AL 35173
(205) 655-4041, FAX 655-2316
Andy Hartley & Harry Higdon

Furniture
Offers handsome **garden furniture** made from southern cypress in a number of classic styles -- even a bed headboard copied from the famous Lutyens garden bench. They make benches, tables, planters, daybeds and headboards, and can make them to custom sizes. (1989)
❒ Catalog: Free, R&W, CAN/OV

Elisabeth Woodburn
P.O. Box 398
Booknoll Farm
Hopewell, NJ 08525
(609) 466-0522
Bradford Lyon & Joanne Fuccello

Books ✍ Services
The happy news is that Elisabeth Woodburn's long-time assistant and a friend have bought and will continue her esteemed business. They are specialists in **horticultural books**, including new, used, out-of-print and very rare books for libraries and serious gardeners; separate catalogs for various categories are $2 each. They do book searches and collection development, too. (1946)
❒ Catalog: See notes, CAN/OV
⌂ Shop: By appointment only

Woodstock Canoe Co.
P.O. Box 118
Woodstock, NH 03293
(800) 362-8804
David & Jack Donahue

Supplies
Bird feeders, bird houses and a bat shelter, all made of 1" thick, rough-sawn northern white cedar for a long lasting, care-free garden attraction. (1991)
❒ Catalog: Free($1 OV), R&W, CAN/OV, $10m

Gary W. Woolson, Bookseller
R.R. 1, Box 1576
Route 9 (Newburgh)
Hampden, ME 04444
(207) 234-4931 TO
Gary W. Woolson

Books
Specializes in **used and out-of-print books** on plants and gardening; also carries used books in many other fields. (1967)
❒ Catalog: Free, R&W, CAN
⌂ Shop: By appointment only

Worm's Way of Indiana
3151 South Highway 446
Bloomington, IN 47401
(812) 331-0300, (800) 274-9676, FAX 331-0854
Claude Eastridge

Supplies
Supplier of a broad range of **hydroponic equipment, indoor growing supplies, pest controls** and even beer making supplies. They have retail stores in Indiana, Missouri, Massachusetts and Florida; call for locations. (1985)
❒ Catalog: Free, R&W, CAN/OV, $10m
⌂ Shop: All year, M-Sa

Yanzum -- Art for Gardens
1285 Peachtree Street N.E.
Atlanta, GA 30309
(404) 874-8063
Douglas Yaney

Ornaments
Offers a broad selection of handsome **planters, statues, birdbaths** and **bird houses**, as well as many other garden ornaments, including works from local artists. Shop is across the street from the High Museum of Art. (1989)
❒ Catalog: Free, R&W, CAN/OV
⌂ Shop: All year, daily

Yonah Manufacturing Co.
P.O. Box 280
Airport Road
Cornelia, GA 30531
(706) 778-8654, (800) 972-8057, FAX 778-9118
Jim Bruce

Supplies
Sell **shade cloth** providing from 30% to 92% actual shade -- used for greenhouses and shade structures, patio covers, etc. Sold with bindings and rust-proof brass grommets custom-sewn to your specifications. They also sell black fabric mulch in 100-foot rolls, 12 feet wide; call for a quote. (1975)
❐ Catalog: Free, CAN/OV
⌂ Shop: All year, M-F, call ahead

© Collector's Nursery
   Artist: William Janssen

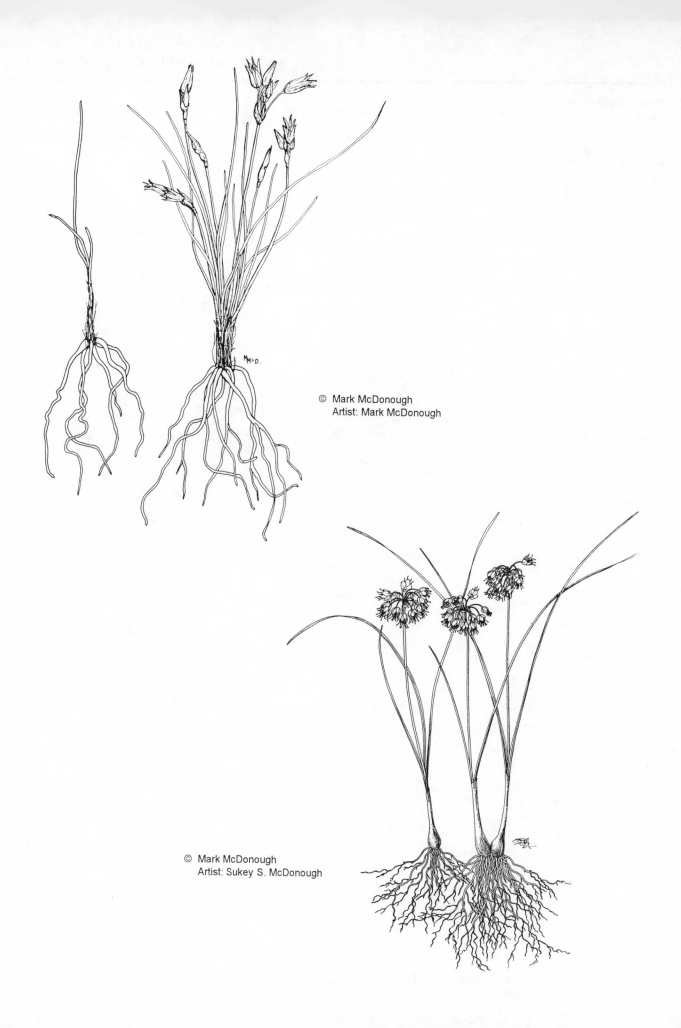

© Mark McDonough
Artist: Mark McDonough

© Mark McDonough
Artist: Sukey S. McDonough

C

Professional Societies and Trade Associations

Professional societies, trade associations and umbrella groups are listed alphabetically.

See the Index section for:

M. Magazine Index: an index to the titles of magazines offered by all societies and professional and trade associations, as well as those horticultural magazines and newsletters available by subscription.

Associations

Except where indicated, membership in these organizations is limited to those in specific trades or professions. Umbrella groups, although not open to general membership, can put you in touch with local affiliates.

Trade associations are listed because they are often excellent sources of information not available elsewhere. Many have useful promotional publications available to anyone, others have active public relations representatives who will field your questions. Dues are not listed because qualifications for membership do not include most people.

Professional societies are listed to help you connect with or get information from groups in fields of professional interest; inquire about membership and dues.

Some of the organizations listed here are groups formed to promote some particular conservation goal and are open to all; dues are listed for these groups.

A table of the symbols and abbreviations used in this book appears
on the bookmark inside the back cover.

Alliance for Historic Landscape Preservation
82 Wall Street, Suite 1105
New York, NY 10005

Write for information.

American Association of Botanical Gardens & Arboreta
Ruth Myers
786 Church Road
Wayne, PA 19087
(215) 688-1120
The Public Garden (4)
AABGA Newsletter (12)

Professional association of botanical gardens, with regional meetings in various locations. Newsletter lists positions available in botanical gardens and they publish an annual Internship Directory.
❒ Annual Dues: $50
❒ Privileges: CONVENTIONS TOURS

American Association of Nurserymen
1250 I Street, Suite 500
Washington, DC 20005
(202) 789-2900
Discover the Pleasure of Gardening

Trade association providing services and information to nurserymen. Publish a directory of the nursery industry with a classified directory of goods and services; it includes many wholesale nurseries.
❒ Privileges: CONVENTIONS

American Community Gardening Association
325 Walnut Street
Philadelphia, PA 19106
Community Gardening Review (1)
ACGA Multilogue (6)

Umbrella association for the community gardening movement; write for information.
❒ Annual Dues: $25
❒ Privileges: CONVENTIONS

American Horticultural Therapy Association
362A Christopher Ave.
Gaithersburg, MD 20879
(800) 634-1603
Journal of Therapeutic Horticulture (1)
People Plant Connection (11)

Professional association devoted to using horticulture to enhance the lives of special populations through therapy and vocational rehabilitation. The annual journal is available by subscription for US$15.
❒ Annual Dues: $50
❒ Chapters: 10
❒ Privileges: CONVENTIONS

American Society of Consulting Arborists
John Duke, Exec. Dir.
5130 W. 101st Circle
Westminster, CO 80030
(303) 466-2722
Arboriculture Consultant (6)

Professional society of qualified arborists; purpose is to educate the public on the value of trees and to refer them to members for consultation on tree care.
❒ Privileges: CONVENTIONS BOOKS

American Society of Landscape Architects
David Bohardt
4401 Connecticut Avenue NW, 5th Fl.
Washington, DC 20008-2302
(202) 686-2752
Landscape Architecture (12)

Professional association; write for information.
❒ Privileges: CONVENTIONS

Assn. of Professional Landscape Designers
Camille G. Chioini
8683 Doves Fly Way
Laurel, MD 20723-1211
(301) 498-8780
APLD News (3)

Formed to create professional guidelines and standards for landscape designers.
❒ Privileges: CONVENTIONS

Associated Landscape Contractors of America
Debra Atkins
12200 Sunrise Valley Dr.
Reston, VA 22091
(703) 620-6363
Landscape Contractors News (12)

Trade association devoted to exchange of business and technical information among its members; they have many educational programs and conferences.

Association for Living Historical Farms & Agricultural Museums
ALHFAM
Route 14, Box 214
Santa Fe, NM 87505
(505) 471-2261
Bulletin (6)

Write for information.
❒ Privileges: CONVENTIONS

Association of Specialty Cut Flower Growers
Judy M. Laushman
M.P.O. Box 268
Oberlin, OH 44074-0268
(216) 774-2887
Cut Flower Quarterly
Proceedings of National Conferences (1)

A group dedicated to growing cut flowers for market.
❐ Annual Dues: in US & CAN $95, OV $115 (PC or IMO)
❐ Privileges: CONVENTIONS EXHIBITS TRIPS

Association of Zoological Horticulture
Jim Martinez, Riverbanks Zoo
P.O. Box 1060
Columbia, SC 29202-1060
(803) 779-8717
Zoo Horticulture (4)

Group of horticulturists at zoos, promoting naturalistic landscaping and botanical collections which suit their animal exhibits.
❐ Annual Dues: $25
❐ Privileges: CONVENTIONS SEEDS

Bedding Plants Foundation, Inc.
Sue Goepp
P.O. Box 27241
Lansing, MI 48909
(517) 694-8537

The Foundation funds research for the greenhouse industry. They publish Final Research Reports of research funded by the BPFI.
❐ Annual Dues: $25
❐ Privileges: CONVENTIONS LIBRARY

California Urban Forests Council
Herb Spitzer, Forestry Div.
1320 N. Eastern Ave.
Los Angeles, CA 90063
(818) 801-5499
Urban Forestry, The Quarterly

A group that works to promote effective urban forestry, through planning, planting, management, research and education.
❐ Annual Dues: $25

Canadian Horticultural Therapy Association
Nancy Lee-Colibaba
c/o Royal Botanical Garden, Box 399
Hamilton, ON, Canada L8N 3H8
(416) 529-7618
CHTA Newsletter (4)

Association provides support and training for people in recreational and occupational therapy programs. It publishes a looseleaf informational guide which is updated with pages that come with the newsletter.
❐ Annual Dues: in CAN C$18, US C$18
❐ Privileges: CONVENTIONS

Canadian Plant Conservation Program
c/o Devonian Botanic Garden
University of Alberta
Edmonton, AB, Canada T6G 2El

Write for information.

Center for Plant Conservation
 Missouri Botanical Garden
P.O. Box 299
St. Louis, MO 63166
(314) 577-5100
Plant Conservation (2-3)

Coordinates the national collection of endangered plants, in cooperation with a consortium of 25 botanic gardens in the continental US and Hawaii. Publishes "Plant Conservation Resource Book," available for $15. Write for membership information.
❐ Garden: 25 gardens; write for list

The Council on Botanical & Horticultural
 Libraries, Inc.
John F. Reed
The New York Botanical Garden
Bronx, NY 10458
(718) 817-8705
Newsletter (3-4)
CBHL Plant Bibliography (occasional)

Association of libraries in the field of botany and horticulture.
❐ Privileges: CONVENTIONS

Garden Centers of America
Clint Albin
1250 I Street Northwest, Suite 500
Washington, DC 20005
(202) 789-2900
GCA Newsletter (6)

The trade association of retail nurseries; has over 3,500 member firms.

The Garden Club of America
598 Madison Avenue
New York, NY 10022
(212) 753-8287
GCA Bulletin (2)
Newsletter (6)

Umbrella organization for 189 local garden clubs; it has programs for awards and scholarships, civic improvement and education to promote the love of gardening.

The Garden Conservancy
Julie Kantor
P.O. Box 219
Cold Spring, NY 10516
(914) 265-2029
Newsletter of the Garden Conservancy (2)

A group devoted to preserving private gardens of particular historical or horticultural interest. Membership open to all.
❐ Annual Dues: $25
❐ Privileges: TRIPS TOURS

Garden Writers Association of America
J.C. McGowan
10210 Leatherleaf Court
Manassas, VA 22111
(703) 257-1032
Quill & Trowel (6)

Association of professional garden writers and broadcasters.
FAX (703) 257-0213
❐ Annual Dues: $75
❐ Privileges: CONVENTIONS EXHIBITS

Great Northern Botanical Association
P.O. Box 362
Helena, Montana 89624
GNBA Newsletter (4)

This is a regional association for growers of specialty crops.
❐ Annual Dues: $25
❐ Privileges: CONVENTIONS

Herb Growing & Marketing Network
P.O. Box 245
Silver Spring, PA 17575-0245
(717) 393-3295
The Herbal Connection (6)
The Herbal Green Pages (1)

Group formed to unite those engaged in the production and marketing of herbs and to educate the public about herbs and herb-related products. "The Herbal Connection" is available by separate subscription, in US & CAN US$28, OV US$38.
❐ Annual Dues: $45

Historic Preservation Committee
  American Society of Landscape Architects
4401 Connecticut Ave. NW 5th Floor
Washington, D.C. 20008-2302
(202) 686-ASLA
Land and History (3-4)

This group is dedicated to the conservation and preservation of historic landscapes of all kinds.
❐ Annual Dues: in US $15, CAN & OV $20
❐ Privileges: CONVENTIONS

Horticultural Research Institute
1250 I Street Northwest, Suite 500
Washington, DC 20005
(202) 789-2900
Journal of Environmental Horticulture (4)

Trade association; this is the research arm of the American Association of Nurserymen.

International Plant Propagation Society
Dr. John A. Wott, XD-10
W.P.Arboretum, University of Washington
Seattle, WA 98195
(206) 543-8602
Proceedings (1)

A professional group devoted to the art and science of plant propagation. Membership is by invitation only.
❐ Annual Dues: Varies with region
❐ Chapters: 7

International Society of Arboriculture
William P. Kruidenier
#6 Dunlap Ct. P.O. Box GG
Savoy, IL 61874
(217) 355-9411
Journal of Arboriculture (6)
The Arborist News (6)

Write for information.

The Irrigation Association
Charles S. Putnam, Exec. Dir.
8260 Willow Oaks Corp. Dr. Suite 120
Fairfax, VA 22031
(703) 573-3551
Irrigation News (6)

Trade association to promote the use of modern irrigation equipment and water and soil conservation. FAX (703) 573-1913.
❐ Privileges: CONVENTIONS BOOKS

Landscape Ontario
  Horticultural Trades Association
1293 Matheson Boulevard East
Mississauga, ON, Canada L4W 1R1
(416) 629-1184
Landscape Trades (9)
Horticulture Review (19)

Association for the horticultural trade in Ontario. Journals are available on subscription (each) for C$30 in Canada, C$40 in the US and overseas.
❐ Privileges: CONVENTIONS EXHIBITS TOURS

The Lawn Institute
James Brooks
1509 Johnson Ferry Rd. NE, Ste. l90
Marietta, GA 30062
(404) 977-5492
Harvests Newsletter (4)

Nonprofit trade association to enhance lawn grass research and education. Periodical is available on separate subscription. FAX (404) 977-8205

Mailorder Association of Nurseries, Inc.
Camille G. Chioini, Exec. Dir.
8683 Doves Fly Way
Laurel, MD 20723-1211
(301) 490-9143
Guide to Gardening & Landscaping by Mail (1)
Mail Order Gardening Reference Guide (1)

Trade association for mail-order nurseries.
❒ Privileges: CONVENTIONS

Master Gardeners
  Cooperative Extension Service
Diane Relf or David McKissack
Dept. of Horticulture, Virginia Tech. Univ.
Blacksburg, VA 24061
(703) 231-6254

The Cooperative Extension Service of Virginia has served as a model for many states that use its concepts and training materials; it serves as a clearinghouse of information on programs in other states. There are now Master Gardeners active in 45 states; to locate a group in your area, or to start one, first contact the Cooperative Extension Service in your home county.

The Gardeners of America
  Men's Garden Clubs of America, Inc.
Carol Donovan, Exec. Sec.
P.O. Box 241; 5560 Merle Hay Road
Johnston, IA 50131
(515) 278-0295
The Gardener (6)
TGOA/MGCA Newsletter (6)

Umbrella organization for local men's garden clubs.
❒ Chapters: 125
❒ Privileges: CONVENTIONS LIBRARY

National Arbor Day Foundation
100 Arbor Avenue
Nebraska City, NE 68410
(402) 474-5655
Arbor Day (6)
Tree City USA Bulletin (6)

A national nonprofit educational organization dedicated to tree planting and conservation; offers special trees to its members. Membership open to all.
❒ Annual Dues: $10
❒ Privileges: PLANTS TOURS

National Council of State Garden Clubs, Inc.
401 Magnolia Avenue
St. Louis, MO 63110
The National Gardener (6)

Umbrella group for state garden clubs, which in themselves are umbrella organizations for 11,000 local garden clubs.

National Garden Bureau
  All America Selections
1311 Butterfield Road, Suite 310
Downers Grove, IL 60515
(708) 963-0770

Introduce the "All-American Selections" each year -- a vegetable and an annual flower. They test new varieties of flowers and vegetables grown from seed. Send a long SASE for their list of trial gardens.

National Junior Horticulture Association
Joe Maxon
401 N. 4th St.
Durant, OK 74701
(405) 924-0771
Going & Growing (3)

Umbrella organization for state and local chapters; students join chapters in their schools or through other local clubs.
❒ Privileges: CONVENTIONS

National Wildflower Research Center
Martha Cavin
2600 FM 973 North
Austin, TX 78725
(512) 929-3600
Wildflower Journal (2)
Wildflower Newsletter (6)

National group to promote conservation and use of native plants in public and private landscapes. Membership open to all.
❒ Annual Dues: $25
❒ Garden: Display/research garden at the Center
❒ Privileges: CONVENTIONS LIBRARY BOOKS EXHIBITS TRIPS TOURS

Northeast Herbal Association
Janice M. Dinsdale
P.O. Box 146
Marshfield, VT 05658
(802) 456-1402

An organization for professional herbalists.
❒ Annual Dues: Sliding scale $30-100.
❒ Privileges: CONVENTIONS SEEDS PLANTS

Ontario Horticultural Association
Mrs. Bonnie Warner
RR #3
Englehart, ON, Canada POJ 1HO
(705) 544-2474
Ontario Horticultural Assn. Newsletter (4)

Umbrella organization for horticultural societies in Ontario; publishes a schedule of agricultural fairs and exhibitions and helps local groups with suggestions for programs and useful resources.
❏ Privileges: CONVENTIONS

People-Plant Council
Dept. of Cons. Hort., VPI & SU
410 Saunders Hall
Blacksburg, VA 24061-0327
(703) 231-8512
People-Plant Council News (4)

An umbrella group which encourages research into the sociological benefits that people derive from working with plants, through therapy, education and community efforts.
❏ Annual Dues: Write for information
❏ Privileges: LIBRARY

Perennial Plant Association
Steven M. Still
3383 Schirtzinger Road
Hilliard, OH 43026
(614) 771-8431
Perennial Plants (4)

Trade association; promotes the development of the perennial plant industry, holds symposia and conferences.
❏ Annual Dues: in US & CAN US$60, OV US$100 (PC or IMO)
❏ Privileges: CONVENTIONS BOOKS TOURS

Professional Plant Growers Association
Darlene Cole
P.O. Box 27517
Lansing, MI 48909-0517
(800) 647-7742
PPGA News (12)

This group provides technical and business information for commercial growers and retailers. They publish a "Buyer's Guide."
❏ Privileges: CONVENTIONS BOOKS TOURS

Soil & Water Conservation Society
Karen Howe
7515 N.E. Ankeny Road
Ankeny, IA 50021-9764
(515) 289-2331
Journal of Soil & Water Conservation (6)

Purpose is to advance the science and art of good land use. Periodical available on separate subscription for US$30 or US$35 overseas. Offers a list of native seed resources for US$3. Membership open to all.
❏ Annual Dues: in US & CAN US$44, OV US$50 (US bank draft)
❏ Chapters: 150
❏ Garden: Native grass meadow, 7515 N.E. Ankeny Road, Ankeny, IA
❏ Privileges: CONVENTIONS BOOKS

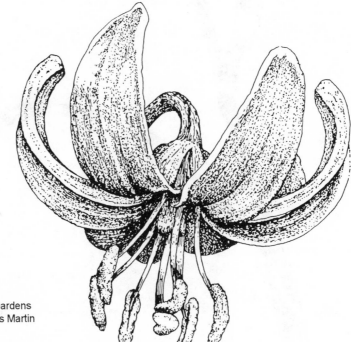

© Ambergate Gardens
Artist: Charles Martin

© Flowerplace Plant Farm
Artist: Lallah Perry

Horticultural Societies

Horticultural societies are listed alphabetically.

See the Index section for:

L. Society Index: an index of horticultural societies listed by plant and/or other special interests.

M. Magazine Index: an index to magazines and other periodicals offered by societies, as well as horticultural and gardening magazines from other sources.

Societies

I have listed only societies that are of international, national or regional interest. There are also local garden clubs, regional chapters of national and state organizations and the "friends" groups at botanical gardens, all of which have activities and programs of interest. Ask at your favorite nursery, city recreation department, chamber of commerce or at the ornamental horticulture department of your local community college to find out about local groups.

If you travel, consider the advantages of joining an international or foreign group a year or so before you go in order to find out about events and places you'd like to include in your plans.

I have to laugh now when I think how shy I was about daring to join the "experts." My experiences have been pure pleasure; I've learned a lot, volunteered time to useful projects, made many new friends—and I usually come home from meetings with a new plant. The gardener's greatest resource is other gardeners; the more you get into the network, the greater your pleasure will be!

Warning

Nothing seems to change more quickly than the addresses of societies. I'd suggest that you write for information about the society before you send off a check. I'd very much appreciate hearing from you if you know of changes for societies listed, or of new societies worthy of inclusion; I'll mention these in my Updates (see Practical Matters).

A table of the symbols and abbreviations used in this book appears
on the bookmark inside the back cover.

Society Abbreviations and Conventions

Society publications are listed after the address with the number of issues per year indicated in parentheses—e.g. (6).

Available membership privileges are indicated as follows:

CONVENTIONS—conferences or annual meetings

LIBRARY—library for use of members

BOOKS—book sales to members

SEEDS—seed exchanges or sales to members

PLANTS—plant sales at meetings

EXHIBITS—plant shows or exhibits sponsored by society

TRIPS—local field trips for members

TOURS—tours or travel program for members

© Robyn's Nest Nursery   Artist: Mari Eggebraaten

African Violet Society of America, Inc.
P.O. Box 3609
Beaumont, TX 77704
(409) 839-4725
African Violet Magazine (6)

❒ Annual Dues: in US $13.50, CAN & OV US$17
❒ Privileges: CONVENTIONS LIBRARY EXHIBITS

African Violet Society of Canada
Mrs. Bonnie Scanlan
1573 Arbourdale Avenue
Victoria, BC, Canada V8N 5J1
Chatter (4)

This is an umbrella group for local clubs.
❒ Annual Dues: in CAN C$12, US US$14, OV C$14
❒ Chapters: 35
❒ Privileges: CONVENTIONS LIBRARY SEEDS EXHIBITS TRIPS

Alabama Wildflower Society
George Wood
11120 Ben Clements Rd.
Northport, AL 35476
(205) 339-2541
Newsletter (2)

❒ Annual Dues: $5
❒ Chapters: 7
❒ Privileges: CONVENTIONS PLANTS EXHIBITS TRIPS

Alaska Native Plant Society
Verna Pratt
P.O. Box 141613
Anchorage, AK 99514-1613
(907) 333-8212
Borealis (9)

❒ Annual Dues: in US $10, CAN C$15, OV $20 (IMO)
❒ Chapters: 2

Aloe, Cactus & Succulent Society of Zimbabwe
P.O. Box 8514, Causeway
Harare, Zimbabwe
(263) 4-39175
The INGENS Bulletin (2)
Excelsa (biennial)

Periodically holds major international conventions; also publishes
the Excelsa Taxonomic Series. Write for information.
❒ Annual Dues: in US & CAN US$20, OV £10, DM30, R40, A$30 (IMO)
❒ Privileges: CONVENTIONS BOOKS SEEDS PLANTS EXHIBITS TRIPS TOURS

Alpine Garden Society
The Secretary
AGS Centre, Avonbank, Pershore
Worcestershire, England WR10 3JP
(0386) 55-4790
Quarterly Bulletin

Publishes a very interesting bulletin.This group has an excellent seed
exchange and an extensive list of alpine and rock garden books for sale
to members.
❒ Annual Dues: in US $30, CAN C$30, OV £16 (IMO)
❒ Chapters: 59
❒ Garden: Display Garden at the Headquarters
❒ Privileges: CONVENTIONS LIBRARY BOOKS SEEDS PLANTS EXHIBITS TOURS

American Bamboo Society
Gerald Bol
666 Wagnon Road
Sebastopol, CA 95472
Journal (occasional)
Newsletter (6)

The purpose of the society is to publish information about bamboo, and to
introduce new species. For information about the society, contact Michael
Bartholomew at (518) 765-3507 or 765-2347.
❒ Annual Dues: $20
❒ Chapters: 7
❒ Garden: Quail Botanical Gardens, Encinitas, CA
❒ Privileges: CONVENTIONS LIBRARY BOOKS SEEDS PLANTS EXHIBITS TRIPS

American Bat Conservation Society
Erin Kelley
P.O. Box 1393
Rockville, MD 20849
(301) 309-6610

Bats, like purple martins, are avid consumers of insects. This organization
is dedicated to education, research and conservation programs for bats.
They encourage bat shelters in the garden.
❒ Annual Dues: $15
❒ Chapters: 2
❒ Privileges: CONVENTIONS LIBRARY BOOKS TRIPS

American Begonia Society
John Ingles, Jr.
157 Monument Rd.
Rio Dell, CA 95562
(707) 764-5407
The Begonian (6)

There are a number of special interest round-robin letter "flights" -- round
robin members meet at conventions.
❒ Annual Dues: in US & CAN US$21, OV US$25 (IMO)
❒ Chapters: 51
❒ Garden: Dallas/Ft. Worth Botanical Gardens
❒ Privileges: CONVENTIONS BOOKS SEEDS PLANTS EXHIBITS TRIPS TOURS

American Bonsai Society
Anne D. Moyle
P.O. Box 358
Keene, NH 03431
(603) 352-9034
Bonsai Journal (4)
ABStracts (3)

❐ Annual Dues: in US $20, CAN & OV US$25 (IMO)
❐ Privileges: CONVENTIONS LIBRARY BOOKS TOURS

American Boxwood Society
Mrs. Joan Butler
107 Cottage Drive
Winchester, VA 22603
(703) 665-5879
The Boxwood Bulletin (4)

Has "Boxwood Workshops" twice a year, annual tour in Mid-Atlantic states. "The Boxwood Handbook" was published in late 1993. Another plant collection at the National Arboretum, Washington, DC.
❐ Annual Dues: $15
❐ Garden: Blandy Experimental Farm, Boyce, VA
❐ Privileges: CONVENTIONS PLANTS TOURS

American Calochortus Society
H. P. McDonald
P.O. Box 1128
Berkeley, CA 94701-1128
Mariposa (4)

A society devoted to both botany and culture of the western Mariposa lilies and other Calochorti. Write for information.
❐ Annual Dues: in US $4, CAN & OV US$6 (IMO)
❐ Privileges: SEEDS PLANTS

American Camellia Society
1 Massee Lane
Fort Valley, GA 31030
(912) 967-2358
The Camellia Journal (4)
American Camellia Yearbook

Offers "Camellia Culture for Beginners" for $2.
❐ Annual Dues: in US $20, CAN & OV US$21.50 (IMO)
❐ Garden: Historic Massee Lane Gardens, Ft. Valley, GA
❐ Privileges: CONVENTIONS LIBRARY BOOKS PLANTS EXHIBITS

American Conifer Society
Nancy B. Akehurst, Exec. Sec.
P.O. Box 314
Perry Hall, MD 21128
(410) 256-5595
Bulletin (4)

❐ Annual Dues: in US $20, CAN & OV US$25 (IMO)
❐ Chapters: 3
❐ Privileges: CONVENTIONS SEEDS EXHIBITS TRIPS TOURS

American Daffodil Society, Inc.
Mary Lou Gripshover
1686 Grey Fox Trails
Milford, OH 45150-1521
(513) 248-9137
The Daffodil Journal (4)

They publish "Handbook for Growing, Exhibiting and Judging Daffodils," available for $7.
❐ Annual Dues: $20
❐ Chapters: 9
❐ Garden: Whetstone Park, Columbus, OH
❐ Privileges: CONVENTIONS LIBRARY BOOKS PLANTS EXHIBITS

American Dahlia Society
Terry Shaffer, Memb. Chair.
422 Sunset Blvd.
Toledo, Ohio 43612
(419) 478-4159
Bulletin (4)
Yearly Classification

"The Judging Manual" is available for $3.
❐ Annual Dues: $20
❐ Chapters: 70
❐ Garden: Trial Gardens throughout US
❐ Privileges: CONVENTIONS BOOKS SEEDS PLANTS EXHIBITS

The American Dianthus Society
Rand B. Lee, Pres.
P.O. Box 22232
Santa Fe, NM 87502-2232
(505) 438-7038
The Gilliflower Times (4)

Published a leaflet "How to Grow Pinks and Carnations: A Practical Introduction" in June, 1993. This leaflet costs US$2.
❐ Annual Dues: in US $10, CAN US$15, OV US$20 (IMO)
❐ Privileges: CONVENTIONS LIBRARY SEEDS

American Fern Society
Richard Hauke
456 McGill Place
Atlanta, GA 30312-1049
(404) 525-3147
American Fern Journal (4)
Fiddlehead Forum (6)

Membership does not include the more scholarly "American Fern Journal," which costs an extra $7 ($9 OV). Spore exchange has fresh spore available by exchange or at nominal cost to society members. Membership is by calendar year only. Also publishes "Pteridologia" (irregular); write for information.
❐ Annual Dues: in US $8, CAN & OV $11 (IMO)
❐ Privileges: CONVENTIONS SEEDS

American Forestry Association
Wendy Newman, Memb. Dir.
P.O. Box 2000
Washington, D.C. 20013
(202) 667-3300
American Forests (6)

This society, which was founded in 1875, is dedicated to balanced forest use. They sponsor tree planting and educational programs about the value of forests.
❐ Annual Dues: in US $24, CAN & OV US$28 (IMO)
❐ Privileges: CONVENTIONS LIBRARY BOOKS EXHIBITS TOURS

American Fuchsia Society
County Fair Building
9th Avenue at Lincoln Way
San Francisco, CA 94122
Bulletin (6)

Has a number of chapters on the Pacific Coast.
❐ Annual Dues: in US $15, CAN & OV US$25 (IMO)
❐ Privileges: CONVENTIONS LIBRARY BOOKS PLANTS EXHIBITS TRIPS

American Gloxinia & Gesneriad Society, Inc.
Jimmy Dates, N.Y. Hort. Soc.
128 West 58th St.
New York, NY 10019
The Gloxinian (6)

Seeds are sold at a nominal cost to members. New members receive a free copy of "How to Know and Grow Gesneriads." "Propagation of Gesneriads and Birds and Bees and Gesneriad Seeds" is available for $2.
❐ Annual Dues: in US $18, CAN $23, OV US$30 (IMO)
❐ Chapters: 40
❐ Privileges: CONVENTIONS BOOKS SEEDS PLANTS EXHIBITS TRIPS TOURS

American Gourd Society
John Stevens
P.O. Box 274 TP
Mount Gilead, OH 43338-0274
(419) 946-3302
The Gourd (4)

Annual meeting at Mt. Gilead Fairgrounds in July; annual show first full weekend in October, same location. Promotes the use of gourds for decorative and useful purposes; magazine shows beautifully decorated gourds.
❐ Annual Dues: in US $5, CAN & OV US$8 (IMO)
❐ Chapters: 7
❐ Privileges: CONVENTIONS BOOKS SEEDS PLANTS EXHIBITS

American Hemerocallis Society
Elly Launius, Exec. Secy.
1454 Rebel Drive
Jackson, MS 39211-6334
(601) 366-4362
Daylily Journal (4)

Has a slide library for members; publishes an extensive source list; has many round-robins on topics of special interest. Also sells "Daylilies: The Beginner's Handbook" for $6.
❐ Annual Dues: in US $18, CAN & OV US$25 (IMO)
❐ Chapters: 15 US, 1 OV
❐ Garden: Many, see publications
❐ Privileges: CONVENTIONS LIBRARY PLANTS TRIPS

American Herb Association
P.O. Box 1673
Nevada City, CA 95959
FAX(916) 265-9552
AHA Newsletter (4)

Publishes a directory of sources as well as a directory of herb gardens and one of herb schools. Emphasis is on medicinal herbs and the healing arts.
❐ Annual Dues: in US $20, CAN US$24, OV US$28
❐ Privileges: BOOKS

American Hibiscus Society
Jeri Grantham, Exec. Secy.
P.O. Box 321540
Cocoa Beach, FL 32932-1540
(407) 783-2576
The Seed Pod (4)

Local chapters have shows, plant sales and exchange scions for grafting; they sell "The Hibiscus Handbook" for $13.
❐ Annual Dues: in US $17.50, CAN & OV US$27.50 (IMO or CC)
❐ Chapters: 21
❐ Privileges: CONVENTIONS BOOKS SEEDS PLANTS EXHIBITS

American Horticultural Society
Membership Dept.
7931 E. Boulevard Drive
Alexandria, VA 22308-1300
(703) 768-5700
American Horticulturist (12)

Has an extensive tour program, a gardener's information service for your plant problems, and plant labels and books for members at special prices. Call toll-free at (800) 777-7931.
❐ Annual Dues: in US $35, CAN & OV US$50 (IMO)
❐ Garden: River Farm, Alexandria, VA
❐ Privileges: CONVENTIONS LIBRARY BOOKS SEEDS PLANTS EXHIBITS TOURS

American Hosta Society
Robyn Duback
7802 NE 63rd St.
Vancouver, WA 98662
Hosta Journal (2)

❐ Annual Dues: in US $19, CAN US$25, OV US$35 (IMO)
❐ Garden: Minnesota Landscape Arboretum, Chanhassen MN
❐ Privileges: CONVENTIONS EXHIBITS

American Iris Society
Marilyn Harlow, Memb. Secy.
P. O. Box 8455
San Jose, CA 95155
(408) 971-0444
Bulletin (4)

Has sections by types of iris; 24 regional affiliates and 127 chapters.
❐ Annual Dues: $12.50
❐ Chapters: Numerous in each state
❐ Garden: Many test gardens, see literature
❐ Privileges: CONVENTIONS BOOKS SEEDS PLANTS EXHIBITS

American Ivy Society
Daphne Pfaff, Memb. Chair.
696 16th Ave. S.
Naples, FL 33940
(813) 261-0388
The Ivy Journal (1)
Between the Vines (2)

Regional display garden at Mendocino Coast Botanical Garden, Fort Bragg, CA. Display garden also at Louis Ginter Botanical Garden in Richmond, VA. There is 1 Ivy plant mailing to all US members. Publications list available from AIS, P.O. Box 520, West Carrollton, OH, 45449-0520.
❐ Annual Dues: in US $15, CAN & OV US$20
❐ Chapters: 4
❐ Garden: AHS Garden, River Farm, Mt. Vernon, VA
❐ Privileges: CONVENTIONS BOOKS EXHIBITS TOURS

American Orchid Society
Victoria Robb Creech
6000 S. Olive Avenue
West Palm Beach, FL 33405
(407) 585-8666
Bulletin (12)

Publishes handbooks on various orchid subjects, including the "Handbook on Orchid Culture." Also publishes "Lindleyana"; see Section E.
❏ Annual Dues: in US $30, CAN & OV US$36 (IMO or CC)
❏ Chapters: 500
❏ Privileges: CONVENTIONS LIBRARY BOOKS TOURS

American Penstemon Society
Ann W. Bartlett, Memb. Secy.
1569 S. Holland Court
Lakewood, CO 80232
(303) 986-8096
American Penstemon Society Bulletin (2)

Publishes a very good "Manual for Beginners."
❏ Annual Dues: $10
❏ Chapters: 3
❏ Privileges: CONVENTIONS LIBRARY BOOKS SEEDS PLANTS TRIPS

American Peony Society
Greta M. Kessenich
250 Interlachen Road
Hopkins, MN 55343
(612) 938-4706
Bulletin (4)

Write for list of publications.
❏ Annual Dues: $7.50
❏ Privileges: CONVENTIONS SEEDS

American Pomological Society
Dr. R. M. Crassweller
102 Tyson Building
University Park, PA 16802
(814) 863-6163
Fruit Varieties Journal (4)

Promotes fruit variety and rootstock improvement through breeding and testing. Open to all; founded in 1848.
❏ Annual Dues: $20
❏ Privileges: CONVENTIONS

American Primrose, Primula & Auricula Society
Addaline W. Robinson
9705 S.E. Spring Crest Dr.
Portland, OR 97225
Primroses (4)

Has slide programs and round-robins, an interesting journal and excellent seed exchanges.
❏ Annual Dues: $15
❏ Privileges: SEEDS EXHIBITS

American Rhododendron Society
Barbara R. Hall, Exec. Dir.
P.O. Box 1380
Gloucester, VA 23061
(804) 693-4433
Journal (4)

Local chapters have active programs and tours; some have libraries.
❏ Annual Dues: $25
❏ Chapters: 70
❏ Garden: Some local chapters maintain gardens
❏ Privileges: CONVENTIONS BOOKS SEEDS PLANTS EXHIBITS TRIPS

American Rock Garden Society
Secretary
P. O. Box 67
Millwood, NY 10546
(914) 762-2948
Bulletin (4)

A very active society, with many local chapters. Holds winter study weekends -- one on the East Coast, one on the West Coast, and an annual spring meeting. Has an excellent bookstore for members.
❏ Annual Dues: in US $25, CAN C$32, OV £17 (IMO or CC)
❏ Chapters: 29
❏ Privileges: CONVENTIONS BOOKS SEEDS PLANTS EXHIBITS TRIPS

American Rose Society
Julia Cecil, Sally Allen
P.O. Box 30,000
Shreveport, LA 71130
(318) 938-5402
The American Rose Magazine (11)
Annual and Handbook

❏ Annual Dues: in US $32, CAN $38, OV US$50 (IMO)
❏ Garden: American Rose Center, Shreveport, LA
❏ Privileges: CONVENTIONS LIBRARY BOOKS

American Willow Growers Network
Bonnie Gale
RD 1, Box 124A
South New Berlin, NY 13843
(607) 847-8264
Newsletter (1)

A new group sharing information and cuttings, and developing new uses for the willow; holds basket-making workshops.
❏ Annual Dues: in US $7, CAN US$8, OV US$10 (IMO)
❏ Garden: South New Berlin, NY, call for information
❏ Privileges: PLANTS

Aril Society International
Donna Downey
5500 Constitution N.E.
Albuquerque, NM 87110
(505) 255-8207
Yearbook

A society for aril iris lovers; write for information.
❏ Annual Dues: $5
❏ Privileges: SEEDS PLANTS EXHIBITS

Arizona Native Plant Society
David Ingram
P.O. Box 41206
Tucson, AZ 85717
Plant Press (4)

Write for information.
❒ Chapters: 5
❒ Privileges: CONVENTIONS SEEDS EXHIBITS TRIPS TOURS

Arkansas Native Plant Society
Rt. 2, Box 256 BB
Mena, AR 71953
(501) 394-4666

Write for information.

Australian Garden History Society
The Secretary
Royal Botanic Gardens, Birdwood Avenue
South Yarra, VIC, Australia 3141
(03) 650-5043
Australian Garden History (6)

Has garden tours, planning a plant collection.
❒ Annual Dues: A$34 (IMO)
❒ Privileges: CONVENTIONS BOOKS EXHIBITS TRIPS TOURS

Azalea Society of America, Inc.
Membership Chairman
P.O. Box 34536
West Bethesda, MD 20827-0536
The Azalean (4)

Local societies have plant shows and sales. There is a slide library.
❒ Annual Dues: $20
❒ Chapters: 8
❒ Privileges: CONVENTIONS EXHIBITS TRIPS

Bio-Dynamic Farming & Gardening Association
Charles Beedy
P.O. Box 550
Kimberton, PA 19442
(215) 935-7797
Bio-Dynamics (6)

Promotes the bio-dynamic method of farming and gardening.
❒ Annual Dues: in US $30, CAN US$42, OV US$48 (IMO)
❒ Chapters: 29
❒ Privileges: CONVENTIONS BOOKS

Bio-Integral Resource Center (BIRC)
P.O. Box 7414
Berkeley, CA 94707
(510) 524-2567
Common Sense Pest Control (4)
The IPM Practitioner (10)

Group devoted to the least toxic methods of pest management. Associate members receive the non-technical "Common Sense Pest Control." Professional members receive "The IPM Practitioner." Dual memberships available.
❒ Annual Dues: Associates: in US $30, CAN US$35, OV US$50 (IMO)
❒ Privileges: LIBRARY BOOKS

Biological Urban Gardening Services
P.O. Box 76
Citrus Heights, CA 95611-0076
(916) 726-5377
BUGS Flyer (4)

Organization devoted to reducing the use of pesticides. "BUGS" offers a professional category of membership for $18 a year in the US, with additional services oriented toward horticultural professionals.
❒ Annual Dues: in US $12.50, CAN US$17.50, OV varies

Bonsai Clubs International
Virginia Ellermann
2636 W. Mission Road, #277
Tallahassee, FL 32304-2556
Bonsai Magazine (6)

A large society, with many local chapters and activities.
❒ Annual Dues: $25
❒ Privileges: CONVENTIONS LIBRARY BOOKS EXHIBITS

© Digging Dog Nursery
Artist: Marsha Mello

Botanical Society of South Africa
Diana Peters
BSA, Kirstenbosch
Claremont, Cape Town, South Africa 7735
(021) 797-2090
Veld & Flora (4)

Personal check in dollars may be sent; inquire first. In addition to Kirstenbosch, the society supports 7 other botanical gardens, promotes the conservation and cultivation of the indigenous flora of South Africa. Also publishes wildflower guides. FAX number is (021) 797-2376.
❏ Annual Dues: in US $22 (IMO or CC)
❏ Garden: Kirstenbosch Botanical Garden
❏ Privileges: LIBRARY BOOKS PLANTS EXHIBITS TOURS

British & European Geranium Society
Mr. Leyland Cox
Norwood Chine, 26 Crabtree Lane
Sheffield, Yorkshire, England S5 7AY
(0742) 426-2000
The Geranium Gazette (3)
The Geranium Year Book

❏ Annual Dues: in US $12.80, UK £8 (IMO)
❏ Chapters: 8
❏ Garden: Fibrex Nurseries, Ltd., Nr. Stratford on Avon
❏ Privileges: BOOKS PLANTS EXHIBITS TRIPS TOURS

The British Cactus & Succulent Society
Mr. P.A. Lewis FBCSS
Firgrove, 1, Springwoods, Courtmoor
Fleet, Hants, England GU13 9SU
British Cactus and Succulent Journal (4)
Bradleya (1)

Members can send personal checks in US dollars for dues; no seed exchange, but seeds are sold to members. "Bradleya" is available on separate subscription.
❏ Annual Dues: US$28 (PC) or £13
❏ Privileges: CONVENTIONS BOOKS EXHIBITS TOURS

The British Clematis Society
Mrs. B. Risdon, Memb. Secy.
The Tropical Bird Gardens, Rode
Nr Bath, Somerset, England BA3 6QW
(0373) 83-0326
The Clematis Journal (1)
The Clematis Supplement (2)

❏ Annual Dues: £12 (IMO)
❏ Garden: Treasures of Tenbury, Worcestershire
❏ Privileges: BOOKS SEEDS PLANTS

British Columbia Fuchsia & Begonia Society
Lorna Herchenson
2402 Swinburne Avenue
North Vancouver, BC, Canada V7H 1L2
(604) 929-5382
The Eardrop (11)
The Annual (1)

❏ Annual Dues: C$10 (IMO)
❏ Privileges: CONVENTIONS LIBRARY BOOKS PLANTS EXHIBITS TRIPS

British Columbia Lily Society
Del Knowlton, Secy.-Treas.
5510 - 239th Street
Langley, BC, Canada V3A 7N6
(604) 534-4729
BCLS Newsletter (4)

❏ Annual Dues: in US & CAN C$5

British Fuchsia Society
Secretary
20 Brodawel, Llannon
Llanelli, Dyfed, Wales SA14 6BJ
Bulletin (2)
Yearbook

Publishes a number of leaflets on fuchsia culture.
❏ Annual Dues: in US & CAN £5 (IMO)
❏ Privileges: CONVENTIONS BOOKS EXHIBITS

British Iris Society
Mrs. E. M. Wise
197 The Parkway, Iver Heath
Iver, Bucks., England SL0 0RQ
The Iris Year Book

❏ Annual Dues: Write for information
❏ Privileges: CONVENTIONS LIBRARY BOOKS SEEDS PLANTS EXHIBITS

British Pelargonium & Geranium Society
Carol & Ron Helyar
134 Montrose Ave.
Welling, Kent, England DA16 2QY
(081) 856-6137
Pelargonium News (3)
Yearbook (1)

See also the Geraniaceae Group for those interested in species geraniums.
❏ Annual Dues: in US & CAN US$12
❏ Garden: Fibrex Nurseries, Ltd., Nr. Stratford on Avon
❏ Privileges: CONVENTIONS BOOKS PLANTS EXHIBITS

Bromeliad Society, Inc.
2488 E. 49th Street
Tulsa, OK 74105
Journal (6)

Local affiliates have exhibits and plant sales, libraries and field trips.
❏ Annual Dues: in US $20, CAN & OV US$25 (IMO)
❏ Chapters: 60
❏ Privileges: CONVENTIONS BOOKS SEEDS EXHIBITS TOURS

Bromeliad Study Group of Northern California
Mary Cottrell
990 Blair Ct.
Palo Alto, CA 94303

Regional group in Northern California devoted to the cultivation, research and conservation of bromeliads.
❏ Annual Dues: $10
❏ Privileges: PLANTS EXHIBITS TRIPS

Cactus & Succulent Society of America
Dr. Seymour Linden
1535 Reeves St.
Los Angeles, CA 90035
(310) 556-1923
Cactus & Succulent Journal (6)

Subscription to the journal is separate from membership; see "Cactus & Succulent Journal" in Section E.
❏ Annual Dues: in US $30, CAN & OV US$35 (IMO or Visa)
❏ Chapters: 80
❏ Privileges: CONVENTIONS LIBRARY BOOKS SEEDS PLANTS EXHIBITS

Calgary Horticultural Society
Membership Chairperson
2405 9th Avenue S.E.
Calgary, AB, Canada T2G 4T4
(403) 262-5609
CHS Newsletter (8)

Monthly meetings with guest speakers.
❏ Annual Dues: in CAN C$20, OV C$25
❏ Privileges: LIBRARY BOOKS PLANTS EXHIBITS TRIPS TOURS

California Horticultural Society
Mrs. Elsie Mueller
1847 - 34th Avenue
San Francisco, CA 94122
(415) 566-5222
Pacific Horticulture (4)
Bulletin (11)

General interest in ornamental horticulture. The society is active in the greater San Francisco Bay area.
❏ Annual Dues: $35
❏ Privileges: SEEDS PLANTS TRIPS TOURS

California Native Grass Association
P.O. Box 566
Dixon, CA 95620
(916) 678-6282
Grasslands (4)

A group dedicated to the preservation of California's native perennial grasses, and restoration of grasslands. CNGA display gardens are at Davis, Winters, Lockeford, Moss Landing, Rio Vista, Santa Ana and Flores; write for addresses.
❏ Annual Dues: $35
❏ Garden: See notes
❏ Privileges: CONVENTIONS EXHIBITS TRIPS

California Native Plant Society
1722 J Street, #17
Sacramento, CA 95814
(916) 447-2677
Fremontia (4)
Bulletin (4)

❏ Annual Dues: in US $25, CAN & OV US$35 (IMO)
❏ Chapters: 30
❏ Privileges: BOOKS PLANTS EXHIBITS TRIPS

California Rare Fruit Growers, Inc.
Kathleen P. Smith
P.O. Box W
El Cajon, CA 92022
(619) 441-7395
The Fruit Gardener (6)

For better understanding of growing subtropical fruits.
❏ Annual Dues: in US $16, CAN US$25, OV US$30 (IMO)
❏ Chapters: 14
❏ Privileges: CONVENTIONS BOOKS PLANTS TRIPS TOURS

Canadian Begonia Society
70 Enfield Ave.
Toronto, ON, Canada M8W 1T9

Write for information.
❏ Annual Dues: C$20

Canadian Chrysanthemum & Dahlia Society
Karen Ojaste
17 Granard Boulevard
Scarborough, ON, Canada M1M 2E2
(416) 269-6960

❏ Annual Dues: C$10 (IMO)
❏ Privileges: PLANTS

Canadian Geranium & Pelargonium Society
Kathleen Gammer, Memb. Secy.
101-2008 Fullerton Ave.
North Vancouver, BC, Canada V7P 3G7
(604) 926-2190
Storksbill (4)

❏ Annual Dues: C$10 (IMO)
❏ Privileges: LIBRARY BOOKS PLANTS EXHIBITS TRIPS

Canadian Gladiolus Society
W.L. Turbuck
3073 Grant Rd.
Regina, SK, Canada S4S 5G9
Canadian Gladiolus Annual
Fall Bulletin (1)

❏ Annual Dues: C$10
❏ Chapters: 10
❏ Privileges: CONVENTIONS

Canadian Iris Society
Verna Laurin
199 Florence Avenue
Willowdale, ON, Canada M2N 1G5
(416) 225-1088
Canadian Iris Society Newsletter (4)

Iris shows and auctions, annual educational and awards program, regional activities.
❐ Annual Dues: C$5 (IMO)
❐ Garden: Laking Garden, Royal Botanical Gardens, Hamilton, ON
❐ Privileges: LIBRARY PLANTS EXHIBITS

Canadian Orchid Congress
Peter Poot
Box 241
Goodwood, ON, Canada L0C 1A0
(416) 640-5643
Canadian Orchid Journal (1)

Umbrella group for orchid societies in Canada. They can help you find a regional group to join.
❐ Privileges: CONVENTIONS PLANTS

Canadian Organic Growers
P.O. Box 6408, Station J
Ottawa, ON, Canada K2A 3Y6
(613) 788-3211
COGnition (4)

Write for information.
❐ Privileges: CONVENTIONS LIBRARY TRIPS

Canadian Prairie Lily Society
M.E. Driver, Secy.
22 Red River Road
Saskatoon, SK, Canada S7K 1G3
(306) 242-5329
Newsletter (4)

Concerned with growing the native prairie lilies of Canada.
❐ Annual Dues: in CAN C$5, US & OV US$5
❐ Garden: U. of Saskatchewan, Saskatoon, SK
❐ Privileges: CONVENTIONS LIBRARY PLANTS EXHIBITS

Canadian Rose Society
Anne Graber, Secy.
10 Fairfax Crescent
Scarborough, ON, Canada M1L 1Z8
416 757-8809
The Rosarian (3)
Canadian Rose Annual (1)

Promotes knowledge of rose-growing in northern climates; has a slide library and annual garden tour. List of demonstration gardens.
❐ Annual Dues: C$18
❐ Chapters: 32
❐ Privileges: PLANTS EXHIBITS

The Canadian Wildflower Society
John Craw, Business Secretary
Unit 12A, Box 228, 4981 Highway #7 East
Markham, ON, Canada L3R 1N1
(416) 294-9075
Wildflower (4)

Society devoted exclusively to the wild flora of North America; interesting to beginners and experts alike; has a handsome magazine.
❐ Annual Dues: in CAN C$30, US $30, OV US$35 (IMO)
❐ Chapters: 5
❐ Privileges: CONVENTIONS SEEDS PLANTS TRIPS TOURS

The Chile Institute
Box 30003, Dept. 3Q, NMSU
Las Cruces, NM 88003
(505) 646-3028
Chile Institute Newsletter (2)

A new organization dedicated to the study of chiles.
❐ Annual Dues: $25
❐ Garden: Fabian Garcia Research Center, Las Cruces, NM

Clivia Club
P.O. Box 6240
Westgate, South Africa 1734
Clivia Club (4)

❐ Annual Dues: US$10 (IMO)

Coastal Georgia Herb Society
Don C. Bass
13 Bransby Drive
Savannah, GA 31406
(912) 354-7299
Coastal Georgia Herb Society Newsletter (4)

This is a regional group. Biblical Garden at St. Thomas Episcopal Church, Savannah, GA is another display garden.
❐ Annual Dues: $10
❐ Garden: Discovery Herb Garden, Savannah, GA
❐ Privileges: SEEDS PLANTS TRIPS

Colorado Native Plant Society
Myrna P. Steinkamp
P.O. Box 200
Fort Collins, CO 80522-0200
Aquilegia (4-6)

Pamphlet "The Prairie Garden" (1991) is available for $4.25. US members only.
❐ Annual Dues: $12
❐ Chapters: 6
❐ Privileges: CONVENTIONS TRIPS

CORNS
Carl and Karen Barnes
Route 1, Box 32
Turpin, OK 73950

This is for people who are dedicated to the preservation of the genetic diversity of open-pollinated corn varieties. For information send a long SASE. Overseas, send US$1.
❐ Annual Dues: See notes
❐ Privileges: SEEDS

Cottage Garden Society
Mrs. C. Tordoff
5 Nixon Close, Thornhill
Dewsbury, W. Yorks., England WF12 0JA
(0924) 46-8469
Cottage Garden Society Newsletter (4)
Cottage Gardens to Visit (1)

Purpose is to keep alive the tradition of gardening in the cottage style
and the use of old-fashioned plants. Arranges garden visits in the summer.
They offer "A Cottage Garden Planner" for £2.50 or $5.
❐ Annual Dues: in US & CAN US$20 (IMO), UK £5, Europe £6
❐ Privileges: SEEDS PLANTS EXHIBITS TRIPS

The Cryptanthus Society
Bob D. Whitman
2355 Rusk
Beaumont, TX 77702
(409) 835-0644
Journal (4)
Yearbook (1)

A cultural flier is available free of charge.
❐ Annual Dues: in US $10, CAN & OV US$15 (IMO)
❐ Chapters: 28
❐ Privileges: CONVENTIONS BOOKS EXHIBITS

The Cycad Society
David Mayo
1161 Phyllis Court
Mountain View, CA 94040
(415) 964-7898
The Cycad Newsletter (3)

They have a seed and pollen bank.
❐ Annual Dues: $15
❐ Privileges: SEEDS

Cyclamen Society
Dr. D.V. Bent
Little Pilgrims, 2 Pilgrims Way East
Otford, Sevenoaks, Kent, England TN14 5QN
(0959) 52-2322
Cyclamen (2)

Society works to preserve and conserve wild species, has an exchange
of viable seed in late summer, offers growing advice from experts.
❐ Annual Dues: in US, CAN & OV £7 (IMO)
❐ Privileges: CONVENTIONS LIBRARY SEEDS PLANTS EXHIBITS

Cymbidium Society of America
Paula Butler
533 So. Woodland
Orange, CA 92669
(714) 532-4719
The Orchid Advocate (6)

❐ Annual Dues: $20
❐ Chapters: 8
❐ Privileges: EXHIBITS

The Daffodil Society (UK)
Don Barnes
32 Montgomery Ave.
Sheffield, England S7 1NZ

Write for information.

The Delphinium Society
Mrs. Shirley E. Bassett
"Takakkaw," Ice House Wood
Oxted, Surrey, England RH8 9DW
Delphinium Year Book

Publishes a basic guide, "Simply Delphiniums" US$6 (£2.50). No
personal checks in US currency.
❐ Annual Dues: in US $10(US bills), CAN & OV £5 (IMO)
❐ Garden: Delphinium Trial Ground, RHS Garden, Wisley, Surrey
❐ Privileges: PLANTS EXHIBITS

Desert Plant Society of Vancouver
6200 McKay Ave. Box 145-790
Barnaby, BC, Canada V5H 4MY
(604) 525-5315

This group is dedicated to growing indoor and outdoor succulent
plants in British Columbia.
❐ Annual Dues: C$15
❐ Privileges: SEEDS PLANTS EXHIBITS

Dwarf Iris Society of America
Lynda S. Miller
3167 E. U.S. 224
Ossian, IN 46777
(219) 597-7403
Dwarf Iris Society Newsletter (3)

A section of the American Iris Society.
❐ Annual Dues: $3
❐ Privileges: CONVENTIONS BOOKS

Eastern Native Plant Alliance
P.O. Box 6101
McLean, VA 22106

Write for information.

Elm Research Institute
Elm St.
Harrisville, NH 03450
(800) FOR-ELMS

Distributes elms resistant to Dutch Elm Disease, primarily through Boy
Scout Troops all over the country. Members receive a free elm tree.
❐ Annual Dues: $25

Epiphyllum Society of America
Betty Berg, Memb. Secy.
P.O. Box 1395
Monrovia, CA 91017
(818) 447-9688
The Bulletin (6)

❐ Annual Dues: in US & CAN US$10, OV Air Mail US$16 (IMO)
❐ Privileges: LIBRARY EXHIBITS

Eucalyptus Improvement Association
P.O. Box 4460
Davis, CA 95617
(916) 753-4535
California Eucalyptus Grower (4)
EIA Annual Report

A group dedicated to the genetic improvement of "eucalyptus as a crop."
Write for information.
❐ Annual Dues: in US $20, CAN & OV US$30 (IMO)
❐ Privileges: CONVENTIONS PLANTS TRIPS

Fava Bean Project
Ross Randrup
P.O.Box 941-SB
Cottage Grove, OR 97424
Fava News (1-2)
Seed offering (2)

Not so much a society as a home grown project. Send long SASE for seed
price list and ask to be put on mailing list for the Fava News.
❐ Annual Dues: Donations with order
❐ Privileges: CONVENTIONS BOOKS PLANTS

Florida Native Plant Society
James D. Lantz
P.O. Box 680008
Orlando, FL 32868
(407) 299-1472
The Palmetto (4)

Other display gardens at Kanapaha Gardens, Gainesville and at Maclay
Gardens State Park, Tallahassee. Write to society for list of publications.
❐ Annual Dues: $20
❐ Chapters: 23
❐ Garden: Heritage Garden in Lev Gardens, Orlando
❐ Privileges: CONVENTIONS BOOKS SEEDS PLANTS EXHIBITS TRIPS

The Flower and Herb Exchange
Diane Whealy
3076 North Winn Road
Decorah, Iowa 52101
Flower and Herb Exchange (1)

A group that is dedicated to the preservation and distribution of heirloom
varieties of flowers. Members receive the annual seed exchange list.
❐ Annual Dues: in US $5, CAN $7, OV $10
❐ Privileges: SEEDS

Garden History Society
Mrs. Anne Richards
5 The Knoll
Hereford, England HR1 1RU
(0432) 35-4479
Garden History (2)
Newsletter (3)

Has excellent tours in Europe and elsewhere.
❐ Annual Dues: in US & CAN £18 (IMO), UK £15
❐ Privileges: CONVENTIONS TRIPS TOURS

Garden Research Exchange
Ken Allan
536 MacDonnell St.
Kingston, ON, Canada K7K 4W7
(613) 542-6547
Vegetable Garden Research Yearbook

A group of devoted vegetable gardeners doing research; they publish a
yearbook with their results, available for $12. (US or CAN $) Write for more
information.

Gardenia Society of America
Lyman Duncan
P.O. Box 879
Atwater, CA 95301
(209) 358-2231
Gardenia News (3)

This group accepts US members only.
❐ Annual Dues: $5

Georgia Organic Growers Association
P.O. Box 567661
Atlanta, GA 31156
(404) 621-4642
GOGA Newsletter (6)
Green Leaf (variable)

This is a regional group.
❐ Annual Dues: $15
❐ Privileges: CONVENTIONS PLANTS EXHIBITS TRIPS

The Geraniaceae Group
Penny Clifton
9 Waingate Bridge Cottages
Haverigg, Cumbria, England LA18 4NF
The Geraniaceae Group News (4)
Group Seed List (1)

The publications "Hardy Geraniums Today" ($2.50) and "Hardy
Geraniums for the Garden" ($6) are available.
❐ Annual Dues: US$16 or £8 (IMO)
❐ Privileges: BOOKS SEEDS TRIPS

Gesneriad Hybridizers Association
Meg Stephenson
4115 Pillar Drive, Route 1
Whitmore Lake, MI 48189
Crosswords (3)

❐ Annual Dues: $5

Gesneriad Society International
Richard Dunn
11510 124th Terr. N.
Largo, FL 34648-2505
(813) 585-4247
Gesneriad Journal (6)

❐ Annual Dues: in US $16.50, CAN & OV US$21.50 (IMO)
❐ Chapters: 20
❐ Privileges: CONVENTIONS SEEDS PLANTS

Hardy Fern Foundation
P.O. Box 166
Medina, WA 98039-0166
(206) 747-2998
Newsletter (4)

Purpose is to test ferns for ornamental value and hardiness. They
are starting test gardens in different areas of the country.
❐ Annual Dues: $20
❐ Garden: Rhododenron Species Foundation, Federal Way, WA
❐ Privileges: CONVENTIONS SEEDS PLANTS TRIPS

Hardy Plant Society (UK)
Administrator
Little Orchard, Great Comberton
Pershore, England WR10 3DP
(0386) 71-0317
The Hardy Plant (2)
Newsletter (3)

Offers seed exchanges, visits to members' gardens. See also Hardy Plant
Society of Oregon and the Hardy Plant Society -- Mid-Atlantic Group (which
offers joint membership).
❐ Annual Dues: in US & CAN £8.50 (IMO)
❐ Chapters: 30
❐ Garden: Pershore Horticultural College
❐ Privileges: CONVENTIONS SEEDS PLANTS EXHIBITS

Hardy Plant Society -- Mid-Atlantic Group
Betty Mackey
440 Louella Avenue
Wayne, PA 19087
The Newsletter (4)

Promotes interest in hardy plants, particularly perennials. Offers membership in the HPS (UK) for an additional $11 a year, must receive application
before November of each year. There is also a list of members' gardens
available to visit.
❐ Annual Dues: in US & CAN US$12
❐ Privileges: CONVENTIONS BOOKS SEEDS PLANTS TRIPS TOURS

Hardy Plant Society of Oregon
Mary Hoffman
P.O. 5090
Oregon City, OR 97045-8090
(503) 656-1575
Bulletin (2)

Hold periodic study weekends in the Northwest, highly recommended!
❐ Annual Dues: $15
❐ Privileges: CONVENTIONS LIBRARY BOOKS SEEDS PLANTS

Hardy Plant Society--Correspondents Group
Jane Lucas
37 Horndean Avenue, Wigston Fields
Leicester, England LE8 1DP
Correspondents Group Newsletter (4)

This group for members of the Hardy Plant Society operates solely
through the mail. It is principally for isolated gardeners who like
to keep in touch with individuals with similar interests.
❐ Annual Dues: £3 (IMO)
❐ Privileges: SEEDS PLANTS

The Heather Society
Mrs. A. Small
Denbeigh, All Saints Road, Creeting St. Mary
Ipswich, Suffolk, England 1P6 8PJ
(0449) 71-1220
Bulletin (3)
Year Book

Has a slide library and a cultivar location service. There is a third display
garden at Cherrybank Gardens, Perth, Scotland.
❐ Annual Dues: in US, CAN & OV £6 (£8 air mail)
❐ Chapters: 14
❐ Garden: RHS Garden, Wisley; NHS Garden, Harlow Carr, Harrogate
❐ Privileges: CONVENTIONS BOOKS EXHIBITS

The Hebe Society
Val Haywood
1 Woodpecker Drive
Hailsham, E. Sussex, England BN27 3EZ
Hebe News (4)

❐ Annual Dues: in US, CAN & OV £5 (IMO)
❐ Garden: Garden being developed at Trewidden, Cornwall
❐ Privileges: CONVENTIONS

Heliconia Society International
David Bar-Zvi
c/o Flamingo Gardens, 3750 Flamingo Road
Ft. Lauderdale, FL 33330
(305) 473-2955
HSI Bulletin (4)

❐ Annual Dues: $35
❐ Chapters: 2
❐ Garden: Flamingo Gardens, FL; Lyon Arboretum, HI
❐ Privileges: CONVENTIONS TOURS

Herb Research Foundation
1007 Pearl Street, Suite 200
Boulder, CO 80301
(303) 449-2265
HerbalGram (4)

Formed to stimulate and support research on both common and uncommon
herbs, with an emphasis on medicinal herbs. Offers botanical literature
searches.
❐ Annual Dues: in US $35, CAN US$40, OV US$45 (IMO)
❐ Privileges: CONVENTIONS

Herb Society of America, Inc.
Headquarters
9019 Kirtland Chardon Road
Mentor, OH 44060
(216) 256-0514
The Herbarist (1)
HSA News   (4)

Society is horticulturally oriented, and seeks to further use and knowledge of herbs. Membership is through sponsorship by a current member; write for information. US members only.
☐ Annual Dues: $35
☐ Chapters: 35
☐ Garden: Herb Garden at The National Arboretum, Washington, DC
☐ Privileges: CONVENTIONS LIBRARY BOOKS SEEDS PLANTS EXHIBITS TRIPS TOURS

Heritage Rose Group
Miriam Wilkins
925 Galvin Drive
El Cerrito, CA 94530
(510) 526-6960
Heritage Rose Letter (4)

Local chapters have meetings and plant sales. Send SASE with two first class stamps for membership information.
☐ Annual Dues: in US $5, CAN & OV US$6 (US$8.50 air mail)
☐ Chapters: 6
☐ Privileges: EXHIBITS

Heritage Seed Program
Heather Apple, President
RR 3
Uxbridge, ONT, Canada L9P 1R3
Heritage Seed Program (3)
Seed Listing (1)

Canadian group interested in saving heirloom and endangered varieties of food crops to guard against the loss of genetic diversity. Their plant collections can be visited at various members' gardens and farms. They are also interested in organic gardening.
☐ Annual Dues: in CAN C$15, US & OV US$18
☐ Garden: Heritage Nursery, Salt Spring Island, BC
☐ Privileges: SEEDS

Historic Iris Preservation Society
Verona Weikhorst
4855 Santiago Way
Colorado Springs, CO 80917
(719) 596-7724
Roots Journal (2)

A section of the American Iris Society.
☐ Annual Dues: $5
☐ Privileges: CONVENTIONS PLANTS

Hobby Greenhouse Association
HGA Membership
18517 Kingshill Road
Germantown, MD 20874-2211
(617) 275-0377
Hobby Greenhouse (4)
HGA News (4)

Publishes a "Directory of Manufacturers: Hobby Greenhouses, Solariums, Sunrooms and Window Greenhouses" which is available for $2.
☐ Annual Dues: in US $12, CAN US$14, OV US$15 (IMO)
☐ Chapters: 3
☐ Privileges: LIBRARY BOOKS

Holly Society of America, Inc.
Mrs. Linda R. Parsons
11318 West Murdock
Wichita, KS 67212-6609
(301) 825-8133
Holly Society Journal (4)

Has holly auctions and cutting exchanges, informative pamphlets, local chapters and annual meetings near notable holly collections.
☐ Annual Dues: $15
☐ Chapters: 8
☐ Privileges: CONVENTIONS PLANTS TRIPS

Home Orchard Society
Winnifred M. Fisher
P.O. Box 776
Clackamas, OR 97015
(503) 630-3392
Pome News (4)

Has scion and rootstock exchanges. For members in the Northwest there are fruit exhibits and various other events.
☐ Annual Dues: $10
☐ Chapters: 4
☐ Garden: HOS Arboretum, Clackamas Comm. Coll., Oregon City, OR
☐ Privileges: CONVENTIONS PLANTS EXHIBITS TRIPS

Horticultural Alliance of the Hamptons
William & Marie Donnelly
P.O. Box 202
Bridgehampton, NY 11932
(516) 537-2223
Newsletter (2)

A rapidly growing and very active group.
☐ Annual Dues: $25
☐ Privileges: LIBRARY PLANTS EXHIBITS TOURS

Horticultural Society of New York
Office Manager
128 W. 58th Street
New York, NY 10019
(212) 757-0915
HSNY Newsletter (4)

Producer of the New York Flower Show, held annually in March.
☐ Annual Dues: $35
☐ Privileges: CONVENTIONS LIBRARY BOOKS PLANTS EXHIBITS TRIPS

The Hoya Society International
P.O. Box 1043
Porterdale, GA 30270
The Hoyan (4)

New members can join for $10.50 for their initial year. Overseas members must pay in US dollars.
☐ Annual Dues: in US $20, CAN & OV US$25
☐ Privileges: CONVENTIONS SEEDS PLANTS

Hydroponic Society of America
Gene Brisbon
P.O. Box 6067
Concord, CA 94524
(510) 682-4193
Soilless Grower (6)
Directory of Suppliers (1)

❒ Annual Dues: in US & CAN US$30, OV US$40 (IMO or CC)
❒ Chapters: 2
❒ Privileges: CONVENTIONS BOOKS TOURS

Idaho Native Plant Society
P.O. Box 9451
Boise, ID 83707
Sage Notes (6)
Sage Briefs (6)

❒ Annual Dues: $8
❒ Chapters: 5
❒ Privileges: CONVENTIONS EXHIBITS TRIPS

**Indigenous Bulb Growers Association
of South Africa**
The Secretary/Treasurer
3 The Bend
Edgemead, South Africa 7441
(021) 58-1690
IBSA Bulletin (1)

Society devoted to the conservation of South African bulbous plants by means of cultivation and propagation.
❒ Annual Dues: in US, CAN & OV US$10 (IMO)
❒ Privileges: CONVENTIONS SEEDS PLANTS EXHIBITS TRIPS TOURS

Indoor Gardening Society of America
Sharon Zentz, Memb. Secy.
944 S. Munroe Road
Tallmadge, OH 44278
(216) 733-8414

Has "Society News" column and "Round Robins" in HousePlant Magazine.
❒ Annual Dues: in US $19.95, CAN US$24.95, OV US$28.95 (IMO)
❒ Chapters: 15
❒ Privileges: PLANTS EXHIBITS

International Aroid Society
Membership Chairman
P.O. Box 43-1853
Miami, FL 33143
(305) 271-3767
Aroideana (1)
IAS Newsletter (6)

Society devoted to members of the arum family (Aroidaceae).
❒ Annual Dues: in US $18, CAN & OV US$25 (IMO)
❒ Privileges: CONVENTIONS LIBRARY BOOKS PLANTS

International Asclepiad Society
L.B. Delderfield
2 Keymer Ct.
Burgess Hill, W. Sussex, England RH15 0AA

❒ Annual Dues: £10 (IMO)
❒ Privileges: SEEDS

International Bulb Society
P.O. Box 4928
Culver City, CA 90230
Herbertia (1)

Formerly the American Plant Life Society, it is devoted to the culture of, research on and preservation of bulbous plants, especially the Amaryllidaceae.
❒ Annual Dues: $30
❒ Privileges: SEEDS

International Camellia Society
Thomas H. Perkins III
P.O. Box 750
Brookhaven, MS 39601-0750
(601) 833-7351
International Camellia Journal (1)
Mid-Year Newsletter (1)

Meets every other year in different host countries; dues may be paid in local currency through regional membership representatives.
❒ Annual Dues: in US $13, UK £8.50
❒ Privileges: CONVENTIONS EXHIBITS

International Carnivorous Plant Society
c/o Fullerton Arboretum, Calif. State Univ.
Fullerton, CA 92634
(714) 773-2766
Carnivorous Plant Newsletter (4)

Has a very interesting magazine with color photographs and articles on plant hunting.
❒ Annual Dues: in US & CAN US$15, OV US$20 (IMO)
❒ Chapters: 3
❒ Garden: Fullerton Arboretum
❒ Privileges: SEEDS

International Geranium Society
Membership Secretary
P.O.Box 92734
Pasadena, CA 91109-2734
(818) 908-8867 eves.
Geraniums Around the World (4)

This is a group for hobby growers who seek growing information.
❒ Annual Dues: $12.50
❒ Chapters: 7
❒ Privileges: CONVENTIONS PLANTS

International Golden Fossil Tree Society
Clayton A. Fawkes, Pres.
201 W. Graham Avenue
Lombard, IL 60148
(708) 627-5636
IGFTS Newsletter (4)

Society for lovers of ginkgo trees.
❑ Annual Dues: $2
❑ Privileges: CONVENTIONS

International Lilac Society
ILS, c/oThe Holden Arboretum
9500 Sperry Road
Mentor, OH 44060-8199
(216) 946-4400
Journal (4)

Publishes a booklet on lilac culture.
❑ Annual Dues: in US & OV US$15 (IMO or US bills), CAN C$15
❑ Privileges: CONVENTIONS BOOKS PLANTS EXHIBITS

International Oak Society
Journal Office
1093 Ackermanville Rd.
Pen Argyl, PA 18072-9670
(215) 588-1037
IOS Journal (2)

A brand-new society formed to increase the number of oak species in cultivation and to encourage the hybridization of oaks. At present it functions
mainly as a seed exchange.
❑ Annual Dues: $10
❑ Privileges: CONVENTIONS SEEDS

International Oleander Society
Elizabeth S. Head, Cor. Secy.
P.O. Box 3431
Galveston, TX 77552-0431
(409) 762-9334
Nerium News (4)

Publishes "Oleanders--Guide to Culture and Selected Varieties on
Galveston Island," available for $10.
❑ Annual Dues: $10
❑ Garden: Moody Gardens, Galveston, TX
❑ Privileges: CONVENTIONS BOOKS SEEDS PLANTS EXHIBITS TRIPS

International Ornamental Crabapple Society
Thomas L. Green
Dept. of Agriculture, Western Illinois Univ.
Macomb, IL 61455
Malus (2)

❑ Annual Dues: $15
❑ Privileges: CONVENTIONS

The International Palm Society
P.O.Box 1897
Lawrence, KS 66044-8897
Principes (4)

Members in eighty countries. Seeds sold to members at a nominal fee.
❑ Annual Dues: in US $25, CAN & OV US$30 (IMO or CC)
❑ Chapters: 20
❑ Privileges: CONVENTIONS PLANTS

The International Ribes Association
Ms. Jeanne Nickless
P.O. Box 428
Boonville, CA 95415
(707) 895-2811
The Ribes Reporter (2-4)

This is a group for growers of edible gooseberries and currants.
❑ Annual Dues: $20
❑ Privileges: CONVENTIONS

International Violet Association
Ms. Elaine Kudela
8604 Main Road
Berlin Heights, OH 44814-9620
(419) 588-2616
Sweet Times (4)

New group interested in preserving old varieties of violets.
❑ Annual Dues: $15
❑ Chapters: 2

International Water Lily Society
Dr. Edward Schneider
Santa Barbara Botanic Gardens
Santa Barbara, CA 93105
(805) 682-4726
Water Garden Journal (4)

❑ Annual Dues: in US $18, CAN US$21, OV £12.50
❑ Garden: Denver Botanic Garden,CO; Burnby Hall, Pocklington, UK
❑ Privileges: CONVENTIONS LIBRARY

Kansas Wildflower Society
Mulvane Art Center,
Washburn Univ., 17th & Jewell
Topeka, KS 66621

Write for information.
❑ Privileges: CONVENTIONS

The KUSA Society
P.O. Box 761
Ojai, CA 93024
The Cerealist (irregular)

A society interested in the preservation of ancient seed crops and their
potential for use as human food. Also sells ancient grain varieties through
the KUSA Foundation; see Section A. Requests for information must be
accompanied by $1.
❑ Annual Dues: various rates

Long Island Horticultural Society
David Carrody
9 Anita Ave.
Syosset, NY 11791
(516) 921-4661
Newsletter (11)

Society has symposia for members, an annual picnic and plant sales and exhibits.
❐ Privileges: PLANTS EXHIBITS

Los Angeles International Fern Society
P.O. Box 90943
Pasadena, CA 91109-0943
LAIFS Journal (6)

Has a spore store and book store. Also holds educational programs.
❐ Annual Dues: in US $20, CAN $23.50, OV $26 (IMO)
❐ Privileges: BOOKS PLANTS EXHIBITS TRIPS

Louisiana Iris Society of America
Elaine Bourque
1812 Broussard Road E.
Lafayette, LA 70508
Newsletter (4)
Special Bulletins (occasional)

A newly reorganized group of lovers of Louisiana irises.
❐ Annual Dues: $7.50
❐ Privileges: CONVENTIONS BOOKS EXHIBITS TRIPS

Louisiana Native Plant Society
Ella Price
P.O.Box 393
Blanchard, LA 71009
Lousiana Native Plant Society Newsletter (4)

❐ Annual Dues: $10
❐ Garden: Caroline Dormon Nature Preserve, Saline, LA
❐ Privileges: CONVENTIONS SEEDS PLANTS EXHIBITS TRIPS

The Magnolia Society, Inc.
Phelan A. Bright
907 S. Chestnut Street
Hammond, LA 70403-5102
(504) 542-9477
Magnolia (2)

❐ Annual Dues: in US $18, CAN & OV US$20 (IMO)
❐ Privileges: CONVENTIONS LIBRARY SEEDS TOURS

Manitoba Regional Lily Society
Jean Atto, Treas.
580 Bardal Bay
Winnipeg, MB, Canada R2G 0J2
(204) 669-2781
Manitoba Regional Lily Society (4)

A society for those interested in members of the genus Lilium.
❐ Annual Dues: C$5
❐ Garden: Plant Science Dept, University of Manitoba
❐ Privileges: CONVENTIONS LIBRARY BOOKS PLANTS EXHIBITS TRIPS

Marigold Society of America, Inc.
Jeannette Lowe
P.O. Box 5112
New Britain, PA 18901
(215) 348-5273
Amerigold Newsletter (4)

Members receive seed of new varieties.
❐ Annual Dues: $12
❐ Privileges: CONVENTIONS SEEDS

© Earthly Goods, Ltd.
Artist: Stephen Brown

Marshall Olbrich Plant Club
P.O. Box 1338
Sebastopol, CA 95473
(707) 829-9189

A regional group that meets 9 times a year in the North San Francisco Bay area; has speakers on a wide variety of horticultural topics.
❏ Annual Dues: $5
❏ Privileges: BOOKS PLANTS

Maryland Native Plant Society
P.O. Box 4877
Silver Spring, MD 20914

Write for information.

Massachusetts Horticultural Association
300 Massachusetts Avenue
Boston, MA 02115
(617) 536-9280
Horticulture (12)

Has sponsored the New England Spring Flower Show in Boston for 123 years.
❏ Annual Dues: $45
❏ Privileges: LIBRARY BOOKS EXHIBITS TRIPS

Master Gardeners International Corp. (MaGIC)
Membership Services
2904 Cameron Mills Road
Alexandria, VA 22302
(703) 920-6677
MaGIC Lantern (4)

Umbrella group for people who have taken the Master Gardening Training. They publish a directory of Master Gardener programs in North America.
❏ Annual Dues: $10
❏ Privileges: CONVENTIONS

Mesemb Study Group
Mrs. Suzanne Mace
Brenfield, Bolney Rd.
Ansty, West Sussex, England RH17 5AW
(0444) 44-1193
Mesemb Study Group Bulletin (4)

❏ Annual Dues: in US & CAN US$15, OV £9 (IMO)
❏ Privileges: CONVENTIONS BOOKS SEEDS PLANTS EXHIBITS

Michigan Botanical Club
Dorothy & Beatrice Sibley
7951 Walnut Ave.
Newaygo, MI 49337
(616) 652-2036
The Michigan Botanist (4)

❏ Annual Dues: $17
❏ Privileges: CONVENTIONS BOOKS TRIPS

Minnesota Native Plant Society
MNPS, 220 BioScience
1445 Gortner Avenue
St. Paul, MN 55108
Minnesota Plant Press (3)

Write for information.
❏ Privileges: CONVENTIONS SEEDS PLANTS TRIPS

Minnesota State Horticultural Society
1755 Prior Avenue North
Falcon Heights, MN 55113
(612) 645-7066
Minnesota Horticulturist (9)

They have a list of display gardens in Minnesota. They also publish "Perennials A to Z" for $5, and the "Minnesota Green Newsletter" (6 issues yearly) for $10. Of interest to all Northern gardeners.
❏ Annual Dues: $25
❏ Chapters: 200
❏ Privileges: CONVENTIONS LIBRARY BOOKS EXHIBITS TOURS

Mississippi Native Plant Society
Victor A. Rudis
P.O. Box 2151
Starkville, MS 39759
(601) 324-0430
Newsletter (4)

Botanical Garden of the South being developed at Sessums, MS. Regional members only.
❏ Annual Dues: $7.50
❏ Garden: Mynelle Gardens, Jackson, MS
❏ Privileges: CONVENTIONS BOOKS SEEDS PLANTS EXHIBITS TRIPS

Missouri Native Plant Society
P.O. Box 20073
St. Louis, MO 63144
(314) 577-9522
Missouriensis (2)
Petal Pusher (6)

❏ Annual Dues: $9
❏ Chapters: 7
❏ Privileges: CONVENTIONS SEEDS PLANTS EXHIBITS TRIPS

National Auricula & Primula Society
Mr. D.G. Hadfield
146 Queens Road, Cheadle Hulme
Cheadle, Cheshire, England SK8 5HY
Yearbook

Write for information.

National Chrysanthemum Society (UK)
H. B. Locke
2 Lucas House, Craven Road
Rugby, Warwicks., England CV21 3HY
(0788) 56-9039
Autumn & Spring Bulletins
Yearbook

Has a second display garden at Brackenhill Park, Bradford (near Leeds).
❏ Annual Dues: £9.75 (IMO)
❏ Garden: RHS Gardens, Wisley, Surrey
❏ Privileges: BOOKS

National Chrysanthemum Society, Inc. (USA)
Galen L. Goss
10107 Homar Pond Drive
Fairfax Station, VA 22039-1650
(703) 978-7981
The Chrysanthemum (4)

❏ Annual Dues: in US & CAN US$12.50, OV US$16.50 (IMO)
❏ Chapters: 45
❏ Privileges: CONVENTIONS BOOKS EXHIBITS

National Fuchsia Society
Agnes Rietkerk
11507 E. 187th Street
Artesia, CA 90701
Fuchsia Fan (6)

❏ Annual Dues: $15
❏ Chapters: 4
❏ Privileges: LIBRARY BOOKS PLANTS EXHIBITS

National Gardening Association
180 Flynn Ave.
Burlington, VT 05401
(802) 863-1308
National Gardening (6)

Dedicated to teaching people to grow plants. Has a seed search service, a members' answer service, group insurance rates, new books at a discount and an interesting magazine for home gardeners. This organization also develops educational curricula about plant growing for teachers.
❏ Annual Dues: in US $18, CAN & OV US$27 (IMO)
❏ Privileges: LIBRARY BOOKS SEEDS EXHIBITS TRIPS

National Hot Pepper Association
Betty Payton
400 N.W. 20th Street
Ft. Lauderdale, FL 33311
(305) 565-4972
Newsletter (4)

A new organization dedicated to growing chiles.
❏ Annual Dues: $20

National Sweet Pea Society
J. R. F. Bishop
3 Chalk Farm Road, Stokenchurch
High Wycombe, Bucks., England HP14 3TB
(0494) 48-2153
Bulletin (2)
Annual

For an extra £4, you can become a vice-president. Members get a free copy of the booklet "How to Grow Sweet Peas."
❏ Annual Dues: in US, CAN & OV £15, UK £11 (IMO)
❏ Garden: Lathyrus species collection being developed in Sussex
❏ Privileges: CONVENTIONS EXHIBITS

Native Plant Society of New Jersey
NPSNJ, Cook College
P.O. Box 231
New Brunswick, NJ 08903-0231

Write for information.

Native Plant Society of New Mexico
Membership Chairperson
443 Live Oak Loop Northeast
Albuquerque, NM 87122
(505) 356-3942
Newsletter (6)

❏ Annual Dues: $10
❏ Chapters: 6
❏ Privileges: CONVENTIONS BOOKS PLANTS TRIPS

Native Plant Society of Oregon
Jan Dobak, Memb. Chair.
2584 NW Savier St.
Portland, OR 97210-2412
(503) 248-9242
Bulletin (12)
Kalmiopsis (1)

❏ Annual Dues: $12
❏ Chapters: 12
❏ Privileges: CONVENTIONS EXHIBITS TRIPS

Native Plant Society of Texas
Dana Tucker
P.O. Box 891
Georgetown, TX 78627
(512) 863-7794
Texas Native Plant Society News (6)

❏ Annual Dues: $20
❏ Chapters: 27
❏ Privileges: CONVENTIONS SEEDS PLANTS EXHIBITS TRIPS

New England Garden History Society
Librarian MHS
300 Massachusetts Avenue
Boston, MA 02115
(617) 536-9280
Journal (1)
Belvedere (2-4)

Write for information.
❏ Annual Dues: $25
❏ Privileges: CONVENTIONS TOURS

New England Wild Flower Society
Georgeanne Roe
180 Hemenway Road
Framingham, MA 01701-2699
(508) 877-7630
Newsletter (3)

Chapters in each state in New England; seed exchanges with botanical gardens.
❏ Annual Dues: $35
❏ Chapters: 5
❏ Garden: Garden-in-the-Woods, Framingham, MA
❏ Privileges: LIBRARY BOOKS PLANTS TRIPS TOURS

New Zealand Camellia Society
C.R. Hurst, Secy.-Treas.
100 Evans Bay Parade
Wellington, New Zealand 6001
(04) 382-8384
New Zealand Camellia Bulletin (3)

You can join through the US agent, Southern California Camellia Society, c/o Mrs. Bobbie Belcher, 7457 Brydon Road, La Verne, CA 91750. The society has published "Growing Better Camellias in the 1990's," available for NZ$7.50.
❏ Annual Dues: NZ$22.50
❏ Chapters: 22
❏ Privileges: CONVENTIONS BOOKS EXHIBITS TRIPS TOURS

New Zealand Fuchsia Society, Inc.
Secretary
P.O. Box 11-082
Ellerslie, Auckland, New Zealand 6
(09) 827-2118
New Zealand Fuchsia Society Newsletter (11)

There is also a garden at Regional Botanic Garden, Manurewa.
❏ Annual Dues: in US & CAN NZ$6 (IMO)
❏ Garden: Eden Garden, Omana Rd, Auckland
❏ Privileges: LIBRARY TOURS

Newfoundland Alpine & Rock Garden Club
Janet Story
c/o Memorial University Botanical Garden
St. John's, NF, Canada A1C 5S7
(709) 737-8590

A chapter of the American Rock Garden Society.
❏ Annual Dues: in CAN C$5
❏ Privileges: SEEDS TRIPS

North American Fruit Explorers
Jill Vorbeck, Memb. Chair.
Route 1, Box 94
Chapin, IL 62628
(217) 245-7589
Pomona (4)

Dedicated home fruit growers who are interested in finding and growing unusual fruits and nuts.
❏ Annual Dues: in US $8, CAN & OV US$12
❏ Privileges: CONVENTIONS LIBRARY

North American Gladiolus Council
William Strawser
701 So. Hendricks Ave.
Marion, IND 46953
(317) 664-3857
Bulletin (4)

❏ Annual Dues: in US & CAN US$10, OV US$11.50 (IMO)
❏ Chapters: 57
❏ Privileges: CONVENTIONS PLANTS EXHIBITS

North American Heather Society
Pauline Croxton
3641 Indian Creek Road
Placerville, CA 95667-8923
Heather News (4)

❏ Annual Dues: $10
❏ Chapters: 5
❏ Privileges: CONVENTIONS LIBRARY PLANTS TRIPS

North American Lily Society, Inc.
Dr. Robert Gilman, Exec. Secy.
P.O. Box 272
Owatonna, MN 55060
(507) 451-2170
Lily Yearbook (1)
Quarterly Bulletin (4)

Introductory publication "Let's Grow Lilies" is available for $3.50.
❏ Annual Dues: $12.50
❏ Chapters: 19
❏ Privileges: CONVENTIONS LIBRARY BOOKS SEEDS EXHIBITS

North American Mycological Association
Executive Secretary
3556 Oakwood
Ann Arbor, MI 48104-5213
(313) 971-2552
The Mycophile (6)
McIlvainea (1)

A group for mushroom growers and enthusiasts.
❏ Annual Dues: in US & CAN US$15, OV US$20
❏ Chapters: 65
❏ Privileges: CONVENTIONS

Rare Fruit Council International, Inc.
Carolyn W. Betts
12255 SW 73 Ave.
Miami, FL 33156
(305) 378-4457
Tropical Fruit News (12)
Membership Directory (1)

Has plant exchanges; publishes a cookbook. Germplasm currently located at a number of Florida locations.
❑ Annual Dues: $35
❑ Chapters: 7
❑ Privileges: LIBRARY BOOKS SEEDS PLANTS EXHIBITS TRIPS TOURS

Rare Pit & Plant Council
Deborah Peterson
251 W. 11th Street
New York, NY 10014
(212) 255-9256
The Pits (8-10)

Society membership is strictly limited because members meet in each others' homes. Their interesting newsletter, devoted to growing exotic fruit and ornamentals indoors, is available by subscription.
❑ Annual Dues: in US $12.50, CAN & OV US$15 (IMO)
❑ Privileges: SEEDS TRIPS

The Reblooming Iris Society
Charles Brown
3114 South FM 131
Denison, TX 75020
Bulletin (2)

A section of the American Iris Society; members are encouraged to join the AIS as well.
❑ Annual Dues: $5
❑ Privileges: PLANTS EXHIBITS

Rhododendron Society of Canada
R. S. Dickhout
5200 Timothy Crescent
Niagara Falls, ON, Canada L2E 5G3
(416) 357-5981
Journal-ARS (4)

This group is affiliated with the American Rhododendron Society.
❑ Annual Dues: in CAN US$25
❑ Chapters: 3
❑ Privileges: CONVENTIONS LIBRARY BOOKS SEEDS PLANTS EXHIBITS

Rhododendron Species Foundation
P.O. Box 3798
Federal Way, WA 98063-3798
(206) 838-4646
RSF Newsletter (4)
Plant Distribution Catalog (1)

Offers classes, lectures and an independent study course by mail, has a rhododendron library and pollen distribution for hybridizers. It has created a living collection of over 1,800 rhododendrons, and also displays the Weyerhaeuser Pacific Rim Bonsai Collection.
❑ Annual Dues: $30
❑ Garden: Rhododendron Species Foundation, Federal Way, WA
❑ Privileges: CONVENTIONS LIBRARY BOOKS PLANTS EXHIBITS TRIPS TOURS

The Rock Garden Club Prague
RNDr. Eva Hanzlíková
Pasteurova 5
Prague 4, Czech Republic 142 00
Prague (47) 14-610
Skalnicky (4)

The journal "Skalnicky" is printed in Czech, with short English or German abstracts.
❑ Annual Dues: in US, CAN & OV US$15 or DM25 (cash)
❑ Garden: Prague 2, Charles Square, during Exhibitions
❑ Privileges: LIBRARY SEEDS PLANTS EXHIBITS TRIPS

Rose Hybridizers Association
Larry D. Peterson
3245 Wheaton Road
Horseheads, NY 14845
(607) 562-8592
Newsletter (4)

Display garden at Gene Boerner Gardens, Hales Corner, WI. Data Base available to members listing back issues, articles and authors.
❑ Annual Dues: $7
❑ Garden: Test Garden, American Rose Center, Shreveport, LA
❑ Privileges: CONVENTIONS

The Royal Horticultural Society
Membership Secretary
80 Vincent Square
London, England SW1P 2PE
(071) 834-4333
The Garden (12)

Frequent plant and flower shows in London, including the best of all, the Chelsea Flower Show. Also has a wonderful library at Vincent Square.
❑ Annual Dues: Write for information
❑ Garden: RHS Garden, Wisley, Surrey
❑ Privileges: LIBRARY BOOKS SEEDS PLANTS EXHIBITS TRIPS TOURS

The Royal National Rose Society
The Secretary
Chiswell Green
St. Albans, Herts., England AL2 3NR
(0727) 50-461
The Rose (4)

Claims to be one of the oldest, largest and friendliest plant societies in the world.
❑ Annual Dues: all members £13.50 (IMO, CC, or PC in US$)
❑ Chapters: 900
❑ Garden: The Gardens of the Rose, St. Albans
❑ Privileges: CONVENTIONS LIBRARY BOOKS EXHIBITS TRIPS TOURS

Sacramento Perennial Garden Club
9498 Alcosta Way
Sacramento, CA 95827

A regional group with an interest in ornamental plants.
❑ Annual Dues: $5
❑ Privileges: CONVENTIONS SEEDS PLANTS TRIPS

The Saintpaulia & Houseplant Society
The Secretary
33 Church Road, Newbury Park
Ilford, Essex, England IG2 7ET
(081) 590-3710
Quarterly Bulletin

They have eleven pamphlets on various plants; write for information.
❑ Annual Dues: in US, CAN & OV £5 (IMO)
❑ Chapters: 3
❑ Privileges: LIBRARY PLANTS TRIPS

Saxifrage Society
Adrian Young, Secretary
31 Edgington Road
London, England SW16 5BS

A new society for the alpine gardener with an interest in saxifrages.
❒ Annual Dues: in US & CAN £10, UK £5

Scottish Rock Garden Club
The Secretary, Dr. Jan Boyd
Groom's Cottage, Kirklands
Ancrum, Jedburgh, Scotland TD8 6UJ
(08353) 354
The Rock Garden (2)
Year Book

Has a very extensive seed exchange, and a good selection of books for sale to members.
❒ Annual Dues: in US & CAN US$20, OV £9 (IMO)
❒ Chapters: 16
❒ Privileges: CONVENTIONS LIBRARY BOOKS SEEDS PLANTS EXHIBITS TRIPS TOURS

The Sedum Society
Micki Crozier
10502 N. 135 W.
Sedgwick, KS 67135-9675
(316) 796-0496
Newsletter (4)

Seed and cutting exchanges. Write for information. Overseas members paying in sterling, send to Prof. Mavis Doyle, 12 Langdale Dr. Gateshead NE1 5RN, England.
❒ Annual Dues: in US & CAN US$17.50, OV £10 (IMO)
❒ Garden: Northumberland, England
❒ Privileges: SEEDS PLANTS

Seed Savers Exchange
Seed Savers Exchange
3076 North Winn Rd.
Decorah, IA 52101
(319) 382-5990
Winter Yearbook
Newsletter (2)

Sells the "Garden Seed Inventory" ($22) and the "Fruit, Berry and Nut Inventory" ($19); these are excellent source books for heirloom varieties.
❒ Annual Dues: in US $25, CAN US$30, OV US$40 (IMO)
❒ Garden: Heritage Farm, north of Decorah, IA
❒ Privileges: CONVENTIONS BOOKS SEEDS

The Sempervivum Society
The Secretary
11 Wingle Tye Road
Burgess Hill, W. Sussex, England RH15 9HR
(0444) 23-6848
Newsletter (3)

Sells a cultural guide, "Houseleeks -- An Introduction," for £1.
❒ Annual Dues: in US & OV, £2.50 (IMO)
❒ Garden: Burgess Hill, West Sussex, England
❒ Privileges: CONVENTIONS BOOKS

Sino-Himalayan Plant Association
Chris Chadwell
81 Parlaunt Rd.
Slough, Berks., England SL3 8BE
Newsletter

Write for information, send 1 IRC.
❒ Privileges: SEEDS

The Society for Growing Australian Plants
SGAP Membership Officer
P.O. Box 410
Padstow, NSW, Australia 2211
(61-2) 528-2683
Australian Plants (4)
Native Plants Newsletter (4)

Magazine available on separate subscription for A$27 a year (IMO).
❒ Annual Dues: in US, CAN & OV A$44 (IMO)
❒ Chapters: 23
❒ Privileges: LIBRARY BOOKS SEEDS PLANTS EXHIBITS TRIPS

The Society for Japanese Irises
Mrs. Andrew C. Warner
16815 Falls Road
Upperco, MD 21155
(410) 374-4788
The Review (2)

A section of the American Iris Society. Private gardens are open to members to display well-grown plants and newer varieties.
❒ Annual Dues: $3.50
❒ Privileges: CONVENTIONS BOOKS PLANTS EXHIBITS TRIPS TOURS

Society for Pacific Coast Native Iris
4333 Oak Hill Road
Oakland, CA 94605
(510) 638-0658
SPCNI Almanac (2)

A section of the American Iris Society.
❒ Annual Dues: $4
❒ Privileges: BOOKS SEEDS TRIPS

Society for Siberian Irises
Howard L. Brookins
N75 W14257 North Point Dr.
Menomonee Falls, WI 53051-4325
(414) 251-5292
The Siberian Iris (2)

A section of the American Iris Society. There is a list of private display gardens available from the membership secretary.
❒ Annual Dues: $5
❒ Privileges: CONVENTIONS BOOKS

South African Fuchsia Society
The Hon. Secretary
P.O.Box 537
Alberton 1450, South Africa
(011) 869-7697 RSA
The South African Fuchsia Fanfare (3)

❒ Annual Dues: R20 (IMO)
❒ Chapters: 5
❒ Garden: Johannesburg Botanical Gardens
❒ Privileges: CONVENTIONS LIBRARY PLANTS EXHIBITS

Southern California Botanists
Alan Romspert
Dept. of Biology, Fullerton State Univ.
Fullerton, CA 92634
(714) 449-7034
Crossosoma (2)
Leaflets (5-6)

Devoted to the study, preservation and conservation of native plants of California. Has an annual symposium and pot luck.
❒ Annual Dues: in US $8, OV US$15 (IMO)
❒ Privileges: CONVENTIONS BOOKS PLANTS TRIPS

Southern California Horticultural Society
Joan DeFato
P.O. Box 41080
Los Angeles, CA 90041-0080
(818) 567-1496
Pacific Horticulture (4)
Monthly Bulletin

This is a regional horticultural group.
❒ Annual Dues: $20
❒ Privileges: BOOKS PLANTS TRIPS

Southern Fruit Fellowship
David E. Ulmer
P.O. Box 14606
Santa Rosa, CA 95402-6606
(707) 778-2362
Southern Fruit Fellowship (4)

US members only.
❒ Annual Dues: $5
❒ Privileges: CONVENTIONS

Southern Garden History Society
Mrs. Zachary T. Bynum, Jr.
Old Salem, Inc., Drawer F, Salem Station
Winston-Salem, NC 27108
(919) 724-3125
Magnolia (4)

Their library is located in the Atlanta History Center, Atlanta, GA.
❒ Annual Dues: $20
❒ Privileges: CONVENTIONS LIBRARY PLANTS

Species Iris Group of North America
Florence Stout
150 No. Main
Lombard, IL 60148
SIGNA (2)

A section of the American Iris Society. Has an excellent seed exchange and periodical.
❒ Annual Dues: $4
❒ Privileges: SEEDS

Spuria Iris Society
Floyd W. Wickenkamp
10521 Bellarose Drive
Sun City, AZ 85351-2241
(602) 977-2354
Spuria Newsletter (2)

A section of the American Iris Society; they publish "The Spuria Irises, Introduction and Varietal Listing" every 5 years.
❒ Annual Dues: $5
❒ Privileges: CONVENTIONS BOOKS

Tennessee Native Plant Society
Dept. of Botany
Univ. of Tennessee
Knoxville, TN 37996-1100
(615) 691-0077
Newsletter (6)

❒ Annual Dues: $15
❒ Privileges: CONVENTIONS EXHIBITS TRIPS TOURS

The Terrarium Association
Robert C. Baur
P.O. Box 276
Newfane, VT 05345
(802) 365-4721
Publications brochure

Not really a society, but a source of information and literature on growing plants in terrariums.

The Toronto Bonsai Society
Eva Rae Davidson
190 McAllister Rd.
Downsview, ON, Canada M3H 2N9
(416) 590-9969
Journal (10)

❒ Annual Dues: C$20
❒ Privileges: LIBRARY

The Toronto Cactus & Succulent Club
David Naylor
9091 Eighth Line Rd., RR 2
Georgetown, ON, Canada L7G 4S5
(416) 877-6013
Cactus Factus (8)

This is a regional group.
❏ Annual Dues: C$20
❏ Privileges: CONVENTIONS LIBRARY SEEDS PLANTS EXHIBITS TRIPS

Toronto Gesneriad Society
Monte Watler
240 Burnhamthorpe Rd.
Etabicoke, ON, Canada M9B I25

Write for information.
❏ Annual Dues: C$15

Tropical Flowering Tree Society
Dolores Fugina
Fairchild Trop. Garden, 10901 Old Cutler Road
Miami, FL 33156
(305) 248-0818
Quarterly Bulletin

❏ Annual Dues: in US $15, OV US$20
❏ Privileges: CONVENTIONS PLANTS EXHIBITS TRIPS

Utah Native Plant Society
P.O. Box 520041
Salt Lake City, UT 84152-0041
Sego Lily (6)

Has an annual mushroom hunt.
❏ Annual Dues: $10
❏ Chapters: 2
❏ Privileges: TRIPS

Victoria Orchid Society
Ingrid Ostrander
P.O. Box 6538 Depot 1
Victoria, BC, Canada V8P 5M4
(604) 652-6133
Bulletin (12)

❏ Annual Dues: C$15
❏ Privileges: CONVENTIONS LIBRARY BOOKS PLANTS EXHIBITS TRIPS

Virginia Native Plant Society
Nicky Staunton
P.O. Box 844
Annandale, VA 22003
Bulletin (4)

Has a good book and gift sales list for members. Offers a list of sources free with a long SASE.
❏ Annual Dues: $15
❏ Chapters: 9
❏ Privileges: CONVENTIONS BOOKS PLANTS TRIPS

Washington Native Plant Society
Shirley Post, WNPS
P.O. Box 576
Woodinville, WA 98072-0576
(206) 485-2193
Douglasia (4)
Occasional Papers

Has annual backpack trips and study weekends.
❏ Annual Dues: $12
❏ Chapters: 11
❏ Privileges: TRIPS

West Virginia Native Plant Society
Corresponding Secretary
P.O. Box 2755
Elkins, WV 26241
Native Notes

❏ Annual Dues: $8
❏ Privileges: CONVENTIONS TRIPS

Western Horticultural Society
Treasurer
P.O. Box 60507
Palo Alto, CA 94306
Pacific Horticulture (4)
Newsletter (10)

Has plant raffles at every meeting. This is a regional organization.
❏ Annual Dues: $25
❏ Privileges: SEEDS PLANTS EXHIBITS TRIPS

Worcester County Horticultural Society
Worcester Co. Hort. Society
Tower Hill Botanic Garden, 11 French Drive
Boylston, MA 01505-1008
(508) 869-6111
Grow with Us (6)

Regional group maintains a display garden and sponsors the Worcester Spring Flower Show annually.
❏ Annual Dues: $25
❏ Garden: Tower Hill Botanic Garden, Boylston, MA
❏ Privileges: CONVENTIONS LIBRARY PLANTS EXHIBITS TRIPS TOURS

World Federation of Rose Societies
Mrs. Jill Bennell
46 Alexandra Road, St. Albans
Hertfordshire, England AL1 3AZ
(0727) 833-648
World Rose News (2)

This is an umbrella group for national societies worldwide.
❏ Annual Dues: £25 (IMO)
❏ Chapters: 27 countries
❏ Privileges: CONVENTIONS

World Pumpkin Confederation
Ray Waterman
14050 Rt. 62
Collins, NY 14034
(716) 532-5995
Cucurbita (4-6)

Promotes the sport/hobby of growing giant pumpkins on a worldwide level.
❐ Annual Dues: in US $l5, CAN US$20, OV US$25 (IMO)
❐ Chapters: 22
❐ Garden: Giant Pumpkin Gardens at Collins, NY
❐ Privileges: CONVENTIONS SEEDS PLANTS EXHIBITS TRIPS

Wyoming Native Plant Society
3165 University Station
Laramie, WY 82071
Newsletter (3)

Write for information. Annual meeting is usually a field trip.
❐ Privileges: CONVENTIONS TRIPS

Xerces Society
10 S.W. Ash St.
Portland, OR 97204
Wings (2-3)

A society dedicated to the preservation of butterflies and their habitats.
Co-authored "Butterfly Gardening, Creating Summer Magic in Your Garden."
List of books available from society office.
❐ Privileges: CONVENTIONS

Gardening On-Line

One of the ways that gardeners are getting together to chat and exchange information is by sitting at their computers and sending messages all over the world to like-minded people. With a good communications program, you can go on-line, send and receive messages, and be off again within a minute or two. You read your mail and write your replies off-line, then go on again for a minute or two to send them. Unless you're a chatterbox, the costs are fairly modest and it's a lot of fun.

The following on-line services have Garden Forums, as well as the ability to send E-Mail to members of other on-line services through Internet. Because fees are constantly changing, call the following services and ask about services, fees, local telephone access, and the necessary computer modem and software to use their services.

America Online	(800) 827-6364
CompuServe	(800) 848-8199
Delphi	(800) 695-4005
GEnie	(800) 638-9636
Prodigy	(800) 776-0836
The Well	(415) 332-4335

You can send me CompuServe Mail at 72330,1665, or E-Mail through Internet at 72330.1665@compuserve.com.

I'd love to hear from you, but I usually pick up my E-Mail only on weekends, so if you expect a reply you won' t receive one right away. Please see the note in the introduction about requesting additional information from Tusker Press; I'm not able to look up specific sources for you.

Magazines

Horticultural magazines and newsletters published in English and available by subscription from all over the world are listed alphabetically by title.

See the Index section for:

M. Magazine Index: an index to horticultural and gardening magazines and newsletters available by subscription, as well as those issued by societies.

Since subscription rates are subject to change, I'd suggest that you write for information before sending payment for a subscription.

The true gardener pulls the gardening magazines out of the mail and flops right down to read them first. They have an alarming way of multiplying—they must have invasive root systems. At any rate, they are very difficult to weed!

Be sure to notice the two indices to gardening magazines listed in this section: *Gardener's Index* and *Garden Literature*. There is also a computerized index listed in Section B called Gardenfind. As soon as you find you can't throw out aging magazines, you'll have to have one of these, and you'll wonder how you ever got along without it.

A table of the symbols and abbreviations used in this book appears
on the bookmark inside the back cover.

© Cricket Hill Garden   Artist: Kasha K. Furman

Agricultural News
Kentucky Dept. of Agriculture
Div. of Comm., 7th Floor, 500 Mero St.
Frankfort, KY 40601

Market bulletin.
❐ Price: Free to KY residents
❐ Issues/Year: 4
❐ Region: Kentucky

Agricultural Report
Connecticut Dept. of Agriculture
Room 234, State Office Building
Hartford, CT 06106

❐ Price: in US $10
❐ Issues/Year: 50
❐ Region: Connecticut

Agricultural Review
North Carolina Dept. of Agriculture
P.O. Box 27647
Raleigh, NC 27611

Market bulletin.
❐ Price: Free to NC residents
❐ Issues/Year: 12
❐ Region: North Carolina

Alabama Farmers'and Consumers' Bulletin
Alabama Dept. of Agriculture & Industries
P.O. Box 3336
Montgomery, AL 36109-0336

Market bulletin.
❐ Price: Free to AL residents, $5 for nonresidents
❐ Issues/Year: 12
❐ Region: Alabama

Allen Lacy's homeground
Allen Lacy
Box 271
Linwood, NJ 08221

❐ Price: in US $38, OV US$50 (IMO)
❐ Issues/Year: 4
❐ Region: East of Mississippi River

The Amateur's Digest
   Cacti - Other Succulents - Caudex Plants
Marina Welham
8591 Lochside Drive
Sidney, BC, Canada V8L 1M5

A magazine written by its subscribers, those interested in cactus
and succulent plants.
❐ Price: in CAN C$17, US US$20, OV US$20 (IMO)
❐ Issues/Year: 6

Arnoldia
Harvard Univ., The Arnold Arboretum
125 Arborway
Jamaica Plain, MA 02130

A scholarly magazine, devoted to all aspects of plants.
❐ Price: in US $20, CAN & OV US$25 (IMO)
❐ Issues/Year: 4

Australian Garden Journal
Australian Garden Journal Pty., Ltd.
P.O. Box 588
Bowral, NSW, Australia 2576

A general-interest magazine on plants, garden design and garden history.
❐ Price: in US, CAN & OV A$36
❐ Issues/Year: 5

Australian Orchid Review
Graphic World Pty., Ltd.
14 McGill Street
Lewisham, NSW, Australia 2049

An attractive magazine for orchid enthusiasts. Subscription can be paid
with a US check.
❐ Price: in US US$34 surface, US$44 Air Mail
❐ Issues/Year: 6

The Avant Gardener
Horticultural Data Processors
P.O. Box 489
New York, NY 10028

Summarizes new information on all phases of gardening. Lists new sources
of garden materials, sometimes has special-interest issues.
❐ Price: in US $18, CAN & OV US$20 (IMO)
❐ Issues/Year: 12

Baer's Garden Newsletter
John Baer's Sons
P.O. Box 328
Lancaster, PA 17608

Folksy newsletter from the editors of Baer's Agricultural Almanac.
❐ Price: in US $4, CAN US$5
❐ Issues/Year: 4

Beautiful Gardens
CMK Publishing
P.O. Box 2971
Dublin, CA 94568

New general interest magazine focuses on the "joy of gardening."
❐ Price: in US $16.97, CAN US$21.97, OV inquire for rate
❐ Issues/Year: 6

Bonsai Today
Stone Lantern Publishing Company
P.O. Box 816
Sudbury, MA 01776

Well illustrated bonsai magazine.
❏ Price: in US $42, CAN US$48, OV US$52.50
❏ Issues/Year: 6

Botanical & Herb Reviews
Steven Foster
P.O. Box 106
Eureka Springs, AR 72632

Reviews of books, periodicals and software related to botany, ethnobotany, taxonomy and herbs.
❏ Price: in US & CAN US$10, OV US$15 (IMO)
❏ Issues/Year: 4

John E. Bryan Gardening Newsletter
John E. Bryan, Inc.
300 Valley Street, Suite 206
Sausalito, CA 94965

A gardening newsletter which focuses on northern California growing conditions, but contains a lot of general information and musings as well.
❏ Price: in US & CAN US$30, OV US$44
❏ Issues/Year: 12
❏ Region: Northern California

The Business of Herbs
Northwind Farm Publications
Route 2, Box 246
Shevlin, MN 56676

Newsletter for the small herb grower and seller, expanding into general articles of "more lasting significance" about herbs.
❏ Price: in US $20, CAN US$23, OV US$28 (IMO)
❏ Issues/Year: 6

Cactus & Succulent Journal
Allen Press
P.O. Box 35034
Des Moines, IA 50315-0301

Journal of the Cactus & Succulent Society available only by subscription.
❏ Price: in US $30, CAN & OV US$35 (IMO)
❏ Issues/Year: 6

California Garden
San Diego Floral Association
Casa del Prado, Balboa Park
San Diego, CA 92101-1619

For gardeners in Mediterranean climates, particularly southern California; information on garden events in the San Diego area.
❏ Price: in US $7, CAN & OV US$13
❏ Issues/Year: 6
❏ Region: Southern California

Canadian Gardening
Camar Publications, Ltd.
130 Spy Court
Markham, ON, Canada L3R 5H6

A general interest magazine that covers all aspects of gardening.
❏ Price: in CAN C$22.95, US US$32.95, OV C$32.95(IMO or CC)
❏ Issues/Year: 7
❏ Region: Canada

Canadian Horticultural History
Royal Botanical Gardens (CHHS)
P.O. Box 399
Hamilton, ON, Canada L8N 3H8

Journal features Canadian gardens, historical restorations, plant collectors, early nurseries, etc. Subscription is for 4 issues, publication temporarily suspended in 1993.
❏ Price: in CAN C$20, US $22, OV US$22
❏ Issues/Year: Irregular

Carolina Gardener
Carolina Gardener, Inc.
P.O. Box 4504
Greensboro, NC 27404

Regional gardening suggestions and information on garden events.
❏ Price: $14.95
❏ Issues/Year: 6
❏ Region: North and South Carolina

Chestnutworks
Chestnut Growers Exchange
Route 1, Box 341
Alachua, FL 32615

Periodical devoted wholly to the chestnut: culture, propagation, research, history, recipes and sources of these magnificent trees.
❏ Price: in US $10, CAN US$15, OV US$20 (IMO)
❏ Issues/Year: 2

Chile Pepper
Robert Spiegel
P.O. Box 70870
Albuquerque, NM 87198

Magazine devoted to spicy foods and to growing and cooking with peppers.
❏ Price: in US $18.95, CAN & OV $24.95 (IMO)
❏ Issues/Year: 6

Chrysanthemum Corner with Peony Highlights
P.O. Box 5635
Dearborn, MI 48128

❏ Price: in US $3, OV US$4
❏ Issues/Year: 6

Convivium
David Wheeler
The Neuadd
Rhayader, Powys, Wales LD6 5HH

This is a new journal for people interested in the growing of fruits and vegetables, and in the appreciation of good food and wine, from the publisher of Hortus. Payment can be made by charge card.
❏ Price: in US $60, CAN $70, UK £30
❏ Issues/Year: 4

Country Journal
Cowles Magazines
P.O. Box 392
Mt. Morris, IL 61054

Generally a magazine on country living, but it has many articles on gardening and fruit growing. For "the person who lives in the country or wishes that they did."
❏ Price: in US $18.95, CAN US$26.70, OV US$24.95
❏ Issues/Year: 6

The Cultivar
UCSC Agroecology Program
Univ. of California
Santa Cruz, CA 95064

Newsletter for researchers, farmers and gardeners interested in agro-ecological approaches to farming and gardening.
❐ Price: Free, donations appreciated
❐ Issues/Year: 2

Desert Plants
Boyce Thompson Southwestern Arboretum
P.O. Box AB
Superior, AZ 85273

Devoted to cultivated and wild desert plants; quite scholarly.
❐ Price: in US & CAN US$15, OV US$20
❐ Issues/Year: 4
❐ Region: Southwest

Bev Dobson's Rose Letter
Beverly R. Dobson
215 Harriman Road
Irvington, NY 10533

Newsletter for the enthusiastic rose lover, full of rose news. Updates her annual "Combined Rose List" (see Books section).
❐ Price: in US & CAN US$12, OV US$15
❐ Issues/Year: 6

Fine Gardening
The Taunton Press
P.O. Box 5506
Newtown, CT 06470-5506

One of the best general-interest gardening magazines.
❐ Price: in US $26, CAN & OV US$32
❐ Issues/Year: 6

Fleurs, Plantes, et Jardins
Editions Versicolores
25, boulevard Taschereau, bureau 201
Greenfield Park, PQ, Canada J4V 2G8

An attractive magazine for the French-speaking hobby gardener.
❐ Price: in CAN C$28.95, OV C$47.95 (IMO)
❐ Issues/Year: 8

The Flora-Line
Berry Hill Press
7336 Berry Hill
Palos Verdes, CA 90274-4404

A newsletter for those in the dried floral trade.
❐ Price: in US $16.95, CAN US$20, OV US$29 (IMO)
❐ Issues/Year: 4

Flower & Garden
KC Publishing
P.O. Box 11230
Des Moines, IA 50340

A general-interest gardening magazine, with articles on all phases of home gardening, regional reports and reports on new cultivars and products.
❐ Price: in US $12.95, CAN $20.28, OV US$18.95
❐ Issues/Year: 6

The Four Seasons
East Bay Regional Park District
Tilden Regional Park, Botanic Garden
Berkeley, CA 94708-2396

Magazine covering all aspects of California native plants, both technical and semipopular articles. For experienced enthusiasts and botanists.
❐ Price: $12
❐ Issues/Year: 1
❐ Region: California

Garden Design
Evergreen Publishing Co.
4401 Connecticut Ave. N.W., Ste. 500
Washington, DC 20008-2302

The only periodical I'm aware of that concentrates on residential garden design -- domestic, international and historical.
❐ Price: in US & CAN US$28, OV US$42
❐ Issues/Year: 5

Garden Literature
Garden Literature Press
398 Columbus Ave., Suite 181
Boston, MA 02116

An index to periodical articles and book reviews about a wide range of topics -- including garden history, horticulture, plants, landscape design and maintenance. This index covers 150 periodicals.
❐ Price: $50, OV add $20 postage
❐ Issues/Year: 4

Garden Railways
Sidestreet Bannerworks
P.O. Box 61461
Denver, CO 80206

Overseas customers may receive their issues via air mail for US$55. Magazine for gardening railroaders -- or railroading gardeners! Emphasis is on railroading, but it's delightful.
❐ Price: in US $21, CAN & OV US$28 (IMO)
❐ Issues/Year: 6

The Gardener's Gazette
Michael Henry
P.O. Box 786
Georgetown, CT 06829

A regional newspaper that covers horticultural and environmental topics, with articles on nature and landscaping.
❐ Price: $15
❐ Issues/Year: 10
❐ Region: New England

Gardener's Index
CompuDex Press
P. O. Box 27041
Kansas City, MO 64110-7041

A combined annual index to "American Horticulturist," "Fine Gardening," "Flower & Garden," "Horticulture," "National Gardening" and "Organic Gardening" -- very thorough and useful. Cumulative issue covering 1986-1990 is available for $18.
❐ Price: $18
❐ Issues/Year: 1

Gardening Newsletter by Bob Flagg
Morningside Associates
5002 Morningside
Houston, TX 77005

A general gardening newsletter oriented to the Sun Belt and Gulf Coast South.
❒ Price: $15.95
❒ Issues/Year: 12
❒ Region: Gulf Coast & Sun Belt South

Gardens Illustrated
John Brown Publishing Ltd.
FREEPOST SW6096
Frome, Somerset, England BA11 1YA

A new, lavishly illustrated magazine for keen gardeners. Credit cards
may be used for payment.
❒ Price: in US $50 or £30, UK £17.70 (IMO)
❒ Issues/Year: 6

Gardens West
Dorothy Horton
Box 2680
Vancouver, BC, Canada V6B 3W8

An attractive magazine with articles on plants and gardening.
Includes a regional calendar of events.
❒ Price: in CAN C$20, US US$25, OV C$28 (IMO or CC)
❒ Issues/Year: 9
❒ Region: Western Canada

G.A.R.L.I.C.
  Growing Alliums & Related Liliaceae in Cult.
Mark McDonough
30 Mt. Lebanon Street
Pepperell, MA 01463

An interesting newsletter on growing ornamental alliums.
❒ Price: in US $20, OV $23
❒ Issues/Year: 4

Green Prints
Pat Stone
P.O. Box 1355
Fairview, NC 28730

A great favorite of mine, it is not a how-to magazine, but charming pieces
short and long about how gardeners feel. Usually funny, sometimes sad,
it's a great shot in the arm each time it comes.
❒ Price: in US $14, CAN US$17, OV US$23
❒ Issues/Year: 4

The Growing Edge Magazine
Tom Alexander
P.O. Box 1027
Corvallis, OR 97339

"Indoor and outdoor gardening for today's high tech grower." This magazine
is concerned primarily with hydroponic and greenhouse growing.
❒ Price: in US $17.95, CAN US$24.95, OV US$45 (IMO)
❒ Issues/Year: 4

Growing for Market
Fairplain Publications, Lynn Byczynski
P.O. Box 365
Auburn, KS 66402

News and ideas for market gardeners.
❒ Price: in US $24, CAN $30, OV US$36 (IMO)
❒ Issues/Year: 12

Growing Native
Growing Native Research Institute
P.O. Box 489
Berkeley, CA 94701

A newsletter of great interest in California & the West; each issue features
a particular type of plant, and articles are frequently written by experts in
Western native plants.
❒ Price: $30
❒ Issues/Year: 6
❒ Region: Western States

Hardy Enough
Hardy Enough Publishing Co.
351 Pleasant Street, Suite 259
Northampton, MA 01060

A newsletter for adventurous gardeners who are trying to grow subtropical
plants north of their usual hardiness range.
❒ Price: in US US$27, OV US$35 (IMO)
❒ Issues/Year: 6
❒ Region: USDA Zones 4 to 8

Harrowsmith: Canada's Magazine of
  Country Living
INDAF, Ltd.
35 Riviera Dr., Unit 17
Markham, ON, Canada L3R 8N4

Originated in Canada, Harrowsmith covers all phases of country living in the
North.
❒ Price: in CAN C$21.38, US C$25, OV C$29 (IMO)
❒ Issues/Year: 6
❒ Region: Canada

Harrowsmith Country Life
Camden House Publishing
Ferry Road
Charlotte, VT 05445

Magazine on all phases of country living; quite a lot of articles on garden-
ing, particularly growing vegetables and fruit. Northeastern emphasis.
❒ Price: in US $18, CAN $24, OV US$30 (IMO)
❒ Issues/Year: 6
❒ Region: US

The Herb Companion
Interweave Press, Inc.
201 E. Fourth St.
Loveland, CO 80537

Very attractive magazine on herbs: growing, history, cooking and crafts.
❒ Price: in US $21, CAN & OV US$26 (IMO)
❒ Issues/Year: 6

The Herb Quarterly
Long Mountain Press, Inc.
P.O. Box 689
San Anselmo, CA 94960

Fine publication devoted to herbs: their culture, history, use and recipes.
❒ Price: in US $24, CAN US$29, OV US$31 (IMO)
❒ Issues/Year: 4

The Herb, Spice and Medicinal Plant Digest
Univ. of Massachusetts Coop. Ext.
Lyle Craker, Dept. of Plant & Soil Sci.
U. of Mass., Amherst, MA 01003

Quarterly for herb growers and those interested in uses of herbs; issues have surveys of recent literature, some technical material -- not for beginners.
❐ Price: in US $10, CAN $15, OV US$17 (IMO)
❐ Issues/Year: 4

Herban Lifestyles
Stone Acre Press
84 Carpenter Road
New Hartford, CT 06057-3003

Newsletter on "herban renewal," or ways to incorporate herbs into your lifestyle.
❐ Price: in US $18, CAN US$22, OV US$33 (IMO)
❐ Issues/Year: 4

High Value Crop Newsletter
Sweet Enterprises
7488 Comet View Court
San Diego, CA 92120-2004

A newsletter for small family farmers and market gardeners in temperate and subtropical regions.
❐ Price: $60
❐ Issues/Year: 12

The Historical Gardener
Kathleen McClelland
1910 North 35th Place
Mt. Vernon, WA 98273-8981

This is a newsletter for museum gardeners, seed savers, landscape designers and backyard gardeners.
❐ Price: in US $12, CAN US$14, OV US$20
❐ Issues/Year: 4
❐ Region: North America

Horticulture
Robert M. Cohn
P.O. Box 51455
Boulder, CO 80323-1455

A fine general-interest magazine devoted to all aspects of gardening and horticulture.
❐ Price: in US $24, CAN & OV US$30 (IMO)
❐ Issues/Year: 10

HortIdeas
Greg & Pat Williams
460 Black Lick Rd.
Gravel Switch, KY 40328

A gardeners' "digest": the latest horticultural research, new sources of plants and supplies, book reviews. Among the best of current reading for all gardeners.
❐ Price: in US $15, CAN US$17.50, OV US$20 (IMO)
❐ Issues/Year: 12

Hortus
David Wheeler
The Neuadd
Rhayader, Powys, Wales LD6 5HH

Quarterly devoted to writings by distinguished British gardeners, with a sprinkling of foreign writers; enough reading for several evenings.
❐ Price: in US & CAN £35 (IMO, CC or PC)
❐ Issues/Year: 4

The Hosta Digest
Jay C. Gilbert
81 Meredith Road
Tewksbury, MA 01876-1333

❐ Price: in US $20, OV US$35 (IMO)
❐ Issues/Year: 4

HousePlant Magazine
HousePlant, Inc., Bonnie Branciaroli
P.O. Box 1638
Elkins, WV 26241

Informative magazine about houseplants, replaced Houseplant Forum.
❐ Price: in US $19.95, CAN $22.95, OV US$24.95 (IMO)
❐ Issues/Year: 4

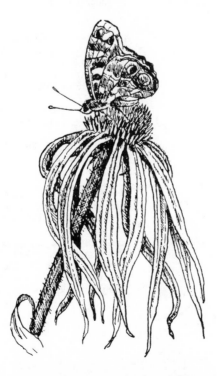

© Holland Wildflower Farm
Artist: Carol Tillery

In Good Tilth
Oregon Tilth
P.O. Box 218
Tualatin, OR 97062

A newspaper for "farmers, gardeners, and consumers working for a sustainable agriculture."
❐ Price: in US $15, OV US$25 (IMO)
❐ Issues/Year: 12
❐ Region: Pacific Northwest

International Bonsai
International Bonsai Arboretum
P.O. Box 23894
Rochester, NY 14692-3894

Quarterly for the serious bonsai enthusiast. Add US$10 to the subscription price for overseas air mail. They also sell video tapes and have a bonsai arboretum; call (716) 334-2595 to arrange a visit.
❐ Price: in US & CAN US$24, OV US$32 (IMO)
❐ Issues/Year: 4

The Island Grower
Greenheart Publications
RR 4
Sooke, BC, Canada V0S 1N0

Canada's oldest gardening magazine; for all types of gardeners. Written by many of the garden experts of British Columbia.
❐ Price: in CAN C$19.26, US $35, OV C$35 (IMO)
❐ Issues/Year: 10
❐ Region: Pacific Northwest

Journal of Garden History
Taylor & Francis, Inc.
1900 Frost Road, Suite 101
Bristol, PA 19007

An international journal with a multi-disciplinary approach to garden history.
❐ Price: in US $70, UK £38, OV US$70
❐ Issues/Year: 4

Lindleyana
American Orchid Society
6000 S. Olive Avenue
West Palm Beach, FL 33405

The scientific journal of the American Orchid Society.
❐ Price: in US $24, CAN & OV US$26 (IMO)
❐ Issues/Year: 4

Living Off the Land, Subtropic Newsletter
Geraventure
P.O. Box 2131
Melbourne, FL 32902-2131

A newsletter oriented toward growing edibles, particularly tropical fruits and crops; list of seeds "wanted" and "available" in each issue.
❐ Price: in US & CAN US$14, OV US$15
❐ Issues/Year: 5

The Maine Organic Farmer & Gardener
Maine Organic Farmers & Gardeners Association
P.O. Box 2176
Augusta, ME 04338

Tabloid periodical for organic gardeners and market farmers, lists gardens to visit, has a calendar of events.
❐ Price: in US $12, CAN US$18, OV US$20
❐ Issues/Year: 6
❐ Region: New England

The Market Bulletin
West Virginia Dept. of Agriculture
1900 Kanawha Blvd. E.
Charleston, WV 25305

❐ Price: Free to WV residents, $5 to subscribers
❐ Issues/Year: 12
❐ Region: West Virginia

Mushroom Growers Newsletter
The Mushroom Company
P.O. Box 5065
Klamath Falls, OR 97601-0017

A newsletter for small scale commercial and specialty mushroom growers.
❐ Price: in US $12, CAN & OV US$30 (IMO)
❐ Issues/Year: 12

Native Notes
Joseph L. Collins
Rt. 2, Box 550
Heiskell, TN 37754

A newsletter devoted to landscaping with native plants of the eastern US. Includes book reviews and a calendar of events.
❐ Price: $15
❐ Issues/Year: 4
❐ Region: Eastern US

**New England Farm Bulletin
 & Garden Gazette**
Jacob's Meadow, Inc.
P.O. Box 67
Taunton, MA 02780

For small farmers and market gardeners; questions and answers, ads for the sale and exchange of farming equipment, animals and plants, calendar of events.
❐ Price: in US $17, CAN & OV US$20
❐ Issues/Year: 24
❐ Region: New England

Northland Berry News
Berry Communications
2124 University Ave. W.
St. Paul, MN 55114-1838

Of interest to all who grow more than a few raspberries, strawberries or blueberries, especially "pick-your-own" operations and market gardeners.
❐ Price: in US $15, CAN $18, OV US$25 (IMO)
❐ Issues/Year: 4

Orchid Digest
Orchid Digest Corp.
P.O. Box 916
Carmichael, CA 95609-0916

A quarterly magazine for orchid enthusiasts; many color photographs.
❐ Price: in US $18, CAN C$18, OV US$18
❐ Issues/Year: 4
❐ Region: worldwide

The Orchid Hunter
Terry Ferraro, Editor
R.R. #1, Box 62-A, Pitts Rd.
Adamsville, PA 16110-8706

Newsletter for orchid hobbyists and professionals.
❒ Price: in US $17, CAN $22, OV US$25 (CC)
❒ Issues/Year: 12

The Orchid Review
The Royal Horticultural Society
80 Vincent Square
London, England SW1P 2PE

The orchid journal of the Royal Horticulture Society; international in scope.
❒ Price: £19.95 (IMO or CC)
❒ Issues/Year: 6

Organic Gardening
Rodale Press, Inc.
33 East Minor Street
Emmaus, PA 18098

The "old standby" was upsized, updated and upscaled; but the homey touch has crept back in.
❒ Price: in US $25, CAN C$32.10, OV US$37
❒ Issues/Year: 9

Pacific Horticulture
Pacific Horticultural Foundation
P.O. Box 485
Berkeley, CA 94701

Published by a consortium of Pacific Coast horticultural societies; a very interesting and beautiful magazine with worldwide readership.
❒ Price: in US $15, CAN US$18, OV US$20
❒ Issues/Year: 4

Phalaenopsis Fancier
Doreen Vander Tuin
1230 Plum Avenue
Simi Valley, CA 93065-4640

A newsletter/round-robin for fanciers of phalaenopsis orchids.
❒ Price: in US & CAN US$15, OV US$20 (IMO)
❒ Issues/Year: 12

Plants & Gardens
  Plants & Gardens News
Brooklyn Botanic Garden
1000 Washington Avenue, Membership Dept.
Brooklyn, NY 11225-1099

Each very informative issue covers one subject in depth: herbs, rock gardens, propagation, shade gardening or other garden subjects. Very good value!
❒ Price: $25
❒ Issues/Year: 4 + 4

The Plantsman
Maxwell Publishing
RHS, 80 Vincent Square
London, England SW1P 2PE

Fairly scholarly coverage of all types of plants in garden use. Scope is international.
❒ Price: in US & OV £19.50, UK £18 (IMO)
❒ Issues/Year: 4

Potpourri from Herbal Acres
Pinerow Publications
P.O. Box 428
Washington Crossing, PA 18977

An herb newsletter from Phyllis Shaudys, author of "The Pleasure of Herbs." It covers all aspects of the herbal life.
❒ Price: in US $20, CAN US$25
❒ Issues/Year: 4

Rocky Mountain Gardener
Susan Martineau
P.O. Box 1230
Gunnison, CO 81230

An attractive magazine that addresses the specific needs of Rocky Mountain gardeners.
❒ Price: $12
❒ Issues/Year: 4
❒ Region: Rocky Mountain States

Seed Exchange Monthly
Peter Collier
56 Red Willow
Harlow, Essex, England CM19 5PD

A new magazine for serious gardeners wanting to share and swap seeds.
❒ Price: Send 2 IRC for information
❒ Issues/Year: 12

Seedling
Univ. of R.I. Cooperative Extension
C.E. Education Center
Kingston, RI 02881

An effort to bring American and Russian gardeners together. They publish a list of Russian pen pals and their gardening interests.
❒ Price: $6.95
❒ Issues/Year: 4
❒ Region: US & Russia

Small Farm News
Small Farm Center
University of California
Davis, CA 95616

❒ Price: $15
❒ Issues/Year: 6
❒ Region: California

Small Farm Today
Ron Macher
3903 W. Ridge Trail Rd.
Clark, MO 65243

A magazine for small farmers and market gardeners.
❒ Price: in US $18, CAN $28, OV $50 (IMO)
❒ Issues/Year: 6

Southern Living
John Alex Floyd, Jr.
P.O. Box 830219
Birmingham, AL 35283

Magazine has frequent articles on gardening in the South.
❒ Price: in US $24.95, CAN & OV US$26.95 (IMO or CC)
❒ Issues/Year: 12
❒ Region: Southeast, TX, OK, MO, DC

Neil Sperry's Gardens
Gardens South
P.O. Box 864
McKinney, TX 75070-0864

An attractive and well-illustrated magazine with articles on all aspects of gardening in Texas.
❏ Price: $21.50
❏ Issues/Year: 10
❏ Region: Texas, Gulf Coast

Sundew Garden Reports
Tom Carey
P.O. Box 214
Oviedo, FL 32765

A newsletter for gardeners in hot weather climates.
❏ Price: in US $15, CAN C$25, OV US$25
❏ Issues/Year: 6
❏ Region: Florida, Southeast US

Sunset Magazine
Sunset Publishing Co.
80 Willow Road
Menlo Park, CA 94025-3691

Familiar to all in the 13 Western states; there are four regional editions, and each issue carries gardening features customized by region.
❏ Price: in US$21, CAN US$33, OV US$41
❏ Issues/Year: 12
❏ Region: Western states

Temperate Bamboo Quarterly
Earth Advocates Research Facility
TBQ, 30 Myers Rd.
Summertown, TN 38483-9768

A newsletter for beginning and experienced growers of bamboo.
❏ Price: in US $24, CAN $32, OV US$36
❏ Issues/Year: 4

Texas Gardener
Chris S. Corby
P.O. Box 9005
Waco, TX 76714-9005

"The magazine for Texas gardeners, by Texas gardeners."
❏ Price: $15
❏ Issues/Year: 6
❏ Region: Texas

TLC ... for plants
Gardenvale Publishing Company, Ltd.
1 Pacifique
Ste Anne de Bellevue, PQ, Canada H9X 1C5

Very nice Canadian garden magazine; includes articles on both indoor and outdoor gardening and plants.
❏ Price: in CAN C$14.93, US $16.95
❏ Issues/Year: 4
❏ Region: Canada & northern US

The Tomato Club
Robert D. Ambrose
114 E. Main St.
Bogota, NJ 07603

A newsletter for "the tomato crowd."
❏ Price: in US $21.95, OV US$28 (IMO)
❏ Issues/Year: 12

The Twenty-First Century Gardener
Growers Press, Inc.
P.O. Box 189
Princeton, BC, Canada V0X 1W0

For greenhouse and hydroponic growers. Foreign subscribers may receive their issues via air mail for US$10 extra. Back issues available.
❏ Price: in CAN C$26, US $24, OV US$24 (IMO or CC)
❏ Issues/Year: 6

Urban Forests
American Forests
P.O. Box 2000
Washington, DC 20013-2000

For those concerned with public tree-planting policy as well as with city beautification and appropriate use of trees.
❏ Price: in US free, CAN & OV US$18 (IMO)
❏ Issues/Year: 6

Weekly Market Bulletin
New Hampshire Dept. of Agriculture
P.O. Box 2042
Concord, NH 03302-2042

Market bulletin.
❏ Price: in US & CAN US$15
❏ Issues/Year: 52
❏ Region: New Hampshire

Libraries

Libraries with special horticultural collections are listed by state or province and then alphabetically by city.

Many public libraries have good collections of books on plants and gardening and will try to borrow books they don't have through interlibrary loan. Some cities, such as Philadelphia (the Library Company of Philadelphia) and San Francisco (the Mechanics Institute), have membership libraries with good horticultural collections. Some colleges and universities will allow alumni and local residents to use their libraries for an annual fee, or you can sign up for a horticultural course and get library privileges for a semester.

Many of the libraries listed, particularly those at botanical gardens, are supported by very active membership groups, horticultural societies or "friends" groups. It is well worth joining such a group to have the use of a good library, to say nothing of all the other interesting activities these groups offer.

Library Abbreviations and Conventions

Available library services are indicated as follows:

MEMBERS ONLY—only members may borrow books

REFERENCE ONLY—books do not circulate

INTERLIBRARY LOANS—other libraries may borrow books

LOANS TO PUBLIC—public may borrow books, subject to library rules

A table of the symbols and abbreviations used in this book appears
on the bookmark inside the back cover.

ALABAMA

Horace Hammond Memorial Library
Birmingham Botanical Gardens
2612 Lane Park Road
Birmingham, AL 35223
(205) 879-1227
Ida Burns

❒ Open: M-F 9-4
❒ Number of Books: 3,500
❒ Periodical Titles: 125
❒ Services: INTERLIBRARY LOANS LOANS TO PUBLIC

ALASKA

Library
University of Alaska Museum Herbarium
907 Yukon Drive
Fairbanks, AL 99775-1200
(907) 474-7108

Call or write for information.
❒ Open: M-F 8-5, by appointment
❒ Services: REFERENCE ONLY

ARIZONA

Richter Memorial Library
Desert Botanical Garden
1201 N. Galvin Parkway
Phoenix, AZ 85008
(602) 941-1225
Jane B. Cole

Public may use books in the library with an admission fee. Particularly strong collection on desert plants; also has a collection of garden catalogs.
❒ Open: M-F
❒ Number of Books: 10,000
❒ Periodical Titles: 65
❒ Services: REFERENCE ONLY

Boyce Thompson Southwestern Arboretum Library
Boyce Thompson Southwestern Arboretum
37615 US Highway 60
Superior, AZ 85273
(602) 689-2723
Shisashi Kokusun

Members and researchers may make an appointment to use the library; call or write for information.
❒ Open: Call for hours
❒ Number of Books: 3,000
❒ Periodical Titles: 40
❒ Services: REFERENCE ONLY

BRITISH COLUMBIA, CANADA

Library
University of British Columbia Botanical Gdn.
6804 S.W. Marine Drive
Vancouver, BC, Canada V6T 1Z4
(604) 822-3928
Judy Newton

Public may use books in the library. Call for appointment.
❒ Open: M-F 8:30-4:30
❒ Number of Books: 1,700
❒ Periodical Titles: 200
❒ Services: REFERENCE ONLY

VanDusen Gardens Library
Vancouver Botanical Gardens Association
5251 Oak Street
Vancouver, BC, Canada V6M 4H1
(604) 266-7194
Barbara Fox

Tu-F 10am-3pm, W 7pm-9pm, Su 1pm-4pm. Best to call for information, as times may vary in future.
❒ Open: See notes
❒ Number of Books: 3,800
❒ Periodical Titles: 50
❒ Services: MEMBERS ONLY

CALIFORNIA

Plant Science Library
Los Angeles State & County Arboretum
301 N. Baldwin Avenue
Arcadia, CA 91007-2697
(818) 821-3213
Joan DeFato

Public may use books in the library.
❒ Open: M-F 9-5
❒ Number of Books: 12,500
❒ Periodical Titles: 100
❒ Services: INTERLIBRARY LOANS

(continued next page)

CALIFORNIA (continued)

Rancho Santa Ana Botanic Garden Library
1500 N. College Avenue
Claremont, CA 91711
(909) 625-8767
Beatrice M. Beck

Library open to researchers only. Collection strong in publications on drought-tolerant plants and water-saving concepts.
❐ Open: M-F 8-5
❐ Number of Books: 25,000
❐ Periodical Titles: 1,000
❐ Services: REFERENCE ONLY

Quail Botanical Gardens Library
Quail Botanical Gardens Foundation
230 Quail Gardens Drive
Encinitas, CA 92024
Druscilla C. Luers

Library is open to members and to researchers by appointment.
❐ Open: W 11-3
❐ Number of Books: 1,536
❐ Periodical Titles: 7
❐ Services: MEMBERS ONLY

Fullerton Arboretum Library
Friends of the Fullerton Arboretum
1900 Associated Road
Fullerton, CA 92631
(714) 773-3579
Joyce Melbinger

Public may use books in the library. Located at the corner of Yorba Linda Boulevard and Associated Road.
❐ Open: Th 12-3
❐ Number of Books: 1,800
❐ Periodical Titles: 25
❐ Services: MEMBERS ONLY

South Coast Plant Science Library
South Coast Botanic Garden
26300 Crenshaw Boulevard
Palos Verdes Penin., CA 90274
(310) 544-1948

This library is for members only.
❐ Open: M-F 9-4
❐ Number of Books: 600
❐ Periodical Titles: 10
❐ Services: MEMBERS ONLY REFERENCE ONLY

Library & Information Center
San Diego Floral Association
Room 105, Casa del Prado, Balboa Park
San Diego, CA 92101-1619
(619) 232-5762

Public may use books in the library.
❐ Open: M-F 10-3
❐ Number of Books: 3,500
❐ Periodical Titles: 20
❐ Services: MEMBERS ONLY

Helen Crocker Russell Library of Horticulture
Strybing Arboretum Society
Ninth Avenue at Lincoln Way
San Francisco, CA 94122
(415) 661-1514
Barbara M. Pitschel

Public may use books in the library.
❐ Open: Daily 10-4
❐ Number of Books: 15,000
❐ Periodical Titles: 400
❐ Services: REFERENCE ONLY

Botanical Library
Huntington Botanical Gardens
1151 Oxford Road
San Marino, CA 91108
(818) 405-2160
Danielle Rudeen

For the use of "qualified researchers, by appointment only."
❐ Open: By appointment
❐ Number of Books: 8,000
❐ Periodical Titles: 150
❐ Services: REFERENCE ONLY

Santa Barbara Botanic Garden Library
Santa Barbara Botanic Garden
1212 Mission Canyon Road
Santa Barbara, CA 93105
(805) 682-4726
Rebecca J. Eldridge

Collection strong in California native plants. Public must make appointments in advance.
❐ Open: Tu-F 10-12, 1-4, by appt.
❐ Number of Books: 8,800
❐ Periodical Titles: 125
❐ Services: REFERENCE ONLY

Wallace Sterling Library
Filoli Center & Friends of Filoli
Canada Road
Woodside, CA 94062
(415) 364-8300
Thomas Rogers

Collection in landscape architecture and garden design; members or researchers may call or write for an appointment.
❐ Open: Tu-Sa, call for appt.
❐ Number of Books: 1,600
❐ Periodical Titles: 10
❐ Services: REFERENCE ONLY

COLORADO

Helen Fowler Library
Denver Botanic Gardens
1005 York Street
Denver, CO 80206-3799
(303) 370-8014
Solange G. Gignac

Public may use books in the library.
❐ Open: M-Su 9-5
❐ Number of Books: 21,000
❐ Periodical Titles: 570
❐ Services: MEMBERS ONLY INTERLIBRARY LOANS

CONNECTICUT

Library
Garden Education Center of Greenwich
Bible Street
Cos Cob, CT 06807
(203) 869-9242

The library is closed July and August.
❐ Open: M-F 9-3:30
❐ Services: LOANS TO PUBLIC

Bartlett Arboretum Library
Univ. of Connecticut at Stamford
151 Brookdale Road
Stamford, CT 06903-4199
(203) 322-6971
Gaye P. Mote

❐ Open: M-F 8:30-4
❐ Number of Books: 3,000
❐ Periodical Titles: 35
❐ Services: LOANS TO PUBLIC

DELAWARE

Delaware Center for Horticulture Library
Delaware Center for Horticulture
1810 N. DuPont St.
Wilmington, DE 19806-3308
(302) 658-1913

Public may use books in the library.
❐ Open: M-F 10-3
❐ Number of Books: 2,000 +
❐ Periodical Titles: 20
❐ Services: MEMBERS ONLY

DISTRICT OF COLUMBIA

Library
Society of American Foresters
5400 Grosvenor Lane
Washington, DC 20814
(301) 897-8720

Write for information.

Gerden Library
Dumbarton Oaks Garden
1703 - 32nd Street N.W.
Washington, DC 20007
(202) 342-3280
Linda Lott

Open to researchers by appointment. Call or write for information.
❐ Open: M-F 9-5, call for appt.
❐ Number of Books: 14,000
❐ Periodical Titles: 42
❐ Services: REFERENCE ONLY

US National Arboretum Library
USDA, Agricultural Research Service
3501 New York Avenue N.E.
Washington, DC 20002
(202) 475-4815
Susan Chapman or Wayne Olson

Public may use books in the library.
❐ Open: By appointment
❐ Number of Books: 7,500
❐ Periodical Titles: 200
❐ Services: MEMBERS ONLY INTERLIBRARY LOANS

Horticulture Branch Library
Smithsonian Institution
Arts & Industries Building, Room 2282
Washington, DC 20560
(202) 357-1544
Susan Gurney or Marca Woodhams

Library has 15,000 nursery and seed catalogs; focus is garden history and
design. Also an excellent Botany Library in the Natural History Museum.
Researchers may make an appointment to use the library.
❐ Open: M-F 10-5
❐ Number of Books: 5,000
❐ Periodical Titles: 300
❐ Services: MEMBERS ONLY INTERLIBRARY LOANS

FLORIDA

Library
Rare Fruit & Vegetable Council
3245 College Avenue
Davie, FL 33314
(305) 941-0668
Frank Moretti

Collection on the use of food-producing plants for permaculture.
❐ Open: Open before meetings
❐ Number of Books: 500
❐ Periodical Titles: 3
❐ Services: MEMBERS ONLY

Montgomery Library
Fairchild Tropical Garden
10901 Old Cutler Road
Miami, FL 33156

Members can borrow from the lending library portion of the collection.
❐ Open: By appointment
❐ Number of Books: 7,000
❐ Services: REFERENCE ONLY

(continued next page)

FLORIDA (continued)

Research Library
Marie Selby Botanical Gardens
811 S. Palm Avenue
Sarasota, FL 34236
(813) 955-7553
Janet Kuhn

Members may use the library for reference by appointment.
❐ Open: By appointment
❐ Number of Books: 5,000
❐ Services: REFERENCE ONLY

GEORGIA

Sheffield Botanical Library
Atlanta Botanical Garden
P.O. Box 77246
Atlanta, GA 30357
(404) 876-5859
Lu Ann Schwarz or Miriam Boland

Open Tu-Su 9-7, April-Oct. Open Tu-Su 9-6, Nov.-March.
❐ Open: See notes
❐ Number of Books: 1,300
❐ Periodical Titles: 25
❐ Services: REFERENCE ONLY

Cherokee Garden Library
Cherokee Garden Club
3101 Andrews Drive N.W.
Atlanta, GA 30305
(404) 814-4040
Anne Salter

Public may use books in the library.
❐ Open: M-F 9-5:30, Sa 9-5
❐ Number of Books: 3,800
❐ Periodical Titles: 50
❐ Services: REFERENCE ONLY

Fernbank Science Center Library
Fernbank Science Center
156 Heaton Park Drive N.E.
Atlanta, GA 30307
(404) 378-4311
Mary Larsen

Public may use books in the library.
❐ Open: M-Sa, call for hours
❐ Number of Books: 15,169
❐ Periodical Titles: 355
❐ Services: REFERENCE ONLY

Library
American Camellia Society
One Massee Lane
Fort Valley, GA 31030
(912) 967-2358
Ann Blair Brown

Collection of books available to members or researchers by
appointment; books do not circulate.
❐ Services: REFERENCE ONLY

HAWAII

Waimea Arboretum Foundation Library
Waimea Arboretum Foundation
59-864 Kamehameha Highway
Haleiwa, HI 96712
(808) 638-8655
Shirley B. Gerum

Call ahead.
❐ Open: 8-4, daily
❐ Number of Books: 500
❐ Periodical Titles: 50
❐ Services: REFERENCE ONLY

Bishop Museum Library
Bernice Pauani Bishop Museum
1525 Bernice Street (P.O. Box 19000-A)
Honolulu, HI 96817-0916
(808) 848-4148
Duane Wenzel

Public may use books in the library. Library includes a horticultural
collection.
❐ Open: Tu-F 10-3, Sat 9-12
❐ Number of Books: 100,000
❐ Periodical Titles: 4,000
❐ Services: INTERLIBRARY LOANS

Research Library
National Tropical Botanical Garden
P.O. Box 340
Lawai, HI 96765
(808) 332-7324
Richard Hanna

A strong collection on tropical plants.
❐ Open: M-F 8-5
❐ Number of Books: 8,000
❐ Periodical Titles: 250
❐ Services: INTERLIBRARY LOANS LOANS TO PUBLIC

ILLINOIS

Library
Field Museum of Natural History
Roosevelt Road & Lake Shore Drive
Chicago, IL 60605-2498
(312) 922-9410

General public may use botanical and horticultural books for reference
in the Reading Room.
❐ Open: M-F 8:30-4:30
❐ Number of Books: 40,000
❐ Services: REFERENCE ONLY INTERLIBRARY LOANS

(continued next page)

ILLINOIS (continued)

Chicago Botanic Garden Library
Chicago Horticultural Society
Lake-Cook Road
Glencoe, IL 60022
(708) 835-8200
Virginia Henrichs

Public may use books in the library.
❏ Open: M-Sa 9-4
❏ Number of Books: 12,000
❏ Periodical Titles: 200
❏ Services: MEMBERS ONLY INTERLIBRARY LOANS

Sterling Morton Library
Morton Arboretum
Route 53
Lisle, IL 60532
(708) 719-2427
Michael T. Stieber or Rita Hassert

Public may use books in the library.
❏ Open: M-F 9-5, Sa 10-4
❏ Number of Books: 23,000
❏ Periodical Titles: 400
❏ Services: MEMBERS ONLY INTERLIBRARY LOANS

Agricultural Library
University of Illinois
1301 W. Gregory Drive (226 Mumford)
Urbana, IL 61801
(217) 333-2416
Carol Boast or Maria Porta

Hours vary, call for information. Public may use books
in the library.
❏ Open: See notes
❏ Number of Books: 220,000
❏ Periodical Titles: 3,000
❏ Services: REFERENCE ONLY INTERLIBRARY LOANS

INDIANA

Horticultural Science Library
  Indianapolis Museum of Art
I.M.A. Horticultural Society
1200 W. 38th Street
Indianapolis, IN 46208
(317) 923-1331
Charles T. Gleaves

Public may use books in the library.
❏ Open: W and Sa 1-4
❏ Services: MEMBERS ONLY

The Hayes Regional Arboretum Library
801 Elks Road
Richmond, IN 47374-2526
(317) 962-3745

❏ Open: Tu-Sa 1-5
❏ Number of Books: 1,000
❏ Services: REFERENCE ONLY

IOWA

Library
Bickelhaupt Arboretum
340 S. 14th Street
Clinton, IA 52732
(319) 242-4771
F. K. Bickelhaupt

❏ Open: Daily, call for hours
❏ Number of Books: 800
❏ Periodical Titles: 20
❏ Services: LOANS TO PUBLIC

(continued next page)

© Caprice Farm Nursery
Artist: Elizabeth Rocchia

IOWA (continued)

Gardeners of America
   Men's Garden Clubs of America, Inc.
P.O. Box 241, 5560 Merle Hay Road
Johnston, IA 50131
(515) 278-0295

The library is open to members, and to researchers by appointment.
❏ Open: M-F 8:30-4:30
❏ Number of Books: 2,000
❏ Services: MEMBERS ONLY

KANSAS

Frank Good Library
Botanica, The Wichita Gardens
701 N. Amidon
Wichita, KS 67203
(316) 264-0448
Amy Kaspar Woolf

Public may use books in the library.
❏ Open: M-F, call for hours
❏ Number of Books: 2,800
❏ Periodical Titles: 25
❏ Services: MEMBERS ONLY

MAINE

Thuya Lodge Library
Asticou Terraces Trust
P.O. Box 625
Northeast Harbor, ME 04662
(207) 276-5130

Public may use books in the library.
❏ Open: July 1-Sept 1, 10-4:30
❏ Number of Books: 1,000
❏ Periodical Titles: 25
❏ Services: REFERENCE ONLY

MARYLAND

The Cylburn Horticultural Library
Cylburn Arboretum Association
4915 Greenspring Avenue
Baltimore, MD 21209-4698
(410) 367-2217
Adelaide C. Rackemann

Public may use books in the library.
❏ Open: Th 1-3, and by appt.
❏ Number of Books: 2,000
❏ Services: MEMBERS ONLY

National Agricultural Library
US Department of Agriculture
10301 Baltimore Boulevard
Beltsville, MD 20705-2351
(301) 504-5204
Joseph Howard

Probably the largest of all the libraries -- the public may use it for reference only. There is a branch reading room in DC, at USDA South, Room 1052; for information call (202) 447-3434.
❏ Open: M-F 8-4:30
❏ Number of Books: 2 mil.
❏ Periodical Titles: 27000
❏ Services: REFERENCE ONLY INTERLIBRARY LOANS

Brookside Gardens Library
Maryland-National Capital Park & Plan. Comm.
1500 Glenallan Avenue
Wheaton, MD 20902
(301) 949-8231

Public may use books in the library.
❏ Open: Tu-Th 10-5, F-M 12-5
❏ Number of Books: 2,500
❏ Periodical Titles: 20
❏ Services: REFERENCE ONLY

MASSACHUSETTS

The Library
The Massachusetts Horticultural Society
300 Massachusetts Avenue
Boston, MA 02115
(617) 536-9280
Walter T. Punch

Public may use books in the library. The collection dates from the 15th century.
❏ Open: M-F 8:30-4:30, Sa 10-2
❏ Number of Books: 45,000
❏ Periodical Titles: 300
❏ Services: MEMBERS ONLY

Library
Worcester County Horticultural Society
Tower Hill Botanic Garden, 11 French Hill Dr.
Boylston, MA 01505-1008
(508) 869-6111
Barbara Trippel Simmons

Hours are M-F 10-5, Nov.-March. Open daily, April-October. Public may use books in the library.
❏ Open: See notes
❏ Number of Books: 7,000
❏ Periodical Titles: 39
❏ Services: MEMBERS ONLY

(continued next page)

MASSACHUSETTS (continued)

The Botany Libraries
Harvard University Herbaria Building
22 Divinity Avenue
Cambridge, MA 02138
(617) 495-2366
Judith Warnement

Library of the Gray Herbarium, Arnold Arboretum, Economic Botany
Library and Oakes Ames Orchid Library; available to serious users
and researchers. Call or write for information.
❐ Open: M-F 9-5
❐ Number of Books: 250,000
❐ Periodical Titles: 1,500
❐ Services: REFERENCE ONLY INTERLIBRARY LOANS

Lawrence Newcomb Library
New England Wild Flower Society
180 Hemenway Road
Framingham, MA 01701-2699
(508) 877-7630
Mary M. Walker or John Benson

Public may use books in the library. Garden is closed Nov. 1 to
April 14, but library is open Tu-F 9-4:30.
❐ Open: Tu-Su 9-4, see notes
❐ Number of Books: 3,000
❐ Periodical Titles: 100
❐ Services: MEMBERS ONLY

Berkshire Botanical Garden Library
Berkshire Botanical Garden
Stockbridge, MA 01262
(413) 298-3926
Dina Samfield

Public may use books in the library. Open Sat. & Sun. 10-4, May-October.
❐ Open: M-F 10-4
❐ Number of Books: 1,500
❐ Services: MEMBERS ONLY

MICHIGAN

Matthaei Botanical Gardens Library
The University of Michigan
1800 N. Dixboro Road
Ann Arbor, MI 48105
(313) 763-7061
Katherine R. French

Public may use books in the library.
❐ Open: M-F, call for hours
❐ Number of Books: 2,100
❐ Periodical Titles: 12
❐ Services: REFERENCE ONLY

Kingman Museum of Natural History Library
Battle Creek Public Schools
West Michigan at 20th St.
Battle Creek, MI 49017
(616) 965-5117
Stacy Mazariegos

Hours are M-Sa 9-5, Su 1-5, Sept.-June.
❐ Open: See notes
❐ Number of Books: 750
❐ Periodical Titles: 50
❐ Services: INTERLIBRARY LOANS LOANS TO PUBLIC

The Detroit Garden Center Library
The Detroit Garden Center
1460 E. Jefferson Avenue
Detroit, MI 48207
(313) 259-6363
Margaret H. Grazier

Public may use books in the library.
❐ Open: Tu-Th 9:30-3:30
❐ Number of Books: 5,000
❐ Periodical Titles: 15
❐ Services: MEMBERS ONLY

Detroit Public Library
5201 Woodward Avenue
Detroit, MI 48202
(313) 833-1400 or 1450

Has a collection on gardening, botany and agriculture.
❐ Open: Tu-Sa 9:30-5:30, W 1-9
❐ Number of Books: 5,500
❐ Periodical Titles: 61
❐ Services: INTERLIBRARY LOANS LOANS TO PUBLIC

Library
Chippewa Nature Center
400 S. Badour Road, Route 9
Midland, MI 48640
(517) 631-0830
Sue McDonald

Public may use books in the library.
❐ Open: M-F 8-5, Sa 9-5, Su 1-5
❐ Number of Books: 2,500
❐ Periodical Titles: 86
❐ Services: MEMBERS ONLY

The Dow Gardens Library
The Dow Gardens
1018 W. Main Street
Midland, MI 48640
(517) 631-2677
Elizabeth Chaussee

Public may use books in the library. Entrance to the library is
through the Information Center, located at the corner of West
Saint Andrews & Eastman Roads.
❐ Open: M-F 10-4
❐ Number of Books: 1,500
❐ Periodical Titles: 50
❐ Services: REFERENCE ONLY

(continued next page)

MICHIGAN (continued)

Fernwood Library
Fernwood Botanic Garden
13988 Rangeline Road
Niles, MI 49120-9042
(616) 683-8653
Eleanor Drew

Public may use books in the library.
❏ Open: M-F 9-5
❏ Number of Books: 3,500
❏ Periodical Titles: 49
❏ Services: MEMBERS ONLY

Hidden Lake Gardens Library
Michigan State University
Tipton, MI 49287
(517) 431-2060
Debbie Cheryl Rittenhouse

❏ Open: M-F 8-4:30, Sa-Su 10-6
❏ Number of Books: 3,500
❏ Periodical Titles: 8
❏ Services: REFERENCE ONLY

MINNESOTA

Andersen Horticultural Library
Minnesota Landscape Arboretum, Univ. of Minn.
Box 39, 3675 Arboretum Drive
Chanhassen, MN 55317
(612) 443-2440
Richard T. Isaacson

Public may use books in the library.
❏ Open: M-F 8-4:30, Sa-Su 11-4:30
❏ Number of Books: 9,500
❏ Periodical Titles: 525
❏ Services: REFERENCE ONLY

MISSOURI

Missouri Botanical Garden Library
Missouri Botanical Garden
4344 Shaw Blvd.
St. Louis, MO 63110
(314) 577-5155
Constance Wolf

The library is open to members and researchers by appointment.
The collection is oriented towards botany.
❏ Open: M-F 8-5
❏ Number of Books: 115,000
❏ Periodical Titles: 1,300
❏ Services: REFERENCE ONLY INTERLIBRARY LOANS

NEW JERSEY

Elvin McDonald Horticultural Library
Monmouth County Park System
Deep Cut Gardens, 352 Red Hill Road
Middletown, NJ 07748
(908) 671-6050
Mae H. Fisher

Public may use books in the library.
❏ Open: M-F 9-4
❏ Number of Books: 3,100
❏ Periodical Titles: 24
❏ Services: MEMBERS ONLY

Elizabeth Donnell Kay Botanical Library
George Griswold Frelinghuysen Arboretum
53 East Hanover Avenue
Morris Township, NJ 07962-1295
(201) 326-7600
Helen Mageau

Public may use books in the library.
❏ Open: M-F 9-4:30
❏ Number of Books: 2,500
❏ Periodical Titles: 24
❏ Services: MEMBERS ONLY

NEW YORK

The New York Botanical Garden Library
The New York Botanical Garden
200th Street & Kazimiroff Boulevard
Bronx, NY 10458-5126
(718) 817-8604
John F. Reed, Bernadette Callery

Public may use books in the library. Academic year hours are Tu-Th 12-6,
Sa-Su 12-4. Call for summer hours.
❏ Open: See notes
❏ Number of Books: 117,400
❏ Periodical Titles: 2,200
❏ Services: REFERENCE ONLY INTERLIBRARY LOANS

Brooklyn Botanic Garden Library
Brooklyn Botanic Garden
1000 Washington Avenue
Brooklyn, NY 11225
(718) 941-4044 ext. 366
Brenda Weisman

Library reopening in 1994 after renovation, call for date. Public may
use books in the library.
❏ Open: Tu-F 9-4, see notes
❏ Number of Books: 15,000
❏ Periodical Titles: 2,800
❏ Services: REFERENCE ONLY

(continued next page)

NEW YORK (continued)

**Buffalo & Erie County
Botanical Garden Library**
Buffalo & Erie Co. Bot. Garden Society
South Park & McKinley Parkway
Buffalo, NY 14128-0386
(716) 828-1040
Florence S. DaLuiso

Public may use books in the library.
❐ Open: M-F 9-4
❐ Number of Books: 450
❐ Periodical Titles: 9
❐ Services: REFERENCE ONLY

George Landis Arboretum Library
P.O. Box 186, Lape Rd.
Esperance, NY 12066
(518) 875-6935

Public may use books in the library.
❐ Open: M-F 8:30-4:30
❐ Number of Books: 8,000

Library
Liberty Hyde Bailey Hortorium
462 Mann Library, Cornell University
Ithaca, NY 14853
(607) 255-2131
Dr. Jerrold Davis

Collection in taxonomic botany. Similar collection in Mann Library.
❐ Open: M-F 9-4
❐ Number of Books: 10,000
❐ Periodical Titles: 350
❐ Services: REFERENCE ONLY

Institute of Ecosystem Studies Library
The Cary Arboretum
P.O. Box AB
Millbrook, NY 12545
(914) 677-5343
Annette Frank

Public may use books in the library.
❐ Open: M-F 8:30-4:30

Garden Club of America Library
598 Madison Avenue
New York, NY 10022
(212) 753-8287
Paula Stewart

Members must pay a fee of $1 to borrow a book. Public may
use books in the library.
❐ Open: M-F 9-4:30, by appt.
❐ Number of Books: 3,000
❐ Services: MEMBERS ONLY

Horticultural Society of New York Library
Horticultural Society of New York
128 W. 58th Street
New York, NY 10019
(212) 757-0915
Katherine Powis

Public may use books in the library. Large collection of seed and
nursery catalogs.
❐ Open: M-F 10-6
❐ Number of Books: 15,000
❐ Periodical Titles: 150
❐ Services: MEMBERS ONLY INTERLIBRARY LOANS

Garden Library
Planting Fields Arboretum
Planting Fields Rd.
Oyster Bay, NY 11771
(516) 922-9024
Elizabeth Reilley

Public may use books in the library.
❐ Open: W 11-4, Sa 10-3
❐ Number of Books: 7,000
❐ Periodical Titles: 60
❐ Services: MEMBERS ONLY

Highland Botanical Park Library
Monroe County Parks Arboretum
180 Reservoir Avenue
Rochester, NY 14620
(716) 244-9023
R. Hoepfl

Public may use books in the library.
❐ Open: By appointment
❐ Number of Books: 680
❐ Periodical Titles: 15
❐ Services: REFERENCE ONLY

Library
Garden Center of Rochester
5 Castle Park
Rochester, NY 14620
Regina Campbell

Public may use books in the library.
❐ Open: Tu-Th 9:30-3:30
❐ Number of Books: 3,500
❐ Periodical Titles: 20
❐ Services: MEMBERS ONLY

NORTH CAROLINA

Addie Williams Totten Library
North Carolina Botanical Garden -- UNC
Campus Box 3375, Totten Center
Chapel Hill, NC 27599-3375
(919) 962-0522
Barbara Emerson

Public may use books in the library. Totten Center is located just
off 15-501/54 Bypass on Laurel Hill Road.
❐ Open: M-F 8-5
❐ Number of Books: 2,000
❐ Periodical Titles: 83
❐ Services: REFERENCE ONLY

OHIO

Hoffman Horticultural Library
Civic Garden Center of Cincinnati
2715 Reading Road
Cincinnati, OH 45206
(513) 221-0981
Jennifer Gleason

Public may use books in the library.
❑ Open: Tu-Sa 9-4
❑ Number of Books: 2,000
❑ Periodical Titles: 30
❑ Services: MEMBERS ONLY

Lloyd Library
917 Plum Street
Cincinnati, OH 45202
(513) 721-3707
Rebecca A. Perry

Open the first and third Saturdays of the month 9-4. Public may
use books in the library.
❑ Open: M-F 8:30-4, see notes
❑ Number of Books: 65,000
❑ Periodical Titles: 600
❑ Services: REFERENCE ONLY

Eleanor Squire Library
The Garden Center of Greater Cleveland
11030 East Boulevard
Cleveland, OH 44106
(216) 721-1600 ext. 22
Joanna C. Bristol

Public may use books in the library.
❑ Open: M-F 9-5, Sa 12-5, Su 1-5
❑ Number of Books: 14,000
❑ Periodical Titles: 200
❑ Services: MEMBERS ONLY

Biological Sciences Library
Ohio State University
200 B & Z Bldg., 1735 Neil Avenue
Columbus, OH 43210
(614) 292-1744

Collection on taxonomic biology, plant geography, and ecology.
Call or write for information. Public may use books in the library.

Cox Arboretum Library
Montgomery County Park District
6733 Springboro Pike
Dayton, OH 45449
(513) 434-9005
Ruth McManis

Public may use books in the library.
❑ Open: M-F 9-5
❑ Number of Books: 2,500
❑ Periodical Titles: 20
❑ Services: REFERENCE ONLY

Kingwood Center Library
Kingwood Center
900 Park Avenue West
Mansfield, OH 44906
(419) 522-0211
William W. Collins

Residents of Richland and five surrounding counties may borrow books.
❑ Open: Tu-Sa 9-5
❑ Number of Books: 8,000
❑ Periodical Titles: 125
❑ Services: INTERLIBRARY LOANS LOANS TO PUBLIC

The Herb Society of America Library
Herb Society of America
9019 Kirtland-Chardon Road
Mentor, OH 44060
(216) 256-0514
Headquarters Office Secretary

Has slide lectures for rent on many aspects of herb history and culture.
❑ Open: M-F 9-12, 1-5
❑ Number of Books: 1,000
❑ Periodical Titles: 13
❑ Services: REFERENCE ONLY

Warren H. Corning Library
The Holden Arboretum
9500 Sperry Road
Mentor, OH 44060
(216) 256-1110 ext. 139
Nadia Aufderheide

Public may use books in the library.
❑ Open: Tu-F 10-5
❑ Number of Books: 7,500
❑ Periodical Titles: 125
❑ Services: REFERENCE ONLY

The Dawes Arboretum Library
The Dawes Arboretum
7770 Jacksontown Road S.E.
Newark, OH 43056-9380
(614) 323-2355
Linda Milligan

Members may use the library for reference; researchers should
make an appointment.
❑ Open: M-F 8-4:30
❑ Number of Books: 5,500
❑ Periodical Titles: 30

Library
Gardenview Horticultural Park
16711 Pearl Road
Strongsville, OH 44136
(216) 238-6653
Henry A. Ross

Library open to members only, by appointment.
❑ Open: See notes.
❑ Number of Books: 4,000
❑ Services: MEMBERS ONLY REFERENCE ONLY

(continued next page)

OHIO (continued)

Horticultural Library
Toledo Botanical Garden
5403 Elmer Drive
Toledo, OH 43615
(419) 536-8365
Janice Lower

Call or write for information on hours.
❒ Open: By appointment only
❒ Services: REFERENCE ONLY

OKLAHOMA

Tulsa Garden Center Library
Tulsa Garden Center
2453 S. Peoria Ave.
Tulsa, OK 74114
(918) 749-6401
Caroline Swinson

Public may use books in the library.
❒ Open: M-F, call for hours
❒ Number of Books: 3,000
❒ Periodical Titles: 20
❒ Services: MEMBERS ONLY

ONTARIO, CANADA

Royal Botanical Gardens Library
Royal Botanical Gardens
P.O. Box 399
Hamilton, ON, Canada L8N 3H8
(416) 527-1158, ext. 159
Ina Vrugtman

Open Sa 9-12 except July and August. Public may use books in the library.
Address is 680 Plains Rd West, Burlington, Ontario. FAX (416) 577-0375.
❒ Open: W-F 9-5, see notes
❒ Number of Books: 12,000
❒ Periodical Titles: 600
❒ Services: MEMBERS ONLY INTERLIBRARY LOANS

School of Horticulture Library
Niagara Parks Commission
Niagara Parkway North (P.O. Box 150)
Niagara Falls, ON, Canada L2E 6T2
(416) 356-8554
Mrs. Ruth Stoner

Open to staff and students daily; researchers may use the library
by appointment.
❒ Open: See notes
❒ Number of Books: 3,200
❒ Periodical Titles: 65
❒ Services: MEMBERS ONLY

Civic Garden Centre Library
The Civic Garden Centre
777 Lawrence Avenue East
North York, ON, Canada M3C 1P2
(416) 397-1340
Pamela Mackenzie

Public may use books in the library. FAX (416) 397-1354.
❒ Open: M-F 9:30-5, Sa-Su 12-5
❒ Number of Books: 7,000
❒ Periodical Titles: 70
❒ Services: MEMBERS ONLY INTERLIBRARY LOANS

Canadian Agriculture Library
Agriculture Canada
Ottawa, ON, Canada K1A OC5
(613) 995-7829

Public may use books in the library.
❒ Open: M-F 8:15-4:30
❒ Number of Books: 800,000
❒ Services: REFERENCE ONLY INTERLIBRARY LOANS

OREGON

Library
The Berry Botanic Garden
11505 S.W. Summerville Ave.
Portland, OR 97219
(503) 636-4112
Janice Dodd

Members may use the library and borrow books.
❒ Open: 8-5
❒ Number of Books: 1,300
❒ Periodical Titles: 40
❒ Services: MEMBERS ONLY

PENNSYLVANIA

Joseph Krauskopf Memorial Library
Delaware Valley College
Route 202
Doylestown, PA 18901
(215) 345-1500
C. Shook, Director

Public may use books in the library. The library is building a collection of
current seed and nursery catalogs; specializes in science and agriculture.
❒ Open: Call for hours
❒ Number of Books: 50,300
❒ Periodical Titles: 662
❒ Services: REFERENCE ONLY

(continued next page)

PENNSYLVANIA (continued)

Longwood Gardens Library
Longwood Gardens, Inc.
Kennett Square, PA 19348
(215) 388-6745 ext. 510
Enola J. N. Teeter

Library is open to researchers by appointment, and to students at the Garden.
❐ Open: M-F 8-4
❐ Number of Books: 20,000
❐ Periodical Titles: 280
❐ Services: REFERENCE ONLY INTERLIBRARY LOANS

Stewart Memorial Library
Academy of Natural Sciences of Philadelphia
1900 Benjamin Franklin Parkway
Philadelphia, PA 19103
(215) 299-1140
Robin Sinn

Large botanical research collection. Horticultural collection focuses on pre-1860 American imprints. Public may use books in the library.
❐ Open: M-F 9-5
❐ Number of Books: 190,000
❐ Periodical Titles: 2,000
❐ Services: MEMBERS ONLY REFERENCE ONLY INTERLIBRARY LOANS

Pennsylvania Horticultural Society Library
Pennsylvania Horticultural Society
325 Walnut Street
Philadelphia, PA 19106-2777
(215) 625-8261
Janet Evans

Public may use books in the library.
❐ Open: M-F 9-5
❐ Number of Books: 14,000
❐ Periodical Titles: 200
❐ Services: MEMBERS ONLY INTERLIBRARY LOANS

Morris Arboretum Library
University of Pennsylvania
9414 Meadowbrook Avenue
Philadelphia, PA 19118
(215) 247-5777
Ann F. Rhoads

Public may use books in the library. Catalog available through Univ. of Pennsylvania On-Line Catalog system.
❐ Open: M-F 9-5
❐ Number of Books: 6,000
❐ Periodical Titles: 60
❐ Services: REFERENCE ONLY INTERLIBRARY LOANS

Library
Carnegie Museum of Natural History
4400 Forbes Avenue
Pittsburgh, PA 15213-4080
(412) 622-3264
Elizabeth Swan

Very large natural history collection; number of books cited are just the botanical books.
❐ Open: M-F 8:30-12, 1-5
❐ Number of Books: 2,800
❐ Periodical Titles: 265
❐ Services: REFERENCE ONLY INTERLIBRARY LOANS

Hunt Botanical Library
Hunt Institute for Botanical Documentation
Carnegie Mellon University, Frew St.
Pittsburgh, PA 15213
(412) 268-2436
Charlotte Tancin

Public may use books in the library; appointments are recommended.
❐ Open: M-F 1-5
❐ Number of Books: 22,000
❐ Periodical Titles: 650
❐ Services: REFERENCE ONLY INTERLIBRARY LOANS

Pittsburgh Civic Garden Center Library
Pittsburgh Civic Garden Center
1059 Shady Ave.
Pittsburgh, PA 15232
(412) 441-4442
Jean Aiken

Public may use books in the library.
❐ Open: M-F 8:30-4:30, Sa 10-4
❐ Number of Books: 2,350
❐ Periodical Titles: 18
❐ Services: MEMBERS ONLY

Scott Arboretum Horticultural Library
Scott Arboretum
500 College Avenue
Swarthmore, PA 19081
(215) 328-8025
Education Intern

Public may use books in the library.
❐ Open: M-F 8:30-4:30
❐ Number of Books: 1,142
❐ Periodical Titles: 46
❐ Services: MEMBERS ONLY

QUEBEC, CANADA

Montreal Botanical Garden Library
Jardin Botanique de Montreal-Bibliotheque
4101 rue Sherbrooke est
Montreal, PQ, Canada H1X 2B2
(514) 872-1824
Celine Arsenault

Public may use books in the library.
❐ Open: M-F 8:30-12, 1:15-4:30
❐ Number of Books: 16,000
❐ Periodical Titles: 500
❐ Services: MEMBERS ONLY INTERLIBRARY LOANS

SOUTH CAROLINA

Orangeberg County Library
P. O. Box 1637
Orangeberg, SC 29115
(803) 531-4636
Paula Paul

Hours are M-Tu 10-9, W-F 10-6, Sa 9-5
❐ Open: See notes
❐ Services: LOANS TO PUBLIC

TENNESSEE

Library
The Dixon Gallery & Gardens
4339 Park Avenue
Memphis, TN 38117
(901) 761-5250
Carol Griffin

Library is open to members only.
❐ Open: Tu-Sa 11-5, Su 1-5
❐ Number of Books: 1,000
❐ Periodical Titles: 40
❐ Services: REFERENCE ONLY

Sybil G. Malloy Memorial Library
Memphis Botanic Garden
750 Cherry Road
Memphis, TN 38117
(901) 685-1566
Ruth Cobb

From March-Oct. hours are M-Sa 9-6, Su 11-6.
From Nov.-Feb. hours are M-Sa 9-4:30.
❐ Open: See notes
❐ Number of Books: 1,000
❐ Periodical Titles: 25
❐ Services: REFERENCE ONLY

The Botanical Gardens Library
Cheekwood
1200 Forrest Park Drive
Nashville, TN 37215
(615) 353-2148
Muriel H. Connell

Public may use books in the library.
❐ Open: M-Sa 9-5, Su 1-5
❐ Number of Books: 3,500
❐ Periodical Titles: 74
❐ Services: MEMBERS ONLY

TEXAS

National Wildflower Research Center Clearinghouse
2600 FM 973 North
Austin, TX 78725-4201
(512) 929-3600
Flo Oxley

Public may use books in the library.
❐ Open: M-F 9-4
❐ Number of Books: 1,500
❐ Periodical Titles: 60
❐ Services: REFERENCE ONLY

W. J. Rogers Memorial Library
The Beaumont Council of Garden Clubs
P.O. Box 7962
Beaumont, TX 77726-7962
(409) 842-3135
Myra Clay

Public may use books in the library. Collection related to plants which thrive on the Gulf Coast.
❐ Open: Daily, by appointment
❐ Number of Books: 1,200
❐ Services: MEMBERS ONLY

Mary Daggett Lake Library
Fort Worth Botanic Garden
3220 Botanic Garden Blvd. North
Fort Worth, TX 76107
(817) 871-7686
Clara Wilson

Public may use books in the library.
❐ Open: M-F 8-5
❐ Services: REFERENCE ONLY

VIRGINIA

Harold B. Tukey Memorial Library
American Horticultural Society
7931 E. Boulevard Drive
Alexandria, VA 22308
(703) 768-5700
Raymond J. Rogers

Members may use the library for reference.
❐ Open: M-F 8:30-5
❐ Number of Books: 2,500
❐ Periodical Titles: 200
❐ Services: REFERENCE ONLY

Blandy Experimental Farm Library
University of Virginia
P.O. Box 175
Boyce, VA 22620
(703) 837-1758
Michael Bowers

Library is open to researchers by appointment.
❐ Open: By appointment
❐ Number of Books: 1,200
❐ Periodical Titles: 20
❐ Services: REFERENCE ONLY

(continued next page)

VIRGINIA (continued)

Crawford Reid Memorial Library
The Irrigation Association
8260 Willow Oaks Corp. Dr., Ste. 120
Fairfax, VA 22031
(703) 573-3551
Charles Putnam, Exec. Dir.

Call for information on the collection.
❒ Open: M-F 8-5
❒ Number of Books: 700
❒ Periodical Titles: 25
❒ Services: REFERENCE ONLY

Huette Horticultural Library
Norfolk Botanical Garden
Azalea Garden Road
Norfolk, VA 23518
(804) 441-5380 ext. 8
Lois Leach

Public may use books in the library.
❒ Open: M-Sa 10-4, Su 12-4
❒ Number of Books: 2,500
❒ Periodical Titles: 13
❒ Services: MEMBERS ONLY INTERLIBRARY LOANS

WASHINGTON

Lawrence Pierce Library
Rhododendron Species Foundation
P.O. Box 3798
Federal Way, WA 98063
(206) 927-6960
Mrs. Richard B. Johnson

Public may use books in the library.
❒ Open: M-F 8-4:30
❒ Number of Books: 1,000
❒ Services: REFERENCE ONLY

Elisabeth C. Miller Library
Center for Urban Horticulture
University of Washington, GF-15
Seattle, WA 98195
(206) 543-8616
Laura Lipton or Valerie Easton

Public may use books in the library.
❒ Open: M-F 9-5
❒ Number of Books: 7,000
❒ Periodical Titles: 350
❒ Services: REFERENCE ONLY

Walker Horticultural Library
Yakima Area Arboretum
1207 Arboretum Drive
Yakima, WA 98901
(509) 248-7337
Cathy Peters or Rita Pilgrim

Public may use books in the library.
❒ Open: Call for hours
❒ Number of Books: 2,000
❒ Services: MEMBERS ONLY

WEST VIRGINIA

Wheeling Civic Garden Center Library
Wheeling Civic Garden Center, Inc.
Oglebay Park
Wheeling, WV 26003
(304) 242-0665
Phyllis Brown

Public may use books in the library.
❒ Open: M-F 10-5
❒ Number of Books: 1,200
❒ Periodical Titles: 7
❒ Services: MEMBERS ONLY

WISCONSIN

Reference Library
Boerner Botanical Gardens
5879 S. 92nd Street
Hales Corners, WI 53130
(414) 425-1131

Hours are March-October, daily, 8-sunset; November-February, daily 8-4. Public may use books in the library.
❒ Open: See notes
❒ Number of Books: 2,000
❒ Services: REFERENCE ONLY

Schumacher Library
Olbrich Botanical Garden
3330 Atwood Ave.
Madison, WI 53704-5808
(608) 246-5805
Dorothy Whitcomb

Public may use books in the library.
❒ Open: 10-4 daily
❒ Number of Books: 1,000
❒ Periodical Titles: 40
❒ Services: MEMBERS ONLY

Books

Useful books on plants and gardening, for reference and daily use as well as for pleasure, are grouped into general categories by plant groups or plant uses. At the end of the list are "good reads," guidebooks of gardens to visit, and plant-finding source books.

All the books listed in this section are books I consider worthwhile. It's a delight to see all the new books, but it's agony to pare down the list to roughly two hundred. The notes are my own opinions, except as noted, based on my own general garden and plant knowledge and my librarian's critical eye.

There are a lot of exciting and informative new books listed; most are fairly recent and should be available in public libraries, bookstores, from secondhand bookshops or on remainder tables. I'd encourage you to find and read some of the older books, too; I don't think that newest is always best, and looking for older books is part of the fun.

Books have been listed on merit without regard to price. Prices have not been given because books seem to go out of print so quickly. Check *Books in Print* for availability and price.

Mail order sources of new, used and rare books are listed in the Garden Suppliers and Services section. Books on specific plants or areas of horticultural interest are often available from specialist nurseries and seed companies. In addition, many societies sell books to their members, often at special prices; some sell to non-members as well.

You should ask horticultural book suppliers for books not commonly found in local bookstores; bookstores can also special-order such books if they are still in print. Addresses of publishers can be found in *Books in Print* or *Forthcoming Books,* available in most public libraries or bookstores. Society addresses not given with the books are listed in the Horticultural Societies section of this book.

A table of the symbols and abbreviations used in this book appears
on the bookmark inside the back cover.

USEFUL REFERENCE BOOKS

Hortus Third. New York, Macmillan, 1976. A dictionary of plants cultivated in the US and Canada -- which means a very great many! It is the standard North American reference and should be in almost any library.

The New York Botanical Garden Illustrated Encyclopedia of Horticulture. Thomas Everett. New York, Garland, 1982. This 10-volume work is monumental; descriptions are more complete and easier to read than *Hortus Third*. Quite a bit of cultural information; most of the photographs are in black and white.

The Royal Horticultural Society Dictionary of Gardening. Anthony Huxley, ed. New York, Stockton Press, 1992. Completely revised recently, the editors have made an effort to make this reference useful to gardeners world wide. I can't decide whether to take out a second mortgage and buy it, but it's very tempting. Critics tell us it's not perfect, but it has excellent plant descriptions, cultural information, many good line drawings, and many articles of general interest. Enough reading and study for a lifetime! Let's see, amortized over twenty years, it would be only $40 a year!

The Bernard E. Harkness Seedlist Handbook. Mabel G. Harkness. 2nd. ed. Portland, Timber Press, 1993. Originally written for people requesting unfamiliar seeds from seed exchange lists, it briefly describes a huge variety of plants by type, size, flower color and place of origin, and gives references to information about, and illustrations of, each plant in about 1,000 authoritative books and magazine articles.

Dictionary of Plant Names. Allen J. Coombes. Portland, Timber Press, 1985. Handy small book with information on pronunciation and derivation of plant names in concise entries.

Plant Names Simplified. A. T. Johnson & H. A. Smith. London, Hamlyn, 1972. Pocket-sized; gives pronunciation and derivation of plant names and very brief plant descriptions.

Stearn's Dictionary of Plant Names for Gardeners. William T. Stearn. London, Cassell Publishers, Ltd., 1992. Covers over 6,000 plant names, giving the meanings and origins of botanical names.

Botany for Gardeners: an Introduction and Guide. Brian Capon. Portland, Timber Press, 1990. A very well-illustrated guide through basic botany, or botany without tears! You'll pick up a lot of knowledge through osmosis. Available in paperback.

North American Horticulture: A Reference Guide. American Horticultural Society. 2nd ed. New York, Macmillan, 1992. A directory of horticultural societies and organizations, educational institutions and programs, botanical gardens, periodicals, journals and much more.

Healthy Harvest: A Global Directory of Sustainable Agriculture & Horticultural Organizations. Davis, CA, AgAccess, 1992. Lists more than 1,000 organizations and sources, with subject and geographical indexes and a description of each. Includes apprenticeships and internships, consultants, courses and conferences, development organizations, marketing cooperatives, newsletters, volunteer programs and much more. An excellent reference. $23.95 postpaid ($25.40 in CA). See Section B for address.

The Gardeners's Reading Guide: The Best Books for Gardeners. Jan Dean. New York, Facts on File, 1993. Organized by subject, here are about 3,000 books about gardens and gardening, each quite briefly annotated; helpful in finding information on recent books as well as older books you might find in a catalog of used and out-of-print books.

Growing with Gardening: A Twelve-Month Guide for Therapy, Recreation, and Education. Bibby Moore. Chapel Hill, University of North Carolina Press, 1989. A week-by-week guide to horticultural projects for anyone using horticulture in teaching or therapy. Advice on how to develop and budget a program and how to find volunteers, references to further information and useful sources. A wonderful book.

The Able Gardener: Overcoming Barriers of Age & Physical Limitations. Kathleen Yeomans. Pownal, VT, Garden Way, 1992. A general gardening book with suggestions for adapting methods to limitations, and sources of equipment for physically limited gardeners. Her best advice: "relax your standards, you don't have to have a perfect garden." We should all heed that.

ILLUSTRATED BOOKS USEFUL FOR FINDING AND IDENTIFYING PLANTS

The Complete Handbook of Garden Plants. Michael Wright. New York, Facts on File, 1984. A concise guide to popular garden trees, shrubs and flowers, with color paintings of many plants.

The Gardener's Illustrated Encyclopedia of Trees & Shrubs. Brian Davis. Emmaus, PA, Rodale Press, 1987. Concise information; color photos are mostly close-ups, with black & white silhouettes of plants. One of my favorites; a good companion to Dirr's *Manual of Woody Landscape Plants* (see Trees and Shrubs, below).

Hortica: Color Cyclopedia of Garden Flora and Indoor Plants. Alfred B. Graf. E. Rutherford, NJ, Roehrs Co., 1992. Organized like his earlier works, *Exotica* and *Tropica*, this is a collection of 8,100 plant photos, showing garden and greenhouse plants of all kinds. There are some plant descriptions, but you'd use it for the photos.

The 500 Best Garden Plants. Patrick Taylor. Portland, Timber Press, 1993. I don't want someone to tell *me* what's best, but this handy little book describes Patrick Taylor's favorites, among them many very desirable garden plants, and shows them in color photos. Hardiness zones are given.

Blooms of Bressingham: Garden Plants. Alan & Adrian Bloom. New York, HarperCollins, 1992. This is a fine plant encyclopedia, dividing hardy plants into broad categories, and offering very good plant descriptions and many color photos.

BOOKS IN SERIES

A number of publishers issue books on basic gardening and plants, all of which offer good information and value. Some of these books are listed individually here; all are well worth consideration. These publishers include Ortho Books, Sunset Books, HP Books (Price Stern Sloan), Harrowsmith and Garden Way (Storey Communications), and Van Patten Publishing. Slightly more expensive but also very good are the Taylor's Guides of Houghton Mifflin and the Time-Life books. Most have good color illustrations and contain the basic information that gardeners want at reasonable prices; most are readily available in bookstores.

GARDENING ENCYCLOPEDIAS

The Gardening Encyclopedia. Donald Wyman. Updated ed. New York, Macmillan, 1987. My favorite of the popular gardening encyclopedias; easy to read and use, but with a northeastern point of view.

Sunset Western Garden Book. 5th ed. Menlo Park, CA, Sunset Books, 1988. An excellent guide to gardening anywhere in the western US. The West is divided into 24 climate zones, and the excellent plant encyclopedia indicates in which zones each plant will grow -- very useful for choosing plants. This very fine book turns up on lists of favorite books from people all over the country.

The Garden Primer. Barbara Damrosch. New York, Workman, 1988. An excellent basic gardening book, dealing with all aspects of gardening in a sensible and very easy-to-understand manner. Damrosch tells you how to adapt advice to your climate and introduces many useful plants. The perfect gift for a new gardener and useful as a reference to any gardener.

The Big Book of Gardening Skills.. Pownal, VT, Garden Way, 1993. A compendium of useful information on all types of gardening questions: soil, pest control, plants and planting, pruning, garden equipment. Basic training for beginners.

Reader's Digest Illustrated Guide to Gardening. Pleasantville, NY, Reader's Digest Assn., 1981. Still one of the best how-to gardening guides, with lots of illustrations and extensive sections on choosing appropriate plants.

Rodale's All New Encyclopedia of Organic Gardening: The Indispensable Resource For Every Gardener. Fern Bradley & Barbara Ellis, eds. Emmaus, PA, Rodale Press, 1992. Comprehensive guide to organic gardening, methods and crops, easy to read and use.

Organic Gardener's Basics. Barbara P. Lawton & George F. Van Patten. Portland, Van Patten Publishing, 1993. Really, the title says it all -- enough useful information to get you started and prospering in your new garden.

Care and Repair of Lawn and Garden Tools. Blue Ridge Summit, PA, TAB Books, 1992. Most of this book is devoted to the care and repair of small engines, with good diagrams of various makes, but there's also good information on maintaining hand tools.

Organic Gardener's Composting. Steve Solomon. Portland, Van Patten Publishing, 1993. A basic "how-to"' guide to creating good compost and using it in your garden; includes methods useful to those with small lots or fussy neighbors.

Pruning Simplified. Lewis Hill. Updated ed. Pownal, VT, Storey Communications, 1986. A good, easy-to-understand introduction to the principles of pruning.

Sunset Pruning Handbook. Menlo Park, CA, Sunset Books, 1983. A good introduction, with basic principles explained, and an encyclopedia of how to prune many common garden plants.

Down-to-Earth Natural Lawn Care. Dick Raymond. Pownal, VT, Storey Publishing, 1993. By now I guess it's no surprise to you that I favor gardening without chemicals as much as possible, so this book appeals to me for its sensible approach.

The Greenhouse Gardener's Companion: Growing Food & Flowers in Your Greenhouse or Sunspace. Shane Smith. Golden, CO, Fulcrum Publishing, 1992. This thick paperback will really tell you just about all you need to know: how to arrange your greenhouse, selecting the best plants, propagating seeds and cuttings, growing plants on and dealing with pests and problems, and it makes it all sound like fun.

Drip Irrigation for Every Landscape and All Climates. Robert Kourik. 1992. A practical guide to planning and installing a drip system in ornamental gardens, orchards and vegetable gardens. Kourik has designed many systems and really knows his stuff. $16. postpaid ($16.93 in CA) from Metamorphic Press, P.O. Box 1841, Santa Rosa, CA 95402.

GARDEN PROBLEMS

Common-Sense Pest Control: Least-Toxic Solutions for Your Home, Garden, Pets and Community. William Olkowski, Sheila Daar & Helga Olkowski. Newtown, CT, The Taunton Press, 1991. This book appears daunting at first, but it is very useful, readable, and offers advice that most of us can quickly put into action. Highly recommended.

The Ortho Problem Solver. Michael Smith, ed. 3rd ed. San Ramon, CA, Ortho Books, 1989. A color encyclopedia of plant diseases and pest problems, with color photographs of the problem, a discussion of the conditions that cause it, and suggested solutions. Includes some cultural information and suggestions. Problems are entered by plant, making them fairly easy to locate. Available for reference in most garden centers.

The Ortho Home Gardener's Problem Solver. San Ramon, CA, Ortho Books, 1993. Scaled down to about 400 pages, a more manageable size for using at home; the editor tells me that it covers about 75% of the problems covered in the original reference book.

Weeds of the United States and Their Control. Harri J. Lorenzi & Larry S. Jeffery. New York, AVI (Van Nostrand Reinhold), 1987. Color photos, maps, descriptions, habitats and suggested controls.

Rodale's Garden Insect, Disease & Weed Identification Guide. Miranda Smith & Anna Carr. Emmaus, PA, Rodale Press, 1988. Gives illustrations, descriptions, life cycles and organic prevention and controls of common garden pests, diseases and weeds.

Pests of the Garden and Small Farm: a Grower's Guide to Using Less Pesticide. Mary Louise Flint. Oakland, CA, Division of Agriculture and Natural Resources, University of California, 1990. (Pub. #3332) An extremely useful and practical guide to pest control, with good photos of the pests and their damage and suggestions for control, using least toxic methods and beneficial insects. $25 postpaid: ANR Publications, 6701 San Pablo Ave., Oakland, CA 94619.

Pests of the West: Prevention and Control for Today's Garden and Small Farm. Whitney Cranshaw. Golden, CO, Fulcrum Publishing, 1992. A practical handbook covering most of the pest problems from the Rocky Mountains to the Sierras. Information on identification, bug life histories, biological and cultural controls.

Gardening in Deer Country: Some Ornamental Plants for Eastern Gardens. Karen Jescavage-Bernard. Tips for country gardeners, some of the advice would be useful anywhere . This maddening problem has no definitive solution, but here are many ideas to try. Available from The Book Tree, see Section B. $8.95 postpaid (NJ resident add 6% sales tax).

Common Poisonous Plants and Mushrooms of North America. Nancy J. Turner & Adam F. Szczawinski. Portland, Timber Press, 1991. Pieris! Hydrangeas! Clematis! Yes, all poisonous. Good color photos, descriptions, discussions of toxicity and treatment. An encyclopedia of what *not* to plant if you have small children.

PROPAGATION

Seed Germination: Theory & Practice. 2nd ed. Norman C. Deno. 1993. One of the most talked about books to come out in ages; Dr. Deno has tested germination of thousands of alpine and garden plants and suggests methods sometimes very different from conventional wisdom. It's rather technical in content and style, but indispensable to seed list fanatics. Write for price and availability to Norman C. Deno, 139 Lenor Drive, State College, PA 16801; you must send a long SASE for reply.

Secrets of Plant Propagation. Lewis Hill. Pownal, VT, Storey Communications, 1985. Good overview of the subject, easy to understand.

Creative Propagation: a Growers Guide. Peter Thompson. Portland, Timber Press, 1992. A fairly advanced guide to propagation, informative with tables of suggested methods for specific plants.

BOOKS ON PLANTS FOR SPECIFIC CONDITIONS & EFFECTS

Ingwersen's Manual of Alpine Plants. Will Ingwersen. Portland, Timber Press, 1986. Written by one of England's premier alpine plantsmen, this is a good, comprehensive guide to alpines, with fine plant descriptions.

Rock Gardening: A Guide to Growing Alpines & other Wildflowers in the American Garden. H. Lincoln Foster. Portland, Timber Press, 1982. Remains the standard rock garden handbook; it's still in print.

Scented Flora of the World. Roy Genders. New York, St. Martin's, 1977. A very interesting and readable book on scented plants -- the author's nose is very lenient and coverage is broad. There are newer books, but this one's my favorite; watch for it in used book catalogs.

The Fragrant Garden: A Book about Sweet Scented Flowers and Leaves. Louise Beebe Wilder. New York, Dover, 1974. Here's a delightful chance to see why Mrs. Wilder is so often quoted by other garden writers.

The Evening Garden. Peter Loewer. New York, Macmillan, 1993. Peter points out that many people's lives are so busy that evening is the only time they can enjoy their gardens. Why not have a fragrant evening bower in which to sing and chat? A delightful read, with his usual striking illustrations.

The Garden in Autumn. Allen Lacy. New York, Atlantic Monthly Press, 1990. A fresh look at planting specifically for autumn bloom and extending the enjoyment of your garden as long as possible before the first frost. Very well done: it will tear holes in your already-decided garden plans, and have you scrambling for places to put plants which give their best display in the autumn.

The Natural Shade Garden. Ken Druse. New York, Clarkson Potter, 1992. An inspirational guide to creating a "natural" garden under trees or in other shady spots using interesting plants; lovely photos give you lots of ideas.

The Complete Shade Gardener. George Schenk. Boston, Houghton Mifflin, 1984. Written by an experienced plantsman whose style and humor put him high on my list of "good reads."

Shade Gardening. A. Cort Sinnes. San Ramon, CA, Ortho Books, 1990. Good illustrations and plant directory; plenty of help with creative and practical aspects.

The Front Garden: New Approaches to Landscape Design. Mary Riley Smith. Boston, Houghton Mifflin, 1991. An unpretentious little book offering many suggestions as alternatives to the patch of lawn in front of most houses. Lots of good ideas to draw on.

The Heirloom Garden: Selecting and Growing over 300 Old-Fashioned Ornamentals. Jo Ann Gardner. Pownal, VT, Storey Communications, 1992. A well researched study of old varieties, with dates of introduction and sources of plants, and a good bibliography of books on restoring historic gardens, preservation groups, and historic gardens to visit.

Butterfly Gardening: Creating Summer Magic in your Garden. Xerces Society and Smithsonian Institution. San Francisco, Sierra Club Books, 1990. There's a lot of interest in butterfly gardening, and this book will help you understand the life cycles of butterflies, and how to choose plants that they find attractive.

Landscaping with Container Plants. Jim Wilson. Boston, Houghton Mifflin, 1990. If you know Jim Wilson from the *Victory Garden* show, you'll feel as if you're visiting with him -- his book is full of inspirational pictures and practical advice based on using new types of planting media.

The City Gardener's Handbook: From Balcony to Backyard. Linda Yang. New York, Random House, 1990. This is Linda's magnum opus on city gardening -- she covers everything you need to know and consider to have a patch of urban green, gives very practical advice, and writes with style and humor.

The Water Garden. Anthony Paul & Yvonne Rees. New York, Viking Penguin, 1986. Not as practical as the books below, but full of inspirational photos which will spark design ideas.

Water Gardening Basics. William C. Uber. Upland, CA, Dragonflyer Press, 1988. Written by the proprietor of Van Ness Water Gardens for home gardeners and garden designers; a beautiful book that covers all the basics. (See Van Ness Water Gardens, Section A.)

Water Gardens for Plants and Fish. Charles B. Thomas. Neptune City, NJ, TFH Publications, 1988. Written by the proprietor of Lilypons Water Gardens, this book covers everything you need to know to get started and to care for your plants and fish. (See Lilypons Water Gardens, Section A.)

Hedges, Screens and Espaliers. Susan Chamberlin. Los Angeles, Price Stern Sloan, 1982. Well-illustrated guide to choosing and caring for hedges, screens and espaliered shrubs and fruit trees.

Plants for Ground-Cover. Graham Stuart Thomas. Portland, Sagapress/Timber Press, 1990. As with all of Thomas' books, this is an interesting read, and it offers suggestions for many plants not usually thought of as ground covers.

Taylor's Guide to Ground Covers, Vines & Grasses. Boston, Houghton Mifflin, 1987. An excellent introduction to plants used for ground covers, as well as to vines for walls and trellises.

Cutting Gardens. Anne Halpin & Betty Mackey. New York, Simon & Schuster, 1993. All you need to know to choose good flowers to grow for flower arranging, including propagation, garden layout, and conditioning flowers to last well in arrangements.

The Flower Arranger's Garden. Rosemary Verey. Boston, Little, Brown, 1989. The inspiration in this book comes from the arrangements themselves, which use a variety of unusual plants and containers to create charming results.

REGIONAL GARDENING BOOKS

Successful Southern Gardening: A Practical Guide For Year-Round Beauty. Sandra F. Ladendorf. Chapel Hill, University of North Carolina Press, 1989. A fine modern guide to gardening in the hot and humid climate of the South. She offers good practical advice, lists recommended plants and suggests further reading and sources. Her lengthy thank yous are testimony to the joy of gardening friends.

Southern Gardens, Southern Gardening. William L. Hunt. Durham, NC, Duke University Press, 1982. This book is full of good advice on how to grow plants under Southern growing conditions.

A Southern Garden: A Handbook for the Middle South. Elizabeth Lawrence. Rev. ed. Chapel Hill, University of North Carolina Press, 1984. Lawrence's books belong on anybody's list of "good reads" because she gives great pleasure with her information. Also see the Bulbs and Good Reads Sections.

Perennial Garden Color for Texas and the South. William C. Welch. Dallas, Taylor Publishing, 1989. A very fine book for gardeners in difficult garden climates of the South, with good suggestions for plant selection, culture and garden design.

Neil Sperry's Complete Guide to Texas Gardening. 2nd ed. Dallas, Taylor Publishing, 1991. From the flowery cowboy boots on the cover to the last page, it covers everything: it's comprehensive, anticipates every question and recommends suitable plants and landscaping solutions -- all in an easy and friendly manner. I haven't seen the 2nd edition, but I'm sure it's just as good.

Cold Climate Gardening: How to Extend your Growing Season by at Least 30 Days. Lewis Hill. Pownal, VT, Storey Communications, 1987. A guide to "defensive" gardening for cold climates, written with humor and good hard-won advice.

Gardening: Plains & Upper Midwest. Roger Vick. Golden, CO, Fulcrum Publishing, 1991. Written by a Canadian from Alberta, this is a good basic guide to gardening in very cold climates and covers everything from ornamentals to vegetables, and from insect pests to monthly chores. Well done, and fun to read.

The Year in Bloom: Gardening for all Seasons in the Pacific Northwest. Ann Lovejoy. Seattle, Sasquatch Books, 1987. Ann Lovejoy's writing has deservedly carried her to the peaks, but this book is what got her started, and it's a charmer. It was followed by *The Border in Bloom: a Northwest Garden Through the Seasons*, 1990, from the same publisher.

Growing California Native Plants. Marjorie G. Schmidt. Berkeley, University of California Press, 1980. The definitive book on growing California natives, which are different in most respects from the wildflowers and native plants of the rest of the country.

Pat Welsh's Southern California Gardening: a Month-by-Month Guide. Pat Welsh. San Francisco, Chronicle Books, 1992. A very practical guide, full of interesting seasonal tidbits and suggestions, offering a lifeline to gardeners unfamiliar with the many microclimates of Southern California.

Plants for Dry Climates: How to Select, Grow and Enjoy. Mary Rose Duffield & Warren D. Jones. Los Angeles, Price Stern Sloan, 1981. Good information on selecting plants for very dry conditions, especially for the Southwestern deserts.

Gardening in Dry Climates. Scott Millard. San Ramon, CA, Ortho Books, 1989. We're all learning to get along with less water; this book offers good advice on garden strategy and plant selection for dry climates.

The Xeriscape Flower Gardener: A Waterwise Guide for the Rocky Mountain Region. Jim Knopf. Boulder, CO, Johnson Books, 1991. Useful to all who want to do away with water guzzling lawns and start using plants adapted to drier growing conditions; the author is a landscape architect. His advice seems practical and easy to follow.

Waterwise Gardening: Beautiful Gardens with Less Water. Menlo Park, CA, Sunset Books, 1989. Landscaping ideas, irrigation systems and plant selection for gardens that use less water. Before long this won't apply just to western gardeners.

Gardening in the Tropics. R. E. Holttum & Ivan Enoch. 1993. Distributed by Timber Press, Portland. Published in Singapore, this book will be of interest to Hawaiians and those few Floridians who qualify, as well as gardeners anywhere in the world who garden under tropical conditions. Some general cultural suggestions and good information on plant selection; many good color pictures.

TREES AND SHRUBS

Manual of Woody Landscape Plants: Their Identification, Ornamental Characteristics, Culture, Propagation and Uses. Michael A. Dirr. Champaign, IL, Stipes Publishing Co., 1983. I keep this one next to my bed -- it's one of my all-time favorites! Full of excellent information (the title says it all), but also wittily written; until an edition with good color photographs is published, I use it with Brian Davis's excellent book on trees and shrubs (see "Illustrated Books") or *Shrubs* by Phillips & Rix.

Trees & Shrubs Hardy in the British Isles. 4 v. W. J. Bean. 8th ed. rev. London, John Murray, 1976-1980. This is the British standard for looking up trees and shrubs; it lists almost any woody plant hardy enough to grow in some part of Britain, no matter what the origin. Plant descriptions are exhaustive, but there are all too few illustrations. A supplement was published in 1988.

Manual of Cultivated Broad-Leaved Trees & Shrubs. Gerd Krussmann. Portland, Timber Press, 1985-86. Three volume set giving great detail; a very strong challenge to Bean's work; I keep both Bean and Krussmann in my bedroom for winter study.

The Hillier Manual of Trees and Shrubs. 6th ed. Newton Abbot, Devon, David & Charles, 1991. This manual is the outgrowth of the plant catalogs of Hillier's Nursery, which once offered the widest selection of trees and shrubs in the world. It describes over 9,000 plants in 650 genera, with brief descriptions and comments on garden habits; very useful indeed. This new edition is much thicker, but if you have the 5th edition, keep it too; it seems somehow slightly more readable.

Landscape Plants for Western Regions. Bob Perry. Claremont, CA, Land Design Publishing, 1992. An update of Perry's excellent *Trees and Shrubs for Dry California Landscape*s, it discusses drought tolerant plants especially for southern California, and various uses including erosion and fire control. Includes a plant encyclopedia, descriptions of various habitats, and discussions of various plant families.

Plants that Merit Attention: V. 1, Trees. Janet Poor, ed. Portland, Timber Press, 1984. Suggests the use of many beautiful trees not well known or widely used in the past. *V. 2, Shrubs* will be issued in the summer of 1994.

Shrubs. Roger Phillips & Martyn Rix. New York, Random House, 1989. Like their excellent photographic books on roses and bulbs, this book will help you identify and choose among over 1,900 shrubs; the authors are British, and so are many of the cultivars shown. Even J. C. Raulston liked it and could find only two errors!

Ornamental Shrubs, Climbers and Bamboos. Graham Stuart Thomas. Portland, Timber Press, 1992. Organized along the lines of his incomparable book on perennials, and as before, his comments are well worth studying, though it's not quite as charming a read as his perennials book.

Garden Shrubs and their Histories. Alice M. Coats. New York, Simon & Schuster, 1992. A reprint of a 1964 book, it tells of the discovery and introduction of shrubs from all over the world. A perfect bedside book, it's great fun to read and is well illustrated with botanical paintings of the 18th and 19th centuries.

Conifers. D. M. Van Gelderen & J. R. P. van Hoey Smith. Portland, Timber Press, 1986. The heart of this very good book is the section containing many color photographs of conifers growing in gardens and in their natural habitats; there are also brief descriptions of each genera and some of the species.

Flowering Plants in the Landscape. Mildred E. Mathias, ed. Berkeley, University of California Press, 1982. Excellent color photographs of trees, shrubs and vines for subtropical climates, with hardiness indicated.

INDIVIDUAL GROUPS: TREES & SHRUBS

Japanese Maples. J. D. Vertrees. Portland, Timber Press, 1987. Certainly the definitive book on Japanese maples -- at least in English. Well illustrated in color, with excellent plant descriptions and information on culture. A beautiful book in itself, updated from the 1978 edition.

Palms. Alec Blombery and Tony Rodd. Topsfield, MA, Salem House, 1983. Good color photos and plant descriptions of palms from all over the world. There is some cultural and propagation information in a separate section.

The Color Dictionary of Camellias. Stirling Macoboy. Topsfield, MA, Merrimack Pub. Circle, 1983. Fine color photographs of many cultivars, good introductory treatment.

The Book of Bamboo. David Farrelly. San Francisco, Sierra Club Books, 1984. A lovely book, giving an inspiring introduction to bamboo and its many uses.

Bamboos. Christine Recht & Max F. Wetterwald. Portland, Timber Press, 1992. A translated German book on growing bamboo, with emphasis on adaptability to gardens. Descriptions and color photographs of many species.

Azaleas. Fred Galle. Portland, Timber Press, 1987. According to azalea lovers, this is the bible; it is a monumental work, and has not been improved on.

Magnolias. James M. Gardiner. Chester, CT, Globe Pequot, 1989. An introduction to the fabulous magnolias, with cultural information and descriptions of many species and varieties. Neil Treseder's more detailed and technical book, *Magnolias*, has long been out of print. (London, Faber and Faber, 1978)

Willows: the Genus Salix. Christopher Newsholme. Portland, Timber Press, 1992. Get rid of the idea that willows are common; here's a terrific guide to willows that will open your eyes to the possibilities, from creepers to stately trees. Makes me wish for a few acres of bottom land.

Rhododendron Portraits. D. M. Van Gelderen & J .R .P. van Hoey Smith. Portland, Timber Press, 1992. Excellent color photographs of over 1,100 species and hybrid rhododendrons, with name of the hybridizer, parentage, and size where applicable. Introduction gives all you need to understand the basic classification of rhododendrons, and a list of hybridizers past and present.

Success with Rhododendrons and Azaleas. H. Edward Reiley. Portland, Timber Press, 1992. Everything you need to know to get started with these popular plants, and enough information to keep you going all the way to showing and hybridizing. Very useful are his lists of "good doers," cold hardy varieties, and varieties by color.

Hydrangeas: Species and Cultivars. Corinne Mallet, Robert Mallet & Harry van Trier. Varengeville sur Mer, France, Editions Robert Mallet, 1992. Well worth seeking out, terrific color photos of many species and cultivars, very good plant descriptions -- and it's in English. (Editions Robert Mallet, Route de l'Eglise, Varengeville sur Mer, France 76119)

Hardy Heather Species, and some Related Plants. Dorothy M. Metheny. Written by a lifelong heather gardener, this book describes plants suitable for the Temperate Zone very well, illustrates many with botanical drawings, and gives references to other published sources of information. $27.45 postpaid, add 7.8% sales tax in WA. American Heather Society, 1199 Monte-Elma Road, Elma, WA 98541.

BULBS

Bulbs. 2 v. John E. Bryan. Portland, Timber Press, 1989. A monumental work covering everything about bulbs from all over the world. I get a little grumpy because it does not say much about gopher damage, but it should answer just about all your other questions. Quite a few color photos.

All About Bulbs. Rev. ed. San Ramon, CA, Ortho Books, 1986. Color guide to growing bulbs; good cultural advice, broad coverage of Dutch and species bulbs.

Bulbs: How to Select, Grow and Enjoy. George H. Scott. Los Angeles, Price Stern Sloan, 1982. A fine color illustrated introduction to bulbs of all types and seasons.

The Random House Book of Bulbs. Martin Rix & Roger Phillips. New York, Random House, 1989. Good for identification of both plants and bulbs; many are species bulbs shown in their natural habitat, excellent color photos.

The Little Bulbs. Elizabeth Lawrence. Durham, NC, Duke University Press, 1986. A "good read" that contains good information on species bulbs, especially narcissus, growing in both her Southern garden and that of a friend in Ohio.

Narcissus. Michael Jefferson-Brown. Portland, Timber Press, 1991. A very interesting introduction to narcissus and daffodils. Good discussion of both species narcissus and daffodil hybrids, and the people who hybridize them.

Modern Miniature Daffodils: Species and Hybrids. James S. Wells. Portland, Timber Press, 1989. These charming little bulbs may not be everybody's cup of tea, but I absolutely fell in love with them when I opened this book and so will you; they make 'King Alfred' look like Hulk Hogan.

HERBS

Growing and Using Herbs Successfully. Betty Jacobs. Pownal, VT, Garden Way, 1981. An herb maven tells me that this is the best and most informative introduction to herbs and herb growing; it must be, it's on the thirteenth or fourteenth printing. It has growing and propagating information, recipes, even information on starting an herb business.

The Complete Book of Herbs: a Practical Guide to Growing and Using Herbs. Lesley Bremness. New York, Viking, 1988. Another book recommended by my maven for general herbal information -- lots of color photos.

The Pleasure of Herbs: A Month-by-Month Guide to Growing, Using, and Enjoying Herbs. Phyllis Shaudys. Pownal, VT, Storey Communications, 1986. A basic guide to herbs, covering a lot of vital information in a charming manner; an ideal first herb book. Another by the same author is *Herbal Treasures*, Storey Communications, 1990.

All About Herbs. San Ramon, CA, Ortho Books, 1990. Good introduction to herb growing; lots of color pictures and useful information.

Rodale's Illustrated Encyclopedia of Herbs. C. Kowalchik & William H. Hylton, eds. Emmaus, PA, Rodale Press, 1987. Color photos and drawings; history, uses and cultivation, index of botanical names and medicinal uses, bibliography of books and newsletters.

Herb Garden Design. Faith Swanson & Virginia Rady. Hanover, NH, University Press of New England, 1984. Full of plans and suggestions for planting herb gardens of all kinds and styles.

Using Herbs in the Landscape: How to Design and Grow Gardens of Herbal Annuals, Perennials, Shrubs and Trees. Debra Kirkpatrick. Harrisburg, PA, Stackpole, 1992. I can't add much to that title!

HOUSE & GREENHOUSE PLANTS

How to Select and Grow African Violets and Other Gesneriads. Theodore James, Jr. Los Angeles, Price Stern Sloan, 1983. A nice introduction to what seem to be the most popular plants in America.

The Essence of Paradise: Fragrant Plants for Indoor Gardens. Tovah Martin. Boston, Little, Brown, 1991. A lovely book, beautifully illustrated, guiding enthusiasts through a year of fragrant indoor plants. Tovah writes with great charm, gentle humor and a sense of history.

Growing Beautiful Houseplants: an Illustrated Guide to the Selection and Care of more than 1,000 Varieties. Rob Herwig. New York, Facts on File, 1992. A lavishly illustrated and very informative guide to growing houseplants; it should answer all your needs.

Foliage Plants for Decorating Indoors. Virginie & George Elbert. Portland, Timber Press, 1989. Of interest to both indoor plant professionals and hobbyists, this book is packed with essential information and includes an excellent indoor plant encyclopedia; it will be a standard for years to come.

Cacti: Over 1,200 Species Illustrated and Identified. Clive Innis & Charles Glass. New York, Portland House, 1991. A very useful guide to cacti, with keys, good color photos, and cultivation symbols for growing guidelines. Though I don't grow any, I love cacti and find them irresistible when looking through such a book.

Fuchsias for Greenhouse and Garden. David Clark. Portland, Timber Press, 1992. There are very few places in this country where one can grow fuchsias outdoors, but they make lovely greenhouse plants, and this little book contains a lot of information about growing them, and descriptions of many cultivars.

The Illustrated Encyclopedia of Orchids: over 1100 Species Illustrated and Identified. Alec Pridgeon, ed. Portland, Timber Press, 1992. What an inspiration it is to look through this book! If lush hybrid orchids are too flamboyant for your taste, here are many hundreds of more modest and charming species orchids, all interesting in their own way, and many irresistible!

All About Growing Orchids. Rick Bond. San Ramon, CA, Ortho Books, 1988. There are zillions of orchid books -- this is a good place to start learning the basics.

Home Orchid Growing, 4th ed., 1990 and *Orchids as House Plants*. Rev. ed., 1976. Both published in New York by Dover. Rebecca Northen. Northen's books come highly recommended by several orchid nurseries for their easy to understand information. She takes a very sensible approach to growing orchids, which many people assume are very difficult to handle.

PERENNIALS

Perennials. 2 v. Roger Phillips & Martyn Rix. New York, Random House, 1991. Wonderful color photos of thousands of perennial plants, many are species plants growing in the wild and not at all common to gardens, with good descriptions and some cultural notes. It's arranged by season of bloom and general plant families instead of alphabetically by botanical name, which slows you down since you have to refer to the index for every plant you want to look up. Still, well worth using!

Hardy Herbaceous Perennials. 2 v. Leo Jelitto & Wilhelm Schacht. Portland, Timber Press, 1990. This is a very fine work, updated from an earlier German edition; the plant descriptions are very good, there are some cultural notes and many black and white and color photographs. More scientific in tone than Phillips & Rix, this does not have color photographs of each plant, but it's arranged in encyclopedic alphabetical order, making it easier to use.

Perennial Garden Plants or The Modern Florilegium. Graham Stuart Thomas. 3rd Ed. Portland, Sagapress/Timber Press, 1990. Written by one of the great English plantsmen, this is a "good read" with sound advice on plant selection. Also try to find his *The Art of Planting.* Boston, Godine, 1984.

Perennials for American Gardens. Ruth Rogers Clausen & Nicolas H. Ekstrom. New York, Random House, 1989. A wonderful encyclopedia of perennial plants, including many that are too little known, with good general cultural information and many excellent color photographs. It has an extensive bibliography.

Herbaceous Perennial Plants: A Treatise on their Identification, Culture and Garden Attributes. Allen M. Armitage. Athens, GA, Varsity Press, 1989. This excellent book should be on every perennial gardener's shelf -- it's beautifully written, has special features such as keys to species for quick identification, information on propagation and references to further reading on many plants. Line drawings, some color photographs.

All about Perennials. A. Cort Sinnes. San Ramon, CA, Ortho Books, 1992. A good introduction to gardening with perennials, with many color photos and a good plant encyclopedia.

Perennials: How to Select, Grow & Enjoy. Pamela Harper & Frederick McGourty. Los Angeles, Price Stern Sloan, 1985. An excellent joint effort by two acknowledged experts, with plant situation and growing well covered; beautiful color photos.

PLANTING DESIGN

Designing with Perennials. Pamela J. Harper. New York, Macmillan, 1991. Pam Harper has two advantages over many garden writers; she really knows her plants, and since she takes her own photos, she's able to illustrate her concepts perfectly. Her text is thoughtful and practical; she's distilled a lifetime of growing experience and plant love into this terrific book.

The American Mixed Border: Gardens for all Seasons. Ann Lovejoy. New York, Macmillan, 1993. I make no secret of my admiration for Ann Lovejoy; she's up there with the very best of garden writers, both for her original ideas and her lovely writing style. This is a book to read for inspiration, new thinking about old ideas, and fresh perspectives on the joys of garden making. The photos by her husband Mark and others are nearly perfect; an essential bedside book.

Perennials and their Garden Habitats. 4th ed. Richard Hansen & Friedrich Stahl. Portland, Timber Press, 1993. When we check to see if a plant likes sun or shade, we're just scratching the surface of the careful study these two Germans have given to placing plants in their optimum locations. For the gardener who loves to study garden making and diagramming plant placement; there's a good deal of interesting plant lore.

Gardening with Perennials Month by Month. Joseph Hudek. 2nd ed. Portland, Timber Press, 1993. A useful guide to garden planning for a long season of bloom; perennials are described at their peak season, with useful lists by color of bloom, preferred growing conditions, foliage, ornamental fruit and seed heads, and drought tolerance. Probably most useful in the Northeast.

Gardening with Color. Mary Keen. New York, Random House, 1991. Thoughtful observations, and excellent photos, on color combinations and the effects of light, seasonal effects and suggestions for unusual combinations. A good plant directory, and lists of plants by color.

Color in your Garden. Penelope Hobhouse. Boston, Little, Brown, 1985. Ways to extend your garden pleasure through the use of plants to provide interest at different seasons of the year. Worth study.

The Well-Chosen Garden. Christopher Lloyd. New York, Harper & Row, 1984. Advice on choosing garden plants from a well-known British plantsman. Also watch for his *The Well-Tempered Garden* and *The Adventurous Gardener* (both New York, Random House, 1985).

The Green Tapestry: Choosing and Growing the Best Perennial Plants for your Garden. Beth Chatto. New York, Simon & Schuster, 1989. This is the sort of book I love, showing how plants look in combination. This book is full of inspiring ideas and color photos. What an eye she has!

Stonescaping: a Guide to Using Stone in your Garden. Jan Kowalczewski Whitner. Pownal, VT, Garden Way, 1992. A great little book on the use of stones in various styles of gardens, full of useful how-to information.

INDIVIDUAL PLANTS

Clematis. Barry Fretwell. Deer Park, WI, Capability's Books, 1989. Clematis have been underused in American gardens and our choice of species and cultivars has been limited, but the rash of books on clematis will soon change all that. This one has good descriptions and many good color photos. (See Cabability's Books, Section B.)

Making the Most of Clematis. 2nd ed. Raymond J. Evison. Wisbech (UK), Floraprint, 1991. Written by one of England's clematis experts, it contains practical information on growing, pruning techniques, propagation, training on walls and through other plants, and descriptions of many species and cultivars.

Daylilies: the Perfect Perennial. Lewis & Nancy Hill. Pownal, VT, Garden Way, 1991. Nothing's perfect, but even I, the imperfect gardener, have had good luck with daylilies, and I found this book able to answer most of my questions, even what to do with all the seeds I collected.

Ferns to Know and Grow. F. Gordon Foster. 3rd ed. Portland, Timber Press, 1993. This has long been the bible of fern growers, with good plant descriptions and drawings of each species. It has been reprinted with an update of nomenclature.

The Encyclopedia of Ornamental Grasses. John Greenlee. Emmaus, PA, Rodale Press, 1992. If you've ever heard John Greenlee sing the praises of ornamental grasses, you'd know that he'd do a great job spreading the faith. He describes over 250 grasses, gives a good picture and lots of cultural information. You'll start looking around for a place to put ornamental grasses!

The Gardener's Guide to Growing Hellebores. Graham Rice & Elizabeth Strangman. Portland, Timber Press, 1993. One of my favorite new books this year -- if hellebores don't become the rage of the 90's, there's just no good sense left! The photos will convert you to these lovely flowers of late winter and early spring; lots of good advice on growing them.

The Hosta Book. Paul Aden. Portland, Timber Press, 1988. Written by a number of hosta experts, this book will give you an appreciation of the diversity and usefulness of this popular plant.

The Genus Hosta. W. George Schmid. Portland, Timber Press, 1992. The absolutely final word on hostas: descriptions of species, nomenclature, an alphabetical listing of all known cultivars, history of cultivation of hostas, critical analysis of previous writings. Hosta fanatics, and there are many of them, will keep this book next to their beds for the next decade. Some color pictures.

Iris. Fritz Köhlein. Portland, Timber Press, 1987. Iris are a huge and, to me, very confusing group of plants. This book by an eminent German plantsman makes it all easier to understand, and is friendly and packed with information; there are many good color photos. You'll fall in love!

The World of Irises. Wichita, KS, American Iris Society, 1978. A very thorough treatment of a very popular group of plants; it should make all of the confusing categories clear.

The Peony. Alice Harding, updated by Roy Klehm. Portland, Timber Press, 1993. This was originally two books published in 1917 and 1923, but the writing holds up very well both for the history of the peony, and for her love of peonies: she says that no garden is too small to hold a peony! Roy Klehm has added lovely color photos, lists of the best doers, and a bibliography.

Poppies: the Poppy Family in the Wild and in Cultivation. Christopher Grey-Wilson. Portland, Timber Press, 1993. At last, a poppy book, and a very nice one! Covers all members of the poppy family with good plant descriptions and some information on cultivation: color photos and a number of good line drawings.

The Genus Primula in Cultivation and the Wild. Josef Halda. Denver, Tethys Books, 1992. Primulas described by section, with information on distribution, habitat and cultivation. Each is illustrated by a very charming and accurate line drawing by Halda's wife; useful to the amateur gardener who will find illustrations of each species useful when checking seed exchange lists. (Tethys Books, 2735 S. Pennsylvania, Englewood, CO, 80110)

Primula. John Richards. Portland, Timber Press, 1993. More technical than the book above, but readable to the amateur. Illustrated with lovely color paintings and some color photos, but not every species is shown; it will especially interest growers and hybridizers.

ROSES

Roses: How to Select, Grow and Enjoy. Richard Ray and Michael McCaskey. Rev. ed. Los Angeles, Price Stern Sloan, 1981. A good introduction to roses and rose growing, full of general information and color photos, and descriptions of many popular roses.

All about Roses. Rex Wolf & James McNair. San Ramon, CA, Ortho Books, 1990. A good introductory treatment of rose growing, with color photos of many roses; information on pruning, propagating and treating problems.

Growing Good Roses. Rayford C. Reddell. Petaluma, CA, Garden Valley Press, 1993. Good growing advice from a professional rose grower; he gives specifics on particular cultivars, steering the new grower away from those that are fussy or don't perform well. Reprint of a popular book.

Roses. Roger Phillips & Martyn Rix. New York, Random House, 1988. If I only had a dollar for every time I've looked longingly through this book! It is an absolute must for lovers of roses, with good coverage of the increasingly popular old roses. The selection of modern hybrids is biased toward English varieties.

Antique Roses for the South. William C. Welch. Dallas, Taylor Publishing, 1990. There are lots of rose books, but few as much fun to read as this one. A very personal discussion of old roses which have thrived for years in difficult conditions: how to grow them, propagate them, arrange them, and enjoy them.

The Old Rose Advisor. Brent C. Dickerson. Portland, Timber Press, 1992. Given a glowing endorsement by old rose expert Graham Stuart Thomas, this book is a compendium of nineteenth and early twentieth century descriptions of more than 2,300 "old roses," most introduced before 1920. Illustrated with 270 color plates from the *Journal des Roses*, 1877-1914.

Rosa Rugosa. Suzanne Verrier. Deer Park, WI, Capability's Books, 1991. Guaranteed to make rugosa roses much more popular, as they really deserve to be. Candid descriptions of over eighty cultivars and hybrids, photos of many, and a list of sources. The triumph of the tough and healthy!

VEGETABLE & FRUIT GROWING

The Backyard Orchardist: a Complete Guide to Growing Fruit Trees in the Home Garden. Stella Otto. 1993. A terrific guide to growing fruit and helpful to anyone starting a small orchard. Lots of practical advice, advice on treating diseases and insects, and a troubleshooting guide. $17.45 from Ottographics, 8082 Maple City Rd., Maple City, MI 49664 (add 4% sales tax in Michigan).

Kiwifruit Enthusiasts Journal, v. 6. Michael Pilarski. 1992. Another mighty effort from the indefatigable Pilarski, who wrote the amazing *International Green Front Report* listed in earlier editions of GBM. This will tell you everything you need and want to know about kiwifruit growing anywhere in the world; highly recommended. Also lists fruit societies and periodicals, growers and sources; published irregularly. Available for $17.20 postpaid from Friends of the Trees, P.O. Box 1064, Tonasket, WA 98855.

Uncommon Fruits Worthy of Attention: a Gardener's Guide. Lee Reich. Reading, MA, Addison-Wesley Publishing Company, 1991. Here are good cultivar descriptions, growing and harvesting suggestions and propagation information on many off-beat fruits: pawpaws, kiwis, medlar, jujubes, persimmons and other fruiting trees and berrries suitable for growing in most of the US and southern Canada.

Seed to Seed: Seed Saving Techniques for the Vegetable Gardener. Suzanne Ashworth. 1991. Offers both general seed saving techniques and variety-by-variety instructions, with information on seed viability, storage, and germination testing. Available from the Seed Savers Exchange, see Section D.

Field and Garden Vegetables of America. Fearing Burr. Chillicothe, IL, American Botanist, 1988. Originally published in 1863, this book describes nearly 1,100 vegetable varieties in cultivation at that time; it is an invaluable source of information to those interested in identifying and preserving heirloom vegetables. Beautifully reprinted, fun to read! (See American Botanist, Section B.)

How to Grow More Vegetables than You Ever Thought Possible on Less Land than You Can Imagine. John Jeavons. 4th ed. Berkeley, Ten Speed Press, 1991. Good book on the bio-dynamic or French intensive method of organic growing by a disciple of Alan Chadwick.

Growing Vegetables West of the Cascades. Steve Solomon. Seattle, Sasquatch Books, 1989. Essential to the northwestern vegetable gardener; everything from start to finish.

Winter Gardening in the Maritime Northwest: Cool-Season Crops for the Year-Round Gardener. Binda Colebrook. Seattle, Sasquatch Books, 1989. How to keep the vegetable plot going; I think they use the term "year-round" just to rile easterners.

The New Organic Grower: A Master's Manual of Tools and Techniques for the Home and Market Gardener. Eliot Coleman. Chelsea, VT, Chelsea Green, 1989. Extremely practical -- the title says it all. Coleman has also written *The New Organic Grower's Four-Season Harvest,* about extending the harvest throughout the year. (Chelsea Green, 1992)

Designing and Maintaining your Edible Landscaping Naturally. Robert Kourik. Santa Rosa, CA, Metamorphic Press, 1986. Everything there is to know about growing vegetables and fruit to make your food garden attractive as well. $24 postpaid ($25.45 in CA). Metamorphic Press, P.O. Box 1841, Santa Rosa, CA 95402.

Fruits & Berries For The Home Garden. Lewis Hill. Pownal, VT, Storey Communications, 1992. Practical advice on growing all sorts of fruits, including pruning and controlling diseases and insects; even some recipes.

Citrus -- How to Select, Grow, and Enjoy. Richard Ray and Lance Walheim. Los Angeles, Price Stern Sloan, 1980. An informative and well-illustrated book on growing all sorts of citrus, including unusual kinds.

All about Citrus & Subtropical Fruits. San Ramon, CA, Ortho, 1985. A book that covers citrus and other fruits for warmer climates. Good color photographs and information on growing.

Red Oaks & Black Birches: the Science and Lore of Trees. Rebecca Rupp. Pownal, VT, Garden Way, 1990. Sure, it's about trees, but it's a terrific read, and so full of interest and history that you'll wallow in it. Her book about vegetables, *Blue Corn and Square Tomatoes* is equally interesting (Garden Way, 1987).

The Opinionated Gardener: Random Offshoots from an Alpine Garden. Geoffrey B. Charlesworth. Boston, Godine, 1988. Very amusing essays on gardening, not just of alpines, by a man who admits that he loves to weed. He can also write with the best of them.

The Gardener's Bed-Book. Richardson Wright. New York, PAJ Publications, 1988. Humorous short essays make it perfect for the bedside. Same publisher reissued his *The Gardener's Day Book* in 1989.

Thyme on my Hands. Eric Grissell. Portland, Timber Press, 1987. The trials and travails of a garden maker, amusingly written and well worth his trouble if the photo on the cover is any proof. Well-developed appreciation of the garden cat.

The Gardener's Year. Karel Capek. Madison, University of Wisconsin, 1984. Proof that gardening knows no boundaries, this little book written in Prague in the 1930s will make you laugh out loud -- his wry observations are timeless.

The Greek Plant World in Myth, Art and Literature. Hellmut Baumann. Translated and augmented by William T. Stearn & Eldwyth Ruth Stearn. Portland, Timber Press, 1993. From earliest times, Greece has been a center of botanical interest: this is a fascinating account of historical botanical lore.

The American Gardener: A Sampler. Allen Lacy, ed. New York, Farrar, Straus & Giroux, 1988. A wonderful way to become acquainted with good garden writers. The selections are loosely arranged by subject and date from the nineteenth and twentieth centuries.

American Garden Writing: Gleanings from Garden Lives Then and Now. Bonnie Marranca, ed. New York, PAJ Publications, 1988. Another omnibus of garden writing. Her selections differ from Lacy's, so you can profitably read both.

By Pen & By Spade: an Anthology of Garden Writing from Hortus. David Wheeler, ed. New York, Summit Books, 1990. A good way to sample the type of articles appearing in Hortus before you pop for a subscription; a showcase for the best contemporary British garden writing.

GUIDES TO GARDENS

Complete Guide to North American Gardens. 2 v. William Milligan. Boston, Little, Brown, 1991. Not complete, these two volumes cover the Northeast (from Canada to Pennsylvania) and the West Coast, with good garden descriptions. Perhaps more volumes are in the works.

Travelers' Guide to Herb Gardens: over 500 Gardens in the United States and Canada Featuring Herbs. 3rd ed. Compiled by The Herb Society of America. Mentor, OH, 1992. Brief descriptions of gardens, open days and hours, and maps of each state and province give location of a variety of public and private herb gardens. Write or call for price: see Section D.

Herb Gardens in America: a Visitor's Guide. Karen S.C. Morris & Lyle E. Craker. 1991. A directory of herb gardens divided into two main sections, one giving detailed descriptions of major gardens, the other giving brief descriptions of "all known herbs gardens open to the public." $11.70 postpaid. HSMP Press, 176 Heatherstone Road, Amherst, MA 01002 .

The Garden Tourist: a Guide to Garden Tours, Garden Days and Special Events. Lois G. Rosenfeld, ed. Portland, Timber Press, 1993. This is a neat idea, a schedule of special events, flower shows, plant society conventions and such, listed regionally so that you can find out what's going on near you, or where you want to visit. Includes major events overseas as well.

Garden Touring in the Pacific Northwest: a Guide to Gardens and Specialty Nurseries in Oregon, Washington, and British Columbia. Jan Kowalczewski Whitner. Seattle, Alaska Northwest Books, 1993. Essential to the gardener traveling in the Northwest, this book gives good descriptions of the gardens and nurseries there, and an idea of how many there are! Buy a copy as you cross into the territory, or to study before you travel.

The Traveler's Guide to American Gardens. Mary Helen Ray & Robert P. Nicholls, eds. Chapel Hill, University of North Carolina Press, 1988. A state-by-state guide to gardens of interest; each is briefly described, those of special merit are starred.

Gardens of North America and Hawaii: A Traveler's Guide. Irene & Walter Jacob. Portland, Timber Press, 1986. Very useful; small enough to take with you on a trip; it rates the gardens. Gardens don't move around, so older books still serve pretty well.

Beautiful Gardens: Guide to over 80 Botanical Gardens, Arboretums and More in Southern California and the Southwest. Eric A. Johnson & Scott Millard. Tucson, Ironwood Press, 1991. Complete information for visiting public gardens in Arizona, Nevada and New Mexico as well as southern California.

Collins Book of British Gardens: A Guide to 200 Gardens in England, Scotland & Wales. George Plumptre. London, Collins, 1985. Organized by region, then by county; black and white photos, regional maps, a page or two on each garden.

The Good Gardens Guide. Graham Rose & Peter King. London, Barrie & Jenkins, annual. Lists over 1,000 gardens open to the public in Greaat Britain and Ireland, with lots of information for visitors (teas, dogs on lead, and much more) and descriptions of the gardens. There are many good guides to gardens in Great Britain, but this one and the one above are comprehensive, light enough to carry, and paperback, so you'll feel free to take them with you.

The Gardens of Europe. Penelope Hobhouse and Patrick Taylor, eds. New York, Random House, 1990. Too heavy to carry with you on a trip, this book makes good study before you go to Europe. It covers 700 gardens in Britain, Europe, and the former Eastern Bloc countries. Essentials for visiting are given, as are special features of the gardens; some of the gardens are private and you must write ahead for an appointment.

PLANT-FINDING SOURCEBOOKS

One would think that through the magic of computers, it would be easy to compile directories of sources by botanical name. *Au contraire!* Such magic takes endless hours of inputting and checking; sources come and go, catalogs change every year; people spending endless hours at the computer turn to stone and their tempers grow very short! It seems to me that the best solution is to divide the job into much smaller, specialized pieces; an ideal project for plant societies. Listed below are some fine efforts.

Andersen Horticultural Library's Source Llist of Plants and Seeds. 3rd ed. 1993. Completely indexes over 400 retail and wholesale catalogs; lists over 47,000 plants by botanical name; the 1993 edition was compiled from 1990-92 catalogs. This is the first place to start looking for an elusive plant. $34.95 postpaid. Anderson Horticultural Library, Minnesota Landscape Arboretum, P.O. Box 39, Chanhassen, MN 55317-0039.

The Plant Finder: 60,000 Plants and Where to Buy Them. Chris Philip. An annual plant source book for Great Britain; lists plants by botanical name with source symbols, indicates which nurseries sell by mail order (but not those which ship overseas), lists plant groups held in national collections of the National Council for the Conservation of Plants & Gardens, and includes an excellent bibliography of articles and books about all kinds of plants. A model sourcebook in every way!

The Canadian Plant Sourcebook, 1992/93. Anne & Peter Ashley. Lists over 15,000 plants of all kinds available from over 110 Canadian nurseries, with keys to sources. $16 postpaid from The Canadian Plant Sourcebook, 93 Fenitman Avenue, Ottawa, ON, Canada K1S 0T7.

The Combined Rose List. Beverly Dobson & Peter Schneider. This is a tour de force: a yearly list of every species and hybrid rose cultivar listed by dozens of rose nurseries in the US, Canada and overseas. They are listed by cultivar name, with brief information on year of introduction, breeder, color of flower and where you can get it. You can't grow roses and not have it! The 1994 edition is $18 postpaid Available from P.O. Box 16035, Rocky River, OH 44116. OH residents add 7% sales tax.

Nursery Sources, Native Plants and Wild Flowers. Framingham, MA, New England Wild Flower Society, 1993. A list of wholesale and retail nurseries that specialize in native plants and wild flowers, listed by region, with notes as to plant and seed sources. Write or call for price; see Section D.

Sources of Native Seeds and Plants. Ankeny, IA, Soil and Water Conservation Society, 1994. A sourcebook for plants to use in conservation and restoration work -- native plants, grasses and trees, both seed and plants. Sources listed by state. Write or call for price; see Section C.

Nursery Sources for California Native Plants. G. S. Newton et al. Sacramento, California Division of Mines and Geology, 1990. Publication 90-04. $8 postpaid. (801 K Street, MS 14-33, Sacramento, CA 95814-3532).

Hortus Northwest: A Pacific Northwest Native Plant Directory. 4th ed. 1993. Dale Shank, ed. Lists native plant nurseries in the Northwest and northern California. $9 postpaid from Hortus Northwest, P.O. Box 955, Canby, OR 97013.

The Northwest Gardeners' Resource Directory. Stephanie Feeney. An annual directory to nurseries, seed sources, plant sales, gardens to visit, flower and garden shows, clubs and societies, organizations that help gardeners, libraries and book shops, and workshops, lecture series and short courses. It covers southern British Columbia to Vancouver WA, and it's terrific -- a model for what can be done with regional information. In local bookstores, or $11.50 postpaid ($12 in WA) from Stephanie Feeney, 59 Strawberry Point, Bellingham, WA 98226.

Hortus Source List. Ithaca, L.H. Bailey Hortorium, 1992. Indexes the catalogs of 63 nurseries, mostly in New York state, by botanical name. Available for $13 from the Hortorium, 462 Mann Library, Cornell Univeristy, Ithaca, NY 14853. Make checks out to Cornell University.

North Carolina Grown: The Source List of Ornamental Plants Available from N.C. Mail Order Nurseries. 1992. J.C. Raulston. Plants listed by botanical name, index to 15 mail order nursery sources in North Carolina. Sadly it will be much thinner when they take out the entries from Montrose Nursery, now closed. $6 postpaid from The NCSU Arboretum -- Source Guide, Box 7609, NCSU, Raleigh, NC 27695-7609.

Boxwood Buyer's Guide. American Boxwood Society. Boyce, VA, 1993. A guide to retail, mail order and wholesale sources of boxwood. A model for society plant source lists, indexed by cultivar and location of source. Write or call for price information. See Section D.

Eureka! 1994 National Daylily Locator. Ken & Kay Gregory. A very useful finding list for daylilies in commerce, giving many sources and comparative prices, as well as lists of award winners and new introductions. $17.90 postpaid from 5586 Quail Creek Dr., Granite Falls, NC 28630-9538. NC residents add $.90 sales tax.

Herb Gardener's Resource Guide, 1994-95. Paula Oliver. Over eleven hundred sources of herbs, herb supplies and products, herb gardens and more; particularly interesting to small herb businesses. $12.95 postpaid (add $2 to Canada, $4 overseas) from Northwind Farm, Route 2, Box 246, Shevlin, MN 56676.

Herb Companion Wish Book & Resource Guide. Loveland, CO, Interweave Press, 1992. Lists plant and supply sources, newsletters and societies, and lots of other interesting facts: oriented to home gardeners. $20.70 postpaid from 201 E. 4th Street, Loveland, CO 80537.

Garden Seed Inventory. Kent Whealy, ed. 3rd ed. Decorah, IA, Seed Savers Publications, 1992. Lists every non-hybrid vegetable variety available from seed companies in the US and Canada, with descriptions and sources for each. One of those wonderful original ideas, laboriously and lovingly compiled and extremely useful to the whole world of horticulture. Bravo! (See Seed Savers Exchange, Section D.)

Fruit, Berry and Nut Inventory. Kent Whealy, ed. 2nd ed. Decorah, IA, Seed Saver Publications, 1993. Like the *Garden Seed Inventory,* this book lists fruit and nut varieties, with plant descriptions and sources.

Cornucopia: a Source Book of Edible Plants. Stephen Facciola. Vista, CA, Kampong Publications, 1990. The amount of information in this book is staggering; it lists almost any plant that can or has been eaten, with a source, first by botanical name, and in a separate listing by cultivar name. It includes a directory of sources, a vast bibliography, and indexes of common English and foreign names. Write to publisher for information: Kampong Publications, 1879 Sunrise Drive, Vista, CA 92084.

Taylor's Guide to Specialty Nurseries. Barbara J. Barton. Boston, Houghton Mifflin, 1993. What can I say? The fun of writing this book was having the time to write a little more about the many interesting people that run the nurseries; it features about 300 mail order nurseries specializing in ornamental garden plants.

The American Association of Nurserymen has compiled a list of commercial plant-locating services and state commercial nursery source publications; send a long SASE for their *Guide to Plant Locators.* See Section C for address.

Well, dear gardeners, it's time to say goodbye again for a few years! I hope that you're already planning to try some of the intriguing new sources listed, or have decided to join some societies and buy some books, and feel the juices of garden intoxication racing through your veins. I feel that the greatest rewards I've received from my interest in plants are the friends that I've made both here at home and much farther afield, and I think of all my readers as gardening friends. I'm always afraid that in my enthusiasm I've tried to tell you *too* much, and yet I'm also afraid that tomorrow when I pick up my mail there will be something more I *should* have told you, or even worse, will find a slip of paper with something that I've *forgotten* to tell you! It's time for you to shout "Goodnight, Barbara!" Happy gardening 'till we meet again!!

Indexes

H. Plant Sources Index: an index of plant and seed sources by plant specialties. Two-letter geographical codes are included to help you find the closest source or a source in a similar climate.

J. Geographical Index: an index of plant and seed sources by location. U.S. and Canadian sources are listed by state or province. Overseas sources are listed by country. Within each primary location, cities or post offices are listed alphabetically. Symbols indicate which sources have nurseries or shops and which have plant displays or display gardens to visit.

K. Product Sources Index: an index of suppliers and services listed by specialty. Within categories, sources are listed by location, and a symbol indicates whether they have a shop to visit.

L. Society Index: an index of horticultural societies listed by plant and/or other special interests.

M. Magazine Index: an index of magazines offered by societies, as well as other horticultural and gardening magazines, newsletters and other occasional publications.

Notes on Indexing

Each plant source or supplier is indexed for up to twelve specialties and/or trade names. When sources didn't indicate which specialties they preferred, I have chosen for them from a study of their catalogs. The companies vary from small to large, and their specialties from narrow to very broad.

For those with few specialties, the indexing is very specific, but as offerings become greater, the indexing becomes broader. A small nursery that offers only ivy is listed under "Ivy," but a large nursery that includes ivy as one of its many offerings is listed under "Ground Covers." Similarly, "Sundials" is a specific category, versus the more general "Garden Ornaments."

You should check both the specific category and the general category to be sure you find all possible sources. Where specific plants are indexed—for instance, crabapples—it is because I have found a better-than-usual selection offered by that source.

The notes on catalogs in the alphabetical listings include some specialties that I was unable to index because each "listee" was limited to twelve categories. To jog your memory, you could jot the company name into the index next to the appropriate category.

A table of the symbols and abbreviations used in this book appears
on the bookmark inside the back cover.

PAGE SOURCE

(continued next page)

H 2 PLANT SOURCES INDEX

(continued next page)

(continued next page)

PAGE SOURCE

BONSAI, FINISHED
A 11   The Bonsai Shop, NY
A 14   Brussel's Bonsai Nursery, MS
B 10   Dave's Aquariums & Greenhouse, IA
A 67   Lone Pine Connection, CA
A 70   Matsu-Momiji Nursery, PA
A 72   Miniature Plant Kingdom, CA
A 77   Northland Gardens, NY
A 99   Shanti Bithi Nursery, CT
A 119   Wildwood Gardens, OH

BONSAI, INDOOR
A 6   Artistic Plants, TX
A 11   Bonsai Farm, TX
A 72   Miniature Plant Kingdom, CA

BONSAI, PLANTS FOR
See also specific plants
A 6   Artistic Plants, TX
A 10   Bijou Alpines, WA
B 5   Bonsai Associates, Inc., MD
A 11   Bonsai Farm, TX
A 14   Brussel's Bonsai Nursery, MS
A 21   Coenosium Gardens, OR
A 26   The Cummins Garden, NJ
B 10   Dave's Aquariums & Greenhouse, IA
A 28   Del's Japanese Maples, OR
A 33   Evergreen Gardenworks, CA
A 37   Foliage Gardens, WA
A 37   Forestfarm, OR
A 41   Girard Nurseries, OH
A 53   Jerry Horne -- Rare Plants, FL
A 60   King's Mums, CA
A 61   Michael & Janet Kristick, PA
A 67   Lone Pine Connection, CA
A 67   Loucks Nursery, OR
A 70   Matsu-Momiji Nursery, PA
A 72   Miniature Plant Kingdom, CA
A 73   Mt. Tahoma Nursery, WA
A 74   Mountain Maples, CA
A 77   Northland Gardens, NY
A 78   Northridge Gardens, CA
A 81   Owen Farms, TN
A 82   Pacific Southwest Nursery, CA
A 83   Pen Y Bryn Nursery, PA
B 28   Pine Garden Bonsai Company, WA
A 87   Porterhowse Farms, OR
A 90   Rarafolia, PA
A 90   Rare Conifer Nursery, CA
A 90   Rare Plant Research, OR
A 92   Rhapis Palm Growers, CA
A 99   Shanti Bithi Nursery, CT
A 103   Southern Seeds, Ne
A 104   Springvale Farm Nursery, IL
A 104   Stallings Nursery, CA
A 106   Stubbs Shrubs, OR
A 107   Sunnyslope Gardens, CA
A 111   Trans Pacific Nursery, OR
A 111   Transplant Nursery, GA
A 116   Wavecrest Nursery & Landscaping Co., MI
A 119   Wildwood Gardens, OH

BOUGAINVILLEA
A 2   Air Expose, TX
A 13   Brudy's Exotics, TX
A 25   Crockett's Tropical Plants, TX
A 59   Kartuz Greenhouses, CA
A 87   The Plumeria People, TX
A 104   Stallings Nursery, CA

BOX
A 5   Appalachian Gardens, PA
A 18   Carroll Gardens, MD
A 21   Coenosium Gardens, OR
A 26   The Cummins Garden, NJ
A 28   Daystar, ME

BRODIAEAS
A 93   Robinett Bulb Farm, CA

BROMELIADS
See also specific plants
A 2   Alberts & Merkel Bros., Inc., FL
A 10   Arthur Boe Distributor, LA
A 20   City Gardens, MI
A 24   Cornelison Bromeliads, FL
A 27   Dane Company, TX
A 38   Fox Orchids, Inc., AR
A 41   Glasshouse Works, OH
A 41   Golden Lake Greenhouses, CA
A 45   Growers Service Company, MI
A 51   Holladay Jungle, CA
A 57   Joe's Nursery, CA
A 69   Ann Mann's Orchids, FL
A 69   Marilynn's Garden, CA
A 71   Michael's Bromeliads, FL
A 76   Neon Palm Nursery, CA
A 79   Oak Hill Gardens, IL
A 85   Pineapple Place, FL
A 89   Rainforest Flora, Inc., CA
A 100   Shelldance Nursery, CA
A 103   Southern Exposure, TX
A 111   Tropiflora, FL

BRUGMANSIAS
A 58   Karleens Achimenes, GA

BUCKWHEAT
A 26   Cross Seed Company, KS
A 60   Kester's Wild Game Food Nurseries, WI
A 88   Prairie State Commodities, IL

BULBS, SPECIES
See also specific plants
A 3   Jacques Amand, Bulb Specialists, MD
A 6   Arrowhead Alpines, MI
A 7   Avon Bulbs, En
A 10   Bio-Quest International, CA
A 14   Bundles of Bulbs, MD
A 16   C K S, Cz
A 18   Cape Seed & Bulb, So
A 20   Paul Christian -- Rare Plants, Wa
A 22   Conley's Garden Center, ME
A 26   Cruickshank's, Inc., ON
A 26   The Daffodil Mart, VA
A 30   Jim Duggan Flower Nursery, CA
A 31   Eco-Gardens, GA
A 35   Timothy D. Field Ferns & Wildflowers, NH
A 43   Russell Graham, Purveyor of Plants, OR
A 44   GreenLady Gardens, CA
A 53   Honeywood Lilies, SK
A 61   Kline Nursery Co., OR
A 68   McClure & Zimmerman, WI
A 68   Mark McDonough, MA
A 69   Mad River Imports, VT
A 71   Messelaar Bulb Co., MA
A 73   Monocot Nursery, En
A 74   Charles H. Mueller Co., PA
A 85   Pine Heights Nursery, Au
A 87   Potterton & Martin, En

(continued next page)

PAGE	SOURCE

PAGE	SOURCE

DAHLIAS
A 3	Alpen Gardens, MT
A 5	Antonelli Brothers, Inc., CA
A 9	Bedford Dahlias, OH
A 22	Connell's Dahlias, WA
A 26	Cruickshank's, Inc., ON
A 27	Dan's Dahlias, WA
A 29	Dick's Flower Farm, WI
A 30	Dutch Gardens, Inc., NJ
A 33	Evergreen Acres Dahlia Gardens, NY
A 34	Ferncliff Gardens, BC
A 39	Frey's Dahlias, OR
A 40	Garden Valley Dahlias, OR
A 52	Homestead Gardens, MT
A 74	Charles H. Mueller Co., PA
A 86	Pleasant Valley Glads and Dahlias, MA
A 97	Sea-Tac Dahlia Gardens, WA
A 99	Shackleton's Dahlias, OR
A 108	Swan Island Dahlias, OR
A 112	Van Bourgondien Bros., NY
A 113	Veldheer Tulip Gardens, MI
A 120	Wisley Dahlia Farm, NY

DAPHNES
A 10	Bijou Alpines, WA
A 29	Digging Dog Nursery, CA
A 33	Euroseeds, Cz
A 49	Heronswood Nursery, WA
A 73	Mt. Tahoma Nursery, WA
A 101	Siskiyou Rare Plant Nursery, OR

DAYLILIES
A 1	A & D Peony & Perennial Nursery, WA
A 1	Adamgrove, MO
A 3	Alpine Valley Gardens, CA
A 3	Ambergate Gardens, MN
A 4	American Daylily & Perennials, MO
A 4	Anderson Iris Gardens, MN
A 6	Artemis Gardens, MT
A 7	B & D Lilies, WA
A 7	Balash Gardens, MI
A 9	Big Tree Daylily Garden, FL
A 10	Bloomingfields Farm, CT
A 10	Blossom Valley Gardens, CA
A 12	Borbeleta Gardens, MN
A 14	Bundles of Bulbs, MD
A 15	Busse Gardens, MN
A 16	C & C Nursery, KY
A 18	Caprice Farm Nursery, OR
A 18	Cascade Bulb & Seed, OR
A 19	Champlain Isle Agro Associates, VT
A 20	Clifford's Perennial & Vine, WI
A 21	Coastal Gardens & Nursery, SC
A 21	Coburg Planting Fields, IN
A 22	Comanche Acres Iris Gardens, MO
A 23	Cooper's Garden, MN
A 23	Cordon Bleu Farms, CA
A 25	Crintonic Gardens, OH
A 26	Crownsville Nursery, MD
A 26	Cruickshank's, Inc., ON
A 27	Daylily Discounters, FL
A 27	Daylily World, FL
A 30	Double D Nursery, GA
A 32	Enchanted Valley Garden, WI
A 32	Englearth Gardens, MI
A 34	Ferncliff Gardens, BC
A 37	Floyd Cove Nursery, FL
A 40	Garden Perennials, NE
A 42	Goravani Growers, FL
A 43	Grace Gardens North, WI

DAYLILIES
A 44	Greenwood Daylily Gardens, CA
A 45	Hahn's Rainbow Iris Garden, MO
A 49	Heschke Gardens, MN
A 49	Hickory Hill Gardens, PA
A 51	Holbrook Farm & Nursery, NC
A 51	Holly Lane Iris Gardens, MN
A 52	Homestead Division of Sunnybrook Farms, OH
A 52	Homestead Farms, MO
A 53	Honeywood Lilies, SK
A 54	Iris & Plus, PQ
A 55	Iron Gate Gardens, NC
A 56	Jasperson's Hersey Nursery, WI
A 57	Jernigan Gardens, NC
A 60	Kirkland Daylilies, AL
A 60	Klehm Nursery, IL
A 62	Lady Bug Beautiful Gardens, FL
A 62	Lakeside Acres, TN
A 64	Lee's Gardens, IL
A 66	Little River Farm, NC
A 67	Louisiana Nursery, LA
A 68	McClure & Zimmerman, WI
A 69	McMillen's Iris Garden, ON
A 69	Maple Tree Gardens, NE
A 70	Maxim's Greenwood Gardens, CA
A 70	Meadowlake Gardens, SC
A 72	Miller's Manor Gardens, IN
A 73	Monashee Perennials, BC
A 76	Nicholls Gardens, VA
A 79	Oakes Daylilies, TN
A 79	Olallie Daylily Gardens, VT
A 85	Pinecliffe Daylily Gardens, IN
A 88	Powell's Gardens, NC
A 90	Ramona Gardens, CA
A 93	Rocknoll Nursery, OH
A 93	Rollingwood Gardens, FL
A 96	Savory's Gardens, Inc., MN
A 96	Saxton Gardens, NY
A 98	R. Seawright, MA
A 101	Sir Williams Gardens, MI
A 102	Soules Garden, IN
A 106	Stoecklein's Nursery, PA
A 107	Sunnyridge Gardens, TN
A 108	Swallowtail Garden & Nursery, SC
A 108	Dave Talbott Nursery, FL
A 109	Thomasville Nurseries, GA
A 111	Tranquil Lake Nursery, MA
A 112	Valente Gardens, ME
A 112	Van Bourgondien Bros., NY
A 114	Andre Viette Farm & Nursery, VA
A 118	Gilbert H. Wild & Son, Inc., MO
A 120	Wimberlyway Gardens, FL
A 121	York Hill Farm, NH

DELPHINIUMS
A 27	Daisy Fields, OR
A 28	DeGiorgi Seed Company, NE
A 29	Donaroma's Nursery, MA
A 35	Fieldstone Gardens, Inc., ME
A 46	Harrisons Delphiniums, En
A 47	Hauser's Superior View Farm, WI
A 71	Milaeger's Gardens, WI
A 84	Perpetual Perennials, OH
A 98	Select Seeds -- Antique Flowers, CT
A 116	Weiss Brothers Nursery, CA

DESERT PLANTS
See also specific plants
A 28	Desert Enterprises, AZ
A 28	Desert Moon Nursery, NM

(continued next page)

PAGE	SOURCE

(continued next page)

(continued next page)

(continued next page)

PAGE SOURCE

FUCHSIAS, HARDY
A 17   Canyon Creek Nursery, CA
A 62   Lamb Nurseries, WA
A 91   Regine's Fuchsia Garden, CA
A 103 Southern Seeds, Ne

GARDENIAS
A 25   Crockett's Tropical Plants, TX
A 78   Nuccio's Nurseries, CA

GARLIC
A 26   Dacha Barinka, BC
A 28   Delegeane Garlic Farms, CA
A 35   Filaree Farm, WA
A 38   Fox Hollow Herbs & Heirloom Seed Company, PA
A 39   Garden City Seeds, MT
A 42   Good Seed Co., WA
A 58   Kalmia Farm, VA
A 63   Le Jardin du Gourmet, VT
A 76   Nichols Garden Nursery, Inc., OR
B 27   Peaceful Valley Farm Supply, CA
A 92   Richters Herbs, ON
A 94   Ronniger's Seed Potatoes, ID
A 101 Silver Springs Nursery, ID
A 103 Southern Exposure Seed Exchange(R), VA

GARLIC, SKINLESS
A 87   Plumtree Nursery, NY

GASTERIAS
A 14   Burk's Nursery, AR
A 106 Succulenta, CA

GENERAL NURSERY STOCK
See also specific plants
A 2   Alberta Nurseries & Seed Company, AB
A 12   Bottoms Nursery & Owens Vineyard, GA
A 14   Buckley Nursery Garden Center, WA
A 15   W. Atlee Burpee Company, PA
A 24   Country Heritage Nursery, MI
A 32   Emlong Nurseries, MI
A 34   Farmer Seed & Nursery, MN
A 35   Henry Field Seed & Nursery Co., IA
A 38   Fowler Nurseries, Inc., CA
A 41   Girard Nurseries, OH
A 45   Gurney's Seed & Nursery Co., SD
A 47   H. G. Hastings, GA
A 57   Johnson Nursery, GA
A 58   J. W. Jung Seed Co., WI
A 61   V. Kraus Nurseries, Ltd., ON
A 63   Lawson's Nursery, GA
A 68   McFayden Seeds, MB
A 70   Mellinger's, Inc., OH
A 72   Miller Nurseries, Inc., NY
A 73   Morden Nurseries, Ltd., MB
A 87   Pony Creek Nursery, WI
A 92   Rider Nurseries, IA
A 101 R. H. Shumway Seedsman, SC
A 104 Spring Hill Nurseries Co., IL
A 105 Stark Bro's Nurseries & Orchards Co., MO
A 108 T & T Seeds, Ltd., MB
A 112 Twombly Nursery, CT
A 120 Windy Ridge Nursery, AB
A 121 Womack's Nursery Co., TX

GENTIANS
A 5   Appalachian Wildflower Nursery, PA
A 6   Arrowhead Alpines, MI
A 13   Brookside Wildflowers, NC
A 21   Collector's Nursery, WA

GENTIANS
A 33   Euroseeds, Cz
A 51   Holden Clough Nursery, En
A 56   Jelitto Staudensamen GmBH, Ge
A 75   Nature's Garden, OR
A 86   Plant World, En
A 88   Prairie Moon Nursery, MN
A 88   Prairie Ridge Nursery/CRM Ecosystems, Inc., WI
A 98   Seedalp, Sw
A 108 Surry Gardens, ME
A 118 Wildginger Woodlands, NY

GERANIUMS
A 12   Brawner Geraniums, WV
A 27   Daisy Fields, OR
A 27   Davidson-Wilson Greenhouses, IN
A 62   Lake Odessa Greenhouse, MI
A 64   Lee's Gardens, IL
A 99   Shady Hill Gardens, IL

GERANIUMS, MINIATURE
A 12   Brawner Geraniums, WV
A 27   Davidson-Wilson Greenhouses, IN
A 70   Merry Gardens, ME
A 99   Shady Hill Gardens, IL

GERANIUMS, SCENTED
A 1   Adventures in Herbs, NC
A 12   Brawner Geraniums, WV
A 24   The Country Mouse, WI
A 26   Dabney Herbs, KY
A 27   Davidson-Wilson Greenhouses, IN
A 38   Fox Hill Farm, MI
A 42   Good Hollow Greenhouse & Herbarium, TN
A 47   Hartman's Herb Farm, MA
A 48   The Herb Barn, PA
A 48   Herbs-Liscious, IA
A 50   Hilltop Herb Farm, TX
A 56   It's About Thyme, TX
A 62   Lake Odessa Greenhouse, MI
A 64   Lewis Mountain Herbs & Everlastings, OH
A 65   Lily of the Valley Herb Farm, OH
A 67   Logee's Greenhouses, CT
A 70   Merry Gardens, ME
A 74   Mountain Valley Growers, Inc., CA
A 91   Rasland Farm, NC
A 92   Richters Herbs, ON
A 94   Rose Hill Herbs and Perennials, VA
A 94   The Rosemary House, PA
A 96   Sandy Mush Herb Nursery, NC
A 99   Shady Hill Gardens, IL
A 102 Sleepy Hollow Herb Farm, KY
A 106 Story House Herb Farm, KY
A 107 Sunnybrook Farms Nursery, OH
A 109 The Thyme Garden Seed Company, OR
A 110 Tinmouth Channel Farm, VT
A 114 Village Arbors, AL
A 116 Well-Sweep Herb Farm, NJ
A 120 Wirth's Herbs, PA
A 121 Wrenwood of Berkeley Springs, WV

GERANIUMS, SPECIES
A 12   Brawner Geraniums, WV
A 15   Busse Gardens, MN
A 17   Canyon Creek Nursery, CA
A 20   Clifford's Perennial & Vine, WI
A 25   Cricklewood Nursery, WA
A 29   Digging Dog Nursery, CA
A 35   Fieldstone Gardens, Inc., ME
A 36   Fir Grove Perennial Nursury, WA
(continued next page)

(continued next page)

(continued next page)

(continued next page)

(continued next page)

PAGE SOURCE

LEPTOSPERMUMS
A 31   Eclipse Farms, MO
A 31   Ellison Horticultural Pty., Ltd., Au
A 103 Southern Seeds, Ne
A 109 Tasmanian Forest Seeds, Au

LEUCODENDRONS
A 34   Feathers Wild Flower Seeds, So
A 81   D. Orriell -- Seed Exporters, Au
A 101 Silverhill Seeds, So

LEUCOSPERMUMS
A 34   Feathers Wild Flower Seeds, So
A 101 Silverhill Seeds, So

LEUCOTHOES
A 81   Ben Pace Nursery, GA

LEWISIAS
A 6   Ashwood Nurseries, En
A 21   Colorado Alpines, Inc., CO
A 73   Mt. Tahoma Nursery, WA
A 90   Rare Plant Research, OR
A 91   Redlo Cacti, OR
A 95   Jim & Irene Russ - Quality Plants, CA
A 104 Southwestern Native Seeds, AZ

LILACS
A 4   Ameri-Hort Research, OH
A 8   Bay Laurel Nursery, CA
A 14   Buckley Nursery Garden Center, WA
A 38   Fox Hill Nursery, ME
A 47   Hartmann's Plantation, Inc., MI
A 47   Heard Gardens, Ltd., IA
A 53   Hortico, Inc., ON
A 61   V. Kraus Nurseries, Ltd., ON
A 73   Morden Nurseries, Ltd., MB
A 102 Smith Nursery Co., IA
A 116 Wedge Nursery, MN

LILIES, HYBRID
A 3   Jacques Amand, Bulb Specialists, MD
A 3   Ambergate Gardens, MN
A 7   B & D Lilies, WA
A 12   Borbeleta Gardens, MN
A 14   The Bulb Crate, IL
A 14   Bundles of Bulbs, MD
A 18   Cascade Bulb & Seed, OR
A 20   Clifford's Perennial & Vine, WI
A 26   Cruickshank's, Inc., ON
A 28   Peter De Jager Bulb Co., MA
A 29   Dick's Flower Farm, WI
A 30   Dutch Gardens, Inc., NJ
A 34   Fairyland Begonia & Lily Garden, CA
A 45   Growers Service Company, MI
A 46   Hartle-Gilman Gardens, MN
A 50   Hildenbrandt's Iris Gardens, NE
A 51   Holly Ridge Nursery, OH
A 53   Honeywood Lilies, SK
A 56   Jackson & Perkins Co., OR
A 63   Orol Ledden & Sons, NJ
A 65   The Lily Pad, WA
A 66   Lindel Lilies, BC
A 69   Mad River Imports, VT
A 71   Messelaar Bulb Co., MA
A 73   Monashee Perennials, BC
A 74   Charles H. Mueller Co., PA
A 92   Riverside Gardens, SK
A 96   Saxton Gardens, NY
A 96   John Scheepers, Inc., CT

LILIES, HYBRID
A 101 Skolaski's Glads & Field Flowers, WI
A 113 Van Dyck's Flower Farms, Inc., NY
A 113 Van Engelen, Inc., CT
A 116 The Waushara Gardens, WI

LILIES, SPECIES
A 7   Avon Bulbs, En
A 7   B & D Lilies, WA
A 14   The Bulb Crate, IL
A 18   Cascade Bulb & Seed, OR
A 19   Chadwell Himalayan Seed, En
A 20   Paul Christian -- Rare Plants, Wa
A 43   Russell Graham, Purveyor of Plants, OR
A 46   Hartle-Gilman Gardens, MN
A 61   Kline Nursery Co., OR
A 66   Lindel Lilies, BC
A 93   Robinett Bulb Farm, CA
A 96   Saxton Gardens, NY

LIMA BEANS
A 34   Fern Hill Farm, NJ

LINGONBERRIES
A 28   DeGrandchamp's Blueberry Farm, MI

LIRIOPE
A 30   Double D Nursery, GA
A 88   Prentiss Court Ground Covers, SC
A 109 Thomasville Nurseries, GA

LITHOPS
A 1   Abbey Gardens, CA
A 29   Desert Theatre, CA
A 50   Highland Succulents, OH
A 66   Living Stones Nursery, AZ
A 71   Mesa Garden, NM
A 91   Redlo Cacti, OR
A 95   Doug & Vivi Rowland, En
A 122 Roy Young, Seedsman, En

LOBELIA, PERENNIAL
A 119 The Wildwood Flower, NC

LOBIVIAS
A 16   Cactus by Dodie, CA
A 16   Cactus by Mueller, CA
A 98   The Seed Shop, MT
A 100 Shein's Cactus, CA

LOTUS
A 48   Hemlock Hollow Nursery & Folk Art, KY
A 60   Kester's Wild Game Food Nurseries, WI
A 65   Lilypons Water Gardens, MD
A 73   Moore Water Gardens, ON
A 84   Picov Greenhouses, ON
A 87   Pond Doctor, AR
A 96   Santa Barbara Water Gardens, CA
A 97   Scottsdale Fishponds, AZ
A 102 Slocum Water Gardens, FL
A 106 Stigall Water Gardens, MO
A 110 Tilley's Nursery/The WaterWorks, PA
A 111 Trees by Touliatos, TN
A 111 William Tricker, Inc., OH
A 115 Water Ways Nursery, VA
A 115 Waterford Gardens, NJ
A 118 Wicklein's Water Gardens, MD

LUPINES
A 47   Hauser's Superior View Farm, WI

(continued next page)

PAGE SOURCE

(continued next page)

PAGE SOURCE

PAGE SOURCE

PERENNIALS (continued)

A 106   Stoecklein's Nursery, PA
A 106   Stokes Seed Company, NY
A 107   Sunlight Gardens, TN
A 107   Sunnybrook Farms Nursery, OH
A 107   Sunshine Farm & Gardens, WV
A 108   Surry Gardens, ME
A 108   Swallowtail Garden & Nursery, SC
A 108   T & T Seeds, Ltd., MB
A 109   Thompson & Morgan, NJ
A 111   Tripple Brook Farm, MA
A 112   Otis Twilley Seed Co., PA
A 112   Twombly Nursery, CT
A 113   Vermont Bean Seed Co., VT
A 114   Vesey's Seeds, Ltd., PE
A 114   Andre Viette Farm & Nursery, VA
A 114   Village Arbors, AL
A 116   John Watson & Anita Flores, En
A 116   Wayside Gardens, SC
A 116   We-Du Nurseries, NC
A 116   Weiss Brothers Nursery, CA
A 116   Well-Sweep Herb Farm, NJ
A 117   White Flower Farm, CT
A 119   The Wildwood Flower, NC
A 119   Willamette Valley Gardens Nursery, OR
A 121   Woodlanders, Inc., SC
A 121   Wrenwood of Berkeley Springs, WV
A 121   York Hill Farm, NH

PERSIMMONS

A 8   Barber Nursery, TX
A 17   California Nursery Co., CA
A 19   Chestnut Hill Nursery, Inc., FL
A 31   Edible Landscaping, VA
A 39   Fruit Spirit Botanical Gardens, Au
A 41   Louis Gerardi Nursery, IL
A 42   John Gordon Nursery, NY
A 58   Just Fruits, FL
A 76   Nolin River Nut Tree Nursery, KY
A 78   Northwoods Retail Nursery, OR
A 100   Sherwood's Greenhouses, LA
A 119   Wiley's Nut Grove Nursery, OH

PHILODENDRONS

A 103   Southern Exposure, TX

PHLOX

A 5   Appalachian Wildflower Nursery, PA
A 11   Bluestone Perennials, OH
A 15   Busse Gardens, MN
A 21   Colorado Alpines, Inc., CO
A 26   Crownsville Nursery, MD
A 35   Fieldstone Gardens, Inc., ME
A 40   Garden Perennials, NE
A 40   Garden Place, OH
A 40   Gardens of the Blue Ridge, NC
A 51   Holbrook Farm & Nursery, NC
A 57   Joyce's Garden, OR
A 61   L. Kreeger, En
A 62   Lamb Nurseries, WA
A 71   Milaeger's Gardens, WI
A 78   Northwest Native Seed, WA
A 88   Powell's Gardens, NC
A 88   The Primrose Path, PA
A 93   Rocknoll Nursery, OH
A 114   Andre Viette Farm & Nursery, VA
A 116   We-Du Nurseries, NC
A 116   Weiss Brothers Nursery, CA

PIERIS

A 13   Broken Arrow Nursery, CT
A 28   DeGrandchamp's Blueberry Farm, MI
A 59   Kelleygreen Rhododendron Nursery, OR
A 95   Roslyn Nursery, NY
A 100   Shepherd Hill Farm, NY
A 102   Sorum's Nursery, OR
A 103   Southern Plants, AL

PINES

A 17   Callahan Seeds, OR
A 18   Carino Nurseries, PA
A 37   Forest Seeds of California, CA
A 59   Kasch Nursery, OR
A 90   Rare Conifer Nursery, CA

PISTACHIOS

A 17   California Nursery Co., CA

PLANT FINDING SERVICES

A 24   The Country Mouse, WI
B 16   Greenlist Info Services, VT
A 48   Herbs-Liscious, IA
A 90   Rare Plant Research, OR
A 90   Rare Seed Locators, Inc., CA
A 104   Southwestern Exposure, AZ

PLATYCERIUMS

A 2   Alberts & Merkel Bros., Inc., FL
A 38   Fox Orchids, Inc., AR
A 51   Holladay Jungle, CA
A 53   Jerry Horne -- Rare Plants, FL
A 103   Southern Exposure, TX

PLEIONES

A 7   Avon Bulbs, En
A 16   C K S, Cz
A 87   Potterton & Martin, En
A 91   Red's Rhodies, OR
A 104   Springwood Pleiones, En
A 109   Terrorchids, Ge

PLUMERIAS

A 13   Brudy's Exotics, TX
A 20   Christa's Cactus, AZ
A 69   Marilynn's Garden, CA
A 87   The Plumeria People, TX

PLUMS

A 1   Adams County Nursery, Inc., PA
A 21   Cloud Mountain Nursery, WA
A 26   Cumberland Valley Nurseries, Inc., TN
A 52   Hollydale Nursery, TN
A 55   Ison's Nursery, GA
A 57   Johnson Nursery, GA
A 76   New York State Fruit Testing Coop. Assn., NY
A 78   Northwoods Retail Nursery, OR
A 93   Rocky Meadow Orchard & Nursery, IN
A 96   St. Lawrence Nurseries, NY
A 102   Sonoma Antique Apple Nursery, CA
A 103   Southmeadow Fruit Gardens, MI
A 112   Tsolum River Fruit Trees, BC
A 113   Van Well Nursery, Inc., WA

POLEMONIUMS

A 107   Sunshine Farm & Gardens, WV

POPCORN

A 26   Cross Seed Company, KS
A 34   Farmer Seed & Nursery, MN

(continued next page)

(continued next page)

(continued next page)

(continued next page)

(continued next page)

(continued next page)

PAGE SOURCE

PAGE SOURCE

© Mostly Natives Nursery
Artist: Robert Hockenos

PAGE	CITY/ZIP	⌂ NURSERY ▼ GARDEN	SOURCE

ALABAMA

A 114	Auburn, 36830	⌂ ▼	Village Arbors
A 91	Birmingham, 35206	⌂ ▼	Steve Ray's Bamboo Gardens
A 60	Newville, 36353	⌂ ▼	Kirkland Daylilies
A 103	Semmes, 36575	⌂	Southern Plants

ALASKA

A 98	Kenai, 99611		Seeds of Alaska
A 77	North Pole, 99705	⌂ ▼	North Pole Acres

ALBERTA, CANADA

A 2	Bowden, T0M 0K0	⌂	Alberta Nurseries & Seed Company
A 120	Hythe, T0H 2C0	⌂ ▼	Windy Ridge Nursery
A 23	Sherwood Park, T8G 1B1		The Conservancy

ARIZONA

A 104	Apache Junction, 85220		Southwestern Exposure
A 20	Coolidge, 85228	⌂ ▼	Christa's Cactus
A 106	Flagstaff, 86003	⌂ ▼	Strong's Alpine Succulents
A 52	Glendale, 85311	⌂ ▼	Homan Brothers Seed
A 28	Morristown, 85342		Desert Enterprises
A 6	Phoenix, 85013		Arena's Antique Roses
A 100	Phoenix, 85051	⌂ ▼	Shepard Iris Garden
A 97	Scottsdale, 85257	⌂ ▼	Scottsdale Fishponds
A 118	Tempe, 85285	⌂ ▼	Wild Seed
A 66	Tucson, 85705	⌂ ▼	Living Stones Nursery
A 75	Tucson, 85719	⌂ ▼	Native Seeds/SEARCH
A 104	Tucson, 85703		Southwestern Native Seeds

ARKANSAS

A 14	Benton, 72015	⌂ ▼	Burk's Nursery
A 51	Elkins, 72727	⌂ ▼	Holland Wildflower Farm
A 4	Fayetteville, 72701	⌂	Ames' Orchard & Nursery
A 32	Fouke, 71837	⌂	Enoch's Berry Farm
A 87	Kingston, 72742	⌂ ▼	Pond Doctor
A 38	Little Rock, 72205	⌂ ▼	Fox Orchids, Inc.
A 83	Mountainburg, 72946	⌂	Pense Nursery
A 50	Pettigrew, 72752	⌂ ▼	Highlander Nursery

AUSTRALIA

A 42	Bagdad So., Tasmania, 7030	⌂ ▼	L.S.A. Goodwin & Sons
A 39	Dorroughby, NSW, 2480	⌂ ▼	Fruit Spirit Botanical Gardens
A 12	El Arish, North QLD, 4855		The Borneo Collection
A 85	Everton Hills, QLD, 4053	⌂ ▼	Pine Heights Nursery
A 109	Kingston, Tasmania, 7050	⌂	Tasmanian Forest Seeds
A 31	Nowra, NSW, 2541	⌂	Ellison Horticultural Pty., Ltd.
A 81	Perth, WA, 6060		D. Orriell -- Seed Exporters
A 15	Yanchep, WA, 6035	⌂	Bushland Flora

BRITISH COLUMBIA, CANADA

A 69	Abbotsford, V3S 4N5	⌂ ▼	Mar-Low Epi House
A 117	Aldergrove, V0X 1A0	⌂	Western Biologicals, Ltd.
A 26	Chilliwack, V2P 3T2		Dacha Barinka
A 72	Duncan, V9L 2X1	▼	Millar Mountain Nursery
A 96	Ganges, V0S 1E0	▼	Salt Spring Seeds
A 112	Ganges, V0S 1E0	⌂ ▼	Tsolum River Fruit Trees
A 46	Grand Forks, V0H 1H0	⌂ ▼	Hardy Roses for the North
A 66	Langley, V3A 7N6	⌂ ▼	Lindel Lilies
A 89	Maple Ridge, V2X 7E7	⌂ ▼	Rainforest Gardens
A 34	Mission, V2V 6S6	⌂ ▼	Ferncliff Gardens
A 96	Vancouver, V6M 2N2		Saltspring Primroses

(continued next page)

PAGE	CITY/ZIP	⌂ NURSERY ▼ GARDEN	SOURCE
BRITISH COLUMBIA, CANADA (continued)			
A 73	Vernon, V1T 7Z3		Monashee Perennials
A 15	Victoria, V8X 3X4	⌂ ▼	The Butchart Gardens
CALIFORNIA			
A 29	Albion, 95410	⌂	Digging Dog Nursery
A 78	Altadena, 91003	⌂	Nuccio's Nurseries
A 33	Anaheim, 92817		Evergreen Y. H. Enterprises
A 8	Atascadero, 93422	⌂	Bay Laurel Nursery
A 72	Atascadero, 93423		Mohns Nursery
A 16	Bakersfield, 93312	⌂ ▼	Cactus by Mueller
A 66	Berkeley, 94709	⌂	Living Tree Centre
A 90	Berkeley, 94704		Rare Seed Locators, Inc.
A 9	Blue Lake, 95525	⌂	Bigfoot
A 77	Bodega, 94922		North Coast Rhododendron Nursery
A 63	Bolinas, 94924	⌂ ▼	Larner Seeds
A 81	Campbell, 95009	⌂ ▼	Pacific Coast Hybridizers
A 20	Carlotta, 95528		Choice Edibles
A 10	Carlsbad, 92009	⌂ ▼	Bird Rock Tropicals
A 1	Carpinteria, 93013	⌂ ▼	Abbey Gardens
A 73	Carpinteria, 93014	⌂	Moon Mountain Wildflowers
A 105	Carpinteria, 93013	⌂ ▼	Stewart Orchids, Inc.
A 3	Chino, 91710		Aloha Tropicals
A 82	Chula Vista, 91910	⌂ ▼	Pacific Tree Farms
A 110	Chula Vista, 92010	⌂ ▼	Tiny Petals Nursery
A 60	Clements, 95227	⌂ ▼	King's Mums
A 80	Coarsegold, 93614	⌂ ▼	Orchid Species Specialties
A 32	Cupertino, 95014	⌂ ▼	Epi World
A 37	Davis, 95617	▼	Flowers & Greens
A 10	El Cajon, 92021		Blossom Valley Gardens
A 104	Encinitas, 92024	⌂ ▼	Stallings Nursery
A 117	Eureka, 95503	⌂ ▼	Westgate Garden Nursery
A 23	Fallbrook, 92028	⌂ ▼	Coopers Nut House/Rancho Nuez Nursery
A 100	Felton, 95018	⌂	Shepherd's Garden Seeds
A 17	Forestville, 95436	⌂ ▼	California Carnivores
A 67	Forestville, 95436		Lone Pine Connection
A 91	Fort Bragg, 95437	⌂ ▼	Regine's Fuchsia Garden
A 112	Fountain Valley, 92708	⌂ ▼	Valley Vista Kiwi
A 17	Fremont, 94536		California Nursery Co.
A 38	Fremont, 94539	⌂	Four Winds Growers
A 48	Fresno, 93722	⌂ ▼	Henrietta's Nursery
A 50	Fresno, 93711	⌂ ▼	Hill 'n dale
A 51	Fresno, 93755	⌂ ▼	Holladay Jungle
A 82	Fresno, 93726		Pacific Coast Seed Company
A 49	Ft. Bragg, 95437	▼	Heritage Rose Gardens
A 44	Garberville, 95542	▼	Greenmantle Nursery
A 120	Garberville, 95440		Nancy Wilson Species & Miniature Narcissus
A 89	Gardena, 90249	⌂ ▼	Rainforest Flora, Inc.
A 4	Grass Valley, 95945	⌂	The Angraecum House
A 37	Grass Valley, 95945	⌂ ▼	Foothill Cottage Gardens
A 116	Grass Valley, 95945	⌂	Weiss Brothers Nursery
A 43	Graton, 95444		Gourmet Mushrooms
A 47	Guerneville, 95446		Heirloom Garden Seeds
A 93	Hayward, 94545	⌂	Clyde Robin Seed Co.
A 72	Healdsburg, 95448	⌂	Misty Hill Farms - Moonshine Gardens
A 102	Healdsburg, 95448	⌂	Sonoma Antique Apple Nursery
A 95	Igo, 96047	⌂ ▼	Jim & Irene Russ - Quality Plants
A 58	Ione, 95640		K & L Cactus & Succulent Nursery
A 66	Knights Ferry, 95361		Live Oak Nursery
A 41	Laytonville, 95454	⌂ ▼	Garver Gardens
A 74	Laytonville, 95454	⌂ ▼	Mountain Maples
A 68	Lemon Grove, 91945	⌂ ▼	McDaniel's Miniature Roses
A 30	Leucadia, 92024	▼	Jim Duggan Flower Nursery
A 115	Lincoln, 95648	⌂ ▼	Violets Collectible
A 37	Livermore, 94550	⌂ ▼	Fordyce Orchids
A 16	Lodi, 95242	⌂ ▼	Cactus by Dodie
A 44	Long Beach, 90804	⌂ ▼	Greenwood Daylily Gardens
A 26	Los Angeles, 90041	⌂	Cycad Gardens
A 106	Los Angeles, 90048		Succulenta

(continued next page)

PAGE	CITY/ZIP	⌂ NURSERY ▼ GARDEN	SOURCE

CALIFORNIA (continued)

PAGE	CITY/ZIP	NURSERY/GARDEN	SOURCE
A 100	Marina, 93933	⌂ ▼	Shein's Cactus
A 34	McKinleyville, 95521	⌂	Fairyland Begonia & Lily Garden
A 70	Mendocino, 95460	⌂	Mendocino Heirloom Roses
A 41	Moorpark, 93021		Golden Lake Greenhouses
A 23	Moraga, 94556	⌂ ▼	Copacabana Gardens
A 97	Morgan Hill, 95037	⌂ ▼	Schulz Cactus Growers
A 82	National City, 91951	⌂	Pacific Southwest Nursery
A 38	Newcastle, 95658	⌂ ▼	Fowler Nurseries, Inc.
A 53	North Hollywood, 91607	⌂ ▼	Spencer M. Howard Orchid Imports
A 121	North Hollywood, 91601	⌂	Guy Wrinkle Exotic Plants
A 58	Northridge, 91324	⌂	KSA Jojoba
A 78	Northridge, 91325	⌂ ▼	Northridge Gardens
A 75	Oceanside, 92056	⌂	Nature's Curiosity Shop
A 61	Ojai, 93024		Kusa Research Foundation
A 17	Oroville, 95965	⌂	Canyon Creek Nursery
A 100	Pacifica, 94044	⌂ ▼	Shelldance Nursery
A 66	Paramount, 90723	⌂	Loehman's Cactus Patch
A 87	Penngrove, 94951		Portable Acres
A 40	Petaluma, 94975	⌂ ▼	Garden Valley Ranch
A 37	Placerville, 95667		Forest Seeds of California
A 44	Pomona, 91766	⌂ ▼	Greenlee Nursery
A 90	Potter Valley, 95469	▼	Rare Conifer Nursery
A 90	Ramona, 92065	⌂ ▼	Ramona Gardens
A 70	Redding, 96001	⌂ ▼	Maxim's Greenwood Gardens
A 92	Redlands, 92373	⌂ ▼	Rhapis Palm Growers
A 53	Redwood City, 94064		J. L. Hudson, Seedsman
A 91	Redwood City, 94064		Redwood City Seed Co.
A 71	Sacramento, 95828	⌂ ▼	Mighty Minis
A 94	Sacramento, 95829	⌂ ▼	Roris Gardens
A 94	Salinas, 93912	⌂ ▼	The Rose Ranch
A 5	San Francisco, 94117	⌂	Arbor & Espalier
A 24	San Francisco, 94121	⌂ ▼	Cottage Gardens
A 44	San Francisco, 94132	⌂	GreenLady Gardens
A 107	San Gabriel, 91775		Sunnyslope Gardens
A 60	San Jose, 95126		Kitazawa Seed Co.
A 69	San Jose, 95125	⌂ ▼	Maryott's Gardens
A 81	San Jose, 95132		Ornamental Edibles
A 23	San Marcos, 92079	⌂ ▼	Cordon Bleu Farms
A 59	Sanger, 93657		Kelly's Plant World
A 69	Santa Ana, 92705	⌂	Marilynn's Garden
A 10	Santa Barbara, 93150	⌂	Bio-Quest International
A 96	Santa Barbara, 93111	⌂ ▼	Santa Barbara Orchid Estate
A 96	Santa Barbara, 93108	⌂ ▼	Santa Barbara Water Gardens
A 5	Santa Cruz, 95062	⌂ ▼	Antonelli Brothers, Inc.
A 8	Santa Cruz, 95060		Bay View Gardens
A 63	Santa Margarita, 93453	⌂ ▼	Las Pilitas Nursery
A 1	Santa Rosa, 95403		Adagent Acres
A 3	Santa Rosa, 95404	⌂ ▼	Alpine Valley Gardens
A 62	Santa Rosa, 95406		D.E. Lark Seeds
A 76	Santa Rosa, 95407	⌂ ▼	Neon Palm Nursery
A 102	Santa Rosa, 95403	⌂	Sonoma Grapevines
A 43	Santee, 92072	⌂ ▼	Gray/Davis Epiphyllums
A 8	Sebastopol, 95472		A Bamboo Shoot
A 8	Sebastopol, 95472	⌂ ▼	Bamboo Sourcery
A 72	Sebastopol, 95472	⌂ ▼	Miniature Plant Kingdom
A 93	Sebastopol, 95473		Robinett Bulb Farm
A 114	Sebastopol, 95472	⌂ ▼	Vintage Gardens
A 97	Selma, 93662		Scotty's Desert Plants
A 94	Shingle Springs, 95682		Roses & Wine
A 11	Somerset, 95684	⌂ ▼	Bluebird Haven Iris Garden
A 47	Sonora, 95370	⌂ ▼	Havasu Hills Herbs
A 33	Soquel, 95073	⌂ ▼	John Ewing Orchids, Inc.
A 68	South San Francisco, 94080	⌂ ▼	Rod McLellan Co.
A 74	Squaw Valley, 93675		Mountain Valley Growers, Inc.
A 118	St. Helena, 94574		Wildflower Seed Company
A 66	Stockton, 95201	⌂	Lockhart Seeds
A 108	Studio City, 91614	⌂ ▼	Sunswept Laboratories
A 83	Sun Valley, 91352	⌂ ▼	Theodore Payne Foundation

(continued next page)

PAGE	CITY/ZIP	⌂ NURSERY ▼ GARDEN	SOURCE

CALIFORNIA (continued)

A 75	Tehachapi, 93561	⌂	Native Oak Nursery
A 73	Tomales, 94971	⌂ ▼	Mostly Natives Nursery
A 33	Ukiah, 95482	⌂ ▼	Evergreen Gardenworks
A 113	Upland, 91786	⌂ ▼	Van Ness Water Gardens
A 92	Ventura, 93001	⌂ ▼	Richardson's Seaside Banana Garden
A 99	Visalia, 93292	⌂ ▼	Sequoia Nursery -- Moore Miniature Roses
A 33	Vista, 92085	⌂ ▼	Exotica Rare Fruit Nursery
A 39	Vista, 92084	⌂ ▼	G & B Orchid Lab & Nursery
A 45	Vista, 92084	⌂ ▼	Grigsby Cactus Gardens
A 57	Vista, 92085		Joe's Nursery
A 59	Vista, 92083	⌂ ▼	Kartuz Greenhouses
A 89	Vista, 92084	⌂ ▼	Rainbow Gardens Nursery & Bookshop
A 109	Vista, 92084	⌂ ▼	Taylor's Herb Gardens
A 29	Watsonville, 95076	⌂ ▼	Desert Theatre
A 94	Watsonville, 95076	⌂ ▼	Roses of Yesterday & Today
A 117	Westley, 95387		Westside Exotics Palm Nursery
A 12	Willits, 95490	⌂	Bountiful Gardens
A 85	Yorba Linda, 92686	⌂ ▼	Pixie Treasures Miniature Roses
A 28	Yountville, 94599		Delegeane Garlic Farms

COLORADO

A 21	Avon, 81620	⌂	Colorado Alpines, Inc.
A 31	Bayfield, 81122		Edge of the Rockies
A 67	Boulder, 80306	⌂ ▼	Long's Gardens
A 117	Canon City, 81215		Western Native Seed
A 50	Denver, 80226	⌂ ▼	High Country Rosarium
A 118	Durango, 81302		Wild and Crazy Seed Company
A 114	Englewood, 80110	⌂ ▼	The Violet Showcase
A 17	Glenwood Springs, 81601		Campanula Connoisseur
A 52	Idaho Springs, 80452	⌂ ▼	Homestead Farm
A 3	Kiowa, 80117	▼	Alplains
A 15	Rocky Ford, 81067		D. V. Burrell Seed Growers Co.

CONNECTICUT

A 96	Bantam, 06750		John Scheepers, Inc.
A 67	Danielson, 06239	⌂ ▼	Logee's Greenhouses
A 32	Deep River, 06417	▼	Ericaceae
A 92	East Lyme, 06333	⌂ ▼	Riverhead Perennials
A 56	Easton, 06612	⌂ ▼	J & L Orchids
A 10	Gaylordsville, 06755	⌂ ▼	Bloomingfields Farm
A 97	Greenwich, 06836		Schipper & Co.
A 13	Hamden, 06518	⌂ ▼	Broken Arrow Nursery
A 113	Litchfield, 06759		Van Engelen, Inc.
A 117	Litchfield, 06759	⌂ ▼	White Flower Farm
A 112	Monroe, 06468	⌂ ▼	Twombly Nursery
A 16	Oxford, 06478	⌂	Butterbrooke Farm
A 63	Salisbury, 06068	⌂ ▼	Lauray of Salisbury
A 99	Stamford, 06903	⌂ ▼	Shanti Bithi Nursery
A 64	Storrs, 06268	⌂ ▼	Ledgecrest Greenhouses
A 25	Thomaston, 06787	⌂ ▼	Cricket Hill Garden
A 98	Union, 06076		Select Seeds -- Antique Flowers
A 107	West Hartford, 06133		Sunrise Oriental Seed Co.
A 22	Wethersfield, 06109	⌂ ▼	Comstock, Ferre & Co.

COSTA RICA

A 90	San Jose, 1017		Rainforest Seed Company

CZECH REPUBLIC

A 33	Novy Jicin, 741 01	⌂	Euroseeds
A 16	Ostrava-Poruba, 708 00	⌂	C K S

DELAWARE

A 52	Seaford, 19973		Honeysong Farm

ENGLAND

A 61	Ashtead, Surrey, KT21 1NN		L. Kreeger
A 12	Aylesbury, Bucks., HP22 4QB	⌂ ▼	S & N Brackley
A 95	Bedford, MK42 8ND		Doug & Vivi Rowland

(continued next page)

PAGE	CITY/ZIP	⌂ NURSERY	▼ GARDEN	SOURCE

ENGLAND (continued)

PAGE	CITY/ZIP	NURSERY	GARDEN	SOURCE
A 110	Benenden, Kent, TN17 4LB			Tile Barn Nursery
A 24	Bingley, W. Yorkshir, BD16 4LZ			Craven's Nursery
A 7	Bridgewater, Somerse, TA5 1JE			B & T World Seeds
A 87	Caistor, Lincs., LN7 6HX	⌂	▼	Potterton & Martin
A 54	Chatham, Kent, ME5 9QT	⌂		Brenda Hyatt
A 73	Clevedon, Avon, BS21 6SG			Monocot Nursery
A 51	Clitheroe, Lancs., BB7 4PF			Holden Clough Nursery
A 10	East Grinstead, R19 4LE	⌂	▼	Birch Farm Nursery
A 11	Halstead, Essex, CO9 4BQ		▼	Robert Bolton & Son
A 3	Hassocks, W. Sussex, BN6 9NB			Allwood Bros.
A 122	King's Lynn, Norfolk, PE33 0QH			Roy Young, Seedsman
A 6	Kingswinford, W.Mid., DY6 0AE	⌂	▼	Ashwood Nurseries
A 104	Leeds, LS16 7AB		▼	Springwood Pleiones
A 16	London, SW1V 4QE			CTDA
A 86	Newton Abbot, Devon, TQ12 4SE		▼	Plant World
A 116	Orpington, Kent, BR5 1HB			John Watson & Anita Flores
A 46	Reading, Berks., RG4 9QN	⌂	▼	Harrisons Delphiniums
A 19	Slough, Berks., SL3 8BE		▼	Chadwell Himalayan Seed
A 7	South Petherton, TA13 5HE			Avon Bulbs
A 84	Stockport, Cheshire, SK6 3DS	⌂	▼	Phedar Nursery
A 20	Ulverston, Cumbria, LA12 7PB			Chiltern Seeds

FLORIDA

PAGE	CITY/ZIP	NURSERY	GARDEN	SOURCE
A 19	Alachua, 32615	⌂	▼	Chestnut Hill Nursery, Inc.
A 27	Alachua, 32615		▼	Daylily Discounters
A 121	Archer, 32618	⌂	▼	Tom Wood, Nurseryman
A 21	Auburndale, 33823			Color Farm Growers
A 89	Avon Park, 33825			Rainbow Acres
A 2	Boynton Beach, 33435	⌂	▼	Alberts & Merkel Bros., Inc.
A 58	Crawfordville, 32327	⌂	▼	Just Fruits
A 40	Davie, 33325	⌂	▼	Garden of Delights
A 74	DeFuniak Springs, 32433	⌂		NWN Nursery
A 56	Delray Beach, 33446	⌂	▼	J. E. M. Orchids
A 93	Eustis, 32726	⌂	▼	Rollingwood Gardens
A 83	Fort Lauderdale, 33307			The Pepper Gal
A 110	Fort Myers, 33902			Tomato Growers Supply Company
A 120	Gainesville, 32605	⌂		Wimberlyway Gardens
A 79	Glen St. Mary, 32040		▼	Nurseries at North Glen
A 108	Green Cove Springs, 32043	⌂	▼	Dave Talbott Nursery
A 35	Gulf Hammock, 32639	⌂		The Fig Tree Nursery
A 36	Homestead, 33032	⌂	▼	Florida Colors Nursery
A 64	Homestead, 33031	⌂	▼	W. O. Lessard Nursery
A 64	LaBelle, 33935	⌂	▼	Lee's Botanical Garden
A 9	Longwood, 32750	⌂	▼	Big Tree Daylily Garden
A 85	Longwood, 32779	⌂	▼	Pineapple Place
A 103	Melbourne, 32902			Southern Seeds
A 53	Miami, 33173	⌂	▼	Jerry Horne -- Rare Plants
A 71	Miami, 33170	⌂	▼	Miami Water Lilies
A 80	Miami, 33196	⌂	▼	Orgel's Orchids
A 81	Miami, 33170	⌂		Our Orchids
A 82	Miami, 33155	⌂	▼	Palms for Tropical Landscaping
A 42	Naples, 33964	⌂	▼	Goravani Growers
A 24	North Fort Myers, 33903	⌂		Cornelison Bromeliads
A 91	Oneco, 34264	⌂		Reasoner's, Inc.
A 13	Orlando, 32803	⌂	▼	Brown's Edgewood Gardens
A 58	Orlando, 32856			Just Enough Sinningias
A 43	Palm Harbor, 34682	⌂	▼	The Green Escape
A 36	Pensacola, 32505		▼	Florida Mycology Research Center
A 102	Pompano Beach, 33060	⌂	▼	Winn Soldani's Fancy Hibiscus(R)
A 27	Sanford, 32772	⌂	▼	Daylily World
A 37	Sanford, 32771		▼	Floyd Cove Nursery
A 60	Sanford, 32771	⌂		Kilgore Seed Company
A 111	Sarasota, 34243	⌂		Tropiflora
A 16	Sebring, 33871			Caladium World
A 71	St. Petersburg, 33710	⌂		Michael's Bromeliads
A 114	Tampa, 33610	⌂	▼	Violet Creations
A 56	Weirsdale, 32195	⌂		Ivies of the World
A 32	West Palm Beach, 33413	⌂	▼	Eric's Exotics

(continued next page)

PAGE	CITY/ZIP	⌂ NURSERY ▼ GARDEN	SOURCE
FLORIDA (continued)			
A 67	West Palm Beach, 33415		Paul P. Lowe
A 69	Windermere, 34786	⌂ ▼	Ann Mann's Orchids
A 102	Winter Haven, 33884	⌂ ▼	Slocum Water Gardens
A 62	Winter Springs, 32708	▼	Lady Bug Beautiful Gardens
FRANCE			
A 8	Plouzelambre, 22420	⌂ ▼	Barnhaven Primroses
GEORGIA			
A 84	Albany, 31703		Piedmont Plant Company
A 30	Arnoldsville, 30619		Double D Nursery
A 47	Atlanta, 30310	⌂	H. G. Hastings
A 110	Augusta, 30903		Totally Tomatoes
A 63	Ball Ground, 30107	⌂ ▼	Lawson's Nursery
A 55	Brooks, 30205	⌂ ▼	Ison's Nursery
A 52	Commerce, 30529	⌂	Homeplace Garden Nursery
A 12	Concord, 30206		Bottoms Nursery & Owens Vineyard
A 31	Decatur, 30031	⌂ ▼	Eco-Gardens
A 31	Dry Branch, 31020	⌂ ▼	Eden Exotics
A 57	Ellijay, 30540	⌂	Johnson Nursery
A 37	Flowery Branch, 30542		Flowery Branch Seed Company
A 8	Grayson, 30221	⌂ ▼	Baycreek Gardens
A 111	Lavonia, 30553	⌂ ▼	Transplant Nursery
A 46	Lawrenceville, 30243		James Harris Hybrid Azaleas
A 42	Lexington, 30648	⌂ ▼	Goodness Grows
A 111	Ochlochnee, 31773	⌂ ▼	Travis' Violets
A 81	Pine Mountain, 31822	⌂ ▼	Ben Pace Nursery
A 109	Thomasville, 31799	⌂ ▼	Thomasville Nurseries
A 58	Valdosta, 31601	⌂ ▼	Karleens Achimenes
GERMANY			
A 56	D 3033 Schwarmstedt,	⌂	Jelitto Staudensamen GmBH
A 61	Erzhausen/Darmstadt, D-610		Gerhard Koehres Cactus & Succulent Nursery
A 109	Wolfenbuttel, 38300	⌂	Terrorchids
HAWAII			
A 89	Hilo, 96720		Rainbow Tropicals, Inc.
A 20	Honokaa, 96727	⌂ ▼	Cloud Forest Orchids
A 59	Honolulu, 96816	⌂ ▼	Kawamoto Orchid Nursery
A 90	Honolulu, 96814	⌂ ▼	Rainforest Plantes et Fleurs, Inc.
A 43	Kaaawa, 96730	⌂ ▼	Green Plant Research
A 119	Kaneohe, 96744	⌂ ▼	Wilk Orchid Specialties
A 86	Kurtistown, 96760	⌂ ▼	Plant it Hawaii, Inc.
A 36	Mt. View, 96771	⌂ ▼	Floribunda Palms & Exotics
A 117	Pahoa, 96778		Ken West Orchids
IDAHO			
A 98	Boise, 83706		Seeds Blum
A 108	Challis, 83226		Alfred Swanson
A 49	Hailey, 83333	⌂ ▼	High Altitude Gardens
A 77	Moscow, 83843	⌂	Northplan/Mountain Seed
A 94	Moyie Springs, 83845		Ronniger's Seed Potatoes
A 101	Moyie Springs, 83845		Silver Springs Nursery
A 86	Twin Falls, 83301	⌂ ▼	Plantasia Cactus Gardens
ILLINOIS			
A 99	Batavia, 60510	⌂ ▼	Shady Hill Gardens
A 82	Bourbonnais, 60914		Pampered Plant Nursery
A 60	Champaign, 61921	▼	Klehm Nursery
A 5	Chapin, 62628		Applesource
A 63	Downers Grove, 60517	⌂ ▼	Laurie's Landscaping
A 79	Dundee, 60118	⌂ ▼	Oak Hill Gardens
A 104	Hamburg, 62045	⌂ ▼	Springvale Farm Nursery
A 60	Hampshire, 60140	⌂ ▼	Arnold J. Klehm Grower, Inc.
A 89	Hebron, 60034		The Propagator's Private Stock
A 11	Hillsboro, 62049	▼	Bluestem Prairie Nursery
A 62	Lafayette, 61449		LaFayette Home Nursery, Inc.
A 41	O'Fallon, 62269	⌂ ▼	Louis Gerardi Nursery

(continued next page)

PAGE	CITY/ZIP	⌂ NURSERY ▼ GARDEN	SOURCE

ILLINOIS (continued)

A 13	Peoria, 61656		Breck's
A 104	Peoria, 61632		Spring Hill Nurseries Co.
A 117	Peoria, 61614	▼	White Oak Nursery
A 105	Petersburg, 62675	▼	Starhill Forest Arboretum
A 14	Riverwoods, 60015		The Bulb Crate
A 120	Sycamore, 60178	⌂ ▼	Windsong Orchids
A 64	Tremont, 61568	⌂ ▼	Lee's Gardens
A 88	Trilla, 62469	⌂	Prairie State Commodities
A 80	Villa Park, 60181	⌂ ▼	Orchids by Hausermann, Inc.

INDIA

A 61	Etawah (U.P.), 206121		Kumar International

INDIANA

A 27	Crawfordsville, 47933	⌂ ▼	Davidson-Wilson Greenhouses
A 85	Floyds Knob, 47119	⌂ ▼	Pinecliffe Daylily Gardens
A 54	Huntingburg, 47542	⌂	Indiana Berry & Plant Co.
A 53	Indianapolis, 46278	⌂ ▼	Hoosier Orchid Company
A 102	Indianapolis, 46217	⌂ ▼	Soules Garden
A 30	New Albany, 47150		Earthly Goods, Ltd.
A 93	New Salisbury, 47161	⌂ ▼	Rocky Meadow Orchard & Nursery
A 72	Ossian, 46777	⌂ ▼	Miller's Manor Gardens
A 44	Shipshewana, 46565	⌂ ▼	Greenfield Herb Garden
A 21	Valparaiso, 46383	⌂ ▼	Coburg Planting Fields
A 55	Winamac, 46996	⌂ ▼	Iris Acres

IOWA

A 19	Cascade, 52033	⌂ ▼	Cascade Forestry Nursery
A 102	Charles City, 50616	⌂	Smith Nursery Co.
A 92	Farmington, 52626	⌂	Rider Nurseries
A 47	Johnston, 50131	⌂ ▼	Heard Gardens, Ltd.
A 48	Marshalltown, 50158	⌂ ▼	Herbs-Liscious
A 35	Shenandoah, 51602		Henry Field Seed & Nursery Co.

KANSAS

A 26	Bunker Hill, 67626	⌂ ▼	Cross Seed Company
A 53	Burlington, 66839	⌂ ▼	Huff's Garden Mums
A 99	Healy, 67850		Sharp Brothers Seed Company
A 43	Leawood, 66209		The Gourmet Gardener
A 24	Sedgwick, 67135	⌂ ▼	Country Cottage
A 24	Udall, 67146		Country Bloomers Nursery
A 68	Wichita, 67207	⌂	McKinney's Glasshouse

KENTUCKY

A 100	Frankfort, 40601	⌂	Shooting Star Nursery
A 102	Lancaster, 40444	⌂	Sleepy Hollow Herb Farm
A 26	Louisville, 40252		Dabney Herbs
A 16	Murray, 42071	⌂ ▼	C & C Nursery
A 106	Murray, 42071	⌂	Story House Herb Farm
A 48	Sandy Hook, 41171		Hemlock Hollow Nursery & Folk Art
A 76	Upton, 42784	⌂ ▼	Nolin River Nut Tree Nursery

LOUISIANA

A 3	Baton Rouge, 70821	⌂	Amaryllis, Inc.
A 44	Folsom, 70437	⌂ ▼	Green Valley Orchids
A 101	Gibsland, 71028	▼	Sisters' Bulb Farm
A 24	New Orleans, 70184	⌂ ▼	Creole Orchids
A 67	Opelousas, 70570	⌂ ▼	Louisiana Nursery
A 30	Shreveport, 71133		Donovan's Roses
A 100	Sibley, 71073	⌂ ▼	Sherwood's Greenhouses

MAINE

A 57	Albion, 04910	⌂ ▼	Johnny's Selected Seeds
A 22	Boothbay Harbor, 04538	⌂ ▼	Conley's Garden Center
A 70	Camden, 04843	⌂ ▼	Merry Gardens
A 112	East Lebanon, 04027	⌂ ▼	Valente Gardens
A 2	Falmouth, 04105	⌂	Allen, Sterling & Lothrop
A 38	Freeport, 04032	⌂ ▼	Fox Hill Nursery

(continued next page)

PAGE	CITY/ZIP	⌂ NURSERY ▼ GARDEN	SOURCE

MAINE (continued)

A 30	Georgetown, 04548	⌂ ▼	Eastern Plant Specialties
A 28	Litchfield, 04350	⌂ ▼	Daystar
A 85	New Gloucester, 04260	⌂	Pinetree Garden Seeds
A 37	North Yarmouth, 04097	⌂ ▼	Forevergreen Farm
A 108	Surry, 04684	⌂ ▼	Surry Gardens
A 35	Vassalboro, 04989	⌂ ▼	Fieldstone Gardens, Inc.
A 34	Waterville, 04903		Fedco Seeds
A 73	Waterville, 04903		Moose Tubers

MANITOBA, CANADA

A 68	Brandon, R7A 6N4		McFayden Seeds
A 73	Morden, R0G 1J0	⌂	Morden Nurseries, Ltd.
A 108	Winnepeg, R3C 3P6	⌂	T & T Seeds, Ltd.

MARYLAND

A 11	Baldwin, 21013	⌂ ▼	Kurt Bluemel, Inc.
A 118	Baldwin, 21013	⌂ ▼	Wicklein's Water Gardens
A 62	Baltimore, 21230	⌂	D. Landreth Seed Company
A 71	Baltimore, 21231		Meyer Seed Company
A 48	Brookville, 20833	⌂ ▼	Heritage Rosarium
A 65	Buckeystown, 21717	⌂ ▼	Lilypons Water Gardens
A 26	Crownsville, 21032		Crownsville Nursery
A 75	Dayton, 21036		Native Seeds, Inc.
A 58	Edgewood, 21040	⌂ ▼	Jungle Gems, Inc.
A 2	Fruitland, 21826	⌂	Allen Plant Company
A 94	Galena, 21635	⌂ ▼	Rosehill Farm
A 69	Jarrettsville, 21084	⌂ ▼	Maryland Aquatic Nurseries
A 59	Kensington, 20895	⌂ ▼	Kensington Orchids
A 14	Owings Mills, 21117	⌂ ▼	Bundles of Bulbs
A 3	Potomac, 20859		Jacques Amand, Bulb Specialists
A 13	Salisbury, 21801	⌂	Brittingham Plant Farms
A 119	Severn, 21144	⌂ ▼	Willow Oak Flower & Herb Farm
A 39	West Friendship, 21794	▼	Friendship Gardens
A 18	Westminster, 21158	⌂	Carroll Gardens

MASSACHUSETTS

A 86	Agawam, 01001	⌂ ▼	Pleasant Valley Glads and Dahlias
A 47	Barre, 01005	⌂ ▼	Hartman's Herb Farm
A 121	Boylston, 01505	▼	Worcester County Horticultural Society
A 98	Carlisle, 01741	⌂ ▼	R. Seawright
A 13	East Sandwich, 02537	⌂ ▼	Briarwood Gardens
A 29	Edgartown, 02539	⌂ ▼	Donaroma's Nursery
A 17	Falmouth, 02540		Cape Cod Violetry
A 17	Falmouth, 02540	⌂ ▼	Cape Cod Vireyas
A 22	Ipswich, 01938	⌂	The Compleat Garden -- Clematis Nursery
A 71	Ipswich, 01938	⌂	Messelaar Bulb Co.
A 68	Pepperell, 01463		Mark McDonough
A 111	Rehoboth, 02769	⌂ ▼	Tranquil Lake Nursery
A 77	Rowley, 01969	⌂ ▼	Nor'East Miniature Roses
A 97	Sandwich, 02563		F. W. Schumacher Co., Inc.
A 78	South Deerfield, 01373	⌂ ▼	Nourse Farms, Inc.
A 28	South Hamilton, 01982		Peter De Jager Bulb Co.
A 111	Southampton, 01073	⌂ ▼	Tripple Brook Farm
A 70	Tewksbury, 01876		Meadowbrook Hosta Farm
A 93	Truro, 02666	⌂ ▼	Rock Spray Nursery
A 15	Westford, 01886	⌂ ▼	Burt Associates
A 82	Whitman, 02382	⌂ ▼	Paradise Water Gardens

MICHIGAN

A 7	Albion, 49224	⌂ ▼	Balash Gardens
A 79	Ann Arbor, 48103		Old House Gardens
A 27	Bellevue, 49021	⌂	Corwin Davis Nursery
A 11	Coopersville, 49404		Bluebird Orchard & Nursery
A 61	Dowagiac, 49047	⌂ ▼	Krohne Plant Farms
A 116	Fennville, 49408	⌂ ▼	Wavecrest Nursery & Landscaping Co.
A 6	Fowlerville, 48836	⌂ ▼	Arrowhead Alpines
A 21	Free Soil, 49411		Cold Stream Farm
A 32	Galesburg, 49053	▼	Ensata Gardens

(continued next page)

PAGE	CITY/ZIP	⌂ NURSERY ▼ GARDEN	SOURCE

MICHIGAN (continued)

A 47	Grand Junction, 49056	⌂	Hartmann's Plantation, Inc.
A 24	Hartford, 49057	⌂	Country Heritage Nursery
A 45	Hartland, 48353		Growers Service Company
A 101	Highland, 48356	⌂ ▼	Sir Williams Gardens
A 113	Holland, 49424	⌂ ▼	Veldheer Tulip Gardens
A 32	Hopkins, 49328	⌂ ▼	Englearth Gardens
A 79	Kalamazoo, 49019	⌂ ▼	Oikos Tree Crops
A 62	Lake Odessa, 48849	⌂ ▼	Lake Odessa Greenhouse
A 103	Lakeside, 49116	⌂	Southmeadow Fruit Gardens
A 34	Livonia, 48154		Far North Gardens
A 20	Madison Heights, 48071	⌂ ▼	City Gardens
A 44	Maple City, 49664	⌂ ▼	The Greenery
A 38	Parma, 49269	⌂ ▼	Fox Hill Farm
A 28	South Haven, 49090	⌂	DeGrandchamp's Blueberry Farm
A 32	Stevensville, 49127	⌂ ▼	Emlong Nurseries
A 91	Vulcan, 49892		Reath's Nursery
A 101	Zeeland, 49464	⌂	Siegers Seed Co.

MINNESOTA

A 116	Albert Lea, 56007		Wedge Nursery
A 80	Andover, 55744	⌂	Orchid Gardens
A 15	Cokato, 55321	⌂ ▼	Busse Gardens
A 96	Edina, 55435	⌂ ▼	Savory's Gardens, Inc.
A 12	Faribault, 55021	⌂ ▼	Borbeleta Gardens
A 34	Faribault, 55021	⌂	Farmer Seed & Nursery
A 4	Forest Lake, 55025	⌂ ▼	Anderson Iris Gardens
A 23	Golden Valley, 55427	⌂ ▼	Cooper's Garden
A 49	Hastings, 55033	▼	Heschke Gardens
A 99	Minneapolis, 55409	⌂ ▼	Sevald Nursery
A 51	Osseo, 55369	⌂ ▼	Holly Lane Iris Gardens
A 46	Owatonna, 55060	⌂ ▼	Hartle-Gilman Gardens
A 78	Princeton, 55371	⌂ ▼	Northwind Nursery & Orchards
A 92	Rockford, 55373	⌂ ▼	Riverdale Iris Gardens
A 12	St. Cloud, 56302		Brand Peony Farm
A 62	St. Paul, 55108	⌂ ▼	Landscape Alternatives, Inc.
A 76	St. Paul, 55118	▼	The New Peony Farm
A 77	St. Paul, 55114	⌂	North Star Gardens
A 3	Waconia, 55387	⌂ ▼	Ambergate Gardens
A 99	Waseca, 56093	⌂ ▼	Shady Oaks Nursery
A 19	White Bear Lake, 55110	⌂ ▼	Cascade Daffodils
A 88	Winona, 55987	⌂ ▼	Prairie Moon Nursery
A 57	Woodbury, 55125	⌂ ▼	Jordan Seeds

MISSISSIPPI

A 92	Biloxi, 39532	⌂ ▼	Riverbend Orchids
A 36	Meridian, 39304	⌂ ▼	Flowerplace Plant Farm
A 14	Olive Branch, 38654	⌂ ▼	Brussel's Bonsai Nursery

MISSOURI

A 1	California, 65018		Adamgrove
A 18	Cape Girardeau, 63701	▼	Cape Iris Gardens
A 45	Desloge, 63601	⌂ ▼	Hahn's Rainbow Iris Garden
A 22	Gower, 64454	⌂ ▼	Comanche Acres Iris Gardens
A 4	Grain Valley, 64029		American Daylily & Perennials
A 31	High Ridge, 63049	⌂ ▼	Eclipse Farms
A 6	Holt, 64048	⌂	Arborvillage Farm Nursery
A 106	Kansas City, 64114		Stigall Water Gardens
A 105	Louisiana, 63353	⌂	Stark Bro's Nurseries & Orchards Co.
A 71	New Melle, 63365	⌂ ▼	Midwest Cactus
A 52	Owensville, 65066	⌂ ▼	Homestead Farms
A 118	Sarcoxie, 64862	⌂ ▼	Gilbert H. Wild & Son, Inc.
A 6	Sedalia, 65301		Archias' Seed Store
A 4	St. Louis, 63108	▼	Amberway Gardens
A 2	Waynesville, 65583	⌂	Alice's Violet Room

MONTANA

A 6	Bozeman, 59715		Artemis Gardens
A 103	Bozeman, 59715	⌂ ▼	Sourdough Iris Gardens

(continued next page)

PAGE	CITY/ZIP	⌂ NURSERY ▼ GARDEN	SOURCE

MONTANA (continued)

A 112	Helena, 59604	⌂ ▼	Valley Nursery
A 3	Kalispell, 59901	⌂ ▼	Alpen Gardens
A 52	Kalispell, 59901	▼	Homestead Gardens
A 98	Miles City, 59301		The Seed Shop
A 9	Moiese, 59824	⌂	Big Sky Violets
A 39	Victor, 59875	⌂ ▼	Garden City Seeds

NEBRASKA

A 59	Fremont, 68025	⌂ ▼	Kent's Flowers
A 38	Ft. Calhoun, 68023		The Fragrant Path
A 50	Lexington, 68850	⌂ ▼	Hildenbrandt's Iris Gardens
A 106	Murdock, 68407		Stock Seed Farms, Inc.
A 77	Norfolk, 68701	⌂	North Pine Iris Gardens
A 28	Omaha, 68117	⌂ ▼	DeGiorgi Seed Company
A 85	Pawnee City, 68420		Pinky's Plants
A 69	Ponca, 68770	▼	Maple Tree Gardens
A 40	Wayne, 68787	⌂ ▼	Garden Perennials
A 104	Wisner, 68791	⌂ ▼	Spruce Gardens

NEVADA

A 22	Reno, 98523	⌂ ▼	Comstock Seed

NEW BRUNSWICK, CANADA

A 48	Norton, E0G 2N0	⌂	The Herb Farm
A 23	Petitcodiac, E0A 2H0	⌂ ▼	Corn Hill Nursery

NEW HAMPSHIRE

A 79	East Kingston, 03827		Oakridge Nursery
A 121	Kensington, 03833	⌂ ▼	York Hill Farm
A 68	Nashua, 03062	⌂ ▼	Lowe's own-root Roses
A 35	Newington, 03801	⌂	Timothy D. Field Ferns & Wildflowers

NEW JERSEY

A 30	Adelphia, 07710		Dutch Gardens, Inc.
A 34	Clarksboro, 08020		Fern Hill Farm
A 118	Freehold, 07728	⌂ ▼	Wild Earth Native Plant Nursery
A 106	Glassboro, 08028	▼	Alex Summerville
A 33	Greenwich, 08323	⌂ ▼	Fairweather Gardens
A 109	Jackson, 08527	⌂	Thompson & Morgan
A 26	Marlboro, 07746	⌂ ▼	The Cummins Garden
A 57	Newfield, 08344	⌂	Jersey Asparagus Farms
A 10	Pompton Lakes, 07442		Black Copper Kits
A 116	Port Murray, 07865	⌂ ▼	Well-Sweep Herb Farm
A 115	Saddle River, 07458	⌂ ▼	Waterford Gardens
A 63	Sewell, 08080	⌂ ▼	Orol Ledden & Sons
A 50	Voorhees, 08043	⌂ ▼	Hillhouse Nursery

NEW MEXICO

A 71	Belen, 87002	⌂ ▼	Mesa Garden
A 76	Belen, 87002	⌂ ▼	New Mexico Cactus Research
A 87	Chaparral, 88021	▼	Pleasure Iris Gardens
A 28	Deming, 88030	⌂ ▼	Desert Nursery
A 98	El Prado, 87529		Seeds West Garden Seeds
A 68	Fairacres, 88033	▼	McAllister's Iris Gardens
A 95	Roswell, 88202	⌂	Roswell Seed Co.
A 108	Santa Cruz, 87567	⌂ ▼	Talavaya Seeds
A 49	Santa Fe, 87501	⌂ ▼	A High Country Garden
A 86	Santa Fe, 87501	⌂ ▼	Plants of the Southwest
A 98	Santa Fe, 87501		Seeds of Change
A 28	Veguita, 87062	⌂ ▼	Desert Moon Nursery

NEW YORK

A 42	Amherst, 14228	⌂ ▼	John Gordon Nursery
A 112	Babylon, 11702	⌂	Van Bourgondien Bros.
A 113	Brightwaters, 11718		Van Dyck's Flower Farms, Inc.
A 106	Buffalo, 14240	▼	Stokes Seed Company
A 72	Canandaigua, 14424	⌂ ▼	Miller Nurseries, Inc.
A 84	Canandaigua, 14424		Peter Pauls Nurseries

(continued next page)

PAGE	CITY/ZIP	⌂ NURSERY ▼ GARDEN	SOURCE
NEW YORK (continued)			
A 81	Collins, 14034	▼	P & P Seed Company
A 95	Dix Hills, 11746	⌂ ▼	Roslyn Nursery
A 68	Dolgeville, 13329	⌂ ▼	Lyndon Lyon Greenhouses, Inc.
A 64	East Moriches, 11940	⌂	Henry Leuthardt Nurseries, Inc.
A 25	East Rochester, 14445	⌂ ▼	Crosman Seed Corp.
A 105	Fairport, 14450		Arthur H. Steffen, Inc.
A 67	Flanders, 11901		Long Island Seed Company
A 76	Geneva, 14456		New York State Fruit Testing Coop. Assn.
A 98	Glen Head, 11545	⌂ ▼	Seagulls Landing Orchids
A 33	Greenlawn, 11740	⌂ ▼	Evergreen Acres Dahlia Gardens
A 120	Hammondsport, 14840	⌂ ▼	Wisley Dahlia Farm
A 41	High Falls, 12440	⌂ ▼	Gloria Dei
A 9	Ithaca, 14850		Betsy's Brierpatch
A 99	Locke, 13092	⌂	Sheffield's Seed Co., Inc.
A 92	Naples, 14512	⌂ ▼	Rob's Mini-o-lets
A 87	New Paltz, 12561	⌂	Plumtree Nursery
A 22	North Collins, 14111		Concord Nurseries, Inc.
A 97	Northport, 11768	⌂ ▼	S. Scherer & Sons
A 89	Parish, 13131		Railway Design & Landscape Company
A 5	Pattersonville, 12137	⌂ ▼	Apothecary Rose Shed
A 96	Potsdam, 13676	⌂ ▼	St. Lawrence Nurseries
A 100	Putnam Valley, 10579	⌂ ▼	Shepherd Hill Farm
A 77	Queensbury, 12804	⌂ ▼	Northland Gardens
A 46	Rochester, 14623		Harris Seeds
A 96	Saratoga Springs, 12866	⌂ ▼	Saxton Gardens
A 75	Schenectady, 12309		E. B. Nauman & Daughter
A 83	Shrub Oak, 10588	⌂	Peekskill Nurseries
A 11	Smithtown, 11787	⌂ ▼	The Bonsai Shop
A 18	South Salem, 10590	⌂ ▼	Carlson's Gardens
A 70	Spring Valley, 10977	⌂ ▼	Matterhorn Nursery Inc.
A 50	Sugar Loaf, 10981		Hillary's Garden
A 118	Webster, 14580		Wildginger Woodlands
NEW ZEALAND			
A 103	Canterbury, 8173	⌂ ▼	Southern Seeds
NO. IRELAND			
A 18	Ballymena, Co. Antri, BT43 7HF	▼	Carncairn Daffodils, Ltd.
NORTH CAROLINA			
A 36	Bailey, 27807	⌂	Finch Blueberry Nursery
A 13	Boone, 28607	⌂ ▼	Brookside Wildflowers
A 13	Brown Summit, 27214	⌂ ▼	Breckinridge Orchids
A 6	Bryson City, 28713		Arrowhead Nursery
A 12	Chapel Hill, 27514	⌂	Boothe Hill Wildflower Seeds
A 17	Chapel Hill, 27516	⌂ ▼	Camellia Forest Nursery
A 76	Chapel Hill, 27516	⌂ ▼	Niche Gardens
A 57	Dunn, 28334	⌂ ▼	Jernigan Gardens
A 29	Fairview, 28730	⌂	Donnelly's Nursery
A 109	Fairview, 28730	⌂	Tiki Nursery
A 51	Fletcher, 28732	⌂ ▼	Holbrook Farm & Nursery
A 86	Franklinton, 27525	⌂	Plant Hideaway
A 91	Godwin, 28344	⌂ ▼	Rasland Farm
A 64	Kannapolis, 28081	⌂ ▼	Lenette Greenhouses
A 116	Kill Devil Hills, 27948		Chris Weeks Peppers
A 55	Kings Mountain, 28086	⌂ ▼	Iron Gate Gardens
A 96	Leicester, 28748	⌂ ▼	Sandy Mush Herb Nursery
A 115	Leicester, 28748	⌂ ▼	Washington Evergreen Nursery
A 116	Marion, 28752	⌂ ▼	We-Du Nurseries
A 118	Marshall, 28753	⌂	Wildflower Nursery
A 66	Middlesex, 27557	⌂ ▼	Little River Farm
A 1	Mint Hill, 28227	⌂ ▼	Adventures in Herbs
A 48	Pilot Mountain, 27041		The Herb Garden
A 40	Pineola, 28662	⌂ ▼	Gardens of the Blue Ridge
A 81	Pisgah Forest, 28768	⌂ ▼	Owens Orchids
A 119	Pittsboro, 27312		The Wildwood Flower
A 88	Princeton, 27569	⌂ ▼	Powell's Gardens
A 54	Raleigh, 27607	▼	Hungry Plants

(continued next page)

PAGE	CITY/ZIP	⌂ NURSERY ▼ GARDEN	SOURCE

NORTH CAROLINA (continued)

A 86	Raleigh, 27603	▼	Plant Delights Nursery
A 65	Rocky Point, 28457		Lewis Strawberry Nursery
A 4	Townsville, 27584	⌂	American Forest Foods Corp.
A 110	Tryon, 28782		The Tomato Seed Company, Inc.
A 62	Warrensville, 28693	⌂	Lamtree Farm

NOVA SCOTIA, CANADA

A 91	Truro, B2N 2P6		Rawlinson Garden Seed
A 29	Windsor, B0N 2T0	▼	Howard Dill Enterprises
A 103	Yarmouth, B5A 4B6	⌂ ▼	South Cove Nursery

OHIO

A 22	Athens, 45701	⌂ ▼	Companion Plants
A 9	Bedford, 44146		Bedford Dahlias
A 61	Brecksville, 44141	⌂ ▼	Kuk's Forest Nursery
A 119	Chardon, 44024	⌂ ▼	Wildwood Gardens
A 52	Chesterland, 44026	⌂ ▼	Homestead Division of Sunnybrook Farms
A 107	Chesterland, 44026	⌂ ▼	Sunnybrook Farms Nursery
A 51	Cleveland Heights, 44118	⌂	Holly Ridge Nursery
A 4	Dayton, 45402		American Bamboo Company
A 50	Gallipolis, 45631		Highland Succulents
A 25	Gates Mills, 44040	⌂	Crintonic Gardens
A 41	Geneva, 44041	⌂ ▼	Girard Nurseries
A 69	Hamilton, 45013	⌂ ▼	Mary's Plant Farm
A 93	Hillsboro, 45133	⌂ ▼	Rocknoll Nursery
A 30	Hiram, 44234		Down on the Farm Seeds
A 111	Independence, 44131	⌂ ▼	William Tricker, Inc.
A 11	Madison, 44057	⌂	Bluestone Perennials
A 64	Manchester, 45144	⌂ ▼	Lewis Mountain Herbs & Everlastings
A 119	Mansfield, 44907	⌂ ▼	Wiley's Nut Grove Nursery
A 4	Medina, 44258		Ameri-Hort Research
A 40	Mentor, 44061	⌂	Garden Place
A 41	Metamora, 43540		Glecker Seedmen
A 65	Minerva, 44657	⌂ ▼	Lily of the Valley Herb Farm
A 65	New Philadelphia, 44663	⌂ ▼	Liberty Seed Company
A 70	North Lima, 44452	⌂ ▼	Mellinger's, Inc.
A 50	Painesville, 44077	⌂	Historical Roses
A 41	Perry, 44081	⌂	Gilson Gardens
A 84	Springfield, 45504	⌂ ▼	Perpetual Perennials
A 41	Stewart, 45778	⌂ ▼	Glasshouse Works
A 30	Vincent, 45784	⌂ ▼	Dyke Blueberry Farm & Nursery

OKLAHOMA

A 71	Oklahoma City, 73112	⌂ ▼	Mid-America Iris Gardens
A 83	Oklahoma City, 73176	⌂ ▼	Patio Garden Ponds

ONTARIO, CANADA

A 84	Ajax, L1S 4S7	⌂ ▼	Picov Greenhouses
A 61	Carlisle, L0R 1H0	⌂ ▼	V. Kraus Nurseries, Ltd.
A 100	Cedar Springs, N0P 1E0	⌂ ▼	Sherry's Perennials
A 27	Dundas, L9H 6M1	⌂ ▼	William Dam Seeds
A 81	Eden, N0J 1H0	⌂ ▼	Otter Valley Native Plants
A 29	Georgetown, L7G 5L6		Dominion Seed House
A 92	Goodwood, L0C 1A0	⌂ ▼	Richters Herbs
A 121	Kerwood, N0M 2B0	⌂ ▼	Wrightman Alpines
A 60	Komoka, N0L 1R0	⌂ ▼	Kilworth Flowers
A 41	Marlbank, K0K 2L0		Golden Bough Tree Farm
A 20	Mississauga, L5J 2Y4	⌂ ▼	Clargreen Gardens, Ltd.
A 17	Niagara-on-the-Lake, L0S 1J0	⌂ ▼	Campberry Farms
A 45	Niagara-on-the-Lake, L0S 1J0	⌂ ▼	Grimo Nut Nursery
A 77	Niagara-on-the-Lake, L0S 1J0	⌂ ▼	Northern Kiwi Nursery
A 69	Norwich, N0J 1P0	⌂ ▼	McMillen's Iris Garden
A 40	Ottawa, K1Y 3M8		Gardens North
A 84	Pickering, L1V 1A6	⌂	Pickering Nurseries, Inc.
A 36	Port Stanley, N5L 1C6	⌂	Floridel Gardens, Inc.
A 73	Port Stanley, N5L 1J4	⌂ ▼	Moore Water Gardens
A 40	Thornhill, L3T 4A5	⌂	Gardenimport, Inc.
A 26	Toronto, M4P 2M1	⌂	Cruickshank's, Inc.

(continued next page)

PAGE	CITY/ZIP	⌂ NURSERY ▼ GARDEN	SOURCE

ONTARIO, CANADA (continued)

A 72	Toronto, M8W 1T9	⌂	Miree's
A 9	Trout Creek, P0H 2L0		Becker's Seed Potatoes
A 82	Virgil, L0S 1T0	⌂ ▼	Carl Pallek & Son Nurseries
A 53	Waterdown, L0R 2H1		Hortico, Inc.
A 80	Waterloo, N2J 3Z9		Ontario Seed Company, Ltd.
A 9	Weston, M9L 1X9		Berton Seeds Company, Ltd.

OREGON

A 76	Albany, 97321	⌂ ▼	Nichols Garden Nursery, Inc.
A 109	Alsea, 97324	⌂ ▼	The Thyme Garden Seed Company
A 93	Aurora, 97002		Lon J. Rombough
A 80	Beaverton, 97007	⌂	Oregon Miniature Roses
A 57	Bend, 97701	⌂ ▼	Joyce's Garden
A 55	Brooks, 97305	⌂ ▼	Iris Country
A 78	Canby, 97013	⌂ ▼	Northwoods Retail Nursery
A 108	Canby, 97013	⌂ ▼	Swan Island Dahlias
A 17	Central Point, 97502	⌂	Callahan Seeds
A 67	Cloverdale, 97112	⌂ ▼	Loucks Nursery
A 10	Coos Bay, 97420		Blue Ridge Gardens
A 11	Corbett, 97019	▼	Bonnie Brae Gardens
A 80	Corbett, 97019	⌂ ▼	Oregon Trail Daffodils
A 78	Corvallis, 97330		Northwest Mycological Consultants
A 91	Corvallis, 97330	⌂	Redlo Cacti
A 109	Cottage Grove, 97424	⌂ ▼	Territorial Seed Company
A 46	Donald, 97020	⌂	Hansen Nursery
A 59	Drain, 97435	⌂ ▼	Kelleygreen Rhododendron Nursery
A 114	Eagle Point, 97524	⌂ ▼	Vicki's Exotic Plants
A 89	Eddyville, 97343	⌂	Qualitree Nursery
A 104	Estacada, 97023	⌂ ▼	Squaw Mountain Gardens
A 28	Eugene, 97404	⌂ ▼	Del's Japanese Maples
A 44	Eugene, 97401	⌂ ▼	Greer Gardens
A 110	Gold Beach, 97444	⌂ ▼	Tradewinds Nursery
A 80	Grants Pass, 97527		Oregon Exotics Rare Fruit Nursery
A 59	Gresham, 97030	⌂	Kasch Nursery
A 27	Hillsboro, 97123		Daisy Fields
A 72	Hubbard, 97032	▼	Grant Mitsch Novelty Daffodils
A 119	Lake Oswego, 97034		Willamette Valley Gardens Nursery
A 111	McMinnville, 97128	⌂ ▼	Trans Pacific Nursery
A 56	Medford, 97501	▼	Jackson & Perkins Co.
A 101	Medford, 97501	⌂ ▼	Siskiyou Rare Plant Nursery
A 49	Milwaukie, 97222	⌂ ▼	Hidden Garden Nursery, Inc.
A 90	Milwaukie, 97222	⌂	Rare Plant Research
A 19	Newberg, 97132	▼	Chehalem Gardens
A 39	Philomath, 97370	⌂	Freshops
A 12	Portland, 97219	⌂ ▼	The Bovees Nursery
A 51	Portland, 97214		Hobbs and Hopkins
A 77	Portland, 97286		Northern Groves
A 40	Roseburg, 97470	⌂ ▼	Garden Valley Dahlias
A 43	Salem, 97304	⌂ ▼	Russell Graham, Purveyor of Plants
A 59	Salem, 97305	⌂ ▼	Keith Keppel
A 97	Salem, 97303	▼	Schreiner's Gardens
A 117	Salem, 97304		Whitman Farms
A 21	Sandy, 97005		Coenosium Gardens
A 87	Sandy, 97055	⌂ ▼	Porterhowse Farms
A 57	Scappoose, 97056	⌂ ▼	Joy Creek Nursery
A 75	Scio, 97374		Nature's Garden
A 18	Scotts Mills, 97375		Cascade Bulb & Seed
A 54	Scotts Mills, 97375	⌂ ▼	Ingraham's Cottage Garden Roses
A 18	Sherwood, 97140	⌂ ▼	Caprice Farm Nursery
A 91	Sherwood, 97140	⌂ ▼	Red's Rhodies
A 102	Sherwood, 97140		Sorum's Nursery
A 23	Silverton, 97381	⌂ ▼	Cooley's Gardens
A 42	Springfield, 97478	⌂ ▼	Gossler Farms Nursery
A 63	Springfield, 97478	⌂ ▼	Laurie's Garden
A 47	St. Paul, 97137	⌂ ▼	Heirloom Old Garden Roses
A 19	Tangent, 97389		Chehalem Creek Nursery
A 61	Tigard, 97281	⌂ ▼	Kline Nursery Co.
A 78	Troutdale, 97060	⌂ ▼	Northwest Epi Center

(continued next page)

PAGE	CITY/ZIP	⌂ NURSERY ▼ GARDEN	SOURCE

OREGON (continued)

A 99	Troutdale, 97060	⌂ ▼	Shackleton's Dahlias
A 39	Turner, 97392	⌂ ▼	Frey's Dahlias
A 106	West Linn, 97068	⌂ ▼	Stubbs Shrubs
A 37	Williams, 97544	⌂	Forestfarm
A 42	Williams, 97544	⌂ ▼	Goodwin Creek Gardens
A 31	Wilsonville, 97070	⌂ ▼	Edmunds' Roses
A 58	Wilsonville, 97070	⌂	Justice Miniature Roses

PENNSYLVANIA

A 1	Aspers, 17304	⌂	Adams County Nursery, Inc.
A 14	Aspers, 17304	⌂ ▼	Bull Valley Rhododendron Nursery
A 110	Coopersburg, 18036	⌂ ▼	Tilley's Nursery/The WaterWorks
A 80	Dillsburg, 17019	⌂	Orchid Thoroughbreds
A 8	Easton, 18042	⌂	The Banana Tree
A 83	Forksville, 18616	⌂ ▼	Pen Y Bryn Nursery
A 110	Huntingdon Valley, 19006	⌂ ▼	Tinari Greenhouses
A 18	Indiana, 15701	⌂ ▼	Carino Nurseries
A 74	Indiana, 15701	⌂ ▼	Musser Forests Inc.
A 90	Kintnersville, 18930	⌂ ▼	Rarafolia
A 48	Lancaster, 17601	▼	Heirloom Seed Project
A 49	Loretto, 15940	⌂ ▼	Hickory Hill Gardens
A 38	McGrann, 16226	⌂	Fox Hollow Herbs & Heirloom Seed Company
A 33	Meadville, 16335	⌂	Ernst Crownvetch Farms
A 94	Mechanicsburg, 17055	⌂ ▼	The Rosemary House
A 112	Media, 19063	⌂ ▼	Upper Bank Nurseries
A 74	New Hope, 18938	⌂ ▼	Charles H. Mueller Co.
A 74	North East, 16428	⌂ ▼	Mums by Paschke
A 120	Pen Argyl, 18072	⌂ ▼	Windrose Ltd.
A 70	Philadelphia, 19111	⌂ ▼	Matsu-Momiji Nursery
A 120	Pittsburgh, 15224		Wirth's Herbs
A 65	Port Matilda, 16870	⌂ ▼	Limerock Ornamental Grasses
A 5	Reedsville, 17084	⌂ ▼	Appalachian Wildflower Nursery
A 106	Renfrew, 16053	⌂ ▼	Stoecklein's Nursery
A 36	Sagamore, 16250	⌂	Flickingers' Nursery
A 88	Scottdale, 15683	⌂ ▼	The Primrose Path
A 112	Trevose, 19053		Otis Twilley Seed Co.
A 48	Trout Run, 17771	⌂	The Herb Barn
A 15	Warminster, 18974	⌂	W. Atlee Burpee Company
A 113	Warrington, 18976	⌂ ▼	Varga's Nursery
A 5	Waynesboro, 17268	⌂	Appalachian Gardens
A 61	Wellsville, 17365	⌂ ▼	Michael & Janet Kristick
A 48	West Elizabeth, 15088		Heirloom Seeds
A 60	Wexford, 15090		Kingfisher, Inc.
A 83	Wynnewood, 19096	⌂	Penn Valley Orchids

PRINCE EDWARD ISLAND, CANADA

A 114	Charlottetown, C1A 8K6	⌂ ▼	Vesey's Seeds, Ltd.

QUEBEC, CANADA

A 84	Laval, H7P 5R9		W. H. Perron & Co., Ltd.
A 120	N.D. Ile Perrot, J7V 8P4	⌂ ▼	Windmill Point Farm & Nursery
A 64	Sawyerville, J0B 3A0	⌂ ▼	Les Violettes Natalia
A 1	St-Felix de Valois, J0K 2M0	⌂	A-mi Violettes
A 54	Sutton, J0E 2K0	⌂ ▼	Iris & Plus

RHODE ISLAND

A 70	Wyoming, 02898		Meadowbrook Herb Gardens

SASKATCHEWAN, CANADA

A 88	Cochin, S0M 0L0	▼	Prairie Grown Garden Seeds
A 53	Parkside, S0J 2A0	⌂ ▼	Honeywood Lilies
A 30	Saskatoon, S7J 0S5	⌂	Early's Farm & Garden Centre, Inc.
A 92	Saskatoon, S7K 3J8	⌂ ▼	Riverside Gardens

SCOTLAND

A 66	Caithness, KW2 6AA		Lochside Alpines Nursery

PAGE	CITY/ZIP	⌂ NURSERY ▼ GARDEN	SOURCE

SOUTH AFRICA

PAGE	CITY/ZIP	NURSERY/GARDEN	SOURCE
A 95	Brackenfell, 7560		Rust-En-Vrede Nursery
A 34	Constantia, Cape, 7848	⌂ ▼	Feathers Wild Flower Seeds
A 107	Howard Place, Cape, 7450	⌂ ▼	Sunburst Bulbs C.C.
A 101	Kenilworth, Cape, 7700		Silverhill Seeds
A 18	Stellenbosch, Cape, 7609		Cape Seed & Bulb

SOUTH CAROLINA

PAGE	CITY/ZIP	NURSERY/GARDEN	SOURCE
A 121	Aiken, 29801	⌂ ▼	Woodlanders, Inc.
A 79	Clover, 29710	⌂ ▼	Oak Hill Farm
A 72	Cross Hill, 29332	⌂ ▼	The Mini-Rose Garden
A 101	Graniteville, 29829	⌂	R. H. Shumway Seedsman
A 88	Greenville, 29604		Prentiss Court Ground Covers
A 83	Greenwood, 29648	⌂ ▼	Park Seed Company, Inc.
A 116	Hodges, 29695		Wayside Gardens
A 95	Laurens, 29360	⌂ ▼	Roses Unlimited
A 21	Myrtle Beach, 29575	⌂ ▼	Coastal Gardens & Nursery
A 18	Newberry, 29108	⌂ ▼	Carter & Holmes, Inc.
A 70	Walterboro, 29488	▼	Meadowlake Gardens
A 108	Woodruff, 29388	⌂ ▼	Swallowtail Garden & Nursery

SOUTH DAKOTA

PAGE	CITY/ZIP	NURSERY/GARDEN	SOURCE
A 45	Yankton, 57079	⌂	Gurney's Seed & Nursery Co.

SWITZERLAND

PAGE	CITY/ZIP	NURSERY/GARDEN	SOURCE
A 98	Meyrin, Geneva, CH 1217		Seedalp

TENNESSEE

PAGE	CITY/ZIP	NURSERY/GARDEN	SOURCE
A 107	Andersonville, 37705	⌂ ▼	Sunlight Gardens
A 38	Chattanooga, 37343	⌂ ▼	Forked Deer Farm
A 49	Cookeville, 38501	⌂ ▼	Hidden Springs Nursery -- Edible Landscaping
A 79	Corryton, 37721	▼	Oakes Daylilies
A 38	Dresden, 38225	⌂	Fred's Plant Farm
A 105	Gleason, 38229		Steele Plant Company
A 74	Greenback, 37742	⌂ ▼	Native Gardens
A 97	Hixson, 37343	⌂ ▼	Schild Azalea Gardens & Nursery
A 2	Knoxville, 37917		Alfrey Seeds -- Peter Pepper Seeds
A 9	Knoxville, 37938	⌂ ▼	Beaver Creek Nursery
A 51	Knoxville, 37923	⌂ ▼	Holly Haven Hybrids
A 107	Knoxville, 37914	⌂ ▼	Sunnyridge Gardens
A 26	McMinnville, 37110	⌂	Cumberland Valley Nurseries, Inc.
A 73	McMinnville, 37110	⌂	Mt. Leo Nursery
A 111	Memphis, 38116	⌂ ▼	Trees by Touliatos
A 62	Ooltewah, 37363	⌂ ▼	Lakeside Acres
A 52	Pelham, 37366		Hollydale Nursery
A 67	Red Boiling Springs, 37150	▼	Long Hungry Creek Nursery
A 81	Ripley, 38063	⌂ ▼	Owen Farms
A 74	Summertown, 38483	⌂	Mushroompeople
A 42	Taft, 38488	⌂	Good Hollow Greenhouse & Herbarium

TEXAS

PAGE	CITY/ZIP	NURSERY/GARDEN	SOURCE
A 11	Adkins, 78121	⌂	Bonsai Farm
A 56	Austin, 78748	⌂ ▼	It's About Thyme
A 8	Bastrop, 78602	⌂	Bastrop Botanical
A 103	Beaumont, 77702	⌂ ▼	Southern Exposure
A 112	Breckenridge, 76424	⌂	Turner Seed Company
A 4	Brenham, 77833	⌂ ▼	Antique Rose Emporium
A 86	Brenham, 77833		Pleasant Hill African Violets
A 6	Burleson, 76028	⌂ ▼	Artistic Plants
A 29	Carrizo Springs, 78834		Dixondale Farms
A 27	Corpus Christi, 78411	⌂ ▼	Dane Company
A 2	Dallas, 75228		African Queen
A 53	Dallas, 75381		Horticultural Enterprises
A 115	Dallas, 75219	⌂ ▼	Volkmann Bros. Greenhouses
A 121	De Leon, 76444	⌂	Womack's Nursery Co.
A 119	Eagle Lake, 77434	⌂ ▼	Wildseed Farms
A 29	El Paso, 79927	⌂ ▼	Desertland Nursery
A 74	Flower Mound, 75028		Native American Seed
A 25	Harlingen, 78551		Crockett's Tropical Plants

(continued next page)

PAGE	CITY/ZIP	⌂ NURSERY ▼ GARDEN	SOURCE

TEXAS (continued)

PAGE	CITY/ZIP	NURSERY	GARDEN	SOURCE
A 54	Hico, 76457	⌂	▼	Huggins Farm Irises
A 2	Houston, 77026	⌂	▼	Air Expose
A 8	Houston, 77065	⌂	▼	Barber Nursery
A 13	Houston, 77282			Brudy's Exotics
A 87	Houston, 77282	⌂	▼	The Plumeria People
A 43	Kerrville, 78028	⌂		Green Horizons
A 40	Laredo, 78043	⌂	▼	Garden World
A 107	Leander, 78641	⌂	▼	Sunrise Nursery
A 117	Lindale, 75771	⌂	▼	Bob Wells Nursery
A 16	Nacogdoches, 75961	⌂	▼	Cactus Farm
A 119	Poolville, 76487			Willhite Seed Co.
A 50	Romayor, 77368	⌂		Hilltop Herb Farm
A 59	San Antonio, 78221	⌂	▼	Kay's Greenhouses
A 87	Stephenville, 76401	⌂		Porter & Son
A 109	Tyler, 75708	⌂		Tate Rose Nursery
A 57	Victoria, 77901	⌂		JoS Violets
A 122	Waller, 77484		▼	Yucca Do Nursery

UTAH

PAGE	CITY/ZIP	NURSERY	GARDEN	SOURCE
A 54	Kaysville, 84037	⌂	▼	Intermountain Cactus

VERMONT

PAGE	CITY/ZIP	NURSERY	GARDEN	SOURCE
A 113	Cavendish, 05142			Mary Mattison van Schaik
A 113	Charlotte, 05445	⌂	▼	Vermont Wildflower Farm
A 84	East Hardwick, 05836	⌂	▼	Perennial Pleasures Nursery
A 43	East Monpelier, 05651	⌂		Green Mountain Transplants
A 113	Fair Haven, 05743			Vermont Bean Seed Co.
A 19	Isle La Motte, 05463			Champlain Isle Agro Associates
A 23	Londonderry, 05148	⌂	▼	The Cook's Garden
A 69	Moretown, 05660			Mad River Imports
A 39	Pittsfield, 05762			French's Bulb Importer
A 89	Putney, 05346	⌂	▼	Putney Nursery, Inc.
A 79	South Newfane, 05351	⌂	▼	Olallie Daylily Gardens
A 63	St. Johnsbury Center, 05863	⌂		Le Jardin du Gourmet
A 110	Tinmouth, 05773	⌂	▼	Tinmouth Channel Farm

VIRGINIA

PAGE	CITY/ZIP	NURSERY	GARDEN	SOURCE
A 31	Afton, 22920	⌂		Edible Landscaping
A 94	Amherst, 24521			Rose Hill Herbs and Perennials
A 56	Charlottesville, 22902	⌂	▼	The Thomas Jefferson Center
A 58	Esmont, 22937			Kalmia Farm
A 114	Fishersville, 22939	⌂	▼	Andre Viette Farm & Nursery
A 21	Fredericksburg, 22404			Coda Gardens
A 76	Gainesville, 22065	⌂	▼	Nicholls Gardens
A 26	Gloucester, 23061	⌂	▼	The Daffodil Mart
A 115	Lovettsville, 22080	⌂	▼	Water Ways Nursery
A 55	McLean, 22101		▼	The Iris Pond
A 14	Monroe, 24574	⌂	▼	Burford Brothers
A 103	North Garden, 22959			Southern Exposure Seed Exchange (R)
A 31	Stanardsville, 22973	⌂	▼	Edgewood Farm & Nursery

WALES

PAGE	CITY/ZIP	NURSERY	GARDEN	SOURCE
A 27	Deeside, Clwyd, CH5 4TE			B. & D. Davies
A 6	Dyfed, SA44 5SB			Jim & Jenny Archibald
A 20	Wrexham, Clwyd, LL13 9EP			Paul Christian -- Rare Plants

WASHINGTON

PAGE	CITY/ZIP	NURSERY	GARDEN	SOURCE
A 46	Arlington, 98223	⌂	▼	Hammond's Acres of Rhodys
A 21	Battle Ground, 98604	⌂	▼	Collector's Nursery
A 37	Bellevue, 98005	⌂	▼	Foliage Gardens
A 13	Blaine, 98230	⌂	▼	Brown's Kalmia & Azalea Nursery
A 118	Brinnon, 98320	⌂	▼	Whitney Gardens & Nursery
A 14	Buckley, 98321	⌂	▼	Buckley Nursery Garden Center
A 19	Centralia, 98531			Cedar Valley Nursery
A 19	Chehalis, 98532	⌂		Chehalis Rare Plant Nursery
A 55	College Place, 99324	⌂	▼	Iris Test Gardens
A 7	Edmonds, 98020			Bailey's
A 47	Elma, 98541	⌂	▼	Heaths and Heathers

(continued next page)

PAGE	CITY/ZIP	⌂ NURSERY ▼ GARDEN	SOURCE

WASHINGTON (continued)

A 21	Everson, 98247	⌂	Cloud Mountain Nursery
A 10	Graham, 98338	⌂ ▼	Bijou Alpines
A 51	Graham, 98338		Holland Gardens
A 73	Graham, 98338	⌂ ▼	Mt. Tahoma Nursery
A 52	Humptulips, 98552		Hollyvale Farm
A 49	Kingston, 98346	⌂ ▼	Heronswood Nursery
A 39	Langley, 98260		Frosty Hollow
A 35	Mercer Island, 98040		Field House Alpines
A 54	Montesano, 98563	⌂ ▼	Hughes Nursery
A 90	Morton, 98356	⌂ ▼	Raintree Nursery
A 9	Northport, 99157	⌂	Bear Creek Nursery
A 27	Oakville, 98568	⌂ ▼	Dan's Dahlias
A 35	Okanogan, 98840	▼	Filaree Farm
A 39	Olympia, 98507		Fungi Perfecti
A 65	Olympia, 98502	▼	The Lily Pad
A 14	Onalaska, 98570	⌂	Burnt Ridge Nursery
A 42	Oroville, 98844		Good Seed Co.
A 36	Port Angeles, 98362		Floating Mountain Seeds
A 1	Port Townsend, 98368		Abundant Life Seed Foundation
A 7	Port Townsend, 98368	⌂ ▼	B & D Lilies
A 7	Redmond, 98053	⌂ ▼	Bamboo Gardens of Washington
A 101	Roy, 98580	⌂	Silvaseed Company, Inc.
A 32	Seattle, 98116	⌂ ▼	A. I. Eppler, Ltd.
A 34	Seattle, 98119	⌂ ▼	Fancy Fronds
A 78	Seattle, 98144		Northwest Native Seed
A 97	Seattle, 98198	⌂ ▼	Sea-Tac Dahlia Gardens
A 102	Sequim, 98382	⌂ ▼	Skyline Nursery
A 1	Snohomish, 98290	⌂ ▼	A & D Peony & Perennial Nursery
A 25	Snohomish, 98290	⌂ ▼	Cricklewood Nursery
A 104	Spangle, 99031		Spangle Creek Labs
A 10	Spokane, 99207	⌂ ▼	Blossoms & Bloomers
A 62	Spokane, 99202	⌂	Lamb Nurseries
A 105	Spokane, 99223	⌂	Stanek's Garden Center
A 30	Sumner, 98390		Dunford Farms
A 20	Tacoma, 98406	⌂ ▼	Chieri Orchids
A 22	Tacoma, 98446	⌂ ▼	Connell's Dahlias
A 86	Tekoa, 99033	⌂ ▼	Plants of the Wild
A 2	Vancouver, 98685	⌂ ▼	Aitken's Salmon Creek Garden
A 36	Vancouver, 98682	⌂ ▼	Fir Grove Perennial Nursury
A 93	Vancouver, 98662	⌂ ▼	Robyn's Nest Nursery
A 22	Vashon Island, 98070	⌂	Colvos Creek Farm
A 25	Walla Walla, 99362		C. Criscola Iris Garden
A 113	Wenatchee, 98807	⌂ ▼	Van Well Nursery, Inc.
A 7	Woodinville, 98072	⌂ ▼	Baker & Chantry Orchids

WEST VIRGINIA

A 121	Berkeley Springs, 25411	⌂ ▼	Wrenwood of Berkeley Springs
A 12	Buckhannon, 26201	⌂	Brawner Geraniums
A 46	Cherry Grove, 26804		Hardscrabble Enterprises
A 82	Palestine, 26160	⌂ ▼	Palestine Orchids
A 107	Renick, 24966	⌂ ▼	Sunshine Farm & Gardens

WISCONSIN

A 47	Bayfield, 54814	⌂ ▼	Hauser's Superior View Farm
A 29	Delavan, 53115	⌂ ▼	Dick's Flower Farm
A 120	Eagle, 53119	⌂ ▼	Windy Oaks Daylilies & Aquatics
A 114	Eagle River, 54521	⌂ ▼	Violet Express
A 20	East Troy, 53120		Clifford's Perennial & Vine
A 7	Edgerton, 53534	⌂ ▼	Avatar's World
A 32	Evansville, 53536	⌂ ▼	Enchanted Valley Garden
A 68	Friesland, 53935		McClure & Zimmerman
A 43	Granton, 54436	⌂	Grace Gardens North
A 88	Mt. Horeb, 53572	⌂ ▼	Prairie Ridge Nursery/CRM Ecosystems, Inc.
A 24	Muskego, 53150	⌂ ▼	Country Wetlands Nursery & Consulting
A 88	North Lake, 53064	⌂ ▼	Prairie Seed Source
A 60	Omro, 54963	⌂	Kester's Wild Game Food Nurseries
A 24	Orfordville, 53576	⌂ ▼	The Country Mouse
A 119	Oshkosh, 54903	⌂	Wildlife Nurseries

(continued next page)

PAGE	CITY/ZIP	⌂ NURSERY ▼ GARDEN	SOURCE

WISCONSIN (continued)

A 34	Peshtigo, 54157	⌂ ▼	Field and Forest Products, Inc.
A 116	Plainfield, 54966	⌂ ▼	The Waushara Gardens
A 71	Racine, 53402	⌂ ▼	Milaeger's Gardens
A 58	Randolph, 53957	⌂ ▼	J. W. Jung Seed Co.
A 66	Spring Green, 53588	⌂ ▼	Little Valley Farm
A 3	Stitzer, 53825	⌂ ▼	Alpine Gardens & Calico Shop
A 87	Tilleda, 54978	⌂ ▼	Pony Creek Nursery
A 101	Waunakee, 53597	⌂ ▼	Skolaski's Glads & Field Flowers
A 88	Westfield, 53964	⌂ ▼	Prairie Nursery
A 56	Wilson, 54027	⌂ ▼	Jasperson's Hersey Nursery

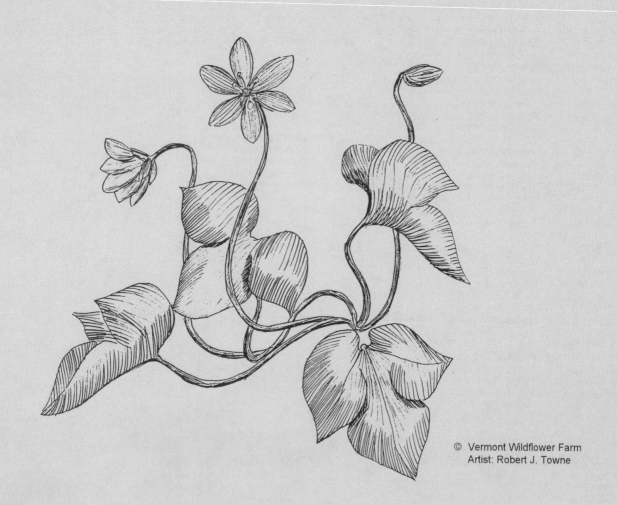

© Vermont Wildflower Farm
Artist: Robert J. Towne

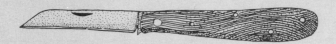

© Collector's Nursery   Artist: William Janssen

PRODUCT SOURCES INDEX K 1

PAGE	STATE	CITY	⌂ SHOP	SOURCE

ADD-IT FERTILIZER INJECTOR (R)

B 33	CA	Monrovia	⌂	TFS Injector Systems

AFRICAN VIOLET SUPPLIES

A 71	CA	Sacramento	⌂	Mighty Minis
A 114	CO	Englewood	⌂	The Violet Showcase
B 36	FL	Gainesville	⌂	The Violet House
A 114	FL	Tampa	⌂	Violet Creations
A 111	GA	Ochlochnee	⌂	Travis' Violets
A 17	MA	Falmouth		Cape Cod Violetry
B 19	MI	Detroit		Indoor Gardening Supplies
A 9	MT	Moiese	⌂	Big Sky Violets
A 68	NY	Dolgeville	⌂	Lyndon Lyon Greenhouses, Inc.
A 110	PA	Huntingdon Valley	⌂	Tinari Greenhouses
A 64	PQ	Sawyerville	⌂	Les Violettes Natalia
A 1	PQ	St-Felix de Valois	⌂	A-mi Violettes
A 86	TX	Brenham		Pleasant Hill African Violets
A 115	TX	Dallas	⌂	Volkmann Bros. Greenhouses
A 57	TX	Victoria	⌂	JoS Violets
A 114	WI	Eagle River	⌂	Violet Express

AGRICULTURAL RESEARCH SERVICE

B 1	CA	Davis	⌂	agAccess

AGROSOKE (TM)

B 16	TX	Ft. Worth		Grosoke, Inc.

ANIMAL REPELLENTS
See also Live Traps

B 28	BC	Delta		Phero Tech, Inc.
B 14	IN	Lawrenceburg	⌂	Gardens Alive!
B 5	NY	Yorkville		Bonide Products, Inc.
B 19	OR	Eugene		International Reforestation Suppliers

ANTIDESICCANTS

B 3	FL	West Palm Beach		Avant Horticultural Products

ARBORS

B 17	BC	Parksville	⌂	Heritage Garden Furniture
B 6	LA	Covington		Bridgeworks
B 6	MA	Bolton	⌂	Bow House, Inc.
B 1	MA	Brewster	⌂	Acorn Services Corporation
B 9	MD	Germantown	⌂	Country Casual
B 17	MI	Lansing	⌂	Heritage Garden Houses
B 34	NC	Saluda	⌂	Taylor Ridge Farm
B 38	NY	Medford		Wood Innovations of Suffolk
B 26	OR	Eugene		Oregon Timberframe
B 20	PA	Point Pleasant	⌂	Kinsman Company, Inc.
B 14	TN	Memphis	⌂	The Garden Concepts Collection
B 28	VA	Orange	⌂	The Plow & Hearth

AUTOMATIC VENT OPENERS
See also Greenhouse Ventilators

B 33	CA	Huntington Beach		Superior Autovents
B 9	MA	Peabody		The Crafter's Garden
B 6	MA	Salem		Bramen Company, Inc.
B 35	NC	Goldsboro	⌂	Turner Greenhouses
B 21	ON	Ottawa	⌂	Lee Valley Tools, Ltd.

(continued next page)

PAGE	STATE	CITY	⌂ SHOP	SOURCE
AUTOMATIC VENT OPENERS (continued)				
B 34	TX	Ft. Worth	⌂	Texas Greenhouse Co.
B 36	VA	Charlottesville	⌂	Victory Garden Supply Co.
B 8	WA	Mt. Vernon	⌂	Charley's Greenhouse Supply
BAMBOO FENCING & MATERIALS				
B 3	NJ	Lakewood	⌂	Bamboo & Rattan Works Inc.
BASKETS				
A 64	OH	Manchester	⌂	Lewis Mountain Herbs & Everlastings
BAT HOUSES				
B 38	NH	Woodstock		Woodstock Canoe Co.
BED & BREAKFAST				
A 47	MA	Barre	⌂	Hartman's Herb Farm
A 84	VT	East Hardwick	⌂	Perennial Pleasures Nursery
BEER MAKING SUPPLIES				
B 23	CO	Pueblo	⌂	Marck Wines
B 38	IN	Bloomington	⌂	Worm's Way of Indiana
BEES AND BEEKEEPING SUPPLIES				
B 20	KY	Clarkson		Walter T. Kelley Co.
A 6	MO	Sedalia		Archias' Seed Store
B 7	NC	Moravian Falls	⌂	Brushy Mountain Bee Farm, Inc.
A 95	NM	Roswell	⌂	Roswell Seed Co.
B 30	OH	Medina	⌂	A. I. Root Company
B 34	OR	Albany		Tec Laboratories, Inc.
B 33	PA	Eighty Four	⌂	Sunstream Bee Supply
BIO-FORCE (TM)				
A 40	TX	Laredo	⌂	Garden World
BIO-GRO (TM)				
A 40	TX	Laredo	⌂	Garden World
BIRD FEEDERS AND FOOD				
B 24	FL	Tallahassee	⌂	Native Nurseries
A 47	GA	Atlanta	⌂	H. G. Hastings
B 38	GA	Atlanta	⌂	Yanzum -- Art for Gardens
A 30	IN	New Albany		Earthly Goods, Ltd.
B 18	MA	Waltham		Hyde Bird Feeder Co.
A 2	ME	Falmouth	⌂	Allen, Sterling & Lothrop
A 116	MI	Fennville	⌂	Wavecrest Nursery & Landscaping Co.
B 21	NC	Colerain		Lazy Hill Farm Designs
B 29	NC	Wilmington	⌂	A Proper Garden
B 3	NH	Dublin	⌂	The Artisans Group
B 10	NH	Penacook		Duncraft, Inc.
B 38	NH	Woodstock		Woodstock Canoe Co.
B 33	NM	Santa Fe	⌂	Stone Forest
B 21	OH	Kidron	⌂	Lehman Hardware & Appliances, Inc.
B 7	OH	Waterville	⌂	Carruth Studio
B 22	OK	Oklahoma City		MAC Industries
B 4	ON	St. Thomas		Berry Hill Limited
A 80	ON	Waterloo		Ontario Seed Company, Ltd.
B 3	PA	Erie		Bruce Barber Bird-Feeders, Inc.
A 30	SK	Saskatoon	⌂	Early's Farm & Garden Centre, Inc.
B 14	TN	Memphis	⌂	The Garden Concepts Collection
B 10	TX	Austin	⌂	De Van Koek
B 28	VA	Orange	⌂	The Plow & Hearth
A 60	WI	Omro	⌂	Kester's Wild Game Food Nurseries
BIRD HOUSES				
B 14	CA	San Francisco		Gardener's Eden
B 37	DE	Dover	⌂	Winterthur Museum & Gardens
B 24	FL	Tallahassee	⌂	Native Nurseries
B 38	GA	Atlanta	⌂	Yanzum -- Art for Gardens
B 2	IL	Galesburg		Alsto's Handy Helpers

(continued next page)

PAGE	STATE	CITY	⌂ SHOP	SOURCE

BIRD HOUSES (continued)

PAGE	STATE	CITY	SHOP	SOURCE
A 30	IN	New Albany		Earthly Goods, Ltd.
B 24	MA	Topsfield		The Walt Nicke Company
B 18	MA	Waltham		Hyde Bird Feeder Co.
A 116	MI	Fennville	⌂	Wavecrest Nursery & Landscaping Co.
A 13	NC	Boone	⌂	Brookside Wildflowers
B 21	NC	Colerain		Lazy Hill Farm Designs
B 29	NC	Wilmington	⌂	A Proper Garden
B 3	NH	Dublin	⌂	The Artisans Group
B 10	NH	Penacook		Duncraft, Inc.
B 38	NH	Woodstock		Woodstock Canoe Co.
B 38	NY	Medford		Wood Innovations of Suffolk
B 21	OH	Kidron	⌂	Lehman Hardware & Appliances, Inc.
B 22	OK	Oklahoma City		MAC Industries
B 20	PA	Point Pleasant	⌂	Kinsman Company, Inc.
B 9	PA	Telford		Dalton Pavilions, Inc.
B 14	TN	Memphis	⌂	The Garden Concepts Collection
B 28	VA	Orange	⌂	The Plow & Hearth
A 7	WI	Edgerton	⌂	Avatar's World
B 5	WI	Edgerton	⌂	Bodoh, Inc.
A 119	WI	Oshkosh	⌂	Wildlife Nurseries

BIRD NETTING

PAGE	STATE	CITY	SHOP	SOURCE
B 14	IN	Lawrenceburg	⌂	Gardens Alive!
B 9	MA	Peabody		The Crafter's Garden
A 24	MI	Hartford	⌂	Country Heritage Nursery
B 16	MI	Vestaburg	⌂	Great Lakes IPM
B 19	MN	Minneapolis	⌂	InterNet, Inc.
B 10	TX	Austin	⌂	De Van Koek
B 19	WA	Wenatchee	⌂	Integrated Fertility Management

BIRD REPELLENTS

PAGE	STATE	CITY	SHOP	SOURCE
A 112	CA	Fountain Valley	⌂	Valley Vista Kiwi
A 15	CO	Rocky Ford		D. V. Burrell Seed Growers Co.
B 11	IN	Jeffersonville		Earlee, Inc.
A 47	MI	Grand Junction	⌂	Hartmann's Plantation, Inc.
A 77	MN	St. Paul	⌂	North Star Gardens
B 6	MT	Bozeman	⌂	Bozeman Bio-Tech

BIRDBATHS

PAGE	STATE	CITY	SHOP	SOURCE
B 14	CA	San Francisco		Gardener's Eden
B 10	NH	Penacook		Duncraft, Inc.
B 13	NY	Long Island City		Florentine Craftsmen, Inc.
B 7	OH	Waterville	⌂	Carruth Studio

BONSAI POTS AND SUPPLIES

PAGE	STATE	CITY	SHOP	SOURCE
B 25	CA	Fairfield		Niwa Tool Co.
A 67	CA	Forestville		Lone Pine Connection
A 99	CT	Stamford	⌂	Shanti Bithi Nursery
B 10	IA	Kelley	⌂	Dave's Aquariums & Greenhouse
A 104	IL	Hamburg	⌂	Springvale Farm Nursery
B 29	IL	Rock Island		Pot Lock
B 9	MA	Andover		Country House Floral Supply
B 27	MA	Sudbury	⌂	John Palmer Bonsai
B 5	MD	Baltimore	⌂	Bonsai Associates, Inc.
A 20	MI	Madison Heights	⌂	City Gardens
A 14	MS	Olive Branch	⌂	Brussel's Bonsai Nursery
A 77	NY	Queensbury	⌂	Northland Gardens
A 11	NY	Smithtown	⌂	The Bonsai Shop
A 119	OH	Chardon	⌂	Wildwood Gardens
A 20	ON	Mississauga	⌂	Clargreen Gardens, Ltd.
B 16	OR	Talent	⌂	Granite Impressions
A 83	PA	Forksville	⌂	Pen Y Bryn Nursery
A 70	PA	Philadelphia	⌂	Matsu-Momiji Nursery
A 11	TX	Adkins	⌂	Bonsai Farm
A 6	TX	Burleson	⌂	Artistic Plants
B 28	WA	Arlington	⌂	Pine Garden Bonsai Company
B 5	WA	Seattle	⌂	Bonsai Northwest

PAGE	STATE	CITY	⌂ SHOP	SOURCE
BONSAI TOOLS				
B 25	CA	Fairfield		Niwa Tool Co.
A 99	CT	Stamford	⌂	Shanti Bithi Nursery
B 10	IA	Kelley	⌂	Dave's Aquariums & Greenhouse
A 104	IL	Hamburg	⌂	Springvale Farm Nursery
B 27	MA	Sudbury	⌂	John Palmer Bonsai
B 5	MD	Baltimore	⌂	Bonsai Associates, Inc.
A 14	MS	Olive Branch	⌂	Brussel's Bonsai Nursery
A 77	NY	Queensbury	⌂	Northland Gardens
B 21	ON	Ottawa	⌂	Lee Valley Tools, Ltd.
A 83	PA	Forksville	⌂	Pen Y Bryn Nursery
B 4	PA	Greeley		Dorothy Biddle Service
A 70	PA	Philadelphia	⌂	Matsu-Momiji Nursery
A 11	TX	Adkins	⌂	Bonsai Farm
A 6	TX	Burleson	⌂	Artistic Plants
B 5	WA	Seattle	⌂	Bonsai Northwest
BOOK CLUBS				
B 26	IA	Des Moines		Organic Gardening Book Club
B 13	NJ	Delran		The Garden Book Club
BOOK SEARCH SERVICE				
B 7	CA	Concord	⌂	Brooks Books
B 15	CA	Santa Barbara	⌂	V. L. T. Gardner Botanical Books
B 29	CA	Stanford	⌂	Quest Rare Books
B 22	En	Kew, Surrey	⌂	Lloyds' of Kew
B 2	IL	Chillicothe	⌂	The American Botanist
B 14	MA	Lincoln	⌂	Garden Works
B 5	MD	Baltimore		Book Arbor
B 32	NH	Bedford		Edward F. Smiley, Bookseller
B 21	NH	Exeter		Landscape Books
B 6	NJ	Englishtown	⌂	The Book Tree
B 38	NJ	Hopewell	⌂	Elisabeth Woodburn
B 6	NY	New York		Bookfinders General, Inc.
B 34	Ne	Hastings	⌂	Touchwood Books
B 28	ON	Rockton	⌂	Pomona Book Exchange
B 4	OR	Portland		Carol Barnett -- Books
B 18	So	Newlands, Cape Town	⌂	Honingklip Book Sales
B 38	WI	Madison	⌂	Wood Violet Books
BOOKS, AFRICAN VIOLETS				
A 114	CO	Englewood	⌂	The Violet Showcase
A 110	PA	Huntingdon Valley	⌂	Tinari Greenhouses
BOOKS, AGRICULTURE				
B 1	CA	Davis	⌂	agAccess
B 2	IL	Chillicothe	⌂	The American Botanist
B 28	ON	Rockton	⌂	Pomona Book Exchange
B 4	PA	Wayne		J. F. Beattie Book Co.
BOOKS, ALPINE & ROCK GARDENS				
A 101	OR	Medford	⌂	Siskiyou Rare Plant Nursery
BOOKS, ARBORICULTURE				
B 3	FL	Fort Lauderdale	⌂	Arborist Supply House, Inc.
B 2	PA	West Chester		American Arborist Supplies
BOOKS, AUSTRALIAN PLANTS				
B 14	Au	Geelong, Victoria		Garden Street Books
A 31	Au	Nowra, NSW	⌂	Ellison Horticultural Pty., Ltd.
B 7	CA	Concord	⌂	Brooks Books
B 15	CA	Santa Barbara	⌂	V. L. T. Gardner Botanical Books
BOOKS, BAMBOO				
A 110	OR	Gold Beach	⌂	Tradewinds Nursery
BOOKS, BEEKEEPING				
B 30	OH	Medina	⌂	A. I. Root Company
B 33	PA	Eighty Four	⌂	Sunstream Bee Supply

PAGE	STATE	CITY	⌂ SHOP	SOURCE

BOOKS, BONSAI

PAGE	STATE	CITY	⌂ SHOP	SOURCE
B 14	Au	Geelong, Victoria		Garden Street Books
A 74	CA	Laytonville	⌂	Mountain Maples
B 15	CA	Santa Barbara	⌂	V. L. T. Gardner Botanical Books
A 99	CT	Stamford	⌂	Shanti Bithi Nursery
B 10	IA	Kelley	⌂	Dave's Aquariums & Greenhouse
B 27	MA	Sudbury	⌂	John Palmer Bonsai
B 5	MD	Baltimore	⌂	Bonsai Associates, Inc.
A 14	MS	Olive Branch		Brussel's Bonsai Nursery
B 14	NH	Hooksett		Gardeners Bookshelf
B 38	NJ	Hopewell	⌂	Elisabeth Woodburn
B 34	NY	Hauppauge		Tiny Trees Book Sales
A 77	NY	Queensbury	⌂	Northland Gardens
A 11	NY	Smithtown	⌂	The Bonsai Shop
B 34	Ne	Hastings	⌂	Touchwood Books
A 83	PA	Forksville	⌂	Pen Y Bryn Nursery
A 11	TX	Adkins	⌂	Bonsai Farm
A 6	TX	Burleson	⌂	Artistic Plants
B 5	WA	Seattle	⌂	Bonsai Northwest

BOOKS, BROMELIADS

PAGE	STATE	CITY	⌂ SHOP	SOURCE
B 14	Au	Geelong, Victoria		Garden Street Books
B 7	CA	Concord	⌂	Brooks Books
B 15	CA	Santa Barbara	⌂	V. L. T. Gardner Botanical Books
A 89	CA	Vista	⌂	Rainbow Gardens Nursery & Bookshop
A 2	FL	Boynton Beach	⌂	Alberts & Merkel Bros., Inc.
A 111	FL	Sarasota	⌂	Tropiflora
B 38	NJ	Hopewell	⌂	Elisabeth Woodburn
B 34	Ne	Hastings	⌂	Touchwood Books

BOOKS, BULBS

PAGE	STATE	CITY	⌂ SHOP	SOURCE
A 69	VT	Moretown		Mad River Imports
A 68	WI	Friesland		McClure & Zimmerman

BOOKS, CACTI & SUCCULENTS

PAGE	STATE	CITY	⌂ SHOP	SOURCE
A 101				Singers' Growing Things
B 20	CA	Azusa		Myron Kimnach
A 1	CA	Carpinteria	⌂	Abbey Gardens
B 7	CA	Concord	⌂	Brooks Books
A 48	CA	Fresno	⌂	Henrietta's Nursery
A 58	CA	Ione		K & L Cactus & Succulent Nursery
A 16	CA	Lodi	⌂	Cactus by Dodie
A 89	CA	Vista	⌂	Rainbow Gardens Nursery & Bookshop
B 20	OR	Newberg		The Ken-L-Questor

BOOKS, CALIFORNIA NATIVE PLANTS

PAGE	STATE	CITY	⌂ SHOP	SOURCE
A 63	CA	Bolinas	⌂	Larner Seeds
B 7	CA	Concord	⌂	Brooks Books
A 83	CA	Sun Valley	⌂	Theodore Payne Foundation
A 75	CA	Tehachapi	⌂	Native Oak Nursery

BOOKS, CARNIVOROUS PLANTS

PAGE	STATE	CITY	⌂ SHOP	SOURCE
A 17	CA	Forestville	⌂	California Carnivores

BOOKS, CHILDREN'S GARDENS

PAGE	STATE	CITY	⌂ SHOP	SOURCE
B 15	CA	Point Reyes Station		Gardens for Growing People

BOOKS, CONIFERS

PAGE	STATE	CITY	⌂ SHOP	SOURCE
A 21	OR	Sandy		Coenosium Gardens

BOOKS, DROUGHT TOLERANT PLANTS

PAGE	STATE	CITY	⌂ SHOP	SOURCE
B 5	CA	San Pedro		Book Orchard

BOOKS, EVERLASTINGS

PAGE	STATE	CITY	⌂ SHOP	SOURCE
A 42	OR	Williams	⌂	Goodwin Creek Gardens

BOOKS, FERNS

PAGE	STATE	CITY	⌂ SHOP	SOURCE
B 20	OR	Newberg		The Ken-L-Questor

PAGE	STATE	CITY	⌂ SHOP	SOURCE
BOOKS, FLOWER ARRANGING				
B 9	MA	Andover		Country House Floral Supply
B 4	PA	Greeley		Dorothy Biddle Service
BOOKS, FOOD PRESERVATION				
B 18	CA	Ramona	⌂	Home Canning Supply & Specialties
B 20	NJ	Mt. Laurel		Kitchen Krafts
BOOKS, GARDEN DESIGN				
B 14	NH	Hooksett		Gardeners Bookshelf
B 7	WI	Deer Park	⌂	Capability's Books
BOOKS, GARDEN GUIDES				
B 7	WI	Deer Park	⌂	Capability's Books
BOOKS, GARDEN HISTORY				
B 21	NH	Exeter		Landscape Books
BOOKS, GREENHOUSE GROWING				
B 8	WA	Mt. Vernon	⌂	Charley's Greenhouse Supply
BOOKS, HEIRLOOM PLANTS				
A 98	CT	Union		Select Seeds -- Antique Flowers
B 2	IL	Chillicothe	⌂	The American Botanist
A 56	VA	Charlottesville	⌂	The Thomas Jefferson Center
A 84	VT	East Hardwick	⌂	Perennial Pleasures Nursery
BOOKS, HERBS				
A 47	CA	Guerneville		Heirloom Garden Seeds
A 47	CA	Sonora	⌂	Havasu Hills Herbs
A 74	CA	Squaw Valley		Mountain Valley Growers, Inc.
A 13	FL	Orlando	⌂	Brown's Edgewood Gardens
A 48	IA	Marshalltown	⌂	Herbs-Liscious
B 2	IL	Chillicothe	⌂	The American Botanist
A 44	IN	Shipshewana	⌂	Greenfield Herb Garden
A 26	KY	Louisville		Dabney Herbs
A 38	MI	Parma	⌂	Fox Hill Farm
A 48	NC	Pilot Mountain		The Herb Garden
B 14	NH	Hooksett		Gardeners Bookshelf
A 116	NJ	Port Murray	⌂	Well-Sweep Herb Farm
A 107	OH	Chesterland	⌂	Sunnybrook Farms Nursery
A 64	OH	Manchester	⌂	Lewis Mountain Herbs & Everlastings
A 65	OH	Minerva	⌂	Lily of the Valley Herb Farm
A 92	ON	Goodwood	⌂	Richters Herbs
A 42	OR	Williams	⌂	Goodwin Creek Gardens
A 94	PA	Mechanicsburg	⌂	The Rosemary House
A 120	PA	Pittsburgh		Wirth's Herbs
B 38	WI	Oregon	⌂	Wood Violet Books
BOOKS, HISTORICAL RESTORATION				
A 84	VT	East Hardwick	⌂	Perennial Pleasures Nursery
BOOKS, HOYAS				
A 50	CA	Fresno	⌂	Hill 'n dale
BOOKS, HYDROPONICS				
B 18	CA	Irvine		Hollister's Hydroponics
B 18	CA	San Rafael	⌂	Hydro-Farm West
B 11	WA	Seattle	⌂	Eco Enterprises
BOOKS, IRIS				
A 55	VA	McLean		The Iris Pond
BOOKS, JAPANESE GARDENS				
B 1	Ja	ichikawa, Chiba	⌂	Albiflora, Inc.
BOOKS, JAPANESE MAPLES				
A 74	CA	Laytonville	⌂	Mountain Maples

PAGE	STATE	CITY	⌂ SHOP	SOURCE
BOOKS, JAPANESE PLANTS				
B 1	Ja	Ichikawa, Chiba	⌂	Albiflora, Inc.
BOOKS, LANDSCAPE ARCHITECTURE				
B 15	CA	Santa Barbara	⌂	V. L. T. Gardner Botanical Books
B 14	MA	Lincoln	⌂	Garden Works
B 21	NH	Exeter		Landscape Books
B 6	NJ	Englishtown	⌂	The Book Tree
B 38	NJ	Hopewell	⌂	Elisabeth Woodburn
B 6	NY	Lansingburgh		Warren F. Broderick -- Books
BOOKS, LILIES				
B 20	OR	Newberg		The Ken-L-Questor
BOOKS, MUSHROOMS				
A 117	BC	Aldergrove	⌂	Western Biologicals, Ltd.
A 78	OR	Corvallis		Northwest Mycological Consultants
B 20	OR	Newberg		The Ken-L-Questor
A 74	TN	Summertown	⌂	Mushroompeople
A 39	WA	Olympia		Fungi Perfecti
A 34	WI	Peshtigo	⌂	Field and Forest Products, Inc.
A 46	WV	Cherry Grove		Hardscrabble Enterprises
BOOKS, NEW				
See also specific subjects				
B 25	AR	Fayetteville	⌂	Nitron Industries, Inc.
B 14	Au	Geelong, Victoria		Garden Street Books
B 7	CA	Berkeley	⌂	Builders Booksource
B 7	CA	Concord	⌂	Brooks Books
B 1	CA	Davis	⌂	agAccess
B 17	CA	Graton	⌂	Harmony Farm Supply
B 7	CA	Marina Del Ray		A.C. Burke & Co.
B 32	CA	Mill Valley	⌂	Smith & Hawken
B 4	CA	Palo Alto	⌂	Bell's Book Store
A 44	CA	San Francisco	⌂	GreenLady Gardens
B 5	CA	San Pedro		Book Orchard
B 15	CA	Santa Barbara	⌂	V. L. T. Gardner Botanical Books
A 74	CA	Squaw Valley		Mountain Valley Growers, Inc.
A 89	CA	Vista	⌂	Rainbow Gardens Nursery & Bookshop
A 107	CT	West Hartford		Sunrise Oriental Seed Co.
B 37	En	Hitchin, Herts.	⌂	Wheldon & Wesley
B 22	En	Kew, Surrey	⌂	Lloyds' of Kew
B 17	En	London	⌂	Hatchard's
B 22	FL	Jacksonville	⌂	McQuerry Orchid Books
A 31	GA	Decatur	⌂	Eco-Gardens
A 98	ID	Boise		Seeds Blum
A 49	ID	Hailey	⌂	High Altitude Gardens
B 33	KY	Williamsburg	⌂	Raymond M. Sutton, Jr.
B 24	MA	Topsfield		The Walt Nicke Company
A 85	ME	New Gloucester	⌂	Pinetree Garden Seeds
A 34	ME	Waterville		Fedco Seeds
B 1	MO	Kansas City	⌂	Acres, U.S.A. -- Book Sales
A 39	MT	Victor	⌂	Garden City Seeds
B 35	NC	Goldsboro	⌂	Turner Greenhouses
B 21	NH	Exeter		Landscape Books
B 14	NH	Hooksett		Gardeners Bookshelf
B 13	NJ	Delran		The Garden Book Club
B 6	NJ	Englishtown	⌂	The Book Tree
B 38	NJ	Hopewell	⌂	Elisabeth Woodburn
A 70	NY	Spring Valley	⌂	Matterhorn Nursery Inc.
B 34	Ne	Hastings	⌂	Touchwood Books
A 70	OH	North Lima	⌂	Mellinger's, Inc.
A 27	ON	Dundas	⌂	William Dam Seeds
A 29	ON	Georgetown		Dominion Seed House
B 22	ON	Scarborough		Linden House
B 4	ON	St. Thomas		Berry Hill Limited
B 21	ON	Toronto	⌂	Laurelbrook Book Services
A 76	OR	Albany	⌂	Nichols Garden Nursery, Inc.
A 109	OR	Cottage Grove	⌂	Territorial Seed Company

(continued next page)

PAGE	STATE	CITY	⌂ SHOP	SOURCE
BOOKS, NEW (continued)				
A 44	OR	Eugene	⌂	Greer Gardens
A 121	SC	Aiken	⌂	Woodlanders, Inc.
B 18	So	Newlands, Cape Town	⌂	Honingklip Book Sales
A 87	TX	Houston	⌂	The Plumeria People
B 24	VA	New Castle	⌂	Necessary Trading Co.
A 90	WA	Morton	⌂	Raintree Nursery
A 1	WA	Port Townsend		Abundant Life Seed Foundation
B 12	WA	Seattle	⌂	Flora & Fauna Books
B 7	WI	Deer Park	⌂	Capability's Books
B 38	WI	Oregon	⌂	Wood Violet Books
BOOKS, ORCHIDS				
A 38	AR	Little Rock	⌂	Fox Orchids, Inc.
B 14	Au	Geelong, Victoria		Garden Street Books
A 105	CA	Carpinteria	⌂	Stewart Orchids, Inc.
B 7	CA	Concord	⌂	Brooks Books
B 15	CA	Santa Barbara	⌂	V. L. T. Gardner Botanical Books
A 96	CA	Santa Barbara	⌂	Santa Barbara Orchid Estate
A 68	CA	South San Francisco	⌂	Rod McLellan Co.
A 2	FL	Boynton Beach	⌂	Alberts & Merkel Bros., Inc.
B 22	FL	Jacksonville	⌂	McQuerry Orchid Books
A 79	IL	Dundee	⌂	Oak Hill Gardens
A 80	IL	Villa Park	⌂	Orchids by Hausermann, Inc.
A 59	MD	Kensington	⌂	Kensington Orchids
B 14	NH	Hooksett		Gardeners Bookshelf
B 38	NJ	Hopewell	⌂	Elisabeth Woodburn
B 34	Ne	Hastings	⌂	Touchwood Books
A 60	ON	Komoka	⌂	Kilworth Flowers
A 91	OR	Sherwood	⌂	Red's Rhodies
BOOKS, ORGANIC GARDENING				
B 5	CA	San Pedro		Book Orchard
B 1	MO	Kansas City	⌂	Acres, U.S.A. -- Book Sales
B 14	TX	Austin	⌂	Garden-Ville of Austin
B 7	WI	Deer Park	⌂	Capability's Books
BOOKS, PALMS				
A 43	FL	Palm Harbor	⌂	The Green Escape
BOOKS, PERENNIALS				
A 60	IL	Champaign		Klehm Nursery
B 14	NH	Hooksett		Gardeners Bookshelf
A 40	ON	Ottawa		Gardens North
B 7	WI	Deer Park	⌂	Capability's Books
BOOKS, PRAIRIE PLANTING				
A 66	WI	Spring Green	⌂	Little Valley Farm
BOOKS, PRAIRIE PLANTS				
A 88	MN	Winona	⌂	Prairie Moon Nursery
BOOKS, PROPAGATION				
A 99	NY	Locke	⌂	Sheffield's Seed Co., Inc.
BOOKS, RARE & ANTIQUARIAN				
B 14	Au	Geelong, Victoria		Garden Street Books
B 7	CA	Concord	⌂	Brooks Books
B 29	CA	Stanford	⌂	Quest Rare Books
B 12	CT	West Cornwall	⌂	Barbara Farnsworth, Bookseller
B 37	En	Hitchin, Herts.	⌂	Wheldon & Wesley
B 22	FL	Jacksonville	⌂	McQuerry Orchid Books
B 2	IL	Chillicothe	⌂	The American Botanist
B 1	Ja	Ichikawa, Chiba	⌂	Albiflora, Inc.
B 33	KY	Williamsburg	⌂	Raymond M. Sutton, Jr.
B 31	MA	Lanesboro	⌂	Savoy Books
B 14	MA	Lincoln	⌂	Garden Works
B 5	MD	Baltimore		Book Arbor
B 32	NH	Bedford		Edward F. Smiley, Bookseller

(continued next page)

(continued next page)

PAGE	STATE	CITY	⌂ SHOP	SOURCE

BOOKS, USED AND OUT-OF-PRINT (continued)

PAGE	STATE	CITY	⌂ SHOP	SOURCE
B 18	NH	Westmoreland	⌂	Hurley Books
B 38	NJ	Hopewell	⌂	Elisabeth Woodburn
B 11	NY	Boiceville		Editions
B 6	NY	Lansingburgh		Warren F. Broderick -- Books
B 6	NY	New York		Bookfinders General, Inc.
B 34	Ne	Hastings	⌂	Touchwood Books
B 7	ON	Picton		Calendula Horticultural Books
B 28	ON	Rockton	⌂	Pomona Book Exchange
B 18	ON	Toronto	⌂	Hortulus
B 4	OR	Gold Hill		B. L. Bibby Books
B 20	OR	Newberg		The Ken-L-Questor
B 4	OR	Portland		Carol Barnett -- Books
B 29	OR	Portland		Larry W. Price Books
B 4	PA	Wayne		J. F. Beattie Book Co.
B 18	So	Newlands, Cape Town	⌂	Honingklip Book Sales
B 12	WA	Seattle	⌂	Flora & Fauna Books
B 38	WI	Oregon	⌂	Wood Violet Books

BOOKS, VEGETABLE & FRUIT GROWING

PAGE	STATE	CITY	⌂ SHOP	SOURCE
A 82	CA	Chula Vista	⌂	Pacific Tree Farms
B 1	CA	Davis	⌂	agAccess
A 102	CA	Healdsburg	⌂	Sonoma Antique Apple Nursery
A 91	CA	Redwood City		Redwood City Seed Co.
A 12	CA	Willits	⌂	Bountiful Gardens
A 103	FL	Melbourne		Southern Seeds
A 63	GA	Ball Ground	⌂	Lawson's Nursery
A 94	ID	Moyie Springs		Ronniger's Seed Potatoes
A 78	MN	Princeton	⌂	Northwind Nursery & Orchards
A 108	NM	Santa Cruz	⌂	Talavaya Seeds
A 96	NY	Potsdam	⌂	St. Lawrence Nurseries
B 28	ON	Rockton	⌂	Pomona Book Exchange
A 42	WA	Oroville		Good Seed Co.

BOOKS, WATER GARDENING

PAGE	STATE	CITY	⌂ SHOP	SOURCE
A 96	CA	Santa Barbara	⌂	Santa Barbara Water Gardens
A 113	CA	Upland	⌂	Van Ness Water Gardens
A 102	FL	Winter Haven	⌂	Slocum Water Gardens
A 82	MA	Whitman	⌂	Paradise Water Gardens
A 118	MD	Baldwin	⌂	Wicklein's Water Gardens
A 65	MD	Buckeystown	⌂	Lilypons Water Gardens
A 115	NJ	Saddle River	⌂	Waterford Gardens
A 111	OH	Independence	⌂	William Tricker, Inc.
A 73	ON	Port Stanley	⌂	Moore Water Gardens
A 110	PA	Coopersburg	⌂	Tilley's Nursery/The WaterWorks

BOOKS, WEATHER

PAGE	STATE	CITY	⌂ SHOP	SOURCE
B 37	CA	Mendocino	⌂	Wind & Weather

BOOKS, WILDFLOWERS

PAGE	STATE	CITY	⌂ SHOP	SOURCE
A 63	CA	Bolinas	⌂	Larner Seeds
B 7	CA	Concord	⌂	Brooks Books
A 83	CA	Sun Valley	⌂	Theodore Payne Foundation
A 13	NC	Boone	⌂	Brookside Wildflowers
A 43	TX	Kerrville	⌂	Green Horizons

BOOT SCRAPERS

PAGE	STATE	CITY	⌂ SHOP	SOURCE
B 10	CA	Placentia	⌂	Denman & Co.
B 21	OH	Kidron	⌂	Lehman Hardware & Appliances, Inc.
B 20	PA	Point Pleasant	⌂	Kinsman Company, Inc.

BOTANICAL PRINTS

PAGE	STATE	CITY	⌂ SHOP	SOURCE
B 22	FL	Jacksonville	⌂	McQuerry Orchid Books
B 31	MA	Lanesboro	⌂	Savoy Books
B 15	Wa	Hawarden, Clwyd	⌂	Gladstone & Jones

BRIDGES

PAGE	STATE	CITY	⌂ SHOP	SOURCE
B 6	LA	Covington		Bridgeworks
B 6	MA	Bolton	⌂	Bow House, Inc.

(continued next page)

PAGE	STATE	CITY	⌂ SHOP	SOURCE
BRIDGES (continued)				
B 33	NM	Santa Fe	⌂	Stone Forest
B 18	NY	Canastota	⌂	Hermitage Gardens
B 38	NY	Medford		Wood Innovations of Suffolk
B 26	OR	Eugene		Oregon Timberframe
B 14	TN	Memphis	⌂	The Garden Concepts Collection
BRUSH CUTTERS				
B 22	OH	London	⌂	Mainline of North America
B 19	OR	Eugene		International Reforestation Suppliers
B 23	TN	Tracy City		The Marugg Company
BULB PLANTING SUPPLIES				
B 7	NJ	Princeton		Bulb Savers
BULB SAVERS (R)				
B 7	NJ	Princeton		Bulb Savers
CALCIUM-25 (TM)				
B 4	VA	Falls Church		Bio-Gard Agronomics
CANNING SUPPLIES				
B 17	CA	Graton	⌂	Harmony Farm Supply
B 18	CA	Ramona	⌂	Home Canning Supply & Specialties
B 14	CT	Farmington		Gardener's Kitchen
A 68	MB	Brandon		McFayden Seeds
B 20	NJ	Mt. Laurel		Kitchen Krafts
A 106	NY	Buffalo		Stokes Seed Company
B 21	OH	Kidron	⌂	Lehman Hardware & Appliances, Inc.
A 29	ON	Georgetown		Dominion Seed House
B 4	ON	St. Thomas		Berry Hill Limited
A 45	SD	Yankton	⌂	Gurney's Seed & Nursery Co.
CARRY-IT CART (R)				
B 20	NY	Saratoga Springs		Kadco USA
CARTS				
B 10	CA	Placentia	⌂	Denman & Co.
B 7	CA	Point Arena	⌂	Cart Warehouse
B 24	CA	San Anselmo	⌂	The Natural Gardening Company
B 10	FL	Miami	⌂	Day-Dex Co.
B 2	IL	Galesburg		Alsto's Handy Helpers
B 6	MA	Salem		Bramen Company, Inc.
B 8	MA	Shelburne Falls		Catamount Cart
B 20	NY	Saratoga Springs		Kadco USA
B 21	OH	Kidron	⌂	Lehman Hardware & Appliances, Inc.
B 21	OH	Piqua	⌂	A. M. Leonard, Inc.
B 21	ON	Ottawa	⌂	Lee Valley Tools, Ltd.
B 14	VT	Burlington	⌂	Gardener's Supply Company
B 25	WI	Stoughton	⌂	Norway Industries
CHILDREN'S GARDEN SUPPLIES				
B 15	CA	Point Reyes Station		Gardens for Growing People
CHRISTMAS WREATHS & GREENERY				
B 16	OR	Grants Pass		Greenleaf Industries
CIDER AND WINE PRESSES				
B 17	KS	Paola	⌂	Happy Valley Ranch
B 21	OH	Kidron	⌂	Lehman Hardware & Appliances, Inc.
B 22	OH	London	⌂	Mainline of North America
B 4	ON	St. Thomas		Berry Hill Limited
A 45	SD	Yankton	⌂	Gurney's Seed & Nursery Co.
A 14	VA	Monroe	⌂	Burford Brothers
COLD FRAMES				
B 16	CA	San Leandro		Green Thumb Industries
B 1	MA	Brewster	⌂	Acorn Services Corporation
B 6	MA	Salem		Bramen Company, Inc.

(continued next page)

PAGE	STATE	CITY	⌂ SHOP	SOURCE

COLD FRAMES (continued)

PAGE	STATE	CITY	⌂ SHOP	SOURCE
B 24	MA	Topsfield		The Walt Nicke Company
A 46	NY	Rochester		Harris Seeds
B 20	PA	Point Pleasant	⌂	Kinsman Company, Inc.
B 34	TX	Ft. Worth	⌂	Texas Greenhouse Co.

COMPOSTING EQUIPMENT

PAGE	STATE	CITY	⌂ SHOP	SOURCE
B 25	AR	Fayetteville	⌂	Nitron Industries, Inc.
B 24	CA	San Anselmo	⌂	The Natural Gardening Company
B 30	CA	San Diego		Reotemp Instrument Corporation
B 1	CO	Boulder	⌂	Age-Old Organics
B 35	ID	Boise	⌂	Tumblebug
B 2	IL	Galesburg		Alsto's Handy Helpers
B 32	IL	Seward		Solarcone, Inc.
B 14	IN	Lawrenceburg	⌂	Gardens Alive!
B 9	MA	Peabody		The Crafter's Garden
B 24	MA	Topsfield		The Walt Nicke Company
B 24	MN	Dundas		Morco Products
B 5	NJ	Princeton		Blue Planet, Inc.
B 21	ON	Ottawa	⌂	Lee Valley Tools, Ltd.
B 20	PA	Lititz	⌂	Kemp Company
B 20	PA	Point Pleasant	⌂	Kinsman Company, Inc.
B 25	PQ	Sherbrooke	⌂	Nova Sylva, Inc.
B 24	VA	New Castle	⌂	Necessary Trading Co.
B 14	VT	Burlington	⌂	Gardener's Supply Company

COMPOSTUMBLER (R)

PAGE	STATE	CITY	⌂ SHOP	SOURCE
B 20	PA	Lititz	⌂	Kemp Company

COMPUTEMP (R)

PAGE	STATE	CITY	⌂ SHOP	SOURCE
B 30	NE	Columbus	⌂	Rodco Products Co., Inc.

COMPUTER PROGRAMS

PAGE	STATE	CITY	⌂ SHOP	SOURCE
B 7	CA	Marina Del Ray		A.C. Burke & Co.
B 10	CT	Eastford		Double-Pawed Software
B 11	FL	Daytona Beach		Economy Label Sales Co., Inc.
B 31	IL	Springfield		Saroh
B 34	MA	Medford		Terrace Software
B 8	MD	Arnold		Computer/Management Services
A 38	MI	Parma	⌂	Fox Hill Farm
B 19	MO	Arcola		Infopoint Software
B 34	NC	Raleigh		Taxonomic Computer Research
B 23	NJ	Andover		Mindsun
B 36	OH	Lima		V-Base
B 1	OR	Eugene		Abracadata, Ltd.
B 30	OR	Portland		Rosebud
B 2	PA	Media		American Weather Enterprises
B 11	UT	Logan		Elemental Software
B 14	WA	Lynnwood		Gardenfind

COMPUTERIZED GARDEN DESIGN

PAGE	STATE	CITY	⌂ SHOP	SOURCE
B 34	MA	Medford		Terrace Software
B 23	NJ	Andover		Mindsun
B 1	OR	Eugene		Abracadata, Ltd.

COMPUTERIZED PLANT SELECTION

PAGE	STATE	CITY	⌂ SHOP	SOURCE
B 31	IL	Springfield		Saroh
B 34	MA	Medford		Terrace Software
B 19	MO	Arcola		Infopoint Software
B 34	NC	Raleigh		Taxonomic Computer Research
B 27	NY	East Hampton		Paradise Information, Inc.
B 36	OH	Lima		V-Base
B 30	OR	Portland		Rosebud

COOKBOOKS (GARDEN PRODUCE)

PAGE	STATE	CITY	⌂ SHOP	SOURCE
A 33	CA	Anaheim		Evergreen Y. H. Enterprises
A 100	CA	Felton	⌂	Shepherd's Garden Seeds
A 102	CA	Healdsburg	⌂	Sonoma Antique Apple Nursery
B 15	CA	Santa Barbara	⌂	V. L. T. Gardner Botanical Books

(continued next page)

PAGE	STATE	CITY	⌂ SHOP	SOURCE

COOKBOOKS (GARDEN PRODUCE) (continued)

A 47	CA	Sonora	⌂	Havasu Hills Herbs
A 107	CT	West Hartford		Sunrise Oriental Seed Co.
A 63	GA	Ball Ground	⌂	Lawson's Nursery
A 94	ID	Moyie Springs		Ronniger's Seed Potatoes
A 54	IN	Huntingburg	⌂	Indiana Berry & Plant Co.
A 43	KS	Leawood		The Gourmet Gardener
B 17	KS	Paola	⌂	Happy Valley Ranch
A 74	TN	Summertown	⌂	Mushroompeople
B 38	WI	Madison	⌂	Wood Violet Books
A 34	WI	Peshtigo	⌂	Field and Forest Products, Inc.

DEHYDRATORS

B 14	VT	Burlington	⌂	Gardener's Supply Company
A 46	WV	Cherry Grove		Hardscrabble Enterprises

DIATOMACEOUS EARTH

B 22	AR	Springdale		Maestro-Gro
B 12	PA	Gap	⌂	Erth-Rite, Inc.

DOG AND CAT PEST CONTROLS

B 25	AR	Fayetteville	⌂	Nitron Industries, Inc.
A 13	FL	Orlando	⌂	Brown's Edgewood Gardens
B 14	IN	Lawrenceburg	⌂	Gardens Alive!
B 6	MT	Bozeman	⌂	Bozeman Bio-Tech
A 39	MT	Victor	⌂	Garden City Seeds
A 48	NC	Pilot Mountain		The Herb Garden
B 5	NY	Yorkville		Bonide Products, Inc.
B 14	TX	Austin	⌂	Garden-Ville of Austin
B 24	VA	Lexington		Naturally Free/Bug-Off, Inc.
B 24	VA	New Castle	⌂	Necessary Trading Co.
B 19	WA	Wenatchee	⌂	Integrated Fertility Management

DOOM (R)

B 12	NY	Clinton Corners		Fairfax Biological Laboratory, Inc.

DRIP IRRIGATION SUPPLIES

B 25	AR	Fayetteville	⌂	Nitron Industries, Inc.
B 30	CA	Chatsworth	⌂	Raindrip, Inc.
A 116	CA	Grass Valley	⌂	Weiss Brothers Nursery
B 17	CA	Graton	⌂	Harmony Farm Supply
B 33	CA	Monrovia	⌂	TFS Injector Systems
B 24	CA	San Anselmo	⌂	The Natural Gardening Company
B 36	CA	San Francisco	⌂	The Urban Farmer Store
B 9	CA	San Marcos	⌂	D.I.G. Corporation
B 10	CA	Willits	⌂	DripWorks
B 19	CO	Colorado Springs	⌂	Hydro-Gardens, Inc.
A 47	MI	Grand Junction	⌂	Hartmann's Plantation, Inc.
B 28	MO	Grover	⌂	Plastic Plumbing Products, Inc.
B 19	NY	Niagara Falls		International Irrigation Systems
B 33	TX	Lubbock	⌂	Submatic Irrigation Systems
A 87	TX	Stephenville	⌂	Porter & Son
A 43	VT	East Monpelier	⌂	Green Mountain Transplants

DRIP IRRIGATION SYSTEMS

A 120	AB	Hythe	⌂	Windy Ridge Nursery
B 30	CA	Chatsworth	⌂	Raindrip, Inc.
A 82	CA	Chula Vista	⌂	Pacific Tree Farms
A 116	CA	Grass Valley	⌂	Weiss Brothers Nursery
B 33	CA	Monrovia	⌂	TFS Injector Systems
B 36	CA	San Francisco	⌂	The Urban Farmer Store
B 9	CA	San Marcos	⌂	D.I.G. Corporation
B 10	CA	Willits	⌂	DripWorks
B 14	IN	Lawrenceburg	⌂	Gardens Alive!
B 28	MO	Grover	⌂	Plastic Plumbing Products, Inc.
B 19	NY	Niagara Falls		International Irrigation Systems
B 21	ON	Ottawa	⌂	Lee Valley Tools, Ltd.
A 15	PA	Warminster	⌂	W. Atlee Burpee Company
B 8	WA	Mt. Vernon	⌂	Charley's Greenhouse Supply

(continued next page)

PAGE	STATE	CITY	⌂ SHOP	SOURCE

FERTILIZERS, ORGANIC (continued)

PAGE	STATE	CITY	⌂ SHOP	SOURCE
B 24	CA	San Anselmo	⌂	The Natural Gardening Company
B 30	CA	San Diego	⌂	Bargyla Rateaver
B 10	CA	San Rafael	⌂	Diamond
A 74	CA	Squaw Valley		Mountain Valley Growers, Inc.
A 12	CA	Willits	⌂	Bountiful Gardens
B 1	CO	Boulder	⌂	Age-Old Organics
A 13	FL	Orlando	⌂	Brown's Edgewood Gardens
A 47	GA	Atlanta	⌂	H. G. Hastings
B 31	IA	Charles City		Sea Born/Lane, Inc.
B 11	IL	Elgin	⌂	Elgin Landscape & Garden Center
B 32	IL	Mendota	⌂	Smith Greenhouse & Supply
B 38	IN	Bloomington	⌂	Worm's Way of Indiana
B 11	IN	Jeffersonville		Earlee, Inc.
B 14	IN	Lawrenceburg	⌂	Gardens Alive!
B 9	MA	Peabody		The Crafter's Garden
B 6	MA	Salem		Bramen Company, Inc.
B 25	ME	Waldoboro		North American Kelp
A 39	MT	Victor	⌂	Garden City Seeds
B 5	NY	Yorkville		Bonide Products, Inc.
B 16	OH	Cleveland		Guano Company International, Inc.
B 26	OH	Hartville	⌂	Ohio Earth Food, Inc.
A 109	OR	Cottage Grove	⌂	Territorial Seed Company
B 12	PA	Gap	⌂	Erth-Rite, Inc.
B 14	TX	Austin	⌂	Garden-Ville of Austin
A 40	TX	Laredo	⌂	Garden World
B 4	VA	Falls Church		Bio-Gard Agronomics
B 24	VA	New Castle	⌂	Necessary Trading Co.
A 23	VT	Londonderry	⌂	The Cook's Garden
B 19	WA	Wenatchee	⌂	Integrated Fertility Management

FERTILIZERS, SEAWEED

PAGE	STATE	CITY	⌂ SHOP	SOURCE
B 1	CO	Boulder	⌂	Age-Old Organics
B 32	IL	Mendota	⌂	Smith Greenhouse & Supply
B 6	MA	Salem		Bramen Company, Inc.
B 25	ME	Waldoboro		North American Kelp

FISH FOR GARDEN PONDS

PAGE	STATE	CITY	⌂ SHOP	SOURCE
A 87	AR	Kingston	⌂	Pond Doctor
A 97	AZ	Scottsdale	⌂	Scottsdale Fishponds
A 113	CA	Upland	⌂	Van Ness Water Gardens
A 102	FL	Winter Haven	⌂	Slocum Water Gardens
A 118	MD	Baldwin	⌂	Wicklein's Water Gardens
A 65	MD	Buckeystown	⌂	Lilypons Water Gardens
A 69	MD	Jarrettsville	⌂	Maryland Aquatic Nurseries
A 115	NJ	Saddle River	⌂	Waterford Gardens
A 97	NY	Northport	⌂	S. Scherer & Sons
A 111	OH	Independence	⌂	William Tricker, Inc.
A 84	ON	Ajax	⌂	Picov Greenhouses
A 110	PA	Coopersburg	⌂	Tilley's Nursery/The WaterWorks
A 111	TN	Memphis	⌂	Trees by Touliatos
A 120	WI	Eagle	⌂	Windy Oaks Daylilies & Aquatics

FLORALIGHT (TM)

PAGE	STATE	CITY	⌂ SHOP	SOURCE
B 13	ON	North York		Floralight Gardens Canada, Inc.

FLOWER ARRANGING SUPPLIES

PAGE	STATE	CITY	⌂ SHOP	SOURCE
B 25	CA	Fairfield		Niwa Tool Co.
B 13	IL	Lombard		The Floral Mailbox
B 9	MA	Andover		Country House Floral Supply
A 14	MD	Owings Mills	⌂	Bundles of Bulbs
A 20	ON	Mississauga	⌂	Clargreen Gardens, Ltd.
B 4	PA	Greeley		Dorothy Biddle Service

FLOWER DRYING SUPPLIES

PAGE	STATE	CITY	⌂ SHOP	SOURCE
B 13	IL	Lombard		The Floral Mailbox
B 9	MA	Andover		Country House Floral Supply
B 4	PA	Greeley		Dorothy Biddle Service
A 103	VA	North Garden		Southern Exposure Seed Exchange(R)

PAGE	STATE	CITY	⌂ SHOP	SOURCE
FOREIGN EXCHANGE SERVICES				
B 31	DC	Washington		Ruesch International Financial Services
B 35	US	Every Town		U. S. Post Office
FORESTRY EQUIPMENT/SUPPLIES				
B 36	CA	Chico		Valley Oak Tool Company
B 3	FL	Fort Lauderdale	⌂	Arborist Supply House, Inc.
B 34	MN	St. Paul		Treesentials
B 21	OH	Piqua	⌂	A. M. Leonard, Inc.
B 33	OR	Corvallis	⌂	Stuewe and Sons, Inc.
B 19	OR	Eugene		International Reforestation Suppliers
B 2	PA	West Chester		American Arborist Supplies
B 25	PQ	Sherbrooke	⌂	Nova Sylva, Inc.
FOUNTAINS				
A 96	CA	Santa Barbara	⌂	Santa Barbara Water Gardens
B 27	CT	Norwalk	⌂	P&R International, Inc.
B 22	CT	Wilton		Kenneth Lynch & Sons, Inc.
B 38	GA	Atlanta	⌂	Yanzum -- Art for Gardens
A 65	MD	Buckeystown	⌂	Lilypons Water Gardens
B 28	MO	Grover	⌂	Plastic Plumbing Products, Inc.
B 6	NC	Hickory	⌂	Andy Brinkley Studio
B 33	NM	Santa Fe	⌂	Stone Forest
B 28	NY	Bronxville		Pompeian Studios
B 18	NY	Canastota	⌂	Hermitage Gardens
B 13	NY	Long Island City		Florentine Craftsmen, Inc.
B 20	NY	Niagara Falls	⌂	Kosmolux & LP, Inc.
A 97	NY	Northport	⌂	S. Scherer & Sons
A 83	OK	Oklahoma City	⌂	Patio Garden Ponds
A 73	ON	Port Stanley	⌂	Moore Water Gardens
B 1	VA	Alexandria	⌂	Adams & Adkins
B 8	VT	Bristol	⌂	Robert Compton, Ltd.
A 7	WA	Redmond	⌂	Bamboo Gardens of Washington
GARDEN BENCHES, METAL				
B 26	CA	Costa Mesa		O'Brien Ironworks
B 22	CT	Wilton		Kenneth Lynch & Sons, Inc.
B 27	DC	Washington	⌂	Park Place
B 29	NC	Wilmington	⌂	A Proper Garden
B 37	NE	Lincoln		Wikco Industries, Inc.
B 28	NY	Bronxville		Pompeian Studios
B 37	PA	Malvern		Windsor Designs
B 8	SC	Charleston	⌂	Charleston Battery Bench, Inc.
GARDEN BENCHES, STONE				
B 27	CT	Norwalk	⌂	P&R International, Inc.
B 22	CT	Wilton		Kenneth Lynch & Sons, Inc.
B 38	GA	Atlanta	⌂	Yanzum -- Art for Gardens
B 33	NM	Santa Fe	⌂	Stone Forest
B 28	NY	Bronxville		Pompeian Studios
B 16	OR	Talent	⌂	Granite Impressions
GARDEN BENCHES, WOOD				
B 38	AL	Trussville		Woodbrook Furniture Manufacturing Co.
B 17	BC	Parksville	⌂	Heritage Garden Furniture
B 1	CA	Fort Bragg	⌂	Adirondack Designs
B 32	CA	Mill Valley	⌂	Smith & Hawken
B 2	CO	Englewood		Alpine Millworks Company
B 27	DC	Washington	⌂	Park Place
B 38	GA	Atlanta	⌂	Yanzum -- Art for Gardens
B 9	MD	Germantown	⌂	Country Casual
B 30	ME	Cape Porpoise		Richardson-Allen Furniture
B 29	NC	Wilmington	⌂	A Proper Garden
B 38	NY	Gardiner	⌂	Wood Classics
B 37	NY	Keeseville	⌂	Willsboro Wood Products
B 33	OK	Tulsa		Sun Garden Specialties
B 9	PA	Carlisle		Cumberland Woodcraft
B 37	PA	Malvern		Windsor Designs
B 14	TN	Memphis	⌂	The Garden Concepts Collection

(continued next page)

PAGE	STATE	CITY	⌂ SHOP	SOURCE

GARDEN BENCHES, WOOD (continued)

PAGE	STATE	CITY	⌂ SHOP	SOURCE
B 1	VA	Alexandria	⌂	Adams & Adkins
B 16	VA	Hamilton		Green Enterprises
B 28	VA	Orange	⌂	The Plow & Hearth

GARDEN CLOTHING
See also Gloves

PAGE	STATE	CITY	⌂ SHOP	SOURCE
B 23	CA	Guerneville	⌂	Emi Meade, Importer
B 10	CA	Placentia	⌂	Denman & Co.
B 14	CA	San Francisco		Gardener's Eden
B 38	ME	York		Womanswork
B 21	ON	Ottawa	⌂	Lee Valley Tools, Ltd.
B 26	ON	Trout Creek		The Original Bug Shirt(R) Company
B 22	WA	Freeland		MN Productions
B 8	WI	Elkhart Lake		Clothcrafters, Inc.

GARDEN DIARIES

PAGE	STATE	CITY	⌂ SHOP	SOURCE
B 10	CT	Eastford		Double-Pawed Software
B 22	ND	Crosby		The Loken Company

GARDEN FURNITURE
See also specific type

PAGE	STATE	CITY	⌂ SHOP	SOURCE
B 38	AL	Trussville		Woodbrook Furniture Manufacturing Co.
B 17	BC	Parksville	⌂	Heritage Garden Furniture
B 26	CA	Costa Mesa		O'Brien Ironworks
B 1	CA	Fort Bragg	⌂	Adirondack Designs
B 32	CA	Mill Valley	⌂	Smith & Hawken
B 14	CA	San Francisco		Gardener's Eden
B 2	CO	Englewood		Alpine Millworks Company
B 22	CT	Wilton		Kenneth Lynch & Sons, Inc.
B 27	DC	Washington	⌂	Park Place
B 37	DE	Dover	⌂	Winterthur Museum & Gardens
B 38	GA	Atlanta	⌂	Yanzum -- Art for Gardens
B 2	IL	Galesburg		Alsto's Handy Helpers
B 1	MA	Brewster	⌂	Acorn Services Corporation
B 6	MA	Salem		Bramen Company, Inc.
B 9	MD	Germantown	⌂	Country Casual
B 30	ME	Cape Porpoise		Richardson-Allen Furniture
B 15	NC	Burnsville	⌂	Gateways
B 6	NC	Hickory	⌂	Andy Brinkley Studio
B 28	NY	Bronxville		Pompeian Studios
B 38	NY	Gardiner	⌂	Wood Classics
B 37	NY	Keeseville	⌂	Willsboro Wood Products
B 13	NY	Long Island City		Florentine Craftsmen, Inc.
A 56	OR	Medford		Jackson & Perkins Co.
B 16	OR	Talent	⌂	Granite Impressions
B 37	PA	Malvern		Windsor Designs
B 9	PA	Telford		Dalton Pavilions, Inc.
B 8	SC	Charleston	⌂	Charleston Battery Bench, Inc.
B 14	TN	Memphis	⌂	The Garden Concepts Collection
B 13	TX	Tyler		French Wyres(R)
B 16	VA	Hamilton		Green Enterprises
B 28	VA	Orange	⌂	The Plow & Hearth

GARDEN MAGAZINE INDEX

PAGE	STATE	CITY	⌂ SHOP	SOURCE
B 14	WA	Lynnwood		Gardenfind

GARDEN MARKERS
See also Plant Labels

PAGE	STATE	CITY	⌂ SHOP	SOURCE
B 12	CA	Cloverdale		Evergreen Garden Plant Labels
A 98	CT	Union		Select Seeds -- Antique Flowers
B 11	FL	Daytona Beach		Economy Label Sales Co., Inc.
A 13	FL	Orlando	⌂	Brown's Edgewood Gardens
B 9	MA	Peabody		The Crafter's Garden
B 27	MI	Paw Paw		Paw Paw Everlast Label Co.
B 14	NH	Barnstead		Garden Fonts
B 17	NJ	Old Tappan		Harlane Company, Inc.
A 116	NJ	Port Murray	⌂	Well-Sweep Herb Farm
B 11	OH	Liberty Center		Eon Industries

(continued next page)

PAGE	STATE	CITY	⌂ SHOP	SOURCE
GARDEN MARKERS (continued)				
B 21	ON	Ottawa	⌂	Lee Valley Tools, Ltd.
B 2	ON	Sydenham		Amaranth Stoneware
GARDEN ORNAMENTS				
See also specific type				
B 26	CA	Costa Mesa		O'Brien Ironworks
B 8	CA	La Honda		Cieli
B 37	CA	Mendocino	⌂	Wind & Weather
B 32	CA	Mill Valley	⌂	Smith & Hawken
B 3	CA	Oceanside	⌂	Asian Artifacts
B 14	CA	San Francisco		Gardener's Eden
B 27	CT	Norwalk	⌂	P&R International, Inc.
B 22	CT	Wilton		Kenneth Lynch & Sons, Inc.
B 27	DC	Washington	⌂	Park Place
B 37	DE	Dover	⌂	Winterthur Museum & Gardens
B 38	GA	Atlanta	⌂	Yanzum -- Art for Gardens
B 2	IL	Galesburg		Alsto's Handy Helpers
B 37	IN	Indianapolis	⌂	Windleaves
A 48	KY	Sandy Hook		Hemlock Hollow Nursery & Folk Art
B 18	ME	Yarmouth	⌂	Heritage Lanterns
B 15	NC	Burnsville	⌂	Gateways
B 21	NC	Colerain		Lazy Hill Farm Designs
B 20	NC	Durham		Kate's Garden & Studio
B 29	NC	Wilmington	⌂	A Proper Garden
B 3	NH	Dublin	⌂	The Artisans Group
B 3	NJ	Lakewood	⌂	Bamboo & Rattan Works Inc.
A 116	NJ	Port Murray	⌂	Well-Sweep Herb Farm
B 28	NY	Bronxville		Pompeian Studios
B 13	NY	Long Island City		Florentine Craftsmen, Inc.
B 7	OH	Waterville	⌂	Carruth Studio
B 33	OK	Tulsa		Sun Garden Specialties
B 2	ON	Sydenham		Amaranth Stoneware
A 56	OR	Medford		Jackson & Perkins Co.
B 16	OR	Talent	⌂	Granite Impressions
B 9	PA	Carlisle		Cumberland Woodcraft
B 29 *	PA	Pittsburgh		Popovitch Associates, Inc.
B 12	PA	Sinking Spring		Escort Lighting
B 3	PA	Somerset	⌂	Baker's Lawn Ornaments
B 14	TN	Memphis	⌂	The Garden Concepts Collection
B 36	TX	Quinlan	⌂	Vintage Wood Works
B 13	TX	Tyler		French Wyres(R)
B 28	VA	Orange	⌂	The Plow & Hearth
B 8	VT	Bristol	⌂	Robert Compton, Ltd.
A 7	WI	Edgerton	⌂	Avatar's World
B 5	WI	Edgerton	⌂	Bodoh, Inc.
GARDEN PLANS				
B 32	MI	Edwardsburg		SeedScapes
A 94	PA	Mechanicsburg	⌂	The Rosemary House
GARDEN RAILWAY DESIGN				
A 89	NY	Parish		Railway Design & Landscape Company
B 1	OR	Eugene		Abracadata, Ltd.
GARDEN STRUCTURES				
B 6	MA	Bolton	⌂	Bow House, Inc.
B 17	MI	Lansing	⌂	Heritage Garden Houses
B 26	OR	Eugene		Oregon Timberframe
GARDEN TROUGHS				
B 26	IN	Carmel		Old World Garden Troughs(R)
A 49	NM	Santa Fe	⌂	A High Country Garden
B 17	NY	Fayetteville		Karen Harris
B 11	WY	Hyattville		Earthworks
GATES				
B 3	CA	Nevada City		David Bacon Woodworking
B 17	MI	Lansing	⌂	Heritage Garden Houses

PAGE	STATE	CITY	⌂ SHOP	SOURCE

GAZEBOS

PAGE	STATE	CITY	⌂ SHOP	SOURCE
B 6	MA	Bolton	⌂	Bow House, Inc.
B 17	MI	Lansing	⌂	Heritage Garden Houses
B 26	OR	Eugene		Oregon Timberframe
B 9	PA	Carlisle		Cumberland Woodcraft
B 36	PA	Elverson	⌂	Vixen Hill Gazebos
B 19	PA	Fairview Village		Ivywood Gazebo
B 9	PA	Telford		Dalton Pavilions, Inc.
B 14	TN	Memphis	⌂	The Garden Concepts Collection
B 36	TX	Quinlan	⌂	Vintage Wood Works

GAZING GLOBES

PAGE	STATE	CITY	⌂ SHOP	SOURCE
B 3	PA	Somerset	⌂	Baker's Lawn Ornaments

GIFTS FOR GARDENERS

See also all other categories

PAGE	STATE	CITY	⌂ SHOP	SOURCE
A 51	AR	Elkins	⌂	Holland Wildflower Farm
B 32	CA	Mill Valley	⌂	Smith & Hawken
B 14	CA	San Francisco		Gardener's Eden
A 117	CT	Litchfield	⌂	White Flower Farm
B 37	DE	Dover	⌂	Winterthur Museum & Gardens
B 24	FL	Tallahassee	⌂	Native Nurseries
B 38	GA	Atlanta	⌂	Yanzum -- Art for Gardens
A 5	IL	Chapin		Applesource
A 104	IL	Hamburg	⌂	Springvale Farm Nursery
B 13	IL	Schaumburg	⌂	Florist Products, Inc.
B 37	IN	Indianapolis	⌂	Windleaves
B 24	MA	Topsfield		The Walt Nicke Company
B 29	NC	Wilmington	⌂	A Proper Garden
B 6	NJ	Englishtown	⌂	The Book Tree
B 7	OH	Waterville	⌂	Carruth Studio
B 16	OR	Grants Pass		Greenleaf Industries
A 56	OR	Medford		Jackson & Perkins Co.
A 94	PA	Mechanicsburg	⌂	The Rosemary House
A 60	PA	Wexford		Kingfisher, Inc.
A 116	SC	Hodges		Wayside Gardens
A 50	TX	Romayor	⌂	Hilltop Herb Farm
B 28	VA	Orange	⌂	The Plow & Hearth
B 8	WA	Mt. Vernon	⌂	Charley's Greenhouse Supply

GLOVES

PAGE	STATE	CITY	⌂ SHOP	SOURCE
B 32	CA	Mill Valley	⌂	Smith & Hawken
B 10	CA	Placentia	⌂	Denman & Co.
B 9	MA	Peabody		The Crafter's Garden
B 6	MA	Salem		Bramen Company, Inc.
B 38	ME	York		Womanswork
B 17	NJ	Old Tappan		Harlane Company, Inc.
B 22	NY	Johnstown		Little's Good Gloves
B 4	PA	Greeley		Dorothy Biddle Service
B 10	TX	Austin	⌂	De Van Koek
B 8	WI	Elkhart Lake		Clothcrafters, Inc.

GLOVES, GAUNTLET

PAGE	STATE	CITY	⌂ SHOP	SOURCE
B 38	ME	York		Womanswork
B 22	NY	Johnstown		Little's Good Gloves
B 10	TX	Austin	⌂	De Van Koek

GOPHER BASKETS

PAGE	STATE	CITY	⌂ SHOP	SOURCE
B 10	CA	Soquel		Digger's Product Development Co.

GRAFTING SUPPLIES

PAGE	STATE	CITY	⌂ SHOP	SOURCE
A 82	CA	Chula Vista	⌂	Pacific Tree Farms
B 25	CA	Fairfield		Niwa Tool Co.
A 93	IN	New Salisbury	⌂	Rocky Meadow Orchard & Nursery
A 78	MN	Princeton	⌂	Northwind Nursery & Orchards
B 21	OH	Piqua	⌂	A. M. Leonard, Inc.
B 19	OR	Eugene		International Reforestation Suppliers
A 14	VA	Monroe	⌂	Burford Brothers
B 19	WA	Wenatchee	⌂	Integrated Fertility Management

PAGE	STATE	CITY	⌂ SHOP	SOURCE
GREEN CONE (TM)				
B 32	IL	Seward		Solarcone, Inc.
GREENHOUSE BUILDING MATERIALS				
B 19	CO	Colorado Springs	⌂	Hydro-Gardens, Inc.
B 35	NC	Goldsboro	⌂	Turner Greenhouses
B 25	ND	Neche	⌂	Northern Greenhouse Sales
B 21	OH	Piqua	⌂	A. M. Leonard, Inc.
B 8	WA	Mt. Vernon	⌂	Charley's Greenhouse Supply
GREENHOUSE CONTROLS				
B 31	CA	Camarillo	⌂	Santa Barbara Greenhouses
B 10	CA	San Rafael	⌂	Diamond
B 19	MD	Laurel		Janco Greenhouses
B 35	NC	Goldsboro	⌂	Turner Greenhouses
B 29	NJ	Princeton	⌂	Qualimetrics, Inc.
B 9	OH	Medina	⌂	Cropking, Inc.
B 33	OR	Portland	⌂	Sturdi-Built Mfg. Co.
B 34	TX	Ft. Worth	⌂	Texas Greenhouse Co.
B 33	WA	Seattle	⌂	Sunglo Solar Greenhouses
GREENHOUSE EQUIPMENT & ACCESSORIES				
B 16	AL	Mobile	⌂	Gothic Arch Greenhouses
B 27	CA	Carmel	⌂	Pacific Greenhouse
B 4	CA	Petaluma		BioTherm Hydronic, Inc.
B 27	CA	Petaluma	⌂	Pacific Coast Greenhouse Mfg. Co.
B 9	CA	San Marcos	⌂	D.I.G. Corporation
B 19	CO	Colorado Springs	⌂	Hydro-Gardens, Inc.
B 13	CT	Rockville	⌂	Fox Hill Farm/Hoophouse
B 26	FL	Miami	⌂	OFE International, Inc.
B 32	IL	Mendota	⌂	Smith Greenhouse & Supply
B 19	MD	Laurel		Janco Greenhouses
B 28	MO	Grover	⌂	Plastic Plumbing Products, Inc.
B 35	NC	Goldsboro	⌂	Turner Greenhouses
B 30	NE	Columbus	⌂	Rodco Products Co., Inc.
B 9	OH	Medina	⌂	Cropking, Inc.
B 33	OR	Portland	⌂	Sturdi-Built Mfg. Co.
A 18	SC	Newberry	⌂	Carter & Holmes, Inc.
B 34	TX	Ft. Worth	⌂	Texas Greenhouse Co.
B 36	VA	Charlottesville	⌂	Victory Garden Supply Co.
B 8	WA	Mt. Vernon	⌂	Charley's Greenhouse Supply
B 25	WA	Redmond		Northwest Eden Sales, Inc.
B 33	WA	Seattle	⌂	Sunglo Solar Greenhouses
GREENHOUSE HEATERS				
B 16	AL	Mobile	⌂	Gothic Arch Greenhouses
B 31	CA	Camarillo	⌂	Santa Barbara Greenhouses
B 27	CA	Carmel	⌂	Pacific Greenhouse
B 4	CA	Petaluma		BioTherm Hydronic, Inc.
B 35	NC	Goldsboro	⌂	Turner Greenhouses
B 9	OH	Medina	⌂	Cropking, Inc.
B 33	OR	Portland	⌂	Sturdi-Built Mfg. Co.
B 34	TX	Ft. Worth	⌂	Texas Greenhouse Co.
B 36	VA	Charlottesville	⌂	Victory Garden Supply Co.
B 33	WA	Seattle	⌂	Sunglo Solar Greenhouses
GREENHOUSE SUPPLIES				
B 16	AL	Mobile	⌂	Gothic Arch Greenhouses
B 13	IL	Schaumburg	⌂	Florist Products, Inc.
B 6	PA	New Brighton		Brighton By-Products Co., Inc.
GREENHOUSE VENTILATORS				
B 16	AL	Mobile	⌂	Gothic Arch Greenhouses
B 31	CA	Camarillo	⌂	Santa Barbara Greenhouses
B 27	CA	Carmel	⌂	Pacific Greenhouse
B 33	CA	Huntington Beach		Superior Autovents
B 19	MD	Laurel		Janco Greenhouses
B 35	NC	Goldsboro	⌂	Turner Greenhouses
B 9	OH	Medina	⌂	Cropking, Inc.

(continued next page)

(continued next page)

PAGE	STATE	CITY	⌂ SHOP	SOURCE

GROWING SUPPLIES, GENERAL (continued)

B 3	OR	Clackamas		Astoria-Pacific, Inc.
A 109	OR	Cottage Grove	⌂	Territorial Seed Company
B 6	PA	New Brighton		Brighton By-Products Co., Inc.
B 20	PA	Point Pleasant	⌂	Kinsman Company, Inc.
A 112	PA	Trevose		Otis Twilley Seed Co.
A 15	PA	Warminster	⌂	W. Atlee Burpee Company
A 114	PE	Charlottetown	⌂	Vesey's Seeds, Ltd.
A 84	PQ	Laval		W. H. Perron & Co., Ltd.
A 101	SC	Graniteville	⌂	R. H. Shumway Seedsman
A 83	SC	Greenwood	⌂	Park Seed Company, Inc.
A 30	SK	Saskatoon	⌂	Early's Farm & Garden Centre, Inc.
A 87	TX	Stephenville	⌂	Porter & Son
B 14	VT	Burlington	⌂	Gardener's Supply Company
A 113	VT	Fair Haven		Vermont Bean Seed Co.
A 58	WI	Randolph	⌂	J. W. Jung Seed Co.
A 87	WI	Tilleda	⌂	Pony Creek Nursery

GROWING SUPPLIES, INDOOR

See also Growing Supplies, General
See also Propagation Supplies

B 10	CA	San Rafael	⌂	Diamond
B 18	CA	San Rafael	⌂	Hydro-Farm West
A 68	CA	South San Francisco	⌂	Rod McLellan Co.
A 89	CA	Vista	⌂	Rainbow Gardens Nursery & Bookshop
A 114	CO	Englewood	⌂	The Violet Showcase
B 36	FL	Gainesville	⌂	The Violet House
B 35	FL	Orlando		Tropical Plant Products, Inc.
A 43	FL	Palm Harbor	⌂	The Green Escape
A 79	IL	Dundee	⌂	Oak Hill Gardens
B 13	IL	Schaumburg	⌂	Florist Products, Inc.
B 2	IL	Streamwood	⌂	Alternative Garden Supply, Inc.
B 38	IN	Bloomington	⌂	Worm's Way of Indiana
A 27	IN	Crawfordsville	⌂	Davidson-Wilson Greenhouses
A 68	KS	Wichita	⌂	McKinney's Glasshouse
A 17	MA	Falmouth		Cape Cod Violetry
B 19	MI	Detroit		Indoor Gardening Supplies
B 28	NY	Buffalo		Plant Collectibles
A 46	NY	Rochester		Harris Seeds
B 5	NY	Yorkville		Bonide Products, Inc.
B 12	OK	Idabel		EZ Soil Co.
A 60	PA	Wexford		Kingfisher, Inc.
A 64	PQ	Sawyerville	⌂	Les Violettes Natalia
B 18	VA	Woodbridge	⌂	Home Harvest(R) Garden Supply, Inc.
B 11	WA	Seattle	⌂	Eco Enterprises

GROWTH STIMULANTS

B 30	CA	San Diego	⌂	Bargyla Rateaver
B 1	CO	Boulder	⌂	Age-Old Organics
B 31	IA	Charles City		Sea Born/Lane, Inc.
A 78	OR	Troutdale	⌂	Northwest Epi Center
B 23	TX	Hondo		Medina Agricultural Products Co.
A 40	TX	Laredo	⌂	Garden World
B 32	TX	Rockport		Spray-N-Grow, Inc.
B 4	VA	Falls Church		Bio-Gard Agronomics

GUANO, BAT

B 25	AR	Fayetteville	⌂	Nitron Industries, Inc.
B 10	CA	San Rafael	⌂	Diamond
B 1	CO	Boulder	⌂	Age-Old Organics
B 38	IN	Bloomington	⌂	Worm's Way of Indiana
B 11	IN	Jeffersonville		Earlee, Inc.
B 16	OH	Cleveland		Guano Company International, Inc.
B 14	TX	Austin	⌂	Garden-Ville of Austin
B 19	WA	Wenatchee	⌂	Integrated Fertility Management

GUANO, SEABIRD

B 16	OH	Cleveland		Guano Company International, Inc.

PAGE	STATE	CITY	⌂ SHOP	SOURCE
HAMMOCKS				
B 14	CA	San Francisco		Gardener's Eden
B 17	CO	Boulder	⌂	Hangouts
B 27	DC	Washington	⌂	Park Place
B 2	IL	Galesburg		Alsto's Handy Helpers
B 29	NC	Wilmington	⌂	A Proper Garden
HANGING BASKETS				
A 5	CA	Santa Cruz	⌂	Antonelli Brothers, Inc.
B 37	DE	Dover	⌂	Winterthur Museum & Gardens
B 26	FL	Miami	⌂	OFE International, Inc.
B 35	FL	Orlando		Tropical Plant Products, Inc.
B 29	NC	Wilmington	⌂	A Proper Garden
B 28	NY	Buffalo		Plant Collectibles
HANGOUTS (R)				
B 17	CO	Boulder	⌂	Hangouts
HASTA GRO (R)				
B 23	TX	Hondo		Medina Agricultural Products Co.
HISTORICAL REPRODUCTIONS, ORNAMENTAL				
See also specific type				
B 26	CA	Costa Mesa		O'Brien Ironworks
B 22	CT	Wilton		Kenneth Lynch & Sons, Inc.
B 15	NJ	Vincentown	⌂	Genie House
B 28	NY	Bronxville		Pompeian Studios
B 13	NY	Long Island City		Florentine Craftsmen, Inc.
B 20	NY	Niagara Falls	⌂	Kosmolux & LP, Inc.
B 9	PA	Carlisle		Cumberland Woodcraft
B 3	PA	Somerset	⌂	Baker's Lawn Ornaments
B 8	SC	Charleston	⌂	Charleston Battery Bench, Inc.
B 14	TN	Memphis	⌂	The Garden Concepts Collection
B 36	TX	Quinlan	⌂	Vintage Wood Works
B 13	TX	Tyler		French Wyres(R)
B 16	VA	Hamilton		Green Enterprises
HONEYDEW (TM)				
B 21	CA	Berry Creek	⌂	The Lady Bug Company
HORTICULTURAL CLIP ART				
B 37	IL	Champaign		Wheeler Arts
HORTICULTURAL TOURS				
B 9	CA	Oakland		Coopersmith's England
B 31	CA	Santa Barbara		Santa Barbara Orchid Garden & Library
B 15	CA	Santa Rosa	⌂	Geostar Travel
B 4	FL	Bay Harbor Islands		Leona Bee Tours & Travel
B 12	NY	New York		Expo Garden Tours
HU MATE (R)				
B 23	TX	Hondo		Medina Agricultural Products Co.
HUMIDIFIERS				
B 31	CA	Camarillo	⌂	Santa Barbara Greenhouses
B 23	CA	San Francisco		Don Mattern
B 35	NC	Goldsboro	⌂	Turner Greenhouses
B 33	OR	Portland	⌂	Sturdi-Built Mfg. Co.
B 8	WA	Mt. Vernon	⌂	Charley's Greenhouse Supply
HUSKY-FIBER (R)				
A 69	FL	Windermere	⌂	Ann Mann's Orchids
HYDROFARM (R) SYSTEMS				
B 18	CA	San Rafael	⌂	Hydro-Farm West
HYDROGELS				
B 20	CA	Davis		Janziker
A 49	NM	Santa Fe	⌂	A High Country Garden

(continued next page)

(continued next page)

PAGE	STATE	CITY	⌂ SHOP	SOURCE
JAPANESE GARDEN ORNAMENTS				
B 3	CA	Oceanside	⌂	Asian Artifacts
B 33	OK	Tulsa		Sun Garden Specialties
JAPIDEMIC (R)				
B 12	NY	Clinton Corners		Fairfax Biological Laboratory, Inc.
LANTERNS, STONE				
B 3	CA	Oceanside	⌂	Asian Artifacts
B 27	CT	Norwalk	⌂	P&R International, Inc.
A 99	CT	Stamford	⌂	Shanti Bithi Nursery
B 22	CT	Wilton		Kenneth Lynch & Sons, Inc.
B 33	NM	Santa Fe	⌂	Stone Forest
B 16	OR	Talent	⌂	Granite Impressions
A 7	WA	Redmond	⌂	Bamboo Gardens of Washington
LAWN VACUUMS				
B 27	NC	Arden		PeCo, Inc.
B 20	PA	Lititz	⌂	Kemp Company
LIGHT FIXTURES, OUTDOOR				
B 8	CA	Concord		Classic & Country Crafts
B 14	CA	San Francisco		Gardener's Eden
B 36	CA	San Francisco	⌂	The Urban Farmer Store
B 27	DC	Washington	⌂	Park Place
B 19	ID	Sandpoint		Idaho Wood
B 18	ME	Yarmouth	⌂	Heritage Lanterns
B 6	NC	Hickory	⌂	Andy Brinkley Studio
B 15	NJ	Vincentown	⌂	Genie House
B 29	PA	Pittsburgh		Popovitch Associates, Inc.
B 12	PA	Sinking Spring		Escort Lighting
LIGHTING SYSTEMS, OUTDOOR				
B 36	CA	San Francisco	⌂	The Urban Farmer Store
B 27	DC	Washington	⌂	Park Place
LIVE TRAPS, ANIMALS				
See also Animal Repellents				
B 16	MI	Vestaburg	⌂	Great Lakes IPM
B 4	ON	St. Thomas		Berry Hill Limited
B 19	OR	Eugene		International Reforestation Suppliers
B 8	PA	Latrobe		Chestnut Lane
B 24	VA	New Castle	⌂	Necessary Trading Co.
LOG SPLITTERS				
B 37	NE	Lincoln		Wikco Industries, Inc.
MARKET GARDEN SUPPLIES				
A 35	WA	Okanogan		Filaree Farm
MAXICROP (R)				
B 30	CA	San Diego	⌂	Bargyla Rateaver
B 11	IN	Jeffersonville		Earlee, Inc.
B 12	PA	Gap	⌂	Erth-Rite, Inc.
MEDINA SOIL ACTIVATOR (R)				
B 23	TX	Hondo		Medina Agricultural Products Co.
METERS AND INSTRUMENTS				
B 27	AR	Eureka Springs		Ozark Handle & Hardware
B 7	CA	Marina Del Ray		A.C. Burke & Co.
B 30	CA	San Diego		Reotemp Instrument Corporation
B 19	CO	Colorado Springs	⌂	Hydro-Gardens, Inc.
B 11	FL	Ft. Lauderdale		Environmental Concepts
B 23	MA	New Bedford		Maximum, Inc.
B 19	MI	Detroit		Indoor Gardening Supplies
B 30	NE	Columbus	⌂	Rodco Products Co., Inc.
B 29	NJ	Princeton	⌂	Qualimetrics, Inc.
B 28	NY	Buffalo		Plant Collectibles

(continued next page)

PAGE	STATE	CITY	⌂ SHOP	SOURCE

METERS AND INSTRUMENTS (continued)

PAGE	STATE	CITY	⌂ SHOP	SOURCE
B 26	OH	Hartville	⌂	Ohio Earth Food, Inc.
B 9	OH	Medina	⌂	Cropking, Inc.
B 4	PA	Greeley		Dorothy Biddle Service
B 11	WA	Seattle	⌂	Eco Enterprises
B 19	WA	Wenatchee	⌂	Integrated Fertility Management

MIST IRRIGATION SUPPLIES

PAGE	STATE	CITY	⌂ SHOP	SOURCE
B 9	CA	San Marcos	⌂	D.I.G. Corporation
B 19	CO	Colorado Springs	⌂	Hydro-Gardens, Inc.
B 26	FL	Miami	⌂	OFE International, Inc.
B 28	MO	Grover	⌂	Plastic Plumbing Products, Inc.
B 35	NC	Goldsboro	⌂	Turner Greenhouses
B 2	NY	Huntington		Aquamonitor
B 33	OR	Portland	⌂	Sturdi-Built Mfg. Co.
B 34	TX	Ft. Worth	⌂	Texas Greenhouse Co.
B 33	TX	Lubbock	⌂	Submatic Irrigation Systems
B 10	WI	Manitowoc		The Dramm Corporation

MIST IRRIGATION SYSTEMS

PAGE	STATE	CITY	⌂ SHOP	SOURCE
B 31	CA	Camarillo	⌂	Santa Barbara Greenhouses
B 9	CA	San Marcos	⌂	D.I.G. Corporation
B 10	CA	Willits	⌂	DripWorks
B 28	MO	Grover	⌂	Plastic Plumbing Products, Inc.
B 2	NY	Huntington		Aquamonitor
B 8	WA	Mt. Vernon	⌂	Charley's Greenhouse Supply

MOISTURE MIZER (R)

PAGE	STATE	CITY	⌂ SHOP	SOURCE
B 24	TN	Chattanooga		Multiple Concepts

MULCHES, FABRIC/PAPER/PLASTIC

PAGE	STATE	CITY	⌂ SHOP	SOURCE
B 39	GA	Cornelia	⌂	Yonah Manufacturing Co.
B 13	IL	Schaumburg	⌂	Florist Products, Inc.
B 14	IN	Lawrenceburg	⌂	Gardens Alive!
B 6	MA	Salem		Bramen Company, Inc.
A 85	ME	New Gloucester	⌂	Pinetree Garden Seeds
A 57	MN	Woodbury	⌂	Jordan Seeds
A 46	NY	Rochester		Harris Seeds
B 19	OR	Eugene		International Reforestation Suppliers
B 6	PA	New Brighton		Brighton By-Products Co., Inc.
B 25	PQ	Sherbrooke	⌂	Nova Sylva, Inc.

MUSHROOM GROWING SUPPLIES

PAGE	STATE	CITY	⌂ SHOP	SOURCE
A 117	BC	Aldergrove	⌂	Western Biologicals, Ltd.
A 36	FL	Pensacola		Florida Mycology Research Center
A 78	OR	Corvallis		Northwest Mycological Consultants
A 74	TN	Summertown	⌂	Mushroompeople
A 39	WA	Olympia		Fungi Perfecti
A 34	WI	Peshtigo	⌂	Field and Forest Products, Inc.
A 46	WV	Cherry Grove		Hardscrabble Enterprises

NATURE'S WAY (R)

PAGE	STATE	CITY	⌂ SHOP	SOURCE
B 11	IN	Jeffersonville		Earlee, Inc.

ORCHARD SUPPLIES

PAGE	STATE	CITY	⌂ SHOP	SOURCE
A 14	VA	Monroe	⌂	Burford Brothers

ORCHID SEED FLASKING

PAGE	STATE	CITY	⌂ SHOP	SOURCE
B 17	OR	Portland		Halcyon Laboratories

ORCHID SUPPLIES

PAGE	STATE	CITY	⌂ SHOP	SOURCE
A 38	AR	Little Rock	⌂	Fox Orchids, Inc.
A 105	CA	Carpinteria	⌂	Stewart Orchids, Inc.
A 80	CA	Coarsegold	⌂	Orchid Species Specialties
A 33	CA	Soquel	⌂	John Ewing Orchids, Inc.
A 68	CA	South San Francisco	⌂	Rod McLellan Co.
A 39	CA	Vista	⌂	G & B Orchid Lab & Nursery
B 26	FL	Miami	⌂	OFE International, Inc.
B 35	FL	Orlando		Tropical Plant Products, Inc.

(continued next page)

(continued next page)

PAGE	STATE	CITY	⌂ SHOP	SOURCE

PEST CONTROLS, ORGANIC (continued)

PAGE	STATE	CITY	⌂ SHOP	SOURCE
B 30	CA	San Diego	⌂	Bargyla Rateaver
B 10	CA	Soquel		Digger's Product Development Co.
B 36	FL	Gainesville	⌂	The Violet House
B 11	IL	Elgin	⌂	Elgin Landscape & Garden Center
B 38	IN	Bloomington	⌂	Worm's Way of Indiana
B 11	IN	Jeffersonville		Earlee, Inc.
B 14	IN	Lawrenceburg	⌂	Gardens Alive!
B 16	MI	Vestaburg	⌂	Great Lakes IPM
A 78	MN	Princeton	⌂	Northwind Nursery & Orchards
B 6	MT	Bozeman	⌂	Bozeman Bio-Tech
A 39	MT	Victor	⌂	Garden City Seeds
B 12	NY	Clinton Corners		Fairfax Biological Laboratory, Inc.
B 5	NY	Yorkville		Bonide Products, Inc.
B 26	OH	Hartville	⌂	Ohio Earth Food, Inc.
B 24	OR	Medford	⌂	Nature's Control
A 64	PQ	Sawyerville	⌂	Les Violettes Natalia
B 14	TX	Austin	⌂	Garden-Ville of Austin
B 24	VA	Lexington		Naturally Free/Bug-Off, Inc.
B 24	VA	New Castle	⌂	Necessary Trading Co.
B 14	VT	Burlington	⌂	Gardener's Supply Company
B 19	WA	Wenatchee	⌂	Integrated Fertility Management
A 116	WI	Plainfield	⌂	The Waushara Gardens

PESTICIDES, LYME DISEASE TICKS

PAGE	STATE	CITY	⌂ SHOP	SOURCE
B 11	MA	Boston		EcoHealth, Inc.

PHEROMONE TRAPS

PAGE	STATE	CITY	⌂ SHOP	SOURCE
B 28	BC	Delta		Phero Tech, Inc.
B 16	MI	Vestaburg	⌂	Great Lakes IPM
B 6	MT	Bozeman	⌂	Bozeman Bio-Tech

PHOTOGRAPHS, HORTICULTURAL

PAGE	STATE	CITY	⌂ SHOP	SOURCE
B 12	En	Uxbridge, Middlesex	⌂	Floracolour
B 17	VA	Seaford		Harper Horticultural Slide Library

PLANT FINDING SERVICES

PAGE	STATE	CITY	⌂ SHOP	SOURCE
A 104	AZ	Apache Junction		Southwestern Exposure
A 48	IA	Marshalltown	⌂	Herbs-Liscious
A 90	OR	Milwaukie	⌂	Rare Plant Research
B 16	VT	Randolph		Greenlist Info Services
A 24	WI	Orfordville	⌂	The Country Mouse

PLANT HANGERS

PAGE	STATE	CITY	⌂ SHOP	SOURCE
B 24	MA	Topsfield		The Walt Nicke Company
A 103	TX	Beaumont	⌂	Southern Exposure
B 24	WA	Bainbridge Island		Mitchells & Son

PLANT LABELS

See also Garden Markers

PAGE	STATE	CITY	⌂ SHOP	SOURCE
A 16	CA	Lodi	⌂	Cactus by Dodie
B 11	FL	Daytona Beach		Economy Label Sales Co., Inc.
B 26	FL	Miami	⌂	OFE International, Inc.
A 2	ME	Falmouth	⌂	Allen, Sterling & Lothrop
B 27	MI	Paw Paw		Paw Paw Everlast Label Co.
A 3	MN	Waconia	⌂	Ambergate Gardens
B 14	NH	Barnstead		Garden Fonts
B 28	NY	Buffalo		Plant Collectibles
A 52	OH	Chesterland	⌂	Homestead Division of Sunnybrook Farms
B 11	OH	Liberty Center		Eon Industries
B 2	ON	Sydenham		Amaranth Stoneware
B 31	OR	Junction City	⌂	S & D Enterprises
A 11	TX	Adkins	⌂	Bonsai Farm
A 43	WI	Granton	⌂	Grace Gardens North

PLANT LIGHTS

PAGE	STATE	CITY	⌂ SHOP	SOURCE
B 10	CA	San Rafael	⌂	Diamond
B 18	CA	San Rafael	⌂	Hydro-Farm West
B 36	CA	Vallejo		Verilux, Inc.

(continued next page)

PAGE	STATE	CITY	⌂ SHOP	SOURCE
PLANT LIGHTS (continued)				
A 114	CO	Englewood	⌂	The Violet Showcase
A 111	GA	Ochlochnee	⌂	Travis' Violets
B 2	IL	Streamwood	⌂	Alternative Garden Supply, Inc.
B 19	MI	Detroit		Indoor Gardening Supplies
B 28	NY	Buffalo		Plant Collectibles
B 29	NY	New York		Public Service Lamp Corp.
B 18	VA	Woodbridge	⌂	Home Harvest(R) Garden Supply, Inc.
PLANT STANDS				
B 26	CA	Costa Mesa		O'Brien Ironworks
B 14	CA	San Francisco		Gardener's Eden
A 114	CO	Englewood	⌂	The Violet Showcase
B 10	FL	Miami	⌂	Day-Dex Co.
B 26	FL	Miami	⌂	OFE International, Inc.
A 111	GA	Ochlochnee	⌂	Travis' Violets
B 2	IL	Galesburg		Alsto's Handy Helpers
B 13	IL	Schaumburg	⌂	Florist Products, Inc.
B 1	MA	Brewster	⌂	Acorn Services Corporation
B 19	MI	Detroit		Indoor Gardening Supplies
B 28	NY	Buffalo		Plant Collectibles
B 13	ON	North York		Floralight Gardens Canada, Inc.
A 110	PA	Huntingdon Valley	⌂	Tinari Greenhouses
A 115	TX	Dallas	⌂	Volkmann Bros. Greenhouses
B 13	TX	Tyler		French Wyres(R)
PLANT SUPPORTS				
B 12	CA	Cloverdale		Evergreen Garden Plant Labels
A 3	En	Hassocks, W. Sussex		Allwood Bros.
B 6	MA	Salem		Bramen Company, Inc.
B 24	MA	Topsfield		The Walt Nicke Company
B 20	PA	Point Pleasant	⌂	Kinsman Company, Inc.
PLANTERS				
See also Terra Cotta Pots/Planters				
B 38	AL	Trussville		Woodbrook Furniture Manufacturing Co.
B 17	BC	Parksville	⌂	Heritage Garden Furniture
B 26	CA	Citrus Heights		Out of the Woods
B 26	CA	Costa Mesa		O'Brien Ironworks
A 74	CA	Laytonville	⌂	Mountain Maples
B 3	CA	Nevada City		David Bacon Woodworking
B 14	CA	San Francisco		Gardener's Eden
B 2	CO	Englewood		Alpine Millworks Company
B 27	CT	Norwalk	⌂	P&R International, Inc.
B 27	DC	Washington	⌂	Park Place
B 37	DE	Dover	⌂	Winterthur Museum & Gardens
B 38	GA	Atlanta	⌂	Yanzum -- Art for Gardens
B 2	IL	Galesburg		Alsto's Handy Helpers
B 26	IN	Carmel		Old World Garden Troughs(R)
B 1	MA	Brewster	⌂	Acorn Services Corporation
B 9	MD	Germantown	⌂	Country Casual
B 30	ME	Cape Porpoise		Richardson-Allen Furniture
B 33	NM	Santa Fe	⌂	Stone Forest
B 17	NY	Fayetteville		Karen Harris
B 38	NY	Gardiner	⌂	Wood Classics
B 37	NY	Keeseville	⌂	Willsboro Wood Products
B 18	NY	Lake Peekskill	⌂	Hollowbrook Pottery and Tile
B 13	NY	Long Island City		Florentine Craftsmen, Inc.
B 38	NY	Medford		Wood Innovations of Suffolk
B 28	OH	Cleveland Heights	⌂	Planters International
B 7	OH	Waterville	⌂	Carruth Studio
B 37	PA	Malvern		Windsor Designs
B 14	TN	Memphis	⌂	The Garden Concepts Collection
B 1	VA	Alexandria	⌂	Adams & Adkins
B 30	WA	Airway Heights		Redwood Arts
B 24	WA	Bainbridge Island		Mitchells & Son
B 11	WY	Hyattville		Earthworks

PAGE	STATE	CITY	⌂ SHOP	SOURCE

PLANTERS, HYDROPONIC

B 10	CA	San Rafael	⌂	Diamond
B 18	CA	San Rafael	⌂	Hydro-Farm West
B 19	CO	Colorado Springs	⌂	Hydro-Gardens, Inc.
B 11	WA	Seattle	⌂	Eco Enterprises

PLANTERS, SELF-WATERING

B 36	FL	Gainesville	⌂	The Violet House
A 9	MT	Moiese	⌂	Big Sky Violets
B 28	OH	Cleveland Heights	⌂	Planters International

PLAY STRUCTURES

B 26	OR	Eugene		Oregon Timberframe
B 9	WI	McFarland		Creative Playgrounds, Ltd.

POISON OAK/IVY CLEANSER

B 34	OR	Albany		Tec Laboratories, Inc.

POLE PICKER (FRUIT)

B 36	CA	Ventura		Vista Products

POLYETHYLENE, WOVEN

B 27	AR	Eureka Springs		Ozark Handle & Hardware
B 25	ND	Neche	⌂	Northern Greenhouse Sales

POND LINERS

A 97	AZ	Scottsdale	⌂	Scottsdale Fishponds
A 96	CA	Santa Barbara	⌂	Santa Barbara Water Gardens
A 113	CA	Upland	⌂	Van Ness Water Gardens
B 10	CA	Willits	⌂	DripWorks
A 102	FL	Winter Haven	⌂	Slocum Water Gardens
A 82	MA	Whitman	⌂	Paradise Water Gardens
B 30	MD	Baltimore	⌂	Resource Conservation Technology
A 65	MD	Buckeystown	⌂	Lilypons Water Gardens
A 106	MO	Kansas City		Stigall Water Gardens
A 73	ON	Port Stanley	⌂	Moore Water Gardens

PONDS AND POOLS

A 97	AZ	Scottsdale	⌂	Scottsdale Fishponds
A 96	CA	Santa Barbara	⌂	Santa Barbara Water Gardens
A 113	CA	Upland	⌂	Van Ness Water Gardens
B 22	CT	Wilton		Kenneth Lynch & Sons, Inc.
A 118	MD	Baldwin	⌂	Wicklein's Water Gardens
A 65	MD	Buckeystown	⌂	Lilypons Water Gardens
A 69	MD	Jarrettsville	⌂	Maryland Aquatic Nurseries
A 106	MO	Kansas City		Stigall Water Gardens
A 115	NJ	Saddle River	⌂	Waterford Gardens
B 18	NY	Canastota	⌂	Hermitage Gardens
A 97	NY	Northport	⌂	S. Scherer & Sons
A 111	OH	Independence	⌂	William Tricker, Inc.
A 84	ON	Ajax	⌂	Picov Greenhouses
A 73	ON	Port Stanley	⌂	Moore Water Gardens
A 110	PA	Coopersburg	⌂	Tilley's Nursery/The WaterWorks
A 120	WI	Eagle	⌂	Windy Oaks Daylilies & Aquatics

POTPOURRI SUPPLIES

A 47	CA	Sonora	⌂	Havasu Hills Herbs
A 48	IA	Marshalltown	⌂	Herbs-Liscious
A 26	KY	Louisville		Dabney Herbs
A 47	MA	Barre	⌂	Hartman's Herb Farm
A 48	NB	Norton	⌂	The Herb Farm
A 91	NC	Godwin	⌂	Rasland Farm
A 48	NC	Pilot Mountain		The Herb Garden
A 116	NJ	Port Murray	⌂	Well-Sweep Herb Farm
A 107	OH	Chesterland	⌂	Sunnybrook Farms Nursery
A 65	OH	Minerva	⌂	Lily of the Valley Herb Farm
A 92	ON	Goodwood	⌂	Richters Herbs
A 76	OR	Albany	⌂	Nichols Garden Nursery, Inc.
A 94	PA	Mechanicsburg	⌂	The Rosemary House

(continued next page)

PAGE	STATE	CITY	⌂ SHOP	SOURCE

POTPOURRI SUPPLIES (continued)

A 42	TN	Taft	⌂	Good Hollow Greenhouse & Herbarium
A 24	WI	Orfordville	⌂	The Country Mouse

POTS

B 23	CA	Buena Park		Malley Supply
A 58	CA	Ione		K & L Cactus & Succulent Nursery
A 16	CA	Lodi	⌂	Cactus by Dodie
A 114	CO	Englewood	⌂	The Violet Showcase
B 36	FL	Gainesville	⌂	The Violet House
B 26	FL	Miami	⌂	OFE International, Inc.
B 35	FL	Orlando		Tropical Plant Products, Inc.
B 13	IL	Schaumburg	⌂	Florist Products, Inc.
B 19	MI	Detroit		Indoor Gardening Supplies
A 13	NC	Brown Summit	⌂	Breckinridge Orchids
B 28	NY	Buffalo		Plant Collectibles
B 33	OR	Corvallis	⌂	Stuewe and Sons, Inc.
A 57	TX	Victoria	⌂	JoS Violets

POTTING BENCHES

B 31	CA	Camarillo	⌂	Santa Barbara Greenhouses
B 1	CA	Fort Bragg	⌂	Adirondack Designs
B 1	MA	Brewster	⌂	Acorn Services Corporation
B 34	TX	Ft. Worth	⌂	Texas Greenhouse Co.
B 36	VA	Charlottesville	⌂	Victory Garden Supply Co.

PROPAGATION SUPPLIES

See also Growing Supplies, General
See also Growing Supplies, Indoor

B 4	CA	Petaluma		BioTherm Hydronic, Inc.
B 16	CA	San Leandro		Green Thumb Industries
B 13	CT	Rockville	⌂	Fox Hill Farm/Hoophouse
B 32	IL	Mendota	⌂	Smith Greenhouse & Supply
B 13	IL	Schaumburg	⌂	Florist Products, Inc.
B 38	IN	Bloomington	⌂	Worm's Way of Indiana
B 1	MA	Brewster	⌂	Acorn Services Corporation
B 6	MA	Salem		Bramen Company, Inc.
B 24	MA	Topsfield		The Walt Nicke Company
B 19	MI	Detroit		Indoor Gardening Supplies
B 35	NC	Goldsboro	⌂	Turner Greenhouses
B 28	NY	Buffalo		Plant Collectibles
B 2	NY	Huntington		Aquamonitor
A 65	OH	New Philadelphia	⌂	Liberty Seed Company
A 70	OH	North Lima	⌂	Mellinger's, Inc.
B 12	OK	Idabel		EZ Soil Co.
B 3	OR	Clackamas		Astoria-Pacific, Inc.
B 33	OR	Corvallis	⌂	Stuewe and Sons, Inc.
B 33	OR	Portland	⌂	Sturdi-Built Mfg. Co.
B 6	PA	New Brighton		Brighton By-Products Co., Inc.
A 83	SC	Greenwood	⌂	Park Seed Company, Inc.
A 11	TX	Adkins	⌂	Bonsai Farm
A 121	TX	De Leon	⌂	Womack's Nursery Co.
B 34	TX	Ft. Worth	⌂	Texas Greenhouse Co.
B 18	VA	Woodbridge	⌂	Home Harvest(R) Garden Supply, Inc.
B 14	VT	Burlington	⌂	Gardener's Supply Company
A 101	WA	Roy	⌂	Silvaseed Company, Inc.
B 33	WA	Seattle	⌂	Sunglo Solar Greenhouses

PUMPS

B 7	CA	Point Arena	⌂	Cart Warehouse

PUSH MOWERS

B 24	CA	San Anselmo	⌂	The Natural Gardening Company
B 28	IN	South Bend		C. K. Petty & Co.
B 21	NJ	Blairstown		Langenbach Fine Tool Co.
B 21	ON	Ottawa	⌂	Lee Valley Tools, Ltd.

QUICK ART (TM)

B 37	IL	Champaign		Wheeler Arts

PAGE	STATE	CITY	⌂ SHOP	SOURCE

RACHET-CUT (R)

B 2	CT	Southington	⌂	American Standard Co.

RAIN BARRELS

B 16	MA	East Boston		Great American Rain Barrel Co.

RAIN-O-MATIC (R)

B 30	NE	Columbus	⌂	Rodco Products Co., Inc.

ROOT GUARD GOPHER WIRE BASKETS (TM)

B 10	CA	Soquel		Digger's Product Development Co.

ROSE GROWING SUPPLIES

B 12	CA	Cloverdale		Evergreen Garden Plant Labels
A 40	CA	Petaluma	⌂	Garden Valley Ranch
A 50	CO	Denver	⌂	High Country Rosarium
A 37	ME	North Yarmouth	⌂	Forevergreen Farm
B 38	ME	York		Womanswork
B 17	NJ	Old Tappan		Harlane Company, Inc.
B 5	NY	Yorkville		Bonide Products, Inc.
A 31	OR	Wilsonville	⌂	Edmunds' Roses

ROW COVERS

A 120	AB	Hythe	⌂	Windy Ridge Nursery
B 27	CA	Grass Valley	⌂	Peaceful Valley Farm Supply
A 103	FL	Melbourne		Southern Seeds
A 34	ME	Waterville		Fedco Seeds
B 16	MI	Vestaburg	⌂	Great Lakes IPM
A 57	MN	Woodbury	⌂	Jordan Seeds
A 65	OH	New Philadelphia	⌂	Liberty Seed Company
A 80	ON	Waterloo		Ontario Seed Company, Ltd.
A 109	OR	Cottage Grove	⌂	Territorial Seed Company
A 48	PA	West Elizabeth		Heirloom Seeds
A 114	PE	Charlottetown	⌂	Vesey's Seeds, Ltd.
B 25	PQ	Sherbrooke	⌂	Nova Sylva, Inc.
B 14	VT	Burlington	⌂	Gardener's Supply Company
A 43	VT	East Monpelier	⌂	Green Mountain Transplants
B 19	WA	Wenatchee	⌂	Integrated Fertility Management
B 8	WI	Elkhart Lake		Clothcrafters, Inc.

SCANMASK (R)

B 4	PA	Willow Hill	⌂	BioLogic

SCYTHES

B 23	TN	Tracy City		The Marugg Company

SEED CLEANERS

A 88	IL	Trilla	⌂	Prairie State Commodities

SEED ENVELOPES

B 35	OR	Portland		Twinholly's

SEED SAVER (R)

B 32	ID	Idaho Falls		Seed Saver(R)

SEED SAVING SUPPLIES

B 35	OR	Portland		Twinholly's
A 103	VA	North Garden		Southern Exposure Seed Exchange(R)

SEED SEARCH SERVICES

A 90	CA	Berkeley		Rare Seed Locators, Inc.

SEED STORAGE SYSTEMS

B 32	ID	Idaho Falls		Seed Saver(R)

SHADE CLOTH

A 120	AB	Hythe	⌂	Windy Ridge Nursery
B 16	AL	Mobile	⌂	Gothic Arch Greenhouses
A 12	CA	Willits	⌂	Bountiful Gardens

(continued next page)

PAGE	STATE	CITY	⌂ SHOP	SOURCE
SHADE CLOTH (continued)				
B 19	CO	Colorado Springs	⌂	Hydro-Gardens, Inc.
B 10	FL	Miami	⌂	Day-Dex Co.
B 39	GA	Cornelia	⌂	Yonah Manufacturing Co.
B 35	NC	Goldsboro	⌂	Turner Greenhouses
B 9	OH	Medina	⌂	Cropking, Inc.
B 33	OR	Corvallis	⌂	Stuewe and Sons, Inc.
B 2	PA	West Chester		American Arborist Supplies
B 34	TX	Ft. Worth	⌂	Texas Greenhouse Co.
B 8	WA	Mt. Vernon	⌂	Charley's Greenhouse Supply
SHREDDERS				
B 32	CA	Mill Valley	⌂	Smith & Hawken
B 37	NE	Lincoln		Wikco Industries, Inc.
B 21	OH	Piqua	⌂	A. M. Leonard, Inc.
B 23	PA	Huntingdon Valley	⌂	Mantis Manufacturing Co.
B 20	PA	Lititz	⌂	Kemp Company
B 20	PA	Point Pleasant	⌂	Kinsman Company, Inc.
B 14	VT	Burlington	⌂	Gardener's Supply Company
SICKLE-BAR MOWERS				
B 22	OH	London	⌂	Mainline of North America
SLUG & SNAIL KILLER				
B 32	OH	Cuyahoga Falls		Slugbuster
SNAIL BARRIERS				
B 24	CA	San Anselmo	⌂	The Natural Gardening Company
B 26	FL	Miami	⌂	OFE International, Inc.
SNAIL REPELLENTS				
B 6	MT	Bozeman	⌂	Bozeman Bio-Tech
SOIL AMENDMENTS				
B 25	AR	Fayetteville	⌂	Nitron Industries, Inc.
B 22	AR	Springdale		Maestro-Gro
A 104	AZ	Apache Junction		Southwestern Exposure
B 17	CA	Graton	⌂	Harmony Farm Supply
B 30	CA	San Diego	⌂	Bargyla Rateaver
A 68	CA	South San Francisco	⌂	Rod McLellan Co.
B 31	IA	Charles City		Sea Born/Lane, Inc.
B 32	IL	Mendota	⌂	Smith Greenhouse & Supply
B 11	IN	Jeffersonville		Earlee, Inc.
A 57	ME	Albion	⌂	Johnny's Selected Seeds
B 25	ME	Waldoboro		North American Kelp
A 95	NM	Roswell	⌂	Roswell Seed Co.
B 5	NY	Yorkville		Bonide Products, Inc.
B 26	OH	Hartville	⌂	Ohio Earth Food, Inc.
B 12	PA	Gap	⌂	Erth-Rite, Inc.
B 14	TX	Austin	⌂	Garden-Ville of Austin
B 16	TX	Ft. Worth		Grosoke, Inc.
B 23	TX	Hondo		Medina Agricultural Products Co.
A 35	WA	Okanogan		Filaree Farm
SOIL TESTING BY MAIL				
B 27	CA	Grass Valley	⌂	Peaceful Valley Farm Supply
B 8	NY	Lowville		Cook's Consulting
B 26	OH	Hartville	⌂	Ohio Earth Food, Inc.
B 12	PA	Gap	⌂	Erth-Rite, Inc.
B 1	TN	Memphis		A & L Analytical Laboratories, Inc.
B 24	VA	New Castle	⌂	Necessary Trading Co.
B 19	WA	Wenatchee	⌂	Integrated Fertility Management
A 116	WI	Plainfield	⌂	The Waushara Gardens
B 21	WY	Laramie		LaRamie Soils Service
SOIL TESTING PRODUCTS				
B 11	FL	Ft. Lauderdale		Environmental Concepts
A 60	FL	Sanford	⌂	Kilgore Seed Company
A 24	MI	Hartford	⌂	Country Heritage Nursery

(continued next page)

PAGE	STATE	CITY	⌂ SHOP	SOURCE
SOIL TESTING PRODUCTS (continued)				
B 16	MI	Vestaburg	⌂	Great Lakes IPM
B 26	OH	Hartville	⌂	Ohio Earth Food, Inc.
B 21	OH	Kidron	⌂	Lehman Hardware & Appliances, Inc.
B 2	PA	West Chester		American Arborist Supplies
B 24	VA	New Castle	⌂	Necessary Trading Co.
SPRAY-N-GROW (TM)				
B 32	TX	Rockport		Spray-N-Grow, Inc.
SPRAYERS				
A 111				Tregunno Seeds
B 26	FL	Miami	⌂	OFE International, Inc.
A 57	GA	Ellijay	⌂	Johnson Nursery
B 28	MO	Grover	⌂	Plastic Plumbing Products, Inc.
B 6	MT	Bozeman	⌂	Bozeman Bio-Tech
B 27	NC	Arden		PeCo, Inc.
B 21	NJ	Blairstown		Langenbach Fine Tool Co.
B 21	OH	Piqua	⌂	A. M. Leonard, Inc.
B 19	OR	Eugene		International Reforestation Suppliers
B 23	PA	Huntingdon Valley	⌂	Mantis Manufacturing Co.
B 2	PA	West Chester		American Arborist Supplies
B 25	PQ	Sherbrooke	⌂	Nova Sylva, Inc.
A 121	TX	De Leon	⌂	Womack's Nursery Co.
B 10	WI	Manitowoc		The Dramm Corporation
SPRINKLERS				
See also Irrigation Supplies				
B 17	CA	Graton	⌂	Harmony Farm Supply
B 9	MA	Peabody		The Crafter's Garden
B 28	MO	Grover	⌂	Plastic Plumbing Products, Inc.
B 21	NJ	Blairstown		Langenbach Fine Tool Co.
B 21	OH	Piqua	⌂	A. M. Leonard, Inc.
B 34	TX	Ft. Worth	⌂	Texas Greenhouse Co.
B 33	TX	Lubbock	⌂	Submatic Irrigation Systems
STATUES				
B 8	CA	La Honda		Cieli
B 3	CA	Oceanside	⌂	Asian Artifacts
B 27	CT	Norwalk	⌂	P&R International, Inc.
B 22	CT	Wilton		Kenneth Lynch & Sons, Inc.
B 27	DC	Washington	⌂	Park Place
B 37	DE	Dover	⌂	Winterthur Museum & Gardens
B 38	GA	Atlanta	⌂	Yanzum -- Art for Gardens
B 15	NC	Burnsville	⌂	Gateways
B 28	NY	Bronxville		Pompeian Studios
B 13	NY	Long Island City		Florentine Craftsmen, Inc.
B 20	NY	Niagara Falls	⌂	Kosmolux & LP, Inc.
A 97	NY	Northport	⌂	S. Scherer & Sons
B 7	OH	Waterville	⌂	Carruth Studio
STEPPING STONES				
B 20	NC	Durham		Kate's Garden & Studio
STORAGE BUILDINGS				
B 17	MI	Lansing	⌂	Heritage Garden Houses
B 26	OR	Eugene		Oregon Timberframe
SUNDIALS				
B 37	CA	Mendocino	⌂	Wind & Weather
B 14	CA	San Francisco		Gardener's Eden
B 27	CT	Norwalk	⌂	P&R International, Inc.
B 22	CT	Wilton		Kenneth Lynch & Sons, Inc.
B 27	DC	Washington	⌂	Park Place
B 38	GA	Atlanta	⌂	Yanzum -- Art for Gardens
B 13	NY	Long Island City		Florentine Craftsmen, Inc.
B 2	PA	Media		American Weather Enterprises
B 28	VA	Orange	⌂	The Plow & Hearth

PAGE	STATE	CITY	⌂ SHOP	SOURCE
SUPERSORB (R)				
B 20	CA	Davis		Janziker
SWINGS AND GLIDERS				
B 17	BC	Parksville	⌂	Heritage Garden Furniture
B 1	CA	Fort Bragg	⌂	Adirondack Designs
B 27	DC	Washington	⌂	Park Place
B 9	MD	Germantown	⌂	Country Casual
B 38	NY	Gardiner	⌂	Wood Classics
B 14	TN	Memphis	⌂	The Garden Concepts Collection
B 16	VA	Hamilton		Green Enterprises
B 28	VA	Orange	⌂	The Plow & Hearth
TECNU (R)				
B 34	OR	Albany		Tec Laboratories, Inc.
TERRA COTTA POTS/PLANTERS				
See also Planters				
B 7	OH	Waterville	⌂	Carruth Studio
TERRARIUMS				
A 71	CA	Sacramento	⌂	Mighty Minis
A 68	KS	Wichita	⌂	McKinney's Glasshouse
A 10	NJ	Pompton Lakes		Black Copper Kits
A 84	NY	Canandaigua		Peter Pauls Nurseries
THERMAFOR (R)				
B 6	MA	Salem		Bramen Company, Inc.
TIER BENCHES				
B 10	FL	Miami	⌂	Day-Dex Co.
TILLERS				
B 37	NE	Lincoln		Wikco Industries, Inc.
B 22	OH	London	⌂	Mainline of North America
B 23	PA	Huntingdon Valley	⌂	Mantis Manufacturing Co.
TISSUE CULTURE SUPPLIES				
A 70	MA	Tewksbury		Meadowbrook Hosta Farm
TISSUE CULTURE, CUSTOM				
A 117	BC	Aldergrove	⌂	Western Biologicals, Ltd.
A 20	CA	Carlotta		Choice Edibles
A 54	IN	Huntingburg	⌂	Indiana Berry & Plant Co.
B 17	OR	Portland		Halcyon Laboratories
A 19	VT	Isle La Motte		Champlain Isle Agro Associates
A 19	WA	Centralia		Cedar Valley Nursery
TISSUE CULTURE, ORCHIDS				
B 26	NY	Burdett		Orchis Laboratories
TOOL HANDLES, REPLACEMENT				
B 27	AR	Eureka Springs		Ozark Handle & Hardware
B 25	PQ	Sherbrooke	⌂	Nova Sylva, Inc.
TOOLS				
B 27	CA	Grass Valley	⌂	Peaceful Valley Farm Supply
B 17	CA	Graton	⌂	Harmony Farm Supply
B 32	CA	Mill Valley	⌂	Smith & Hawken
B 24	CA	San Anselmo	⌂	The Natural Gardening Company
A 35	IA	Shenandoah		Henry Field Seed & Nursery Co.
A 49	ID	Hailey	⌂	High Altitude Gardens
B 2	IL	Galesburg		Alsto's Handy Helpers
B 24	MA	Topsfield		The Walt Nicke Company
A 57	ME	Albion	⌂	Johnny's Selected Seeds
B 21	NJ	Blairstown		Langenbach Fine Tool Co.
A 70	OH	North Lima	⌂	Mellinger's, Inc.
A 29	ON	Georgetown		Dominion Seed House
B 21	ON	Ottawa	⌂	Lee Valley Tools, Ltd.

(continued next page)

PAGE	STATE	CITY	⌂ SHOP	SOURCE
TOOLS (continued)				
B 4	ON	St. Thomas		Berry Hill Limited
B 20	PA	Point Pleasant	⌂	Kinsman Company, Inc.
A 15	PA	Warminster	⌂	W. Atlee Burpee Company
A 30	SK	Saskatoon	⌂	Early's Farm & Garden Centre, Inc.
B 10	TX	Austin	⌂	De Van Koek
A 87	TX	Stephenville	⌂	Porter & Son
B 14	VT	Burlington	⌂	Gardener's Supply Company
TOOLS, HAND				
B 25	CA	Fairfield		Niwa Tool Co.
B 32	CA	Mill Valley	⌂	Smith & Hawken
B 10	CA	Placentia	⌂	Denman & Co.
B 14	CA	San Francisco		Gardener's Eden
A 117	CT	Litchfield	⌂	White Flower Farm
B 2	CT	Southington	⌂	American Standard Co.
B 2	IL	Galesburg		Alsto's Handy Helpers
B 13	IL	Lombard		The Floral Mailbox
B 9	MA	Peabody		The Crafter's Garden
B 24	MA	Topsfield		The Walt Nicke Company
A 71	MD	Baltimore		Meyer Seed Company
A 85	ME	New Gloucester	⌂	Pinetree Garden Seeds
B 21	NJ	Blairstown		Langenbach Fine Tool Co.
A 63	NJ	Sewell	⌂	Orol Ledden & Sons
A 52	OH	Chesterland	⌂	Homestead Division of Sunnybrook Farms
B 21	OH	Kidron	⌂	Lehman Hardware & Appliances, Inc.
B 21	OH	Piqua	⌂	A. M. Leonard, Inc.
B 21	ON	Ottawa	⌂	Lee Valley Tools, Ltd.
B 20	PA	Point Pleasant	⌂	Kinsman Company, Inc.
B 2	PA	West Chester		American Arborist Supplies
B 10	TX	Austin	⌂	De Van Koek
B 14	TX	Austin	⌂	Garden-Ville of Austin
B 31	TX	Ft. Worth		Rudon International Trading Company
B 28	VA	Orange	⌂	The Plow & Hearth
TOOLS, PRUNING				
B 25	CA	Fairfield		Niwa Tool Co.
B 10	CA	Placentia	⌂	Denman & Co.
B 2	CT	Southington	⌂	American Standard Co.
B 3	FL	Fort Lauderdale	⌂	Arborist Supply House, Inc.
A 57	GA	Ellijay	⌂	Johnson Nursery
B 13	IL	Schaumburg	⌂	Florist Products, Inc.
B 17	KS	Paola	⌂	Happy Valley Ranch
B 9	MA	Andover		Country House Floral Supply
B 9	MA	Peabody		The Crafter's Garden
B 6	MA	Salem		Bramen Company, Inc.
B 24	MA	Topsfield		The Walt Nicke Company
B 21	NJ	Blairstown		Langenbach Fine Tool Co.
B 17	NJ	Old Tappan		Harlane Company, Inc.
A 96	NY	Potsdam	⌂	St. Lawrence Nurseries
B 21	OH	Piqua	⌂	A. M. Leonard, Inc.
B 21	ON	Ottawa	⌂	Lee Valley Tools, Ltd.
B 19	OR	Eugene		International Reforestation Suppliers
A 31	OR	Wilsonville	⌂	Edmunds' Roses
A 1	PA	Aspers	⌂	Adams County Nursery, Inc.
B 4	PA	Greeley		Dorothy Biddle Service
B 2	PA	West Chester		American Arborist Supplies
B 25	PQ	Sherbrooke	⌂	Nova Sylva, Inc.
B 10	TX	Austin	⌂	De Van Koek
A 121	TX	De Leon	⌂	Womack's Nursery Co.
A 9	WA	Northport	⌂	Bear Creek Nursery
TOPIARY FRAMES				
B 12	CA	Friant	⌂	Cliff Finch's Zoo
B 22	CT	Wilton		Kenneth Lynch & Sons, Inc.
B 34	FL	Tampa		Topiary, Inc.
B 29	NC	Wilmington	⌂	A Proper Garden
B 13	TX	Tyler		French Wyres (R)
B 34	VT	Pownal		Topiaries Unlimited

PAGE	STATE	CITY	⌂ SHOP	SOURCE
TRAKE (TM)				
A 5	PA	Waynesboro	⌂	Appalachian Gardens
TREE SHELTERS				
A 75	CA	Tehachapi	⌂	Native Oak Nursery
B 34	MN	St. Paul		Treesentials
TRELLISES				
B 9	GA	Atlanta		Cross VINYLattice
B 1	MA	Brewster	⌂	Acorn Services Corporation
B 9	MD	Germantown	⌂	Country Casual
B 34	NC	Saluda	⌂	Taylor Ridge Farm
B 38	NY	Medford		Wood Innovations of Suffolk
B 13	PA	Philadelphia	⌂	The Garden Architecture Group
B 14	TN	Memphis	⌂	The Garden Concepts Collection
TRUBLOOM (R)				
B 36	CA	Vallejo		Verilux, Inc.
TUBEX (R) TREE SHELTERS				
A 75	CA	Tehachapi	⌂	Native Oak Nursery
B 34	MN	St. Paul		Treesentials
VIDEO CASSETTES				
B 30	CA	Chatsworth	⌂	Raindrip, Inc.
B 29	CA	Corralitos		Purple Sage Productions
B 31	CA	Los Osos		San Luis Video Publishing
B 7	CA	Marina Del Ray		A.C. Burke & Co.
B 26	CA	San Francisco		One Up Productions
B 36	CA	San Luis Obispo		Visual Education Productions
A 16	CT	Oxford	⌂	Butterbrooke Farm
B 23	CT	Southport		The Matrix Group
A 38	MI	Parma	⌂	Fox Hill Farm
B 7	NC	Moravian Falls	⌂	Brushy Mountain Bee Farm, Inc.
A 111	OH	Independence	⌂	William Tricker, Inc.
A 74	TN	Summertown	⌂	Mushroompeople
A 37	WA	Bellevue	⌂	Foliage Gardens
VIDEODISCS				
B 23	CT	Southport		The Matrix Group
VIRUS TESTING				
B 26	NY	Burdett		Orchis Laboratories
WATER BASINS, STONE				
B 16	OR	Talent	⌂	Granite Impressions
WATER GARDEN SUPPLIES				
See also Fish for Garden Ponds				
See also Ponds and Pools				
A 87	AR	Kingston	⌂	Pond Doctor
A 97	AZ	Scottsdale	⌂	Scottsdale Fishponds
A 96	CA	Santa Barbara	⌂	Santa Barbara Water Gardens
A 113	CA	Upland	⌂	Van Ness Water Gardens
A 102	FL	Winter Haven	⌂	Slocum Water Gardens
A 82	MA	Whitman	⌂	Paradise Water Gardens
A 118	MD	Baldwin	⌂	Wicklein's Water Gardens
B 30	MD	Baltimore	⌂	Resource Conservation Technology
A 69	MD	Jarrettsville	⌂	Maryland Aquatic Nurseries
A 20	MI	Madison Heights	⌂	City Gardens
B 2	MN	White Bear Lake	⌂	Aquacide Company
A 106	MO	Kansas City		Stigall Water Gardens
A 115	NJ	Saddle River	⌂	Waterford Gardens
B 18	NY	Canastota	⌂	Hermitage Gardens
A 97	NY	Northport	⌂	S. Scherer & Sons
A 89	NY	Parish		Railway Design & Landscape Company
A 70	NY	Spring Valley	⌂	Matterhorn Nursery Inc.
A 111	OH	Independence	⌂	William Tricker, Inc.
A 83	OK	Oklahoma City	⌂	Patio Garden Ponds

(continued next page)

PAGE	STATE	CITY	⌂ SHOP	SOURCE

WATER GARDEN SUPPLIES (continued)

PAGE	STATE	CITY	⌂ SHOP	SOURCE
A 84	ON	Ajax	⌂	Picov Greenhouses
B 21	ON	Ottawa	⌂	Lee Valley Tools, Ltd.
A 73	ON	Port Stanley	⌂	Moore Water Gardens
A 110	PA	Coopersburg	⌂	Tilley's Nursery/The WaterWorks
A 111	TN	Memphis	⌂	Trees by Touliatos
A 120	WI	Eagle	⌂	Windy Oaks Daylilies & Aquatics
A 24	WI	Muskego	⌂	Country Wetlands Nursery & Consulting
A 119	WI	Oshkosh	⌂	Wildlife Nurseries

WATER PURIFIERS

PAGE	STATE	CITY	⌂ SHOP	SOURCE
B 25	AR	Fayetteville	⌂	Nitron Industries, Inc.
B 21	OH	Kidron	⌂	Lehman Hardware & Appliances, Inc.

WATER STORAGE TANKS

PAGE	STATE	CITY	⌂ SHOP	SOURCE
B 7	CA	Point Arena	⌂	Cart Warehouse
B 10	CA	Willits	⌂	DripWorks

WATERING CANS

PAGE	STATE	CITY	⌂ SHOP	SOURCE
B 21	NJ	Blairstown		Langenbach Fine Tool Co.
B 20	PA	Point Pleasant	⌂	Kinsman Company, Inc.
B 10	TX	Austin	⌂	De Van Koek
B 10	WI	Manitowoc		The Dramm Corporation

WEATHER INSTRUMENTS

PAGE	STATE	CITY	⌂ SHOP	SOURCE
B 37	CA	Mendocino	⌂	Wind & Weather
B 13	IL	Schaumburg	⌂	Florist Products, Inc.
B 23	MA	New Bedford		Maximum, Inc.
B 30	NE	Columbus	⌂	Rodco Products Co., Inc.
B 29	NJ	Princeton	⌂	Qualimetrics, Inc.
B 19	OR	Eugene		International Reforestation Suppliers
B 2	PA	Media		American Weather Enterprises
B 25	PQ	Sherbrooke	⌂	Nova Sylva, Inc.

WEATHERVANES

PAGE	STATE	CITY	⌂ SHOP	SOURCE
B 37	CA	Mendocino	⌂	Wind & Weather
B 16	CT	Stamford		Good Directions
B 22	CT	Wilton		Kenneth Lynch & Sons, Inc.
B 37	IN	Indianapolis	⌂	Windleaves
B 29	NC	Wilmington	⌂	A Proper Garden
B 13	NY	Long Island City		Florentine Craftsmen, Inc.
B 21	OH	Kidron	⌂	Lehman Hardware & Appliances, Inc.
B 4	ON	St. Thomas		Berry Hill Limited
B 2	PA	Media		American Weather Enterprises
B 20	PA	Point Pleasant	⌂	Kinsman Company, Inc.

WEED CUTTERS, GAS/ELECTRIC

PAGE	STATE	CITY	⌂ SHOP	SOURCE
B 21	OH	Piqua	⌂	A. M. Leonard, Inc.
B 19	OR	Eugene		International Reforestation Suppliers
B 2	PA	West Chester		American Arborist Supplies

WEED CUTTERS, HAND

PAGE	STATE	CITY	⌂ SHOP	SOURCE
B 23	TN	Tracy City		The Marugg Company

WEEDERS, HAND

PAGE	STATE	CITY	⌂ SHOP	SOURCE
B 36	CA	Chico		Valley Oak Tool Company
B 25	CA	Fairfield		Niwa Tool Co.
B 10	CA	Placentia	⌂	Denman & Co.
B 24	MA	Topsfield		The Walt Nicke Company
A 77	MN	St. Paul	⌂	North Star Gardens
B 6	MT	Bozeman	⌂	Bozeman Bio-Tech
B 29	OR	Jacksonville		RNM Sales
B 31	TX	Ft. Worth		Rudon International Trading Company

WHEEL HOE

PAGE	STATE	CITY	⌂ SHOP	SOURCE
B 36	CA	Chico		Valley Oak Tool Company

WHEELBARROWS

PAGE	STATE	CITY	⌂ SHOP	SOURCE
B 10	CA	Placentia	⌂	Denman & Co.

(continued next page)

PAGE	STATE	CITY	⌂ SHOP	SOURCE
WHEELBARROWS (continued)				
B 10	FL	Miami	⌂	Day-Dex Co.
B 21	NJ	Blairstown		Langenbach Fine Tool Co.
B 21	OH	Piqua	⌂	A. M. Leonard, Inc.
B 2	PA	West Chester		American Arborist Supplies
B 10	TX	Austin	⌂	De Van Koek
B 37	WI	Janesville	⌂	Wisconsin Wagon Co.
WHIRLIGIGS				
B 38	GA	Atlanta	⌂	Yanzum -- Art for Gardens
A 6	MT	Bozeman		Artemis Gardens
WINDOW BOXES				
B 3	CA	Nevada City		David Bacon Woodworking
B 13	TX	Tyler		French Wyres(R)
B 24	WA	Bainbridge Island		Mitchells & Son
WINE MAKING EQUIPMENT				
B 23	CO	Pueblo	⌂	Marck Wines
B 17	KS	Paola	⌂	Happy Valley Ranch
B 4	ON	St. Thomas		Berry Hill Limited
WONDERLITE (R)				
B 29	NY	New York		Public Service Lamp Corp.
WORM CASTINGS				
B 25	AR	Fayetteville	⌂	Nitron Industries, Inc.
B 29	CA	Lake Elsinor		Rainbow Red Worms
B 26	CA	Los Angeles	⌂	Organic Control, Inc.
B 24	CT	Avon		Mother Nature's Worm Castings
B 38	IN	Bloomington	⌂	Worm's Way of Indiana
B 7	MA	Buzzards Bay		Cape Cod Worm Farm
B 16	OH	Cleveland		Guano Company International, Inc.
B 14	TX	Austin	⌂	Garden-Ville of Austin
B 18	VA	Woodbridge	⌂	Home Harvest(R) Garden Supply, Inc.

© The Fragrant Path
Artist: Christine Rasmussen

SOCIETY INDEX L 1

AFRICAN VIOLETS

D 1   African Violet Society of America, Inc.
D 1   African Violet Society of Canada
D 21 The Saintpaulia & Houseplant Society

AGRICULTURAL HISTORY

C 1   Association for Living Historical Farms
D 8   CORNS
D 12 Heritage Seed Program
D 22 Seed Savers Exchange

ALOES

D 1   Aloe, Cactus & Succulent Society of Zimbabwe

ALPINE PLANTS

D 1   Alpine Garden Society
D 4   American Rock Garden Society
D 18 Newfoundland Alpine & Rock Garden Club
D 21 The Rock Garden Club Prague
D 22 Saxifrage Society
D 22 Scottish Rock Garden Club

AMARYLLIDS

D 13 International Bulb Society

AQUATIC PLANTS

D 14 Water Lily Society

AROIDS

D 13 International Aroid Society

ASCLEPIADS

D 13 International Asclepiad Society

AUSTRALIAN PLANTS

D 22 The Society for Growing Australian Plants

AZALEAS

D 4   American Rhododendron Society
D 5   Azalea Society of America, Inc.
D 21 Rhododendron Society of Canada
D 21 Rhododendron Species Foundation

BAMBOO

D 1   American Bamboo Society

BEGONIAS

D 1   American Begonia Society
D 6   British Columbia Fuchsia & Begonia Society
D 7   Canadian Begonia Society

BONSAI

D 2   American Bonsai Society
D 5   Bonsai Clubs International
D 23 The Toronto Bonsai Society

BOXWOOD

D 2   American Boxwood Society

BROMELIADS

D 6   Bromeliad Society, Inc.
D 7   Bromeliad Study Group of Northern California
D 9   The Cryptanthus Society

BULBOUS PLANTS

D 2   American Calochortus Society
D 2   American Daffodil Society, Inc.
D 6   British Columbia Lily Society
D 7   Canadian Gladiolus Society
D 8   Canadian Prairie Lily Society
D 8   Clivia Club
D 9   Cyclamen Society
D 9   The Daffodil Society (UK)
D 13 Indigenous Bulb Growers Association
D 13 International Aroid Society
D 13 International Bulb Society
D 15 Manitoba Regional Lily Society
D 18 North American Gladiolus Council
D 18 North American Lily Society, Inc.
D 20 Pacific Northwest Lily Society

BUTTERFLIES

D 25 Xerces Society

CACTUS

D 1   Aloe, Cactus & Succulent Society of Zimbabwe
D 6   The British Cactus & Succulent Society
D 7   Cactus & Succulent Society of America
D 9   Desert Plant Society of Vancouver
D 24 The Toronto Cactus & Succulent Club

(continued next page)

(continued next page)

PAGE	TITLE	ISSUER
C1	AABGA Newsletter	American Association of Botanical Gardens & Arboreta
D2	ABStracts	American Bonsai Society
C1	ACGA Multilogue	American Community Gardening Association
D1	African Violet Magazine	African Violet Society of America, Inc.
E1	Agricultural News	Kentucky Dept. of Agriculture
E1	Agricultural Report	Connecticut Dept. of Agriculture
E1	Agricultural Review	North Carolina Dept. of Agriculture
D3	AHA Newsletter	American Herb Association
E1	Alabama Farmers' and Consumers' Bulletin	Alabama Dept. of Agriculture & Industries
E1	Allen Lacy's homeground	Allen Lacy
E1	The Amateur's Digest	Marina Welham
D2	American Fern Journal	American Fern Society
D2	American Forests	American Forestry Association
D3	American Horticulturist	American Horticultural Society
D4	American Penstemon Society Bulletin	American Penstemon Society
D4	The American Rose Magazine	American Rose Society
D15	Amerigold Newsletter	Marigold Society of America, Inc.
D17	Annual	National Sweet Pea Society
D4	Annual and Handbook	American Rose Society
D19	Annual Report	Northern Nut Growers Association
C1	APLD News	Assn. of Professional Landscape Designers
D8	Aquilegia	Colorado Native Plant Society
C4	Arbor Day	National Arbor Day Foundation
C1	Arboriculture Consultant	American Society of Consulting Arborists
C3	The Arborist News	International Society of Arboriculture
E1	Arnoldia	The Arnold Arboretum, Harvard Univ.
D13	Aroideana	International Aroid Society
D5	Australian Garden History	Australian Garden History Society
E1	Australian Garden Journal	Australian Garden Journal Pty., Ltd.
E1	Australian Orchid Review	Graphic World Pty., Ltd.
D22	Australian Plants	The Society for Growing Australian Plants
E1	The Avant Gardener	Horticultural Data Processors
D5	The Azalean	Azalea Society of America
E1	Baer's Garden Newsletter	John Baer's Sons
D6	BCLS Newsletter	British Columbia Lily Society
E1	Beautiful Gardens	CMK Publishing
D1	The Begonian	American Begonia Society
D18	Belvedere	New England Garden History Society
D3	Between the Vines	American Ivy Society
D5	Bio-Dynamics	Bio-Dynamic Farming & Gardening Association
D2	Bonsai Journal	American Bonsai Society
D5	Bonsai Magazine	Bonsai Clubs International
E2	Bonsai Today	Stone Lantern Publishing Company
D1	Borealis	Alaska Native Plant Society
E2	Botanical & Herb Reviews	Steven Foster
D2	The Boxwood Bulletin	American Boxwood Society
D6	Bradleya	The British Cactus & Succulent Society
D6	British Cactus & Succulent Journal	The British Cactus & Succulent Society
E2	John E. Bryan Gardening Newsletter	John E. Bryan, Inc.
D5	BUGS Flyer	Biological Urban Gardening Services
D2	Bulletin (ACS)	American Conifer Society
D2	Bulletin (ADS)	American Dahlia Society
D3	Bulletin (AFS)	American Fuchsia Society
D3	Bulletin (AIS)	American Iris Society
D4	Bulletin (AOS)	American Orchid Society
D4	Bulletin (APS)	American Peony Society
D4	Bulletin (ARGS)	American Rock Garden Society

PAGE	TITLE	ISSUER
D12	Heritage Rose Letter	Heritage Rose Group
D12	Heritage Seed Program	Heritage Seed Program
E5	High Value Crop Newsletter	Sweet Enterprises
E5	The Historical Gardener	Kathleen McClelland
D12	Hobby Greenhouse	Hobby Greenhouse Association
D12	Holly Society Journal	Holly Society of America
E5	Horticulture	Robert M. Cohn
E5	HortIdeas	Greg & Pat Williams
E5	Hortus	David Wheeler
E5	The Hosta Digest	Jay C. Gilbert
D3	Hosta Journal	American Hosta Society
E5	HousePlant Magazine	HousePlant, Inc.
D12	The Hoyan	The Hoya Society International
D11	HSI Bulletin	Heliconia Society International
D12	HSNY Newsletter	Horticultural Society of New York
D13	IBSA Bulletin	Indigenous Bulb Growers Association
D14	IGFTS Newsletter	International Golden Fossil Tree Society
E6	In Good Tilth	Oregon Tilth
D1	The INGENS Bulletin	Aloe, Cactus & Succulent Society of Zimbabwe
E6	International Bonsai	International Bonsai Arboretum
D13	International Camellia Journal	International Camellia Society
D14	IOS Journal	International Oak Society
D5	The IPM Practitioner	Bio-Integral Resource Center
D6	The Iris Year Book	British Iris Society
C3	Irrigation News	The Irrigation Association
E6	The Island Grower	Greenheart Publications
D3	The Ivy Journal	American Ivy Society
D1	Journal (ABS)	American Bamboo Society
D4	Journal (ARS)	American Rhododendron Society
D6	Journal (BS)	Bromeliad Society, Inc.
D9	Journal (CS)	The Cryptanthus Society
D14	Journal (ILS)	International Lilac Society
D18	Journal (NEGHS)	New England Garden History Society
D23	Journal (TBS)	Toronto Bonsai Society
C3	Journal of Arboriculture	International Society of Arboriculture
C3	Journal of Environmental Horticulture	Horticultural Research Institute
E6	Journal of Garden History	Taylor & Francis, Inc.
C5	Journal of Soil & Water Conservation	Soil & Water Conservation Society
C1	Journal of Therapeutic Horticulture	American Horticultural Therapy Association
D17	Kalmiopsis	Native Plant Society of Oregon
D15	LAIFS Journal	Los Angeles International Fern Society
C3	Land and History	Historic Preservation Committee
C1	Landscape Architecture	American Society of Landscape Architects
C1	Landscape Contractors News	Associated Landscape Contractors of America
C3	Landscape Trades	Landscape Ontario Horticultural Trades Association
D18	Lily Yearbook	North American Lily Society, Inc.
E6	Lindleyana	American Orchid Society
E6	Living Off the Land, Subtropic Newsletter	Geraventure
D15	Lousiana Native Plant Society Newsletter	Louisiana Native Plant Society
D16	MaGIC Lantern	Master Gardeners International Corp. (MaGIC)
D15	Magnolia	The Magnolia Society, Inc.
D23	Magnolia	Southern Garden History Society
E6	The Maine Organic Farmer & Gardener	Maine Organic Farmers & Gardeners Association
D14	Malus	International Ornamental Crabapple Society
D15	Manitoba Regional Lily Society	Manitoba Regional Lily Society
D2	Mariposa	American Calochortus Society
E6	The Market Bulletin	West Virginia Dept. of Agriculture
D18	McIlvainea	North American Mycological Association
D19	Mentzelia	Northern Nevada Native Plant Society
D16	Mesemb Study Group Bulletin	Mesemb Study Group
D16	The Michigan Botanist	Michigan Botanical Club
D13	Mid-Year Newsletter	International Camellia Society
D16	Minnesota Green Newsletter	Minnesota State Horticultural Society
D16	Minnesota Horticulturist	Minnesota State Horticultural Society
D16	Minnesota Plant Press	Minnesota Native Plant Society
D16	Missouriensis	Missouri Native Plant Society

PAGE	TITLE	ISSUER
D23	Monthly Bulletin	Southern California Horticultural Society
E6	Mushroom Growers Newsletter	The Mushroom Company
D18	The Mycophile	North American Mycological Association
C4	The National Gardener	National Council of State Garden Clubs, Inc.
D17	National Gardening	National Gardening Association
E6	Native Notes	Joseph L. Collins
D24	Native Notes	West Virginia Native Plant Society
D22	Native Plants Newsletter	The Society for Growing Australian Plants
D14	Nerium News	International Oleander Society
E6	New England Farm Bulletin	Jacob's Meadow, Inc.
D18	New Zealand Camellia Bulletin	New Zealand Camellia Society
D18	New Zealand Fuchsia Society Newsletter	New Zealand Fuchsia Society, Inc.
D1	Newsletter (AWS)	Alabama Wildflower Society
D1	Newsletter (ABS)	American Bamboo Society
D4	Newsletter (AWGN)	American Willow Growers Network
D8	Newsletter (CPLS)	Canadian Prairie Lily Society
C2	Newsletter (CBHL)	Council On Botanical & Horticultural Libraries
D10	Newsletter (GHS)	Garden History Society
D11	Newsletter (HFF)	Hardy Fern Foundation
D11	Newsletter (HPS-UK)	Hardy Plant Society (UK)
D11	Newsletter (HPS-Mid Atlantic)	Hardy Plant Society - Mid-Atlantic Group
D12	Newsletter (HAH)	Horticultural Alliance of the Hamptons
D15	Newsletter (LIHS)	Long Island Horticultural Society
D15	Newsletter (LISA)	Louisiana Iris Society of America
D16	Newsletter (MNPS)	Mississippi Native Plant Society
D17	Newsletter (NHPA)	National Hot Pepper Association
D17	Newsletter (NPS-NM)	Native Plant Society of New Mexico
D18	Newsletter (NEWFS)	New England Wild Flower Society
D19	Newsletter (NCWFPS)	North Carolina Wild Flower Preservation Society
D19	Newsletter (NNNPS)	Northern Nevada Native Plant Society
D19	Newsletter (NSWFS)	Nova Scotia Wild Flora Society
D20	Newsletter (PSI)	Passiflora Society International
D20	Newsletter (PSA)	The Plumeria Society of America, Inc.
D20	Newsletter (RCF)	Rare Conifer Foundation
D21	Newsletter (RHA)	Rose Hybridizers Association
D22	Newsletter (SS)	The Sedum Society
D22	Newsletter (SSE)	Seed Savers Exchange
D22	Newsletter (SS)	Sempervivum Society
D22	Newsletter (SHPA)	Sino-Himalayan Plant Association
D23	Newsletter (TNPS)	Tennessee Native Plant Society
D24	Newsletter (WHS)	Western Horticultural Society
D25	Newsletter (WNPS)	Wyoming Native Plant Society
C3	Newsletter of the Garden Conservancy	The Garden Conservancy
D19	Northern Gardener	Northern Horticultural Society
E6	Northland Berry News	Berry Communications
D19	Nutshell	Northern Nut Growers Association
D24	Occasional Papers	Washington Native Plant Society
C5	Ontario Horticultural Assn. Newsletter	Ontario Horticultural Association
D9	The Orchid Advocate	Cymbidium Society of America
E6	Orchid Digest	Orchid Digest Corporation
E7	The Orchid Hunter	Terry Ferraro
E7	The Orchid Review	The Royal Horticultural Society
E7	Organic Gardening	Rodale Press, Inc.
E7	Pacific Horticulture	Pacific Horticultural Foundation
D10	The Palmetto	Florida Native Plant Society
D6	Pelargonium News	British Pelargonium & Geranium Society
C1	People Plant Connection	American Horticultural Therapy Association
C5	People-Plant Council News	People-Plant Council
C5	Perennial Plants	Perennial Plant Association
D19	The Perennial Post	Northwest Perennial Alliance
D16	Petal Pusher	Missouri Native Plant Society
E7	Phalaenopsis Fancier	Doreen Vander Tuin
D20	PHS News	Pennsylvania Horticultural Society
D21	The Pits	Rare Pit & Plant Council
D20	Plant Amnesty	Plant Amnesty
C2	Plant Conservation	Center for Plant Conservation

PAGE	TITLE	ISSUER
D5	Plant Press	Arizona Native Plant Society
E7	Plants & Gardens	Brooklyn Botanic Garden
E7	The Plantsman	Maxwell Publishing
D12	Pome News	Home Orchard Society
D18	Pomona	North American Fruit Explorers
E7	Potpourri from Herbal Acres	Pinerow Publications
C5	PPGA News	Professional Plant Growers Association
D20	PPS Newsletter	Pioneer Plant Society
D4	Primroses	American Primrose, Primula & Auricula Society
D14	Principes	The International Palm Society
C3	Proceedings	International Plant Propagation Society
D20	PSDA Bulletin	Puget Sound Dahlia Association
D2	Pteridologia	American Fern Society
C1	The Public Garden	American Association of Botanical Gardens & Arboreta
D1	Quarterly Bulletin (AGS)	Alpine Garden Society
D18	Quarterly Bulletin (NALS)	North American Lily Society, Inc.
D21	Quarterly Bulletin (SHS)	The Saintpaulia & Houseplant Society
D24	Quarterly Bulletin (TFTS)	Tropical Flowering Tree Society
C3	Quill & Trowel	Garden Writers Association of America
D22	The Review	The Society for Japanese Irises
D14	The Ribes Reporter	The International Ribes Association
D22	The Rock Garden	Scottish Rock Garden Club
E7	Rocky Mountain Gardener	Susan Martineau
D12	Roots Journal	Historic Iris Preservation Society
D8	The Rosarian	Canadian Rose Society
D21	The Rose	Royal National Rose Society
D21	RSF Newsletter	Rhododendron Species Foundation
D13	Sage Notes	Idaho Native Plant Society
E7	Seed Exchange Monthly	Peter Collier
D3	The Seed Pod	American Hibiscus Society
E7	Seedling	Univ. of Rhode Island Cooperative Extension
D24	Sego Lily	Utah Native Plant Society
D22	The Siberian Iris	Society for Siberian Irises
D23	SIGNA	Species Iris Group of North America
D21	Skalnicky	The Rock Garden Club Prague
E7	Small Farm News	Small Farm Center
E7	Small Farm Today	Ron Macher
D13	Soilless Grower	Hydroponic Society of America
D23	South African Fuchsia Fanfare	South African Fuchsia Society
D23	Southern Fruit Fellowship	Southern Fruit Fellowship
E7	Southern Living	John Alex Floyd, Jr.
D22	SPCNI Almanac	Society for Pacific Coast Native Iris
E8	Neil Sperry's Garden	Gardens South
D23	Spuria Newsletter	Spuria Iris Society
D7	Storksbill	Canadian Geranium & Pelargonium Society
E8	Sundew Garden Reports	Tom Carey
E8	Sunset Magazine	Sunset Publishing Co.
D14	Sweet Times	International Violet Association
E8	Temperate Bamboo Quarterly	Earth Advocates Research Facility
E8	Texas Gardener	Chris S. Corby
D17	Texas Native Plant Society News	Native Plant Society of Texas
C4	TGOA/MGCA Newsletter	The Gardeners of America/ Men's Garden Clubs
E8	TLC ... for plants	Gardenvale Publishing Company, Ltd.
E9	The Tomato Club	Robert D. Ambrose
C4	Tree City USA Bulletin	National Arbor Day Foundation
D20	Trillium	Ohio Native Plant Society
D21	Tropical Fruit News	Rare Fruit Council International, Inc.
E8	The Twenty-First Century Gardener	Growers Press, Inc.
C2	Urban Forestry, The Quarterly	California Urban Forests Council
E8	Urban Forests	American Forests
D10	Vegetable Garden Research Yearbook	Garden Research Exchange
D6	Veld & Flora	Botanical Society of South Africa
D14	Water Garden Journal	International Water Lily Society
E8	Weekly Market Bulletin	New Hampshire Dept. of Agriculture
D8	Wildflower	The Canadian Wildflower Society
C4	Wildflower Journal	National Wildflower Research Center

© Larner Seeds
Artist:Terry Bell

© Native Seeds/SEARCH
Artist: Bill Singleton

Practical Matters

This section contains some practical forms which I hope you will find useful. All can be removed or photocopied for your use. As a matter of "good formsmanship" and to be sure you get what you request, carefully print or type your name and address.

❀ **Catalog and Information Request:** use this form to request catalogs or ask for information from societies and magazines, or to ask companies if they can supply specific items on your "want list."

The best use of this form is to photocopy it once, print or type in your name and address, and then photocopy it again as many times as you like. You can then check off the appropriate boxes for each specific request. If you don't use this form, please mention *Gardening by Mail*.

❀ **Reader Feedback and Update Order Form:** I'm eager to hear your opinions of and suggestions for *Gardening by Mail*. Please let us know what you like and don't like, any improvements you'd like to see—readers have suggested many improvements.

Please list sources and organizations that you think we should list on a *separate sheet*. Before you recommend a source, please check to see if it sells by mail order; Weston Nurseries and Western Hills Nursery do not!

You can subscribe to the updates in advance. Changes to the listings in this edition are cumulative, so you only have to order the latest update to be current. New sources and books received will be mentioned on a separate sheet, and will not be cumulative.

❀ **Listing Request and Update of Current Listing:** if you feel your company, society, publication or library should be listed in the next edition of *Gardening by Mail*, please let us know by filling in and sending us this form as soon as possible. The information requested on the form is the minimum we need to know about you. Companies and organizations already listed in this edition may use this form to update their listing; all information will be verified before the publication of the next edition. We include changes and new sources in our periodic updates; it helps to send your current catalog or other information with the form.

❀ **Changes and Corrections:** room has been left at the back of the book for including changes and corrections in subsequent printings.

❀ **Mailing Labels:** Tusker Press will rent mailing labels for the various listings in this book; each set of labels is rented for one time use only. Unauthorized use of labels will be invoiced for the full amount. Inquire about prices.

Readers are reminded that photocopying, scanning or storing the information in this book into a computer for any personal or business use is against copyright law.

THE WISDOM OF TUSKER PRESS

Having just finished six months of intensive study of many, many hundreds of nursery and garden supply catalogs, I've decided to sit down and write up some informal thoughts and suggestions for the people who write mail order catalogs, plant lists and sales brochures, which are probably the most important point of contact you have with many or all of your customers. If you're thinking of starting a plant or garden related business, or already have one, and would like to know what an experienced catalog reader thinks, I'd be glad to share my thoughts with you.

This distilled wisdom of Tusker Press is about the length of a magazine article, and will be sent to anyone interested for a long stamped self-addressed envelope and $3 to cover my costs.

Tusker Press
Wisdom Department
P.O. Box 1338
Sebastopol, CA 95473

Catalog and Information Request Form

Date: _____

To: _____

☐ Please send me your free catalog.

☐ I enclose a long self-addressed envelope with $ _____ postage.

☐ Please send me your catalog, for which I enclose $ _____.

☐ You did not provide the price of your catalog; please send me one or advise me of the cost.

☐ Please send me information on joining your society.

☐ I'd like to subscribe to your periodical; please tell me your current rates.

☐ Please let me know if you have _____

_____

☐ Other information I need: _____

_____

— —

My name and address are:

Name: _____

Mailing Address: _____

City and State: _____

Country: _____ Postal Code: _____

Daytime Phone: _____ Evening Phone: _____

I found you in
Gardening by Mail: A Source Book
by Barbara J. Barton
Published by Houghton Mifflin Company
Boston & New York

Reader Feedback & Update Order Form

Date: _____

What I like about *Gardening by Mail*

_____

_____

_____

_____

_____

What I don't like about *Gardening by Mail*

_____

_____

_____

_____

_____

Suggestions for improvements in the next edition

_____

_____

_____

_____

_____

Please list your recommendations for new plant and product sources, societies, magazines, etc. on a separate sheet of paper.

By identifying your special interests, the following information will help us improve the contents of the book.

I am a	☐ home gardener	☐ professional/commercial horticulturist	☐ both
	☐ new gardener	☐ experienced gardener	☐ very experienced gardener
I have a	☐ small garden	☐ medium-sized garden	☐ large garden (acre or more)
I grow	☐ lawn	☐ flowers	☐ vegetables
	☐ fruit	☐ ornamental shrubs	☐ trees
	☐ greenhouse plants	☐ indoor plants	☐ special interests (list below)

_____

_____

Please send this form to

Please continue on back. ⟶

Tusker Press, Database Department
P.O. Box 1338, Sebastopol, CA 95473

I use *Gardening by Mail* for:

☐ mail orders

☐ finding local sources

☐ visiting display gardens

☐ reference when traveling

☐ finding plants by climate zone

☐ finding products/services

☐ finding gardening books

☐ finding magazines

☐ Other uses: _____

_____

Name: _____

Mailing Address: _____

City and State: _____

Country: _____ Postal Code: _____

Daytime Phone: _____ Evening Phone: _____

☐ finding societies

☐ finding libraries

☐ making professional contacts

☐ buying plants/products for resale

☐ selling plants/products to retailers

☐ compiling a mailing list for prospects

☐ finding unusual plants or products for customers

Order for Updates to *Gardening by Mail*

Over the years that we have been collecting information about horticultural sources, we have learned one sobering lesson: things change—and rapidly. As fast as we gather information, our listees are changing their names, addresses and ownership, going out of business or ceasing to fill mail orders. We try to keep current and we're constantly on the lookout for changes, but it's like trying to catch sand in a hairnet.

In addition, we are continually finding new and exciting sources of plants and supplies, new societies, libraries, magazines and books which we'd like to share with our readers.

Tusker Press issues periodic updates to *Gardening by Mail* which include any name and address changes that **we know about** for the listings in the book, and new sources on a separate sheet. Updates are cumulative, so order **only** the most recent or future issues:

To order updates, sent **U.S. $2.00 for each update desired** to Tusker Press and check the updates you wish.

☐ September 1994   ☐ September 1995

☐ January 1995   ☐ January 1996

☐ May 1995   ☐ May 1996

Total enclosed: $_____

Please put your name and address on this form and let us know if you move.

Request for Listing in
Gardening by Mail
or Update of Current Listing

If you would like to be listed in the next edition of *Gardening By Mail*, please return this form as soon as possible. **We also list new sources in our regular updates as space allows.**

Current listees: Please use this form to notify us of any changes. **Changes, except catalog prices, will be included in our updates.**

To be listed in *Gardening By Mail*:

Seed companies, nurseries, other plant suppliers, and garden suppliers must sell direct by mail order to buyers in the U.A. and/or Canada and **must enclose their most recent catalog with this request**.

Plant and horticultural societies must welcome members for the U.S. and/or Canada and **must include a current issue of their periodical with this request**.

Libraries must allow member of their sponsoring organizations and/or the public to use their facilities for reference.

Questionnaires will be sent when a new edition is planned. Those listed in the current edition will automatically receive one but must meet the same conditions AND return the completed questionnaire and their catalog or literature to be listed again.

Questionnaires vary by type of company or organization. Please specify your **primary** category:

Date: _____

☐ Seed company   ☐ Plant or horticultural society

☐ Nursery   ☐ Horticultural library

☐ Garden suppliers   ☐ Gardening/horticultural magazine or newsletter

☐ Trade, professional or umbrella   ☐ Other (be specific and indicate why you should be listed):
      organization

_____

Final selection of those listed is at the discretion of the author.

- -

Please type or print—if we can't read it, we can't use it.

☐ Request for listing   ☐ Current listing update (provide current listing name, and new name, if changed).

Name of Business or Organization: _____

Proprietor/Manager: _____

Mailing Address: _____

City and State: _____

Country: _____ Postal Code: _____

Phone Number(s): _____

Please send this form to   Please continue on back. ➡

Please continue on back. ➡

Tusker Press, Database Department
P.O. Box 1338, Sebastopol, CA 95473

☐ We have added Tusker Press to our mailing list.

☐ Name of the individual who will promptly complete and return your future questionnaires.

_____

The following information is the **minimum** Tusker Press needs to know now:

The price of our catalog is $ _____ ☐ Long SASE   ☐ Free

☐ Minimum retail order is $ _____

☐ Telephone orders accepted with credit cards—$ _____ minimum.

☐ We sell wholesale AS WELL AS retail by mail order.

☐ We ship to (   ) USA   (   ) Canada   (   ) overseas.

☐ We ship live/perishable materials in the months _____

☐ We sell MAIL ORDER ONLY (no nursery or shop/sales location).

☐ We also sell at this sales address: _____

☐ We have a display garden or many plants/products on display at sales location.

The twelve most important plants/products that we sell are:

_____

_____

_____

_____

_____

Comments/other information.

_____

_____

_____

_____

_____

_____

_____